ETHNICITY, NATIONALISM AND VIOLENCE

Ethnicity, Nationalism and Violence

Conflict management, human rights, and multilateral regimes

CHRISTIAN P. SCHERRER
Hiroshima Peace Institute, Japan

ASHGATE

Published by
Ashgate Publishing Limited
Gower House
Croft Road
Aldershot
Hants GU11 3HR
England

Ashgate Publishing Company
Suite 420
101 Cherry Street
Burlington, VT 05401-4405
USA

Ashgate website: http://www.ashgate.com

British Library Cataloguing in Publication Data
Scherrer, Christian P.
  Ethnicity, nationalism and violence : conflict management,
  human rights, and multilateral regimes
  1. Ethnic conflict 2. Nationalism 3. Conflict management
  I. Title
  305.8

Library of Congress Cataloging-in-Publication Data
Scherrer, Christian P.
  Ethnicity, nationalism, and violence : conflict management, human rights, and
  multilateral regimes / Christian P. Scherrer.
    p. cm.
  Includes bibliographical references and index.
  ISBN 0-7546-0956-1 (alk. paper)
    1. International relations and culture. 2. National state. 3. Ethnic conflict. 4. Human
  rights. I. Title.

JZ1251 .S34 2002
303.6--dc21

2002074711

ISBN 0 7546 0956 1

Printed and bound by Athenaeum Press, Ltd.,
Gateshead, Tyne & Wear.

Contents

List of Tables

The Author

Christian P. Scherrer (Dr. phil., University of Bern 1985) is professor for Peace Studies at *Hiroshima Peace Institute* (HPI) of Hiroshima City University, Japan. He is the head of the *Ethnic Conflict Research Project* (ECOR), an independent research project, since its foundation in 1987, and conducted 1986–2002 field research in a number of areas of violent conflicts on four continents. He also worked for international organizations (ICRC, UNCHR) and contributed expertise to a number of institutions, among them the Conflict Prevention Network of the European Commission and the Development Assistance Committee of the OECD. For the UN High Commissioner for Human Rights he conducted genocide investigation in Rwanda's southern Butare province and elaborated a study on *Justice-in-Transition and Conflict Prevention in Post-Genocide Rwanda*. He is the editor of the ECOR studies and compiler series and the author of the first ever series of handbooks on ethnicity and state in conflict (*Ethno-Nationalism*, vols. 1–2. Münster: agenda 1996–7; IFEK-IRECOR 1998–2003). From 1997–1999 he was senior researcher at *Copenhagen Peace Research Institute*, responsible for building up the new project on 'Intrastate Conflicts and Peace Strategies', and from 1999–2001 he was research director at the *Institute for Research on Ethnicity and Conflict Resolution* (IRECOR). In recent years he contributed to a new multi-dimensional theory for a better understanding of contemporary mass violence as well as to policies and procedures for its prevention (*Structural Prevention of Ethnic Violence*. Palgrave 2002). In a book on the Rwandan genocide from a comparative perspective he discussed possible responses to genocide (Campus 1997), followed by a totally revised English version *Genocide and Crisis in Central Africa* (Praeger 2002) and a volume on *Responses to Genocide* (forthcoming).

Preface

Since 1945, more than 300 wars have taken place worldwide—most of them, until the end of the 1980s, in the Third World. The claims of so-called nation-states in regard to the nationalities, which they claim as their own citizens, and in regard to ethnic minorities and indigenous peoples, became increasingly aggressive. On the view presented here, this state of affairs is, in empirical-cum-historical terms, the most dangerous potential and actual source of conflicts and wars both in the former Third World and, since 1989–90, in the former nominally socialist multinational states. Almost two-thirds of current violent conflicts are susceptible of ethnic interpretation. It was only when the Janus-like countenance of nationalism reappeared in Europe that the Western media and broad sections of the public became aware of this global trend towards ethno-nationalism, of which there had been evidence since half a century, more precisely since the period of decolonization. Ethno-nationalism, this last wave of nationalism, has been in different stages of the process of reviewing the situation left behind by the colonial world-order. Its duality has to do with an inherent dichotomy between liberation and oppression, between emancipation and barbarity.

Against the background of media discovery of the ethnic phenomena and of the general inadequacy of research into the forgotten conflicts raging in many parts of the world, this study first attempts (in part I) to work out some key elements of a new comprehensive theory of non-Clausewitzean warfare, ethno-nationalism and contemporary mass violence. The aim is to investigate their causes, to distinguish their many different manifestations, to highlight their potential, to analyse their structural characteristics and the driving forces, and to set the phenomenon of violent conflict in a global context. In searching for the root-causes of today's violent conflicts it becomes clear that the career of the nation-state has had momentous reper-cussions in the formerly colonized world. Where the retreat of the colonial powers was followed by internal colonization future conflicts were pre-programmed. Separatism and ethno-nationalism have become a built-in, long-term problem in the 'Third World' since 1948 and more recently, in the 1990s, also in the erstwhile nominally socialist world. A comprehensive typology of contemporary violent conflict is presented, the world's conflicts are indexed, results drawn and trends identified. Part I extensively deals with the challenge ethno-nationalism poses to the nation-state and the danger emanating from the ethnicization of social or political conflict.

Part II critically reviews the activities undertaken by international and humanitarian organizations in ethnic conflicts and also the efforts of the United Nations, such as the Human Rights Commission and the International Labour Organization (ILO) to work out minimum standards for the rights of minorities and indigenous peoples. The observations on multilateral regimes are confined, for the most part, to the 'human dimension'—that is to say, to human-rights mechanisms and minority rights issues. New paths in this direction have been embarked on within the framework convention of the Council of Europe and the Organization for Security and Cooperation in Europe (OSCE, formerly the CSCE process). However, speculations about the transposability of European 'models' must be viewed with scepticism. Reflection on increasing calls since the early 1990s for the United Nations to become involved, or to intervene militarily, in zones of war and non-war mass violence, genocide in particular, underlines the primary need for structural prevention and for an expansion in the choice of non-military options. To round off this part of the discussion, a few observations are made about a possible new role for the United Nations in the 21st century.

This choice of objectives necessitates an interdisciplinary approach and moving beyond a narrowly defined standpoint. As a field of study, ethno-nationalism and ethnicization embrace the disciplines of social anthropology, the humanities, human geography, political science, international relations, and constitutional and international law. At present, the needs created by interdisciplinary co-operation have still only very limited institutional possibilities corresponding to (or rather conflicting with) them. The use of concepts borrowed from several disciplines is a necessity in the area of peace research, but it does not in itself constitute interdisciplinarity.

Another study named Structural Prevention of Ethnic Violence (Scherrer 2002b) outlines and compares various regional and local attempts at conflict resolution within the framework of state policies on minorities and nationalities. An attempt is made to give a conceptual account of the phenomenon of ethnicity. A planned additional volume will illustrate the mapping of contemporary conflict and their possible or intended resolution by means of comparing examples from four different continents.

The need for peace and conflict research for reorientation towards the 'real existing' conflict-formations—and the intensification of international attempts to find methods of preventing and resolving conflict—has been recognized by more major actors in recent years. One factor that is of crucial importance in the prevention of ethno-national conflicts is the extension not only of international norms and standards of protection for non-dominant minorities and indigenous peoples but also of the rights of these groups in regard to autonomy and self-governance. In the current debate, normative and structural dimensions of conflict prevention (better: prevention of violence) are often neglected in favour of technical aspects, despite the fact that techniques of preventive diplomacy, such as mediation, facilitation, good offices, arbitration, etc., and other forms of peaceful conflict settlement by go-betweens can only be of secondary importance compared with a long-term policy for the prevention of violent intra-state conflict. Some observers see the current proliferation of states as a form of 'conflict resolution' and by others as a dangerous fragmentation and a slide into chaos. The mentioned second study includes an account of applied forms of self-governance; to provide a global comparison of nationality policies based on a set of evaluative/quality criteria for self-governance agreements is something that could only be attempted in outline.

This book and the mentioned second study are also the fruits of several years of field-research in ethno-national war-zones and of collaboration with representatives of indigenous and endangered peoples. For some of the cases mentioned, the author can call not only on a wealth of documentation, but also on first-hand information and personal on-the-spot observation. During the period 1987-95, I conducted field research on ethnic nationalism in the Horn of Africa (focusing on Ethiopia, Eritrea and Sudan), Southeast Asia (mainly Burma, Thailand and Yunan, China) and Central America (Nicaragua, Panama, Guatemala) and Mexico, and I investigated genocide in Rwanda in 1994-95 for the UN High Commissioner for Human Rights.

By experiencing life in the world's most deadly conflict areas I learned that there is nothing more valuable than peace and justice. But it was in Rwanda in 1994 where I investigated the worst crime against humanity in the late 20th century. This deeply shocking experience changed my life; ever since I tried to contribute to the prevention of violence and genocide and to the peaceful resolution of conflict—not only on a theoretical level, and by publishing studies like this one, but also in practical activities.

On the basis of extensive empiric research I started to re-evaluate and revise global conflict indexes, definitions and theoretical approaches. Recently, I proposed a wholesale reorientation of peace research, which aims at constructing a new comprehensive theory of contemporary mass violence and which involves of a fusion of polemological research with comparative genocide research, studies into mass murder, and what has been named 'democide' and 'politicide', i.e., terrorism and slaughter by government. Peace and conflict-research are a fundamentally problem-oriented field of social and political sciences. The themes and methods of research into nationalism, ethnicity and violent conflict overlap with similarly problem-oriented areas of research dealing with major issues such as migration, racism, and multiculturalism. Preoccupation with topical prob-lem-areas has become a common feature of the studies, concepts, and analyses of peace and conflict research since the Cold War. The analytical framework has long become trans-disciplinary; the specializations of the individual disciplines must be linked up to themes and issues of general interest. It is in this area that peace and conflict research could exercise one of its most important functions within the academic enterprise.

The presupposition of states as the primary political actors became an obstacle due to the tendency to exclude or neglect the part played by other actors. An exclusively state-centred orientation has to be rejected. Nations without states look for means that will secure them protection and guarantees within the community of nations. For indigenous peoples and endangered nationalities the quest to secure an improvement in their legal status and recognition as political entities is a matter of survival.

We live in the third era of globalization. The principle of non-interven-tion in internal affairs is now being negated by the existence of global players. Among them are international regimes and multilateral organiza-tions, the UN system, powerful institutions such as the IMF and World Bank, the financial markets, the activities of international banks and multi-national concerns, and the omnipresence of the electronic media, with their disregard for national frontiers. The territorial integrity of the 194 states is also being called into question by the existence of up to 10,000 distinct entities. Many nationalities aspire to separate statehood or respond to the particular configuration of power by seeking a free association with existing states; some already enjoy a form of autonomy or self-governance, others have fought for and secured a *de facto* autonomy based on arms.

For a long time concepts such as 'ethnic conflict' or 'ethno-nationalism' were avoided as far as possible or, depending on the situation and area of the world, were replaced by misleading euphemistic (or demonizing) expressions such as 'miscellaneous conflicts', 'ethnic cleansing', or 'tribalism'. Because of considerable stigmatization of the subjects mentioned, there has been little incentive to try to fill the gaps in research on ethno-nationalism and on the ways of resolving ethno-national conflicts and preventing the ethnicization of political conflict. Some of these themes were taken up by second-class journalists, propagandists, and bar-room politicians. As a result of the frequently distorted depiction of ethnicity and nationalism in the media and under the influence of confused categorization of horrendous images of war, the scientific discourse on this subject is scarcely audible. This study is part of an overdue attempt to address one of the major issues of our time from a multi-dimensional perspective.

Christian P. Scherrer   Hiroshima Peace Institute, HPI

Acknowledgements

I should like to preface this work with some words of thanks to friends and colleagues. I am very grateful to Johan Galtung, Kader Asmal, the late Bernard Nietschmann, Dieter Senghaas, Henry Huttenbach, Jehuda Bauer, the late Howard R. Berman, Ted R. Gurr, Judy Butler, Mohamed A. Teisir, Kumar Rupesighe, Jannis Markakis, Mohamed Sahnoun, Julian Burger, Michael van Walt, Onno Seroo, Matthias Stiefel, Patrick Mazimhaka, Lorenz Löffler, Joseph Nsengimana, Mohamed Suleiman, Nadir Bekirov, Khaw Tho, the late General U Twin, Dima Noggo Sarbo, Thuingaleng Muivah, Armando Rojas, the late Leonidas Valdez, Stephen Ryan, Hans Petter Buvollen, Willem J. Assies, Patricia van Nispen, Uwe Markino, Dietrich Jung, Norbert Ropers, Christoph Schwager, Alexander Sutter, Regine Mehl, Martin Bondeli, and Tobias Debiel for their advice, comments and criticisms, and especially to Siglinde Gertschen and Sigrid Szczepanski for further suggestions and reading through the manuscript. I am indebted to Margaret Clarke, for her careful and competent translation of large sections of my German writing.

I am particularly indebted, also, to all the representatives and champions of indigenous and endangered peoples whose acquaintance I have made over the last dozen years. They have opened my eyes to the abysses, sufferings, and fighting spirit that exist on the periphery of the world's states and systems. Their resistance and their struggle for their historic rights, and for the right to be different, deserve our sympathy and support.

Abbreviations and Glossary

ACP	States of African, Caribbean, and Pacific having privileged relation with EU
ACS	Association of Caribbean States (25 members and eight associates)
ADB	African Development Bank
AFB/PRIUB	Arbeitsstelle Friedensforschung Bonn, Peace Research Information Unit Bonn (http://www.priub.org)
AFDL	Alliance des Forces Démocratiques de Libération (Congo-DRC)
Afronet	Zambian NGO promotes human rights in Africa, network, http://www.zamnet.zm/zamnet/afronet/afrohome.htm)
AGKED	Arbeitsgemeinschaft Kirchlicher Entwicklungsdienste / Workgroup of Church-based Development Agencies (Germany)
AGP	Assam Gana Parishad (India)
AHRRC	African Human Rights Resource Center (website on human rights in Africa http://www.umn.edu/humanrts/africa/index.html)
AI	Amnesty International (largest voluntary organisation dealing with human rights; http://www.amnesty.org)
AIM	American Indian Movement (USA, http://www.aimovement.org/)
AIPP	Asian Indigenous Peoples Pact
AJSU	All Jharkhand Students Union (India)
AKUF	Arbeitsgemeinschaft Konfliktursachenforschung / Workgroup for Research on Conflict Causes (University of Hamburg, Germany)
AN	Aymara Network (Andes, www.aymaranet.org/map.html)
ANC	African National Congress (South Africa)
APEC	Asia Pacific Economic Co-operation (21 member economies representing 47% of global trade; http://www.apecsec.org.sg/)
APPRA	Asia-Pacific Peace Research Association
ASEAN	Association of South-East Asian Nations
ASEN	Association for the Study of Ethnicity and Nationalism
ASSR	Autonomous Soviet Socialist Republic
AU	African Union (regional community decided in Abuja 1991, implemented from 2002 onwards; potentially 53 member states)
AWEPA	Association of West European Parliamentarians concerned with Africa (http://www.awepa.org/)
BIA	Bureau of Indian Affairs (USA government institution)
BJP	Bharatiya Janata Party (India)

BWC	Biological and Toxin Weapons Convention (of 1972 and its successive Review Conferences)
CARICOM	Caribbean Common Market (community and market of 15 Carribbean island states; Haiti might join; www.caricom.org)
CCA	Carter Center in Atlanta, Georgia (USA, www.cartercenter.org/)
CCM	Chama Cha Mapinduzi (Tanzania)
CCW	Convention on Prohibition or Restrictions on the Use of Certain Conventional Weapons Which May be Deemed to be Excessively Injurious or to Have Indiscriminate Effects (in force since 1983)
CDI	Center for Defense Information (USA, www.cdi.org/)
CDR	Coalition pour la Défense de la République (Rwanda)
CEEAC	Communauté Economique des Etats de l'Afrique Centrale / Economic Community of the Central African States
CEPGL	Communauté Economique des Pays des Grands Lacs / Economic Community of the Great Lakes Countries
CIA	Central Intelligence Agency (USA)
CIDA	Canadian Development Agency (resources on conflicts and prevention http://www.synapse.net/~acdi20/)
CIDCIM	Center for International Development and Conflict Management (University of Maryland, USA)
CISA	Congreso Indígena del Sur de América (www.puebloindio.org)
CLADHO	Collectif des Ligues et Associations pour les Droits de l'Homme (Rwanda)
CMG	Conflict Management Group (Harvard)
CMM	Chattisgarh Mukti Morcha (India)
CNDD	Conseil National pour la Défense de la Démocratie (Burundi)
CNI	Congreso Nacional Indígena (Mexico)
CoE	Council of Europe
COMESA	Community of Eastern and Southern Africa (19 member states from Eastern and Southern Africa, from Sudan to Angola including all GLR countries; http://www.comesa.int/)
COPRED	Consortium on Peace Research, Education and Development (http://www.igc.apc.org/copred/)
CORPI	Coordinación Regional de Pueblos Indígenas (South America)
COW	Correlates of War Project (University of Michigan, USA)
CPB	Communist Party of Burma
CPC	Conflict Prevention Centre (OSCE)
CPSID	Convention on the Peaceful Settlement of International Disputes
CRCII	Conflict Resolution Center International, Inc (http://www.igc.apc.org/crcii/)
CRLK	Conseil de Resistance et de Liberation du Kivu (DRC, S-Kivu)

CSCE	Conference on Security and Co-operation in Europe (now OSCE)
CTBT	Comprehensive Nuclear Test Ban Treaty (adopted on 10 September 1996 by the United Nations General Assembly; has not yet been ratified by a sufficient number of the 44 nuclear-capable States)
DAB	Democratic Alliance of Burma
DEZA	Dienst für Entwicklungszusammenarbeit (Swiss Development Agency)
DGFK	Deutsche Gesellschaft für Friedens- und Konfliktforschung (German Society for Peace and Conflict Research)
doCIP	Documentation Centre for Indigenous Peoples (Geneva)
DPCR	Department of Peace and Conflict Research (Uppsala, Sweden)
DRC	Democratic Republic of Congo
EBLUL	European Bureau of Lesser Used Languages (CoE)
ECA	Economic Commission for Africa (UN, http://www.uneca.org/)
ECOR	Ethnic Conflicts Research Project (Tegelen, Netherlands)
ECOSOC	Economic and Social Council (UN)
ECOWAS	Economic Community of West African States (regional-level organisation, 16 members, based in Nigeria, www.ecowas.int/)
ELN	Ejército de Liberación Nacional (Colombia)
EPCPT	European Platform for Conflict Prevention and Transformation (Netherlands, network of European NGOs, www.euconflict.org/)
EPLF	Eritrean People's Liberation Front
EPRDF	Ethiopian Peoples Revolutionary Democratic Front
ESN	Ethnic Studies Network (Univ. Ulster, Northern Ireland)
ETA	Euzkadi Ta Askatasuna (Basque Fatherland and Liberty/Freedom, Basque Country, Spain/France, since 1959, violent since 1968)
EZLN	Ejercito Zapatista de Liberación Nacional / Zapatista Army for the National Liberation (Mexico/Chiapas)
EU	European Union (15 members; union to be enlarged eastwards from 2004 to as many as 25 members; earlier European Community, EC)
FAC	Forces Armées Congolaises (Congo-DR)
FAR	Forces Armées Rwandaises (Rwanda; genocide army)
FARC	Fuerzas Armadas Revolucionarias de Colombia (Columbia)
FAZ	Forces Armées Zairoises (Zaire, defeated army of Mobutu)
FDD	Force pour la Défense de la Démocratie (Burundi; *Intagohekas*)
FGN	Federal Government of Nagaland (India)
FIER	Foundation for Inter-ethnic Relations
FLEC	Frente para a Liberataçao do Enclave de Cabindo (Angola)
FLNC	Front de Libération National du Congo (Congo-DR)
FLNK	Front de Libération National du Katanga (Congo-DR)

FMLN	Frente Farabuno Martí para la Liberación Nacional (El Salvador)
FP	Front Populaire (Burundi)
FPR	Front Patriotique Rwandais (Rwanda)
FRELIMO	Frente de Libertacão de Moçambique
FRODEBU	Front pour la Démocratie au Burundi
FROLINAT	Front de Libération Nationale (Burundi)
FSLN	Frente Sandinista de Liberación Nacional (Nicaragua)
GfBV	Gesellschaft für bedrohte Völker (Germany)
GNLF	Gorkha National Liberation Front (India / West Bengal)
GOMN	Groupement des Observateurs Militaires Neutres / Group of Neutral Military Observers
Group of 77	G-77 established in 1964 by 77 developing countries at the first session of UNCTAD in Geneva, has increased to 133 countries; in alliance with China; G-77 dominates the UN General Assembly
HCNM	High Commissioner on National Minorities (OSCE)
HIIK	Heidelberg Institute for International Conflict Research
HPI	Hiroshima Peace Institute (Japan)
HRFOR	Human Rights Field Operation in Rwanda (run by UN-HCHR)
HRW	Human Rights Watch (http://www.hrw.org/)
HSM	Holy Spirit Movement (Uganda)
IA	International Alert (http://www.international-alert.org)
IBRD	World Bank (http://www.worldbank.org/)
ICAR	Institute for Conflict Analysis of George Mason University (http://www.gmu.edu/departments/ICAR/)
ICC	International Criminal Court (to be established; www.iccnow.org)
ICC	Inuit Circumpolar Conference (Arctic)
ICCPR	International Covenant on Civil and Political Rights (UN)
ICESCR	International Covenant on Economic, Social and Cultural Rights
ICJ	International Court of Justice (The Hague)
ICRC	International Committee of the Red Cross (http://www.cicr.org)
ICTR	International Criminal Tribunal for Rwanda (Arusha, Tanzania, www.ictr.org)
ICTY	International Criminal Tribunal for the Former Yogoslavia (Hague, Netherlands, http://www.un.org/icty/)
IDP / IDPs	internally displaced person/s
IGCC	Institute on Global Conflict and Coperation at University of California (http://www-igcc.ucsd.edu)
IITC	International Indian Treaty Council (USA, American Indian)
ILO	International Labour Organization (part of UN system)

ILRC	Indian Law Resource Center (American Indian resource org.)
IMEMO	Institute for World Economy (Russian Federation)
IMF	International Monetary Fund (http://www.imf.org/)
INCORE	Initiative on Conflict Resolution and Ethnicity (N-Ireland, Derry; http://www.incore.ulst.ac.uk/)
INEF	Institut für Entwicklung und Frieden, at University of Duisburg
INGOs	International Non-Governmental Organisations
INN	International Negotiation Network (USA; Carter Center)
Intagohekas	'Those who never sleep' (Burundi, genocidal militia)
Interahamwe	'Those who strike together' (Rwanda, genocidal militia)
IPA	International Peace Academy (http://www.ipacademy.org/)
IPN	Indigenous Peoples Network (http://lanic.utexas.edu/la/region/indigenous/)
IPRA	International Peace Research Association (http://www.human.mie-u.ac.jp/~peace/about-ipra)
IRA	Irish Republican Army (Northern Ireland/UK, peace treaty)
IRECOR	Institute for Ethnicity Research and Conflict Resolution / Institut für Ethnizitätsforschung und Konfliktbearbeitung IFEK (Germany)
IRIN	Integrated Regional Information Network for Central and Eastern Africa IRIN-CEA (UN OCHA on http://www.reliefweb.int)
IRIPAZ	Instituto de Relaciones Internacionales y de Investigación para la Paz
IUPIP	International University of Peoples' Initiative for Peace (http://www.unimondon.org/iupip)
IWGIA	International Work-Group for Indigenous Affairs Indigenous (umbrella resource org., based in Copenhagen, Denmark)
JEEAR	Joint Evaluation of Emergency Assistance to Rwanda (International consortium set up by DANIDA, reported in 1996)
KANU	Kenya African National Union (Kenya; governing party)
KIA/KIO	Kachin Independence Army/Organization (N-Burma; rebels, truce)
KNU	Karen National Union (SE Burma; rebels, no cease-fire)
KOSIMO	Konfliktsimulationsmodell / Conflict Simulation Model (HIIK)
LLDC	least developed country
LNO	Lahu National Organization (Northern Burma; rebels, cease-fire)
LRM	Lord's Resistance Army (N-Uganda, armed sectarian fundamentalist)
LTTE	Liberation Tigers of Tamil Eelam (Sri Lanka; rebel army)
Maji-Maji	gangs and militia group among Nande, Tembo, Hunde, Nyanga, a/o (DRC, Noth Kivu; 'traditional warriors', two factions)
MAR	Minorities at Risk project (at CIDCM; Maryland, USA)
MCAC	Mediation, Conciliation and Arbitration Committee (OAU)
MCC	Maoist Communist Centre (India, armed group)

MCTK   Movimiento Campesino Tupak Katari (Bolivia, civil group)

MDR   Mouvement Démocratique Républicain (Rwanda; political party, Hutu party; 1994 genocidal Hutu power faction)

MERCOSUR Mercado Común del Sur, (Common Market of the South), economic integration project of four members: Argentina, Brazil, Paraguay and Uruguay; two associates: Chile and Bolivia; and interested states: Colombia, Perú and Venezuela; http://www.mercosur.org

MIAND   Ministry for Indian Affairs and Northern Development (Canada)

MINURSO   United Nations Mission for the Referendum in Western Sahara

MLC   Mouvement de Liberation Congolais (Congo DRC, Equateur, rebel army, supported by Uganda; alliance with both RCD-factions),

MNC-L   Mouvement National Congolais/Lumumba (DRC; opposition party)

MRND   Mouvement Révolutionnaire National pour le Développment / la Démocratie (Rwanda: former single party; genocidal)

MSF   Médecins Sans Frontières (INGO, http://www.msf.org)

MTA   Mong Tai Army (S-Burma/Shan State; rebel group, drug warlords)

NAC   National Aboriginal Conference (Australia; indigenous organization)

NADECO   National Democratic Coalition (Nigeria; civic organization)

NAFTA   North American Free Trade Agreement (USA, Canada, and Mexico)

NAI   Nordiska Afrikainstitutet (Sweden; www.nai.uu.se/indexeng.html)

NAILS   National Organization of Aboriginal and Islander Legal Services (Australia; resource organization)

NAM   Non-Aligned Movement (most representative organization of the developing countries; composed of 113 member states; last XII Summit in Durban 1998; http://www.nam.gov.za/)

NCGUB   National Coalition Government of the Union of Burma (Burma; provisional rebel government)

NCIV   Nederlands Center for Inheemse Volken (Dutch support group)

NDA   National Democratic Alliance (Sudan; umbrella organization of all opposition groups, based in Asmara)

NIOD   Nederlands Instituut voor Oorlogsdocumentatie / Netherlands Institute for War Documentation (Amsterdam)

NNA   neutral and non-aligned states

NNC   Naga National Council (NE-India; former armed rebel organization)

NPT   Treaty on the Non-Proliferation of Nuclear Weapons (signed 1968)

NRM   National Resistance Army / Movement (Uganda; in power since 1986)

NSCN   National Socialist Council of Nagaland (NE-India; armed rebel group)

OAS   Organization of American States (http://www.oas.org/)

OAU   Organisation of African Unity (African regional organization of 53 member states; http://www.oau-oua.org/)

OBK	Organisation pour l'amenagement et le développement du Bassin de la rivière Kagera / Organization for planning and development of the Kagera river basin
OCHA	UN Office for the Coordination of Humanitarian Affairs (runs the Integrated Regional Information Network, IRIN, and the Reliefweb on http://www.reliefweb.int)
ODA	Official Development Assistance
ODIHR	Office for Democratic Institutions and Human Rights (OSCE)
OLF	Oromo Liberation Front (Ethiopia; liberation movement)
OSCE	Organization for Security and Co-operation in Europe (formerly CSCE)
ÖSFK	Österreichisches Studienzentrum für Frieden und Konfliktlösung (Stadtschleining; EPU)
OWO	One World Online (network of 250 NGOs, www.oneworld.org/)
OXFAM	British development, advocacy and relief agency; www.oxfam.org
Palipehutu	Parti pour la Libération du Peuple Hutu (Burundi; extremist)
PALU	Parti Lumumbist (Congo-DR; civil org.)
PARENA	Party for National Recovery (Burundi; Tutsi party)
PBI	Peace Brigades International (www.igc.apc.org/pbi/)
PCA	Permanent Court of Arbitration (The Hague)
PHR	Physicians for Human Rights (NGO; http://www.phrusa.org/)
PIF	Pacific Island Forum (16 member countries are all independent and self-governing Pacific Island countries, Australia and New Zealand)
PIOOM	Interdisciplinary Research Programme on Causes of Human Rights Violations (www.fsw.leidenuniv.nl/www/w3_liswo/pioom.htm)
PL	Parti Libéral (Rwanda; political party; also in Burundi)
PLA	Peoples Liberation Army (India)
PRIO	International Peace Research Institute, Oslo (http://www.prio.no/)
PSLF	Palaung State Liberation Front (N-Burma; rebel org.)
PTA-ESA	Preferential Trade Area for Eastern and Southern Africa
RCD	Rassemblement Congolais pour la Démocratie (DRC; rebel alliance)
RENAMO	Resistência Nacional Moçambicana (rebel group; integrated)
RGN	Revolutionary Government of Nagaland (NE-India; rebel group)
RPA	Rwandese Patriotic Army (Rwanda: 1990 guerrilla, 1994 state army)
RPF / FPR	Rwandese Patriotic Front (Rwanda: 1990 guerrilla party, 1994 political party; coalition)
RSS	Rashtriya Swayamsevak Sangh (India; extremist org.)
RTLM	Radio Télévision Libre des Milles Collines (Rwanda, hate radio 1994)
SAARC	South Asian Association for Regional Co-operation
SADC	Southern African Development Community (www.sadcexpo.org/)

SAP   Structural Adjustment Programme (IMF)
SIPRI   Stockholm International Peace Research Institute (Sweden)
SLORC   State Law and Order Council (Burma; military junta, renamed SPDC)
SOJEDEM   Solidarité Jeunesse pour la Défense des Droits des Minorités
              (Burundi; wing of Tutsi militias 'sans échec' and 'sans défaite')
SPDC   State Peace and Development Council (Burma/Myanmar: regime)
SPLA / M   Sudanese People's Liberation Army / Movement (guerrilla, NDA)
SSP   Shiv Sena Party (India; extremist political party)
SUA   Shan United Army (Burma; rebel group)
SWF   State of the World Forum (http://www.worldforum.org/); State of
              the World CoExistence Network (http://www.co-net.org/index.html)
TFF   Transnational Foundation for Future and Peace Research, Lund
              (www.transnational.org/)
Tigres   Tigres du Katanga (DRC; former Katangan gendarmes)
TNC   Transnational Corporation (global player)
TPB   Terrorism Prevention Branch of UNODCCP (Vienna, Austria;
              http://www.undcp.org/terrorism.html)
Transcend   Peace and Development Network (http://www.transcend.org)
UÇK / KLA   Ushtria Çlirimtare e Kosovës / Kosovo Liberation Army
UDPS   Union pour la Démocratie et le Progrès Social (Congo-Zaire,
              opposition party, led by E. Tshisekedi)
ULFA   United Liberation Front of Assam (India; rebel force)
UNAMIR I-II   United Nations Assistance Mission for Rwanda (UN troops sent Oct.
              1993 and pulled out in April 1994, 2.500; resent mid 1994, 5.500)
UNAR   Union Nationale Rwandaise (Rwanda; party 1959, later guerrilla)
UNCTAD   United Nations Conference on Trade and Development (10 global
              conferences, last in Bangkok 2000)
UNDP   United Nations Development Programme (http://www.undp.org/)
UN-DPKO   United Nations Dep. for Peacekeeping Operations (information on
              UN operations. http://www.un.org/Depts/dpko/)
UNESCO   United Nations Educational, Scientific and Cultural Organisation
              (http://www.unesco.org/)
UNFCCC   United Nations Framework Convention on Climate Change (adopted
              9 May 1992 and its additional Kyoto Protocol of on 11 December
              1997; http://unfccc.int/)
UNHCHR   United Nations High Commissioner for Human Rights
UNHCR   United Nations High Commissioner for Refugees (www.unhcr.ch)
UNICEF   United Nations Children's Fund (http://www.unicef.org/ ; formerly
              UN International Children's Emergency Fund)
UNICRI   United Nations Interregional Crime and Justice Research Institute
              (Turin, Italy; http://www.unicri.it)

UNITA	Uniâo Nacional para Independência Total de Angola (W-Angola, large rebel army, led by J, Savimbi)
UNLF	United National Liberation Front (India; rebel army)
UNODCCP	UN Office for Drug Control and Crime Prevention
UNPO	Unrepresented Nations and Peoples Organization (The Hague)
UNRISD	United Nations Research Institute for Social Development (Geneva
UNU	United Nations University, UNU, Tokyo (http://www.unu.edu/)
UNWGIP	United Nations Working Group on Indigenous Populations (Geneva)
UPRONA	Union pour le Progrès National/Union for National Progress (Burundi)
US-AID	Development agency of the United States of America
US-IP	United States Institute of Peace (http://www.usip.org/)
US-SD	US State Department (www.state.gov/www/regions.html)
UWSA	United Wa State Army (Burma: rebel force)
WCIP	World Council of Indigenous Peoples (indigenous umbrella group)
WNBF	Western Nile Border Front (N-Uganda, Muslim guerrilla)
WSP	War-torn Societies Project (UNRISD, UN Geneva)
WTO	World Trade Organization (established 1995, 144 member states, successor of GATT deals with global rules of trade)
WWI	Worldwatch Institute (http://www.worldwatch.org/)
YATAMA	Yapti Tasbaya Masrika (Eastern Nicaragua; Miskitu Indian movement; earlier rebel force)

Introduction

Ethno-nationalism in the International System

Efforts by, on the one hand, the community of states, and, on the other, non-governmental organizations to work out internationally binding standards on the ethno-national issue have not progressed very far. In order to be able to respond properly to the national question in general and to the ethno-nationalist challenge in particular, regimes for secession should be made a subject of international law and part of regional regimes. At the level of the international system, the current proliferation of states is taking place in 'uncontrolled' fashion. The process of fragmentation in the former Eastern block has led to a large number of warlike conflicts in the former republics of the USSR and Yugoslavia from 1990 to 2002, the last being the Kosovo crisis followed by a NATO war against Yugoslavia, which triggered the spread of violence to Macedonia. In the case of the Third World, it has become clear that warlike conflicts that have been going on for decades can probably only be ended through the creation of new states.

In 1990, the end of the Cold War in Europe, the upheavals in the Soviet Union (and, following this, in the whole of the 'Eastern bloc'), changes of regime in Latin America, and the crisis of military dictatorships and one-party regimes in Africa during the early 1990s, all led to illusory hopes of democracy and freedom on a global scale. Although the community of states has steadily expanded the codified protection of human rights and shifted it both from the intra-state to the international level and into the Law of the Nations, this has so far had little effect on the actual situation.

In the majority of states, the bases of legitimate rule are not present or are very weak, and basic political rights are daily violated or threatened.[1] Multi-ethnic states are ruled over by ultra-nationalist regimes who equate nation and state absolutely with one another, by 'total states', and by brutal dictatorships. Political repression is aimed not only at individual dissidents, but very often also against members of ethnic and national minorities. In parallel with this, the 'erosion of basic social rights' (Nuscheler) and mass impoverishment are assuming alarming proportions. The number of impoverished people in the world has increased to over 1.5 billion. The situation of the poorest of the poor—an estimated 900 million 'absolute poor'—is characterized by such catastrophic living conditions that human dignity, the cornerstone of all human rights, is nullified. According to the Human Development Report 2001 some 968 million people survive without access to clean water; 854 million are illiterate adults; 1.2 billion people living on less than $1 a day, 2.8 billion on less than $2 a day.[2]

Dramatically growing inequality characterizes many countries in the South, especially Latin American and Caribbean countries have the world's highest income inequality, as well as the countries in Eastern Europe and the CIS that suffered low or negative growth in the 1990s;[3] here, a time bomb is ticking due to the fact that much inequality develops according to ethnicity, not only according to class. On a global scale North-South inequality reached extreme proportions.[4] In most southern regions the struggle against poverty seems lost. Many ethnic minorities are systematically impoverished and become second and third class citizen. In the long run inequality will exacerbate the effects of policy failures.

In the era of neo-liberal globalization, with rising social inequality, death and despair is also growing. Most people who die an unnatural death are not killed in violent conflict but they die from diseases that could be prevented and from famine. The structural violence of poverty is the deadliest force: 100,000 people die every day of famine and its related effects. In the year 2000, according to Jean Ziegler, the UN Special Rapporteur on the right to food, 36 million people were starved to death. Every seven seconds a child dies. 826 million of 6.2 billion people are permanently and severely undernourished. Figures of horror, with no progress reported,[5] though the eradication of poverty and the prevention of violence are key tasks of global governance and declared objectives of the United Nations.

The contribution which interstate regimes make to the solution of violent conflicts is currently a modest one, but could become more significant in future. The instruments of conflict management should be further developed within the framework of regional regimes and within the UN system. The Kosovo crisis 1998–1999 became a front-page conflict and has drawn the full attention of the international news media on a case of ethno-nationalism—once again in Europe, although many other ethno-nationalist conflicts, among the currently 40 plus conflicts world-wide, are much worse (in terms of fatalities). The disproportionate strike, the selective approach, and the ignorance for humanitarian problems elsewhere pose serious ethical problems.[6] Despite the urgency of the situation, given the monumental problems we face today, most of the initiatives launched within the framework of the United Nations, the Organization for Security and Co-operation in Europe (OSCE) or the Council of Europe have so far been unsuccessful. Because of their state-centred nature, the efforts made to date have been marked by inherent weaknesses. It was only in 1991 that the

OSCE (then CSCE) concluded for the first time that minority policies could be a legitimate cause of international dispute and therefore could not be a purely internal affair of individual states.

At the level of the international system, legitimate demands for self-determination should be brought before the International Court of Justice in The Hague, as a procedure for averting conflict.[7] The budgets which the United Nations, the OSCE, and other regional organizations currently set aside for violence prevention, including preventive diplomacy, mediation, and monitoring, are minimal and seem ridiculous compared to military expenditure—less than 0.001 percent. For instance, the entire OSCE budget is less than a third of the cost of a single B-2 'Stealth' bomber, the U.S. air force lost in the NATO war against Yugoslavia 1999.[8] The priority of the OSCE Office for Democratic Institutions and Human Rights is the building of civil society and democratic institutions, which indeed contributes chiefly to peace and security. The ODIHR shall also assist the OSCE states to implement their human dimension commitments. For this important task it got 2001 just 6.5 million Euro (of the OSCE annual budget of 209 million Euro) or 3.1 percent, which is only slightly more than the 2.8 percent this institution got in 1998. The key institution of the OSCE for preventive diplomacy, the High Commission for National Minorities, only got 2 million Euro or 1 percent of the total budget, which is still very low but more than the 0.65 percent it got 1998.

The OSCE budget reflects the return of war and mass violence to Europe and the efforts to contain it. The questions to asked here: are these efforts effective and do they produce sustainable situations? The budget rapidly rose from 1 million Euro in 1991 to 24 million Euro in 1995, doubled to 48 million in 1997, tippled the next year (1998) to 148 million and passed the mark of 200 million Euro in 2000.[9] Although, within a decade, the OSCE budget has greatly increased from one to meanwhile over 200 million Euro, it is still inappropriate, especially regarding the distribution of the funds for the different tasks. If these figures are meant to show what value the major contributors (the Western industrial nations) really attach to violence prevention, this bodes ill as regards the political will to pursue what these nations themselves acknowledge is one of the most important goals of international diplomacy.

A debate has recently begun about whether the United Nations should become more involved or intervene more in the case of internal conflicts. It took Saddam Hussein's persecution of the Kurds and the civil wars in the former Yugoslavia to trigger this debate and to enable us belatedly to see that ethnic conflicts inside sovereign states must be regarded as a threat to international security. In Afghanistan the world community could again (as already in the end 1980s) observe that a thin layer of religious ideology, in this case Islamic fundamentalism propagated by the Taliban, covered an essentially ethnically determined conflict formation. One of the main tasks, if UN peacekeeping and UN sponsored political change ought to be successful, is to work for all inclusive and ethnically balanced governance in Afghanistan—as well as in the Congo—in order to end deadly conflict.

In the more than fifty years since the United Nations came into existence, there have been repeated object lessons demonstrating the persistent nature of ethnic conflicts. Violent conflicts are ethnicized and militarized from above and ethno-nationally charged up and responded to from below. The consequences are horrendously widespread suffering, death on a massive scale, and the destabilization of entire regions.

Notes

1. *Amnesty International Report* var. years; Freedom House var. years. Also, 'The Map of Freedom', *Freedom Review*, 26 (1995), 1: 40–1; UNDP var. years. A comparison of these sources is not possible (Nuscheler 1992: 272).
2. Table 1.1 on 'Serious deprivations in many aspects of life', in UNDP: *Human Development Report*, 2001: 9–10 (on www.undp.org/hdr2001/complete.pdf); for the development of poverty since the mid 1990s compare SEF 1995: 2. 'A study of 77 countries with 82% of the world's people shows that between the 1950s and the 1990s inequality rose in 45 of the countries and fell in 16.' HDR 2001, 17.
3. 'In 13 of the 20 countries with data for the 1990s, the poorest 10% had less than 1.20 of the income of the richest 10%. This high income inequality places millions in extreme poverty and severely limits the effect of equally shared growth on poverty.' Ibid., 17.
4. 'The richest 1% of the world's people received as much income as the poorest 57%. The richest 10% of the US population (around 25 million people) had a combined income greater than that of the poorest 43% of the world's people.' UNDP 2001, 19.
5. Reports by Jean Ziegler are available on www.unhchr.ch/html/menu2/7/b/mfood.htm.
6. Kosovo 1999 highlighted the danger of a new era of 'anarchy in the international system', provoked by breaches and violations of several instruments of international law and the way the aerial bombing of Yugoslavia was conducted, hitting scores of civilian targets, which is outlawed by conventions and pacts signed by most of the fifteen NATO states. The arbitrary choice of one particular conflict among others also raises questions.
7. As recommended by the Dutch Centre for Indigenous Peoples long ago: NCIV 1993.
8. The OSCE has today 55 participating States and spans almost the entire northern part of the world, a geographical area from Vancouver to Vladivostok. The self-declared aim of OSCE is truly ambitious: 'As a regional arrangement under Chapter VIII of the Charter of the United Nations, the OSCE has been established as a primary instrument in its region for early warning, conflict prevention, crisis management and post-conflict rehabilitation in Europe' (www.osceprag.cz/info/facts/factshet.htm). Compared to this task, the budget and its distribution seem inappropriate. The bulk of it goes to OSCE long-term missions (above 80%), mainly in Former Yugoslavia. To give a telling comparison: The entire OSCE budget is less than a third of the cost of one single B-2 'Stealth' bomber, as the one shot down by the Yugoslav army during the months of NATO bombardments in 1999.
9. 'OSCE budget 1991 – 2001', see chart on http://www.osce.org/general/budget/.

PART I

ETHNO-NATIONALIST CHALLENGE WITHIN THE NATION-STATE

Chapter 1

The Nation-State Project:
Colonial Export and 'Mother of Disorder'

The European colonisation of the world in the last 500 years and the three waves of proliferation of capitalist production resulted—on the level of political organisation—in widespread, coercive and rapid change. This first phase of globalization was first based on raw military violence, followed by political domination and economic exploitation. Following the geopolitical changes of 1990 the new area of capitalist globalization is characterised by high dynamics in a number of world regions.

Today the globalization process is far from having achieved a degree of homogenisation and having produced the *global village*. Conspicuous and ongoing contradictions prove that there is no homogenous linear dynamic. It seems that an equally powerful process of fragmentation permanently counteracts the process of globalization, with both being at odds with the key political actor of modern times: the nation-state.

The emergence of ethnic and nationalist warfare started with the decolonisation after 1945. It is simply one of the most popular misconceptions to link the emergence of ethno-nationalism with the end of the Cold War. Since World War II more than 200 wars and explosions of mass violence took place. Almost all violent conflicts were fought in the Third World. The majority of contemporary violent conflicts are intra-state wars or acts of genocide. Ethnicity and the struggle against the colonial world order play a dominant role.

The Colonial Clash of Civilizations

Colonialism brought about a rigid reduction of the number and the diversity of pre-colonial political systems, in some cases 'only' an alteration of the originality and peculiarities of indigenous political systems. Such enduring systems were part of distinct social formations, today renamed civilizations:[1] irrigation-based societies with strong central states; other states based on 'slavery'; tributary and feudal systems; agricultural proto-states, and other 'traditional societies'. The latter notion has usually escaped the attention of political science.

Enduring sustainable political systems were also developed in traditional societies. This includes the type of *acephalous societies* that means previously stateless egalitarian societies without central organisation and dominance. So-called *primitive* societies co-existed peacefully with irrigation-based *high* cultures. Boundaries were fluid. Stateless spaces, currently rather unthinkable, posed 'security problems' but were part of normality in pre-colonial times.

The global change of this diverse structure materialised as a result of European colonial expansion, accelerated by the genesis of the modern state in the Europe, following the era of absolutism. European militarism clashed with the old civilizations of the Far East and the civilizations of the South. Resistance against European penetration and hostility took different forms. In the first phase of out-right violence the European expansion clashed with indigenous societies, for example Spain versus American Indian or the Portuguese in Africa. The resistance of highly centralised indigenous states (Aztecs, Incas) was broken in astonishing short time while the subjugation of decentralised and acephalous societies took centuries of colonial warfare. The second phase of expansion to the West (North America), to the East (India, Island Asia, Far East), and to the South (Africa, Arabia) was less violent. Strong military resistance of established empires and kingdoms modified the agenda of the European powers. The goal of establishing trade links and spreading unequal exchange contributed to a more sophisticated agenda.

Resistance against attempts to coerce ancient state society into the colonial system of Indirect Rule necessarily took different forms. These attempts were of shorter duration (India) or remained superficial (Japan) and territorially limited (China). In the case of traditional societies, with the exception of gatherers and hunters societies, stateless societies mobilised a high degree of ongoing, armed resistance against intruders of all types, be it colonial powers, new states or settlers.[2]

Irrigation-based societies produced the most stable states characterised by sustainable development. Both, the mode of production as well as the administrative structure of the state and the cultural ideological scope, were determined by the logic of constructing large irrigation systems (mainly for wet rise agriculture). The construction of such systems is a regional or district activity. Large-scale public works need a strong central state as managing instance. Public works such as irrigation constituted a state-owned managerial and true form of political economy.[3]

Irrigation-based states developed a system of regulatory mechanisms for securing the long-term reproduction of 'the entire system'. Strong internal orientation was predominant and internal conflict settlement was fairly well established. Other types of political systems (such as slave-based societies, despotic or feudal states) were more aggressive and therefore unstable.

Traditional unilinear hypotheses of the development of regional and global society formations reflect, in no way, the richness in form and diversity of formerly autonomous socio-political systems.[4] Unilinear development became realised through colonial capitalist expansion, and it is an illusion that there were any 'white spots' on the map of the colonial expansion.

The 'historic revenge' of the colonised, feared by Huntington and other authors, who remain slaves of the military thinking and the mentality of the Cold War, shall materialise in the 21st century.[5] It already showed its first expressions. However this 'revenge' came in a very different form as expected in the West. On the one side the September 11 attack on America was perceived as a 'clash of civilizations' or as an outright challenge for 'civilization' as such, with a US president calling for a new 'crusade' against Islamists and terrorists. On the other side, as a peaceful but powerful challenge, capitalist production forces as well as new sophisticated technologies and the advancement of science were rapidly developed in several East Asian countries. And they were long used more efficiently, with much innovation and in a so far less war-oriented way (arguably with the exception of Japan until 1945) as in Europe and its former settler colonies earlier.

The European Idea of the Nation-State and its Ambivalence

At the birth of the modern state several elements were constitutive: the absolutist state and the radical break with the monarchic clerical world. This became possible with the revolution in philosophy (during the era of enlightenment) and the national movement of the bourgeoisie with its idea of a nation state. Both, the impetus of revolutionary emancipation and Hobbesian pessimism were midwives of the project of modernism. The European idea of the 'nation state' proved to be an ambitious and not very peaceful endeavour.

Conditions for the Making of Nation-States

Since the French revolution the nation has been seen as a horizontal relationship of brotherhood (*fraternity* in *liberty* and *equality*). This important element may explain why masses of people were ready to die in the name of their nation.[6] Even in Europe itself several notable deviations from above seven preconditions were occurring. This also concerns the way

ethno-national unification processes have been structured. My key
hypothesis is that for most conditions for the idea of the nation-state there
was no correspondent adequate base outside of Europe. There were a series
of (pre-) conditions for the making of nation-states:

1. A nation with potentially unified ethnic base
2. An often violent process of unification, which results in ethno-cultural
    homogenisation
3. A demarcated and limited territory
4. Ideally geographical and ethnic boundaries are congruent
5. A national bourgeoisie and a political will to struggle for so-called
    national interests (allegedly not identical with class interests)
6. The claim of national sovereignty, as usage of the collective key
    principle of freedom, directed against the predominance of supra-
    national religious beliefs
7. The element of formal equality of all members of an imagined nation,
    independent of real equity and divorced from the exploitation of
    farmers and workers.

The concept of the nation has shown fairly early its ambivalence as a political category. During the area of enlightenment the nation was seen as a
state erecting community of people. The French revolution brought as a
result the constitution of a class, the *Thiers État*, as a nation. Further
development sprung from the nation to the Unity State. All so-called backward local identities could only be violently subjugated to the hegemony of
the emerging nation state. In some areas violent resistance was the order of
the day. In the rural region of the Vendée for instance a rebellion of the
lower gentry against the revolution (having its base among the urban
sectors of the French society) was violently repressed. The Vendée-
syndrome but was positively turned upside down: the nation emerges in
violent struggles. The French nation came into being under the influence of
revolutionary changes resulting from its opposing parts, a violent process
that is until today not a closed process (as violent resistance in Corsica,
civil resistance in Brittany and cultural resurgence in the South of France
might show).

   The European nationalism of the 19th century was the political expression of the emerging bourgeoisie and the liberal citizen movements. Its
degeneration into national chauvinism turned Europe into killing fields. In a
global perspective Europe was the main theatre of wars since 1500.[7]
Europe accounts for two third of all war-related victims. In total close to
hundred million people died in European 'tribal wars' or became victims of
so-called 'ethnic cleansing'.

The Career of an Export Product

Regarding the impact of the idea of nation state on the political organisation and statehood elsewhere we may only speak of in the framework of asymmetrical relationships of power. The proliferation of stereotypical integration forms of the modern nation state outside Europe began with military force and was imposed by violent means. The definition of the political realm was done under condition of exclusion or with marginal participation of educational elites of the subjected society societies.

The new states of the colonised World were subsequently enlarging the exclusive club of sovereign states. From the mid 19th century the new states of Latin America became part of the sovereign states, followed by some by a few nominally socialist states of the Second World (from 1917 onwards) and followed in the mid 20th century by the Afro-Asiatic states of the Third World. These cases of state building do not exclude latecomers. The unity states in Germany and Italy only were only erected after the first wave of Latin American states joining the club. No state, not even the huge Chinese Empire, could sustain totally outside of these processes of colonial subjugation and separation of the world.[8] The first capitalist globalization, the European colonial expansion, did not succeed to penetrate as deep into the subjected societies of Asia and Africa as in the Americas. Colonialism failed to end the existence of several social formations. However, it succeeded in modifying indigenous forms of statehood.

In all rule the colonisers and the large colonial companies had no interest in a total control as long as the foreign economies could the streamlined according to their economic interest, their claim of sovereignty and colonial mastery. Reflecting the different conditions of the genesis of modern statehood in Europe and its resulting immediate consequences for the Colonial World, different colonial trajectories can be distinguished.

Diverse political systems of subjected nations and nationalities were the reason for structurally different forms of resistance against military penetration by European powers:

- Formerly acephalous societies had a leading role in anti-colonial movements (compare the works of Amilcar Cabral) and continued to resist in a bitter and ongoing struggle against assertions by post-colonial states.
- Transitional societies often revolted in anarchic resistance.
- Societies with relatively weak states (e.g., sacred kingdoms) organised resistance if a strongman (chief, *mtemi* or king) or a spiritual leader gave the order.

- Other historic types of statehood produced different forms of resistance that was ranking from the sustained resistance of ethnically almost homogeneous, irrigation-based societies of Eastern Asia against foreign intruders, as in China, Japan and Vietnam, to the defenceless collapse of ethnically heterogeneous tributary systems, as in Mexico and Peru.

One of the most revealing observations in my research into ethno-nationalism has been the repeated indication of massive support for (or the actual creation of) ethnic resistance-movements by members of previously stateless societies. It is my thesis that the dichotomy between (formerly) acephalous and centrally organized peoples persists. The differing capacities for opposition of acephalous and centrally organized peoples are empirically on solid basis. It manifests itself in a much greater participation in ethno-national movements and anti-regime struggles by, for example, members of segmentary pastoral societies in Africa, acephalous Hill Tribes in South-East Asia, or indigenous egalitarian-communitarian communities in America, than in societies with a centralized system of rule either in the more restricted region concerned or in the same country. The resistance of acephalous nations, as contrasted with the collaboration of chiefs and kings, is illustrated by the struggle of the Ogoni in Nigeria and of the Konkomba in Ghana.[9]

Rigidly centralised state societies, especially those with far reaching ethnical homogeneity and long state traditions, staged successful resistance; such states command over high organisation, internal coherence and a disciplined population. The Confucian-Buddhist cultural complex plays a decisive role.[10] A few pre-colonial states could survive. In the Third World the identity of pre-colonial and post-colonial states could only exceptionally be seen.[11]

Post-colonial Legitimacy Crisis in the New States

The post-colonial adoption and utilisation of the colonial repressive apparatus by the new elites remains to be interpreted as result of an integrated concept and the principle of political dominance. The new raison d'état grew out but this relationship in natural form since the existence of stateless spaces was not foreseen in the colonial design. The new states' crisis of legitimacy was pre-programmed: states as the expression of nations interpreted as imaginary political communities (Anderson) were not invented in the sense of non- real but produced. Such states were obligatory repressive communities of distinct peoples, by design (as Anthony Smith would put it). They produced separatism as a logical reaction on series of assertions such as absolute national sovereignty, control of civil society, the constitutive monopoly of legitimate violence, and the right to expropriate economic resources.[12]

Emergency Cases in the New World Disorder: Separatism and State Failure

Separatism as an emergency case and security threat within the structure of the colonial world order became one of the dominant political problems of our times. The process of state foundation and nation building in the Third World is 'an important dimension for the explanation of military conflicts'.[13] Senghaas saw separatism not as a typical problem of the Third World alone, as it can be seen in parts of the Second World (e.g. in the Former Soviet Union and in Yugoslavia). Many authors tend to forget that the upsurge of separatism and warfare is nothing unknown to Europe. The state building was a process of unequal timing and dominated the grand lines of development over centuries. The so-called 'nation building' was an extremely violent process.

The emergency case of separatism began immediately after an often very short process of decolonisation. In several cases secession took place at the same time the new states were in the making. The most illustrative example is arguably the separation of British India in autumn 1947, ending in a disastrous slaughter. The imaginary linked with new statehood—in a multi-national setting characterising India—might be seen in the figure of Cyril Radcliffe, the man 'who knew nothing about India', but decided with his drawing of state boundaries about the plight of entire peoples.[14]

Decolonisation and the Rise of Internal Strife

Some violent conflicts obviously would not have broken out without conflict potentials accumulated in pre-colonial times. Such dormant conflicts were not only revived in South Asia but in other regions of the Third World, sometimes immediately after the retreat of the colonial powers. Today's 55 states of Africa are almost without exception pure colonial creations. Internal strife broke out in an astonishing short time. Where the decolonisation has been delayed—as in the Portuguese colonial empire—several versions of state collapse were significant. In the Portuguese colonies the anti-colonial liberation wars of the 1960s began in the mid-1970s (without noticeable breaks but superficially) to mutate into ideologically caused civil wars and Cold War proxy conflicts, until they became protracted ethno-national conflicts (as in Angola), or foreign instigated bloody de-stabilisation wars (as in Mozambique). Both countries are illustrative for what is called state failure.[15] In Angola successive government has never been able to control the entire country, including the strongholds of the UNITA, and it was only after the UNITA head Savimbi was killed in action early in 2002 and a truce signed that Angola would finally become one country. Foreign state aggression by regional powers (as Indonesia under the Suharto dictatorship and in complicity with USA) subdued and occupied former colonial territories such as East Timor and West Papua. Many of the mentioned Separation and partition of 'what does not fit together' often takes place after a few years of independence (as the secession of Bangladesh or the partition of Guinea-Bissau and Cap Verde).

In the Third World there is no place and no society not having suffered from colonial legacies and the deformation of indigenous structures by colonialism.[16] This is equally true for nominally non-colonised areas such as Ethiopia. The colonial legacies are often present in such a way, that even today we get the impression, as if the colonial occupants would have left just yesterday. Internal colonialism began right from the beginning. In many new states the indigenous clients of the colonials were drawn from privileged ethnic groups which have in the colonial plan and under the policy of divide and rule been created as dominant groups. These client political classes clung to the power they inherited from their masters.

The colonial powers left ethnocratic and authoritarian regimes as their successors. In a few colonies genuine liberation movements came to power. The vertical integration of colonial economies into the world market conserved relationships of dependency in many states, as it may seem, 'for ever'. Under-development is in some world regions a condition and not a phase. Incomplete and asymmetric economies that are mainly export oriented run high risk. They tend to reproduce and aggravate harsh social contradictions and ethnic cleavages. Under-development combined with ethnic cleavages produces permanent political instability.

In the 1980s the complex combination of partly contradictional developments aggravated the crisis of many new states. A number of countries were weakened by the debt crisis and changing geopolitical constellations, resulting from attempts to reform the nominally socialist block during Gorbachov's *Perestroika*. Increasingly higher pressure for democratisation in the South caused deeper conflicts between state and civil society.[17] Besides conflicts, which are notorious for their particularistic character, such as nationalist, ethnic, religious, ideological, and racial conflicts, two other main types of intra-state conflicts were developed. These types are the anti-regime conflicts as well as conflicts caused by economic under development, unequal resource distribution and ecological destruction, aggravated by an increasing confrontation of winners and losers of the globalization process.

The Democracy Deficit

The democracy deficit in a large number of Third World countries did not get much attention by the Western media and the political class until recently—with the notable exception of human rights organisations. Such deficits were seen as secondary to the imperatives of development. In the case of pro-Western development dictatorships the former colonial powers were keeping silence on human rights violations, even massive ones. Democracy and respect for human rights were sacrificed for the 'higher goals' of development and future prosperity. However, the abysmal failure of development aspirations in most Third World countries finally deprived the political class of the very basis of their ideology of 'development first'.

Perestroika launched under Gorbachev culminated in democratic change in the Soviet Union and put Western donors under pressure. From 1990 Western type democratisation was increasingly demanded, and, from 1993 onwards, the West increasingly put pressure on Third World regimes in an attempt to force them to introduce democratic procedures. This became an official policy after the Francophone summit in La Baule 1990. The so-called *Paristroika*, a democratisation from above, dictated by Paris to the West African states, had an ambiguous impact. Its effects were of a very contrary nature.

'Democratisation' in situation of high tension can lead to new spirals of violence. Slavish copies of Western democracy and freedom of expression can have most disastrous impacts, as illustrated in the most shocking way by the example of Rwanda.[18] Civilian opposition and popular movements accuse democracy deficits in Third World states. Euro-centric schools of political science are still taking the nation state as civilization progress and guarantee for institutionalised democracy. Most scholars failed to recognise the fundamentally despotic character of most postcolonial states. Amnesty International in its annual reports frequently accuses almost two thirds of all states of gross human rights violations. Masses of citizens are becoming vulnerable to be victimised by arbitrate state repression and they are forced to survive in conditions of total of lawlessness and insecurity.

The National Dilemma, Hybrid Nationalism and Failed Development

The career of a successful concept (Anderson) was having series of negative impacts. The 'imagined communities' and the making of the nation state seem to have produced more problems than it was able to solve, particularly in the Third World as well as in parts of the former socialist world. The export of the European concept of nation-state to the former colonies has created enduring and great difficulties. Much of these difficulties are inherent to the concept as such. Or were been produced by its imposition on conditions which were not conductive or receptive for the idea of a nation state. Additional difficulties resulted from lack of adoption of the concept by the new state class as well as. The undermining of the base of legitimacy was crucial. Development nationalism without development has to lose its legitimacy within short periods of time.

On the level of political economy the claim for total sovereignty by the new nation states proved as a particular dilemma. Such claims became hollow after propagandistically induced expectations of future prosperity were pitilessly dashed by the continuation of colonial dependency and the integration into a hierarchical alien world economy. On the level of geo-political structures the nation states are confronted with the practical impossibility of modifying or reforming their political core structure. Key concepts remained without solid base in their respective culture. However, the structural characteristics had developed and became an unmoveable object. The irreversibility of state structures has more to do with its logic then with its concrete form. The term of irreversibility carries no judgement on the sustainability and viability of state structures.

The debate about the dilemma of nationhood, nationalism and nation-state is far from being a closed issue.[19] The process of assimilation and military subjugation in the making of homogeneous ethnic substrate of nations remained even in Europe incomplete, in most Third World countries a homogeneous ethnic basis of the nation state remains in most cases simply an illusion.

In reality, nation building was since 1945 no more than state building. The 'official nationalism' (Seton-Watson) or they 'secondary development nationalism' (Senghaas) was a systematic and even a 'Macchiavelistic ideology' (Anderson). They nationalist enthusiasm in the first euphoric phase of independence not of long duration in most new states. Models of official nationalism or development nationalism followed European blueprints to different degrees. An acquired somewhat own character based on its own grammar developed as a totalising screen was put on everything considered to be 'under the real or possible control of the state'.[20]

The Official Nationalism and Its Sacred Cows

European ideas of the nation, the modern state and the nation state became a reality on word scale not because such abstract collective units have been seen as 'modern' beyond its euro-centric signification. Gellner qualified the definition of the state by Weber as euro-centric, seen as agency above society and in possession of the monopoly of legitimate violence.[21]

The most trivial reason for military violence and superior technology with the help of which the European powers introduced their ideas during 500 years in other places on earth, in crude way in the first phase and later be deploying more sophisticated colonial techniques. Colonial rule had to be legitimised, increasingly so after the upsurge of anti-colonial nationalism. The nationalists not only wanted to takeover the colonial state but also its techniques and its symbols of power.[22] Imported European ideologies of legitimacy were instrumental for smoke-screening the class interests of the new state leadership—but proved to be fragile.

Anti-colonial nationalists were almost always ready to identify with the European model of the nation state as long as it concerned the sacred cows of statehood, namely *national sovereignty*, *territorial integrity*, more or less consequent *secularity* and the constitutive ideology of *modernity*. Claims to total control and absolute sovereignty launched by local elites were legitimised by efforts for nation building and the struggle for modernity.

The official nationalism in the South was formed as a product of negative dialectics between own elements and mixed forms. In many cases the 'product' would have had the approval of the colonial administration. But some of the strongest nationalist movements in the Third World were either rejecting colonial designs or shifting away from the European colonial blueprints, in order to increase adaptation to local conditions. In the case of pre-colonial empires the attempts of modelling own brands of nationalism were fairly significant.

Failure of Collective Efforts to Overcome the Nation-State Project

For the nationalist movements in the South, then called the Third World, the European imagination prevailed in its model character simply because attractive alternatives failed. This failure restrained the political and economic space of manoeuvre for most new states, especially in Africa.[23] Following the Second World War the system confrontation between East and West increasingly narrowed the political space. Alternatives to the European colonial legacy had already taken shape from the 1840s, with the plan of Simon Bolivar to unify the entire Hispanic America.

The character of alternative roads to self-centred development began to change fundamentally with the global confrontation of the Cold War and its ideological battles. Anti-colonial alternatives such as Panafricanism in the 1950s, the idea of uniting the Arab nation and other regional projects failed repeatedly. The same happened to economic alternatives. Some countries in the Third World took independent non-capitalist roads to development. Mostly they were following the Chinese or Soviet model—with limited success. The Non-aligned Movement (NAM), a broad coalition of 113 developing countries with differing ideologies and purposes, and its attempts for an economic pact among UN member states from the South were sabotaged by the western powers. Many projects for collective self-reliance as well as other South-to-South-relations failed, often after the first lukewarm attempts, a few succeeded. ECOWAS, SADC and COMESA in Africa, MERCOSUR in South America and (to a lesser degree) ASEAN in Southeast Asia were relatively successful. It remains to be seen if the stepwise implementation of the 1991 Abuja treaty for the African Economic Community will be successful and realize the ambitious project of an African Union. Such types of regional co-operation schemes were in contradiction to the existing vertical structure of the post-colonial world economy. The export orientation of most Third World countries, the particular self-interest of the new state classes, the institutional links to the former colonial mother states and ongoing 'imperial interests' were all standing against attempts of regional co-operation.

The failure or the weakness of many projects of regional integration was even more deplorable as such forms of multilateral or supra-state co-operation could have developed as a veritable counter weight to the multiplication and fragmentation of the post-colonial new states. The influence of the fatal failure of radical alternatives, such as forms of regional integration and co-operation in the South, were seen as complementary to the fragmentation of the new states. It was not until the 1990s, and the ever increasing constitution of regional blocks, which ironically seemed to give the developed countries a lead again, that the developing world understood the necessity of South-South cooperation. The implementation of the North American Free Trade Agreement (NAFTA) since early 1994 and the removal of most barriers to trade and investment among the United States, Canada, and Mexico, and the even more far-reaching transformation of the European Community into the European Union, a common marked and a monetary union, with the Euro as new currency for most European countries since January 2002, and the enlargement process towards the East, put the North-North cooperation ahead of attempts to South-South cooperation.

The East Against the Trend: Emerging Asia and the Chinese Wonders

Apart from Europe and its settler colonies (USA, Australia, New Zealand) only Northeast Asia (Japan, South Korea and China since mid 1980s) has achieved high economic growth and political stability over a longer period. Vietnam joined that trend after overcoming its socio-economic crisis looming from mid 1980s onwards. There is a degree of correlation between prosperity and stability on one side and relative ethno-national homogeneity, indigenous state-building and certain civilizational pre-dispositions on the other side.[24] To a lesser degree and on the base of a much more heterogeneous ethno-national composition the Indian Union also achieved steady economic growth and relative political stability despite internal conflicts and ongoing increasing confrontation with Pakistan, due to the Kashmir issue, rising nationalism and the extremely dangerous nuclearization of the subcontinent.

The anti-colonial movement in British India had a pan-ethnic, secular character. However, this could not prevent the disastrous partition of British India. Subsequently the Indian Union gained political profile. India invented a policy of self-reliance and self-centred development while Pakistan failed to develop an equally stable identity. The South Asian Regional Co-operation (SARC) developed some dynamics and could well become a common project of economic pacification between the Indian Union, Pakistan, Bangladesh and some smaller states. Since the late 1980s India is enjoying a moderate but constant growth. India will be among the giant economies of the future. According to estimates India's economy might rank fourth in 2030, after China, the EU and the USA, and ahead of Japan.

The nationalist movement and the socialist revolution in China forged the combination of elements such as an adapted Western-type of modernity with their own band of specific Chinese cultural and state traditions. Confucianism was amalgamated with capitalist management methods and produced the 'Chinese economic wonder'. The 'One Child Policy' was largely successful and enabled faster development. The transformation to a socialist market economy since 1978 and sustainable economic growth at a staggering high rate (partly double-digit growth rates and above ten percent average growth per annum 1982–2002) have also accelerated certain negative dynamics. China continued to prosper throughout the 1990 and became the world economy's strongest driving force, even in times of the 'Asian crisis' 1997, which hit Southeast Asia and Korea, while Japan's economy has stagnated and contracted since the early 1990s and most Western countries also saw negative growth. End 2001 China joined the WTO, an overdue step for the world's largest producer of consumer goods. Especially the highly developed coastal regions saw an unprecedented boom based on an ever more dynamic economy of scale, the interlinkage of industrial clusters and the rapid use of advanced technologies, transforming China's coastal regions into the 'factory of the world'.[25]

However, some of the growth works to the detriment of cultural self-reliance and the originality of the Chinese way to industrial and high tech development. The expanding gap between the richer Western and Southern regions and the poorer and partly underdeveloped Eastern and Northern regions poses a long-term threat if ethnicized. Mounting differences between social classes unknown a decade ago, including immense corruption and enrichment of a few, as well as large East-West migration of workers and super-exploitation by rogue entrepreneurs pose short-term threats for social peace and stability. However, there is awareness of these problems, which are exposed and debated publicly. The two Chinese economies might be unified in the year 2020, at a time when China will make-up the world's largest market.[26]

The revolutionary anti-colonial movement in Vietnam proved one of the most powerful world-wide. It was able to win costly wars against some of the strongest nations (France and USA) as well as to defend the country against China's brief military aggression. After its victory in 1974 and the end of the disastrous war against USA the Vietnamese people had to rebuild their devastated country. The serious economic crisis of stagnation and hyperinflation (1987: 774 percent) was tackled by introducing *Doi Moi*, a reform policy of renovation.[27] A successful land reform made Vietnam the world's third largest rice exporter.[28] Controlled democratisation was part of the change.[29] Since 1991 Vietnam is enjoying constant growth (of eight percent per annum) and has regained political stability. The country will be among the *new tigers* and the most driving economies of ASEAN in the future.

After giving up their relative isolation and their narrow special relations to the former USSR, India and Vietnam introduced reforms and both countries reached stable development and political stability in the 1990s. Newly industrialised countries in Southeast Asia, namely the three Chinese tiger economies of Taiwan, Singapore and Hong Kong (until reunification in 1997), as well as South Korea, remained politically and economically closely linked to the West, though Taiwan developed strong economic relations with mainland China. From the 1970s onwards they achieved a visible economic success. Three medium-size tigers, Malaysia, Thailand and Vietnam as well as the giant *tiger candidate* named Indonesia, all seem to follow their tracks.[30]

The great dragon (China) has well understood the lesson the tigers were teaching it but since 1997 it is the tigers' turn to learn their lesson. China gave new meaning to official language of *Newly Industrialising Countries* (NIC). Notably, one of China's specifics is that its growth was never dependent from Western capital, thus, it did not suffer from the 1997 Asian crisis, it did also not devaluate its currency and it was even ready to help badly hit Thailand out wit loans. The bulk of China's growth was self-generated. The Overseas Chinese community, Taiwan and South Korea accounted for most foreign investment until the late 1990s, and foreign investment remained of modest size compared to China's giant and fast growing economy.

After the 1997 crash in Asia's stock markets, devaluation of currencies and ecological devastation caused by Indonesia's burning rainforests the *Asian Miracle* seemed to have lost its nimbus. Additionally Japan's severe economic problems had already started to appear since the early 1990s. The fear that Asia's growth might not be sustainable was caused by several deficiencies. First, the depletion of resources proved economically short-sighted; the cost of rapid industrial growth in terms of environmental damage will prove too high. Second, growing inequality might develop into a dangerous threat for the social fabric and long-term political stability across South-East Asia and well into China. Third, the peripherization of some regions already led to large-scale migration of workers and will further increase massive cross-boundary migration in Asia. Easy access privileged certain geographical areas. The coastal areas of China boom at the detriment of the western rural areas. Growing income gaps will further increase migration, within China as well as across Southeast Asia. More future mega-cities with some 20 million inhabitants (like Tokyo and soon Shanghai) will deeply impact on culture and lifestyles and may affect the quality of life for hundreds of millions.

Some of the current trends may become socially disruptive. This would have particular impacts since the continuation of the *Asian Miracle* in China, Southeast Asia and parts of South Asia is entirely linked to the human factor: a flexible and hardworking labour force, well educated, motivated, apt to adapt to changes brought by globalization, with a lively entrepreneurial spirit and a high acceptance of world market discipline.[31]

Business leaders and international bankers seem to have learned some lessons. In the wake of all-out globalization there seems more acceptance for the 'invisible hand' and the social role for the state in Asia.[32] Taxation can again be seen as a legitimate social-political instrument.[33] The debate on *Asian Values* in the late 1990s has reflected the fact that rapid change and high rates of economic growth are threatening traditional values (based on Confucianism or Hinduism)[34] and are about to change 'virtually every dimension of life'.[35] Meanwhile the talk about *Asian Values* had to be differentiated since Asia is far from being a homogenous world region.

Weak Self-reliance and Embryonic Regional Co-operation in the South

A few historic examples may illustrate the negative dialectics between official nationalism and the failure of non-conform alternatives. Such political models were designed in order to overcome the ideological, political and economic limitations of the nation state project in the South.

The liberation struggles in Latin America from 1809 to 1824 did not lead to the rise of a Latin American common identity but to the endless search of such an identity. In the struggle of Bolivarism versus Monroeism the latter remained victorious. Until the present day Europe still provides the main model for the ruling elites in most Latin American countries. For centuries Europe was slavishly imitated. It was because of this adherence to Europe why most new Afro-Asiatic states saw Latin America as being an integral part of the West (means the Christian Occident).

Latin America was not represented in Bandung 1955 as the 'third path' of non-alliance was taken enthusiastically by most liberated countries, under the leadership of Nasser, Tito and Nehru. Accordingly the Latin American states were not seen as part of the Third World and they did not easily identify themselves as part of it.[36] Attempts to establish regional co-operation were welcomed by most states but had limited follow-up.

As for Eurasia the modernising effect of the Russian revolution was characterised by forceful and rapid development of industrial production. Despite devastation suffered in two world wars stunning rates of industrial growth sustained from the 1920s until the 1960s. The Soviet Union was almost approaching the industrial and technological level of Western countries; in some areas, such as space technology (the Sputnik shock), the USSR remained competitive until the 1970s. The price for the rapid rise of the USSR to become an industrial and great power was the prevalence of an authoritarian political regime.

The Soviet type of nationhood and the Leninist nationality policy were defining the way the union disintegrated (according to its ethno-political structure) at the end of the 1980s, without determining future developments in the non-Russian republics. In the new post-Soviet states an awful wave of discriminating new minorities began immediately after the dissolution of the Soviet Union. The present political fragmentation was essentially the result of a long period of economic and political stagnation since the 1970s (the Brezhnev era). But stagnation was followed by the introduction of wild capitalism, resulting in a devastating crash of the industrial and agrarian production and a free fall of almost all economies in the CIS and in Eastern Europe. Industrial production shrunk by an average of 50 percent and Third World style mass poverty became the lot of millions.[37]

After having escaped the turmoil of decolonisation, Indonesia until the military coup in 1965, Vietnam, Ghana, Tanzania, Algeria after 1956 and some other Afro-Asian countries were changing directions, as the Turkish state did earlier under Mustafa Kemal (Ataturk) in the 1920s and the Arabic world started during Nasser's rule in Egypt in the 1950s. Most mentioned countries have developed their own brand of official nationalism and self-centred politics without separating from European-based models of modernity. With the exception of some Asian countries their economic performance was much less successful than their political appeal to self-reliance.

Anti-colonial movements in the rest of the Third World, mainly in Sub-Saharan Africa, the Caribbean, Central Asia and Melanesia (Western Asia-Pacific), has since 1950 only exceptionally revived own state traditions and amalgamated them with European models. Most new states at the periphery are ethnically extremely diverse; their political systems are heterogeneously structured. As states they remained rather hybrid. Compared to East Asia these states have mostly been under a longer period of European colonial influence. The conditions of take-off for such states (with the possible exception of a few Caribbean mini-states and Arabian oil emirates) were economically rather unpromising. A change of status from a dependent periphery to become a pro-active independent actor was attempted by some governments with limited success.

Summary and Conclusions

Most developing countries of the southern hemisphere remained for the most part without any successful self-controlled economic growth as base for political stability. The official nationalism failed to satisfy its own aspirations of achieving an acceptable degree of development and to safeguard peace and security. In most countries the struggle against poverty was lost in the 1990s. At the start of the 21st century the UN Millennium Summit declared the eradication of poverty, 'War No More', and the protection of the environment as priority goals of combined efforts by civil society, governments, and the United Nations in this century.[38]

The sacred cows of statehood have been slaughtered: IMF dictate of economic policies undermined *national sovereignty*. Rebel movements perforated *territorial integrity*. *Secularity* was given up in many countries that feared religious fundamentalism; some were giving in to demands of conservative or fundamentalist religious movements. The ideology of *modernity* proved hollow compared to the harsh conditions of survival.

Exceptions from the rule are China first, then India, some Asian tiger economies (riddled by the 1997 crisis but rapidly recovering) and socialist Vietnam. The rate of savings is most impressive in East Asia, and it is very high compared to Africa and Latin America. Today the former Third World is far from representing a unitary block. Differences between the world regions in the South seem to become greater rather than to diminish.

The magic term of *self-reliance* is today not often heard; the term of collective self-reliance has bluntly disappeared. Projects such as an *African Economic Community* (possibly in the framework of the OAU's project of an African Union) or of an *Islamic Common Market* from Turkey to Pakistan are in an embryonic state and both might not be viable concepts.

To unite Africa it would need a different set of leaders and a strong grass-roots movement for an African renaissance. Disorder in Africa and the Islamic world seems in striking contrast to the high and ever increasing degree of co-operation in the framework of the European Union.

Notes

1. Large formations, today—on a macro level—with somewhat more appeal renamed civilizations (Huntington 1993), were existing over ages and centuries.
2. Subtypes of acephalous egalitarian or stateless societies: 1) Vigilant segmentary societies such as nomadic pastoralists in Africa, hill tribes of South East Asia and hunters in the Americas. 2) Peaceful, defenceless or retreating societies such as communitarian indigenous peoples of the Americans and the Nordic areas of Russia as well as hunters & gatherers e.g. pygmies, K'hoi, Negritos, rainforest peoples of South East Asia, Africa and the Americas.
3. For 'hydro societies' Karl Wittfogel introduced the notion of *Oriental Despotism*, based on the so-called Asian Mode of Production. See: Wittfogel 1977, 47
4. As a concept and as political belief unilinearism was inspired by the historically unprecedented colonial expansion of the 19th century. The concept has failed, including the political church it submitted, no matter if affirmative or not. The summary of this historic debate was given by Gianni Sofri in his work 'On the Asian mode of production' (Frankfurt (EVA) 1972).
5. For a thorough critique of Samuel P. Huntington's concepts, including a revealing re-evaluation of his empirical data, see 'The Fairytale of the Clash of Civilization' in Scherrer 1997: 47–99.
6. In former Yugoslavia there was again a struggle for the 'nation' in the narrow sense. People were willing to give their lives for such an abstract idea.
7. Of 142 million casualties from 1500 to 1990 there were 93.3 million people dying on European Killing Fields. 50 million people died as a result of the European expansion. (Eckhardt 1991, 20).
8. Great powers and empires such as Tsarist Russia or China had themselves colonial or other influence areas in their neighbourhood. However both could not remain outside of the historical process dominated by the West European powers. Territorial and influence boundaries were internment from the 19 centuries by Western powers. Great China lost all vassal states to France (Vietnam and the whole of Indochina), Great Britain (Tibet, parts of Burma), Portuguese (Macao) and temporary to the German empire (only a coastal strip). China and Japan had to open exterritorial trade areas; they had to face interference in their own affairs and even all-out aggression (the Opium War against China). Perhaps the West will one day pay for the oppression of the past centuries (Galtung, in: Scherrer 1991 a, 12).
9. See chapter 5 in Scherrer 1997, 194–275.
10. Compare: Galtung, in: ECOR paper 3 / 1990, Scherrer 1991a.
11. Continuous statehood is most notably in the case of Asia's irrigation-based societies (China, Vietnam, Java, India, Sri Lanka, etc). The latter ones are part of the most endurable states of the old and new history. In Africa the durability of irrigation-based states can be maintained in the case of Egypt. See: Smith 1991, Nations by design?, 99–122; Wittfogel 1977, 513 f.
12. In view of Benedict Anderson's provocative thesis Ruth McVey named separatism a 'figment of the imagination of the nation-state' (McVey 1984, 3). See: 'Separatism and

the paradoxes of the nation-state in perspective'. In: Lim Joo-Jock and Vani (eds.): Armed separatism in South-east Asia. Singapore (ISAS) 1984, 3–29.

13. Senghaas 1988, 165
14. Collins, Larry and Dominique Lapierre: Freedom at midnight. New York (AVON) 1975.
15. See Bayart *et al.* 1999.
16. The social and economic structures of most societies in the Third World were deeply deformed by colonialism and the neo-colonialism of 'Structural Adjustment Programmes' of IMF.
17. To monopolize the concept of civil society for the West could only be an expression of arbitrary assessment and misconception. Civilian popular movements have forced the fall of dictatorship in many Third World countries. Compared to the militarism and to the repressive character of many periphery states their societies seem to appear even more 'civilian'.
18. For the devastating impact of democratization from above in Central Africa, mainly in Rwanda and Burundi, see: Scherrer 2002a (*Genocide and Crisis in Central Africa*), 43–48, 70, 78–79, 88–89, 97, 122, 128, 179, 201–3, 222, 354; concerning the escalation dynamics in Rwanda from 1990 to 1994, which led to the total genocide in that country, see ibid., 87–92.
19. E.g., Rocker, Gellner, Seton-Watson, Anderson, Senghaas, Satha-Anand, and Smith.
20. Anderson 1991, 209
21. Gellner calls Weber's definition 'valid now, however strangely ethno-centric it may be as a general definition' (Gellner 1983, 4).
22. In his essay on English and Dutch colonial tactics Anderson wrote in 1989 about the role of the colonial state in producing official nationalism. He was looking at different fields of activity, such as the categorisation of census (taken the Malay example, which became increasingly racist), the demarcation of borders, the 'logification' of territories and symbols of history, as well as the archaeological archiving of ancient monuments, material culture and their usage for legitimising colonial and post-colonial rule.
23. See Bayart *et al.* 1999. Chabal and Daloz titled 'Disorder as political instrument'.
24. Japan and Korea are among the largest nation-states with ethnic homogeneity of some 97 percent each while China (with 93 percent Han Chinese) is certainly a multi-ethnic state but only at its peripheries. All three countries are ancient states and are culturally embedded in long traditions of Buddhism and Confucianism.
25. See the highly interesting article by Kojima Akira ('Return of the Dragon: China, factory of the world', in Japan Echo, February 2002, 34–37), with recurs on scholarly debate on economy and analysis and findings of the May 2001 White Paper by the Japanese Ministry of Economy, Trade and Industry (METI, former MITI); see http://www.meti.go.jp/english/report/data/gWP2001cpe.html.
26. China is understood as composed of the mainland (incl. Hong Kong) and Taiwan.
27. With *Doi Moi* Vietnam changed from a centrally planned economy with 12,000 highly subsidised state companies to a mixed market economy. Today there are five sectors (instead of 2): pubic sector, co-operatives, rural economy (with 10 million households getting using right for land), state capitalist sector (6,000 companies) and private capitalist sector (incl. foreign companies). Compare: Nguyen Duy Quy: 'Renovation in Vietnam'. Copenhagen (NIAS) 10/1997.
28. In 1999 some 70 percent of Vietnam's labour was still linked to agriculture, artisanal fisheries and forestry. Today Vietnam produces around 30 million tons of rice (compared to 20 m tons previously). The land reform provided ten million households with the rights of usage, transfer, land exchange, leasing, getting credit for production and the right to grow what can be sold on the free market. The success in production had

positive impacts on the wellbeing of the population (still suffering from massive devastation induced by the war) and the environment (massive reforestation projects).

29. Vietnam has still got a one-party-system, seen by some as 'presently quite suitable' (Dui Quy). After changing the constitution in 1992 the Vietnamese got the right to elect their representatives on all levels. From 450 MPs of the National Assembly 26 percent are women and 20 percent are not members of the unity party, e.g. representatives of religious communities such as Buddhists, Christians, Muslims or Traditionalists (Gadism and Wa How). Some 34 of the country's 54 official minorities and ethnic groups are represented.

30. The *Newly Industrialising Countries* in South-east Asia have in some industrial fields draw near to reach the level of the OSCE-countries (Nohlen/Nuscheler 1992, 15) and have taken over the former Socialist World, as well as some EU countries such as Portugal, Ireland and Greece, according to per-capita income.

31. Asian Development Bank: Emerging Asia. Chances and challenges. Manila (ADB) 1997. Bruce Koppel: 'Submerging Asia? Policies, politics, and the future of the Asian Miracle'. Copenhagen (Mimeo). Pierre Uhel: 'Challenges for Asia in the next 30 years'. Copenhagen (NIAS) 10/1997.

32. Joseph Stiglitz, chief economist of the World Bank, pointed out—in a World Bank publication—that 'in East Asia the basis for the amazing achievements and the miracle, which has no precedent, is that governments took major responsibility for the promotion of economic growth, abandoning the religion that markets know best, and intervening to enhance technology transfer, relative equality, education, health, along with industrial planning and coordination, and in fact strict capital controls until they were forced to relinquish them in the last few years' (Noam Chomski: 'Whose World Order: Conflicting Visions', University of Calgary, Sept 1998, www.zmag.org/chomsky/).

33. 'The World Bank just discovered the state six months ago' (Pierre Uhel in his speech at NIAS, Copenhagen, 31 October 1997.

34. Kanishka Jayasuriya: 'Approaches to the Asian values debate'. Murdoch: Asia Research Centre, Murdoch University 1997

35. 'Asia is in the midst of an economic and social transformation unrivalled in history. In East Asia especially, stunning rates of economic growth sustained over many years and have changed virtually every dimension of life.' ADB 1997, p 1.

36. Until today some Latin American countries are not members of the Non-Aligned Movement (NAM). However, the Afro-American dominated Caribbean states and Cuba are members of NAM, but not the largest Hispano-American states of Brazil, Mexico, Argentine and Venezuela, smaller states such as Uruguay, Paraguay, Dominican Republic and some of the Central American States remain outside NAM (exceptions are the Black American dominated Belize and Guyana; Columbia, Nicaragua under the Sandinistas, later followed by Guatemala and Honduras; Bolivia, Peru and Panama).

37. 'Many of the countries with rising inequality are those in Eastern Europe and the CIS that suffered low or negative growth in the 1990s' (2001 Human Development Report).

38. See Millennium Forum 2000. UNDP 2000. In the UN declaration 'WE, the peoples' the key appeals for consideration by the summit were 'We must spare no effort to free our fellow men and women from the abject and dehumanizing poverty'. 'We must spare no effort to free our fellow men and women from the scourge of war' ... 'to free humanity from the danger of living on a planet irredeemably spoilt by human activities', e.g., by adopting 'a new ethic of conservation and stewardship' (ibid., 28–23); and, as first steps, adopting the 1997 Kyoto Protocol, with the 2001 Marrakesh compromise, ratifying it so that it can enter into force before the World Summit on Sustainable Development in Johannesburg, September 2002, and the 10th anniversary of the Earth Summit in Rio and the adoption of the UN Framework Convention on Climate Change (UNFCCC).

Chapter 2

Intra-state Conflicts and Disappearance of Clausewitzean Warfare

False nation-states and ethnocracies are ruled by dominant ethnic groups who have acquired 'possession' of the state. Their claims in regard to ethnically distinct nationalities have proved to be one of the major sources of violent conflicts since 1945. An urgent need for research is evident in the case of every subspecies of ethnically interpretable conflict—and, depending on the source consulted, these account for around two-thirds of the dominant component of all violent conflicts. In some indexes of contemporary conflict, those with an ethnic content are still listed under the shameful rubric of 'miscellaneous' or 'internal' conflicts. This is an attempt to get round the basic problem of there apparently being no clear definition of what would be an 'ethnic conflict'.

Ethnic or ethnicized conflicts may take various forms; this points to the need for some kind of classification. The ethnic factor *in itself* not only has a perplexing number of dimensions; it can also claim to be quasi-ubiquitous, in so far as it plays some sort of role in almost all multi-ethnic and pluri-cultural societies. On top of this, it often figures in combination either with conflicts between different religious communities (as in the Sudan, in the northern Nigerian pogroms, in northern Ghana, and in the struggle of the ethno-national rebels in Burma and north-east India) or—in all sorts of permutations—with various forms of anti-regime war. Mainstream conflict theory has failed to understand the power and the multi-dimensionality of the ethnic phenomena or of what is commonly called by the sociological term of 'ethnicity'. One of the traditional tasks of theory has been to classify a particular subject matter. In conflict theory the elaboration of comprehensive typologies are a requisite for advances in understanding contemporary mass violence, in times characterized by the near disappearance of the Clausewitzean warfare type of 'classic' interstate conflicts and the tremendous multiplication of intrastate conflicts. Unfortunately, conventional political science and conflict research have long failed to abandon their predominantly state-oriented view and proved unable to deliver the required typologies of war and non-war types of conflict that dominate contemporary mass violence.

For a descriptive purpose the specifically 'ethnic' element of a conflict has to be highlighted by reference to concrete examples. This is what I shall also do in the course of the next chapters. However, the general question of whether there are ethnic conflicts *per se* leads on to consideration of how such conflicts have evolved and what structural features they display. Conflicts can only be understood in their historic context, and 'ethnic conflicts', particularly ethno-nationalist conflicts, have a history, which is very often longer or much longer than the lifespan of the post-colonial states they have been challenging so fundamentally.

'Ethnic' and other Intra-state Conflicts: Chronic and Forgotten

What has been termed 'ethnic conflict' by the media has in fact little common characteristics. One type of 'ethnic conflict', what the ECOR typology defines as *interethnic conflict*, does not really challenge the state since the state is mostly not a party to it.[1] Similarly, the *gang wars and warlordism*, which are also 'ethnic' (in the common understanding) but account for a limited number of conflicts, are structurally different from the higher number of interethnic or communal conflicts; both subspecies of 'ethnic conflicts', again, are very different from the ethno-nationalist conflicts, which also recruit among disadvantaged ethnic groups but their political configuration has much more in common with the type of anti-regime conflict. All of these three types are again very different from a forth type of 'ethnic conflict', which (at least in its total and most virulent form of *genocide*) is entirely state organized and chooses members of a particular racial, national or ethnic group as victims. The lethality of this ultimate form of mass violence is the highest of all. As a result of decades of ethnicization three times more people died in the smallish state of Rwanda in 100 days than in all wars in the Former Soviet Union and Yugoslavia together since 1989.

For the purpose of conflict analysis, which goes beyond the descriptive stage of understanding conflict, the history of conflict and its root causes and mediate causes (apart from triggers) are a primary focus of research interest. Some of the basic concepts have been misunderstood; one chapter of this study is dedicated to the search for causes. What has been named 'root causes' of violent conflicts in the recent debate about complex emergencies, namely poverty and bad governance, are rather part of the general conditions or mediate causes for conflict Galtung would call structural violence. Cause and effect must be related. For instance, one integral element of colonial techniques for maintaining power was the pursuit of a policy of segregation and the preferential treatment of particular ethnic groups—with devastating effects that continue to be felt today. Since the decolonisation period, separatism and ethno-nationalism have become a pre-programmed and enduring problem in the Third World—and recently also in the former nominally socialist world.

That violent ethno-national conflicts can in most cases be traced back to the arbitrary colonial creation of new states, to the colonial policy of giving preferential treatment to, or discriminating against, particular ethnic groups, and to the post-colonial installation of ethnic power-élites, is capable of empirical demonstration and statistical expression. The fact that the colonial policy of segregation became the breeding-ground for a whole range of violent post-colonial conflicts is therefore no longer a secret. The apologists of the nation-state complain that since decolonisation, ethno-nationalism has become a real threat to survival for some Third World states. But ethno-national violence in our time is generally not only a cause but also a product of the inherent instability and precarious existence of many peripheral states.

There is a considerable dearth of research into the various subtypes of ethno-national conflict. Ethno-national conflicts are the forgotten wars, despite the fact that they make up the majority of all violent conflicts. My analysis of them takes into account: the potential for such conflicts; the actors involved in them; the history of their development; their causes; the triggers to them and the matters in contention; the shape they take; the aims of the anti-state opposition and the way this is organized; the course followed by the conflict; the resources and available military means (including weapons); and the question of outside involvement. To illustrate particular situations of conflict, I refer in each case to a range of relevant examples.

One of the most revealing observations in what will soon be ten years of research into ethno-nationalism has been the repeated indication of massive support for ethnic opposition-movements amongst members of (formerly) stateless societies. The actors involved are not only to be found amongst small communities. It is my thesis that the dichotomy between formerly acephalous and centrally organized peoples persists, and I verified this using a number of examples (Scherrer 1997, 193–275). I include in this process transitional societies that tend towards one type or the other.

Most of the fashionable new theories about 'new war' are neither based on hard evidence, for instance empiric quantitative or qualitative data, nor on sufficient understanding of the multi-dimensionality of contemporary mass violence but are rather speculative and conjunctural, exhibiting less than medium reach and use mono-causal explanations. Practical knowledge of the real conflicts would certainly contribute to inhibit overly simplistic general analysis. This is not merely a problem of lacking scientific coherence and seriousness but could well have consequences in deforming responses to violence. How one understands mass violence and war causing humanitarian crisis also determines for a good part the response to it. Much of the past failures of UN peacekeeping and humanitarian responses to complex emergencies could have been avoided if better knowledge of the nature, causes and dynamics of contemporary violence were at hand.

The post-Cold War period has seen a significant overhaul and beginning transcendence of the former war theory. Until 1998 the threat of a nuclear war seemed diminishing. Conventional war lists and the concentration of theory on war between states became gradually obsolete. The knowledge that many more people die in organized mass murder, genocides and other crimes against humanity, such as *democides, politicides* and *ethnocides*, than in wars was not yet given its proper value (in war theories). But the need to understand new forms of *civil war* (rather 'uncivil wars'), communal violence and state organized mass violence has been recognized.

In times of change the grand theories, which promise spectacular new insights, face a rapid decrease of explanation value after short periods of time. Some of the rather dubious theories such as Samuel P. Huntington's clash of civilization hardly survive the day. In a simple re-evaluation of his interpretation of empiric datasets I made rather reversed conclusions about alleged Islamic war-mongers (being in a future alliance with China against the West), and I doubt very much that future violence will occur along what Huntington calls the 'fault line' of civilizations (Scherrer 1997, 72–98). Besides theories of civilizational fault-lines, the alleged political and economic rationale of post-modern conflict, and some more intelligent variations of older big power theories there is a growing body of theory focusing on the 'problem' of ethnicity and identity as critical determinant of contemporary mass violence and civil wars. Theories of identity conflict have perhaps become the most popular of conflict theories in the 1990s, even thought that the concept of 'identity' is often an empty box.

Today the term 'ethnic', for anthropologists a fundamental category and a technical term, became an acceptable word for the common citizen if not a politically correct way to talk about tribalism, racial conflicts and that more. But some stigmatisation of the term did not disappear with its inflationary use. The rediscovered term of ethnic in combination with conflict became so popular that it was used by journalists and 'common people' for almost all conflicts, also those where one would hardly believe that ethnicity is at work. Politicians were using the talk about allegedly primordial ethnic conflicts in order to explain why 'nothing can be done'; such conflicts were seen as irrational and pre-modern if not barbaric.

New versions of the old resource competition theory, the manipulation of evil leaders and psycho-economic theories of deprivation (among small elites) as the main cause of conflict are still used to explain what ethnicity and conflict is all about. Fashionable theories of shorter reach often generalize certain features of 'new wars', for instance the phenomena of warlordism (analysed by Duffield, Elwert and others) and the 'unstoppable' decay of states, which—based on a few spectacular examples such as Somalia and Liberia—have been declared the dominant new forms and results of 'post-modern conflict'. Although the empiric evidence was narrow, and the state in Liberia has since been revived by a former warlord 'elected' as normal president, such adventurist 'theories' were willingly accepted as explanations of the phenomena of 'post-modern conflicts'.

The political-humanitarian concern to find ways of avoiding violent forms of ethno-nationalism leads on to the questions of (1) how ethnic and cultural difference can be understood and acknowledged, and what role ethnic and cultural otherness (and the threats against it imposed by the states) plays in the formation of ethnic nationalism, (2) how destructive forms of interaction between states and nations or nationalities can be prevented, and (3) which institution and which political and legal measures are appropriate for that purpose. This chapter tries to answer the first cluster of questions and only develops some general ideas regarding the questions of 'what to do?'.[2] The characteristics exhibited by different types of society have, corresponding to them, different types of ethno-nationalist claims to autonomy and regulatory mechanisms, ranging from cultural autonomy, through regional self-governance and power-sharing, to *de facto* sovereignty. In a few cases the struggle for self-determination may lead to the creation of more states.

Towards a Typology of Forgotten Wars and Mass Violence

According to the ECOR world conflict index a majority of all conflicts that have occurred in the past twenty years have been ethnic in character or have been ethnicized. From 1995 to 2000 there was a light reduction to just below 60 percent of all violent conflicts having dominant ethnic components (see Tables 2.2 and 2.3). The most frequently dominant conflict type continued to be the ethno-nationalist (31.8 percent), followed by inter-ethnic wars (23.4 percent), the latter with a strong increase, followed by anti-regime wars (19.6 percent) and gang wars (14 percent, doubling compared to 1995–6, including warlordism and international terrorism), decolonization wars and interstate conflicts (4.7 percent). Genocide (1.9 percent) remains the rarest type of violent conflict but the one with a high mortality. Conflicts that acquired a dominant ethnic character (types B, D,

E and G) account for 61.7 percent (down from two thirds or 66.2 percent in the decade 1985–94) of all contemporary violent conflicts since mid 1990s.

On the one hand, *ethno-nationalism from below* is carried by a multitude of political movements at the grass roots and armed parties and groups, with the support of large sections of the civilian society of the respective entity, aiming at the liberation or emancipation—often acting in self-defence—of a particular ethnic entity threatened by hostile governments or state-organized onslaught. On the other hand, *ethnicization from above* is usually carried out by the leaders of an alleged nation state with the intent to single out members of a particular national group, in order to exclude them from the mainstream society or even threaten their existence. In the worst case, ethnicization is a preparatory stage for genocide.

The ECOR conflict index is based on a seven-type classification of contemporary wars and mass violence (in a short overview):

A   Anti-regime-wars, political conflicts; state versus insurgents

B   Ethno-nationalist conflicts, mostly as intra-state conflicts (state versus nation), often cross-border or spill-over effects

C   Interstate conflicts, state versus state, seen as 'classic wars'

D   Decolonisation wars or Foreign State Occupations

E   Inter-ethnic conflicts, predominantly non-state actors (exclusively so in communal conflicts)

F   Gang wars, non-state actors (warlords, religious extremists and terrorists, mixed with organised criminal elements), esp. in situations of state failure or state collapse

G   Genocide, state-organised, mass murder and major crimes (including forms called 'democide' and 'politicide').

The heterogeneous dynamic character of contemporary violent conflicts has to be expressed adequately. In the ECOR index this has been solved as such: besides pointing at a dominant type secondary and tertiary components were also codified. Thus the ECOR world conflict index makes secondary and tertiary ascriptions, in addition to the primary one (see appendices, pages 331–344).[3]

The global increase in the frequency of wars and non-war types of mass violence has to do with, amongst other things, a significant increase in duration, and a sizeable proportion of that increase is accounted for by ethno-national wars, in their capacity as 'chronic' or protracted conflicts. In the case of these types of conflicts, negotiations and third-party mediation are generally extremely difficult: the longer a conflict goes on, the slimmer the chances of success appear to be for any outside attempt at mediation or peaceful intervention.[4] The ending of the Cold War has further reinforced the tendency to ethnic (counter-) violence. Depending on the source used, other indexes of war confirm that about two-thirds of all wars exhibit the characteristics of ethnic conflicts, or that a large number of wars are susceptible of ethnic interpretation.

Ethno-national conflicts are products as well as causes of the instability of states. And the general conflict-situation and external conditions could become even worse for many states if the mega-trends of Second-World marginalization and of the impoverishment of broad sections of the Third World persist as a result of capitalist globalization. New states have generally worse starting-conditions now than at the time of decolonisation (in the 1960s). As regards the increase in the number of states that has been observable since 1990, it must be emphasized that many of the underlying problems remain unsolved. To view the new state-entities blanket-fashion as so-called ethno-states is quite arbitrary and, in many cases, demonstrably false. Those who define ethnic entities as authentic and schematically contrast their traditionalism with the modernity of the new states fall prey to the temptation to interpret the current proliferation of states as a coming-into-being of *ethno*-states.[5]

Definitions

Wars and non-war types of mass violence, such as genocide or large-scale massacres, have to be clearly defined and distinguished. Actors and driving forces have to be named and explained.

Major wars and mass violence are distinguished from other armed conflicts or massacres by various degrees of medium or high intensity, claiming usually more than an estimated 1,000 victims per annum or as an average during the course of the conflict (see CoW, SIPRI, and others). In many cases the numbers of victims are contested or otherwise questionable. Governments tend to reduce the number of victims while rebels usually inflate numbers. Additionally, in most wars the adversaries exaggerate enemy casualties. Verification of numbers of battle-related deaths and (even more so) of massacre-related deaths is an awesome task.

War is defined as a violent mass conflict involving two or more armed forces as combatants/actors in warfare. Not in all cases are regular state armed forces (such as military, police forces, militias and other paramilitary troops) involved. Not-state actors are mainly so-called liberation movements having regular guerrilla or partisan armies, often recruiting along ethnic, national or social class lines. Tribal militias, gangs, and other irregular forces have different agendas; they have less (or no) centralised control nor identifiable lines of command. In most types of contemporary warfare violent clashes and combat between the warring parties take place with some degree of continuity. Ethno-nationalist wars especially tend to become *protracted conflicts*.

Terrorism is sporadic, repeated or almost systematic violent action by clandestine gangs or by state elites who pursue illegitimate demands/aims and/or criminal interests by employing unjustifiable and criminal means, characterized by serious violations of human rights, committing war crimes (as defined by the Geneva conventions) or even crimes against humanity, whereby spreading fear and horror amongst defenceless populations by randomly or selectively targeting predominantly civilian victims.

Non-war types of mass violence are characterized by a separation of perpetrators of mass murder and their victims. In most cases the victimization and aggression is organised, supported, or tolerated by state actors. As compared to asymmetries in many types of wars (regarding quality of weaponry, availability of resources, and level of training), in non-war mass violence there is a clear difference to be made between armed perpetrators and victimised non-armed civilians, which are by definition defenceless. The worst type of mass violence is genocide.

Genocide is defined as state-organized mass murder and crimes against humanity characterised by the intention of the rulers to exterminate individuals because of belonging to a particular national, ethnic, 'racial' or religious group. Definitions different from the binding one made in the UN Anti-Genocide Convention of 1948 are not relevant and shall be rejected.

Mass murder committed against members of a particular political group (called *politicide* by Barbara Harff) or of a social group (called *democide* by Rudolph Rummel) also constitutes a horrifying crime but does not legally fall under the UN Anti-Genocide Convention of 1948.

Most deadly regimes in the 20th century have all committed total genocide against domestic groups, mainly their barbarian attempt to exterminate domestic national, ethnic or religious minorities.

Dominant groups got into positions of command over the so-called monopoly of violence. Their assertive relationship toward ethnically distinct nationalities (*nations without their own state*) became the most important dangerous source of violent conflict since 1945, increasingly so with each cycle of decolonization.

Ethnic communities can be defined as historically generated or (in some cases) rediscovered communities of people that largely reproduce themselves. An ethnic or communal group has a distinct name, which often simply signifies 'person' or 'people' in the ethnic community's language, a specific heterogeneous culture, particularly, a distinct language, and a collective memory or historical remembrance, including community myths (myths of foundation or emergence relating to shared ancestry). This is producing a degree of solidarity between members, generating a feeling of belonging.

Ethnicity as a term is used to describe a variety of forms of mobilization, which ultimately relate to the autonomous existence of specifically ethnic forms of socialization. However, no clear-cut distinction can be made between struggles by social classes and struggles by ethnic groups. To talk about the politicization of ethnicity seems tautological. Different types of actors such as states, transnational corporations, liberation movements, migrants' organizations, political parties, pressure groups, strategic groups, military leaders, and populists all seek to make political capital out of 'ethnic identity'. Some actors deliberately try to influence and manipulate the identity set-up.

Typology of Mass Violence

A typology allows an analysis of global trends in warfare and non-war types of mass violence, which is otherwise not readable. Methods and techniques applied to read the database of traditional registers must be able to detect the most disturbing trends and extreme problems the victims of conflict and the international community are facing today.

A Anti-regime wars or political and ideological conflicts: State versus Insurrection (SvI). There are different forms: liberation movements versus colonial powers; popular movements and/or social-revolutionary movements versus authoritarian state; destabilization or re-establishing a *status quo ante*. The aim is to replace the government of the day or to change the socio-political system. Destabilization conflicts started in the framework of the Cold War can be very violent and have long duration; exemplary cases are groups like RENAMO in Mozambique or UNITA in Angola, Mujaheddin (until 1991) and Taliban in Afghanistan and *Contras* in Nicaragua. All of these groups were supported by the USA and its client states (White South Africa, Saudi Arabia and Pakistan among others). Although configured differently from ethno-nationalist conflicts some conflicts exhibit common dimensions. Former destabilization conflicts and proxy wars of the Cold War period have mutated and became dominantly ethno-nationalist or ethnic-*tribalist* (e.g., in Afghanistan and Angola).

B Ethno-nationalist conflicts: there are diverse forms, mostly as intra-state conflicts opposing states and national groups (State versus Nation, SvN); sometimes as interstate conflicts (MSvN). Ethno-nationalist SvN-conflicts are the most frequent type of contemporary armed conflicts and wars; such conflicts are generally of long duration (decades). The root causes of current incompatibilities are often perceived as 'ages-old'; there is a history of past threats, discrimination, targeted repression and violence.

The aim is self-defence; in extreme cases as a struggle for survival against aggressive state policies and outright threats of extermination. Conflict resolution would only in a few cases afford to create new states. Possibilities for conflict resolution and preventive measures range from concessions regarding cultural autonomy and diverse degrees of autonomy and self-governance to (con-) federal solutions and sovereign statehood.

   C   Interstate conflicts: State versus State (SvS): earlier seen as the 'classic type' of warfare. Cases: war in the Persian Gulf between Iraq and Iran (1980–88), the 11 Days War between Mali and Burkina Faso (Dec. 1985) or the invasion of the USA in Panama (Dec. 1989). The number is limited; according to the ECOR-Register during the decade 1985–94 there were only 12 cases (of 102). 1995 a brief border war occurred between Peru and Ecuador. One later case was costly: from March 1998 to mid 2000 an increasingly bloody war between Eritrea and Ethiopia was not stopped until a disengagement plan in mid 2000 was signed.[6] 1998–99 the Kargil war occurred between Pakistan and India in Kashmir. (This was followed by nuclear threats between the two powers in May 2002). In all three cases the primary incompatibility was about (mutual) territorial claims. Before 1990 coalitions or war alliances used to be rather seldom: multi-state versus one state (MSvS); multi-state versus nation/nationality (MSvN); several states vs. several other states (MSvMS). Since quite a few MSvS or MSvN cases occurred, all opposing Western powers and smaller states or nations. The MSvMS subtype was the classic World War constellation. Since 1990 there are already five examples of the MSvS subtype: USA, UK, France, and others vs. Iraq 1990–91 (second Gulf war); the NATO intervention against Serbs in Bosnia 1995; new sustained bombardments of Iraq by USA and UK as an attempt of destabilizing Saddam Hussein, end 1998–2000 (with new threats of a US attack on Iraq issued since April 2002); 75 days of NATO bombing raids against FR Yugoslavia in 1999; and, the US-led coalition supporting the Northern alliance against Taliban and al-Qaeda in Afghanistan, starting in October 2001, with an ongoing US military presence in the area. In type C the application of international law (e.g., the Geneva Conventions) seems unproblematic but is often violated (e.g. by massive bombardments of civilian targets in Yugoslavia 1999 and Iraq 1991–95). Contrary to common belief, since 1945, with the exceptions of the Chinese revolution (type A), the interstate wars in Korea, Vietnam and the Gulf (Iran vs. Iraq), the mortality in B and G cases is generally higher than in C.

   D   Decolonization wars or Foreign-State-Occupations (FSO): Eritrea became a sovereign state in 1991–92 and East Timor in 2002, after a UN peace-enforcement operation. There are still a number of Afro-Asiatic cases: Western Sahara, West Papua and Palestine; additionally, due to internal colonization by ethnocratic regimes, many ethno-nationalist movements claim that their cases were decolonization issues. Most examples of type D have a dominant ethno-national character. Because of its privileges in international law type D is different from type B; this is of decisive influence for a possible conflict resolution. Essentially former European colonial territories were occupied or annexed by non-European regional powers; the occupied peoples have a good case if the United Nations adopts it and does not delay or mismanage the solution.

E   Inter-ethnic conflicts: Type E is, together with types B, D and most G cases, part of the 'ethnic' or ethnicized conflicts in a broad sense. Type E is different regarding actors and aims; the latter are characterized by particular collective (non-private) interests. The issues are narrowly defined: particular interests, *tribalism*, clan disputes, chauvinism, and *narrow nationalism*. Economic aspects play a role but cultural and political aspects dominate. As in type B the militants use their own ethnic group as recruiting and support base (contrary to B, in most cases exclusively). E actors are not forced to develop a war economy above normal levels. Such conflicts are often fought without a state actor intervening directly in combat; foreign covert intervention can play a role.

F   Gang wars: Non-state actors are mixed with criminal elements, especially in situations of state collapse. They act according to particular or even private interests. Economic aspects are dominant; a particular type of war economy is developed. Gang wars are fought over valuable resources (diamonds, gold, precious stones, drugs, etc.), land, or control of markets. Even 'modern' slavery is possible (e.g., in Sudan). Type F developed a variety of characteristics. Actors can be rather diverse, such as village militias, demobilised soldiers, or mercenaries (*contras, re-contras, re-compas*), so-called 'dead squads', the Mafia, (drug) syndicates (e.g., in Columbia or in the Golden Triangle of SE Asia), professional groups (e.g., *Garimperos* vs. Indians in the Amazon), private armies of warlords (e.g., in Afghanistan, Liberia, Sierra Leone and Somalia), terrorist groups or networks (such as al-Qaeda and Hamas), big landowners (in Latin America: *hacienderos* vs. landless *campesiños*), or settlers or migrants vs. indigenous peoples, for example, in mountain areas of Bangladesh, the NE Indian states of Tripura and Assam, the Kenyan Rift Valley and so on.[7]

G   Genocide: State-organised mass murder and crimes against humanity characterised by the intention of the rulers to exterminate individuals belonging to a particular national, ethnic, 'racial', or religious group (genocide) as a whole or in parts. Genocide is the worst type of mass violence and has to be clearly distinguished from warfare. Targets and victims are civilians (non-combatants) including old people, children, and even babies. Recent cases of large-scale genocide were the exterminations committed by states. The Khmer Rouge regime in Cambodia, during 1975–

1979, exterminated Vietnamese, Cham Muslim, and Chinese minorities; mass murder was also committed against ethnic Khmer (*auto-genocide*).[8] Rwanda's Hutu power regime overkilled almost the entire remaining Tutsi branch of the Banyarwanda in 100 days (from April 7 to July 15, 1994); massacres were repeatedly committed against Tutsi since 1959 (half of the Tutsi group had to flee to all neighbouring states) and against three other minorities (Gogwe, Mbo, and Hima).[9] Sudan's NIF regime has committed genocide against the Nuba in Central Sudan and Dinka civilians in South Sudan since the early 1990s; this genocide continues to the present day.[10] Many of the 50 non-signatory states of the anti-genocide convention are potentially genocidal.[11] In a few other countries non-state actors are the culprits of genocidal acts, as for instance in Somalia, Sierra Leone, and Tajikistan. Organized forms of communal violence can be genocidal.

A tentative attempt to introduce an eighth type (H for Homicide) was given up.[12] On the basis of these seven core-types of conflict diverse mixed forms can be identified.[13] Their characteristics and main impulses can be analysed, starting with their historical and regional backgrounds. The task of conflict research remains a Herculean one: to detect the roots, genesis, and dynamics of intra-state conflicts. The aim is to give a survey of conflict potentials, to identify belligerent actors and their goals, to analyse characteristics of rebel forces, and to research the course of a conflict case and its means (domestic resources and external support) as well as possible foreign involvement. Furthermore, the task for peace research is to think about ways of structural prevention, transformation, and peaceful resolution.

Lacunae of Global Surveys on Mass Violence

A comprehensive typology of violent conflicts is indispensable for any useful survey of conflicts. Surveys and registers are again necessary for assessing possibilities for responses. There are abundant difficulties inherent in the subject matter. Most conflicts are extremely dynamic and can change their 'face' over time. In order to register violent conflict comprehensively ECOR first re-evaluated existing typologies and subsequently developed a sophisticated methodology to codify conflicts in such a way that changes are indicated and become visible. Credible work needs hard empirical data. The ECOR typology was elaborated after intensive experience with armed conflicts and mass violence in the real world.[14] Four main lacunae of global surveys on mass violence could be identified:

1) Present war registers 'overlook', deliberately ignore or even exclude certain categories and types of mass violence such as genocide (as well

as the subtypes of *democide* and *politicide*), other state sponsored mass murder, communal violence, and post-modern types of conflicts.

2) Some conflict types do not necessarily involve state actors, such as gang wars (warlordism, terrorism and organised crime) and most inter-ethnic conflicts, contrary to ethno-nationalist conflicts, which always include state actors vs. ethnic rebels.

3) Most registers are constructing static entities instead of expressing the permanent mutation of conflicts in the real world. Conflicts develop over time and may change in quality, with a new type becoming dominant over the other(s).

4) External factors cannot be ignored; in fact, contrary to common belief, their importance increased in recent periods. Unfortunately there are no up-dated compilations of overt and covered foreign interventions.[15]

Such shortcoming and gaps have serious implications: A critical limitation occurs if compilations exclude non-war types of mass violence. This necessarily results in radically reduced explanatory power since the latter (genocide and *democide*) account for a much higher number of casualties than wars in recent years. According to Rummel 'roughly four times as many people have been killed by their governments (or in killings *sponsored* by their governments) as have died in war'.[16] While flaws in Rummel's methods and exaggerated death toll figures have been criticized, the fact that many more people die from (state-)organized mass murder then in wars is hardly contested.

Recent examples highlight that the impact of genocides is many times deadlier than that of wars. War and genocide are often confused. As a general rule it can be said that genocides take place in situations of war and crisis but have nothing to do with the war effort as such or even hamper it. Wars serve as a smoke-screen for much larger crimes. For instance the war that began in Rwanda in 1990 should divert the attention from the planned extermination of an entire population group. In Rwanda 1994, a state-organized genocide killed three times as many people as all wars in the former Soviet Union and Eastern Europe since the end of the Cold War.[17]

Drawing from fifteen years of fieldwork and conflict analysis, ECOR developed the, at present, most advanced survey (see Tables A.1 and A.4 in the Appendices), based on a typology and codifying conflict cases according to a dynamic model featuring multiple components, thus reflection both, complexity and change in contemporary mass violence. Analysis illustrates that conflicts change over time and can have two or more different layers. Secondary and tertiary components have to be identified in order to understand changes and provide analytic insight for responses to conflict.[18]

Differences and Limited Comparability of Conflict Indexes

One well-known index of wars is that of the AKUF in Hamburg.[19] The classification used to be based on four types of war but avoided a category for ethnic conflicts.[20] Reacting to thorough criticism, AKUF—having retained this division against all odds for a good while[21]—introduced a new category of 'wars for autonomy and secession' in its more recent reviews of wars.[22] (This compromise raises new questions: Peoples go to war for self-determination but who goes to war for autonomy? What kind of autonomy?) A closer examination of 1992 AKUF data already produced a proportion of 62.2 percent predominantly ethnic conflicts.[23] According to Nietschmann, over three-quarters of all conflicts involving state agencies had an ethnic dimension even before the end of the 1980s (and the collapse of the USSR and Yugoslavia).[24] Nietschmann's compilation cannot easily be compared with other indexes, because tribal and other conflicts not involving states (no matter how deadly they might be) are not listed by many indexes. Such serious shortcoming is caused due to fixation on war, erroneous definitions and neglect of non-war mass violence.

Regarding the number of violent conflicts the available indexes differ largely, according to specific methodologies, particularistic definitions and their limitations.[25] Some examples for lacunas are, indexes differentiates between war and genocide, an absolute and fundamental difference, ignoring that more people die in genocides and genocidal violence than in wars. Some indexes count states (where conflict occurs) instead of conflicts; often there are several in one state or one involving several states. Some indexes (e.g. AKUF and HIIK) falsely maintain that one party to a conflict must be a state, ignoring that many conflicts do not involve a state but cause thousands of victims. Most indexes 'overlook' certain conflicts, which escape their definitions and codes.

Table 2.1: Comparison of World Conflict Indexes

period	AKUF				KIIK-Kosimo				SIPRI-DPCR			
	1997	1998	1999	2000	1997	1998	1999	2000	1997	1998	1999	2000
violent conflict	46	49	48	47	27	31	36	36	25	27	27	25
most deadly	25	32	34	35	9	9	13	12		14	14	12
least deadly	21	17	14	12	18	22	23	24		13	13	13

The discrepancies make comparison of conflict indexes difficult. There are several reasons for diverging results: 1) the simple fact that the figures arrived at clearly depend from the criteria used to define conflict, 2) the different methods for the evaluation of the available data, 3) the counting done country-wise instead of counting different conflicts in one location, and 4) ideological block-out of particular forms of mass violence. SIPRI saw a fluctuation in the number of major armed conflicts with a significant medium term decline since the early 1990s—indicating a downward trend starting 1989, with a recent moderate increase; SIPRI was counting 33 in 1992, 34 in 1993, 31 in 1994, 30 in 1995, and between 27 and 25 1996–2000. HIIK counted 124 in 1997, 128 in 1998 and 81 conflicts in 1999 (of which nine were new). Both, AKUF and HIIK detected an increase of most deadly conflicts in the period of 1997 to 1999.

The ECOR World Conflict Index (Tables A.1 and A.4) does not see a medium term decline in the number and the intensity of conflict and has registered an increase in the number of conflicts since 1995, which is not due to longer duration of violent conflicts but due to the occurrence of new conflicts. Contrary to this CIDCM (Gurr *et al.*) saw a marked and constant decrease of conflict 1990–2000.[26] CIDCM claims that in 2001 we would have 'a world more peaceful than at any time in the past century' (ibid., 1).[27] Contrary to that, PIOOM and ECOR detect an increase in the number of conflicts in general and of the most deadly conflicts in particular in recent years, mainly ravaging in Africa, making-up a world more violent then most decades of the 20th century since 1945.[28] Since mid 1998 probably as many as two million people died in the Congo alone, most of them from slaughter in the eastern part of the country and from violence-induced famine and ailment.[29] Mass deaths continued to occur in Sudan, Congo, Angola, Ethiopia-Eritrea (until 2000), Afghanistan (increase since the October 2001 US-led attack), Burundi, Columbia and Burma.

Contemporary Mass Violence: Trends and Perspectives

From 1995 to 2000 some 107 cases of mass violence occurred (1995–1996: 80). Of these 107 conflicts 73 cases continued (1995–1996: 75 of 80), 34 ended and 26 were new cases. (1995–1996: only five new conflicts were started). Contrary to other compilations ECOR found no significant decline in the number of the world's violent conflicts. This is partly due to the way of identifying and counting conflict: ECOR counts violent conflicts according to instances of organized mass violence between the mentioned conflict actors (including alliances) in a particular conflict and not according to countries/territories.

Due to the complexity of contemporary mass violence, several violent conflicts can occur in the same country during the period of observation. For instance in the 6–years period of 1995–2000 ECOR identified seven conflicts in the ex-Zaire/Democratic Republic of Congo and as many involving India on its territory, five conflicts in Sudan, four which involved Ethiopia, Burma, Indonesia or Iraq, three in Nigeria, Uganda, Somalia, Yugoslavia/Serbia, and two conflicts in a larger number of states. Conflicts are identified and codified according to a dynamic model featuring multiple components, the base of which is a combination of the dimensions of actor-orientation and driving forces (reflecting the basic incompatibility) of a particular conflict. Actor and place is not counted the same way. For instance, USA and UK were directly involved in four respectively three conflicts in recent years—not as a theatre of conflict but as actors elsewhere—in Somalia, Bosnia, Iraq and Serbia / FRY.

Some results are significant: The over-all frequency of violent conflicts was higher in recent years (107 in the six years from 1995 to 2000 compared to 102 in the decade before) but their duration was shorter compared to the decade 1985–1994. Regarding a conflict settlement the result shows that 61 violent conflicts were settled or ended otherwise within the 16–year-period since 1985 (1985–1996: 27). However, in some of these conflicts the end of the violence came to a comprehensive solution while in a number of other cases the end or the cease-fire remain precarious and violent conflict might re-ignite in the future.

High Frequency and Dominance of Ethno-nationalism

The results show some clear trends: in the 16–year period from 1985 to 2000 ethno-nationalist wars and interethnic conflicts were more dominant than anti-regime wars, gang wars or interstate wars. Dominance and frequency are roughly balanced regarding interstate wars, decolonization wars, and interethnic wars. The tables 2.2 and 2.3 show dominance and frequency of conflict types in the recent six years period from 1995 to 2000.

Table 2.2: Frequency of Types and Dominance 1995–2000

Type	A	B	C	D	E	F	G	Total
dominant	21	34	5	5	25	15	2	107
secondary	34	10	15	1	18	14	4	96
tertiary	4	1	8	4	6	8	4	35
Frequency	59	45	28	10	49	37	10	238

Particularly significant is the result concerning the most frequent types A, B and E: The world's violent conflicts contain most frequently an anti-regime component, followed by interethnic and ethno-nationalist components. According to dominance the ethno-nationalist conflicts (34 cases) are well ahead of interethnic (25) and anti-regime wars (21). Most significant is the result that ethno-nationalist wars are much more frequently in a dominant position compared to anti-regime wars (31.8 percent : 19.6 percent); this result is as a trend in line with the results from the decade 1985 to 1994 (44.1 : 19.6) but ethno-nationalist conflicts— though still the most frequent dominant conflict type—lost ground to the interethnic conflicts, which in recent years became the second most dominant type ahead of the anti-regime wars (1985–94 the second type).

Table 2.3: Correlates of Conflict Frequency and Dominance

Correlates	Dominance & Frequency		Quotas	
Period	1985–1994	1995–2000	1985–94	95–2000
Anti-regime wars	19.2 : 30.7	19.6 : 24.8	0.63	0.79
Ethno-nationalism	44.1 : 29.3	31.8 : 18.9	1.51	1.68
Inter-ethnic wars	13.7 : 17.3	23.3 : 20.6	0.79	1.13

Source: Scherrer / ECOR © 2001

Conclusion: The most frequently dominant conflict type continued to be the ethno-nationalist (31.8 percent), followed by inter-ethnic wars (23.3 percent), the latter with a strong increase, followed by anti-regime wars (19.6 percent) and gang wars (14 percent, almost doubling compared to 1995–96), decolonization wars and interstate conflicts (4.7 percent). Genocide (1.9 percent) remains the rarest type of violent conflict but the one with the highest mortality. Conflicts with a dominant ethnic character (types B, D, E and G) account for 61.7 percent (down from almost two third or 66.25 percent in the decade 1985–94) of all contemporary violent conflicts in recent years. According to the number of mentioning per type of conflict the ethnic components appeared in 47.9 percent of all cases (earlier above 50 percent). Regarding the dominance quota, ethno-nationalist conflicts were still twice as often dominant as the anti-regime conflicts.

Reduction of Interstate Wars—Increase of Interventions

Shocking for mainstream security studies and conflict research is the fact that the Clausewitzean type of inter-state conflict has practically disappeared. The most significant trend in recent years shows a decline of the absolute number (and proportion) of inter-state conflicts; according to dominance there are less than one in 20 conflicts. Since the late 1990s there were only a few cases of 'classic' interstate conflicts: Eritrea vs. Ethiopia 1998–2000; Pakistan vs. India 1998; NATO vs. Yugoslavia 1999; the US-led coalition vs. the Taliban regime in Afghanistan and the al Qaeda terrorist network. The conflict in the Congo, with eight states intervening in August 1998 and some still being actively involved up to 2002, is not a 'classic' interstate conflict since intra-state conflict issues dominate.[30]

In utter contradiction to much of the traditional polemological research and contemporary conflict analysis, my provocative assessment is that interstate conflict character may increasingly become a component of other types of conflicts. In the period of observation 1995–2001 we find only six interstate conflicts. The latest example is already in the grey area of categorization: In the case of current conflict in Afghanistan the foreign intervention by a US-led coalition since October 2001 did not really change the rules of the internal conflict beyond succeeding, towards the end of 2001, to add to the demise of the Taliban regime, which was (on the ground) brought about by the Northern alliance. Currently it is the UN that is trying to rebuild governance and helping to resolve the Afghan conflict.

In 23 cases in from 1996 to 2000 the inter-state conflict character clearly became a secondary component of intra-state types of conflict, most prominently in Africa. My hypothesis is that today interstate conflicts increasingly mutate into a sub-component or an extension of intra-state wars. In Africa this new pattern can be demonstrated in several recent cases occurring in the years 1996–1998.[31] The military involvement of eight African states and a dozen non-state actors in the new war in the Democratic Republic of Congo between the Kabila regime and the RCD-rebels since August 1998 (joined by MLC rebels later on) is only the latest and most complex example.[32] Contrary to the *classic* type of inter-state conflict, different types of ethnic conflicts and disputes could be compared to rhizome plants growing for decades, nearly impossible to up-root, growing 'everywhere', and surfacing where and when one would not expect.

1995–2000 foreign state participation increased to 26 cases (of 107 conflicts; there were 17 of 80 conflict cases 1995–1996).[33] In the decade of 1985–1994 there had been 27 cases of foreign state intervention; in 15 of those 27 cases the intervention occurred in the last phase of the conflict, while in 12 cases the former state intervention took place in the 1980s. Hence the number of recent foreign state interventions is on rise and became extraordinary high. Since the 1990s foreign military intervention was ever increasing. A few interventions even occurred in types B and E.[34] The question of foreign state intervention is to be distinguished clearly from support by foreign states for one or more conflict actors (e.g., by providing hinterland or weapons).[35]

Decrease of Conflicts in Asia—Increase in Africa

The distribution of conflicts according to world regions shows the following picture. Today 44 percent of all violent conflicts are taking place in Africa, which is a significant increase of more than 50 percent compared to the decade 1985–1994 (Table 2.4). During the period from 1985 to 1996 the regional distribution of violent conflicts was largely modified. The proportion of Latin America remained constant, those of Asia and Europe were declining and Africa's share of violent conflicts was greatly increasing.

In the mid 1990s the share of Africa in the world's conflicts became the largest. Further increase to about half of all conflicts was avoided by some increase in Asia. However, according to the number as well as the mortality of violent conflicts Africa has become the most war-thorn continent in recent years, ahead of Asia (with West Asia and Southeast Asia accounting for over half of Asia's share); see Tables 2.4 and 2.5.

Table 2.4: Regional Distribution of Contemporary Mass Violence

Distribution	1985–1994	(1995–1996)	1995–2000
Asia	42.2 %	(33.7 %)	37.4 %
Africa	**29.4 %**	**(45.0 %)**	**43.9 %**
Europe	14.7 %	(7.5 %)	8.4 %
Americas	13.7 %	(13.7 %)	10.3 %

Source: Scherrer / ECOR © 2001

Changes in the Regional Distribution of Conflicts

After 1990 Europe became once again one of the major theatres of war. The talk but 'Europe as island of peace' in the midst of a war-thorn world was abruptly silenced in 1991. The most peaceful world regions were East Asia and North America (the latter without taking into account high rates of urban violence and criminality). Six years later violent conflicts in Europe were reduced almost by half and conflicts in Asia decreased by some 10 percent. Only on the African continent the number of violent conflicts increased dramatically by almost 50 percent; the increase started already from the early 1990s and continued during the mid-1990s. Parallel to the increase in the number conflict also their intensity increased. In recent years Africa has the highest share of most deadly conflicts—more than the rest of the world combined.

Dramatic Increase of Most Deadly Conflicts in Africa

In Africa the civilian population suffered heavy losses by exterminatory mass violence, warfare and war-induced famine. Since the mid 1990s there are three macro trends regarding violent conflicts in Africa: (1) Africa's share of the world's conflicts is increasing, (2) inter-state conflicts are increasingly mutating into subcomponents or extensions of intra-state conflicts, and (3) the overall conflict situation in Africa has developed increasingly towards higher intensity conflicts—which means from armed conflict to major armed conflict (defined as claiming more than 1.000 lives).[36] Especially the increase of major armed conflicts and mass slaughter in Africa is a matter of great concern.

Table 2.5: Regional Distribution and Change

Regional Distribution and Change	*1985–1994*	*percent*	*1995–2000*	*percent*	*Change*
Latin America	**14**	**13.7**	**11**	**10.3**	**–**
Central America	7		4		–
South America	7		7		**none**
Europe	**15**	**14.7**	**9**	**8.4**	**– –**
Western Europe	3		3		**none**
Eastern Europe	5		5		**none**
South East: Caucasus	7		1		**– –**
Africa	**30**	**29.4**	**47**	**43.9**	**+ +**
North Africa	5		9		**+ +**
West Africa	5		12		**+ +**
Central Africa	5		11		**+ +**
East Africa	10		12		**+**
Southern Africa	5		3		**–**
Asia	**43**	**42.2**	**40**	**37.4**	**–**
West Asia	11		11		**none**
Central Asia	3		4		**+**
South Asia	7		7		**none**
South East Asia	15		10		**– –**
East Asia	1		0		**–**
Island Asia/Pacific	6		8		**+**
World's conflicts	**102**	**100%**	**107**	**100%**	**– / +**

Source: Scherrer / ECOR © 2001   Remark: **+ +** or **– –** means a significant change

The provisional compilation reviewing the world conflict situation in the years 1996–2000 in regard to conflict intensity (according to the definition of 'major armed conflicts' as claiming more than 1,000 violence-related deaths) exhibits a dramatic trend: Since 1997 the number of most deadly conflicts was generally higher in Africa then in the rest of the world.[37]

Currently, the world's most deadly conflict, which claimed already an estimated number of two million victims since August 1998, and the most complex of all contemporary conflicts (due to the large number of actors, issues and incompatibilities, as well as due to large-scale outside interference) is the one in the Democratic Republic of Congo.[38]

Increase of Complex Crisis Situations, Terrorism and State Collapse

Genocide and mass murder of defenceless victims account for around 2 percent of all conflicts in the respective periods. This is an alarming sign and a matter of most serious concern. The number of victims of genocide and mass violence in the period from 1985 to 2000 is much higher than the frequency would suggest. The small numbers of genocidal mass violence show a higher mortality than those of all other conflicts combined. The state-organised genocide in Rwanda 1994 alone took one million lives in a period of 99 days. This incredible number of victims is more than twice the number of victims caused by all violent conflicts in the former Soviet Union and in the former Yugoslavia 1989–2000 combined. In the 20th century the number of battle-related victims was much less than the number of victims of genocide and mass murder.[39] Genocide prevention is among the most urgent tasks for the new 21st century.

In the 1990s a dramatic increase of extreme crisis situations and complex emergency cases led to an alarming increase of conflict-induced mortality in cases of protracted conflicts. The most deadly contemporary case of mass violence—in a cumulative count since 1954—ravages Sudan. An estimated 2.5–3 million people became the victims of genocide, war, and famine, as consequences of successive Sudanese regimes' onslaught in southern Sudan. At present this large-scale conflict is going on unabated.

Another matter of concern is the proportion of gang wars (warlordism, (inter-) national terrorism, international gangsterism and other organized crime) that grew exponentially, first almost doubling from 3.9 percent to 6.25 percent in a period of less than ten years and then further rising to one out of seven conflicts or 14 percent of all recent conflicts. Until the mid 1990s 'chaos power' and warlordism characterised only a small number of all conflicts (every 16th), but gang wars increased even further, as I predicted some years ago, based on data covering the period up to 1996 (see Scherrer 1999: 398). This concern was based on the evidence that the higher proportion of mentioned cases compared to the proportion of dominance of this type of post-modern conflict indicates a trend toward further increases in dominance and frequency.

Additionally, one of the components and manifold actors of gang wars are terrorist organizations and this sub-type was recently undergoing a qualitative change. Though in the 1970s this sub-type of gang wars was quite prominent in several world regions (mainly in the Middle East but including Europe with the German RAF and the Italian Red Brigades and Japan with the Japanese Red Army) and even developed into some sort of transcontinental networks it was not until the 1990s when a new type of terrorist network developed into a global threat. Growing out of covert action against the Afghan communist-oriented regimes of Taraki and Amin by the Carter Administration, including actions to provoke a Soviet military intervention (as disclosed by one of the chief instigators)[40] and the build-up of a radical Mujaheddin front against the Soviet military presence in Afghanistan (end of 1979 to early 1989), sponsored by the USA under Reagan and Bush Sr., Saudi Arabia and Pakistan, an highly organized extremist Islamist movement developed.

The al-Qaeda ('the base') organization, trained by US-special forces, became a multi-national terror organization built up for the task to destabilize the Central Asia republics of the Soviet Union. Al-Qaeda was soon led by the charismatic Osama bin-Laden, who had been closely working with the CIA for more than a decade. After the Soviet retreat from Afghanistan US-support dwindled. The former allies subsequently turned into enemies, provoked by the US military presence in Saudi Arabia since 1991 and the failed US policy in the Middle East. A series of terrorist attacks on the US presence in East Africa and the Middle East culminated in an attack on symbols of America's power in the USA itself, on September 11, 2001.

Loss of Hegemony of State Actors: Further Fragmentation

In the case of most ethno-nationalist types of conflict the conspicuous silence of the Western mass media is even more suspicious; such conflicts account for about a third of all violent conflicts. The ethno-nationalist character is undoubtedly the dominant component of contemporary conflicts. Adding to that, the type of interethnic conflict grew to another quarter of all conflicts. One of the particularities of these conflict types is the relatively low chance for peaceful conflict settlement. This was one of the main causal reasons for the steady increase (up to 1995) of durable protracted conflicts, which again contributed significantly to the increase of the total number of wars since 1945. The related type of decolonization conflict is continuously accounting for one of 20 wars. Such conflicts received more attention by Western media (e.g., Palestine and East Timor).

Already in the mid 1990s I pointed to the fact that the rising number of inter-ethnic conflicts—that is to say, conflicts between ethnic groups, mostly without the involvement of state actors—is a cause for alert. Such conflicts, in most cases, occur in the particular form that generally called 'communal violence' between warring ethnic groups, though this term tends to banalize rather sophisticated and extremely brutal forms of mass violence (for instance those occurring in parts of Central and West Africa). Comparing results in the most recent period of observation from 1995 to 2000 with those of the decade 1985–94, these conflicts (as dominant type) increased by not less than 170 percent, from 13.7 to 23.4 percent of the world's violent conflicts, and will—in all probability, taken its frequent appearance as secondary or tertiary component in many other ongoing violent conflicts—continued to grow in numbers.

Current trends point toward a further fragmentation within existing states. In many countries of the Southern Hemisphere this results in a loss of hegemony of state actors. Failed states are dangerous states. The scourge of genocide is intrinsically associated with state failure. Embattled states and warlordism may produce ideal conditions and hide-outs for other gangs, such as terrorist gangs. Following some of these main themes will be further analysed. State failure, protracted warfare and other forms of mass violence are inextricably linked.

The Challenge of Ethno-nationalism
and the Tendency of Peripheral States to Conflict and Collapse

The causes of the unstable nature of statehood in the Third World, and more recently also in parts of the former Second World, are many and varied. The critical situations in which states find themselves, and the challenge posed to them by ethno-nationalism, are rooted in the history of the last 500 years and have developed regionally distinct momentums. The present structure of less than 200 state-entities for between 2,500 and 6,700 peoples of extremely varied size[41] came into being in two major thrusts: from the 1950s onwards, as a result of the re-styling of the old colonies as new Third World states; and at the beginning of the 1990s, as products of the collapse of the Eastern bloc. This state-structure is inherently unstable. The number of independent states will rise yet further as a result of conflictual processes—without this resolving any of the underlying problems.

A complex reciprocal relation exists between some of the major causes of peripheral states' proneness to crisis and conflict and some of the roots of ethno-nationalism. Ethno-nationalism therefore appears to be both a product and a cause of the formation and unstable existence of states. But it is not in essential contradiction to the idea of statehood; it is merely directed at the particular concrete embodiment of it.

I shall here divide the most conflictual causes of peripheral states' proneness to crisis and violence into twelve thematic areas. Half of them fall under colonial causes of violent ethno-national conflicts and half of them are socio-economic and political causes of violent conflicts. Taking into account a number of virulent causes of violent conflict the initial question would be: Will modern statehood consolidate or will we see a disintegration of weak states at the peripheries?

Colonial Causes of Violent Ethno-national Conflicts

Most of the following six categories comprise direct socio-cultural and political causes of violent ethno-national conflicts:

- the forcible imposition, in the wake of colonial expansion, of the European idea of the nation-state onto areas where there was no infrastructure for it;
- the destruction of the many different pre-colonial regulatory spheres through disregard for traditions and through the elimination or devaluation of endogenous political systems;
- the arbitrary creation of new states—either through the division or forcible incorporation of peoples and ethnic entities in the colonies, or through the resettlement, regrouping, and autonomization of peoples within the framework of the ethnicized political system of the now-defunct USSR;
- the interest of the former colonial powers, for reasons of power-politics or economics, in having a fragmented, controllable periphery, to the extent of promoting, or tolerating, the emergence of post-colonial ethnocracies, and of supporting secession;
- the encouragement of rivalry between different ethnic groups as part of cleverly devised colonial techniques of rule involving either the creation and establishment in power of local (indigenous, settlers or mixed) élites whose power-base was often ethnically determined, or the ethnicization of strategic groups[42] who would vie with one another for possession of common goods and the usurpation of surplus; and
- the post-colonial subjection of ethnic minorities (and, more rarely, majorities) to discrimination, repression, or actual persecution at the hands of dominant ethnic groups in the new states.

Socio-economic and Political Causes of Violent Conflicts

The latter six categories relate to the proneness of peripheral states and societies to crisis and conflict; they comprise indirect socio-economic and political causes of violent conflicts of both an ethnic and anti-regime kind:

- the failure of most socialist and 'auto-centred' modernization-projects based on self-reliance or collective self-reliance—a failure manifested in the weakness of regional and South–South co-operation—which meant the only route left open was that of peripheral-capitalist 'modernization'; the upheavals wrought on traditional societies since colonial times, which have led to profound dislocations, social inequality, and political conflicts;
- the negative changes in the general economic situation in most Third World countries, as a result of an aggravation of dependency-based underdevelopment triggered by the oil crisis and recession of the mid-1970s onwards, by the debt-trap of the 1980s, with its continuing, accelerated transfer of value from South to North, by the 'uncoupling' of whole regions of the world from any kind of process of development, and by deregulation and downward adjustment in the wake of the globalization of the 1990s;[43]
- global development of an uneven kind, which is not a process of transformation but in most countries of the South is actually cementing a situation of permanent underdevelopment[44] characterized by top-down globalization—with, on the one hand, processes of unification and concentration in what will in future be three major centres, and, on the other, even greater degrees of fragmentation on the periphery;[45]
- the lack, or collapse, of public services in many Southern countries—in some cases to the extent of, on the one hand, a total disintegration of traditional statehood, and, on the other hand, inordinate privilege, corruption, mismanagement, and abuse of power among the ruling élites
- the absence of democracy and the rule of law, and the repeated violation of elementary human and minority rights by many Third World regimes and some new states in the former Second World;
- the severe crisis of legitimacy facing many peripheral states, accelerated by state repression and economic regression (mass poverty) and resulting in hopelessness and an increased readiness on the part of the population to resort to violence.

In these negative overall conditions, and where ethnic difference is politicized, the direct causes of, and triggers to, conflict make themselves comprehensively felt. Ethnicized conflicts thus often have underlying causes other than ethno-national ones in the narrower sense. Where this is the case, mobilization along ethnic lines acquires added political virulence on account of its tendency to reduce complexity and enhance emotion.[46]

Consolidation of Modern Statehood or Disintegration of the State?

Whilst the trend to the formation of new states continues, the picture conveyed by the three to four decades of supposedly independent existence by what were then *new states* is an unremittingly awful one. In recent years there is more attention for the phenomena of *state collapse* and *state failure*. Whether the failure of the modern nation state at the peripheries is ultimately due to bad governance, whether the lack of legitimacy, the irreparably inadequate state of affairs or the non-existing legitimacy of state rule has proved a decisive factor, or whether the institutions of the post-colonial states have not been adequate to deal with existing potentials for conflict (as many writers suppose), can only be decided on a case-by-case basis. However, some of the causes of crisis and violent conflict are of a systemic nature and thus lie outside the ambit of governments and govern-ance. Such causes are inherent to the very nature of most impoverished, peripheral nation states.

What has in general been the violent exercise of the state's legitimate monopoly on force—which many writers deem to have been an great achievement (albeit conflictual) in terms of integration and equality of citizens, thus seen as a civilizatory step forward—does in too many instances lead to the opposite situation—namely, wars, disintegration and barbarity—when new states' monopolies on force come into the hands of a dominant ethnic minority or an ethnocratic-despotic elite. Whether the state's monopoly on force could generally be called legitimate and a 'civili-zatory achievement' (Senghaas), seems in my view as a peace researcher to be a very debatable question.

The peace of Westphalia did not solve the malady of warfare in Europe, in fact quite to the contrary, the state's jus ad bellum lead to the most bloody wars humanity has ever seen. Europe has by far been the continent with the world's most deadly battle-fields and massacre-sites. Outside of the historically rather recently 'civilized parts' of Europe and its settler colonies only the old civilizations in Asia, Africa, and South and Meso America were able to maintain the state's monopoly on force in their influence areas over long periods. Without these important corrections Senghaas' idea might be called a euro-centric idea. The idea then gets into trouble if applied universally. If protracted violence, disintegration and barbarity are realistically the consequence of the use of the state's monopoly on force in dozens of countries in all world regions except for

East Asia and North America then Dieter Senghaas' argument in his thoughts about a 'civilizatory hexagon' is untenable. His hexagon should rather be an octagon that would include minority rights and ethnic balance as well as a culture of peace (negatively speaking: violence prevention) as civilizatory elements of truly universal importance.[47]

The belief in Western-style modern statehood—a hallmark of which, according to Max Weber, is a legitimate monopoly on the use of force—can be severely shaken by a reading of the annual reports of human-rights organizations. In the face of the reality of totalitarian dictatorships, incompetent regimes, corrupt state leaders, and marauding troops, the idea of a 'legitimate monopoly on the use of force' turns out to be one of the seriously erroneous euro-centric thoughts. Weber's misconception (if not heterodoxy) was of grave consequences for millions of civilians in weak or repressive states. In a number of Third World countries, the claims of a consolidation of modern statehood have actually been realized, on the basis of economic success and political prudence. Conversely, in other new states—so far on a one-off basis—there has been a widespread collapse of the state and a chaotic disintegration of the monopoly on the use of force.

The genocide in Rwanda was the most extreme example to date of the disintegration of a repressive 'strong-arm state' and the reconstruction of state structures elsewhere—in nearby countries; prior to this, the state leadership's genocidal policy had operated a downward 'delegation' of the monopoly on force.[48] When the state monopoly on force is transformed into an 'ethnic-cum-racist' one, the situation becomes extremely grave. Such states are indeed the most dangerous states one can imagine. State structures in an advanced state of collapse and the chaotic disintegration of the monopoly on force are hallmarks of most areas in which violent conflicts on a mass scale occur.

In the former Italian colony of (southern) Somalia, as a result of clannish fighting in 1993, the state disappeared completely; first attempts of re-establishing a central administration were made in 2000 but are far from being successful. In Liberia the state disintegrated (until the strongest 'war lord' was elected president); in Afghanistan during the 1990s, it was repeatedly re-divided. In the former Zaire of dictator Mobutu as well as in today's Democratic Republic of Congo, in Sudan since 1955, in Burma since 1948, and in a fluctuating number of other countries much of the claimed state territory is not under control of the central government and rival governments are sometimes formed. In all mentioned cases, the ethnic dimension of the collapse of the state was unmistakable.

International Terrorism: A Provisional Assessment

In an immediate response on September 12, and a week later, I developed some concrete thoughts and strategies of how to combat terrorism.[49] What we witness is the results of failed prevention efforts, missed opportunities, or quite the opposite of it, the results of decades of denial of development, democracy, freedom, and human rights to people in the South by the West, especially in places where rich resources are abundant or in places, which were considered strategically important. The legacy of neo-colonialism is lasting and destructive. For decades the USA deposed popularly elected leaders and replaced them with puppet military dictators in countries it considered as its backyard, which is all of Latin America and beyond, and in countries it considered as of strategic interest, such as the oil states in the Middle East.

Democidal Attack Against America

We all saw the same images.[50] When I turned on the TV on September 11 all stations showed the same horrific images. Time and time again I watched collapsing buildings, deliberately hit by airplanes, huge explosions, firestorms, desperate people jumping from high towers into certain death, huge structures in Manhattan collapsing one by one, the Pentagon burning, scenery like in a war—but it was not war. Thousands of people died. The symbols of America's global power were attacked. The world's mightiest state seemed defenceless and confused.

The world's politicians appeared on the screen. A deeply shocked Arafat—in the name of the Palestinian people—offered his condolence to the American government and the people, and Arafat set the tone for others. Some Palestinians, however, seemed full of joy about the tragedy. President Bush appeared on television several times, leaving a helpless impression. Instinctively I understood that he did the wrong thing. Instead of expressing shock about the tragedy and condolence with the victims and their families he vowed to hit against the perpetrators of these heinous crimes without knowing who they were. He called them cowards and flew through half of the country into hiding. The United States was without leadership.

What was the aim of the aggressors? They attacked the most powerful symbols of America, its dominance of world trade and the headquarters of its mighty army, though the crashed airplane was nowhere to be seen. The airspace over Washington, and the Pentagon in particular, was not as tightly controlled as we were told for decades. The aim of the attackers was to strike decisively and scare a whole nation by leaving as much destruction as possible in terms of human lives, economic and symbolic value.

How did they do it? Several aspects remain in the dark.[51] The suicide bombers must have been armed and equipped with instruments to instantly open locked cockpit doors, without giving the crew a chance to send an SOS (which must have alerted the US air force). A comparison with Pearl Harbor was being made (but contributed to confusion). The attackers must have been trained to manoeuvre the particular airplanes they brought under their control. It remains to be explained how several groups of attackers managed to pass controls and checks with all the necessary equipment without even one group being discovered (which would trigger an alert).

Who were the aggressors? The highjackers were no cowards but fanatics—fully determined to fulfill a carefully planed suicide attack. Their mission was different from all previous highjackers we know so far. They were not fleeing after aggression nor did they want to take hostages for exchanging them against comrades and 'prisoners of war'. They did not make any statements about their aims and objectives. They did not want to make a statement at all. Those unknown attackers were ready to commit mass murder and mass destruction, and they did it in the most ruthless way. They never planned to survive the mission which was nothing less than transforming a civilian plane into a living bombshell.

Indeed, there are only a few ideologies capable of turning individuals into suicide warriors. Fanatism must be based on belief and belonging, no matter if the belief system is religion, its modern surrogate of nationalism or both of it. In contemporary history suicide bombing was rarely used by ethno-nationalists (except by the Tamil Tigers, LTTE) but rather often by religious fundamentalists (Islamists, Hinduists and potentially also Christians), whereby religious and nationalist ideologies may mix.[52] Even states used this tool, as Japan did with the kamikaze pilots in World War II.

Sustained Structural, Cultural and Direct Violence Breeds Terrorism

Galtung accused structural violence, after mentioning some '230 US military interventions abroad, the near extermination of native Americans, slavery, the CIA's responsibility for 6 million killed 1947–87, according to CIA dissidents, and the 100,000 dying daily at the bottom of an economic system identified by many with US economic, military and political power. Given the millions of victims, not thousands, it has to be expected that this generates a desire for retaliation somewhere, some time'.[53]

The personalization of evil in the person of Osama bin Laden (following Muhamar Qaddafi, Saddam Hussein and Slobodan Milosevic) is constructed according to the very same simple logic—while bin Laden's ten years of narrow collaboration with the CIA is rarely mentioned. Bowman wrote that the aim of the present war effort will backlash: 'To kill bin Laden now would be to make him an eternal martyr. Thousands would rise up to take his place. In another year, we would face another round of terrorism, probably much worse even than this one'. This is the type of analysis you will not find in the Western mass media.

Difficulty to Differentiate Terrorism from Legitimate Struggles

The contradiction between the viewpoints that one state's terrorist is another's freedom fighter has not died with the Cold War. The question 'How to differentiate terrorism from struggles for self-determination and combat against foreign occupation?' makes it almost impossible to find an international consensus on how to define non-state terrorism—and even worse so for state terrorism. This does not mean that we have no way of distinguishing heinous terrorist acts from liberation struggles. Terror acts violate international humanitarian law, especially international humanitarian law such as the Geneva conventions, since they target the defenceless civilian population (not combatants and other military targets), but so did many acts of dirty war committed by a number of UN member states.

The fear that the US military response, which was in the making since September 11, would develop out of proportion, did not materialize, though cluster bombs and the use of depleted uranium bombs became a matter of great concern.[54] We have witnessed that sort of 'punishments' in the past (with a rather long list of US military interventions and strikes since the times of Monroe). The combination of US airpower and Northern alliance ground forces brought down the Taliban regime faster than expected.

Policy Failures Breed Terrorism

The United States is certainly a superpower in regards to military might and economic wealth. In the political scope America was unable to match any expectations of global leadership—rather the contrary. Narrow designs and short-sightedness characterize US policy in many areas. The country seems isolated with regard to global issues and a number of major policy failures occurred in recent years such as in the domains of justice (alone in the campaign against the ICC), human rights (the failure in Durban), ecology (going against the Rio summit and the Kyoto protocol) and its role in policing the world without UN mandate (military interventions and the mess caused in Iraq and the former Yugoslavia). Worse than that, the United States' exorbitant military spending is about to cause a new arms race and fears of nuclear war (START disaster, the undermining of the NPT and the nuclear test ban). No lessons were learned from Somalia and the failure to prevent genocide and crisis in Rwanda and all of Central Africa.

Embarrassing US policy failures occurred most notably in the Middle East. The weak resolve of the Clinton administration in bringing the Oslo peace process back on track, since Sharon's Temple Mountain provocation, was followed by a non-response to the escalation of violence in Israel and in the occupied territories. As no other country the United States could be able to play a critical role in calming the situation in the Middle East. The present administration has utterly failed to tame Israel's new aggressive policy that is arguably bordering to state terrorism. As abuse of power, injustice and sustained oppression continue unchecked in the Middle East—and are allowed to reproduce political violence and terrorism—more 'democidal' attacks against America are likely to occur in the future. In recent debates on international terrorism it has not become clear what actually is the new threat added by September 11 and how terrorism would impact on the existing arsenal of preventive measures, schemes and policies.[55]

What is New About the September 11 Attack?

First it should be exposed what is truly new about the threat of highly organized international terrorism. My assessment is that only the direction / target of this form of terrorism is new. It points against the West and against the leading power of the West, the USA. This type of terrorism has been invented and financed to go against the East, now it goes against the West. Obviously something went wrong.

The former Iranian president Bani Sadr called on the US political class to stop lying to its own people and to the world about the origins of September 11. Ahmed Rashid and others have revealed that the United States has built up Islamist terrorism over decades. In 1998 it was disclosed by the security adviser of former US president Jimmy Carter allocated some US$500 million to provoke a Russian intervention in Afghanistan as and to build up an Islamist 'response' to it. We knew already that this engagement was maintained (and greatly increased in size) under US presidents Reagan and Bush Senior. Despite abundant evidence that Osama bin Laden and his al-Qaeda ('The base') organization are a creature of the United States in its Cold War against the Soviet Union, the denial of the facts continues. Bin Laden and his lieutenants were some ten years on the 'payroll' of the CIA; in the 1970s his family's construction company had built a good deal of those caves he later used for hiding and that were being bombed by US airplanes—using dangerous bombs containing depleted uranium that set free large amount of toxic uranium-plutonium dust.[56]

Knowledgeable journalists and scholars (like Ahmed Rashid) have given detailed descriptions about developments in Afghanistan, when in 1986, CIA boss William Casey stepped up the war against the USSR by taking significant top-secret measures, such as providing the Mujaheddin with US-made Stinger anti-aircraft missiles to shoot down Soviet planes, providing US advisers to train the guerrillas, to launch guerrilla attacks into the Islamic belt of Soviet Republics such as Tajikistan and Uzbekistan, to disrupt supplies for the Soviet troops in Afghanistan, and, finally, with CIA support, to recruit radical Muslims from around the world to come to Pakistan and fight with the Afghan Mujaheddin. The Pakistani secret service ISI had encouraged this since the early 1980s.

The United States and Saudi Arabia have financed the infrastructure to built up an Islamic fundamentalist threat against the Central African republics of the former USSR as well as against China. Among other nationalities tens of thousands of Uzbeks, Kazaks, Kyrgyz and Tajiks from the Central Asian republics of the former Soviet Union, as well as Uyghurs from China, Chechens from Russia, other Turks and Arabs from different countries, mainly from Algeria, Saudi Arabia and the Gulf states, all went through training courses of al-Qaeda and started with the destabilization of their respective countries. The potential threat seems large and hardly measurable. Rashid wrote that more than some 100,000 Muslim radicals had direct contact with Pakistan and Afghanistan and were influenced by the *jihad* (holy war) ideology; an unknown percentage of them had a regular training as terrorists. Additionally, a few thousand were trained as special commandos. Probably several hundreds have learned secret service skills. To advance global jihad al Qaeda has trained a large number of sleepers for potential new strikes world-wide. From the technical point of view these type of terrorist network is only comparable with highly-organized secretive organizations such as the German RAF, Red Brigades in Italy and Japan, and their respective alliances with left-wing fighters in several countries in the Middle East, Southeast Asia and Latin America. The difference and advantage compared with left-wing terrorist networks is that the jihadists had secret and massive support by a dozen states. Until 1989 (and probably even longer, until the Gulf war in 1991, the jihadists were supported by the United States, Saudi Arabia, the Gulf states and Pakistan. A key figure was general Hameed Gul, an ethnic Pashtun, head of Pakistan's ISI secret service and 'most fervent Islamic ideologue in the army after Zia's death' (Rashid 2000: 129). Gul's aim was to build up Islamic international brigades.

Many areas of the world had suffered from US overt or covert state terrorism, as Blum has reminded us. Latin America stands out: the role of USA in deposing democratically elected governments (e.g. in Guatemala and Chile, resulting in genocide and mass murder in these countries). The rounding up, torturing and killing (called disappearances) of the opposition to US client regimes became known facts virtually around the globe. The

School of the Americas was one of the knots in the US network to train local staff in repressive tactics and measures. Sometimes the USA was unable to go to war against unfriendly states (or to win the war, as in Vietnam) or failed to destabilize a regime it disliked, as e.g. Sandinista Nicaragua, but the USA always made life for the local people difficult or unbearable. While hundreds of millions of people suffer under Western and US imposed structural violence several millions died by direct violence in which the West was involved, directly or indirectly. Is it among those people suffering most that hatred against the West is breeding and that another wave of terrorism is in the making. If such hatred is additionally mixed with religious connotations then it becomes even more serious. In a Gallup poll among nearly 10,000 Muslims in nine countries—five from the Arab world—respondents overwhelmingly described the United States as 'ruthless, aggressive, conceited, arrogant, easily provoked, biased'.[57] Saudi Arabia was among the countries where people registered the most negative views. This reflects the fact that 15 Saudis were involved on September 11.

What Could Have Prevented September 11?

Many scholars were pondering about what would or could have prevented the September 11 attacks. Some of the ideas were rather about who would be well situated to do something (e.g., experts advising politicians and NGOs engaging in dialogue and peace-building) than about what could have been done. In a violent conflict it is usual practice to listen to all sides and get their point of view. In the case of Osama bin Laden and the al-Qaeda network the key question has not been asked: What made them turn against their masters?

Al-Qaeda people were trained enough to use the media for spreading their demands. Their demands were known and publicly expressed. Years ahead of September 11 this Islamic network warned the United States' governments and made several demands; these were ignored. The response were bomb attacks against US troops in Saudi Arabia, terror attacks such as the embassy bombings in East Africa and a bomb attack against USS Cole in Yemen. What were the demands? Why was there no action?

Most commentators say that the demands of al-Qaeda were impossible to fulfill—without some major policy changes. This point of view is contested. Generally speaking, the demands were limited, concise and legitimate. The two main demands could have been fulfilled, without major problems seen from the US security angle. What was asked for was the retreat of the US military presence from the *holy lands* of Saudi Arabia and a settlement of the Israeli-Palestine conflict, whereby the Palestinian right of self-determination, including an own state, is to be honoured. It was only during the military campaign against the Taliban regime that president Bush Jr. was—all of a sudden—talking about a Palestinian state. His U-turn was later compensated by attacks on Arafat who became already physically a hostage of the Israeli army.

Indeed the US-military presence on the holy lands of Saudi Arabia represents an insult for all Muslims, and it was easy for bin Laden to capitalize upon. The troops were stationed there against the 'threat of military aggression' from Iran. That threat has gone if it ever existed. As for the Israeli-Palestine question it was the USA that passively sabotaged the implementation of the 1993 Oslo accord, giving chances and even a carte blanche to the extreme right-wingers and Ariel Sharon to strike against Palestinian occupied territories and use sophisticated weapons and excessive force against defenceless civilians. Possible solutions for the Palestine question are on the table; one recent proposal, the unexpected peace plan launched in February 2002 by Saudi Prince Abdullah in the *New York Times*, came in the midst of a dangerous escalation in Middle East.[58] It would be inadequate to oversee that bin Laden and al-Qaeda have mass support in many Muslim countries, and it was precisely for the legitimacy of their demands that they got supported and will continue to pose a threat to the security of the United States. Without a political solution there will be no end of this kind of violence.

Terrorism Calls for a Multi-dimensional Response

The United States are firm in the fight against terrorists. Many believe that fighting terrorism is a military venture. Any narrow security concept in the fight against terrorism is bound to fail. By their complexity and openness all modern societies are at risk. We know that terrorism poses a challenge on a global scale. However, nobody knows how many determined fanatics are still waiting somewhere in Western countries, on the soil of the United States, waiting for the next violent campaign. The improvement of security on the airports was the first logical step in preventing such attacks. But total security is impossible. It would hurt the daily functioning of modern society. All of a sudden we became aware of the strange vulnerability of even the mightiest nation on earth.

The USA might strike with cruse missiles and bombs against targets in Afghanistan, Iraq, Somalia or Sudan, as we have witnessed in the past. The impact on curbing terrorism will be limited but destruction will be great. So far US forces failed to capture bin Laden, Mullah Omar or anyone of significance among the al-Qaeda and Taliban leaders. Preventing future terrorist attacks needs more sophistication than being employed for policing airports, launching cruise missiles and dropping bombs on 'rogue states'.

Political means are of cardinal importance if the root causes of terrorism are to be taken into account. Addressing the root causes of terrorist forms of political violence does not exclude international law enforcement against those who instigated the crimes we witnessed and those who supported the perpetrators to commit their crimes. To bring them to justice is the work of FBI, Interpol, Europol and domestic police forces—in joint-venture with the respective intelligence establishments. We should keep in mind that 'sleepers' of international terrorist networks may be waiting for the next round of violence—in the USA and European countries.

Preventing terrorism and political violence in general can only be countered by an integrated approach, combining different means. If abuse of power, power imbalance, injustice and sustained oppression have created political violence, and terrorism in particular, then any attempt for meaningful prevention would need to address the root causes of such violence. Political solutions are called for.

Notes

1. Contemporary types of mass violence (wars and non-war violent conflicts) according to the ECOR typology A–G: A = anti-regime, B = ethno-nationalism from below, C = inter-state, D = decolonisation, F = inter-ethnic, E = 'post-modern wars': gang wars and war-lordism, and G = genocide, democide, massacres and organized mass murder.
2. Extensive elaborations on the subject see Scherrer 2002b (*Structural Prevention of Ethnic Violence*). Outlines were given in Scherrer 1999 ('Structural Prevention and Conflict Management'; Encyclopedia of Violence. Peace and Conflict, vol. 3, 381–429).
3. See the ECOR indexes of contemporary mass violence and some results in Tables A.1–4 in the appendices on pages 331–344.
4. This negative conclusion was arrived by Bercovich *et al.* (1991) in an article about the likely success of attempts at mediation. Only in 22 percent of all cases (284 wars and crises reviewed by the authors) peaceful intervention was successful. See also Tobias Debiel (INEF), 'Kriege', in SEF 1993, 177–97.
5. For more detail on legitimate resistance in the unequal struggle for survival and on efforts to create a secession and recognition regime for new states, see Scherrer 2002b.
6. Mediation and outside intervention are much more successful in C type cases than in any of the other conflict types. In the case of Ethiopia vs. Eritrea there was a conspicuous lack of success. From May 1998, Colonel Ghaddafi, Hassan Gouled of Djibouti, Italy, Rwanda, the US, Zimbabwe and others rushed to intervene and mediate in this absurd war. Amid a famine both countries spent scarce resources for war, continued the spiral of escalation and even exported proxy conflict to neighbouring states. Only with the Cessation of Hostilities Agreement (18 June 2000) the war died down, followed by the Peace Agreement (12 Dec 2000), disengagement and the rapid deployment of UN troops. The war took a high toll (according to new estimates over 100,000), if compared with other type C cases in the 1990s.
7. Some of the frequent clashes between settlers and indigenous do not include criminal elements (at least with no higher participation of criminal actors as in other types of conflicts). However, such conflicts become gang wars and not 'normal' inter-ethnic conflicts because the settlers would often not be grouped together and armed without the

support of the state they belong to. Individual settlers conceive indigenous territories as *terra nullius*, as settler states have done during the past five centuries.

8. Compare the authoritative work of Kiernan 1996.

9. Rwanda genocide compare: African Rights 1995, ECOR 1995*a*, Prunier 1995, Scherrer 1995, 1997*a*, 2002*a* and 2003*b*; JEEAR 1996, Human Rights Watch 1999.

10. The perpetrators of genocide in South and Central Sudan are the Sudanese Army and tribal Arab militias. Irregular forces were armed and recruited by central governments since the reign of Sadiq al-Mahdi. In Oct 2000 the United States Holocaust Memorial Museum' committee of conscience issued a (late) genocide alert regarding Sudan.

11. Amongst over fifty non-signatory states are many weak, dangerous or war-thorn countries, such as Angola, Central African Republic, Chad, Congo, Equatorial Guinea, Eritrea, Guinea, Indonesia, Japan, Kenya, Mauritania, Niger, Nigeria, Paraguay, Sierra Leone, Somalia, Sudan, Tajikistan, Uzbekistan, and others. In many or by many of the above-mentioned states, genocide or crimes against humanity have been committed in the past. In some cases governments are committing such crimes, as recently in Congo, Equatorial Guinea, Indonesia, and Sudan.

12. *Homicide:* mass murder and crimes on scale characterised by the intention of the perpetrators / a group of perpetrators to kill individuals belonging to a particular social group; homicide, as configured as organized criminal violence of some degree of duration and intensity, thus having structural aspects and a particular unique configuration. Type H had been in discussion for some time; the type was not included into the ECOR typology but also not finally rejected.

13. Mixed types such as AB, BA, BC, CB, AC, CA, AE, EA, ABC, BAC, etc. The first mentioned letter indicates the type which in a given period is the dominant type in combination with a less influential secondary type and an less influential tertiary type.

14. ECOR conflict index in Kurtz *et al.* 1999, vol. 3, 381–430.

15. States of the North were 88 times (of 363) directly involved in wars. SEF 1993: 181.

16. See Allen D. Grimshaw: 'Genocide and Democide', in Kurtz *et al.* 1999, vol. 2, 53–74, 53. In the past 20th century, according to Rummel, the number of victims of slaughter was four times higher than war-related fatalities. See Rummel 1994. 2–3.

17. For Rwanda see note 9. Not at all a viable solution is to register (for the sake of a narrow definition of war) non-war violence such as massacres only if they constitute 'mass murder or exterminatory actions occurring during a war or in close relation to a war' (Gantzel 1997, 259). As an example Rwanda 1994 was mentioned!

18. This of course makes conflict analysis a complex task. In order to allow comparison with other compilations the ECOR register somewhat follows (in types A—D) standards set by AKUF, corrected by Nietschmann's early works.

19. AKUF stands for 'Arbeitsgemeinschaft Kriegsursachenforschung' (which translates as *Workgroup for Research on Conflict Causes*) / Institute for Political Science, University of Hamburg. The AKUF is active since the 1980s; e.g. its index of armed conflicts in the period 1985 to Sept. 1992 lists 68 wars. See Gantzel *et al.* 1992. AKUF data is not collected in field research (as it is the case for most indexes). Criteria of their compilation are somewhat outdated and partly non-operational.

20. A = anti-regime wars, B = miscellaneous intra-state wars, 'mostly…wars involving a struggle by an ethnic-cultural minority' (Gantzel *et al.* 1992).

21. See Scherrer 1993 and Scherrer 1997, 145, also 120, 124, 152, 159–160.

22. In recent compilations and definitions AKUF used the term 'wars for autonomy and secession' (*Autonomie- und Sezessionskriege*) in order to point to aims/objectives of ethnic rebel. AKUF retained its former type B of 'miscellaneous conflicts' as type E = other intrastate conflicts (*sonstige innerstaatliche Kriege*). AKUF also admitted mixed types; see AKUF 2000, 1999, www.sozialwiss.uni-hamburg.de/Ipw/Akuf/home.html).

For older compilations see Gantzel/Schlichte 1994: 7 and 13 ff; Gantzel 1997: 257–66; and Rabehl/Trines (eds.) 1997.

23. For a more detailed comment on the AKUF index, see Scherrer 1997: 145. A close examination of the 1992 index reveals (AKUF data together with details about other wars/parties to the wars listed) that 40 of the 68 'wars' have ethno-national components, as do seven out of ten other 'armed conflicts' which receive only a mention.

24. This applies to 86 of the 108 wars in progress in 1987. See Nietschmann 1987: 1–16, 7. The AKUF-register excludes whole sections of contemporary violent conflicts (analysed by Nietschmann more than a decade ago). Of the total of 120 wars for that year, only 108 can be compared with the AKUF material (NvN not listed by the AKUF). According to Nietschmann, of all those wars that involved one or more states, 75.9 percent were intra-state ethnic conflicts (cf. Scherrer 1997: 145).

25. The indexes of AKUF, SIPRI and HIIK can only tentatively be compared. All three differentiate intensity of conflict: Though ECOR only counts violent conflicts causing 1000 death per annum or cumulatively over several years, its index cannot be compared. AKUF counts wars (probably >1000 victims, one side a state) and armed conflicts (<1000), SIPRI counts 'major armed conflicts' and differs in >1000 victims and <1000. HIIK counts 'war' (systematic, collective use of force by regular troops, one side a state) and 'severe crisis' (sporadic, irregular use of force, 'war-in-sight' crisis) and further differentiates crisis (mostly non-violent) and latent conflict (completely non-violent). All three compilations do not use the concept of mass violence as including war, genocide, politicide and democide but use the concepts of armed conflict and war which are fully inadequate to index current mass violence. Nevertheless, the ECOR and AKUF methodology have some similarities; the two databases share four conflict types (of seven for ECOR and five for AKUF). SIPRI and HIIK do not use a typology at all. SIPRI publishes the war-lists of the Uppsala DPCR study group (Wallensteen et al). The HIIK conflict barometer is built according to a 'conflict simulation model' (KOSIMO, the name of the HIIK database), which is coding conflicts using 28 variables. HIIK counted (end 1999) 693 'political conflicts' in the period 1945–1999.

26. See Figure 1 in Gurr *et al.* 2000: 7. CIDCM talks about 'warfare' being either 'societal' or interstate. Societal probably means intra-state. The possibilities are that non-war types of conflicts are either not counted or declared as 'war'.

27. For the same period ECOR had covered (1985–94) Gurr compiled 70 ethnic groups in armed struggle, identifying in 1990 some 233 minorities at risk in 93 countries, with almost a billion people or 17.3 percent of the world's population (Gurr 1993, 11). 1945–9 some 26 *ethno-political* groups were in violent conflict, in the 1950s there were 36 groups in conflict, in 1960s the same number, in the 1970s the number rose to 55, in the 1980s it reached 62, and in the mid 1990s 70 ethnic groups were in violent conflict. (Gurr 1994). These findings seem to contradict some conclusions in Gurr *et al.* 2000.

28. In the mid 1990s the share of Africa in the world's conflicts became the largest. Currently 44 percent of the world's mass violence is occurring among the 11 percent of the world population living in Africa. The threat of a further increase to about half of the world's conflicts was avoided by some increase in Asia. PIOOM 2001 detected 12 of 23 high-intensity conflicts, 30 of 79 low-intensity conflicts as well as nine of 38 violent political conflicts in Africa.

29. 'On average, 62 million people die each year (an unnatural death), of whom probably 36 million (58 percent) directly or indirectly as a result of nutritional deficiencies, infections, epidemics or diseases which attack the body when its resistance and immunity have been weakened by undernourishment and hunger.' (See: The Right to Food. Report by the Special Rapporteur on the right to food, Mr. Jean Ziegler, submitted

in accordance with Commission on Human Rights resolution 2000/10. E/CN.4/2001/53. Geneva: UNCHR, 7 February 2001, p 5.)

30. Latest cases of dominant inter-state conflicts in the past five years: (1) the war between Pakistan and India in Kargil/Kashmir 1998–9; (2) continuous US bombardments in Iraq; (3) the war between Ethiopia and Eritrea, being fought with increasing intensity since March 1998, with spillover effects on Southern Somalia during 1999, cease-fire and the deployment of UN peacekeepers late in 2000; (4) the 78–days air war of the NATO alliance against the Federal Republic of Yugoslavia 1999, resulting in ongoing violence and reversed 'ethnic cleansing' in Kosovo in 2000; (5) the attack of the allegedly disarmed UÇK on Macedonia in 2000—under the eyes of NATO-KFOR troops in Kosovo—and the subsequent intervention of NATO forces, pressing for policy changes in Macedonia and (only partial) disarmament of UÇK; and, (6) the September 11, 2002 terrorist attack (on Manhattan/New York and the Pentagon in Washington) drawing a US-led retaliation against al-Qaeda and the Taliban regime in Afghanistan. The most costly of these wars and acts of violence was the war at the Horn of Africa; the original issue allegedly was territory but under-cover there was a power struggle between competing leaders and former liberation movements. The most frequent directly involved state actors were the United States (in 4 of 7 cases) and UK (in 3 of 7 cases).

31. The new trend is most evident in Africa of the later 1990s, though there is ample evidence for it in Asia too. In 1996 and 1997 there were several cases: Angolan military involvement 10/1997 gave decisive support for Sassou Nguesso's 'cobra' militia who tried since 6/1997 to seize control over Congo-Brazzaville from the Lissouba government. The intervention of Rwanda and Uganda in Nov 1996 helped AFDL-rebels to topple the Mobutu regime in May 1997. Rwandan troops were crossing August 1998 again into Congo DR to support the anti-Kabila revolt. The result was a rapid inter-nationalization of the new war in Congo, which is currently the world's most deadly and most complex war. RPA was followed by troops of seven other states, five of them joining Kabila's camp. Sudanese state army battalions are fighting an 'endless' civil war in South Sudan and violate the borders to Congo and Northern Uganda 'in hot pursuit' since 1996. The same does the Ethiopian EPRDF-army when fighting Ethiopian Somali rebels (Ogadeni) across the border in stateless Southern Somalia since 1996/97.

32. There is a talk about 'Africa-War-I' regarding Congo-DR. Angola, Zimbabwe, Sudan (unofficially), Namibia and Chad (until May 1999) propped-up the faltering government army (dominated by Kabila's Lubakat officers and the main faction of the Katanga tigers/gendarmes along with FAR-Interahamwe and FDD as troops) while Uganda, Rwanda, Burundi and the SPLA supported the RCD rebels (dominated by the Banyamulenge). Some of the involved states are only interested to clear the hinterland of their respective insurgencies, e.g. Angola vs. UNITA, Uganda vs. LRA, ADF, and WNB, Rwanda vs. FAR-Interahamwe and Burundi vs. FDD. Some dozens of militias and gangs in Congo-DR struggle in changing alliances with state actors and rebel armies. Most groups and gangs undergo frequent splits.

33. From 1995 to 1996 the number of foreign state interventions was 23 cases, whereby in six cases the intervention started before the mentioned period. The number of interventions has further increased since.

34. In all rule no so-called 'Third Parties' take immediate part in combat in case of ethnic conflicts. Exceptions from the rule are such ethno-national conflicts that have earlier been named 'regional conflicts' or proxy wars during the Cold War period (escalated by intervention of super powers).

35. All successful rebel organizations have or had their hinterland in one or more neighbouring states. This fact will be officially denied by the respective states out of diplomatic necessity. Depending from political conjunctures and the current state of

interests a number of states provided resistance movements of neighbouring countries with hinterland. Such support has a long tradition and even includes criminal organization (organised crime, e.g. drug cartels and terrorist groups)

36. A quantitative criterion such as 1.000 victims per annum remains a tentative criterion. Contrary to the *Correlates of War Project* and others, AKUF/Gantzel refused to apply (mechanic) quantitative criteria and followed Istvan Kende's definition of warfare (Gantzel 1997, 259). The way Small and Singer apply their criteria showed some inconsistencies of a marked quantitative approach. Wallensteen *et al.* (see chapter on 'Major armed conflicts' in various SIPRI yearbooks 1994–9) used the 1.000 victims' criteria to distinguish *intermediate armed conflicts* (1.000 'battle-related deaths' for the entire course of conflict) and *wars* (1.000 during a particular year). But the cardinal problem is beyond the 1.000 victims' criteria and remains unsolved for most conflict indexes: Genocide-related deaths can not be classified as battle-related and are by definition excluded in so-called war indexes. As discussed already this makes such indexes almost useless, considering that in any period between two and four times more people died from genocide and slaughter than from war. Indeed, it is worse than war.

37. In 1996 seven African countries were among the 15 countries affected by major armed conflicts: Algeria, Burundi, Congo-Zaire, Ethiopia, Somalia, Sudan and Uganda; outside Africa eight major conflict were being fought in Afghanistan, Burma, Chechnya / RF, Columbia, India, Philippines, Sri Lanka, and Turkey/ Kurdistan. In 1997 the number of African countries with major conflicts claiming more than 1.000 violence-related deaths rose to ten (Angola again, Rwanda again, Sierra Leone again and Congo-Brazzaville) compared to seven other cases in the rest of the world (the above mentioned without Chechnya). In 1998 already thirteen major armed conflicts occurred in Africa: Algeria, Angola, Burundi, Congo-DR, Congo, Ethiopia vs. Eritrea, Guinea-Bissau, Rwanda, Senegal, Sierra Leone, Somalia, Sudan, and Uganda; seven major conflicts were fought in the rest of the world: Afghanistan-Tajikistan, Burma, Colombia, Sri Lanka, Turkey-Kurds, US-UK vs. Iraq. In 1999 again thirteen major armed conflicts occurred in Africa: the above mentioned with Nigeria new, Senegal less; eleven major conflicts were fought in the rest of the world: the above mentioned, less US-UK vs. Iraq, and five new or newly igniting conflicts: NATO vs. FRY-Kosovo, Kargil-Kashmir (Pakistan vs. India), Lebanon/Israel, Indonesia/E-Timor and Russia vs. Chechnya. In 2000 some eight major armed conflicts occurred in Africa: Angola, Burundi, Congo-DR, Ethiopia vs. Eritrea, Sierra Leone, Somalia, Sudan, and Uganda (the conflicts in Algeria, Congo-Brazzaville, Guinea-Bissau and Rwanda were less deadly); six major conflicts were fought in the rest of the world: in Afghanistan, Burma, Colombia, Sri Lanka, Turkey-Kurds and Israel. In 2001 some six major armed conflicts continued in Africa: Angola, Burundi, Eastern Congo-DR, Somalia, Sudan, and Uganda (the war in the Horn between Ethiopia and Eritrea had died down from mid 2000; Sierra Leone became less deadly) six major conflicts were fought in the rest of the world (USA-UK and others vs. Afghanistan from Oct 2001, Burma, Colombia, Sri Lanka, Turkey-Kurds and Israel (second Intifada).

38. The regional war in Congo broke out in mid–1998; eight states and two dozen armed non-state actors are fighting each other. Only African actors are directly involved. Observers talk about an 'Africa War I'; its outcome will be decisive for the new order in Africa. Two alliances with some in-between parties are fighting it out. 'The Kabila regime survived since August 1998 due to marginal or non-existent links between the internal political opposition and the armed groups, because of their influence areas and ethnic base being apart or their differences too great. The power struggle in Central Africa became truly regional. The old Franco-phone networks were revived by Kabila, reinforced by several SADC countries, against the axis Uganda-Rwanda-Burundi, backed by most East African states' (ECOR 1999: 130). The Lusaka peace agreement of

July 1999 was seen as a turning-point in the war and called for a UN peace enforcement operation. For the implementation of the agreement, however, there was no political will by the UN Security Council; a proposed African peace force did not materialize for long and remains a tiny force of 2.500 in a country of Western Europe's size.

39. Rudolph Rummel's estimates conclude that four times as many people were murdered by their states then killed in war. See: Rummel 1994*a*. 2–3; also 1994 and 1997. For a good presentation of the issue compare Grimshaw 1999.

40. Covert action by the CIA to build-up a force of radical Islamist *agents provocateurs* was a long-guarded 'open secret' used by the Soviets to justify intervention. Indeed, the CIA began to aid the Mujaheddin in Afghanistan some six months before the Soviet intervention. It only became public knowledge when leaked by the former director of the CIA, Robert Gates, in his memoirs. The shocking news was leaked early in 1998, when the former US president Jimmy Carter's security advisor, Zbigniew Brzezinski, boasted about it in an interview given to a French weekly ('Les Revelations d'un Ancien Conseiller de Carter: 'Oui, la CIA est entrée en Afghanistan avant les Russes'', *Le Nouvel Observateur* (Paris), Jan 15–21, 1998: 76). On July 3, 1979, president Carter signed the first directive for secret aid to the opponents of the 'pro-Soviet regime in Kabul'. Brzezinski added that 'Et ce jour-là, j'ai écrit une note au président dans laquelle je lui expliquais qu'à mon avis cette aide allait entraîner une intervention militaire des Soviétiques' ('And the same day, I wrote a note to the president in which I explained to him that in my opinion this aid was going to result in a Soviet military intervention'). On the journalists question if he, looking at the massive devastations created, regretted his action, Brzezinski cynically stated that there was no regret and that this covert action planned to provoke the USSR into intervening in Afghanistan was 'an excellent idea', for the very purpose to experience 'their own Vietnam' ('Nous avons maintenant l'occasion de donner à l'URSS sa guerre du Vietnam.', ibid.). Brzezinski even made the equally outrageous but exaggerated statement that the resulting conflict would have caused the demise of the Soviet Union due to demoralization ('conflit qui a entraîné la démoralisation et finalement l'éclatement de l'empire soviétique'). 'If there had been no intervention here by the West (i.e. the U.S.A.), there would have been no war at all', wrote Phillip Bonosky in 'Washington's Secret War Against Afghanistan'. Until its backlash on September 11 the costs of whole action for the American tax payers were some US$ 3 billion, which caused the death of hundred thousands, the despair of millions of refugees, and, many years later, the death of 2.800 people in New York and another war in Afghanistan.

41. The figure clearly depends on the criteria used to make the calculation.

42. Evers/Schiel 1988, esp. on South-East Asia (30 ff., 48 ff., 134 ff)

43. Nohlen/Nuscheler 1992–3: 50–1. 'For the majority of the developing countries, foreign trade turned out to be not a motor to development, but a cul-de-sac for it.'

44. For Galtung (1972: 29), the two most spectacular features of this world are 'the colossal inequality in and between nations' (in regard to conditions of life, decision-making power, etc.) and the resistance of these inequalities to change.

45. The three centres of the world society are the European Union (today economically the most powerful block), the USA (currently militarily no. 1) and Eastern Asia (seen as the future no. 1). A future Asian Union composed of China, Japan and the Koreas is the most populous block among the three. China will be the world's largest economy by 2025. A union among the culturally similar East Asian nations would make it the world's gravity center in the middle of the 21st century; for the argument see Scherrer in 'Dialectics of Civilization and Barbary'. IFEK Arbeitspapier 2, 1997.

46. Müller spoke of a 'regression to simplistic patterns of interpretation' and even speculated about a general 'anthropological conformity to natural law' (Müller 1994: 7).

He saw ethno-nationalism, tribalism, and fundamentalism as a 'socio-cultural guerrilla-movement against the presumptions of a liberal economic world-order' (13).

47. See the contribution of Senghaas 1997a, my argument and the minutes of a conference on the 'Civilizatory Hexanon' in Calließ, Jörg (Ed): *Wodurch und wie konstituiert sich Frieden? Das zivilisatorische Hexanon auf dem Prüfstand.* Loccum: EAL 1998.

48. State bodies co-ordinated the preparations for the genocide; the challenge presented to the state and its monopoly on force by the countrywide build-up of the (party) militias belonging to the former state-party MRND (*Interahamwe*) and the fascist CDR (*Impuzi*) was only apparent; in reality, the aim was to strengthen the state and 'ethnic' monopoly on force. See Scherrer 2002a and 1997a: 72 (an answer to Neubert's views on the legitimacy/illegitimacy and undermining of the monopoly on force in Rwanda in from 1991 to 1994). Earlier works on Rwanda, see also African Rights 1994, Prunier 1996.

49. Both documents can be found on www.dwcw.org/cgi/wwwbbs.cgi?Terrorist-Attack (JCPF-DWCW, section 'US under terrorist attack'). To analyse the September 11 attack in terms of a *democide* is probably the adequate way of understanding what has happened. I have done so on September 12, 16:00, after thinking about what we all saw on television the day and night before (please see below). The contribution was sent to TFF as an urgent commentary (but they decided not to publish it). The text contains some errors but still reflects my basic thinking.

50. On 11 September 2001 I was called to switch on my TV immediately. My friend calling me seemed to be in shock. I could not believe what she said. Unknown aggressors had declared 'war' on America. Several sites were attacked from the air, among them allegedly the Pentagon and both of the twin towers of the World Trade Center, several airplanes had crashed, and the expectation—shortly afterwards—was that probably tens of thousands of people had died in a matter of hours. Others called me in anger and shock, asking me for an analysis. I could not figure out who the aggressor was. When I started to make sense out of the horror I found out that the tragedy could not be named a 'war'. Unknown perpetrators had not really staged a military attack on US forces.

51. On 11 September four or more fully tanked airplanes on long distance lines were simultaneously taken over shortly after the start from several East coast airports by an unknown number of attackers. The attackers first killed everyone standing in their way, in particular pilots and security guards, taking innocent civilians as hostages on their deadly attack on basically civilian targets.

52. Even in the so-called civilized world people are still ready to die for an 'idea'. The nation and most religions (especially Islam and Christianity) have been seen as a horizontal relationship of brotherhood (fraternity and equality). This important element may explain why masses of people were ready to die in the name of their nation/religion. In former Yugoslavia there was and is again a struggle for the 'nation' in the narrowest sense. For centuries abuse of power, power imbalance, injustice and sustained oppression has created political violence, terrorism in particular. In the past, people were willing to give their lives for an abstract idea if they felt threatened in their belief and belonging, if they saw their nation or religion being humiliated and devalued. The question was: which groups among the many nations and peoples of the world feel suppressed and humiliated by the United States and would be capable of 'retaliating' (as they see it) and to strike in such a ruthless way as we have witnessed in New York?

53. See 'The United States, the West and the Rest of the Wold' by Johan Galtung, 24 September 2001, on www.transcend.org. Robert M. Bowman, Lt. Col., USAF, ret.. wrote 'the seeds our policies have planted have borne their bitter fruit' (see 'What Can We Do About Terrorism?' on http://www.rmbowman.com/ssn/terror3.htm).

54. There may yet be other indiscriminate attacks, e.g., with cluster bombs (as admitted by the Pentagon), as a sort of punishment for 'rogue states' such as Iraq or Sudan. It was

clear that bombs are almost certainly not going to hit the Taliban ruling elite and al-Qaeda bosses bin Laden *et al.* but the Afghani population at large. Except for the demise of the Taliban, thanks to good cooperation by the Northern Alliance, Washington's war aims have not been realized.

55. My original text 'What is new? What could have prevented September 11?' was written as a contribution for the e-symposium on 'The Future of Conflict Prevention in the Post September 11 World', February 6–14, 2002, on the website of the Japan Center for Preventive Diplomacy (http://www.dwcw.org/). Amazed by the inability of most participants to focus on the salient issues involved and about the inability to formulate a comprehensive reply I sent a text on February 13, 2002 6:44 PM ET, apparently too late to be included. Replying to the moderator, it was my wish to place it on the same website in the section 'US under terrorist attack'; this was only honoured after my reminder and with two days delay.

56. In the March 2002 issue of *Le Monde Diplomatique* (LMD), a startling and frightening vision of war, both in Afghanistan and in the future, was reported by Robert J. Parsons ('Depleted Uranium in Bunker Bombs. America's big dirty secret'). The US is waging a secret radioactive war. There were warnings in 1999 about the use of depleted uranium-plutonium during NATO's war against Yugoslavia. A serious investigation was never conducted. The article in *LMD* is based on the report of Dai Williams and tells why WHO and UNEP mismanaged a serious investigation. In Afghanistan possible health hazards are going to be of a far greater dimension, several hundred times greater as in Yugoslavia. The bunker breaking bomb GBU–31, carrying a BLU–109 warhead, can weigh as much as 1.5 metric tons (so-far the maximum weight used in SE Europe may have been five kilos used in 120mm rounds), greatly increasing nuclear waste from US nuclear plants used in these bombs, thus multiplying the amount of toxic uranium-plutonium dust affecting wide areas in Afghanistan. Already last October, Afghan doctors, citing rapid deaths from internal ailments, were accusing the US-led coalition of using chemical and radioactive weapons. Among the symptoms they reported were haemorrhaging, pulmonary constriction and vomiting, which could have resulted from radiation contamination. This frightening vision of a kind of local-level nuclear seems to be part of the Pentagon's new aggressive strategy for US supremacy: 'America's big dirty secret', http://MondeDiplo.com/2002/03/03uranium.

57. Report by Serge Schmemann in the *New York Times*, March 3, 2002.

58. The peace plan proposed by the Saudi crown prince Abdullah, revealed spontaneously to Thomas L. Friedman, a New York Times columnist, is widely seen as asking concessions from both sides. The plan does not insist on the abolition of weapons for mass destruction by Israel, keeping in mind that Israel is the world's only undeclared nuclear power and the only nuclear power in West Asia; no Arab state is balancing this threat. The proposal is built on full withdrawal from all the occupied territories, in accordance with U.N. resolutions, including East Jerusalem, in exchange for full normalization of relations between Israel and the Arab world. The most comprehensive proposal focussing on long-term impact is probably the one elaborated by Johan Galtung / TRANCEND (see www.trancend.org).

Chapter 3

Genocide as the Ultimate Crime

Documenting genocide in the modern age is one of the most delicate and sensitive matters. Those who work on projects such as documenting modern genocides are aware of the fact that they are dealing with one of the most important and virulent themes of our times. Unfortunately genocide is not something of the past. Today gross human rights violations, atrocities and in some cases outright genocide cause havoc in many regions of the world and result in whole populations being petrified in fear and traumatization. Violence not only kills humans but also life chances for those surviving.

The worst kind of destructive interaction of different ethnic or national groups (one of them in possession of the state machinery) is genocide and mass murder.[1] Genocide is the most barbaric crime and has long-term effects. Cold-blooded state-organized mass murder is not an exceptional crime. Though genocides and mass murder of defenceless victims account for 2 percent of all conflicts, this is an alarming sign and a matter of most serious concern.[2] The number of victims of genocide and mass violence is much higher than the frequency suggests; the small numbers of genocidal mass violence show a higher mortality than those of all other conflicts combined. The illustrative example given was that the state-organised genocide in Rwanda 1994 alone took one million lives in a period of 99 days; this incredible number of victims is more than three times the number of victims caused by all violent conflicts in the former Soviet Union and in the former Yugoslavia 1989–2000 combined.[3] Genocide is the most severe type of violent conflict and has to be clearly distinguished from warfare; its victims are civilians, including old people, children, and even babies.

Today gross human rights violations, genocidal atrocities and in some cases outright genocide cause havoc in many regions of the world and result in whole populations being petrified in fear and mass traumatization. Contemporary mass violence is intrinsically linked with the ethnicization-from-above and the ongoing wave of *ethnic* nationalism-from-below. Unlike most new types of warfare, such as gang wars (by warlordism, organized crime and international terrorism), communal strife and most interethnic conflicts, genocide is always a state-organized crime. If attempts to prevent mass violence and genocide are to be successful then the quest for understanding has to concentrate on inter-linking fields:

First, the secrets of ethnicity and the process of ethnicization have to be uncovered. We are dealing with a powerful source of deep-rooted conflict, often nourished by destructive interaction in the past. If ethnicity is combined with domination then things become dangerous. Second, the phenomenon of weak or *failed states* became more salient in the 1990s. Awareness is growing that such failed states are the most dangerous states, especially ethnocracies. Losing out to globalization and economic decline add pressure. The wellbeing, security, and sometimes the very survival of non-dominant groups are put at the disposition of states. Failed states threaten to become genocidal states. Third, meaningful prevention of violent conflict has a very strong structural component. Such structural prevention aims at safeguarding inter-group balance and an accommodation of just demands on a sustainable base, providing protection and 'save space' for non-dominant and vulnerable groups. Fourth, the timing of conflict management is crucial. If conflicts break out violently then it is already too late for most peaceful solutions. Successful prevention of violent conflict cannot be reactive, as a response to crisis and violent conflict, but has to be anticipative. Fifth, the best prevention is *prophylactic* promotion and institutionalization of constructive relationships between different groups. There is no simple cure-all. The problem is that today there are still only a few research projects operating on a larger scale attempting to relate the development of theoretical findings with empirical studies and vice-versa, not talking about the step beyond—into practical action of early warning and genocide prevention and peace-building.[4]

Genocide has a long and dreadful history. One of the most important observations is that genocide and colonization were always closely linked. The largest ever genocide in modern history was committed by half a dozen European states in what was later called the Third World. Large-scale genocide was committed against American Indians, against Africans and Afro-Americans, against the Australian Aborigines and against a large number of subjugated peoples in European colonies.

According to Darcy Ribero the Indians of the Americas were reduced by the Spaniards in the South and European settlers in the North from 80 million in 1492 to 3.5 million in 1750. Genocide against Indians continues today, for example. in Paraguay, Guatemala, and Brazil. From 1500 onwards Africa lost 100 million people to European slavery. Most enslaved Africans died under genocidal conditions during mass transport from Africa to Americas. Genocide against Africans was continued by infamous lynching campaigns in Southern USA. It is important to understand that genocide was an inherent part of general practice employed by virtually all European powers throughout the colonial period, with Belgium, Germany and Britain ranking after Spain. In the late 19th and early 20th centuries the largest genocide went on for decades in the Congo Free State; heinous techniques used by the Germans against the Herero and Nama in Southwest Africa and against the peoples of South Tanganyika became part of modern genocide.[5]

The 20th century is called the 'Age of Genocide'. From 1910 onwards, genocide underwent a paradigmatic change towards the type of total genocide involving aggression of dominant group vs. domestic minorities.

Defining Genocide and Mass Murder

Genocide is a phenomenon known since ancient times; it means actions carried out by a state or ruler with the intent to systematically kill a particular community of people or social collectivity, resulting in destroying the targeted group in whole or in part.

Modern genocide is state-organized mass murder and crimes against humanity characterized by the intention of the rulers to exterminate individuals because of belonging to a particular national, ethnic, religious or 'racial' group (genocide). Victims belonging to a particular cultural group (*ethnocide*), to a particular political group (*politicide*) or to a particular social group (*democide*) or not equally well protected by the UN Anti-Genocide Convention of 1948. Genocide is a premeditated mass-crime that has been systematically planned, prepared, and executed.

Massacres and pogroms are acts of mass murder committed by different types of perpetrators such as state agents, security forces, political extremists and interest groups against vulnerable groups, which have been excluded from main-stream society. Pogroms are usually committed by a mob of incited thugs while massacres can well be premeditated and may include state agents or are ordered by political and state leaders.

Partial genocide means that the perpetrators aimed at destruction-in-part of a particular community or group of people in order to dominate the group. This was the case regarding genocide and slavery against Africans and Afro-Americans committed by European colonial powers and settlers.

Total genocide means that the perpetrators aimed at the complete extermination and destruction-in-whole of a particular community or group of people, with the intent to destroy its members, its reproduction (as a group) as well as its culture and institutions.

The Authoritative Definition by the Anti-Genocide Convention

Scholars do not have to define genocide. This worst possible crime is defined and codified in the UN *Convention on the Prevention and Punishment of the Crime of Genocide* of 9 December 1948, which entered into force on 12 January 1951. The definition reads in Article 2 as follows:[6]

... 'genocide means any of the following acts committed with intent to destroy, in whole or in part, a national, ethnical, racial or religious group, as such: (a) Killing members of the group; (b) Causing serious bodily or mental harm to members of the group; (c) Deliberately inflicting on the group conditions of life calculated to bring about its physical destruction in whole or in part; (d) Imposing measures intended to prevent births within the group; (e) Forcibly transferring children of the group to another group.'

In Article 1 the convention declares that 'The Contracting Parties confirm that genocide, whether committed in time of peace or in time of war, is a crime under international law which they undertake to prevent and to punish.' In Article 3 the punishable acts are listed: 'The following acts shall be punishable: (a) Genocide; (b) Conspiracy to commit genocide; (c) Direct and public incitement to commit genocide; (d) Attempt to commit genocide; (e) Complicity in genocide.'

Basic Standards Concerning Genocide and Its Application

A short note about what is underpinning definitions can be added, keeping in mind that there are different starting points and points of consideration:

1. Genocide is not a matter for interpretation. The definition the international community is obliged to use (and most genocide scholars stick to) is the codification of the crime of genocide in the Anti-Genocide Convention of 1948, defining scope, intent and four victim groups.
2. War and genocide are not the same and have to be strictly separated.
3. The UN defines genocide on the base of a procedure (UN Human Rights Commission, Special Rapporteurs and on-the-spot inquiries by experts). The regime is slow; it did not prevent Cambodia, East Timor, Rwanda.
4. The term 'genocide' shall not be abused as a political propaganda tool.

Any exercise of defining genocide must be aware of the fact, if we like it or not, that genocide is already defined and that the UN definition is policy relevant, e.g., the only definition relevant in prosecuting the crime of genocide, currently by the UN International Criminal Tribunal for Rwanda (ICTR) and in future by the International Criminal Court (ICC).

Who is Who: Perpetrators and Victims

There is some agreement in the question of defining the victim group largely following Raphael Lemkin's definition of genocide and the wording of the anti-genocide convention of 1948.[7] The convention partly goes further than the present minimal consensus, especially concerning the grey area of 'indirect' genocidal practices and measures (Article 2 c–e).

Particular national, ethnic or political groups rule a state in crisis, often as ethnocracy. Such dominant groups—no matter if they are demographically in a majority or minority position—were under particular historic circumstances able to bring the *new* state into their 'property', often as a consequence of colonial legacies, wars or crisis. Dominant groups got into position of command over the so-called monopoly of violence; they exercise firm control (total state). Assertive relationships towards minority groups, the political opposition, religious communities and ethnically distinct nationalities (*nations without own state*) became a dangerous source of violent conflict for a long period of time, since 1945 mainly in the South and since 1990 also in Eurasia (ex-USSR, Yugoslavia), increasingly so with each cycle of decolonization. Exclusion of minorities and their persecution by dominant groups commanding the states' monopoly of violence became the single most dangerous source of destructive violence in modern times. In situations of exclusion there is a high risk of genocide.

Distinguishing Genocide from other Destructive State Interventions

Other forms of destructive interaction between states and nations, nationalities and peoples are to be considered. Destructive interaction took the form of forced assimilation of non-dominant groups; territorial invasion of minority areas by state actors; settlement policy in indigenous territories, infiltration of homelands of minorities or indigenous groups; forced massive transfer of populations, forced resettlement, 'ethnic cleansing', expulsion, and deportation.[8] The so-called ethnic cleansing and other above mentioned forms of aggression against non-dominant groups are often falsely equated with genocide. This is an unfortunate and fully inappropriate use of terms; obviously the intent guiding the above destructive forms of interaction was not to murder or exterminate a national or ethnic group but to drive it out, deport it or forcibly transfer it to a different location.

In all cases genocide was committed in a situation of crisis, internal turmoil or civil war, as for instance in Burma, Sudan, Central Africa, Bangladesh, Cambodia and Indonesia. As the latter case, genocide (against Chinese 1965) is often combined with crimes against humanity, such as mass murder of the opposition. The Rwandan genocide is only the most extreme case. Defencelessness of the victims or lack of attempts to resist—as witnessed in Rwanda—has been analysed as contributing to the likelihood of genocide.[9] The Hutu extremists were killing for 100 days; in 2001 the Rwandan government conducted a country-wide survey and the provisional result showed a death toll of over one million Rwandans killed during the genocide in 1994.[10] This represents four times more victims then in all violent conflicts of the 1990s in the ex-USSR and in Yugoslavia combined.[11]

Defining and distinguishing genocide and mass murder are difficult tasks due to fragmented and complex realities in the world's most deadly conflicts. It needs more than to differentiate into what is called 'ethnic cleansing' (a very odd term indeed) and genocide. The question is which incidents can be defined as such; in the reality out there we deal with different degrees of gross human rights violations (1–2), war crimes (3), crimes against humanity (4–8), among them genocide (7–8). Such gross violations and crimes are ranged on a scale from 1 to 8—with increasing degree, intensity and magnitude of the crimes committed:

1. 'ethnic cleansing' or expulsions;
2. mass deportations, euphemistically called 'population transfers';
3. war crimes and crime of aggression, now being codified by the ICC;
4. pogroms, crimes against humanity not organized by the state;
5. massacres, crimes against humanity, often state-organized / in wars;
6. large-scale atrocities, crimes against humanity, often during wars;
7. partial genocides, usually using a war as a front; and
8. total genocides, 'genocide-in-whole' according to the UN anti-genocide convention, with four total genocides in the 20th century (Armenian Aghet, Holocaust, Cambodia, Rwanda); another one started in the 19th century (in the Congo Free State, 1835–1909).[12]

Only the last two crimes are defined as genocide; they are by definition organized by a state or other authority. Another issue is to what extent it is necessary to educate a mass audience in these definitions. A broad public in the West may understand as genocide what was misleadingly called 'acts of genocide', for instance atrocities committed in ex-Yugoslavia, which comes in only in the points 5 to 6 (Srebrenica)—not under points 7 and 8.

Four Cases of Total Genocide in the 20th Century

Total genocide means that the perpetrators were aiming at destruction-in-whole of a particular community of peoples (not genocide-in-part) and the result was accordingly. There were only very few cases of total genocide before the 20th century, namely the largest ever genocide committed 1492–1750 by the Iberians (Spanish and Portuguese) against the American Indians and the genocide against North American Indians by European powers and settlers. In the 20th century alone there were four cases of total genocide, causing more victims than in any previous period.

1. the *Aghet*: Turkish genocide 1914–1923 against the Armenians
2. the Holocaust: genocides committed 1933–1945 by the fascist German state and its allies and collaborators against the European Jews (*Shoah*),

the Roma (*Porrajmos*), Poles, Russians, Serbs and other Slavs, as well as democide against POWs, foreign slave workers, domestic disabled people and homosexuals, and politicide of domestic/foreign opposition

3. the Khmer Rouge genocide in Kampuchea 1975–1979 against the Vietnamese, the pre-Khmer Cham nation (Muslims), Chinese minorities and Buddhist monks, as well as democide against the Khmer urban classes

4. the Hutu-power genocide in Rwanda 1994 committed by the *akazu* elite, their state machinery, Hutu-power militia and factions of political parties and a huge number of common people against the Tutsi branch of the Banyarwanda, as well as politicide against the Hutu opponents.[13]

The most deadly regimes of the 20th century have all committed total genocide against domestic groups—the barbarian attempt to exterminate *their* minorities—often combined with democide (murder of social groups).[14]

Genocide in the 20th Century

The most infamous cases of state-organized crimes in *modern* Europe are large-scale genocide committed during both World Wars. The willing executioners of the Holocaust were not only Germans but also local collaborators among different nations in occupied countries all over Europe; the executioners of the Armenian genocide were also recruited among non-Turkish peoples of the Ottoman Empire. Both large-scale genocides were committed under the cover and during periods of warfare. However, the genocidal agenda of the perpetrators was known, e.g. in the case of German fascism openly announced by Hitler well in advance.

War as a Smokescreen for Slaughter

War provided a smoke screen for the slaughter of millions of civilian victims. After reaching the height of power in the moribund empire in 1914, the Young Turk military elite (originating entirely from the European part of the Ottoman Empire) began with systematic preparation for the genocide against the Armenians. On August 2, 1914, a secret German-Turkish agreement on the entry of Turkey at the side of Germany into World War I was signed. The situation was similar concerning the fascist genocides: Since 1939 Germany was at war with its neighbors, starting with Poland where in the following years alone 4.4 million civilians perished. Genocide was one of the means totalitarian regimes in Europe used against national, ethnic or religious minorities, which played leading roles in the economy and culture of their respective countries.[15]

The Holocaust as Model Genocide

Genocidal atrocities started with a politicide (state-organized mass murder of the political opposition). Violence was first directed against communists, trade unionists and socialists. Mass executions and slaughter was executed by special task forces and SS paramilitary, the main instrument of fascist terror policy, under direct command of the *Führer* and the Nazi power elite, based on the *National Socialist German Workers Party* (NSDAP) party.

When World War II was started with Hitler's *Blitzkrieg* against Poland, mass executions began in 1939. Following the occupation of large parts of Eastern Europe, mass murder against the European Jews, Roma, Poles, Russians and other peoples was ordered immediately and took the form of full-scale genocide. Units of the German army (*Wehrmacht*) and special battalions executed the mass murder. The infamous *Einsatzgruppen A–D* partly consisted of police reserve battalions of 'normal Germans'. Finally the civilian population and prisoners of war (POWs) from the USSR were targeted. The overkill of prisoners and millions of slave workers through hard labor and inhumane conditions in the concentration camps was organized parallel to the killings in war zones.

The Nazi terror reign was culminating in 'industrial genocide' in places like Auschwitz and in other extermination factories, especially constructed for the execution of the 'final solution' (*Endlösung*), by gazing and cremating millions—separated many different categories of victims—throughout the years 1942–1945. 50 millions died in WW2, among them the victims of the Nazi genocide and 'total war' fascist Germany brought over eastern Europe, southeastern Europe and Northern Africa. German fascism murdered 6 million Jews (the *Shoah*), 1.5 million Roma and Sinti (the *Porrajmos*), 3.3 million Soviet POWs (besides 12 million Russian civilians), 3 million Poles, 1 million Serbs and millions others.

The indirect death toll among the civilian populations (*democide*) was enormous: seven million people died of hunger during the German extermination war in the hinterlands of FSU only. These were cases of intentional mass murder, as H.H. Nolte pointed out.[16] In both cases (Germany 1930s-40s; Turkey 1910s) the exterminatory ideologies used were an inherent part of pre-modern ethnicist or racist theories.[17]

Modern Genocide in the South: Ongoing Legacies of Colonialism

Examples of more than 50 years of modern post-colonial genocide are manifold. Legacies of colonialism led to genocide or genocidal atrocities in different parts of the world since 1948. Some of the crimes (listed hereafter) were supported or covered up by Western powers:

- Burma since 1948: ethnic Burman (Bamar) vs. 70 minorities.
- Southern and Central Sudan since 1956 until today: 3.5 million victims; Arabs / Arabized Northerners vs. Dinka, Nuer, Shilluk, Nuba, a/o.
- Rwanda since 1959 and Burundi since 1964: Hutu vs. Tutsi branch of Banyarwanda and Hima-Tutsi vs. Hutu branch of Barundi.
- Indonesia 1965–6: against alleged communists; upheaval of 1993-4, with many victims among members of the Chinese minority; renewed chasing of Chinese in 1998 during fall of dictatorship and turmoil.
- Genocide against American Indians: continued in the 1970s against the Aché in Paraguay, in the 1980s by the regime of General Rios Montt against Guatemala's indigenous Mayan majority (mainly against Quiche, Ixil, a/o.), in the 1990s against the Yanomami and other low land Indian peoples in the Brazilian Amazon region.
- East Timor from 1975: Indonesian invaders vs. Timorese; the USA gave the green light to the military rulers; in a full-scale genocide from end 1975 until 1999 a third of the population perished; the Portuguese colony was annexed, until TNI had to pull out 1999, and the UN came.[18]
- Irian Jaya/West Papua: Indonesian invaders and settlers against Papuans.
- Pol Pot's Cambodia in the 1970s.
- Burundi's selective genocide in 1972: Hima-Tutsi army killing over 100,000 among the educated Hutu and Tutsi-Banyaruguru opposition.
- Burundi's second partial genocide in 1993: premeditated by Frodebu leaders and perpetrated by Hutu thugs, killing Tutsi farmers in almost all prefectures following Ndadaye's assassination; 'revenge killings' were carried out by the Hima-Tutsi army against Hutu; communal violence continued, even after the strengthening of the peace process in 1998.
- Bangladesh 1971: two to three million people perished in a partial genocide perpetrated by the West Pakistani army to prevent the secession of former *East Pakistan*, which was carved out by the British colonizers from the Bengal region of British India to become part of the Muslim state of Pakistan,[19] as a result of massive terror against dissent among Bengali and supporters of the Awami League as well as large-scale communal strife and a parallel attempt by Muslim Bengali and Muslim Bihari to exterminate the large Hindu minority.[20]
- Congo-Zaire since the 1970s: Mobutu's ethno-politics had a genocidal agenda; Congo-Zaire since 1993: genocidal atrocities increased in the three Kivu provinces, partly as spill-over of the crisis in Burundi 1993 and the aftermath of the genocide in Rwanda 1994.
- Rwanda 1994: among the four total genocides of the 20th century.
- Democratic Republic of Congo: ongoing slaughter since 1996;[21] very high death toll (estimated 2.5 million victims from mid 1998 to end of

2001) in Eastern Congo due to support of *génocidaires* and militias by the Kinshasa regime and the inability of UN peace keeping (MONUC) to enforce disarmament and disbanding of irregular 'negative forces'.

Genocide and Crimes Against Humanity during the Cold War

Some of the mentioned cases were facilitated or directly caused by the Cold War confrontation. The Cold War remained only cold on the territories of the superpowers and in Europe, formerly the worst theatre of wars and genocide, but the Cold War became 'hot' everywhere else and dismembered whole nations, killing tens of thousands up to several millions in wars and slaughters one superpower—the United States—started, provoked, instigated and/or funded. Direct US military aggression caused 3 million victims in Korea, 3.5 million in Vietnam, 2.5 million in Cambodia (including victims of Pol Pot's Khmer Rouge, which the USA supported even after they committed genocide) and hundreds of thousands in Laos.

Declassified documents prove that USA gave the 'green light' or was accomplice to mass murder committed by client regimes. Cases of genocide and mass murder in Indonesia 1965 and 1975 are well documented.[22]

As a consequence of US supported destabilization and proxy wars 1.5 million Afghans, 1.2 million Angolans, almost 1 million in Mozambique, and hundreds of thousands in Guatemala, Columbia and El Salvador died. Tens of thousands died, were tortured or disappeared in Chile, Argentine and Uruguay in the 1970s, in Nicaragua in the 1980s and in dozens of other countries in Latin America and beyond; they were considered (pro-) communists or they simply dared to engage in independent nation building.

A Typology of Genocide

The distinction of scale shall be introduced. The wording of the Anti-genocide convention of 1948 suggests genocide-in-whole and genocide-in-part, thus total or full-scale genocide and partial or large-scale genocide. Robert Melson combined this distinction of scale (total / partial) with the equally obvious distinction of place (domestic / foreign).[23]

This also calls in the type of victims targeted. Modern full-scale genocide in the 20th century, such as the ones committed by the Young Turks, the Nazis and their allies, the Khmer Rouge and the Hutu power regime in Rwanda, were *all* directed against a domestic component of the respective societies or against several components at once. In *all* four cases the state machinery was used extensively.

The type of perpetrator, being state and non-state actors therefore defines an obvious distinction and third dimension of the crime of genocide. In order to broaden the picture I include other types of mass murder, such as pogroms and massacres, to be distinguished from total or partial genocide. The resulting 12-types scheme in Table 3.1 is still simple.

Table 3.1: Genocide and Mass Murder in a 12-Types Scheme

	full-scale genocide	partial genocide	mass murder (pogroms, massacres)
domestic state actors	total domestic state genocide	partial domestic state genocide	domestic state mass murder
domestic non-state actors	total domestic non-state genocide	partial domestic non-state genocide	domestic non-state mass murder
foreign state actors	total foreign state genocide	partial foreign state genocide	foreign state mass murder
foreign non-state actors	total foreign non-state genocide	partial foreign non-state genocide	foreign non-state mass murder

The table becomes more illustrative with reference to structural situations (3.2). This typology of genocide is illustrated with a series of cases (3.3).

Table 3.2: Genocide and Mass Murder as Structural Situations

	full-scale genocide	partial genocide	mass murder (pogroms, massacres)
domestic / state actors	extreme worst case: total extermination of a minority planed and executed by the state	destruction of a minority perpetrated by the state	massacres against a minority organized by state agents / agencies
domestic / non-state actors	European adventurers and invaders against indigenous groups in settler colonies of the Americas and Australia	genocidal atrocities directed against a minority committed by extremists / interest groups	genocidal atrocities directed against a minority committed by extremists / interest groups
foreign / state actors	genocides committed by European colonial powers against indigenous peoples (mainly Spain, Britain, Portugal, Germany)	colonial genocides and slavery committed by European powers against indigenous and rebellious groups	massacres committed by invaders against civilian populations and rebellious or resisting groups
foreign / non-state actors	no evidence found / probably invalid	colonial genocides and slavery committed by European settlers and colonial companies against victim groups	massacres committed by invading settlers against local populations and resisting groups

Referring to cases can test the validity of the resulting scheme, as elaborated in Table 3.3.

Table 3.3: Typology of 20th Century Genocide and Mass Murder

	total genocide	partial genocide	mass murder (crimes against humanity and war crimes)
genocide and mass murder/ state actors until 1945	colonial genocide of USA against Indian peoples extending into 20th century; Aghet 1914–23; Shoah, Roma & POWs 1939–45	during WW1 and WW2: Serbs vs. Albanians 1912; Japanese Nanjing massacre 1937–38; German army's 'total war' and collaborators in FSU, Balkan and Greece; Croatian Ustasha vs. Serbs, Roma; Jews a/o 1940s;	Hundreds of cases: 1898–1900 European powers massacre boxer uprising in China; US army vs. Creek Indians 1901; Japanese war crimes across Asia; Stalin's gulags, mass death in Ukraine; A-bombs on Hiroshima & Nagasaki 1945
domestic genocide and mass murder / state actors after 1945	four cases of total full-scale genocide in the 20th century (incl. Aghet and Nazi Holocaust); Cambodia: Khmer Rouge vs. Cham, Chinese, Monks, Vietnamese and urban Khmer classes 1975–9; Rwandan Hutu power vs. Tutsi April-July 1994 [see description in the main text]	Indonesian army and mob vs. Chinese 1965; Bangla Desh 1971: Pakistani & others vs. Bengali Hindu; Burundi 1972 army vs. Hutu elites & Tutsi-opposition; Sudan's regimes (1954–72; 1984 until today) vs. Nuba in Central Sudan and vs. Dinka, Nuer in South Sudan; Burma: army vs. Mon, Karen, Tai a/o; Paraguay vs. Aché in 1970s; Indonesian army vs. West Papuans 1970s to 1990s; Guatemalan military regimes vs. Mayan majority (Quiche, Ixil, a/o.) in 1980s; Iraq vs. Marsh Arabs and Kurds 1980s (Halabja 1988)	over hundred cases since 1945: KMT massacres in Taiwan March 1947; Cheju island in 1948–9; Burma: military vs. minorities ever since 1948; Zionists against Palestinians in 1948 (e.g., Deir Yassin); 1965 Indonesian army mass murder of 'communists'; series of Apartheid crimes in South Africa 1961–92; May 1980 Kwangju massacre in South Korea; IDF and Phalangists in Sept 1982 in Shatila and Sabra near Beirut; Burma vs. students in 1988; China's Tien-An-Men massacre 1989; IDF in Jenin camp April 2002
domestic genocide and mass murder/ non-state actors	European settlers vs. American Indians; landless peasants vs. low Indian peoples in the Amazon	in the 1990s by *Garimperos* against the Yanomami and other low land Indian peoples in the Brazilian Amazonia; SE Asia: Filipino, Malay, Thai a/o vs. Negritos a/o	several hundred cases: pogroms against Jews and Roma in several states of Eastern and Western Europe; lynching of Blacks in USA; settlers vs. indigenous groups
foreign genocide and mass murder / state actors	total genocide in the Congo Free State 1877–1909; genocide of the colonial German army vs. Herero & Nama 1904–7	foreign state occupation and genocide of Indonesia against East Timorese 1975 to the 1980s (US complicity; green light to Suharto regime) / new mass killings by Indonesian-supported militias in 1999	USA in Indochina 1960–75: Vietnam, Laos, Cambodia: 'carpet-bombings', massacres, nuclear threats, 4.5 million civilians died; US covert actions; USSR dirty war in Afghan / US support terrorists
foreign / non-state actors	no case	Transnational Corporations vs. indigenous groups in the Brazilian Amazon	Mercenaries in Third World conflicts; TNCs against marginal groups; other cases

Patterns of Total Genocide and Indicators of Alert

The elaboration of a comprehensive typology of genocides, based on the definition of clear-cut criteria, is a demanding task. Identification of key elements of comparison and of general patterns of genocides may help to reduce the voids of comparative genocide research. This will contribute to the key objective of such research endeavors, the prevention of future genocide and mass violence. Barbara Harff and Robert Melson have both identified a number of common patterns of modern genocides.[24] Harff's early warning model is based on six key elements: exclusionary ideology, character of the elite, upheaval, autocratic regime, religious divisions, and degree of interdependence.[25]

An integrated warning process is needed. In 1999 I have proposed such a process based on twelve indicators of alert deduced from detailed escalation model, which is exploring both, six indicators each for warning and red alert; the first six are deducted from the fields of genocidal society, development of an exterminatory ideology, the construction of the victim group by the perpetrators, the process of victimization the making of a genocidal state and the development of a conductive social-political environment; the second six indicators of red genocide alert are deducted from the dynamics of totalitarism, the development of a genocidal environment, the establishment of a totalitarian state and total control, the preference for the option of outright violence and extermination, war and crisis as a smoke-screen, and misinformation and denial (see Scherrer 2002b: 214–219).

Indicators of genocide alert are (1) reinforcement and manipulation of old stereotypes, (2) construction of dichotic collectivities: us/them and nationals/vermin, (3) ensuring and reinforcing defencelessness of victims, (4) dehumanising of the victims, (5) impunity for crimes against the victims, and, (6) appeals to complicity and supply of more privileges. The *indicators of red alert* are (7) recruiting, indoctrinating and training of a 'willing executioner' force separate from army/police, (8) surge of hate propaganda in the state controlled media, such as gossip, lies, and fabrications about victim group, (9) liquidation of the political opposition, (10) breaking resistance among the national population, (11) skilful use of framework in producing a smoke-screen of 'crisis', and, (12) pre-emptive launch of well-prepared cover-up operations.

The framework conditions are of crucial importance. Melson saw 'four tidal waves of ethno-national conflict and genocide in the wake of crushing or crumbling states and empires'.[26] The progressive disintegration of the Ottoman Empire produced the first of the four total domestic genocides in this century, the *Aghet*, the destruction of the Armenians in Anatolia by the regime of the Young Turks. The collapse of the German and Austro-

Hungarian empires in WW1 produced instability and the growth of fascism in Germany since 1920. Under the cover of WW2 the Nazis and their willing local supporters committed large-scale genocide at home and in the occupied countries. By 1945 this had resulted in the intended total extermination of the European Jews and the Roma. Partial genocide was committed against a large number of Slavic peoples. Large-scale mass murder was committed against millions of slave workers and prisoners of war (POWs).

Decolonization and Derailed Nation-building as Triggers of Violence

The decolonization period was earmarked by artificial and weak states searching for ways of nation building, which were often very violently directed against non-dominant groups and the political opposition. 'Endless' ethnic civil wars, liberation wars, secessions and slaughter of populations began soon after WW2 in the Afro-Asian space. In Former British India the separation of India and Pakistan ended in large scale communal violence and horrible bloodshed. Internal wars in Burma since 1948, the secession of Eastern Pakistan and the civil war in Ceylon/Sri Lanka crippled South Asia. Africa was paralyzed by endemic mass violence in Sudan, Algeria, Indochina, Nigeria/Biafra, Indonesia, Uganda, Rwanda-Burundi, Former Portuguese Africa and the Horn of Africa.

In the 1990s the collapse of the federations of the USSR and Yugoslavia led to the latest violent wave of wars, 'ethnic cleansing', and communal violence. During this period the last and most rapid genocide of the 20th century occurred in Rwanda 1994. The Rwandan genocide resulted in much higher destruction in terms of loss of human lives than the ongoing instability, crisis and warfare in parts of the Former Soviet Union and Yugoslavia. Extermination in Rwanda exhibits unique features unknown to previous genocides: the objective difference between the perpetrators and the victims was minimal, it was the first genocide in modern history characterized by a massive participation of common people and it was the first ever genocide to divide families. Its destructive power was enormous due to masses of the majority population mobilized by the state to become the executioners of the minority. More than a million of ordinary Hutu men (even women and children) followed the orders of government functionaries and were involved in slaughtering one million Tutsis at a rate much faster than during the Nazi Holocaust.

Common Elements and Patterns of Genocidal Processes

Analyzing and comparing the total and partial 'modern' genocides of the 20th century produces a set of common elements and patterns of genocidal processes. Patterns can be found by looking at the perpetrators and their environment. Comparative research identifies and explores:

- the contexts in which genocidal escalation processes take place,
- the role of the elite, the core organizers, legitimizers and perpetrators of genocide, and their relations to the 'willing executioners' (Goldhagen),
- the internal and external conditions genocidal elites find and create,
- the political environment in which they take the decision to destroy,
- the way genocidal extremists gain the state power and transform it,
- the type of victims they chose and how they stigmatize them,
- the politics of exclusion and the exterminatory ideology they use,
- the reaction they get from the neighbours / the international community,
- the way they prepare and execute the crime of genocide, and
- the type and extent of denial the perpetrators employ.

Elites, Perpetrators, Objectives, and the Context of the Crime

The perpetrators, their ideology, the process of victimization, and the way they executed the crime of genocide are the first focus of attention. Coherent and vicious elites are more likely to gain state power in situations of deep historic changes. Under certain internal and external conditions they succeed in imposing their genocidal and destructive aims. The agendas of such elites are to destroy specific domestic groups, which as a rule are *always* in a non-dominant and minority position.

Genocidal elites try to penetrate and dominate the state. Their objective is to impose their aims on the state machinery they have conquered and on the majority people of their respective societies. The modern nation state is the 'predominant culprit in genocides' (Harff). Evidently the likelihood to realize such aims are much higher in a totalitarian system then in a democratic one. However, periods of imposed democratization can be conductive to genocide, as the case of Rwanda exhibits in the most drastic way.

The context is characterized by rapid political, social and structural changes which were described by the context of 'national upheaval' (Harff), separatist conflict, internal strife, rebellion or 'revolution' (Melson). What is meant are rapid or abrupt historic changes following an extended period of crisis. The aim of genocide is part of a larger project of the nation state formation or its revision. This includes all the different processes of changing regimes, moving of boundaries or loss of territory, warfare (especially lost wars) or security threats resulting from (or perceived as) challenges to the dominant groups identity and to the identity of the 'national' political community.

Narrow Nationalism, Exterminatory Ideology, and Victimization

The redefinition or mystification of 'national' identity by the power-elites is a central point. The perceived 'struggle for national survival'—against internal and external enemies—has to become somewhat plausible for the majority group. The 'foreign' minorities shall function as scapegoats. The 'nation' needs to be purified. The elimination of so-called '*foreign* elements from within' (Harff) is one of the common denominators of total modern genocide.[27] In reality all total domestic genocides were preceded not so much by real challenges to national identity rather than by challenges to the dominant power strata, having won, consolidated or maintained its power by use of force in an outright unstable situation.

The intentions of the killers are expressed in their exterminatory ideology. This ideology will always take up older stereotypes. The aim of the power elite is to single out and exclude a group as 'enemy of state and society'. Extremist regimes are essentially combining militarism, xenophobia, ethno-chauvinism and ultra-nationalism—a dangerous brand of militant narrow nationalism—with promises for the majority population's 'bright future'. They try to revamp the allegedly threatened identity of their political constituency on a narrow hybrid base. The result is the ethnicization of the nation. If any of its key elements came under heavy internal or external pressure for change then the reaction was fierce and in the end self-destructive.

Support for the genocide aim by a minority—and more important: the indifference of the majority—can ultimately be won if victimized groups are presented as 'racially', ethnically, religiously or morally different from the dominant group. The 'most *different* groups' (Harff) become scapegoats for losses and 'national frustrations' and finally the targets of destruction. Most successful proved the construction of close links between domestic 'enemies' and external 'aggressors' by the genocidal elites. Individual victims may often not be easily identifiable, and there is usually a large 'grey area' calling for arbitrary solutions. As a result the target group becomes visible and easily identifiable—as an imagined entity of domestic 'enemies' seen as 'foreigners' or 'fifth column of the enemy'.

Extremist Elites, Willing Executioners, and Lack of External Constraints

Decisive elements are the exacerbation of existing internal cleavages, the lack of external constraints in implementing so-called 'final solutions' or/and foreign support for it, and the shaping of the state by the power-elites in order to function as a genocidal state. Such a state needs willing executioners. Of utmost importance is a subservient state bureaucracy and obedient or extremist sections of armed forces or special troops. Contributing to the genocidal aim is the great fear and confusion among the 'national population', the well-organized massive support by their core political constituencies and the at least lukewarm support among larger sections of the grassroots. To describe the genocidal elites as 'power-mad' is not sufficient. There are structural reasons for their drive to state-centrism and extreme centralization of power, often symbolically in one person with a single cadre-party as platform. Obviously such a scheme is bound to end in totalitarism and self-destruction. Often there is little or no external pressure to prevent the worst.

The Problem of Enforcing the Anti-Genocide Convention

The challenges of genocide prevention are great and the matter is urgent. Many states have not ratified the convention, among them a number of dangerous states.[28] Today effective instruments, practical procedures and respected institutions necessary to achieve these noble goals are only partly in place: most instruments and institutions for averting, preventing and outlawing genocide have yet to be created.

Genocide prevention is a task for global governance: global monitoring of gross human rights violations is a task that has to be coordinated by a special UN branch. The UN system is called to implement the recommendations made by the remarkably candid and forward looking Carlsson inquiry report 1999. Deadly threats and the vulnerability of civilian populations in intra-state conflicts and genocides were growing at a fast rate in the 20th century.

Civilians are seen by many actors as soft targets, easy to assault; they are murdered, tortured, terrorized, starved, pillaged, put at high risks for their health, chased, expulsed, displaced, rather than protected. Violence is more often used without any purpose other than destruction of lives and livelihood. The international law and the international humanitarian law are not enforced. There are often no sanctions linked to gross violations of international law. The perpetrators of large crimes often get away with it. This is an invitation for others to act the same way.

However, changes are under way. On 11 April 2002, the world's first permanent International Criminal Court (ICC) was established at an historic UN treaty event. The simultaneous deposit of ten ratifications of the Rome Statute brought the number of countries formally supporting the establishment of the Court from 56 to 66, which is more than the 60 ratifications required for the treaty to enter into force. As of 1 July 2002, the ICC will have permanent jurisdiction over genocide, crimes against humanity, war crimes and other serious breaches of international law.[29]

Notes

1. Burger, Julian: Report from the frontier. London: Zed 1987, 37f, 83–84. Ryan, Stephen: Ethnic conflict and international relations. Aldershot: Dartmouth 1990, 11–12. Ribero, Darcy: The Americas and civilization. London: Allen 1971.

2. For proportion and cases see the ECOR Index of Mass Violence 1985–2000; index 1985–1994 in Tables A-1 (pages 380–4) and index 1995–2000 in A.4 (pages 386–91).

3. The numbers apply to the period of 1985–2000; see ECOR 29 (World Conflict Index), forthcoming; Scherrer 1999*d*. Rudolph Rummel has argued that the death toll of what he calls *democide* (e.g. includes genocide) was much higher than that of wars in the the past 20th century; see Rummel, R.J.: 'Power, genocide and mass murder', JPR 31:1. 1994. 2-3.

4. The particular character of a conflict situation has to be assessed and analyzed in radical contextualization (historical and regional context) of individual case studies / monographs. One of the pertinent limits of research in this area is the difficult relationship between theory and empirical studies. Theorist often talk about genocide committed elsewhere and wars been fought in far away places -- without ever acquiring practical knowledge about a given conflict, thus without knowing about the horrors of mass violence. On the other hand empiricists tend to extrapolate too much from particular experience. An appropriate approach is trying to realize a genuine relationship by combining these two spheres of research.

5. On genocide in the Congo Free State see: Hochschild, Adam: *King Leopold's Ghost: A Story of Greed, Terror, and Heroism in Colonial Africa*. Houghton Mifflin 1998. On genocide in German South-West Africa see Trotha, Trutz von: 'Kolonialgenozid an den Hereros und Namas in 'Deutsch-Süd-West' Afrika' (conference paper 1997).

6. Free download of the text of the convention and the status of ratifications and reservations from http://www.unhchr.ch/html/menu3/b/p_genoci.htm on the website of the UN High Commissioner of Human Rights.

7. 'Genocide means ... acts committed with the intent to destroy, in whole or in part, a national, ethnic, racial or religious group as such' (article 2). United Nations: Convention on the Prevention and Punishment of the Crime of Genocide 1948. U.N.T.S. no. 1021, vol. 78 (1951), p.277. The convention was adopted by UN General Assembly (resolution 260 (III) A) on 9 Dec. 1948.

8. Examples for massive population transfer: Soviet Union deportations of a dozen nationalities from 1943 and to a lesser degree in the Baltic states from 1945, China in Tibet and Eastern Turkestan (Xinjiang) since the 1950s, Indonesia with its policy of transmigration in West Papua, Moluccas and Aceh, Bangla Desh in the Chittagong Hill Tracts 1979–92, Ethiopia under Mengistu in Oromia, in Gambella lowlands and the inter lake area (until 1990), Iraq and Iran in Kurdestan. (The destruction of hundreds of Kurdish villages in Turkey/Anatolia constitutes a crime against humanity and is beyond population transfer or deportations.)

9. Fein, Helen: 'Genocide. A sociological perspective'; Current Sociology 38: 1. 1990. However, the notion of defencelessness of the victims is not relevant to genocide alone but also plays a role in war crimes against civilians and POWs; see Tanaka 1998 and 2002.

10. A preliminary report released by Rwanda's Ministry of Local Government and Social Affairs says that 1,074,017 people were killed in massacres and genocide between 1 October 1991 and 31 December 1994. The ministry's report, the result of a recent census, showed that 66 percent of genocide victims were male, people aged between one and 21 years had been the most affected age group for both sexes, and of those killed, 97.3 percent were Tutsi. UN OCHA: 'Rwanda: Government puts genocide victims at 1.07 million'. Nairobi: IRIN 19 December 2001.

11. Victims were the entire Tutsi minority and the political opposition among the Hutu.

12. The genocide in the Congo Free State of Belgium king Leopold II was probably the largest but definitely the largest ever in Africa (atrocities continued for decades in the Belgian Congo, a Belgium state's colony, 1909–1960; see Hochschild 1998).
13. Rwanda genocide see: African Rights 1994. Joint Evaluation of Emergency Assistance to Rwanda / Millwood, D. (chief ed.) 1996. Prunier 1995. Scherrer 1997, also: 'The Rwanda genocide' in Förster/Hirschfeld 1999; and Scherrer 2002*a*.
14. Cases of large-scale genocide since 1945 were the extermination committed by the Hima-Tutsi army in Burundi (1972) against the Hutu elites and Tutsi-Banyaruguru opposition, the Khmer Rouge (1975–9), the Barundi Hutu against their Tutsi neighbors in October/November 1993, Rwanda's Hutu regime against the Tutsi (4–6/1994) and Sudan's Arab or Arabized regimes (1954–1972; 1984 until today) against the Nuba in Central Sudan and against Dinka, Nuer and other nation peoples in Southern Sudan.
15. Genocide, totalitarism and the 'national idea' in Turkey 1915: Armenians as all others of the more than 150 communities of the huge Ottoman Empire were organized under the *millet*-system that was providing for religious freedom and self-administration of their own affairs. With the disintegration of the empire the Armenians became the targets of persecution more than any other non-Muslim minority (such as Greeks and Arameans, while Jews were never persecuted). This stood in stark contrast to their situation in Eastern Armenia, which was part of the Russian Tsarist Empire. Genocide against the Armenians started with systematic liquidation of Armenian leaders in Anatolia, in autumn 1914, to become exterminatory deportations and hunger marches in Spring 1915, continued throughout 1916, restarted after the armistice in 1918 with 500.000 more Armenians perishing 1918–1923. The latter period overlapped with Ataturk's raise to power. The *Aghet* claimed the death of more than 1.5 million Armenians, exterminated during the whole period from 1915 to 1923. — Comparative research of the Aghet, has been conducted by Helen Fein ('A formula for genocide: Comparison of the Turkish genocide (1915) and the German Holocaust (1939–1945)'; in: Comparative Studies in Sociology, 1, 1978) and Robert Melson (Revolution and genocide: On the origins of Armenian genocide and the Holocaust. Chicago: CUP 1992). Also: Taner Akçam, Mihran Dabag, Bernhard Lewis, Vahakan N. Dadrian, a/o.
16. Nolte, Hans-Heinrich: 'Der Krieg im Osten als Vernichtungskrieg'; in: Landtag Niedersachsen: Ausstellung ‚Vernichtungskrieg, Verbrechen der Wehrmacht 1941–1944'. Hannover: LGN 1999,43–68. Nolte, H.H: 'Völker- und Massenmorde im 20. Jahrhundert: Zur Problematik des Vergleichens'. Potsdam: FES 1997
17. In the case of the Young Turks it was the re-discovering of Pan-Turkism and the construction of Turanism combined with late nationalism. In the case of the Nazis it was the superiority of pure Aryan race, derived from both, false myths about heroic German tribes and the incredible race theories of the 19th century. Such racist myths were combined with both, age-old Anti-Semitism harbored chiefly by the catholic church and other churches deeply involved in collaborating with the Nazis, and the 'idea' of *Volksgemeinschaft*—a homogenous or rather homogenized all-German nation; it included the Austrians and most German minorities in a dozen occupied countries. Despite its pre-modern ideologies both genocidal processes were embedded in the discourse of modernity and late European nationalism. It was executed within a specific rationality of bureaucratic pedantry and militarized perfection, by using the latest technological means—in the case of German fascism, thus aiming at a complete fusion of genocide and modernity.
18. In the example of East Timor the US acted indirectly. Declassified documents (see http://www.gwu.edu/~nsarchiv/NSAEBB/NSAEBB62/) prove that US president Ford and his anti-communist *superman*, Henry Kissinger, after just having lost their 'total

war' against the Vietnamese people, feared the spread of 'communism' and gave Indonesian general Suharto the green light to overrun East Timor and annex it.

19. The differences between the two parts were extreme in all aspects (geography, culture, language, ethnicity, economy and history); religion could not work as a substitute in the long run. The only thing in common was the fear of Hindu domination.

20. Twelve million Hindu Bengali fled to India and it was only due to the intervention by the Indian army in Dec. 1971 that the mass murder of 15 percent of population of Eastern Pakistan was stopped. Leo Kuper 1981: 76–80 discusses the case of East Pakistan, based on the *prima facie* assessment made by the International Commission of Jurists 1992.

21. Self-defense by the victimized group of Banyamulenge Tutsi in eastern Congo-Zaire was supported by Rwanda. It kicked off an effort of some six countries to dump the Mobutu dictatorship was successful in 1996/7 but subsequently led to a new (more costly) war from August 1998.

22. For declassified documents see *Digital National Security Archive*; it contains file collections on US involvement in Afghanistan, Cuba, El Salvador, Iran-Contra Affair, Nicaragua, Philippines, South Africa and East Timor. The case of East Timor was added in December 2001. The East Timor question was part of the continuous 'strategic relationship with the anticommunist Suharto regime, especially in the wake of the communist victory in Vietnam, when Ford and Kissinger wanted to strengthen relations with anticommunists and check left-wing movements in the region,' according to Burr and Evans: DNSA Briefing Book 62 (www.gwu.edu/~nsarchiv/NSAEBB/NSAEBB62/).

23. Table: Genocide and mass murder (Melson 1997)

Genocide	total (full scale)	partial (lower scale)
domestic / intra-state	total domestic genocide	partial domestic genocide
foreign / (neo-) colonial	total foreign genocide	partial foreign genocide

See: Melson, Robert: Problems of comparative genocide. Paper. Stuttgart: BfZ 1997

24. Harff, Barbara: 'The Ethiology of Genocides'; in: Wallimann, Isidor and Michael N. Dobkowski: Genocide in the Modern Age. Ethiology and case studies of mass death. New York/London: Greenwood 1987, 41–60. Melson 1992, op.cit. (footnote 15).

25. Harff developed an early warning system of genocide and mass violence for the previous US government; the project was supported by then vice-president Al Gore. See: Harff, Barbara: *Strategic approaches to genocide prevention*. AGS conference 'The Future of Genocide' paper. Madison: University of Wisconsin 1999.

26. These waves followed during WW1, WW2, the decolonization period and the collapse of USSR and Yugoslavia, which has led to the end of the Cold War. See Melson, Robert: *Twentieth century genocide*. PIOOM award ceremony. Leiden 12/1993

27. The elites need to 'reconstruct society, (and) revitalize support for the state by way of a new system of legitimization' (Melson). Melson 1997, 17. Genocidal aims, although pathological and anti-human as they might appear, are part of larger political aims.

28. Some 56 states are not yet party to the UN Genocide Convention. Among them are genocidal states such as Sudan, the Democratic Republic of the Congo and Indonesia, as well as violence-prone states such as Tajikistan, Angola, Uzbekistan and Bolivia.

29. The first meeting of the assembly of states parties to the Rome treaty is expected to convene in September 2002. Early in 2003 the judges will be elected and the ICC, based in The Hague, Netherlands, will get operational probably mid-2003. The ICC is expected to realize universal justice and to have preventive force by contributing to discourage massive human right violations in the future.

Chapter 4

Structural Features of Ethno-nationalist Conflicts

To deny the ethnic factor does not seem serious to me, and is also becoming increasingly difficult. The other, equally dubious, approach is to name every intra-state conflict to be an 'ethnic conflict'. For some authors the term 'ethnic' is almost self-explicatory; others use the term when they are unable to otherwise explain the driving force of a conflict. Others again use the term to indicate that any attempt to conflict resolution would be futile.

Some denounce the ethnic factor as 'pathological' and 'barbaric'. Ethnic strife is described as pathological by more than a few authors; but what they actually mean by this is (a) symptomatic of some underlying 'disease', (b) deviant, and, (c) compulsively (or rather instinctively) motivated violence, seen as atavistic.[1] The same authors would probably be unable to make a difference between ethnicity and ethnicization. The prophecies of doom and gloom about challenges to the state's monopoly on force often care little with what legitimacy certain states (such as Burma and the Sudan) claim this kind of monopoly, or how arbitrarily and violently it is used against the population. Restyling ethno-national conflicts as wars of secession or struggles for autonomy does not get us much further either; such wars are often (as in Eritrea) political ventures by multi-ethnic movements of liberation, which do not want to have anything to do with ethnicity, or such wars occur in multi-ethnic regions (e.g., eastern Nicaragua).

Reference to major objects of contention and to the difficult processes involved in state formation, or to the competition for scarce resources, is not, of itself, sufficient. The question of state formation simultaneously and immediately also raises the crucial question of control of the state as a new instrument of power.[2] Indeed, state formation has generally been, and still generally is, ethnicized—over and above the many cases of manifestly ethnocratic rule; it can, at all events, not be separated from ethnic factors. The same applies to the distribution of resources, which often follows ethnic criteria. The colonially pre-resolved question of which ethnic or national group would 'carry' the state, or of which would be the state-nation—a question to which there was often a variety of possible answers—determined whether people lived or died.[3]

An excellent example of this is the historical gaffe committed by the Colonial Office in London in regard to the future of the Sudan. The obvious option of granting separate statehood to African, Christian-Animist Southern Sudan was rejected by the desk-bound powers-that-be in the Colonial Office. The worst possible variant—that of linkage to Arab-Muslim Sudan—was eventually also preferred to the second option of fusion with northern Uganda, with which Southern Sudan was in an ethnic continuum. This error of power politics—with predictably dramatic consequences, of which the trauma of the Arab slave-hunts in the south should have served as a clear warning—led to a permanent state of war in the south of Sudan. As a result of failure in decision-making amongst two factions of colonial bureaucrats, the Sudanese civil war that has been going from 1955 to the present day—with a single interruption, from 1972 to 1984—has cost an estimated three million lives.

The core causal elements of ethnic conflicts include the Eurocentric or alien nature of modern nation-statehood and the inadequate degree of integration in the post-colonial states. Appropriation of the state by a dominant ethnic group, and the use of the state-apparatus as a tool for enforcing ethnic dominance or particularistic interests, lead inexorably to opposition, which, in its turn, is often mobilized along ethnic lines. The modern state has seldom revealed itself as a 'legitimate order' or a 'conflict-mediating institution' in the Third World.

Even if the phenomenon of 'politicized ethnicity'—probably a tautological concept—is 'only' an expression of fragmentation into social groups and of institutional weakness and lacking integrating force on the part of political systems associated with peripheral (and some other) states, it still ought to be taken seriously as such, and investigated. More detailed research could show what role ethnic difference plays in the composition or decomposition of large social groups (such as socio-economic classes), of abstract collectivities, and of putative communities.

Is There Such a Thing as an Ethnic Conflict *Per Se*?

That ethnicity and ethnic otherness may not only be an 'expression' but also a cause of conflictual processes of fragmentation has been more than amply demonstrated by my own research. However, a larger group of colleagues, who are measuring social differentiation—exclusively or mainly—on an economic scale, are predisposed to underestimate (or sometimes even to deny) the importance and acuteness of ethnic or cultural difference.[4]

Ethnic Identity between 'Fiction' and 'Illusion'?

Many European conflict-researchers have competed in their neglect of ethnicity. To justify this, some take refuge in feeble claims that there is no scientifically reliable definition of ethnicity; others assert that the concept of ethnicity has only 'limited explanatory value'. This latter stance is justified by reference to the alleged 'fiction' or 'illusion' of the 'supposed authenticity' of ethnic identity and its politicization in ethno-nationalism.[5]

The key issue is generally overlooked. It is precisely what is inadequately named and claimed to be the 'illusion', in other words the fictitious, putative, and allegedly primordial element of ethnicity, that contributes in great part to the physical violence associated with the ethnic factor and that gives ethnic mobilization added thrust. That is why, the 'illusion' and its complexity-reducing mechanism must be scientifically deconstructed down to its very detail—not with a view to re-mythologizing the world but, on the contrary, as a de-mythologizing enterprise. Any attempt to generalize from the illusoriness, abstractness, and unappetizing character of European nationalism, and to label all ethnic identities *per se* as 'fictions', must be rejected as an example of Eurocentric presumption and crass ignorance.

Another frequently heard objection to the concept of ethnic conflict is based on a non-dialectic mechanic separation of form and content. According to this, ethnicity is not the real cause of the particular conflict concerned, but 'only' the form it assumes.

The Search for the True Cause

Political, economic, or (more recently) ecological causes—which those involved have '*unfortunately* overlooked' as the 'true cause'—are seen to be operating; or else the ethnic, ethno-centric interpretation (often traceable to 19th century racial theories), and in some cases even the top-down state-driven ethnicization that may become deadly relevant for all involved, are 'objectified' (as power struggle, resource competition, battle for political survival, etc.).[6] The physical violence resulting from state ethnicization in Rwanda, and the attempts at explanation offered by Rwanda 'experts', who themselves were part of the problem, have been discussed by me elsewhere.[7]

Yet another objection sees ethnicity not as (false) 'authenticity', but, trivially, as 'the result of a prior process'—hence, almost as a secondary phenomenon. This would no doubt be applicable to other causes or forms of conflict, given that, of course, every cause of conflict is the result of a historical process.

The issue of ethnicity as resulting from, or being entailed by, something else should be put aside in favour of an analysis of the dominant elements in a conflictual formation. Almost every conflict is made up of a number of causal strands. Given that this is so, the question is then which elements have primary, secondary, or tertiary dominance—not from the point of view of the outsider, the quasi-objective observer, but from a standpoint that takes into account the views and experiences of the actors in the conflict. It is the perception of those involved in the conflict (not ascription by conflict researchers) that is ultimately the deciding factor. Analysis of war propaganda may be one valid area of operation for the researcher in this connection, but the main task is empirical fact-finding on the ground. Allegedly objective causes of conflict are of little relevance if they are not socially transmitted and communicated and if such causes are not perceived to be what they claim to be by those affected.[8] Uncoupling the causal explanation of a conflict from the consciousness of the actors can be seen as presumptuous and is certainly misleading.

Ethnic bones of contention, and those that are subjected to ethno-centric interpretation (and we Europeans are past-masters in this art), overlap with one another and form a complex and often tangled mixture. Ethnicity is therefore necessarily an 'ill-defined concept'. Nevertheless there is a number of objective and subjective criteria what an ethnic group is all about. To anyone who considers ethnicity merely as a blanket term covering every manner of affiliation, the specifically ethnic permutation of socialization will remain a mystery.

Ethnicity is not an 'Explanatory Factor' in Armed Conflicts

The concepts of 'minority' and 'ethnic group', which are often used in connection with ethno-national conflicts, are in need of elucidation. Similarly, the almost customary confusion of the concepts of 'nation', 'state', and 'nation-state' indicate a need for a thoroughgoing definition of terms. Colonial expansion put an end to the autonomous existence of a variety of social formations and political systems. 'Concepts' and reality were homogenized. The export of the nation-state model to the colonies ran into a host of difficulties, because no appropriate foundations for this kind of construct existed in the extra-European world.

Characteristics that define an ethnos or indigenous people as a nationality or as a nation without its own state continue to be a subject of dispute, for power-political (not analytical) reasons. Nowadays, however, stipulations are acquiring greater political relevance. The relationship between national minorities, nationalities, and nations on the one hand, and recognized states on the other can no longer be declared to be solely an internal matter of states; it is increasingly being viewed as part of international relations.

Reference to ethnicity simplifies the search for the causes of conflict not one jot. Ethnicity is not an 'explanatory factor' in armed conflicts, nor should it be pressed into service as one because other explanations fail.[9] Often—as in the case of Yugoslavia—one can talk of a hybrid ethnicization of religious groups.[10] The violent conflict in Kosovo 1998/99 was the first war in the region showing a clear-cut ethnic component, with Serbian armed elements (army, police and paramilitary gangs) versus Albanian Kosovar civilians, and from May 1999 UCK elements versus Serbian and Roma civilians (after 78 days of NATO bombing of the Federal Republic of Yugoslavia). The hope is that such practises will be stopped by an administration dominated by the party led by the veteran leader Ibrahim Rugova, which won elections held in Kosovo 2000 and in 2002.

To call for such 'ethnic conflicts' to be labelled blanket-fashion as 'identity conflicts' because there is nothing very ethnic about them is simply playing with words. Amnesia about historical developments, and a lack of understanding for the justified fears of non-dominant minorities, made comprehension of the wars in the Balkans impossible and encouraged the grotesquely distorted and more or less unquestioned coverage of them in the mass media.

The Concept of the Ethnos and the Nation-without-State

Some of the problems already discussed crop up from the fact that the basic concept of the ethnos is not clearly defined. In ethnology it is delimited, but contentiously, within certain boundaries.[11] The variety and number of categorizations offered by the different ethnological schools is very great; but any combination of the more accessible definitions is not really possible, given the differing approaches and standards. The most frequently mentioned factors are shared origin and similar culture, religion, class, and language.[12] However, two of these (class and religion) are not apposite.

The Ethnic Form of Socialization

The ethnic form of socialization must be distinguished from socialization into social classes. The extent and boundaries of the two are often congruent, but they can also overlap, as in more complex societies, or exclude one another, as in egalitarian societies. Religion must be rejected totally as a criterion, since it is an ideological domain, which, within the framework of colonialism, was mostly externally directed and fortuitously selected.

Imported religions and syncretistic variants are more common and/or more dominant than indigenous religions among the 2,500 to 6,500 ethnic groups world-wide.[13] The term of 'ethnic groups' ought to be used as a technical term. According to linguists there are some 6,500 ethnic core groups worldwide. The general supposition is that religions, like nationalisms, generate a transcendent identity-forming link, whereas ethnicity, though identity-forming, has a divisive effect. This supposition does not seem generalizable. Connections (or rather conflicts) between religion, nationalism, and ethnicity ought not to be denied.[14] One of several possible approaches to the subject focuses on attributes based on clusters of special features or social specializations, which are both seen as constituting 'ethnic markers'.

Ethnic makers are only relevant within the framework of inter-ethnic relations. Often they only become a major focus of perception when situations of conflict arise. The attributes of an ethnic community include, as a minimum a self-reproducing community with a name, a culture, a distinct language, a memory and solidarity between its members.[15] These attributes by no means constitute a definitive checklist; they are, rather, an attempt to get closer to the problem of ethnicity, the individual elements of which need to be examined more closely and be defined in detail for each concrete instance.[16] Over-emphasising individual elements, such as participation in a shared culture or the social dimension (which sees ethnic groups as a particular form of social organization), would appear to be problematic.[17]

The Conceptual Shift to National Minorities and Nationalities

In the concrete hostile conditions of internal or external colonization (with its unconditional claims of state sovereignty) an ethnos that does not reshape itself into a nation/nationality risks destruction as an independent unit. An ethnic community in the position of a non-dominant group may be regarded as a national minority or nationality—a nation without an own state—if, despite the claims to dominance and sovereignty from outside, it constitutes a distinct space of communication and interaction, i.e. it is able to form or maintain a public sphere of its own; it has a particular mode of production and life identifiable with it, and is able to reproduce it; it maintains some form of political organization; it has settled an identifiable area of land (more than a neighbourhood) or a demarcated territory; it is distinctive, i.e. its members identify themselves or are identified by others as members of this particular community.[18]

In the case of *migrant communities* several of these attributes do apply while others are obviously obsolete due to changed life conditions. Ethnicized or radicalized characteristics are only relevant within the framework of inter-ethnic relations and it is primarily in conflict situations that they become a major focus of perception. The same characteristics—particular socio-cultural practices, for example—may be totally unimportant in various situations of interaction, but in a different context they may suddenly acquire huge significance. For example, skin color and other phenotypic features are of secondary importance in most societies of the Southern hemisphere; but in Western societies, physical characteristics are one of the main distinguishing features.[19]

Ethnic communities may be imagined (Anderson) but as imagined entities they can appear to be significantly more concrete and more tangible than that of the nation. There are differences in perspectives: from the point of view of those concerned, in their *emic* view as opposed to the *etic* view of the outsiders, most ethnic groups—a technical term for scientific purpose—see themselves as a people or as a nation. Ethnic affinity is generally (*emically* speaking) not perceived in any way as ideologically generated or as primordial.[20] (See discussion of primordialism vs. constructivism in anthropological theory.) The hypotheses on this subject are unusually far removed from one another. In a situation of threat, individual elements of personal and collective identity can become enhanced or diminish in influence. Political instrumentalization of mechanisms of demarcation (for the purposes of discrimination and exclusion) plays a role here, as does recourse to socially unconscious elements of group identity. Identity constitutes itself via processes of demarcation that do not occur within a non-discriminatory space and whose modalities cannot be determined freely and independently. The abstract difference of others poses no problem. The experience of real threat from others, or a construed feeling of superiority *vis-à-vis* others, are, in contrast, results of processes of exclusion and polarization. Constant injury to central elements of identity, either from within or from without, elicits specific forms of resistance in each particular case, ranging from withdrawal to rebellion.

Within the framework of socio-political or international legal categorization, an ethnic minority or an indigenous people may be viewed as a nationality. This conceptual shift should essentially be seen as the result of a political process, which, in most cases, has followed a conflictual course. The analysis of competing appellations (such as minority, people, nationality or nation) is not sufficient if no account is made of social judgements, appropriateness, or the power question. The conquest and dominance aspect is of central importance. This constitutive aspect has been acknowledged, notably in the definition of minorities and in particular in the elaboration of new instruments of international law designed to protect them.[21]

An ethno-national community that possesses some crucial attributes develops a distinct collective identity; it could, in political contention, invoke the international legal principle of self-determination. This in no way implies a right to secession—something never acknowledged by the community of states. The creation of new states occurs in accordance with political opportunity. International law speaks of 'nations' but actually means states; most states are multi-ethnic.

In actual political/legal practice, the right to self-determination is often not applied, even in the form of internal self-administration, because in these cases it is (allegedly) not linked to territoriality and because most peoples are generally not recognized as peoples but as minorities. The relevant legal basis is then human rights, which are generally individual rights. As a consequence, the rights of ethno-national communities are located in a precarious 'grey area' between collective international law and individual human rights.

Whether affiliation to an ethnic community becomes politicized and whether the right to self-determination is demanded depend on a large number of factors. It may be said, however, that the fundamental right to self-determination is generally in antagonistic relation to the 'inviolability of the borders' of existing state entities. In the Third World, state territory only rarely corresponds to ethnic territory. State borders, often traced out with a ruler at some official's desk, cut across ethnic borders.

The politicization of the ethnic (or ethnicity) is often seen as a precondition for conflictual processes between states and distinct ethnic groups. From the perspective of any ethno-national community, however, such politicization is, as a rule, not a precondition, but a *result* of conflictual processes. Politicization of the ethnic is one of several possible lines that may be followed by macro-social processes that may develop as a reaction, but not an automatic one, to changes in social surroundings.

Ethno-politicization is thus one possible (but not necessary) consequence of external interference. Such interference can either be destructive in its ultimate effects, as, for example, the preferential treatment of a particular ethnic group by colonial powers. Interference can be destructively structured from the outset, as a form of external aggression, like the invasion of an ethnic territory for the purposes of exploiting resources or of expelling an ethno-national community from its ancestral lands.

False Theses Concerning Ethnicity, Ethnicization, and Ethno-nationalism

In what follows here, I provide an outline rebuttal of the seven most familiar false theses concerning this complex of issues. The detailed analysis of ethnic and ethno-nationalist conflicts, which then follows, should be read as a 'hypertext' to the observations made below. I begin by replying to the most fundamental of the seven erroneous theses.

False thesis No. 1: According to the prognoses of the established political and social sciences concerning modernization and the development of modern societies, ethnicity is generally declining in importance.

Correction No. 1: Contrary to all expectations, the importance and the degree of politicization of ethnicity in violent conflicts, civilian disputes, and social exclusion and demarcation, right down to questions of status and classification, has increased over the last few decades. Ethnicity has increased in importance all over the world. Ethnicity continues to be an element in social contention, not just of a conflictual kind; it seems still (or again) to be an integral factor in many forms of status-allocation.

As a part of state policies of ethnicization-from-above, ethnicity or rather the guided ascribed ethnic identity of non-dominant groups functions as a vehicle for their social exclusion or demarcation and discrimination. In the worst case, ethnicization by the state results in organized mass murder and outright genocide (as in Rwanda 1994).

Pathologization and Accusations of Irrationality

False thesis No. 2: Ethno-nationalism should be viewed either as an expression of backward tribalism, in the form of tribal wars, and as a quasi-natural constant of history, or as a political pathology. The concept of ethnicity therefore has a predominantly negative connotation. The ethnic itself, and the concept of ethnicity, are primitive and backward. Ethno-national movements make use of an irrational ideology.

Correction No. 2: The very idea of ethno-nationalism often causes consternation. Studies on it are suspected by many governments of being politically motivated or of providing a kind of 'guerrilla' back-up by seeking to create identities, shape myths, or offer other legitimacy. In fact, research into the causes of conflict seeks, for analytical purposes, to highlight the conditions under which collective identities and potentials for mobilization emerge.[22] Ethno-nationalism is one of the most contradictory and complex political ideologies of contemporary times. A distinction should be drawn between: 1) ethno-nationalism from below, which sees itself as a civilian political, social, or cultural liberation movement or as an armed movement of resistance against the persecution and endangerment of an oppressed nation/nationality; and 2) destructive ethno-nationalism from above, as part of state strategies designed to consolidate the power of dominant ethnic groups.

Concepts of tribalism, by contrast, are mostly (post-) colonial fabrications, which overlook the fact that ethnicity and ethno-nationalism (particularly in its militant form) are modern concepts and ideologies that contradict the notions of primitivity and backwardness often associated with it. Hence, ethnicity and ethno-nationalism might well be bearers of progressive contents that represent a rational answer to a perceived or real threat. Evidence of the functionality and relativity of ethno-nationalism offered by contemporary examples demonstrates that ethnic-cum-national patterns of thinking and action are not quasi-natural, unchanging historical phenomena but develop from specific social constellations and power-political situations.[23]

Ethno-nationalism as an Element in the World Order

False thesis No. 3: The Cold War has given way to a 'new chaos'. 'Chaos power' is gaining ground, often in 'ethnicized' form. Internal wars have taken the place of inter-state wars as the crucial destabilizing factor in the global order.[24] Within the model of the world of states and the societal world, societal actors have a 'chaoticizing' effect. This order and state claims to sovereignty are being jeopardized by rebels (and not, for example, by internationally active big business).

　　Correction No. 3: Anyone who makes this claim has misconstrued developments since 1945. Internal wars (civil wars) and other internal conflicts have long since become the predominant type of conflict. Through repressive modernization, colonial expansion had relativized ethnic identity in some societies and activated it in others. Opposition to colonial subjection had sometimes organized itself along ethnic lines. Opposition to internal colonization by the new states organized itself from the very outset mainly along ethnic lines (ethno-nationalism from below). Internal conflicts erupted even before, or during, the transition to political independence (as in India and Burma). Compared with the destabilizing effect of ethno-nationalism, the global disruptive threat which international commercial concerns and the power of the financial markets and speculators poses to the sovereignty of most states (not only in the Third World) is far greater.[25]

War-Lordism and Gang Wars as a 'New' Phenomenon?

False thesis No. 4: The new phenomenon of the war lord is a typical expression of our age. More and more contemporary wars are taking the form of hostilities between sub-state organizations, and this will be true of the wars of the future.

　　Correction No. 4: War-lordism, terrorism, organised crime and other types of gang wars are not a new phenomenon; they existed right from the early centuries of feudal Europe (between the Middle Ages and early modern times); and rule by princes of war was a frequent occurrence in Chinese history, in transitional phases after peasant uprisings and/or after the collapse of individual dynasties.[26] Chaotic gang-wars involving warlords and mafia-like interests have occurred in ten states of Africa, Asia, and Latin America were affected, four of them badly; Somalia, Liberia, and, in the wake of the latter, Sierra Leone, were dominated by gang wars, as well as Afghanistan (since the 1970s) and Burma (since the 1950s); to a lesser degree Pakistan, the southern Philippines, parts of Indonesia, Colombia and Peru were also affected.[27] In the 1990s international terrorist gangs of the al-Qaeda network extended their operation area from Afghanistan and Central Asia to West Asia, East Africa and finally to the territory of the United States (September 11, 2001).[28] However, the great majority of wars are still fought out between states and their recalcitrant nationalities, or between states and political opposition-movements.

False thesis No. 5: It is not heavy weapons and regular armies that predominate; mafia-like ethnic-tribal, religious or even 'ethno-fascist' war lords and their gangs are battling it out with one another using light arms and irregular troops.

Correction No. 5: Gang wars have until the mid 1990s been a rather peripheral phenomenon. According to the ECOR index of conflicts (see also the appendices), they were the dominant type in only 3.9 percent of cases (accounting for 7.7 percent of mentions) in 1985–94, though they did rise to 6.25 percent dominance (8.5 percent of mentions) in 1995–96. However, the significant increase of gang wars further continued 1997–2000 (reaching 14 percent, doubling compared to 1995–96). A breakdown of the data indicates that there is a grey area between ethno-national wars and gang wars, and between anti-regime wars and gang wars. It is within this grey area where modern and international forms of terrorist organisations developed. Looking at all the seven types of violent conflict, gang wars occupied the penultimate position in terms of frequency in the decade 1985–94; in 1995–96, however, they moved up to fourth place and increased their share further in 1997–2000. Given the shortness of these latter periods, upward or downward movements are possible. It is therefore too early to talk about a firm long-term trend—though the tendency to gang warfare and globally active terrorism is worrying indeed. This *post-modern* and globalized warfare acquired its own symbols and media-attractive presentations. War lords and their armies besieged the capital cities or fought each other at the centres, in front of TV-cameras (as in Somalia, Liberia, or Afghanistan) or sent video tapes to TV-stations that were eager to show them to the large public (as al-Qaeda's leader bin-Laden). The *CNN-ization* became a constitutive element of post-modern warfare.

False thesis No. 6: As a result of 'tribal' wars, war-lordism, terrorism and gang wars, whole societies and states are being destabilized. A large number of states will collapse and dissolve into chaos.

Correction No. 6: It is true that since 1985 there has been an increase in predominantly inter-ethnic wars (from 13.7 percent to 20 percent) and in gang wars that are waged, mainly without state involvement, between war lords, clan chiefs, tribal princes, drug barons and terrorist gangs (from 3.9 percent to 14 percent), and it is also true that such wars are particularly problematic. Somalia, Liberia/Sierra Leone, Afghanistan, Bosnia, the Caucasus, the Shan state in Burma, Columbia, Peru, and the Lebanon serve as admonitory examples. Of these states, 'only' the first three have largely collapsed and only one state (Somalia) has fully disintegrated and disappeared; in other words, there are still 190 other states in existence. Ethno-nationalist wars, that is to say wars between states and nations or nationalities, have decreased from 44.1 percent of all wars in the decade 1985–94 to 32.7 percent in 1995–2000 (but still remain the most frequently dominant type) while anti-regime wars stood at close to 20 percent during the entire period since 1985. In other words, violent conflicts in which states are the major players (types A, B, C, D and G)—and mostly the aggressors—are twice as frequent as interethnic conflicts and gang wars, which involve predominantly non-state actors (types E and F). Though their impact on the state structure has been vastly exaggerated, the rise of 'tribal' wars, war-lordism, terrorism and other gang wars is nevertheless a matter of great concern in terms of death toll, devastation and destabilization.

False thesis No. 7: Multi-ethnic states will inevitably disintegrate, as has happened with the multi-ethnic states of Europe.

Correction No. 7: There is no automatic link between the frequency and intensity of conflicts and the degree of ethnic homogeneity in a particular region. In many regions of the earth, distinct ethnic groups have lived in peace for centuries. Some of the longest-established states in the world have, at least on their peripheries, tolerated the existence of conglomerates of distinct peoples who were unwilling to be assimilated. Since formal decolonisation started, ethnic nationalism developed to the level of becoming an existential threat to the unitary state system in a large number of countries in the South. For some observers this remained a 'secret' until the first states collapsed; many states did so but 'only' at their peripheries.

Structural Features

Typologies of violent conflicts are generally drawn up according to the criterion of major driving forces or of actors involved (sponsors of the conflict or parties carrying it out). The main types of violent conflict can generally be derived from the constellation of major sponsors pitted against one another.[29] In this context, ethno-national conflicts in the narrower sense are the real forgotten wars: the Western media give them only selective publicity.[30] Conflicts and state-organized mass murder (such as that in Rwanda in 1994) often continue to be portrayed as 'ethnic problems', or indeed as 'tribalism', even where it is quite evident that the underlying lines of conflict have been artificially ethnicized (as in Bosnia, for example).

A schematic classification of armed conflicts in Third World countries according to sponsors of, or parties to, the conflict is a sensible and practical method of division, but as it stands it might convey a static, model-type picture of the situation. As in the case of a typology based on driving forces, it will be brought to life by including structural and classificatory features. My *deconstruction* of violent ethno-national conflicts will here be carried out on the basis of a list of structural features as follows:

1. Potential for such conflicts; number of conflicts within a longish determined period
2. Sponsors of/actors in the conflict and their conflictual relations
3. History of the conflict: background and causal factors
4. Causes of the conflict
5. Triggers to the conflict and relationship of these to the causes
6. Matters in dispute and classification by urgency
7. Aims (purpose, military objectives), programme of conflict sponsors
8. Opposition organizations as representatives of the interests of the parties to the war: leadership, recruiting base, troops, influence of leadership / leaders and possible (counter-) élites
9. Course of the conflict, conduct of the war and resources used: form and legitimation of the violence, duration and intensity of the hostilities, military organization, arms, supplies
10. Resources, hinterland and the question of outside involvement
11. Possible solutions and mechanisms of regulation aimed at preventing violence and dealing with the conflict constructively[31]
12. Examples[32]

These features, as they appear in all subspecies of conflicts between Third World states and the nations/nationalities whom they view as citizens, will be examined in what follows here. There continues to be an urgent need for research into the nature and structural features of ethno-national conflicts. Taken together, conflicts with ethno-national, inter-ethnic, communal or 'tribal' components account for two-thirds of all current conflicts worldwide. Multi-sided conflicts are proliferating in over-determined, highly complex conflict-formations—notably as a dangerous legacy of disintegrating post-colonial multi-nation states with systems of ethnicized class-rule, and also in a number of minority ethnocracies.[33]

Statistical Conflict Potential

The number of ethno-nationalist or ethicised conflicts is huge but largely under-researched. According to Nietschmann, in 1978–88, out of a total of 120 armed conflicts, 72 percent were susceptible of ethnic interpretation.[34] The number of states and ethnic groups involved in violent conflicts has multiplied since 1945.[35] In the decade from 1985 to 1994, the ECOR World Conflict Index shows 66 violent conflicts with a predominant role of ethnos, ethnicity or ethnicization (types B, D, E and G, 66.25 percent out of a total of 102; see Table A.3). This high share sank in the period 1995–2000 considerably to 61,7 percent. In other words, the various subtypes of 'ethnic conflicts' together made a solid majority of well over 60 percent of all current wars and mass violence. By far the most frequent dominant conflict type is violent ethno-nationalism, accounting for dominance in 31,8 percent (1985 to 1994: 44.1 percent) of all cases, followed by the inter-ethnic type, which rose to 23.3 percent dominance (up from 13.7 percent).

According to the ECOR Index the most frequently dominant conflict type for the period of 1995 to 2000 continued to be the ethno-nationalist (31.8 percent), followed by inter-ethnic wars (23.3 percent), the latter with a strong increase, followed by anti-regime wars (19.6 percent) and gang wars and terrorism (14 percent), which were almost doubling compared to the mid-1990s, decolonization wars and interstate conflicts (4.7 percent). Genocide (1.9 percent) remains the rarest type of violent conflict but the one with the highest mortality. Those conflicts that acquired a dominant ethnic character (types B, D, E and G) account for 61.7 percent, which is noteworthy less then the two third or 66.25 percent in the decade 1985–1994 of all contemporary violent conflicts in recent years.

Historically, the increase in the number of violent ethno-national conflicts occurred in the wake of particular phases of decolonisation and affected the particular continents in varying ways. It was the *new states* of the Third World, first in Asia since 1948 and then in Africa from the 1960s —often under chaotic circumstances 'released' into independence—that became the main theatre for ethno-nationalist and inter-ethnic conflicts. In the 1970s, violent ethno-national conflicts once again began to occur in Europe—in the Basque country (Euskadi, north-west Spain and south-west France), in Northern Ireland (part of the United Kingdom), and on Corsica (part of France). In Eastern Europe, the ethnic potential for conflict became more and more evident from the mid 1980s, and more and more dramatic from 1989–91. Towards the end of the 1980s, the same was true in the southern parts of the USSR—in Tajikistan and the South Caucasus—and, from 1991, in the collapsing Yugoslavia (Serb minorities in Slavonia and Krajina vs. Croatians, multi-cultural Bosnia, Kosovo, which was *de facto* disconnected from Serbia by the 1999 NATO intervention, and finally the export of the Kosovo crisis by the UCK-KLA to Macedonia in 2000–1).

Until the mid 1990s the global ethno-national trend has grown almost continually since the World War II. The number of ongoing major violent conflicts has risen from five cases in 1948 up to 54 violent conflicts during the 1990s. In recent years there was a general but slow decrease of the number of ethno-nationalist conflicts (and an increase of interethnic conflicts and gang wars) but the conflict panorama remained contradictory: decrease in Asia and the Orient (North Africa and Middle East) versus increase in Africa. In contrast to inter-state wars, ethno-national conflicts are generally of longer duration—another reason why the total annual number of wars waged is constantly increasing. Numbers about the current trends differ a lot. CIDCM (Gurr et al 2000) was alone to prospect a substantial decrease in terms of numbers and intensity of armed conflicts during the 1990s.[36] AKUF, HIIK and SIPRI-DPCR present much lower figures and detected stagnation of numbers or a slight increase in recent years (see Table 2.1), while PIOOM and ECOR registered an increase in numbers and intensity of violent conflicts in recent years.

Since 1953, the number of newly started wars has stood at between one and ten per year; since the mid–1990s there was a slow decline due to the combination of less new conflicts and more ongoing old conflicts (temporarily) resolved. The increase in the number of wars has been the result of various phases of decolonisation and began as early as 1948 with the start of decolonisation in British India. The largest increases occurred: between 1962 and 1965 (Afro-Asian decolonisation); in the mid-1970s (second phase of decolonisation following the revolution in Portugal); and in 1990 (upheavals in the USSR and Eastern Europe). Ethno-nationalism is thus by no means a new phenomenon; it has merely come to greater attention in the West because of the end of the Cold War.

Various so-called regional conflicts or 'proxy wars' were resolved during the 1980s, that were conflicts exacerbated by the Cold War divide; others were not resolved but mutated to 'ordinary' interethnic or ethno-nationalist conflicts, such as the high-intensity conflicts in Angola and Afghanistan, thus putting some question marks to the applicability of the concept of 'proxy wars'. Such wars could have taken the forms of inter-state conflicts (type C), anti-regime wars (A) or wars of destabilization (D), or political-cum-ideological insurrections involving outside actors (A+).[37] By contrast, ethno-national conflicts (B) are mostly of long duration and, in addition, generally do not—unlike decolonisation conflicts (D)—admit to third-party mediation, United Nations dispute-settlement, or internationally monitored peace-agreements.

The Actors Involved and Their Conflicting Relations

Using the sponsors of conflict as a basis, seven forms of ethno-national conflict between states and nations can be distinguished. The conflictual relations between states and nations/nationalities in state versus nation conflicts (SvN) are generally characterized by imbalance in military strength, resources, and the numerical size of the recruiting base. The 'majority versus minority' constellation dominates totally in Europe, but only to a limited extent in the Third World. In Africa, most states have a dominant group, but it is often only a quasi-majority or a minority. Instead of everything being geared purely to numerical relations, the questions of power and dominance should also be posed. International structural framework conditions favour—often ethnocratically ruled—states (as the major actors in the world system), whilst working to the disadvantage of non-dominant peoples, whose struggle to survive, to deter, and to defend by appealing to the 'international order' is delegitimised.

In the list below, the types of conflict A-G (A = anti-regime insurgency, B = ethno-nationalism from below, C = inter-state war, D = decolonisation, F = inter-ethnic or communal violence, E = gang wars, terrorism and war-lordism, and G = genocide, massacres and organized mass murder), as detailed in chapter 2 and in the indexes of contemporary violent conflicts (Tables A1–4 in the Appendices), are included in parentheses:[38]

1. State versus Nation/Nationality, SvN (Type B und G): The state orders the execution of genocide against a minority or/and members of a distinct ethnic, national, racial or religious group with the intent to destroy the groups in whole or in part (Type G, e.g. Rwanda 1994). The Central government sends the army out against armed elements fighting 'in the name' of a distinct nationality; in this case a mostly lengthy conflict of varying intensity ensues (e.g. Burma v. Karen since 1948). About half of all current conflicts are ascribable to this type. The application of international law is problematic. The aim of the nation/nationality waging the struggle is autonomy, a federal or confederal solution, or independence. A solution can in certain circumstances be achieved through cultural, geographical, or regional autonomy, frequently also through political reforms (including reforms of the structure of the state), and in some cases only through independence and separate statehood—in other words, through secession.

2. Several States versus One Nation, SSvN (Type BC): Starting-position similar to that in classic SvN conflicts but more complex; currently there are about ten SSvN conflicts in progress. The most important example is the conflict of the states of Turkey, Iran, Iraq, and Syria against the Kurds. Kurdistan has been divided since 1637; since the 1920s (uprisings in Turkey), the conflict has claimed 500,000 victims. The strongest force was

until its sudden demise some years ago the PKK (founded 1978, engaged in hostilities from 1984 to 1998), which competed with older organizations which, for tactical reasons, have collaborated with successive central governments of one or more of the four states where the Kurds met hostile governments.

3. State versus Several Nations, SvSN (Types B, BA): This is the typical form of conflict in multi-national states: Indonesia, India, Burma, the Sudan, Ethiopia, etc. Minorities under threat from central governments often form alliances with other ethno-national rebel-groups or politically/ideologically motivated insurgents in order to be able to co-ordinate their military and political operations.

4. Insurrection versus Nation(s)/Nationality(ies), IvN/NvI (Types BA, BF and incl. F elements): Since 1985 there have only been a few cases of this type—e.g. the FDN versus the Miskitu and Sumu in Nicaragua. Conflicts between rebel and ethnic movements are often halted only on tactical grounds, or else break out again later, when the rebels take over the state, or even earlier.

5. Nation/Nationality versus Nation/Nationality, NvN (Type E): The classic form here is the so-called tribal conflict. There were only a small number of armed NvN conflicts until the 1990s when a marked increase took place; such conflicts often take the SvN form due to the fact that the state is in the 'possession' of a dominant ethnic group. At present, there are fifteen cases and 37 or 238 mentionings (see Table 2.2). Their character emerges most clearly in conflict situations characterized by disintegration or collapse of the state (as in Liberia, Southern Somalia, and Afghanistan) due to communal strife or interethnic conflict and often—additionally— mixed up with different forms of gang wars.

Political conflicts can assume the character of NvN conflicts if at least some of those sponsoring them are guided by a tribal consciousness (e.g. the Inkatha in South Africa) or by religious affiliations (as in Northern Ireland, Bosnia, the Lebanon and Afghanistan). Class conflicts can also be ethnicized and assume a hybrid form of NvN conflicts (e.g., the Hima-Tutsi and/or the state of Burundi versus the Hutu or the converse constellation, of Hutu versus Tutsi, in Rwanda in 1959–94).

6. Multi-sided Wars/Conflicts, SvI+SvN (Types A+B), sometimes IvN (Type E): These involve ethno-national, rebel, and state actors in every combination, and they produce complex situations of conflict. A few examples from Burma, Ethiopia, the Philippines, Indonesia, and India will illustrate these conflict constellations—which are extremely resistant to constructive treatment, for which the ECOR series provide insider views.[39]

In Burma (Myanmar), four sides, each comprising between one and a dozen actors, are fighting one another: the military junta versus the

Communist Party of Burma (CPB) until 1989, and versus the ethnic rebel alliance of the National Democratic Front (NDF) and the pan-ethnic opposition-movement the Democratic Alliance of Burma (DAB) from 1988. The CPB and NDF sometimes co-operated and sometimes fought with one another. The nominally pan-ethnic CPB is now neutralized, having dissolved into seven ethnic-cum-tribal armies, some of which co-operate, or have concluded cease-fires, with the junta (SLORC, renamed SPDC). Some sections of rebel armies are identical with the drug guerrillas (MTA, UWSA); others are fighting it (NDF, DAB). From 1993, DAB members came under increasing pressure (including from the neighbouring states of China and Thailand) to come to an arrangement with the regime.

In Ethiopia, the Mengistu regime, until its collapse and the defeat of its army in May 1991, was waging several wars simultaneously against the four large-scale opposition organizations of TPLF (changing to EPRDF), OLF, EPLF, and EPRP, as well as several smaller ones. The Ethiopian People's Revolutionary Democratic Front (EPRDF), which is now the party of government and is dominated by the Tigrai people (TPLF), is an alliance of ethno-national (TPLF, OPDO) and left-wing 'pan-Ethiopian' thus Amhara rebels (EPDM). After one year of broad multi-party governance in Ethiopia the EPRDF wanted all powers and continued Mengistu's war against the ethno-national Oromo Liberation Front (OLF), which is the most important of several organizations of the Oromo majority (about 50 percent of the population). In addition, soon after taking the capital in May 1991, the EPRDF started fighting against the formerly Maoist EPRP, with which the TPLF had already engaged in a bloody 'fratricidal struggle' in the 1980s. The EPLF became the party of government in liberated Eritrea. The former rebels became oppressors; since mid 1992 the OLF and other liberation movements are fighting the new Abyssinian minority regime of EPRDF. From spring 1998 to 2000 an intra-Abyssinian war started between Eritrean and Ethiopian Tigrai; the pretext was a piece of dry land but the underlying issue is a struggle for hegemony between EPLF and TPLF.

In the Philippines, the armed forces of the state are battling on the one hand against the pro-communist New People's Army (NPA), which is allied with the ethno-national Cordillera, and, on the other, against the Islamic resistance-organization on Mindanao and the Sulu archipelago (MNLF and many splinter groups), which are fighting for independence.

In Indonesia, the Javanese-dominated army was fighting against several ethno-national and rebel groups (FRETELIN in East Timor, OPM in West Papua, GAM in Aceh, Moluccas, and others); after the fall of dictatorship and the 1999 crisis and an autonomy law came in force early 2001. In the Indian Union, a larger number of SvI and SvN conflicts are taking place simultaneously, with up to ten conflicts being waged at the time.[40]

7. Decolonisation Conflicts (Type D): These are political-cum-nationalist conflicts. A foreign state occupation of a (former) colonial territory (FSO). Such (post-) colonial occupations of internationally recognized territories always have an ethno-national component. Resistance to such occupations, carried out in violation of international law, is generally armed and often extends over a long period of time, for instance since 1948 in Palestine (Oslo treaty of 1993 not implemented), about 30 years in Eritrea (liberated in May 1991) and West Papua (autonomy law passed Oct 2001); genocide in the mid 1970s in East Timor (full independence in May 2002), Diego Garcia (unsolved) and Western Sahara (UN resolutions not implemented).

In all, a dozen cases were regarded as decolonisation conflicts: Palestine–Israel (West Bank, Gaza, Golan); Eritrea and Namibia (both independent); Western Sahara (subject of unsuccessful UN mediation); East Timor (referendum, massacre and UN intervention 1999); West Papua; the Chagos Island chain (which includes Diego Garcia, the Indian Ocean atoll used as the main base for the USA in the region, e.g. from October 2001 for the bombardments in Afghanistan); and other countries and terrirtories.

Recently there were new developments in two decolonization cases. It was only in March 2002 that the United Nations took a stronger stance on Palestine (in the Security Council Resolution 1397, 2002), adopted by a vote of 14 in favour to none against), 'affirming a vision of a region where two States, Israel and Palestine, live side by side within secure and recognized borders' (ibid.), and Secretary-General Kofi Annan calling on Israel to end its illegal occupation of Palestine and the use of excessive force against civilian populations. As a response Ariel Sharon, an indicted war criminal (Beirut 1982), ordered an all-out invasion March-April 2002 against refugee camps, where Palestinians fought with guns against jets, helicopters and tanks. It was also recently that a British court found the occupation of the island of Diego Garcia by the USA illegal and the Chargossians filed charges against the US government in December 2001.[41]

Additionally to these internationally recognized cases a number of ethno-national movements, such as the Oromo OLF in Ethiopia, the YATAMA in Nicaragua, the Karen KNU, KNPP and Mon NMSP in Eastern Burma, and the Naga NSCN in north-east India, see their struggle as a decolonisation conflict; they accuse the respective governments of (internal) colonization.

The History of a Conflict: Background and Causal Factors

Every conflict has its own history and is an expression of social relations:

- Most ethnic conflicts evolve over a long period of time lasting decades or, in some cases, centuries (e.g., in pre-colonial conflict-formations).

- Every conflict-formation involves a multiplicity of factors, large numbers of actors with varying influence, a range of conflict-generating structures, as well as negative external framework-conditions, with colonial distortions playing a central role at the causal level.
- It is often difficult to determine the main cause of a violent conflict, or which causes and triggers have fused to escalate a conflict. Deeper causal factors (root causes of conflict) often combine with current triggers and escalators in such a way that they are not detected.
- External and internal causes combine with, and reinforce, one another.
- Internal colonialism as one of the major direct causes of conflict displays a number of regional permutations but a terrifying uniformity in the repressive measures it uses.
- Armed conflicts do not arise 'spontaneously'. Individual structural elements can only be properly analysed in their particular contexts.

Aggressive claims by peoples in control of states are sometimes the continuation of pre-colonial conflict-formations by other means. More often, negative interaction between states and 'their' peoples has its origin in colonial distortion. The correlation between particular techniques of rule in the former colonial territories and the frequency of potential and actual conflicts in the *new states* is significant.[42]

Ethnicization from above, which often began with the creation and establishment in power of local ethno-élites in the colonies, led to competition between ethnic groups within the framework of colonial techniques of rule and to the formation of ethnically based strategic groups during decolonisation. In many cases, the colonial discrimination against particular majorities led, after decolonisation, to the oppression or actual persecution of minority ethnic groups by the dominant ethnic group(s) in the new states.

Causes of a Conflict

The causes of ethno-national SvN conflicts are many and varied. The complex interplay of individual causes is often difficult to disentangle. In many cases, outsiders see only the immediate triggers, not the deeper causes. Methodologically speaking, it is possible to distinguish abstract from concrete, direct from indirect, and primary from secondary causes. We need to begin by considering the 'climb' from abstract to concrete.

The main abstract socio-cultural and political causes of violent ethno-national conflicts are the imposition of the nation-state and the destruction of endogenous political systems. Direct conflictual elements such as the arbitrary creation of new states by division, or the enforced incorporation of peoples, combine with indirect or concrete destructive forms of interaction between states and peoples. These forms of interaction include resettlement and regrouping, colonial interest in peripheral fragmentation, the encouragement or toleration of post-colonial ethnocracies, and (selective) support for secession. Such activities have led to the build-up of explosive conflict-potentials and the creation of breeding-grounds for ethno-nationalism from below. Hence, a regime for peaceful secession remains to be elaborated and sanctioned internationally.

As response to some of the root-causes of violent conflict several proposals for a Secession Regime were elaborated as a joint international effort of peace researchers in responding to the Balkan crisis. Consensus is that secession would be justified in three cases:

(1) where there is 'massive and prolonged violation' of human rights, with no prospect of change;
(2) where there are gross structural inequalities in living-standards based on ethnic/national discrimination; and
(3) where one state has been annexed by another (Eritrea, East Timor, West Sahara and others) and this is to be reversed—in other words, in the case of a decolonization conflict.

As regards the last point, legal guarantees already exist in the international system, within the framework of self-determination for colonized peoples. The other two grounds for legitimate secession—namely, massive violations of human rights and gross socio-economic asymmetries—may apply to many ethno-national trouble-spots in the Third World. In many cases, the new state-classes act/have acted—in the manner of the former colonial powers—by calling upon an arsenal of repressive measures. Direct administrative repression, the persecution of individual ethnic groups, the military invasion of settlement-areas belonging to minorities defined by the state as nationalities, demographic outnumbering by settlers and by forcible resettlement, etc. are widespread. Violation of elementary human and minority rights become 'the norm'.

Negative interaction is often associated with economic exploitation of natural resources, of cheap labour, and of allegedly empty territories in the minority areas; indiscriminate plundering produces ecological degradation. Cultural discrimination, up to and including forms of ethnocide, racist repression, religious persecution, and genocide, are some of the destructive types of intervention engaged in by new states or the state-classes running them. State repression by dictatorial regimes combined with economic regression (mass poverty) lead to crises of legitimacy in many peripheral states, and to an increased propensity to violence on the part of the repressed and disadvantaged.

Negative external framework-conditions such as the failure of many modernization projects, weak regional co-operation, underdeveloped South–South co-operation, transfer of value to the North, the cementing of conditions of permanent underdevelopment, and the aggravation of dependency-based underdevelopment (by the debt crisis, for example), are often combined with negative internal developments such as deep distortions resulting from upheavals wrought on traditional societies, social inequality, and the lack or collapse of public services. In individual cases, criminal activity by the government, privilege, corruption, mismanagement, abuse of power by the ruling élites, in combination with ethnicization from above, have triggered conflicts and gone so far as to cause the disintegration of traditional statehood. Where conflicts are continuously militarized by weak or new states, ethno-nationalism from below frequently leads to protracted conflicts, which in many cases cannot be won militarily by any of the parties and negotiations are refused by one party (usually the state party) or by several actors.

The Triggers to a Conflict and Their Relationship to the Causes

The major triggers to a conflict are directly related to the causes of the conflict, which in most cases consist in colonial subjection by the dominant ethnic group (internal colonialism) or in the division, separation, and regrouping of peoples by European colonialism. Colonial intervention led to a loss of original pre-colonial autonomy as a result of increased colonial control, invasion of indigenous territories, subjugation of resisting populations and continuous occupation. Loss of autonomy always and first bears a close relation to the past (e.g. because there was formerly some form of independent statehood or an independent existence as an acephalous society) or an existing autonomy regulation was abrogated, e.g. after a province or sub-state became an independent state; the latter was the immediate reason for several wars after the collapse of federations (USSR and Yugoslavia) and the following narrow nationalism of new ethnocratic rulers.

Internal colonialism as a major cause of conflict exists in several regional permutations: attempts at enforced integration by the state; increased assimilation (e.g. Hispanization, Burmanization, Amharization); settler-immigration; long periods of oppression and/or political exclusion, a snapping-point where there is upheaval or where a regime is in crisis, etc. The objects of contention in these cases vary greatly; they mostly relate to continuing collective discrimination (against ethnic groups), systematic repression, the recollection of, or excessive insistence on, an earlier separate history (as in eastern Nicaragua), the loss of traditional forms of autonomy (e.g. by the Frontier Areas in Burma), etc.

A number of very varied aggressive state measures or events can trigger a conflict that has been 'ripening' over a very long period. The triggers are always specific to the situation. Due to the diversity of possible triggers it is (unlike as with causes) difficult to identify any actual trends. Some examples for conflict triggers shall be mentioned: measures to outlaw a particular symbolism (cultural prohibitions), an act of repression and persecution, individual elements of an overall policy of repression (including in the form of ethnic-religious oppression) that are experienced as particularly aggressive, or single events of high importance such as passing of a decree or law infringing severely on the human rights and life of a particular group, faking election results causing riot, revolt or even regime change (as seen in Yugoslavia/Serbia and Ivory Coast in the same year 2000), criminalizing an opposition organization, political assassinations (e.g. the murder of a charismatic popular leader), massacres, pogroms, etc.. More general developments as, for example, the intensification of the narrow nationalism of the state-classes, the will to social insurrection, anti-colonial struggles in the neighbourhood or other developments can rapidly culminate and trigger violence.

Medium-term developments produce a whole range of specific triggers. In concrete situations, these may take the form of individual measures or steps such as the cancellation of a land reform, the foundation of an irredentist party or the upsurge of a movement amongst members of the same ethnic group in several countries (e.g. Barré's aggressive pan-Somalism; the PKK among Turkish Kurds), outside support for one group can enrage another, state measures to strangulate a nomad economy, e.g. an attempt by agents of central government to impose exhaustive taxes, etc.

Triggers are called escalators if their effect has been a direct one, according to a stringently experienced manner. Escalators have an even more immediate effect than triggers. The difference is basically the speed of changes; additional aggressive action in an existing already very tense situation can result in an explosion of violence. There are many examples of individual events that lead to rapid conflicts escalation in a highly charged situation. Events, which can become escalators from latent to violent conflict, include: massacres (like that of the Christian Delta Karen in Burma 1948); the use of weapons of annihilation (like the use of poison gas against the Iraqi Kurds); a military coup; attacks on symbols for a culture, such as a mosque, a temple, a library, etc.; the loss of power by a party; the 'betrayal' by another party; power struggle culmination in political assassinations, etc.

Matters in Dispute Classified by Urgency

The objects of contention in the ethnic conflicts in the CIS overlap to some extent with those in similar conflicts in the Third World. They include: historically disputed territories; loss of autonomy by a formerly self-ruled territory, or the question of its status;[43] a threat of the population in indigenous areas being outnumbered by settlers and migrants;[44] and the continuing belated repercussions of Stalin's deportations.[45] A number of ethnic conflicts in the CIS had been tranquillized by the *pax sovietica*—that is to say, 'put on ice' without the underlying causes of the conflict being eliminated—only to erupt again, sometimes in violent form, after 1989.

The key issues in ethnic conflicts in the Third World are a great deal 'tougher' (compared with the situation in Europe and the CIS). In terms of classification by urgency, key issues can be reduced to the following basic elements, in decreasing order of urgency and virulence from 1 to 8:

1. Threat of annihilation (genocide, extermination)
2. Threat to existence (state-organized mass murder and massacres, question of survival as a group)
3. Warding off direct physical threat (territorial invasion, persecution and expulsion, enforced resettlement, enslavement; massive human rights violations)
4. Warding off indirect physical and psychological threat (outnumbering in indigenous territories, settler colonialism, forcible assimilation, sporadic or repeated acts of violence, climate of psychological and physical terror)
5. Issues and conflicts of identity (assimilation measures and resistance to them, oppression and injurious treatment, racism in everyday life and in politics)
6. Political disputes (historically disputed territories, administrative status of an ethnic territory, threat of outnumbering, resistance to swamping)
7. Political demands (special rights, affirmative action)
8. Conflicts of interest (mostly of an economic kind, particularistic interests of élites, resources and their distribution, safeguarding ownership).

Often, a simplistically economistic perspective or an exclusively psychologizing approach is adopted and the real matters in contention are concealed through concentration primarily on conflicts of identity (issue 5) and conflicts of interest (issue 8). In the overall picture, however, these issues are of secondary importance. Threats of annihilation by genocide, threats to existence, and resistance to direct physical aggression are obviously 'far away' from conflicts of identity, which might be threatening but not life-threatening, and 'worlds apart' from conflicts of interest, which—under civilized conditions—would hardly become militarised and explode violently but can be solved at the negotiation table.

Aims and Demands of the Parties to the War

The aims of ethno-national movements of resistance and liberation are:

1. Territorial (or only cultural) autonomy, with independent administrative structures or self-government estimated (over 60 percent of all cases)
2. Quasi-total autonomy, with self-rule or internal self-determination or as a constituent state within a federal scheme (about 20 percent)
3. Separate statehood (full sovereignty as an independent state) or large-scale sharing of sovereignty in a genuine federation or federated supra-state is sought in less than 20 percent of cases.

The list of potential states, either independent of federal states, is a long one and overlapping with the list of ongoing violent conflicts (see Table 6.2). The status of the actors in international law plays an important role here: on account of their legally privileged status, indigenous peoples and nations have more of a chance than non-indigenous peoples of seeing aims within the first two categories realized (struggle for autonomy or federalization);[46] movements whose struggle can be legally interpreted as falling within the ambit of decolonisation have better prospects of achieving independent statehood than do other movements of secession.

Aims are set out in the programmes of the organizations conducting the war and determine the latter's strategic plans. Programme goals can be changed in bilateral negotiations between nations/nationalities and states but are rarely reversible. Programmatic statements are often coded, or necessitate some kind of prior knowledge in order to be understood. Many rebel organizations have a civilian administration in the areas under their military control. The rebel governments issue statements, draw up state budgets, and produce papers and documents, all of which can serve as research sources.

Opposition Organizations, Recruiting Base, and Leadership

Opposition organizations that claim to represent the interests of a particular nation, nationality, or ethnic group have their social basis in one ethnic group and draw their resources from it; in particular, they recruit their 'foot soldiers' and cadres from it. The leadership is generally drawn from the (educated) élite, the intellectuals (students, academics, teachers), and the free-floating so-called middle classes.[47] Because of its educational standard, its social status, and its political motivation, it is able to produce a multiplier effect.[48] No matter that leaders often come 'from the fringes of the postulated unity'.[49] What is important is that leadership needs to be legitimate and the ethno-nationalist ideology, its aims and objectives, need to be supported by the masses of a particular ethnic or national entity; if not, the guerrilla cannot move among the populace 'like a fish in the water'.

One important criterion is possession of the 'saviour knowledge' of political nationalism (as it has been broadly developed and experienced in Europe) and of the ability not only to demonstrate knowledge of the Western-cum-colonial discourse about nation, nationalism, ethnicity, and the nation-state, but also to modify that discourse in a plausible way and apply it to one's own conditions. Ideological about-turns—'changing the wheels of a moving train'—are quite possible, but this cannot hide the fact that there are certain 'basics'.[50] In a situation of threat, ethnic nationalism has its task—apart from all simplification—to create awareness of the situation, teach about a particular view of the nationals history, preferably in popular ways and in the groups own language, formulate aims and objectives for the betterment of the situation, build up national institutions, open-up perspectives for emancipation, arouse hope, protect the groups cultural heritage and moral values, promise security, build confidence, enhance solidarity amongst group members and create expectations.

The interaction between elites and their ethnically determined social (recruiting) base is not a random matter structurally. Manipulative actions by élites that have been 'short-changed' (e.g. in relation to the privilege they previously enjoyed as part of deliberate techniques of rule applied by colonial powers), the rise of warlords, competition over resources, and the hunger for power of neo-colonial strategic groups—these are not in themselves sufficient explanation; nor can they replace investigation into the deeper causes, into what, in the eyes of those affected, are the most important issues, and into more distant or more immediate triggers.

Warlords, in the sense of autocratic or even sometimes mafia-like leaders, are the rare exception in ethno-national movements. New war-waging organizations such as international terrorist organizations, organized crime, drug-mafias, 'clan militias', and fundamentalists of every colour are a marginal reality (of 3.9 percent of all violent conflicts); the overlap between these and ethno-national movements is limited. The horrendous vision of states 'everywhere losing their monopoly on the use of armed force'[51] as a result of gang wars and terrorism, as van Creveld has put it, seems implausible and interest-led.

Young rural workers form the main recruiting base for ethno-national movements, or, sometimes, young people from the urban *lumpenproletariat* (ex-schoolchildren, students, workers). The rural guerrilla-force wages sustained low-intensity war. The recruits are often very young. A frighteningly high proportion of young people and children fight in the ranks of almost all parties to these conflicts; women seldom form part of the fighting forces.

The fighting forces of individual nations and nationalities are mostly highly motivated, disciplined, and determined, and know their way around the terrain—all of which makes them a dangerous adversary. I make this statement on the basis of long experience of ethno-national guerrilla-armies; it is an account that conflicts with the common picture of undisciplined, marauding militias looting and pillaging their way across the countryside. Quasi-total breakdowns of social rules originate in most cases in (weak) governments. Contemporary civil wars are often wars without rules. State-organized terrorism against the civilian population, and the brutalization of internal wars, are not 'spontaneous' phenomena; they are organized and deliberate.[52]

Members of various minority nations were formerly used as élite troops by the colonial powers—for example, against the nationalist movements amongst the particular majority nations concerned—and/or were put to use in a number of successor states with no dominant ethnic group. There are many examples of this in South and South-East Asia. Colonial recruitment for military service is something that affected the Ghurkhas,[53] who are the classic example of mercenary recruitment along ethnic lines. Even today, they continue to be recruited for military service not only by Britain, but also by India and Nepal; many of the UN peacekeeping troops of these latter countries are Ghurkhas. Other prominent examples are the Sikhs, Naga, and Chin.[54] The latter still number amongst Burma's best troops. Colonial recruiting of soldiers (and later mercenaries) along ethnic lines also included the Karen, Hmong, Hima-Tutsi, Tuareg, and others.[55]

Conflict Formation: Course of the Conflict, Legitimating Violence, Conduct of Hostilities, Weaponry

Protracted wars waged by new Third World states against those nationalities within them that reject the state's absolute claims to sovereignty make up the majority of current conflicts. Armed interventions by the state against nationalities and nations occur in a variety of domains and take diverse forms. As a rule, violent internal ethno-national conflicts are of lengthy duration and claim a high toll of lives, particularly amongst the civilian population. State armies deliberately strike against soft targets (the sedentary civilians they accuse of supporting the guerrilla); against a better equipped enemy the ethno-nationalist insurgents use hit-and-run tactics, strike, disappear and being permanently on the move.

The question of the legitimating armed resistance as an integral element in the formation of ethno-national movements is closely bound up with the causes of these types of conflicts and the matters in contention; the use of violence is seen by the non-dominant, generally minority nationalities, ethnic groups, and peoples concerned essentially as legitimate resistance to oppression and attack by the state.

The question of legitimating armed violence becomes more complicated in the case of movements that are not genuinely ethno-national—notably new types of revolutionary movements which have only recently emerged (particularly during the 1980s) from radical left-wing organizations or from the Maoist-Stalinist Left (some as break-away groups) and which combine political programmes and positions from the classical Marxist-Leninist Left with an ethnic discourse. A number of these movements tend towards sectarianism, factionalism, rigid actionism, and revolutionary voluntarism. Certain actions, because of their brutal and illegitimate nature, fall within the murky ambit of warlordism, terrorism, and pointless of violence.

Ideology-wise classic ethno-nationalist movements aim at the creation of an own nation state thus they share the basics of revolutionary 18th to 19th century European nationalism. At this point there is formally no difference from the declared 'values' of state elites they are fighting. This is of particular relevance in regard to the issues I once described as the four 'holy cows' of revolutionary European (e.g. French) nationalism: national sovereignty, territorial integrity, secularity and the constitutive ideology of modernity. The realities of the official nationalism of periphery states are different: state sovereignty—not of a sovereign people possessing the democratic decision powers of elections and referenda (possibly law initiatives as in Switzerland) but rather as covering control of the so-called nation-state over its citizen, without respecting their citizen rights—the state's territorial integrity, its often illusionary secularity due to practical collusion with the leaders of the accepted religious communities, and its ideology of state-driven modernization.

Repression, exclusion, and assimilation (not just exploitation) by the neo-colonial state, and also the emptiness of state promises in regard to development, the failure of industrialism, of progress, of social justice, etc., have been major indicators of the disintegration of the central state-driven narratives of modernity. The ethno-nationalists aspire to do it better, as say the revolutionary insurgents against the clientelist-cum-capitalist state.

Movements that are not genuinely ethno-nationalistic can act in an extremely violent manner—not only towards their true adversary, the colonial state (or internally colonialist state), but also against rival movements (some of which they have eliminated by violent means), against so-called traitors and collaborators in their own ranks, and against their own population, in whose name and for whose liberation they are (allegedly) fighting. The motives and themes of sectarian leftist-nationalist movements lie somewhere between the better known basic concerns of the left-wing rebel and liberation movements of the Third World and those of the ethno-nationalist opposition-movements—in other words, such movements agitate both against exploitation and repression and against the assimilation or exclusion of particular ethno-social groups.[56] The following are examples, from various regions of the world, of this special type of Maoist-oriented ethno-nationalist movement: the PKK in Kurdistan (Turkey, Iraq, Syria); the Tamil Tigers and Singhalese JVP in Sri Lanka; the Tigrai TPLF (in northern Ethiopia); some factions of the SPLA in Southern Sudan; and, in my view, the Shining Path in Peru. The problem is that many writers treat this type of movement as an example—or indeed as an 'ideal type'—of ethno-nationalist movements at large, though the above-mentioned organizations are more like revolutionary armies with a standardized revolutionary discourse and a more or less hidden ethno-nationalist agenda; some use pieces of the ethnic discourse merely for recruiting purposes.

Other differences are observable in the recruiting base of radical left-wing movements that engage in an ethnic discourse: they use young farm workers or peasants, who form the main recruiting base for ethno-national movements, only as second-line troops (e.g., Sendero Luminoso in Peru); the main recruits are young people from the urban *lumpenproletariat*. Recruits are also very young. Many women belong to the left-wing-cum-ethnic guerrilla-forces. In authentically ethno-nationalist movements, women do rarely form a part of the fighting force. However, recruits (but not so much leaders) can also belong to an ethnic group other than the one being represented.

When I refer to ethno-nationalist conflict-formations, I am talking of periods of time stretching over decades. Militant national opposition to state intervention or to the instrumentalization of the state by the dominant ethnic group is often organized as a kind of protracted guerrilla-war. During the course of a conflict—which, for the purpose of the analysis, has to be reconstructed—several phases of escalation are worked through, and it is possible to analyse the triggers to these. Such triggers effect the escalation from latent conflict to armed hostilities.

Ethno-nationalist conflicts, at least in their initial phase, may generally be characterized as wars of low to medium intensity. The concept of warfare that lies behind them is, in my observation, comparable to that of the 'people's war' in insurrection conflicts. There are similarities with the strategy of the protracted people's war; this is a strategy, originally used by Maoist guerrilla-groups, whereby 'the guerrilla moves amongst the people like a fish in the water', using small-scale, highly mobile fighting units.

Adoption of the concept of the 'people's war' focuses on the military tactics and strategy associated with it; the adoption or assimilation, by ethno-national rebel-organizations, of the associated political ideologies of the classical Left (of Marxist-Leninist, Maoist, or Trotskyist bent), or of independent left-wing groups, has been a frequent—though by no means necessary—concomitant. Rejection of it has occurred even in regions or cases where, in the period of bloc confrontation, such a step (tantamount to an ideological profession of faith) would have brought with it the possibility of backing and supplies from outside.[57]

In terms of their form and means, ethno-national wars generally rank as protracted guerrilla-wars. The laying of ambushes is a favourite tactic (hit and run tactics); encounters with large-scale enemy-units are avoided. Political agitation is often given priority. Ideally, military actions are undertaken that have high symbolic content (in terms of target, timing, and circumstance); such actions are regarded as so-called armed propaganda.

Weaponry generally consists of light infantry weapons, and more rarely heavy artillery. Recently, highly developed mobile equipment such as anti-tank grenade-launchers (rare) and even anti-aircraft missiles (very rare) have been observed, but often the items in question are mainly confiscated weapons—second-hand or almost run-down military hardware. Many military actions are carried out primarily in order to capture weapons and munitions from the reserves of the opposing (government) forces. In most cases, the adversary is many times superior to the rebels in terms of fire-power and equipment.

The opponent's material and technical superiority can only be offset by high motivation, precise knowledge of the locality and terrain, a combination of resourceful tactics and a solid long-term strategy, and the involvement of the rebels' own population in every guise (as payers of levies, scouts, suppliers, and other facilitators). Shortage of resources means that purchases generally have to be made on the open arms-market—often at inflated prices (because of the increased risk to the arms-dealers), in small quantities, and on a limited scale as measured both against troop-strength (in the SPLA in Southern Sudan in 1991 and in the OLF in Ethiopia there was one gun to every three men) and against recruiting potential.

The conflicting links between ideology, strategy, military resources, and outside support can be illustrated by a three examples from one of the most conflict-prone regions of the world, the mountain areas of mainland South-East Asia. (1) In Burma, for instance, there is no doubt that the Karen (KNU a/o) have made use of the 'people's war' concept, in some cases without flirting with socialism; some of their leaders were actually of a strongly anti-communist bent or belonged to Christian fundamentalist sects. (2) The Naga (NSCN) in north-east India brought Christianity, socialism, and nationalism into intimate combination and for a long time enjoyed generous support from China; they allied themselves with left-wing rebel-movements. (3) The Kachin (KIO) in northern Burma combined British World War II guerrilla-tactics (all the veterans had fought against the Japanese) in virtuosic fashion with Mao's 'people's war' concept and at one point were receiving almost all their military equipment from China. From the time of the hostilities with the Communist Party of Burma (CPB), this source dried up, and the KIO at various junctures even affiliated itself with the anti-communist world league; under pressure from China, the Kachin 'moderated' their position and put the emphasis on the nationalist aspect, withdrawing the ideological and Christian elements.

Resources, Hinterland, and the Question of Outside Involvement

The question of support must be distinguished from that of outside involvement. As a rule, no third parties are directly involved in hostilities in ethno-national SvN conflicts. Exceptions to this are the ethno-national conflicts, which, in the guise of so-called regional conflicts and proxy wars, were previously fuelled by the East–West conflict and the intervention of the superpowers.

Only in a few cases have regular troops from third states participated directly in hostilities in ethno-national conflicts; involvement by foreign secret services, special troops, mercenaries, and so-called 'military advisers', however, has been frequent. A general overview reveals that, given a total number of involvements in war of 363 between 1945 and 1992, the states of the North have, to date, been directly involved 88 times: 52 times as a directly affected power—mostly as a (former) colonial power—and 36 times as an intervening power.[58] In the period between 1945 and 1991, there were 690 open military interventions, mainly by former colonial powers such as Britain, France, and Portugal, by the super-powers (USA, China, India), and by aggressive regional powers such as Israel, apartheid South Africa, and Iraq.[59]

All successful rebel-organizations have, or had, a 'hinterland' in one or more neighbouring states. Because of diplomatic conventions, this is in most cases officially denied by the state or the states concerned. Depending on the political climate and the prevailing situation in regard to interests, individual states will each offer hospitality to the respective rebel move-ments of the neighbouring country.[60] This is a continuing tradition and even

encompasses criminal organizations, as in the case of the Rwandan perpetrators of genocide (the former national army, FAR, and the Interahamwe
party militias) in the refugee camps in Kivu province in eastern Zaire.

Depending on (global) political interests, the rebels have obtained, and
continue to obtain, support from the West (USA, South Africa, Pakistan,
Saudi Arabia, Brunei), the East (mainly China, the former USSR), and
Third World countries (mainly Cuba, Iran, Libya). The previous massive
support given to a few socialist rebel-movements in Third World countries
by the former USSR decreased greatly in 1989–90 and has since ceased.
Ethnically organized parties to a war have often obtained support from
China; in destabilization conflicts (contra-phenomenon in Nicaragua,
Afghanistan, Angola, etc.), they have obtained support from the USA and
interested regional powers.[61]

Rebel movements have their own economy. Some exploit natural
resources and export them, e.g. diamonds, precious stones, gold, other
metals, minerals, hardwood (e.g. teak, mahogany), rubber, etc. Warlords
always preferred high-value items such as diamonds or drugs;[62] other
warlords trade with humans (mainly young girls for prostitution). Examples
for such warlordism and gansterism are Taylor (became 'president' of
Liberia), Kabila, (first AFDL, 1997–2001 'president' of Congo DR,
assassinated 16 Jan 2001), Foday (RUF, Sierra Leone; now arrested,
accused of crimes against humanity), Savimbi (UNITA in Angola, for years
escaping government offensives was killed by the FAA on 27 Feb 2002),
Khun Sa (MTA in Burma, famous drug kingpin, long protected by the
SPDC military regime but finally put under 'house arrest') or Lo Hsing
Han (a Kokang leader and drug baron who served another faction of the
Burmese junta). The death of the two most powerful warlords (Kabila Sr.
and Savimbi) changed the course of the wars in the DRC and in Angola.

Organizations trading in drugs and sex slaves commit criminal acts and
have to deal with international networks involving criminal syndicates such
as the Italo-American mafia, the Cali cartel or Chinese triads and secret
societies, some of which were collaborating with state secret services (e.g.
CIA, KGB, a/o) at different points of time. Recently conflict diamonds
became a big issue starting with the United Nations banning arms and
diamond deals with the UNITA. The hold on the diamond-rich provinces of
Kasai and Katanga was securing and fuelling the Kabila regime's war effort
in the Congo; his Zimbabwean allies became companions in exploiting the
Congo's riches. The Congolese rebels and their foreign state supporters
also want to finance a part of their war with exploiting natural resources.

Normally ethno-nationalist organizations levy taxes and duties, have an
active diaspora-community whom they can call on, or receive financial
donations from third parties (INGOs, solidarity and support groups,

neighbouring states). Opposition groups are able to obtain any type of weapon that they can afford, in any quantity they desire, on the open arms-market. Where there is war, arms-dealers are never far away.

Understanding the Problem is the First Step to its Solution

Apologists of the *modern* nation state decry what they used to call 'ethnic fragmentation'. Social science expected the dying away of the *ethnic* factor. The 'problem' should have been solved quasi automatically by modernisation. Accordingly some states tried to undermine ethnic identity by repressive modernisation. But what actually happened was just about the contrary: In a number of cases the reaction was that ethnic identity instead of becoming relative and softer turned out to be activated and strengthened.

On the other hand sub-states of multi-ethnic federations used the power of politicised ethnicity in order to reach full sovereignty as independent states, claiming being oppressed. Some of the new states began to oppress their own minorities' rights after having gained international recognition. In the early 1990s, narrow-nationalist leaderships were abrogating autonomy for national minorities in almost all new states of the former Soviet Union and Yugoslavia. The result was predictable. Abrogation of autonomy led or contributed to 17 episodes of wars and genocidal atrocities in Eastern Europe and Eurasia, with deadly conflicts in the Caucasus and the Balkans.

Today gross human rights violations, atrocities and in some cases out-right genocide are intrinsically linked with the third contemporary wave of *ethnic* nationalism. Unlike some types of warfare, genocide is always a state-organised crime. If attempts to prevent mass violence and genocide ought to be successful then the quest of understanding has to concentrate on the following inter-linked areas: The secrets of ethnicity have to be uncovered; we are dealing with a powerful source of deep-rooted conflict, often nourished by destructive interaction in the past. If ethnicity is combined with domination then things become difficult. Ethnicity has to be de-constructed; the *ethnos* became a resource for political manipulation and vested interests; we may talk about the hybridisation of the ethnos. The phenomenon of weak or failed states became more salient in the 1990s. Awareness is growing that *failed states* are the most dangerous states. The well being, security, and sometimes the very survival of non-dominant groups are put at the disposition of states. Failed states threaten to become genocidal states—if only political conjunctures or regional powers allow it.

Meaningful prevention of violent conflict has a very strong structural component. Such structural prevention aims at safeguarding inter-ethnic balance and an accommodation of just demands, providing protection and 'safe havens' for the self-controlled development of non-dominant and vulnerable groups. The timing of conflict management is crucial. If conflicts break out violently then it may already be too late for most peaceful solutions. As a response to crisis successful prevention of violent conflict cannot be reactive but anticipative.

The best prevention is prophylactic promotion and institutionalisation of constructive relationships between different groups. In most cases the combination of different schemes and procedures such as minority protection, power sharing, internal self-determination (e.g. self-governance and forms of autonomy) is successful. In some cases only independence solves the problem (e.g. Bangladesh, Eritrea, partition of Czechoslovakia, East Timor, etc.), often after violent conflicts. A larger number of different ways of violence prevention have been realized in different word regions. Large differences between such 'success stories' and the varying principles for averting conflict reflect the fact that there is no simple cure-all.[63]

Notes

1. Atavistic is commonly used for recent cases in the Third World but not so much for the behaviour of European colonizers in the same Third World.
2. Lentz (1995: 14–17) summarized Anglo-Saxon research on ethnicity, put the thesis of the colonial 'invention' of ethnic groups into perspective, and demonstrated clearly that the processes by which ethnic identities come into being are 'historically and regionally specific'. She critically observed that a one-dimensional understanding of ethnicity that reduced it to 'a political resource used by élites in their competition with the state for the fruits of modernity' was inadequate, indeed so. Ethnicity, she said, could become 'a resource for clientelist networks and political mobilization'. However, these findings are not applied to the state itself, taking the evidence that the peripheral state only too often assumes an ethnocratic character. The critique is that in Lentz' view the state remains 'isolated', and the interaction between state and ethnic groups is ignored.
3. Chrétien 1988, Horowitz 1985, Ryan 1990, Smith, Anthony D. 1992.
4. The thesis that the parties to a conflict have a greater tendency to form 'along linguistic, confessional, or kinship lines' the smaller the 'degree of internal social differentiation' (Gantzel and Schlichte 1994: 4) is not tenable. It is precisely when social and economic inequalities become more acute that religious or sectarian conflicts tend to break out. Language and kinship are indeed important attributes of the ethnic, but, taken in isolation, they are only of secondary significance as far as the development of armed conflicts is concerned. Gantzel and Schlichte also overlook the fact that in the Third World, societies cannot be divided into internal and external along state borders. Of all possible cases, the authors picked that of the Jumma in the Chittagong Hill Tracts. The ethnic difference between Jumma and encroaching Bengali settlers is undeniable and the brutal policy of the Bengali state (Bangladesh) is well documented. Massive resettlement-programmes were being carried out to the detriment of the indigenous mountain-peoples. But the authors talk about 'other factors' and 'economic conflicts of interest'.
5. Despite the Marxist language, the authors fail to recognize the power of 'illusions' and 'deceptive appearance' masses of people 'believe in', as opposed to objective reality.

6. To some naïve observers, the genocide in Rwanda in 1994 was not a massacre planned and organized by the state, nor an ethnicized conflict driven by power politics, but an ecologically 'induced' conflict that erupted because of the scarcity of land (more an economic criterion) and the high population density.

7. See Scherrer 1997b: 8 ff., 39, 64 ff., 76, 79, 99 ff, 104, 110 ff., 113, 161 ff., 165–73.

8. The interpretations offered by some Western conflict-researchers can be extremely particularistic (in that they stress isolated elements); in other words, they are not connected in any way to the perceptions of those involved, or they are presumptuous or guided by prejudices—e.g. with claiming an 'unawareness of the true causes'.

9. In the non-aligned Yugoslavia, there was no fighting or dying for the nation—a concept that appeared to have been surmounted. The media coined terms such as 'ethnic cleansing'. Religious communities were ethnicized on the basis and in recollection of the last chapter in a barbaric externally imposed history of genocide scarcely two generations old. According to my definition of an ethnos (see next section), the parties to the conflict in Bosnia are lacking certain major objective attributes that would justify speaking of a nation of Croats as distinct from that of the Serbs or Muslims. The differences between the Slav peoples of Yugoslavia lie at the level of confession/religion and (concomitant) colonial history and of the affiliation to two empires—the Habsburg and the Ottoman. The crucial objective attributes of language, and many cultural features of the parties to the conflict, are largely identical (= Serbo-Croat). Talk of 'ethnic cleansing' makes little sense in this context.

10. The example of Yugoslavia involves a hybrid ethnicization of religious groups (Muslims, Roman Catholics and other Christians, etc.) that accelerated or was revitalised as the conflict escalated. The existing group-cohesion (however weak) was 'confirmed' by the traumatic events of the Second World War, or was reinforced by ongoing atrocities. This form of ethnicization of political and social conflicts became a vehicle through which the ex-Communist élite maintained power.

11. The saying that there are as many definitions of an ethnos as there are ethnologists is exaggerated, given that many ethnologists show no interest in having an easy-to-handle definition; too narrow a definition would entail a risk of abuse in the political domain.

12. For a detailed definition, see Zimmermann 1992: 75–118. Isajiw investigated 27 definitions of an ethnos, involving up to 12 characteristics: see Wsevolod Isajiw, 'Definitions of Ethnicity', in Bienvenue and Goldstein (eds.) 1980.

13. Recently a figure of 10,000 or more ethnic groups has been mentioned. The variation in figures is due to the differences in the criteria or attributes used to define an ethnos.

14. There are two opposing points of view on this. 1) Religion is tantamount to a marker of ethnic identity, because it gives the individual a collective identity and security (Durkheim's 'religion as social cement'); in this scheme, functional and structural implications remain obscured. 2) Religion is an instrument of social control that works in a subtle way through internalised value- and belief-systems, cosmologies, and so on, or that secures subjection and obedience/provides the powerful with a justification for their power, through direct commands and instructions from authoritative institutions. This second point of view does not deny the power of religion to form identities and to confer authoritarian structure on sectarian factions in politics.

15. The attributes of an ethnic community cannot be regarded as uncontroversial. P. Smith (1991: 21) lists six: distinct name, myths about origin, historical memory, shared culture, 'homeland', and a feeling of solidarity amongst significant sectors of the population. Barth (1969: 10 ff.) names four groups of attributes: biological reproduction, shared cultural values, shared area of interaction, self-identification, and distinctiveness.

16. Maintaining ethnic borders—and thus also being able to delimit different ethnic groups—has its problems, for various reasons. Despite this, many ethnologists seem to

regard peoples defined thus as a kind of 'island' in themselves (Barth), which can be arbitrarily wrenched from its social context and removed from the area of enter-ethnic communication for the purposes of description.

17. To put the cultural aspect first would interfere with the chronological continuity of an ethnic group (which we presuppose as one of the most enduring forms of social organization) and with those factors that determine its form. One-sided concentration on the social aspects, for its part, would result in too great an emphasis on the identification of Self and Other.

18. These definitions consist of about half (inter-) subjective and half objective features. The disputed point with some of the named features is whether they can be described as 'objective'. Name-giving, certain cultural aspects (especially language), the association with a particular territory as a settlement area and site of economic activity (not with a mythical primeval homeland), and the mode of production can, at least, be regarded as objective, empirically verifiable characteristics.

19. In Western societies physical characteristics are one of the main distinguishing features at home (in relation to migrants and asylum-seekers) and abroad (e.g. in holiday resorts).

20. From an *emic* point of view, shared origin is crucial. The fact that this does not have to be 'real origin', and is usually putative-cum-mythical or fictitious in nature, is often overlooked. Other central elements that determine affinity to an ethnically constituted group—the capacity to reproduce as a group, for example, or common cultural configurations, or a so-called 'feeling of belonging' that implies group solidarity—may be regarded as too general to be able, ultimately, to provide precise empirical insights into the ethnic dimension of political processes in a conflict situation. Constant injury to central elements, either from within or from without, elicits specific forms of resistance in each particular case, ranging from withdrawal to armed rebellion.

21. The authoritative six-point definition of an indigenous people given by Burger (1987: 9) allows for the conquest and dominance aspect but imposes unnecessary restrictions (nomadism, acephalousness, 'different world-view').

22. On the scientific concepts, methods, and theories of interdisciplinary research into nationalism, see Berding (ed.) 1994, who seeks to 'highlight the diversity, changeability, and transitoriness' of national consciousness and particular manifestations of nationalism. On the relationship between ethnic consciousness and forms of national identity, see the observations, in the same work, by Claus Leggewie and Gisela Welz on the state of research and on the ethno-social concepts used in analysing integration and differentiation/multi-culturalism.

23. See the individual investigations into nationalism in general and into particular examples of it from Eastern and Western Europe in Estel/Mayer (eds.) 1994.

24. Kumar Rupesinghe, preface in Ropers/Debiel 1995: 7. Rupesinghe claimed that the expansion of the world of states in the last 50 years reflects 'the trust placed in this system as a means of preserving international stability' (ibid. 8). This development has probably little to do with 'trust' but more to do with colonial strategy and group interests of state-classes. With 50 wars in progress, it is impossible to talk of 'stability'. The actors of the societal world, says Rupesinghe, are the link between peoples (according to the UN Charter 'all peoples have the right to self-determination'), states, and the international system (ibid.10). Rather than simply being a 'link', civil actors ought to be a 'corrective'; especially Human Rights NGOs ought to be 'watchdogs'.

25. The 'world of states vs. societal world' model needs to be defined in more detail: transnational companies (TNCs) ought not to be classified as part of the societal world (they are, after all, often 'states within states'); in my view, they should form a separate category. TNCs have much do with globalization and little with democracy. An example of the scale involved: the world's largest company in terms of turnover at that time, in

the mid 1990s and before the end of the Japanese 'bubble economy', was Mitsubishi. This company had a workforce of 360,000 and a turnover of $US185 billion, equivalent to the GPD of Austria, three times that of the 'tiger' Malaysia, and eight times that of Bangladesh with its 120 million inhabitants. (*Der Spiegel* 39/1996, 80–95, this ref. 85).

26. On war-lordism, see AGKED 1995: 5–83, on China see Osterhammel, ibid., 38–40.

27. In all three African cases and in Afghanistan, the state was used as a tool by a particular (in all cases small and minoritarian) ethnic group (clan): in Somalia it was the Marehan-Darod (2 percent, for the duration of the Barré regime), in Liberia it was the tiny US-African upper class (3 percent, since the foundation of the state), in Sierra Leone it was the Limba (8 percent) and Creoles (2 percent), and in Afghanistan it were the manifold Pashto-speaking clans (but mainly the Durrani Pashtuns, to which the royal aristocracy, some communist leaders as well as the Taliban top leaders around Mullah Mohammed Omar belong). All of Afghanistan's rulers until the 1978 Marxist coup were from Durrani's Pashtun tribal confederation, since 1747, when Ahmad Shah Durrani, the founder of what is known today as Afghanistan, established his rule, and after 1818 all were members of that tribe's Mohammadzai clan (2 percent). In both West African mini-states, the fact that the mineral resources (mainly diamonds) and raw materials (rubber, coffee, cocoa, etc.) were exploited by the 'governments' or 'war-lords' helped prolong the war. In (South-) Somalia international aid prolonged the war and the following crisis; the region became essentially stateless (since the fall of the Barré regime).

28. In Afghanistan foreign aid (mainly disaster relief) and military support for the Islamist forces by the USA (before and during the invasion by the USSR) and by Pakistan (with strong support for extremist Pashtun warlords and later the Taliban) prolonged the war and included support for non-Afghan gangs of Mujaheddin from Arab countries, Turkic-speaking countries (including the Muslim-dominated Central Asian states of the USSR and China's Uyghurs) and other Islamic states or communities. It was from among these gangs of Arab Mujaheddin that the al-Qaeda group, led by Saudi Arabs from the extreme Wahabbist sect (such as bin Laden), emerged and continued to exist after the withdrawal of USSR from Afghanistan in February 1989 (see Rashid 2000 and 2001). These former clients of the USA turned violently against their paymasters, extending the Central Asian gang wars to Africa and West Asia and finally, on September 11, 2001, to US territory.

29. These are: the state, several states, the nation/nationality, several nations, rebel groups or insurgents, the counter-insurgency phenomenon, and organized gangs; in addition there are generally unarmed actors such as mass movements (in conflicts about authority or power), migrants, and refugees. As an example: the vague term 'rebel' (revolutionaries, contras and Mafiosi may meet the criteria all together) highlights the limits of a system of classification based solely on the actors concerned.

30. Despite the outbreak of hostilities in Yugoslavia, and the massive media presence on the ground, this has not changed much in regard to other trouble spots.

31. See Scherrer 2002*b* and 1997.

32. For detailed case studies see broad resource materials in the ECOR book series (ECOR 1–28, compiler of interviews and studies, ISBN 3–932446–) and the IFEK Reports 2–6 exemplifying ethno-national or ethnicized conflicts in Nicaragua, Horn of Africa, Burma/Myanmar, NO-India, and Central Africa.

33. One example is the ruling class in Burma: since 1948 it has consisted, almost without interruption, of the army leadership and a few civilian assistants. The army also dominates part of the economy. Ethnically speaking, the regime is regarded as Burmese, although it also recruits members of minority nationalities. Even the rebel communists were viewed as Burmese, despite the fact that the 'foot soldiers' of the CPB were

recruited mainly from amongst the minorities of the so-called hill tribes. The CPB split up into seven ethnic sections in 1989. The minorities had/have concluded various alliances with one another and with the internal Burmese opposition.

34. Nietschmann 1987. This includes some conflicts in which no state actors are involved. Comparability with the AKUF data is therefore precluded, given that the latter are based on the definition of war posited by Istvan Kende, according to which, when it comes to actors in a war (as opposed to in any other 'mass conflict'), at least one of the sides must be made up of a 'regular army or other government troops' (Kende 1982). In many wars this is not applicable anymore.

35. Gurr cites the following figures: in 1945–9, 26 ethno-political groups were involved in conflicts, in 1950–9 it was 36, and similarly in the 1960s; in 1970–9 the number climbed steeply to 55, in the 1980s it reached 62, and in 1994 70. See Ted R. Gurr, 'Peoples against States', unpublished manuscript, Maryland 1994, taken from Ropers 1996: 7. If the number of ethnic groups (not states) involved were counted, the actual figures would probably be some ten times greater than this. In Burma alone, there were sometimes over 20 ethnic groups and a far greater number of individual actors involved in the war with the central government.

36. See Gurr et al/CIDCM 2000 (Peace and Conflict 2001 report).

37. These often have ethnic components, but not such that they predominate.

38. Contemporary types of mass violence (wars and non-war violent conflicts) according to the ECOR typology. B+D+F+G have a dominant 'ethnic/ethnicized' component. Almost all conceivable combinations actually exist.

39. For authentic material such as compilers of interviews with conflict actors and case studies see Ethnicity and State (ISSN 1430-8428 or ISBN 3-932446-...), the ECOR books series, vols. 1–28, 1989–2002; issues 29 and 30 are in preparation.

40. Troops of the Indian Union and police-forces from various individual states fight against ethno-nationalist, insurgents, other rebels: Bihar State vs. Naxalites insurgency (SvI), Sikhs (KLF, KCF, etc.) vs. India, Kashmir-Muslims vs. India, Naga vs. India, Kuki vs. Naga, Mizo, Bodo vs. Assam State, ULFA vs. Indian troops in Assam, Ghurkha vs. West Bengal, Naga vs. Manipur, Tripura vs. Bengalis, Tripura vs. CPI militia, etc..

41. See Lobe, Jim: 'Diego Garcia Islanders Contest Rights of U.S. Military Base Used in Afghanistan Air War,' FRIP, Jan. 2002, www.selfdetermine.org/news/0201chagos.html.

42. On the special effects of British divide-and-rule policy as compared with the colonial policies of France, Russia, Portugal, Spain, and other colonial or regional powers, see Scherrer 1996, 60–65.

43. CIS: conflicts between Ingushetians and Ossetians, Armenians and Azeris, and Ossetians and Georgians (south Ossetia). Question of status/loss of autonomy became virulent in Abkhazia, Gagausia, Pridbestrovye, Chechnya, etc.

44. E.g. in the Baltics, in Moldova, in some Russian republics, and in Abkhazia (Georgia).

45. The Uzbek pogrom against the Meshketian Turks in June 1989 in the Ferghana valley; the pogrom against Caucasians in Novy Usen (Kazakhstan); no solution or compensation for the Crimean Tartars, only belated repatriation and hostile treatment for this non-rehabilitated, victimized group—despite various promises and despite demonstrations by them in Moscow in July 1987.

46. In relation to the legal status of (indigenous) peoples, Rehof (1992, quoted in Assies 1993) gives a list of six hierarchical levels: independence, federal sub-state (or quasi-state), constitutional recognition of a distinct state, statutory autonomy, *de facto* accords, non-recognition. On systems of indigenous self-government, see, amongst others, Assies 1993, Stavenhagen 1991, Minugh, Morris and Ryser 1989.

47. The educated élites are often socio-economically pauperized.

48. This effect is often purely destructive. Even the ultra-nationalist leadership of the fascist genocidal Khmer Rouge must be seen as belonging to the educated élite: almost all of them studied in France—some of them (like Khieu Samphang) actually got doctorates.

49. Elwert cites the examples of Dr Sun-Yat-sen (the 'father of modern China'), who was born in Hawaii, or Mustafa Kemal, later Attaturk (father of Turkey), who was born in present-day Saloniki in northern Greece (see Elwert 1995: 18–19). Saloniki mirrored the multi-ethnic character of the Ottoman Empire (and in those days was by no means on the 'fringes' of the empire, though it later fell outside the new Turkey); before the Balkans war of 1912–13, it was a city with population made up mainly of Jews, Slavs (Macedonians), Thracians, and Turks.

50. In the former USSR, almost all the erstwhile party-bigwigs and apparatchiks became 'businessmen' and 'nationalists'; the same set of people now manages the 'Wild West' capitalism there.

51. Ludermann refers to the military historian Martin van Creveld (Ludermann/AGKED 1995: 5), who talks about the difficulties faced in combating sub-state adversaries. Creveld's allegedly 'path breaking' and often quoted assessment is such that he envisages states either retreating before this new challenge—which is in my assessment in the great majority of intra-state conflicts extremely unlikely—or 'adopting [the] fighting methods [of such organizations] and thus becoming more like them' (*ibid.*)— which is nothing new but something that has long been on the record as being carried out by secret-service circles and state-organized death-squads.

52. The most horrendous example is the so-called 'four-cut operation' of the Burmese military junta. 'The four-cut operation is: First cut communication with the revolution. Second, cut all information. That means our troops are not given any information. We were totally separated from the Karen villages. Three, cut the economy. And four, cut the heads of all the revolutionaries. In the black area is where they can do anything; there they don't respect any rules or regulations. The Burmese troops have raped a lot of women in many villages. There is so much abuse that they have done. Raping, violations and other brutalities.' See Major Ganemy Kunoo, 'Gross Human Rights Violations Committed by the Burmese Army' ECOR 9, 1995*b*: 132.

53. Ghurkhas were used by the British in the war about the Malvinas/Falklands, in Hong Kong, against rebellious Vietnamese refugees, etc.

54. Sikhs: Sikhs are very well represented in India's army and government, despite the existence of militant and violent Sikh independence-movements (with links to the Pakistani secret services). Naga: Having previously been wooed as 'noble savages' by the British and recruited into the Assam Rifles as an auxiliary force, the Naga guerrilla-force began the fight for independence against the Indian troops. After the creation of a constituent state for the Naga, within the framework of the Indian Union (Nagaland, the 22nd union state), some Naga guerrilla-groups continued the fight for independence; the only force still defiant is the National Socialist Council of Nagaland (NSCN). Zo/Chin: The Chin had been recruited by the British; nowadays, some of them are organized into the Chin National Front, and some are fighting rebels alongside the Burmese army.

55. Karen: the troops used behind the Japanese lines in the Second World War consisted mainly of Karen; even before this, they had been used by the British colonial masters to fight the anti-colonialism of the Burmese majority. The Karen National Union, KNU, has been fighting against successive central governments and military regimes since 1949. Hmong (Meo): Having once been armed and equipped by the USA as jungle fighters against the Vietmin or Vietcong, the Hmong now form a Mafia-like drug-based guerrilla-force (LLA) opposed to the Tai-Lao-dominated state of Laos (see AKUF 1992: 51). Tuareg (an Amasir or Berber people): During the French colonial period, particularly after the beginning of the Algerian liberation-struggle in 1954, recruitment

of Tuareg was stepped up. Later on, from 1980 to 1990, about 20,000 Tuareg were trained in Libya or performed military service for other Arab states (such as the Lebanon and Iraq). See Klute 1995: 146–61, this ref. 148.

56. Werner Schiffauer's thesis about what such movements have in common (Schiffauer 1996) is essentially that they are a response to the collapse of modernity (ibid. 44). Schiffauer is controversial in his treatment of the PKK ('pure adventurism'); the PKK certainly does not represent a 'minority' but one of the largest nations without own state.

57. The states that supported ethno-national rebel-movements for one reason or another— usually to do with power politics—were: on the Eastern side, first and foremost China, then the USSR, and, in individual cases, Cuba; on the Western side, above all the USA, Britain, France, Israel, and South Africa (plus a few conservative Arab or Islamic regimes); and on the Third World side, it was mainly Libya and Iran, along with Iraq, Algeria, Egypt, India, and Pakistan.

58. Unfortunately there are no recent compilations on foreign war involvement, interventions and direct participation with troops (often only so-called experts or military trainers). The mentioned figures based on SEF 1993: 182.

59. On interventionism and outside participation by foreign states, see also Ch. 2.

60. e.g. Ethiopia and the Sudan continued to try to destabilize one another until 1991; the same was true of Ethiopia and Somalia until the fall of Siad Barré.

61. As in the case of the Miskitu vs. Nicaragua, the Ovimbundu (UNITA) vs. the Angolan government (panethnic MPLA), the Bakongo (FNLA) vs. Angola, the fundamentalist Taleban vs. Afghanistan (today Tajiks against Taleban-run Afghanistan) , the Hmong vs. Laos and Vietnam, the Montagnards (hill tribes, now FULRO) vs. Cambodia, Laos, and Vietnam, the Kurdish PKK vs. Turkey and Agas, etc.

62. Warlords make life dangerous for scores of people; rarely were they 'paid back' in the same currency: Khun Sa has always been a unscrupulous businessman and known for his brutal methods of eliminating opponents and competitors. His pact with the Burmese government has not loosened his close ties with many officials in other countries. One never knows. The Burmese Army's entry into Ho Mong, headquarters of Khun Sa's Mon Tai Army (MTA), in January 1996, took experts on Burmese affairs by complete surprise. The move proved a shock for certain officers of the Opium King's own organization. Accusations of 'treason' put forth by some of Khun Sa's more nationalistic lieutenants resulted from a series of events which seriously damaged Khun Sa's excessive ambition. Pressure from Washington led to the drying up of part of Khun Sa's support from neighboring Thailand, reinforced by that country's near-total blockade of its border with the Shan State. The June 1995 a mutiny had already sparked the dissidence of several thousand men and was the precursor of the disintegration of the Mong Tai Army. Thus the MTA suffered a dramatic sapping of manpower, losing about 6,000 men in the space of three months. Their boss, however, made another lucrative deal with the Burmese military junta.

63. For principles see 'Constructive structural elements for multi-ethnic states', in: Scherrer 2002*b*: 142–147; cases for successful prevention of ethnic and nationalist conflicts see *Ibid.*, 148–210.

PART II

RESPONSES OF THE INTERNATIONAL SYSTEM

Chapter 5

Options for Preventing Violence and Resolving Conflict

Internal social peace—and that is what it is all about in today's world—is a process of *rapprochement*. The path to it is a rocky one. The various players are constantly seeking to ensnare one another. Partial solutions and instances of 'imperfect peace' are also worth documenting as learning processes.[1] Some of the deliberations and findings in this area are usefully summarized in typologies of peace (see Tables 5.1–5.3). Since the mid-1990s prevention has become very topical and it was translated into state policies. It has become clear that the prevention of violent conflicts is in every case far cheaper than any so-called humanitarian intervention. However, the politicians still have not acted comprehensively on this state of affairs. Budgets for conflict-prevention measures and for the peaceful settlement of disputes are still infinitesimal compared with the high costs of military intervention. Structurally preventive measures and interventions applied over a long period have much more value than all the many mediation attempts that have purely reactive character.

Boutros-Ghali's *Agenda for Peace* of January 1992 was the first authoritative treatment, within the UN system, of approaches to prevention (albeit in the context of classical diplomacy) and to peacemaking and peacekeeping. That said, the UN's range of instruments is geared to inter- rather intra-state conflicts. The 1989–91 C/OSCE Documents on the Human Dimension suffered from the same defect. Since then 'conflict prevention'—correct term: violence prevention—became part of the official policy of many states, supra-states and international organizations. The contribution of the sciences in the critical transitional phase since the end of the Cold War has been a modest one. The new unintelligibility that has prevailed since 1989–90 and new challenges—which were 'new' only in so far as they had been largely ignored up till then, and this applies to 'new' terrorism as well—have generated increasing anxiety and uncertainty. The shortcomings of established peace and conflict research, now laid bare, have undoubtedly been recognized, but by no means eliminated yet. Interim periods are always 'periods of prophetism'; in the sciences such periods are triggered by a lack of empirically substantiated findings.

The actionist approach to peace pursued by states and the United Nations within the framework of preventive diplomacy, and the increasing importance of civilian third parties and go-betweens—either international NGOs or individuals such as the Carter Center—are a much better and cheaper alternative to military intervention and to strangulation by economic embargoes that often cause much more harm to the population than to the bellicose state-classes. These latter measures are reactive, are geared to ongoing conflicts, mostly so-called 'headline conflicts', are short- (or medium-) range, and generally combat symptoms rather than causes.

The task of peace building is most effectively approached by various ways to structurally prevent violence on different levels. This includes different actors or institutions and can be achieved by using various means. In the enclosed general survey of types of crisis prevention and conflict management I tried to specify some aspects of my typology of peace in order to give a structural view of existing procedures, and instruments for peaceful coexistence and interethnic balance (compare Table 5.1). In much the same way possibilities for prevention of troubles are listed on one page (see Table 5.2). Ways of achieving crisis prevention and peaceful coexistence are given in a systematic overview (Tables 5.3).

Change of Perspective after the Rwanda Shock

It took the 'Rwanda shock' to bring about a change in attitudes regarding prevention amongst the political classes and multilateral organizations.[2] The utter failure of the international community in regard to the state-organized genocide in Rwanda in 1994 was an incomprehensible scandal. UN peacekeeping troops were present at the scene of events—and looked on without intervening.[3] The helplessness of the response to the refugee drama, the haphazard actions of the UN, of humanitarian organizations, hundreds of NGOs, and the high consequential costs prompted reflection as to how such a disaster might be prevented in future. In this regard, it is a couple of years ago when leading EU politicians started to sum up the goals; one did it in the key expression of 'structural stability'.[4]

Initial steps towards preventive measures have been developed within the framework of the European Union.[5] In 1996 a remarkable study was compiled that contained an outline of options for an EU conflict-prevention procedure.[6] What is envisaged is the creation of a kind of linked think-tank offering a basis for information and political consultation. Within the framework of a 'conflict-prevention network', NGOs and peace and conflict research institutes are called upon to help to drafting, discussing and monitoring the implementation of EU conflict-prevention measures.[7]

Table 5.1: Peaceful Coexistence through Violence Prevention and Interethnic Balance: A Typology

coexistence	scope, realm	principle	period	Characteristics / phenomena	aims / objectives / results
negative peace **by threat of aggression** *pax americana / sovietica*	global state system – global economy	deterrence (external) and internal control	short and medium-term	Northern states or regional powers against weaker Southern states; exception: mutual deterrence of the super powers (Cold War)	imposition of interest / containment /economic interest; result: hegemony
negative peace **by military intervention falsely named 'humanitarian'**	state system (often against civil society); UN	external; state-centred; powered by legacy of Euro-colonialism	short-term; since colonialism	usually colonial powers, Northern states or regional powers against weaker states at the peripheries; expression of (post-)colonial dependency (*dependencia*); toppling of unfriendly governments, e.g., US-interventions in Latin America since the era of President Monroe	often ultimate with no agreement proposed; control / imposition of 'solutions'; result: conflict of interests; partial, non-sustainable effect, perpetuation of dependency
coexistence and peace by arbitration and settlement of disputes	state system	external potentially also internal	since 1899 First Hague Peace Conference	establishment of the *Permanent Court of Arbitration* (PCA) 1899; Convention for the *Peaceful Settlement of International Disputes* (CPSID) provide for legal base	peaceful settlement of disputes is a good old idea (reaffirmed by the UN-Charter 1945, Article 33c); result: PCA had little impact
coexistence by agreements	state system (primary); TNCs	internal expansive state-centred; *colonialism*	since the early 19th century	settlers vs. indigenous nations / weak settler states; conflict reduction by treaties, mostly broken after changes of the balance of power	treaties were made regulate territorial invasion, for the purpose of control over lands, resources and populations

Table 5.1: Peaceful Coexistence through Violence Prevention and Interethnic Balance (continued; part 2)

coexistence	scope, realm	principle	period	Characteristics / phenomena	aims / objectives / results
coexistence through **welfare state policies and limited-scope agreements**	state system (primary); economy; civil society	internal state-centred; expansive, *internal colonialism*	longer periods; since the early 20th century	*mainstream*-societies vs. indigenous groups / strong settler states; attempted reduction of conflict, post-colonial *trusteeship* ideology; limited agreements with indigenous groups; reservation-type of system complemented by affirmative action (USA, Australia, New Zealand)	alien control of most indigenous lands and resources; population control
internal peace and coexistence by means of **modern treaties**	state system economy; civil society	internal and state-centred; softened *internal colonialism*	undefined periods; since the 1980s	*mainstream*-societies, indigenous and other minorities / strong settler states; conflict prevention through treaties and agreements with indigenous peoples; partial to full self-governance (Canada, Denmark, Sweden)	control and internal peace as aim; result: hopeful beginnings in Kalaallit Nunaat; Nunavut, Dené NWT, Hudson Bay Cree of Quebec; Saami Land in the Nordic European countries
coexistence by means of **autonomy and conservation** (in Southern neo-liberal states)	state system (primary); civil society (only corporate)	internal state-centred; internal colonialism by other means	shorter and longer periods	*Mestizo* societies vs. manifold indigenous communities / weak states (periphery); agreements with selected communities; type: *comarca* (Panama since 1920s), *resguardo*; non-integration often broken by attempts of assimilation; self-rule in Eastern Nicaragua, flawed by neglect / paternalism	traditional institutions (*caciques / congreso*-system); control by concession of self-rule; aim to avoid structurally induced conflicts by territorial autonomy regulations (by law or constitutional, often *ad hoc*); real autonomy needs an economy

Table 5.1: Peaceful Coexistence through Violence Prevention and Interethnic Balance (continued; part 3)

coexistence	scope, realm	principle	period	Characteristics / phenomena	aims / objectives / results
peaceful coexistence by **self-rule and free association** (Northern welfare states as a base)	state system and civil society	associative non-expansive, internal and external	medium and longer periods after 1945	enlightened / libertarian societies, indigenous minorities / social welfare states; structural conflict avoidance, conflict regulation through rights and concessions, self-governance (Føroyar or Faeroe Islands' home rule 1948)	security through respect for others; high degree of organization; development and prosperity for many; realized solid models for indigenous and minority self-governance
peaceful coexistence by **neutrality and welfare**	state (primary) civil society	external and internal	Austria, Malta a/o for 50 years	liberal social-democrat societies, protection for minorities / welfare states; structural conflict avoidance, prosperity for many still the ideal but steady reduction of welfare levels	conflict regulation through welfare state; proportional representation in parliamentary democracy; non-allied policy in crisis
peaceful coexistence by **neutrality and (con-) federation**	state system and civil society	stable; self-centered	Swiss model for 400 years (?)	decentralization in multi-ethnic pluri-cultural Switzerland: confederation since 1848, linked with a big-party coalition in the central government (leaving no real opposition); respect for other indigenous languages and cultures, but no inclusion of migrants; prosperity for many ran into crisis	conflict regulation / solution by self-rule (canton system) and proportional / regional representation; elements of direct democracy formally exist but are in reality over-powered by corporatist interests; serious abuse of federalism
peace through involvement / **peaceful intervention**	state system / UN-System, OSCE, OAU-AU, etc.	(re) active; civil actors marginally included	since 1945, on the rise since 1990, short term	divided societies / states; UN-operations; OSCE-missions; in between intervention and mediation / facilitation	conflict regulation/solution through agreements between all parties to the conflict; security through inter-ethnic balance and protection of minorities

The danger is that the long-term and proactive structural prevention of violent conflicts, the creation of appropriate instruments within the framework of development co-operation and multilateral organizations, and back-up for existing mechanisms (e.g. for violence prevention within the framework of the OAU) might be neglected in favour of short-term emergency-prevention and dubious forms of actionist crisis-management. The 'Rwanda crisis' also led to the formulation of proposals for reform within development co-operation (development for peace) and in regard to reconstruction in war-torn countries.[8] The Amsterdam Appeal for the promotion of conflict prevention, issued in February 1997 and directed at the European Union, called for a coherent programme of action to prevent war and violence.[9]

An ability to moderate conflicts, reconcile differing interests, and maintain a properly functioning administration (good governance) is in the interests not only of the societies concerned, but also of the state-classes and of the international community as a whole. In conditions of economic dependence and underdevelopment, statehood in ravaged societies can only be kept functioning if there is a minimum consensus in regard to the rules governing its operation. The kind of contribution, which a newly oriented peace and conflict research community could make following the end of the Cold War, is particularly urgently needed in this area.[10]

From Conflict Research to Peace Research

Up to now, the irenological perspective has only been dealt with in passing. Irenology must be systematically pursued as a necessary complement to what has so far been the exclusively polemological orientation of research.[11] Peace itself, and different forms of peaceful co-existence, must be subjected to a greater degree of systematic documentation and analysis. The positive effect of references to functioning models (even if incomplete) and to successes in resolving conflicts should not be underestimated.

Realization of the need for a shift of perspective, from conflict research to peace research, was almost 'forced' upon me between 1987 and 1992 by the historical process attendant on dramatic changes in two areas of acute conflict in the South. This happened when I was carrying out on empirical investigations into ethno-nationalism—out in the field. Regional and local schemes for the structural prevention of future conflicts were developed on the ground and went far beyond so-called peace talks (involving local and Western mediators). Demands made by the parties to the conflict were worked into a politically viable shape and then implemented within the framework of a reform of the constitution and of state structures. But scientific interest in this process was relatively meagre, as was clear from two examples.

Once hostilities in Nicaragua had died down, almost no one seemed interested in the promising new beginnings that had been made in the 'other half' of the country. The war was over, or 'in its last throes', and, compared with the spectacular armed hostilities and subsequent peace-negotiations at the highest levels, peace soon came to appear not particularly attractive, indeed 'run of the mill'. The change in the peace and war situation in Ethiopia in March 1991 was even more unexpected and dramatic.[12] I was witness, during this initial period, to the start of the 'struggle over the post-war order' that was waged over the next few months, admittedly not with arms, but definitely 'with gloves off'.

The Ethiopian charter, a transitional government, and the planned new order were elements of a unique experiment in Africa. For the first time, the ethnic-national question was brought out 'onto the table'—almost, as it were, from the bottom of the pile. The conflict between the Abyssinians and Oromo that is of such crucial significance for Ethiopia has remained unresolved; to many observers, it seems unfounded, and it fails to be given the attention it deserves in EU diplomacy and foreign policy.

The major regulations aimed at preventing violence affect the rights of the various non-dominant ethnic groups, particularly their rights in regard to autonomy and participation, and also the distribution of public goods. The aim is to seek out an equitable arrangement amongst the ethno-social groups involved. This necessitates getting rid of the dominant-groups' monopolies and channels of influence. Power sharing and respect for distinct cultures are amongst the core elements of any policy for preventing violence. Through bilateral negotiations between states and nations, preferably with the involvement of a go-between or a third party, possible solutions can be discussed in a mutually acceptable fashion. With the Permanent Court of Arbitration in The Hague, there is an independent institution available that could also become competent to deal with 'intra-state' disputes and whose rulings the parties can accept without loss of face.

In my view, in 60 to 80 percent of ethno-national conflicts, solutions could be found through negotiations. 'Minority rights', affirmative action, autonomy arrangements, nationality policies, self-administration, and free association are some of the possible concrete solutions on offer. (See the Table 5.2: Violence Prevention and Inter-Ethnic Balance). Frequently, there is a lack of will on the part of states to prevent violence or settle a dispute peacefully, e.g., by granting autonomy rights, power sharing, self-governance, or federal solutions. In a few cases, the end-result has been the formation of new states. Where this happens, it does so in two forms:

1. *De jure*, in the sense of a true secession regime or as an upgrading of status within the framework of nationality-policy structures; this was the case with the successor states of the USSR (15 Soviet republics became sovereign states) and with Yugoslavia (five new states so far).
2. In the South, as a belated decolonization, as it was the case in Namibia and Eritrea (type D). Somaliland (BA) and 'liberated areas' in Columbia (A) or Burma (B) provide examples of *de facto* proto-states.

According to UN resolutions, a referendum is to be held in Western Sahara (type D). In two major regional conflict (Middle East 1993), mediation by a third party (Norway) has produced an agenda for peace, which has faced too many obstacles since. In Palestine (type D), the promise of autonomy and self-governance (Oslo peace accords between the Israeli government and the PLO) seemed to prepare the way to a partial solution; however, the implementation of the accords has been delayed and sabotaged by successive Israeli governments. In the case of Sri Lanka (type B) the Norwegian initiative has proved successful so far. The United Nations ought to play a more active part—in the sense of peaceful intervention—among others in Palestine, West Papua, Western Sahara, Kurdistan, and Kanaky.

Positive Peace: Between Past, Present and Utopia

According to Kant positive peace needs constant efforts. For every society the understanding of peace has its own meaning and its own taste. Today Kant's thoughts seem very modern: He mentioned the central problem, which are the nation states' claims for absolute sovereignty, and resulting from that the permanent threat of war. In 1795 Kant proposed to establish a League of Nations to end war. Reason shall triumph over the anarchy of warfare. He wrote that at the place of the positive idea of a veritable world republic only the negative surrogate of a league of all peoples could prevent war and contain lawless hostility. Galtung rediscovered Kant for peace research. While negative peace would only mean the absence of violence, *positive peace* would be in its own right and represent a new quality of social interaction. Positive peace only exists as an incessant effort to approach it.

Peace researchers have been busy elaborating the typology of wars. Implicitly they deal with peace as a mere *normal situation*. Almost nobody thought of the advantage of distinguishing different forms of peaceful coexistence, which have a real existence today, existed in the past or shall exist in the future, to describe and analyse them, and, based on this work, to elaborate a typology of preventing troubles (see Table 5.2) for peaceful coexistence (Table 5.3) or a typology of the different types of peace.

Table 5.2: Prevention of Troubles by Peaceful Interethnic Coexistence: Types, Instruments and Models

type / instrument	scope, realm	principle	period	models, processes, deficits	needs for studies and application
interethnic coexistence by granting of **minority rights**	states multilateral regimes	active preventive internal rule of law	since 1980s; increasingly since 1990	protection of the rights of non-dominant groups (OSCE HCNM); standard setting by UN-CHR towards a *Declaration of the Rights of Indigenous Peoples*	internal peace and external security through inter-ethnic balance and protection of new minorities; application of international law
peaceful interethnic coexistence by **power sharing**	states regimes civil actors	active preventive innovative	since many centuries; more cases still to be established	lessons to be learned from experience with existing models of power sharing, representation, ethnically mixed elites and their co-operation (Lebanon, Malaysia, Benin, Nigeria); models of limited attraction	comparison of existing models and their performance; development of new instruments for power-sharing and balancing of different ethnic and national groups
interethnic peace and coexistence by granting the **right to self-determination and free association**	co-operation of involved state(s) and peoples; facilitation by UN, regional regimes, NGOs	interactive preventive innovative	increasingly since 1945; still to be established on larger scale	'lessons learned?' from experiences with autonomy and self-governance in all continents; large-scale models: *korenisazia* and autonomization in FSU and China; creation of new states in India, quotas for scheduled castes/tribes ; autonomy regulations in Europe	comparison of existing models and their performance; development of new instruments with the objective to promote constructive interaction between states and nation(alitie)s; establishment of international regimes in high demand; problem of lack of implementation
interethnic peace and coexistence by establishing **(con-) federal schemes**	co-operation of pluralist people(s); facilitation by relevant actors	interactive preventive	increasingly since 1945; still to be established	lessons to be learned from experiences with federal schemes in all continents; models (also incomplete): FSU/RF, India, Nigeria, Tanzania, Ethiopia, new South Africa, Switzerland, Spain, etc.	comparison and evaluation of already existing models and their performance; development of new elements of (con-) federal and regional schemes and prevention of its abuse

Table 5.3: Types and Ways of/for Crisis Prevention and Conflict Management

types and ways	scope, realm	principle	period	models, processes / deficits / needs	aims / objectives / expectations
preventing violence by **early warning linked to early action**	UN, INGOs, regional regimes, states, civil actors	active preventive	still to be established	improving capabilities of early warning; best use of violence prevention networks to be built-up jointly by multilateral regimes, research institutes and INGOs / NGOs	top priority for bridging the gap between early warning and early action
transforming ethnic violence by **preventive diplomacy**	state system primary; civil actors such as INGOs	state-centred regime building	on the rise since 1990; medium term	multi-ethnic states; from actionist activities to mediation; conflict regulation as agreements; reactive. limited impact; often successful	*protection* / minimal rights for non-dominant groups; security through respect for others, recognition of multiplicity
inter-ethnic coexistence by **enforcing accountability & compliance** by states	United Nations regimes under monitoring by NGOs / INGOs	interventive, rule of (inter-)national law	long-term approach; still at point zero	enlightened civilized state leaders and civic organizations pushing for change; over-all promotion of standard-setting in international law aimed at forcing states to obey to the rules / comply with international law	humanitarian minimum, respect of human and minority rights; no double standards; clear-cut sanctions to be introduced against crimes by repressive and intransigent state governments
peace by peaceful intervention: **mediation / facilitation**	civil society actors, NGOs / INGOs, some states	reactive-activist interactive preventive	since the 1980s; short to long term	multi-ethnic societies / states; actionistic mediation / facilitation, conflict regulation / solutions through agreements between in-side parties facilitated by out-side parties	*empowerment* for non-dominant groups; security through respect for others, recognition of multiplicity / promotion of minorities' issues
peace building by **constructive dialogue**	states external and local civil actors	active, processual preventive innovative	on the rise; medium term	improvement of overall relationships in multi-ethnic societies; recognition and awareness about hidden agendas / perceptions of involved parties	discovering shared needs; focusing on the future; translating common needs into 'joint actions as stepping stones to agreements' (Weeks)

Table 5.3: Types and Ways of/for Crisis Prevention and Conflict Management (continued; part 2)

types and ways	scope, realm	principle	period	models, processes / deficits / needs	aims / objectives / expectations
peaceful coexistence by **structural prevention** of destructive interaction	United Nations regional regimes, states, societies, NGOs	Interactive preventive rule of law	increasingly since 1945; still to be enforced	application of existing instruments / laws (international pacts, conventions, declarations) as well as development of new instruments in international law; problem: how to break the resistance of states?	new instruments to combat destructive interaction between states and nation(alitie)s; rapid establishment of international criminal justice in high demand; lack of enforcement
coexistence by rules for implementing **full right to self-determination**	co-operation of involved state(s) and international community	interactive preventive innovative	still to be established	consequences to be drawn from experiences with destructive ethno-nationalist civil wars in all continents; deficit of shared norms / standards for secession; global governance	rules for the creation of new states; regimes for recognition of claims; new instruments to promote constructive transition
peace building by constructive **conflict resolution** approaches	states external and local civil actors	active processual preventive innovative	still to be established	facilitation of conflict resolutions through negotiation about binding agreements as constructive medium and long term approaches	shared needs and joint plans for the future; securing accountability of all parties and building sustainability
peace by peaceful means: education, **culture of peace** by lively cross-cultural communication	civil society civilized states	active interactive preventive innovative	medium periods	enlightened libertarian sectors of societies / civilized states pushing for change; prevention of violence by getting to know each-other (multiculturalism vs. daily racism; travelling, cultural contacts and exchanges, arts, etc.)	conflict regulation through rights for non-dominant groups (citizenship for 2nd generation migrants); respect for other societies and different cultures / life styles

Peaceful coexistence can be approached by using existing means and knowledge. Before creating new instruments the application of existing instruments should be guaranteed. International law is to safeguard international security as well as internal peace. The critical factor in international law—in general, and in regard to human and minority rights in particular—is the lack or fragmentary nature of mechanisms and procedures for enforcing legal instruments such as declarations, conventions, covenants, and treaties.

Building on the typologies of peaceful coexistence in the modern age I went into further more fundamental reflections on the nature of peace. In an attempt to elaborate a socio-historical typology of peace, I identified twenty-one such types. Although some of them might only be considered as cases of more or less fruitful peaceful coexistence or as transitional stages of a peace not yet achieved, I nevertheless took a closer look at their particular scope, key principle, time frame or period of existence, their characteristics and aims.

Any typology of peaceful coexistence will probably be considered as far from being complete but might well be a source of inspiration. I tried to include social-historic types of peace taken from different periods of history and regions of world; two types belong to utopia. (See Table A.5: Social-historical Typology of Peace, in the Appendices.) At present many of these types have their place in reality in somewhat modified form. For instance, one could relate traditional societies of less 'extreme kind' as the case of the !Khoi to (post-) modern sub-cultures. Through the course of human history different forms and ways of peaceful coexistence of peoples, nations, cultures and civilisations have been experienced.

Conclusions

As a guide on how to approach the complex field of 'politicised ethnicity', I shall here make a number of further general observations. These are initially of a negative nature: first and foremost, modes of investigation that distort or hamper access to the issues must be avoided. The appeal to objectivity, freedom from prejudice, and impartiality in research is particularly important in situations that are emotionally highly charged or seem in some way alien. Yet in some of the literature to date, denunciation rather than analysis has been the dominant feature.

- Accusations of manipulation against the leaderships of ethno-national movements and the imputation of particularistic economic interests are two of the commonest 'explanatory models' in use; they almost always fall short of the mark. In many cases, such accounts are merely an attempt to deflect attention from the real situation.

- Care should be taken to avoid the 'traps' laid by the adversary—in other words, deliberate attempts to mislead in regard to what triggers or shapes ethnic conflicts. There are at least two sides to every conflict, and there are always at least two—often completely divergent—accounts of the situation.
- Ethno-nationalism from below and ethnicization from above must be kept separate; confusing the two phenomena, or failing to distinguish clearly between them, hampers understanding of ethno-national opposition and 'pathologizes' legitimate ethnic demands.
- The 'lack of clarity' in regard to the major bones of contention in, causes of, and triggers to ethnic conflict is generally due not so much to the allegedly 'intangible' or 'irrational' element in such conflicts, but to deliberate attempts to mislead on the part of states and other actors.
- Laying emphasis on resistance and preservation as motives for ethno-national movements is aimed at portraying them as 'backward-looking' and opposed to the 'inevitability' of modernization.
- Attempting to fathom complex realities by having recourse to 'purified forms' of ethnic conflict is doomed to failure. This kind of approach often has a lot in common with the obfuscating strategies employed by individual actors in conflicts.
- Active denial of the true driving forces of ethno-national movements distorts access to an understanding of them. Abstracting the basic asymmetry present in most ethnic conflicts, and blocking out relationships of power and dominance also distorts findings.
- Adopting a state-centred interpretation results in many theoretical models of, and findings about, ethnicity being one-sided, incomplete, and 'wrong', and leads to a distorted account of particular examples.

Some theoretical approaches lack any empirical substrate; others continue to be applied without regard for empirical findings. What dominates such attempts to tackle the ethno-national phenomenon is not understanding or the desire to understand but prejudice, myth-building, and artificially constructed approaches. Ethno-national conflicts of a violent kind are a response to deeply rooted crises and dislocations—and not only in the decolonised states of the Third World and former Eastern bloc. Such conflicts become comprehensible when they are seen as processes of resistance and self-identification. Their social, cultural, and economic aspects must be investigated from both horizontal and vertical perspectives, and from the point of view of their depth or intensity. Social science studies of ethno-nationalism will in future make an important contribution to the grand theory of social transformation.

The most important prerequisites if research into ethnicity in general and the analysis of ethno-nationalism in particular are to be made fruitful in terms of the theory of social transformation are:

- A process-based and empirical (rather than an aetiological and 'theoretically' fully pre-defined) approach, in which violence does not appear as anomie, ethnicity does not appear as 'primitive', and ethno-nationalism does not appear as a pathological reaction to conditions of oppression and violent subordination.[13]
- A dynamic type of analysis rather than a static and isolating mode of observation. Such analysis would embrace the causes and objects of ethno-national conflict-formations and would cover all the actors involved, along with their interests, divergent discourses, goals, resources, etc.; it would distinguish between the various phases of escalation, would acknowledge any outside elements and external factors (including macro-political ones), and would be able to point up options for de-escalation and peaceful resolution.
- Situating the analysis—in other words exploring violent conflicts in their historical and regional contexts.
- A comprehending, critical (not denunciatory) intent, which takes the form of a dialectical relation between the *emic* and *etic* perspectives, not denying differences but discussing them.

Conflict researchers, political ethnologists, and development sociologists cannot come to terms with the fact that peace research has not as yet developed its own heuristics worthy of this name. At the level of international politics, it would be particularly useful in terms of actual practice, if a framework of recognized socio-political structural analysis were established that could act as a guide in defining properly planned, reflective and responsible conduct in political decision-making processes. This kind of recognized unitary framework does not exist today. Questions of crucial nature remain unclarified because problems are imported from the disciplines involved rather than being resolved.

Rigid subject-based division, with its differing perspectives and traditional areas of operation, would result in a fragmentation of the research-field and would hamper the prospect of understanding. On the other side the objective cannot be to 'know a little bit about everything'; what we need to do, rather, is to flesh out those issues and methods that have to do with current social problems or can be brought into some kind of relation with them. The separate disciplines can only be linked to current issues—such as forced migration, racism and intra-state conflicts—when peace research has completed the process of reorientation that has been on the agenda since 1990, and when it has developed its communication skills and is able to promote issue-centred dialogue between various disciplines. But establishing an interdisciplinary dialogue is a demanding process. Where networking goes well, it does so only on a discrete basis. Up to now it has been too little structured, very much tied to individuals, and, in terms of practical application, restricted to conferences, workshops, the occasional public debate, and—a trend that is no doubt likely to increase even more in future—online debates and conferences via the internet.

Dividing off causes of conflict and processes is wrong, because then the antinomy between social science and historiographical modes of research and thought that we want to eliminate just waltzes back in 'through a different door'. Past causes, whose histories often stretch back over decades or even longer periods of time, may be difficult to identify in terms of their bearing on current processes of violence, or may have 'only' an indirect effect—compared to manifest triggers to conflict; but they are ultimately crucial for the (re)cognition and understanding of conflictual processes. The historical amnesia not only of Western European politicians but also of political scientists in regard to the Yugoslavian conflict is only the most recent of many examples of this disregard of the past.

Division of the totality of a conflict into neat analytical compartments of structural and other causes, economic and political (power) structures, and socio-cultural processes is also to be rejected. Western-style terms and concepts can often be traced back to long-lived 19th-century paradigms.[14] In this connection, concepts such as those popular export-items the 'nation-state', 'development', and 'sovereignty' must be critically put into perspective, adapted, or, if that is not possible, rejected.

The seemingly permanent establishment and the globalization of ethno-nationalism in the last fifty years dictate that research efforts be multiplied. But there is a real cognitive problem here, in that many sociologists, ethnologists, and conflict researchers 'have never experienced [the horror of war or of mass violence] at close quarters and have no realistic prospect at all of going through a trauma of this kind'.[15] The overstated contrast between modern and non-modern societies implies different potentials for violence. It was the modern societies who waged the most violent of wars against one another and in the colonies.[16]

Only detailed, empirical-cum-practical knowledge of the causes of war, its structural characteristics and the forces that drive it—ideally first-hand information combined with personal experience—will turn up the kind of solid findings that are a prerequisite for practical action in concrete instances. Otherwise, well-meaning attempts at prevention, containment, or peaceful intervention by the international community risk failing. That said, it would be naïve to believe that the series of recent cases in which the spectacular failure of the international community was repeatedly and amply demonstrated were due 'only' to deficiencies in fact-finding and poor implementation. Knowledge and interests are seldom compatible in international politics. But ignorance and inadequacy did contribute to the political failure.

The threat to the world order emanating from ethno-nationalism will make increased efforts to identify and deal with the underlying wrongs unavoidable—within the limitations imposed by practical politics, big-power interests, and the crumbling principles of non-intervention in the 'internal affairs' of sovereign nation-states. The success of attempts at solution depends on whether states can be civilized—that is to say, whether states, which up to now have been the universally privileged protagonists, can be forced to share the sovereignty to which they lay claim with 'their' peoples. Ethno-national conflicts can only be resolved by political, not military means.

Notes

1. See IFEK report 3, 2001 (Indigenous peoples and the state. The case of Nicaragua).
2. 'April 1994 saw the start of the long-heralded, long-prepared genocide against the Rwandan Tutsi and of the massacre of the Hutu opposition. Despite prior warnings, the United Nations remained inactive. In order to preserve their power and privileges, Rwandan leaders decreed that the Tutsi minority be wiped out. The assassination of Dictator Habyarimana served as the trigger for organized massacre. The whole state-apparatus was mobilized for murder. Foreign development-workers were evacuated; the victims were abandoned to their fate. Every day, radio-stations incited 'loyal citizens' to go out and murder the Tutsi' (Scherrer 1997*d*: 177).
3. The 2,500 UN peacekeeping troops (UNAMIR I) present in the country looked on as civilians were massacred. They were actually withdrawn at the height of the massacre. Any kind of rapid or sensible response from the UN was blocked by the big powers in the Security Council.
4. See the remarks of Luis de Almeida Sampaio, a member of the cabinet of then EU Commissioner João de Deus Pinheiro, in the opening address of the European Congress on Conflict Prevention in Amsterdam, Feb. 1997. Sampaio stressed that stability (a core concept of security policy) embraced the notion of dynamism.
5. The EU Commission's response of late 1995 to the Rocard report and the advances in the European Parliament (Resolution on Conflict Prevention, 5 June 1995) were drawn up in the language of the UN Secretary-General of the time (see Commission of the European Communities, 'Preventive Diplomacy, Conflict Resolution and Peace-Keeping in Africa', Brussels, 4 Dec. 1995).
6. A few months later, on the basis of the guidelines and principles (e.g. drawn up in the above mentioned document), a remarkable study was compiled by the Directorate-

General VII, written by Martin Landgraf (Development Co-operation/Africa) (Commission of the European Communities 1996). It contained the first outline of options for an EU conflict-prevention procedure.

7. Under pressure from the European Parliament and the governments of certain individual member-states, the Commission arranged for a pilot project to be done within the framework of DG IA, as a way of enhancing EU competence in the prevention of violence. A Conflict Prevention Network (CPN) and a data bank for crisis prevention were created by the end of 1997 but not filled with life; CPN remained under-organized and rather inactive. Detailed analyses are to be made of violent conflicts, assessing both potential and actual threats, in trouble-spots near to Europe (with special reference to the causes of conflict as insisted upon in the DG VII study mentioned earlier), and options for action are to be worked out, thus enabling the political decision-makers in the EU to act preventively and to respond appropriately to situations of crisis.

8. See the remarks of Jan Pronk on the role of development co-operation (conflict-prevention measures, peace-keeping, reconstruction) and on the reform of the UN system, 'Towards New Policies for International Cooperation with Countries in Conflict', speech, The Hague, 1997.

9. The appeal was adopted by the world's largest conference on conflict prevention (Amsterdam, 27–8 February 1997, attended by some 1,200 people). See NCDO 1997 and 1997*a*.

10. Years ago I have commented on the shortcomings and new tasks (Scherrer 1996).

11. The Greek term *polemos* was translated with 'war' / warfare; originally the old Greeks meant 'struggle', mainly the 'exchange of ideas' (not the exchange of fire), as the term polemic reveals.

12. I learned of Mengistu's flight via the BBC in the liberated region of the Oromo rebels. My heavily armed escorts remained sceptical and at first believed this to be deliberate disinformation—'just another trick of the government'. However, the news reports were correct, and the largest army in Black Africa collapsed within weeks.

13. The term 'aetiological' contains the idea of 'social disease', i.e. a concern with pathological phenomena (analogous to the pathogenesis of visible phenomena in medicine). In many cases, it would be the absence of violent conflicts that would be pathological.

14. See Wallerstein 1995.

15. The discourse about war and violence is now concerned 'not with truth but with suitability'. Researchers, it is said, lack experience of on-site observation; they find the topic 'fascinating' and so work on it. They do this in a 'sanitized language'; they impose 'thought restrictions' on themselves; and even the empirical material (deriving from the small handful of people with first-hand knowledge of the violent conditions on the ground) appears 'in a very curious way, not to have been penetrated, theoretically and conceptually, beyond particular points' (Rottenburg 1996: 8).

16. Anyone who sees the modern age as 'non-violent', and associates violence with 'primitiveness, the archaic, and nature' must be turning a blind eye to the everyday racism in modern industrial states. Was the industrial-style annihilation in Auschwitz not 'modern'?

Chapter 6

Minorities, New States, and Human Rights

Since 1990, over 20 new states have been admitted to the United Nations. The total number of independent states with UN membership now stands at 193. As regards this proliferation, there are, as I see it, two contrary processes at work. On the one hand, the creation of new states seems in many cases to be unavoidable as a way of bringing armed conflicts in the Third World to an end. On the other hand, similar creation in the Second World has actually led to armed follow-on conflicts, as in Yugoslavia and the South-western and Central Asian republics of the former USSR. Within a framework of regional bloc-formation, or of regimes tailored to the particular regions involved, the propagation of states could be organized as a process of decentralization, without any obviously destructive fragmentation.

The 'community of nations', which in reality is a community of states, faces a fundamental dilemma: only from time to time has it managed to make a choice between two antagonistic principles—the right of peoples to self-determination on the one hand, and state sovereignty and territorial integrity on the other. Often, depending on political expediency, it was the principle of *uti possidetis* that triumphed. A deviation from previous practice, which as a rule accorded sovereignty to states rather than people, was the recognition of the successor states of the USSR and Yugoslavia. Typically, however, this occurred on the basis of the 'unalterable nature' of the internal administrative borders drawn by Stalin and Tito, fraught with potential for conflict.

Existential issues that are perceived by a distinct group of people as a threat to their identity are not negotiable; they are one of the primal preconditions of constructive interaction between states and nations. Some forms of interaction that have destructive patterns of progression have yet to be systematically investigated. Nor does the international community have any consistent policy in regard to them—in the form, for example, of regimes of recognition or secession. Efforts by the community of states and by non-state actors to elaborate internationally binding standards on the ethnic question are a novelty. In order to measure up to the ethnic challenge, classical minorities politics must be reformed and be made a subject of international law and international relations.

The Propagation of States as a Form of Conflict Resolution

The contradiction between the Third World crisis of the state and the creation of new states is only an apparent one: besides economic impoverishment, indebtedness, and mismanagement, the critical situation in which many states find themselves has to do, chiefly, with the artificial nature of these states' foundation in colonial times and the ethnic tensions resulting from this—tensions which in some cases could evidently be eliminated or reduced by the creation of new states. To conclude from this that secession is *per se* a successful method of resolving conflicts, would, however, be rash. The creation of new, potentially ethnically homogeneous (small-scale) states would be expedient and defensible only within the framework of supra-state co-operation, within—to take Africa as an example—a Pan-African Community.[1]

A substantial increase in the number of sovereign, internationally recognized states, and their admission to multilateral institutions—as the Baltic states were admitted to the United Nations and the OSCE—is apparently unstoppable. This applies in particular to some of the fifty-eight or more territories annexed by colonial powers, big powers, or neighbouring countries.[2] The proliferation of states affects not only eastern and south-eastern Europe and Africa, but also Asia and Oceania. Worldwide, this inexorability of state propagation applies to conflicts involving both separatist and irredentist interests. In Europe, prime examples in this connection are the constituent states of the CIS and Yugoslavia: the new Second World states spawned by these either resulted from ongoing violent conflicts or actually triggered such conflicts by their emergence. On the other hand, there are certain (Third World) cases that should be mentioned where the creation of new states seemed the only means of bringing to an end lengthy wars involving great loss of life.

Liberation and the Pitfalls of Self-Determination

It has mainly been in Asia and Africa that secession—often under the banner of decolonization—has brought armed conflicts to an end. In 1971 this was achieved in Bangladesh, following the mass murder by the Pakistani military of the oppressed Bengalis and the Hindu minority in East Bengal (1.5–2.5 million victims between 1970 and 1971). This secession only succeeded due to massive military intervention by India (Rummel 1994*a*: 5). In 1991, secession was achieved in Eritrea due to the military/political strength of the EPLF liberation movement, which had the backing of the people. Some recent examples of potentially conflict-resolving processes in the Third World did not develop as expected:

- the liberation of Eritrea, a multinational state comprising ten nationalities, after thirty years of war, was followed by an intensive and costly new war with Ethiopia 1998–2000, which ended with the deployment of a UN peace-keeping force, with mutual territorial claims remaining unsolved
- the breaking-away of Somaliland, formerly British Somalia, which is dominated by the Isaaq clan, further fragmented the former Somalia, while in the Southern part (Somalia proper) the collapse of the state remained the state of the affairs, despite international and domestic efforts to establish a transitional authority, which is in place but only commands little authority
- the creation of an independent nation-state of Western Sahara— ethnically not homogeneous due to the presence of Moroccan settlers— under the supervision of the United Nations has been delayed and the relevant UN resolutions, namely the return of the Saharawi refugees, fair elections and a referendum were sabotaged by Morocco (with support by USA and France) and remained unimplemented by the UN
- the decolonization of East Timor, after the UN failure to supervise its transition in 1974–75, the crime of genocide committed by Indonesia in 1975–78 and new Indonesia-sponsored violence by militias to prevent self-determination as a result of a referendum held fall 1999, finally took place under protection by a UN peace-enforcement mission and a UN transitional administration, and became effective in May 2002.

In contrast to Somaliland, which emerged almost unnoticed as a by-product of the military confusion that accompanied the collapse of Siad Barrés' minority dictatorship, the independent Eritrea, still-occupied Western Sahara and East Timor are the products of decolonization conflicts stretching back over decades. In April 1993, under the supervision of the United Nations and the OAU, Eritrea held a referendum presenting the people with the alternatives of independence or federation with Ethiopia. The overwhelming majority voted for independence and separate statehood. Ethiopia's provisional parliament had already issued a resolution assenting to this as early as 1991. Eritrea concluded agreements on economic co-operation with the new Ethiopia.[3] But the massive *fratricide* launched by two governments dominated by the very same ethnic group, the Tigrean (or Tigrai), showed dramatically that some of the underlying incompatibilities had not been resolved, with the border issue (though decided by the PCA in April 2002) still being used as a pretext for a political and power struggle.

In the case of Western Sahara, the process is deadlocked. The conflict between the Frente Polisario (representing the Saharawis) and the Kingdom of Morocco is ethno-national in character. The UN mission to Western Sahara is developing into more and more of an incomprehensible disaster. As East Timor the Western Sahara was occupied by a foreign state. The United Nations should have tried-and-tested strategies at the ready to deal with these kinds of conflicts—strategies that enforce or complete decolonization in accordance with international law.

A comparison of violent conflicts in Africa and south-eastern Europe shows up contrary developments (mentioned at the start of this chapter). On the African continent, some wars of longish duration, most of them falling into the category of conflicts with ethno-national dimensions, have been brought to an end (but remained partly unsolved). Some have reignited several times (Angola, West Africa). In addition to the above-mentioned wars in Somaliland (1991) and Western Sahara (1992), this seemed to apply to the liberation of Namibia (1988), and long-standing civil wars in Zimbabwe (1988), Uganda (1991–2) and Mozambique (1992), and Angola (1994–5; truce 2002). However, all of the mentioned countries (except for Mozambique) became involved on different fronts in the second war in the Congo, which started in mid 1998 and is still going on as the currently most deadly conflict, despite the disengagement of the state armies, due to the not implemented disarming of various government-aided militia forces.

Some wars were ended by the secession of parts of internationally recognized states as a result of decolonization or through power sharing and democratization consequent upon anti-regime wars with ethno-national components.[4] In eastern and south-eastern Europe, similar circumstances have given rise to eleven new armed conflicts since 1990/1991; eight of these are regarded as settled. Other deadly wars have not yet been brought to an end; these include two large 'protracted conflicts' of ethno-national and anti-regime character: Sudan, Africa's bloodiest war (in cumulative count), and the Congo crisis; ethnic gang-warfare in West Africa (in Sierra Leone and Liberia, with spill-over effects into Guinea) only died down.

Which Matters Most: Size or Quality of Life?

To single out the size of new states—that is to say, their population and territorial extent—as a central criterion of their viability, seems inappropriate. Even smaller autonomous entities could, as in the idea of a Europe of the Regions, fulfil the functions expected of them in terms of cultural independence and economic niche-activity without eliciting the negative effects of political weakness and economic dependency. The mini-states of Liechtenstein, Monaco, and Luxembourg have provided sufficient proof of this. The myth of the 'impossibility' or 'non-viability' of smaller states is constantly being invoked by supporters of the 'strong state'. Amidst all this, the comfortable existence of a series of independent mini-states in the Third World—in the Caribbean, the Indian Ocean, and the Pacific (Barbados, for instance, or the Seychelles, the Maldives, and Tonga)—is passed over in complete silence. Small states frequently offer their citizens a much higher quality of life (measured in terms of life-expectancy, literacy, and per capita income) than neighbouring states of middling to large size. This is easily demonstrated by a non-analytic but, to my mind, more revealing comparison of the smallest states with the largest respective neighbouring states in various parts of the world.[5]

It is difficult to establish a lower limit, or indeed any fixed limit, for the level of population, territorial dimensions, and economic power required to enable a state to be created.[6] The notion of the sectoral completeness of a domestic economy is open to varying interpretations, but points to the essential problem. However, 'completeness' does involve a certain degree of internal centring.[7] The following comparisons between four small states and the large state nearest to each of them makes no claim to be systematic.

Table 6.1: Small States Offer Higher Quality of Life than Large States

World Region	*State or Country*	*Population (estimates)*	*M/F Life-expectancy*	*Literacy (percent)*	*Income PCI in $*
Caribbean	Barbados	255,000	78/62	99	6,340
S. America	Brazil	153,322,000	69/63	76	2,690
Africa	Seychelles	67,000	66	69	1,400
Africa	Nigeria	108,542,000	54/51	25–40	470
South Asia	Maldives	215,000	57	82	1,320
South Asia	India	843,931,000	60/54	36–43	350
Polynesia	Tonga	103,000	?	99	1,100
Oceania	Papua/NG	3,699,000	57/55	45	860

The results are surprising: in the small states, which are mostly composed of islands, life expectancy can be up to ten years greater (except in the case of South Asia); literacy in mini-states can probably be estimated to be consistently far higher—between 25 percent and 40 percent more people can read; and income in small states can be anything from one half to many times greater than the average income in large states.

The Long List of Potential States

The following list of potential (part-) states and (part-) states that already are *de facto* or *de jure* existent is neither complete nor conclusive. The entries run from west to east within the respective region. I begin with a few preliminary remarks.

In Africa, I have listed Western Sahara as well as Eritrea (*de jure* since 1993) and Somaliland (*de facto* since 1990). The UN peace plan for Western Sahara, adopted at the beginning of 1991, provides for a plebiscite on the future of the former Spanish colony. Since its adoption, Morocco's King Hassan has been blocking the UN referendum on the legalization of independent statehood.[8] Of the remaining areas named in the list, only Darfur (a province of western Sudan) and Shaba/Katanga exist as part-states or recognized territories, but not Luba and Bakongo,[9] Natal/Kwa Zulu (a province of South Africa), Oromia (region 12 in Ethiopia), Zanzibar, the Yoruba (administrative units in south-west Nigeria but not in Benin), the Hausa-Fulani (northern states of Nigeria), and the Tuareg lands (only an autonomous area in northern Mali).

In Asia, many of the potential states named in the list already enjoy a form of statehood: Palestine (self-government in Gaza from 1994 and on the West Bank from 1995–6); Kurdistan (self-government only in northern Iraq, forced from outside since 1991, not in Turkey nor Iran); Pan-Turkestan (states or partially autonomous areas extending from Azerbaijan to Xinjiang-Eastern Turkestan in north-west China); Tuva, the Bashkir Republic, Udmurtiya, etc. (autonomous republics in Russia); Pashtunistan, Baluchistan, and Sind (administrative areas of Pakistan); the Punjab, Kashmir, Nagaland, and Mizoram (constituent states of the Indian Union) and Bodoland; Karen, Kachin, and Kayah States (administrative units of Burma); Tibet (autonomous republic of China).

In the Asia-Pacific region, potential new states are: the Cordillera peoples and the Moro in Mindanao (Philippine regions with limited autonomy); Bougainville (with *de facto* independence from Papua-New Guinea); and Hawaii (a US state).

In Europe, there has been secession by the former seven Yugoslavian and 15 Soviet constituent states. Further instances of secession or irredentism will probably follow: Catalonia and Euskadi (autonomous regions of Spain), the four autonomous Russian republics in the Caucasus—Kabardino-Balkar, Karachi-Cherkess, Tatarstan (Russian Federal Republic), and Abkhazia (*de facto* independence since 1993, having broken away from Georgia). All last-named are located in the European part of the south-western part of the Russian Federation. (See Table 6.2: Secession and Autonomy, on the next two pages).

Table 6.2: Secession and Autonomy: A Global Conflict Potential

Africa*	Asia	Asia–Pacific	Europe	America
• Western Sahara	• Palestine	• Aceh (Sumatra)	• Tamazgha (Berber on the Kanarian Islands)	• Inuit country (Alaska, Nunavut-Canada, Kalaallit Nunaat or Greenland, N.E. Siberia)
• Tamazgha (Berber peoples in Morocco, Algeria, Tunisia, N. Libya, NW Egypt)	• Assyria (N Iraq, N Iran, SE Turkey and S Syria	• Aboriginals (Queensland / Australia)	• Reunification of Ireland and N-Ireland / Ulster	
• Bambara (Mali)	• Kurdistan (SE Turkey, N Iraq, W Iran, NE Syria)	• Cocos and Christmas Islands (Australia)	• Scotland (now Brit.)	• Dene Nation (W. USA and Canada)
• Ewe (Ghana, S. Togo)	• Pan-Turkestan (from Turkey to Xinjiang, China)	• Cordillera Peoples and Moro / Mindanao (Philippines)	• Catalonia, Basque country, Canary Islands	• Rapa Nui (Chile)
• Kabylei (Algeria)		• Moluccas (Indonesia)	• Flanders and Valonie (Belgium)	• Lakota Nation (USA)
• Imâzighen (Tuareg country: Burkina Faso, Mali, Niger, S. Algeria)	• United Pan-Tajikistan (CIS Tajikistan with parts of Afghanistan)	• Belau archipelagos (US protectorate)	• Corsica (now FR)	• Maya state (up to now in 5 states of Mexico and Central America)
• Fulani (N. Nigeria, Niger, much of West Africa)	• Pashtunistan, Baluchistan, Sind (in Pakistan / Afghanistan)	• Guam, Marianans, Carolinians (USA)	• Secession of former federated constituent states of Yugoslavia (began 1991–2)	• Quebec (Canada)
• Fon (N. Benin)		• West Papua (or a United Papua)	• Pan-Albania	• Andean Republic (Quichua and Aymara)
• Yoruba (SW Nigeria, Benin)	• Punjab, Kashmir, (today states of the Indian Union)	• Bougainville (part of Papua New Guinea; possible fusion with Solomon Islands)	• Magyar (Hungary and parts of Romania, Serbia, Slovakia, Ukraine)	• Proto-nations in present-day states of Columbia, Ecuador, Peru, Bolivia, N. Chile)
• St Helena (U.K)	• Tamil Eelam (Sri Lanka)	• Kanaky (Nouvelle Calédonie, France)	• Sanjak (FRY, between Serbia and Montenegro)	• Mapuche state (S Chile, SW Argentina)
• Bakongo (Congo-DR, Congo, and N. Angola)	• Bashkortostan (South Ural mountains, RF)			

* More than a third of all peoples with aspirations to secession/autonomy live in Africa; the list contains only a small proportion.

Source: Scherrer / ECOR © 1995

Table 6.2: Secession and Autonomy: A Global Conflict Potential (continued; part 2)

Africa*	Asia	Asia–Pacific	Europe	America
• Luba (S. DRC) • Shaba/Katanga • Uvimbundu (central and S. Angola) • Darfur (W. Sudan) • S. Sudan (Dinka, Nuer, Shilluk, Anuak, Azande, Nuba, Bari, Ingessana) • Ndebele (Zimbabwe) • Kwa Zulu (South Africa) • Eritrea (de jure since Apr. 1993) • Oromia (S. Ethiopia) • Lake peoples (in Ethiopian Rift Valley) • Zanzibar (union with Tanganyika) • Somaliland (since 1990) • Reunion (FR) • Chagos Island chain • Diego Garcia (UK, leased by USA as base)	• Sakha Jakutia, and others (Republics of the Russian Federation) • Tibet (currently an autonomous republic in China) • Jumma (Chittagong Hill Tracts, Bangladesh) • Nagaland (NE India) • Chinland (W. Burma) • Kawthoolei (Karen State in E. Burma and N. Thailand) • Kachin State (N. Burma and SW China) • Hmong state (in diverse states of Indochina) • Korry (North and South Korea, possibly incl. a small part of E. China) • Ainu-Kurils (Japan / Hokkaido and Russian Kurils)	• Norfolk Islands (Australia) • Wallis and Futuna Islands (now Fr.) • American Samoa (now US protectorate) • Tokelau, Cook and Niue Islands (now NZ) • Kalahui Hawaii (now US state) • Guano Islands (treaty with USA) • Maohi (French Polynesia) • Pitcairn (now Brit.) • Easter Islands (now Chilean)	• Soviet constituent states (took place in 1991) • Abkhazia (de facto independent from Georgia since 1993) • Crimean Tatars (crimea, Ukraine) • Tatarstan and Udmurtia (Russian Federation) • Republics in North Caucasus: Kabardino-Balkaria, Karachai-Cherkessia, Chechnya and Ossetia (all RF) • Carpatho-Rusyns (Ruthenia, W Ukraine) • Scania (Skåneland, S Sweden)	• Puerto Rico (annexed by USA) • Bermuda, Virgin Islands, Anguilla, Chaicos and Cayman Islands (now British) • Aruba, Bonaire, Curaçao (NL) • Federation of indigenous peoples of Amazonia (now parts of Bolivia, Brazil Ecuador, Columbia, Peru, Surinam) • Guadeloupe and Martinique (so-called overseas departments of France) • French Guyana

Source: Scherrer / ECOR © 1995

In the Americas, Quebec (province of Canada) and Nunavut are partly autonomous settlement-areas in Northern Canada and Kalaallit Nunat / Greenland (home rule; part of Denmark); the Lakota and Dene nations only have reservations in the USA and Canada. In the majority of cases—as named in Table 6.2—there have so far been no territorial concessions. The great proto-nations of the Ketchua (Quichua) and Aymara can only claim some limited rights in Bolivia, where they constitute the solid majority, but not in Peru, where indigenous peoples make up half of the population. This questions the very nature of the democratic constitution in these countries.

Differing Chances of Statehood in Three Different Worlds

Different attitudes prevail in the three worlds as to the chances of various forms and degrees of self-determination being realized. Many of the areas mentioned in the list of potential new states have already secured *de facto* autonomy, at least in parts of the territory to which they lay claim; they have done this either via the constitutional route or by means of wars of liberation. The former applies to the areas of Russia listed, the latter to the Caucasian mini-republics now at war, and to most of the Third World territories listed.

- In the Third World, there is already *de facto* autonomy in some of the territories listed; and in certain cases, that autonomy has existed for decades—as in independent Karen State (Kawthoolei) in south-east Burma and in large parts of upland Burma. In other cases, the hard-fought-for *de facto* autonomy has a more or less precarious existence in areas liberated but not permanently controlled by the rebels —e.g. in parts of Oromia, in southern Sudan, lowland Columbia, Tamil Eelam, West Papua, Kurdistan, the Uvimbundu region/southern Angola, and on Bougainville (which may want to join the Solomon Islands).
- In the case of the former Second World, one can say, with certain reservations, that, as in the Third World, the crisis manifests itself primarily as an economic crisis and crisis of legitimacy. But the decay started in 1990 from a degree of economic development that was not comparable to the one in the majority of Third World countries, and from a relatively intact infrastructure and administration.
- In the Western industrial countries of the First World, the extensive economic integration and prosperity and the pacification of ethno-national conflict by means of (sometimes far-reaching) offers of autonomy, are the main reasons for the limited attraction of the option of separate statehood. (The type of autonomy concerned is illustrated by the cases of Euskadi, Catalonia, Corsica, Scotland, Greenland, etc.)

The question of the extent to which the creation of new states in the other two worlds might improve matters or fulfil aspirations of freedom and prosperity seems worthy of further reflection and comment. For the majority of Third World states, the fundamental problem of existence has its roots in colonial times: liberation or the forcible achievement of formal independence by liberation movements in the colonies placed the latter before the problem of how a nation might constitute itself as a state within an ethnic and territorial framework imposed by colonial powers. State traditions had first to be created or invented in many Third World countries.[10] The adoption of the pre-existing state apparatus and of an economy vertically integrated into the world market meant that there were pre-existing constraints which perpetuated dependency and restricted the scope for action. Ethnic, social, and religious differences—which some colonial regimes had suppressed and others had fuelled in a policy of divide and rule—erupted openly in many decolonized new states, and threatened their cohesion.

After throwing off the colonial yoke, many African and Latin American states did what states in conflict situations naturally do: they claimed a monopoly on force and stepped up repression. Many Third World countries ended up with military regimes, mostly as a way of preserving national unity. In Burma, for example, war operations began even before the state had become independent—and the Burmese civil war has continued from 1948 to the present! Only in a very few cases does it seem possible to achieve any reordering of states or reform of statehood *per se* by peaceful means. Threats to national unity and territorial integrity lead to war.

The lack of legitimacy of the new regimes was closely bound up with their failed attempts at modernization. Both the export-oriented development model and the model of development based on the idea of 'catch-up' industrialization (geared to the former USSR or China—an option for liberation movements that had assumed the governmental mantle) failed in most Third World countries, for varying reasons. One lowest common denominator of the state classes, however, is their control of small-scale farmers (peasants) as the major producers in most Third World countries.

But the largest and potentially most powerful social class in Third World countries—the peasantry—is disparate, split, and poorly organized. Peasants do, it is true, often refuse to sustain the state, either by limiting their production or by (temporarily) withdrawing into the subsistence domain; but their opposition, if it receives any political articulation at all, is mostly spontaneous and linked to prevailing economic trends. Their resistance or passivity is logical, given that the state is increasingly disrupting their survival by repeated interventions in their reproduction mechanisms. In addition, the state discriminates against them if they belong to a non-dominant ethnic group; or it declares them backward, trapped in traditionalism and tribal thinking. Ethnic movements can open up a lot of opportunities for recruitment amongst the class of small-scale and subsistence farmers by declaring self-will to be legitimate resistance, and tribalism to be genuine nationalism, and by promising, or pretending, to protect the interests of the peasant classes. Ethno-national liberation or rebel movements are, for the most part, peasant armies. In the name of their oppressed peoples, they link the UN-stipulated right to self-determination for which they resort to arms with the quest to recover their autonomy.

War Without Rules and the Activity of Humanitarian Organizations

Ethno-national and other internal conflicts make up the great majority of present wars and are responsible for most of the millions of refugees and displaced persons in the world. Between 1991 and 1995, the total number of people falling within the UNHCR's ambit rose from 17 million to a record 27 million. This number subsequently decreased—to 22 million on 1 January 1997, was oscillating around 22 million until 2001 and reached some 21 million on 1 January 2002—but one out of every 300 people is still a refugee.[11] Not included in these numbers are Internally Displaced People (IDP), who have not crossed an international boundary; there number is higher than the number of recognized refugees. Not included in the numbers of UNHCR's refugees are 3.8 million Palestinians (as of 2001 the highest number by origin, followed by 3.6 million Afghans); another agency is mandated to care for them.[12] Major conflicts often assume exterminatory proportions (state-organized genocide and mass murder) and develop into complex emergencies, as was the case in Central and North-eastern Africa in the 1990s;[13] since 2000 Asia became again the continent with the highest refugee movement. The ten countries producing most refugees are all violence-prone societies with current or past violent conflicts.[14] In most intra-state conflicts violations of human rights and international law form part of the agenda and force people to seek refuge.

Under the impact of the horrors of the Second World War, International Humanitarian Law was extended.[15] It is important to note that this law historically forms part of the law on warfare, which in principle grants states the right to wage war (*ius ad bellum*) provided this takes the form of legitimate defence against attack or of an anti-colonial war of liberation.[16]

From the second half of the 19th century, various 'minimum rules' for regulating situations of war were introduced by (initially) European states within the framework of diplomatic conference-processes. The various stages included: the declarations of Saint Petersburg in 1868 and Brussels in 1874; the law on warfare agreed at The Hague in 1899 and 1907;[17] the Geneva Conventions of 1864, 1906, and 1929; and the four Geneva Conventions of 1949.[18]

The general trend away from classic inter-state wars to intra-state conflicts such as civil wars (anti-regime and ethno-national), rebel movements, and guerrilla wars began after the Second World War and has gathered momentum since the 1960s. The International Committee of the Red Cross (ICRC) is playing an important role in the regulation of such conflicts; it talks of 'internal disturbances' and 'severe internal disturbances'.[19] However, it was not until 1977 that this highly significant trend was reflected in International Humanitarian Law. IHL should be a globalizing strategy pursued in the name of humanity, which forces states to limit their sovereign rights appropriately.

The Red Cross Movement and the ICRC as Third Parties

After thirty years, under pressure from the states of the Second and Third Worlds, the 1949 Geneva Conventions were adjusted to confirm to the changed realities. In June 1977, a diplomatic conference of 155 invited states that had remained in session over several years (1974–7) adopted two additional protocols drafted by the ICRC:

- Protocol I on the protection of victims extended the term 'international armed conflict' to include national wars of liberation.[20]
- In the case of internal conflicts, the lesser protective provisions of Protocol II apply. Pt. 2, art. 1.1 of this protocol lays down strict requirements for rebel forces, so that those fighting for them can share in minimum humanitarian standards and themselves observe these (treatment of wounded, prisoner-of-war status, etc.).

In this way, armed rebel organizations were indirectly acknowledged—for the first time and without choice—as negotiating partners. This is the main reason why many states continue to resist signing Protocol II. 'Internal unrest' not classified as 'armed conflict' remains outside the ambit of IHL.[21] Protocol I also improved protection of the civilian population and banned certain forms of warfare that are used particularly frequently in ethno-national conflicts—for example, 'indiscriminate attacks', blanket bombing, and other acts of state terror, and also 'scorched-earth' policies.

The International Movement of the Red Cross for a time took over direction of the regulation of violent conflicts from the UN, which had become paralysed by the Cold War. The Red Cross Movement comprises

150 Red Cross or Red Crescent Societies and their umbrella organization, the League of Red Cross Societies, as well as the purely Swiss International Committee of the Red Cross.[22] The ICRC is more than an executive committee or board of trustees. As 'guardian' of the Geneva Conventions and 'overseer' of principles throughout the Red Cross Movement, it has managed, in a situation of global political paralysis, to enhance its role in the struggle to secure respect for humanity.

The ICRC has sole and exclusive responsibility for humanitarian interventions by the Red Cross in armed conflicts. This includes: aid to victims of war (the injured and sick); civilians (refugees, displaced persons, the tracing of missing persons via a central bureau in Geneva), visits to, and care of, prisoners of war and political prisoners by delegates in prisons (including camps, places of torture, etc.). The Committee now boasts a sizeable machinery for executing its many diverse tasks, a good infrastructure, and (because of its reputation) an efficient and lucrative fund-raising system. Until recently it employed only Swiss nationals, and it is managed mostly by elderly retired members of the Swiss power-élite, this character being preserved by a system of co-option. Many of the ICRC's tasks have a strongly political character and are subject to strict confidentiality. Although discretion is not one of the basic principles named, in practice it is treated as one, and it frequently goes too far.

The seven basic principles of the Red Cross as laid down in 1965 are: respect for humanity (aid, understanding, co-operation); impartiality, without distinction of nationality, race, religion, social situation or political affiliation; neutrality; independence; good will; unity (only one Red Cross organization per state); and universality.[23] These basic principles are taken as a guide for all ICRC activities.

The ICRC's discretion is in fact highly problematic in many cases, especially as regards questions of so-called *mauvais traitement*—mostly a euphemistic term for torture—and other serious violations of human rights committed by state forces of repression. By pointing to the presence of the ICRC, a state can claim that such violations are not going on or are being looked into. Conversely, the ICRC argues that the mere presence of its delegates often stops the parties to the conflict, especially the state forces of repression, from engaging in serious human-rights violations.

The work of the ICRC differs from that of international NGOs not only in content but also in form. In order to enable the work of its delegates to go ahead, the ICRC concludes detailed agreements on working conditions with the relevant government. These agreements are the subject of tough negotiations between ICRC emissaries (with diplomatic status) and high-ranking government representatives—mainly departmental heads from the interior ministry. In the numerous cases of internal armed conflict, the

ICRC maintains contact with all the parties to the conflict and often acts as a mediating third party, without this being made known.[24]

Despite this, the ICRC remains constrained in its political work, given that, up to now, only a third of all states have ratified both protocols. Most of the big powers, and many states in crisis regions, are unwilling to accede to Protocol II; and even Protocol I has been rejected by certain major states. This attitude of rejection is logical in terms of *raison d'état*, given that, in both protocols, states' sole right to representation is relativized in line with the actual circumstances in conflict situations. In brief: Protocol II gives international and regional organizations (e.g. the OAU, the OAS, the Arab League) the right to declare nations and nationalities legitimate and thus to make them subjects of international law.[25]

The High Commission for Refugees

The UN High Commission for Refugees (UNHCR) is also subject to tight restrictions, for 'diplomatic' reasons or for reasons of state: only about half the actual refugees and displaced persons from Third World countries are currently recognized as such and supported by the UNHCR. Since 1951 the Commission is under the jurisdiction of the Economic and Social Council. Its history as an organization goes back to the 1920s.

As well as the UNHCR, there are a number of Red Cross organizations and state-run aid-organizations, as well as a large number of private aid-bodies (humanitarian NGOs) looking after the welfare of the 50 million and more people (some estimates put the figure at 70 million) who are currently seeking refuge, internally or cross-boundary.[26] So-called regional conflicts of the Cold War, such as those that were under way in Indochina until 1974 and in Central America and Central Asia until 1989, led, and still lead, to large-scale refugee movements out of war-ravaged states (as in Afghanistan today). But cross-border flows of refugees can generally be monitored more effectively than refugee movements and displacements within states.

Only half of the 50 million and more people in the process of fleeing are recognized as refugees, having crossed a national frontier. The other half are classified as 'internally displaced persons'—in other words, people who usually flee to other parts of a country when there are ethno-national or other internal conflicts, are not categorized as what they are: refugees. Refugee dramas in so-called complex emergencies as the ones in Central Africa (Rwanda, Burundi), southern Africa, north-east Africa, the Middle East (Kurds), the Gulf region, and Central Asia/Afghanistan have assumed unexpected proportions.

All the different scenarios predict an increase in the flows of refugees. Nuscheler cited five reasons for this:[27]

- oppression of national/ethnic groups and insistence on the right to self-determination ('explosive elements in the state system')
- growing conflicts over resources
- conflicts over distribution could end in a 'clash of civilizations'
- population growth and impoverishment increases migratory pressure
- the climatic and environmental catastrophe will, according to Nuscheler, produce millions of environmental refugees; in the desertification belt in the (sub)tropics, 850 million people are, he says, under threat.

It is not just the future scenarios that are worrying; the legal, political, and economic conditions do not lead one to expect that the international community would be able to cope with a large increase in the flows of refugees. Even in countries that take in only a fraction of the global flows of refugees and which, economically, would be well able to care for large numbers of refugees, the political will to become involved in preventive measures is minimal. In many European states, racism and ethno-chauvinism are on the increase. Disturbing findings of the *Eurobarometers* 1997 and 2000, which conducted representative polls in Europe Union member states, ring alarm bells (see EUMC 2001 Measures are directed not against the causes of refugee and migrant movements, but against refugees and migrants themselves.

The basis of international law on refugees is the Geneva Convention on Refugees of 1951, to which a protocol was added in 1953. Only one hundred or so states have signed the convention, and the law codified in the convention is far from being universal. Thailand, for example, which is the target country for flows of refugees from South-East Asia (Burma, Cambodia, Laos, Vietnam), has not ratified the convention and does not worry much about the principle of *non-refoulement* (no forced return)[28] when it comes to dealing with endangered Burmese students; hundreds of Burmese have been sent back to certain death since the crack-down on the democracy movements in 1988 and the killings of more than 2,000 students, monks, and workers by the army in the streets of Rangoon and several other cities in Burma (renamed Myanmar by its military rulers).

Independent Human-Rights Organizations

There are a number of human-rights organizations that play a part in elucidating internal conflicts in so far as they deal with human-rights violations, either in a general way or as parties specifically mandated for this purpose. Their methods differ: the ICRC, for example, is concerned to maintain discretion, neutrality, and impartiality,[29] whereas Amnesty

International seeks publicity and takes sides with the victims—though with self-imposed restrictions in relation to perpetrators of violence, i.e. in the case of armed conflicts. An important function in elucidating internal conflicts is played by the UN Human Rights Commission. In particular, its second sub-committee—on the protection of minorities—and its working-group on indigenous populations serve as forums for non-state actors and afford the United Nations a glimpse into the murky waters of 'forgotten wars' (so-called internal, mainly ethnic, conflicts).

Certain large international non-governmental organizations of high repute, such as the Anti-Slavery Society (ASS), the World Council of Churches (WCC), Amnesty International, Human Rights Watch, and the Russell Tribunal, create publicity in regard to internal conflicts. Regional human-rights organizations and/or political bodies can act as important forums for endangered peoples: on every continent there are regional human-rights organizations trying to monitor and restrict state power in the domain of human rights.

UNPO: The United Nations for Indigenous and Endangered Peoples

There are a many small- and medium-sized peoples who, on the whole, are not recognized as nations by states, in some cases not even by the Unrepresented Nations and Peoples Organization. Founded in 1991, UNPO has over fifty members, representing more than hundred million people.[30] Because of its structure, it is one of the (umbrella) organizations of indigenous and non-dominant peoples that have a good chance of developing.[31] Although its membership is not as great as that of the United Nations (193), it has the potential to grow much larger than the latter.

UNPO members belong to those indigenous or endangered peoples of the earth who have so far lacked a representative forum that could publicize their case and help enhance their standing in the international community. At present, UNPO's geographic distribution is not yet representative and is rather uneven in regional terms. Africa and the Americas are under-represented,[32] and this also true of Asia, in terms of demographic importance; Europe[33] and the Asia-Pacific area, on the other hand, are well represented.[34] Unfortunately the membership of UNPO was stagnating for many years due to financial mismanagement and weak leadership.[35]

Some UNPO members represent nationalities (or organizations) that are engaged in armed resistance or already involved in a violent process of secession and state-formation. According the UNPO statutes, this ought not to be possible, because the UNPO covenant requires its members to foster non-violence. However, a strict requirement to forgo violence would be unenforceable and hypocritical. Many non-dominant nations and peoples have been occupied and colonized by new states; some of them have been oppressed for decades by states to which they do not wish to belong. Opposing ethno-political discrimination and fighting for self-determination generally lead to increased repression by state organs.[36]

The choice of UNPO members sometimes seems to depend to some extent on the political climate, and thus to be questionable.[37] Four former members of UNPO have since become members of the UN. As new members of this state-based federation, they are refusing to grant what they themselves were formerly refused. They now themselves discriminate against minorities, or try to quell the yearning of their minority nationalities (*sic!*) for autonomy—even by means of armed violence: Armenia took over between 25 percent and 30 percent of Azerbaijan and expelled the Azeri minority; Estonia and Latvia discriminate against Russians, Poles, Belarussians, and other minorities; and in 1991 Georgia revoked the autonomous status of four nationalities. The Georgian army fought against the South Ossetians and—with little success—against secession by Abkhazia, which, for its part, became a member of UNPO.

Other members (such as Zanzibar, for example) cannot in any way be regarded as 'unrepresented', or even under-represented.[38] Yet others are represented by organizations that can hardly be regarded as representative or as accepted by the majority of the population. UNPO sent a mission to Zanzibar in 1995, during the period when the opposition party narrowly lost the first multi-party elections, which were held in both parts of the union, on Zanzibar and in mainland Tanganyika, in October 1995.[39] The presidential candidate for the opposition party Seif Sharif Hamad happened to be the then UNPO president. UNPO's engagement for the fairness of elections could not have be seen as truly impartial. Furthermore, contesting the status of Zanzibar in the United Republic of Tanzania does not make sense, since Zanzibar is profiting from it in many ways. A secession of Zanzibar could again lead to massive trouble and pitch Zanzibari against other Zanzibari, as seen in 1964.

Generally speaking, the selection and acceptance of Zanzibar as UNPO member points to defects, which could be eliminated by having stricter admission-procedures. Some of the other UNPO members cannot have been said to adhere to the important principles of the UNPO charter, namely the promotion of non-violence (thus the rejection of terrorism) as well as the principle of democracy and rejection of ignorance.[40] For some members democracy and tolerance seems to be rather alien concepts; for others the Cold War is still not yet over.

The conditions for future UNPO membership should be formulated in more restrictive terms. A real recognition regime should be introduced. Discrimination against new minorities should entail suspension of membership, and violent treatment or persecution of minorities should result in exclusion from the organization. In the case of inter-ethnic conflicts ('in-fighting'), potential and actual members should submit their disputes with other nations/nationalities to a permanent court of arbitration made up of other UNPO members. The court of arbitration would be in a strong position, because members who showed no willingness to accept arbitration would be put in the position of worrying about preserving their prestige-enhancing affiliation to UNPO, the 'alternative UN'.

UNPO should safeguard its status as a representative of oppressed and internationally unrepresented peoples. In so doing, this 'alternative UN' would make a contribution towards civilising international relations and creating a constructive culture of peace—independent of intervention by states, which otherwise are the dominant actors on the international stage.

Indigenous Organizations and NGOs for Endangered Peoples

There are a large number of independent political organizations that make an important contribution to elucidating and publicizing ethnic and other intra-state conflicts:

- First and foremost, there are the indigenous organizations. These began to emerge in the 1970s as umbrella organizations at trans-regional and global level—in top-down fashion, as it were, notably in former North American settler-colonies. They include such bodies as: the International Indian Treaty Council (IITC, 1974), the World Council of Indigenous Peoples (WCIP, 1975), and the Indian Law Resource Center (ILRC, 1978), all based in the USA; and the more recent Asian Indigenous Peoples Pact (AIPP), which has its headquarters in Bangkok.[41] Some trans-regional and regional organizations have consultative status at the United Nations and take part in numerous international congresses, conferences, and forums on indigenous matters.
- Regional indigenous organizations emerged in (former) settler-colonies as early as the 1970s. They included the Inuit Circumpolar Conference (ICC, 1977); the Coordinación Regional de Pueblos Indígenas (CORPI, 1977); the Congreso Indígena del Sur de América (CISA, 1980); the National Aboriginal Conference (NAC, 1981) and National Organization of Aboriginal and Islander Legal Services (NAILS, 1992). In addition to these, there are hundreds of local organizations, which as a rule represent a particular indigenous people or ethnic sub-group.
- Non-governmental organizations working for the protection of endangered peoples also emerged at the beginning of the 1970s, in parallel with the indigenous organizations (and in some cases prior to them).

They appeared in the large urban centres, and were an expression of the growing awareness of the problems of ethnic minorities and indigenous peoples. Almost all of them are based in Europe or the USA; there are just one or two in Asia. Their activities include: creating an infrastructure for indigenous affairs, conducting human-rights campaigns, and producing large numbers of publications. They endeavour to establish links with one another (as is clear from the title of their joint organization, the Indigenous Peoples Network: IPN), in order to increase their chances of exerting influence and in order to cut out duplication.

Among the major organizations working for the cause of indigenous, threatened and endangered peoples in Western countries are: the International Work Group for Indigenous Affairs (IWGIA) in Copenhagen; the Gesellschaft für bedrohte Völker (founded 1970) in Göttingen; the Nederlands Center for Inheemse Volken (NCIV—formerly the Working-Group for Indigenous Peoples (WIP), founded 1972) in Amsterdam; Cultural Survival in Cambridge (Mass.); Survival International in London. In Brussels, support-groups from five countries came together to form a European Alliance, in order to co-ordinate lobby work in the various forums of the European Union. Unfortunately this important project collapsed 1998.

Many support-groups for individual indigenous peoples or particular indigenous movements engage in information-work; in many cases, they provide assistance on the ground. Some organizations also act as arbitrators, third parties, or go-betweens in negotiations between governments and representatives of indigenous and endangered peoples, or in the settlement of disputes between peoples, nationalities, and nations.

Procedures for Enforcing Minimum Human-Rights Standards

The United Nations Universal Declaration of Human Rights of 10 December 1948 has been ratified by every state in the world. It is complemented by the International Covenant on Civil and Political Rights (ICCPR) and the International Covenant on Economic, Social and Cultural Rights (ICESCR). Other important documents are the Convention on the Prevention and Punishment of the Crime of Genocide, the International Convention on the Elimination of All Forms of Racial Discrimination, and various other trans-regional and regional conventions designed to protect human and minority rights. The two covenants named above have been ratified by over hundred thirty states; the two optional protocols to the Covenant on Political Rights, meanwhile, have only been ratified by a very small number of states.[42] In terms of ratification the negative record is held by the convention, which aims at ameliorating the plight of migrant workers. Only a handful of states had ratified the International Convention on the Protection of the Rights of All Migrant Workers and Members of Their Families. On the other hand, the perforation of the Non-Proliferation Treaty (NPT) illustrated that even a virtually universal treaty has limited impact on the arms race and belligerent under-cover developments;[43] this was most shockingly disclosed by the mutual nuclear testing in South Asia 1998 as well as by the alarming nuclear policy and arms race.[44]

The critical factor in international law in general and in regard to human and minority rights in particular is the lack or fragmentary nature of mechanisms and procedures for enforcing legal instruments such as declarations, conventions, covenants, and treaties. The status of some of the instruments that will be mentioned here is essentially that of a declaration of human-rights principles. In international law, a declaration of principles has mainly political-cum-moral force and implies legal obligations.

The total or almost-total absence of sanctions is a phenomenon common to all contractual arrangements in international law. There is no world government that ensures international law is observed. The United Nations is not a world government that could engage in global governance in this sense.[45] Over the last few years, there have been a series of proposals for making states assume greater responsibility in matters relating to human and minority rights. Few of these proposals have been realized, and any kind of optimism would be premature. None the less, there have been one or two positive beginnings within the framework of the Council of Europe, the OSCE, and other regional organizations, and also within the European Union and the United Nations system.[46]

The European Convention on Human Rights and the Council of Europe

The Council of Europe has taken important steps in the direction of establishing workable procedures for enforcing human rights conventions, based on the right of recourse. In November 1950, it drafted a European Convention for the Protection of Human Rights and Fundamental Freedoms (ECHR). This has since been complemented by various protocols and ratified by the member states of the Council of Europe. The ECHR guarantees, amongst other things, personal freedoms, protection against torture, the right to a fair hearing, and freedom of expression.

The unique feature of the convention is that every citizen has the right to take legal action against a state.[47] The Strasbourg-based European Court of Human Rights passes judgements that have practical consequences in the member states. The convention could point the way as regards dealing with discrimination on the grounds of ethnic or religious affiliation (e.g. in the Basque country, Northern Ireland, and, especially, in Turkey). Not only states, but also multilateral entities (such as the EU) can accede to it. The accession of the European Union, although belated, is to be welcomed.

Turkey, for example, was forced to recognize individual right of recourse and thus faces an avalanche of court-cases. Complaints against it for serious and systematic violations of human rights in its south-eastern area, for the persecution of nationalities which the state ostracizes as minorities (notably Kurds, Armenians, and Greeks), and for the lack of minimum standards in regard to the rule of law and humanitarian considerations are turning into a litmus-test of the ECHR. Because of the geopolitical changes and the accession of new members, this positive process of verification in regard to the situation of human rights in the member states could lose some of its momentum. Throughout the 1990s, and most prominently in 1992, Turkey was publicly arraigned as a land of torture. After the second *ad hoc* visit of the European Committee for the Prevention of Torture and Inhuman or Degrading Treatment or Punishment (CPT), the latter issued a very clear public statement on the systematic use of torture in Turkey.[48] The committee has made dozens of periodic and *ad hoc* visits.[49] It has drawn up a package of protective provisions to be observed by all states.[50] The very admission of Turkey to the EU had triggered a debate for the first time about how the European character of the council was to be defined.

The Council of Europe has become the main political focus for cooperation with the countries of Central and Eastern Europe, as and when these have opted for a democratic form of government. By 1996, the council reached a total of forty members (following the admission of Croatia). The admission of states from these regions has pointed up the urgent need for clear standards on the rights of minorities. With the exception of Slovenia, all the new members have had great difficulties and shown scant good will in dealing with their new or old minorities. In the Czech Republic and Romania they are old minorities, like the Roma; in the Baltic states they are new ones, like the Russians, Poles, and Belarussians, and their basic rights were massively violated from 1991 onwards. The multiplication of new states in Eastern Europe presented new challenges as regards the existing role of the Council of Europe, its Western-centred character, its 'themes', and its methods of working. The changed role of the OSCE will force the Council of Europe to redefine its own role, and vice-versa.

Turkey is not the only multinational entity here; so are other existing and potential member states. The views as to the rights of ethnic and national minorities are correspondingly varied. The dividing-lines run along much the same path as in the C/OSCE. The countries that tend to put a brake on the expansion of minority rights are traditionally those that have a high proportion of minorities, notably France, Greece, Spain, and Turkey.

In 1992, the Committee of Ministers of the Council of Europe directed its human-rights committee to determine standards in regard to minority rights ('standard-setting'). Non-governmental organizations may attend the committee's half-yearly sessions as observers. The council has laid down a series of common principles governing the protection of national minorities, actively supported the transition to democracy, and strengthened the machinery it uses to monitor how far its members fulfil their commitments. The Strasbourg summit of October 1997 fixed new priorities for co-operative efforts that will benefit some 800 million Europeans.

In October 1994, the Committee of Ministers of the European Council gave the green light for the first legally binding multilateral instrument on minority protection to be adopted in Europe, namely the so-called Framework Convention for the Protection of National Minorities, which contains thirty-two articles.[51] The convention is intended as a legal back-up to the fight against minority discrimination. It will guarantee the following rights:

- the right to self-identification
- full and effective equality (art. 4, ban on discrimination)
- preservation of culture (arts. 5–6, ban on (enforced) assimilation)
- freedom to organize (arts. 7–8)
- access to the media, and the right to set up independent ones (art. 9)
- the use of minority languages in public life, the education system (arts. 10–14), and ('as far as possible') administrative dealings (art. 10. 2)
- the right to full participation and consultation (art. 15)
- a ban on all transfers of population (art. 16) and provisions requiring the member states to ease contact between relatives across state borders (art. 17–18)

The remaining provisions (arts. 19–32) relate to the translation of these principles into national law, to their validity, and to the monitoring of their implementation in the forty-one member states, once the convention enters into force. A framework convention was the first legally binding multilateral instrument in its field and contains binding principles that have to be translated into domestic law and governmental decrees by the contracting states. Protocols may be added to the convention in future.[52] However, the Convention does not define the concept of national minority.

The Assembly of the Council of Europe made a series of intervention in order to address certain weaknesses.[53] Rapporteur Henning Gjellerod questioned the will of many member states to do the follow-up of the 1993 Vienna Summit. At the post-Cold War summit of the Council of Europe in Vienna in October 1993, the main themes have been: (1) the prevention of ethnic conflicts through the introduction of extensive minority-rights, and (2) a programme of action against the growing racism in Europe. Regarding the first issue taken up in 1993, two new agreements on minority rights were adopted; in addition, in 1993 the Parliamentary Assembly had already asked the Council to act as a third party and mediator in acute, violent minority conflicts.

Racism and the Up-hill Struggle for Justice

States and trade unions of states are extremely reluctant to take action in these fields. Gjellerod recalled in 1997 that, though the Council of Europe, at the assembly's initiative, has prepared legally binding instruments— notably the Framework Convention for the Protection of National Minorities and the European Charter for Regional or Minority Languages— both instruments have not entered into force for three to five years due the slow pace of ratifications.[54] The Framework Convention was open to signature on 1 February 1995 and came into force three years later, on 1 February 1998; the condition for the entry into force was twelve ratifications (of currently 43 member states). As of end 2001 the great majority of the member states were parties to the Convention: the total number of ratifications (accessions to the treaty) is 34 as of early 2002; eight more have signed.

On 1 March 1998, the European Charter for Regional or Minority Languages also entered into force, more than five years after the Charter had been opened for signature in November 1992. The number of ratifications has reached only a quarter of the membership of the Council of Europe (11 of 43). The *Euromosaic* study of the European Commission revealed that of the existing 48 minority languages some 23 are threatened or have 'limited chances for survival'. Some fifty million members of a national minority in the European Union do not speak one of the official languages of the member states and need special protection measures.[55]

With regard to the second issue dealt with by the Council of Europe in Vienna 1993, the European Year against Racism in 1997 brought some limited advances. The 'Political Declaration adopted by Ministers of Council of Europe Member States on 13 October 2000 at the concluding session of the European Conference against Racism, Strasbourg, France' pledged to 'to reinforce European bodies active in combating racism, discrimination and related intolerance, in particular the European Commission against Racism and Intolerance'.

The European Union had already taken the lead during the year 2000, which brought real progress: A first EU Council Directive incorporated the principle of racial equality and a second Directive established a general framework for equal treatment in employment and occupation.[56] The implementation of both directives has to be monitored in all member states. The same applies for the Programme of Action of the 2001 UN World Conference against Racism, Discrimination and Xenophobia; though this important conference was 'highjacked' by the Israel-Palestine question, some advances were made in the acknowledgement of colonialism and slavery as massive racist offences and crimes against humanity.[57]

The Durban programme of action has been adopted thanks to the commitment and diplomatic skills of the South African government, in the absence of United States and with the delegation of the European Union trying to water it down.[58] The victims of decades of European colonial racism were 'assured of having access to justice, including legal assistance where appropriate, effective and appropriate protection and remedies, including the right to seek just and adequate reparation or satisfaction for any damage suffered as a result of such discrimination, as enshrined in numerous international and regional human rights instruments, in particular the Universal Declaration of Human Rights and the International Convention on the Elimination of All Forms of Racial Discrimination'. Individual plaintiffs may try to take chances; the likelihood of adequate reparation as result of civil court cases is low. The latter of the mentioned instruments is legally binding, the other (as all declarations) is not legally binding but may set standards that governments would try to attain. Protection mechanisms provided for by international law often are not translated into legal provisions within the nation states that implement the rules of international conventions; hence they remain without direct consequences.

Discrimination of Minorities

Where discrimination and intra-state conflicts are being discussed, there is often talk of minorities. Underneath the global structure of currently 193 states there are probably some 10.000 ethnic, national, religious, linguistic and other minorities. Additionally to these 'old minorities' thousands of migrant communities constitute 'new minorities' in a very large number of states. To place the content of ethnic, national or religious conflicts on a par with that of minority conflicts is, in many cases, mistaken.

The terms *minorities* and *discrimination* seem in need of elucidation; the main frameworks for it are the nation state and the international community at large. Unfortunately there are only a view studies that compare various regional and local attempts at dispute resolution within the framework of state policies on minorities and nationalities. The states' interaction with the minorities on their territory range, in ascending order, from racial segregation, through unilateral assimilation and ideas about melting-pots (social and racial amalgamation), to purely formally equal integration, to the replacement of unitary-cum-homogenist ideas with the notion of 'diversity in unity', and, ultimately, to inclusion, respect, protection, and encouragement for otherness on an equal basis, e.g., within the framework of multicultural tolerance and affirmative action, and for ethnic and national minorities in the form of autonomy arrangements, free association or federalism. More far-reaching demands by the latter minorities, which claim the status of nations or nationalities, point to structural differences between minority and nationality policy. Generally, the term 'minorities' is applicable in most countries of Asia-Pacific, the Americas and Europe. In most of Africa the term does not make sense since there is no national or ethnic majority; this reflects the fact that Africa is the culturally and ethnically most heterogeneous continent.

The concept of *minority*, and the reality, in which minorities are created and obliged to live, point up a variety of facets that are often ignored in the debate about minority, religious or ethno-national conflicts. The most important seems to be that the concept of minority is essentially ascriptive in nature: as a rule, it is the state that decides what makes a minority and to which circle of people the term will apply. The state itself is often dominated by, or in the ownership of, a particular ethnic group that defines itself as a majority but often is not one in demographic terms. National censuses and demographic statistics are hot issues and often just one more battlefield for all actors concerned. Statistics are usually presented according to predetermined political conditions. In extreme cases, an ethnic group apostrophized as a minority is only a political minority, measured in terms of power, while demographically it constitutes the majority (as in the case with the Oromo in Ethiopia or the Mayan peoples in Guatemala). The case of large transnational minority peoples (such as Berbers in a dozen northern African counties or Kurds in five West Asian countries) seems similar.

In the international discourse about the minority question the dual concept of *national minorities* has come into increasing use in recent years. This is a consequence of the increased attention that has been paid to the contentious minorities issue in post-Cold War Europe and the Former Soviet Union; but it also means that a compromise formula has been found, ostensibly bridging or unifying the varying usages in eastern and western Europe. The concept of minorities requires elucidation for a variety of other reasons as well. Many nationalities that find their rights curtailed by states, or are harassed, discriminated, threatened or persecuted by them, do not regard themselves as minorities; they do not share the socio-psychological characteristics of classic minorities, on the contrary, some even cultivate a robust nationalism.

Forms and Definition of Discrimination

Discrimination means that the dominant ethnic or national majority mostly regards national minorities as subordinate segments of the state's society, whereby denying basic rights and freedoms, impeding their social, cultural and economic development, and obstructing political representation and participation. Minorities have special phenotypic and cultural peculiarities ascribed to them. These kinds of ascribed markers are looked down on by those segments of the state society that are dominant (either in terms of power or numerically). Some traditional societies, among them most indigenous peoples, derive their distinctiveness and reproduce themselves on the basis of their non-integration into market economies; in a few cases they have developed a whole series of autonomous, self-supporting modes of production. But many more minorities are vulnerable and find no way of escaping discrimination.

There is a vast scope of *different forms of discrimination* against minorities. The victims are usually members of a multitude of non-dominant groups. Minorities exist in almost every state, only their composition between indigenous minorities (national or language minorities), religious communities of belief and origin, diverse migrant communities, asylum-seekers and refugee populations, etc., and their proportion of the resident population may change from country to country. Specifically targeted are undocumented migrant workers, Muslim communities in Islam-phobic environments, (semi-) nomadic peoples, and women of minority groups. Gender, ethnicity, belief and illegality are factors that profoundly contribute to appalling situations of *multiple discrimination*.

Discrimination of minorities has structural features that are generated by the way economic, political and social institutions operate. Structural racism categorizes and marks people, makes minority members visible, and denies such people equal access to jobs, education, medical facilities, social welfare, leisure, and habitation. Governments, local and state administrations, the education system, domestic companies and transnational corporations, and (not least) the media are part of the apparatus which form a *dispositif* against different categories of minorities; these are the forces producing *others* and *aliens* and shaping public attitudes towards *others*, such as national minorities, and *aliens*, such as the new minorities of migrants, refugees, asylum seekers, and trafficked people.

The worst form of discrimination is the one based on what is perceived as race or colour. As a rule, racist discrimination in the developed world is not perceived as the splitting-up of a population but as hostility towards an alien group of *others* (as opposed to the own breed of *us*-self); the terms of racialization and scapegoating, coined in a decade-old debate by social scientists, is essentially to understand the nature of new domestic racism that replaced the old colonial racism. With the *increase of new minorities* in the past decades racists found it easier to construct scapegoats and to blame aliens and minorities for socio-economic losses. In the Americas the legacies of racial discrimination against Indians, Blacks and Hispanics are still powerful and destructive; compared with that, the new Asian minorities suffer less discrimination due to above average income and education. In many developing countries the claims of a number of post-colonial states in regard to the nationalities, which they claim (or did not want) as their citizens, and in regard to ethnic minorities and indigenous peoples, seem to become increasingly aggressive in times of changes.

Globalization does not exclude fragmentation, as exhibited by the global trend towards an increase of intra-state conflicts. While the discrimination of ethnic minorities was, in empirical-cum-historical terms, one of the most dangerous sources of conflicts and wars both, in the former Third World (since the period of decolonization) and, since 1989–90, in the former socialist states—with almost two-thirds of current wars being susceptible of 'ethnic' interpretation—violence against minority groups again became a reality in Europe—in its eastern and south-eastern parts, in Yugoslavia and the Caucasus. If we take the examples of Bosnia (Serbs vs. Croats) or Rwanda (Hutu vs. Tutsi) and compare with objective attributes (see chapter 1) we will find very little or no ethnic distinction at all. Often ethnicization and racialization occur on the base of minor differences. Decisive are not the perceived differences but the interest of political elites to use them as resources for their power struggle and as source for mobilizing the mobs. Those conflict types suitable to ethnic and racial interpretation—with ethnicization or racialization as mobilizing forces—seemed to grow fastest in the South, although they have been prominent for quite some time, and appear again in the North, as organized violence against minorities, racial and ethnic discrimination or 'ethnic cleansing'.

In fall 2001 Rwanda's parliament passed a law imposing prison terms and a fine on any person practicing discrimination and segregation. This is one of the lessons drawn from the devastating 1994 genocide. The new law aims at enforcing positive discrimination in favor of vulnerable groups like the Batwa minority (one percent of the populations of both, Rwanda and Burundi). The law gives a comprehensive legal definition of discrimination as 'any act, utterance or writing aimed at depriving a person or group of persons, their rights, by reason of sex, ethnicity, age, race, color, opinion, religion nationality or origin'.

Ways to Combat Discrimination

Combating discrimination, racism and destructive ethnicization and the prevention of violence are political imperatives for the 21st century. The task to explore policy strategies and measures to address these problems starts with rethinking definitions and core concepts. Efforts to accommodate ethno-cultural difference are an essential part of anti-racist strategies; they have conflict preventive force and contribute to the long-term transformation of intra-state conflicts. The main topics are laws against discrimination, cultural and other autonomies, collective rights, self-governance, and nationality policies. The political-cum-humanitarian concern is to ensure that all possible means of avoiding violent forms of multi-ethnic interaction are exploited, strengthened, and made more attractive to the majority populations.

An important approach in improving mutual relations between majorities and minorities is the policy option that discrimination of non-dominant groups should be outlawed and that some measure of temporary and targeted affirmative action should be institutionalized. However, it comes as no small surprise to realize that only a third of the respondents in Eurobarometer polls (regularly made by the EU) agree with outlawing discrimination though 60 percent were classified as more or less tolerant. Nevertheless, in 2000, a EU Council directive incorporated the principle of racial equality and a second directive established a general framework for equal treatment in employment and occupation.

As a rule the victims of discrimination and xenophobia are members from among a multitude of 'minorities-at-risk' (Gurr). When talking about discrimination most West Europeans first think of migrant communities (especially Muslim communities) as victims while people in the Americas, Eastern Europe, Asia and Africa think of indigenous, religious and ethnic minorities, historic nationalities, and other non-dominant groups. But even in the enlarging European Union the population of indigenous non-dominant groups is numerically exceeding that of migrant communities by far. Many minorities are either permanently confronted with everyday discrimination and racism (e.g., the sad example of 15 million Roma all over Europe, 30 million Afro-Americans or 200 million Dalit of India), or they are discriminated upon in different ways by the respective demographic majorities or otherwise dominant groups. Anti-discrimination policies ought to address the rejection of non-dominant groups by large national-chauvinists groups among the majority populations in many states.

The focus should be on activities, which are essential to combat discrimination of manifold minorities. Among others a list of essentials to such policies has to include combating and outlawing militant chauvinism and racism. The conception of new policies for preventing and combating discrimination follows strategies that are targeting its structural, institutionalized and organized forms. The political-humanitarian concern is to find ways of avoiding structural and direct, personal forms of discrimination.

Structural Prevention of Conflicts between Majorities and Minorities

Regarding forms of structural prevention of troubles, the word 'structural' implies that new frameworks and institutions are created to avert discrimination and possible direct violence and reduce structural violence, mainly all forms of discrimination against non-dominant groups. Johan Galtung developed the concept of structural violence in the 1970s, based on his path-breaking distinction between direct personal violence and structural violence; Galtung also reflected on cultural violence, e.g., values that promote/justify violence and superiority complexes that result into aggressive attitudes. Structural prevention aims at ending discrimination, repression, injustice and racism, which are ingrained in many state policies and which are also inherent part of the cultural attitudes held by many dominant groups.

However, there are practical problems politicians face in promoting preventive measures and policies—beyond rhetoric. When it comes to implementing declared policies, the difficulties are threefold: (1) the unspectacular and long-term character of many such measures makes them not really attractive if quick results are required, (2) the difficulty to measure their effectiveness, and (3) a number of rather diverse institutions, measures and policies have preventive character but they often remain unrelated or only partially implemented.

In *preventing discrimination* of minority groups there are no easy solutions. The great diversity of cultural and political characteristics exhibited by different types of minorities demand different regulatory mechanisms. Steps to mitigate and pre-empt destructive forms of interaction between majorities and minorities should be prioritized. The classic solutions for indigenous minorities range from cultural autonomy, special rights and territorial self-governance to forms of *de facto* sovereignty. Protection of ethnic and national minorities by means of a variety of autonomy arrangements did not begin until the 20th century, triggered by a worsening of the so-called minority problem in Europe, as a result of revolutions and the regroupings in the wake of two world wars.

Account should be taken of positive policies of a number of multinational states when it comes to looking for methods of preventing and dealing with latent or open ethno-national conflicts. Many states have been able to pursue active and successful policies of prevention of troubles by making concessions and negotiating offers involving elements of reactive minority protection and proactive nationality policy, in Europe most prominently by granting home rule for the Faeroese and the Inuit in the Kingdom of Denmark from 1948 onwards. Others have—often with limited success—used similar offers to try and resolve armed conflicts that have already escalated (e.g., the regionalization and granting of autonomy to Basques, Catalonians, Andalusians, and Galicians in post-Franco Spain).

Nationality policies are generally conceived of as solutions to discrimination but not to conflicts that are smoldering or have already erupted. Some procedures aim more at containment, or pose the nationality question in a purely socio-political context. But such policies are part of the problem, which they claim to be solving. A detailed comparison ought to be made of the different approaches to nationality policy pursued by selected states such as Denmark, Italy, Spain and the former USSR (maintained in the Russian Federation). This might include comparison with lessons learned from affirmative action in the United States as well as autonomy and constitutional arrangements realized in the past 50 years in China, India and Panama, and, more recently, in Colombia, Australia, Nicaragua and Ethiopia.

One factor of major importance in preventing discrimination of minorities is not only the focus on basic rights of these groups (and the granting of citizenship and autonomy/self-governance) but also the extension of international norms and *standards of protection* for non-dominant minorities. The role of multilateral regimes in preventing discrimination of minorities and resolving latent and violent conflicts should be discussed more systematically in order to draw the 'lessons learned' from it. Critical reviews should focus on the activities undertaken by NGOs in protecting minorities, the efforts of the Council of Europe in regards to national minorities, similar the efforts of the Organization for Security and Cooperation in Europe (OSCE) as well as the efforts of the UN Human Rights Commission to work out minimum standards for the rights of minorities and indigenous peoples.

New paths in this direction have been embarked on with the Framework Convention for the Protection of National Minorities issued by the Council of Europe, which laid great emphasis on the protection of national minorities, and the creation of the institution of a High Commissioner for National Minorities within the OSCE. Legal instruments are not sufficient in themselves in promoting good relations between majorities and minorities. In addition to such standard-setting activities more confidence-building and practical measures at the grass-roots level aimed at increasing tolerance and understanding between citizens belonging to different ethnic communities are required.

The European Anti-racist Movements and their Influence

The first breakthrough in combating racism in Europe was not achieved by the Council of Europe but by the European Union in 2000, based on the 1997 Amsterdam treaty, in which the problem of 'racial discrimination' was for the first time acknowledged and addressed. Prior to the Amsterdam amendments the EC treaty contained a clause prohibiting discrimination on the grounds of nationality as citizenship of one of the member states (Article 12). In Amsterdam a new title VI (incorporating the Schengen *acquis*) was inserted into the EC Treaty, namely related to 'free movement of persons'. Precisely the freedom of movement becomes the sticking point in recasting Europe.[59] The new Article 13 empowered the European institutions to take action in order to combat discrimination based on sex, racial or ethnic origin, religion, etc. Despite some weaknesses in the article this was seen as 'a tremendous step forward' (Chopin and Niessen 2001: 9). Article 14 will have the effect of formally eliminating discrimination between EU citizens and third-country nationals.

Anti-racism appeared formally on the agenda of the European Parliament with the Evrigenis report of 1986; but for the next decade most of its recommendations were ignored although the Parliament continued to press for measures to be taken in Brussels.[60] The 1997 European Year Against Racism passed, several studies were commissioned,[61] and the EU Monitoring Centre on Racism in Vienna was established in 1998[62] but still no major EU decisions against racism were taken; only behind the scenes 'a lot happened'. The agenda-setting strategies of the anti-racist advocacy coalition operating at the EU level came into the decisive phase. Carlo Ruzza examined how decision-making took place in the area of anti-racism regulation in EU institutions, and described how important policy-making emerged 'from a fragmented coalition of NGOs, politicians and civil servants operating in connected but distinct regulative environments'.[63]

Since the mid-1990s a coalition of activists and EU bureaucrats attempted to achieve a strong policy response on the challenges of racism, xenophobia and minority discrimination being felt in most EU member states. Among the most active organisations were the Starting Line group, the European Migrants' Forum, the internationally organized anti-racist movement with SOS *Racisme*,[64] the 1998 formed European Network against Racism (ENAR), the Anti-Poverty Lobby, and also the Youth Forum and the Women's Lobby, representing a broad European movement of several hundred organisations.[65] Combating racism, traditionally an activity of the left, 'has in recent years received attention in the media and mainstream politics as a reaction to substantial advances of the extreme right in several EU countries' (Ruzza 1999: 6).

EC Racial Equality Directive as Acquis Communautaire

The year 2000 was a break-through regarding equal rights and protection of minorities in the European Union. Two directives and a Community Action Programme to Combat Discrimination were the first measures taken under Article 13: the Council Directive of 29 June 2000 implementing the principle of equal treatment between persons irrespective of racial or ethnic origin and the Council Directive of 27 November establishing a general framework for equal treatment in employment and occupation (CM-EC 2000a and b). In this respect the upcoming incorporation of the EC Racial Equality Directive into the national laws of the EU member states and the accession states before July 2003—as an *acquis communautaire*, in other words a mandatory condition for new members—paves the way for meaningful enlargement.

Not only is a further imposition of restrictive and exclusionary immigration policies by host countries being prevented but also EU minimum standards are set. Unfortunately, there are a number of weaknesses;[66] e.g., only discrimination based on racial or ethnic origin is forbidden but not religious belief, as the NGO-based Starting Line group had recommended (Chopin *et al.* 2001: 25). This is by no means binding for national legislation; NGO pressure will still have effects. The European Parliament and the Economic and Social Committee will closely monitor this transposition process and may ask the European Commission for regular reporting.

The European Union (of the 15) has also made the protection of minorities and the incorporation of the racial equality directive into domestic law conditions for future membership for the 12 candidate countries that opted to join the EU from 2004 onwards. The implementation of such positive policies is however seriously hampered by the absence of a comprehensive monitoring mechanism and lack of clarity as to what standards a given country is supposed to respect in the field of minority protection.

Confronted with a Xenophobic Wave—EU on Risk of Losing Social Cohesion?

The challenges of enlargement from 15 to 27 states are great for both, the EU and the applicant states. The EU is at risk of losing social cohesion. The East-West divergence between the socio-economic models in operation, the greatly different levels of economic development, the types of governance, regulatory models and practices are enormous. Income North-South disparities between the 15 EU member states are already considerable and even greater disparities will need to be addressed: the large gap between economic standards in West and East. The GDP in Eastern Europe is below

50 percent of the EU average, with great variations from prosperous Slovenia to impoverished Romania.[67]

The enlargement process called 'differentiation' (admission on own merits, without hard conditionality) followed by the Swedish presidency wants the first accession group—probably Poland, Czech Republic, Hungary, Slovenia, Malta, and possibly Cyprus—to join towards the end of 2003 or early 2004. A decade after the collapse of the Cold War divide there is growing uncertainty about the socio-economic forces to be unleashed soon. While many eastern European fear to be relegated to second-class EU citizenship and are anxious of a brain drain, property buy-out and 'economic invasion' by westerners in the East, expectations of scores of migrating Slavonic workers to the West and the fear of a xenophobic wave among the established West European working classes will put the new EU racial equality and equal opportunity regime on a serious test.

Already strong xenophobia and right-wing agitation is running even stronger in eastern Germany, Austria and northern Italy. The risk of a political backlash of the enlargement has already played to the advantage of populist demagogues in the May 2001 elections in Italy. Pre-emptive moves by EU leaders against the political exploitation of such anxieties by far-right populists in other countries, EU members and candidates the like, are in high demand.

Worrying Levels of Racist Attitudes in EU States

Attitude surveys amongst common folks showed high levels of ethnocentrism, xenophobia and racist mentalities. The results of the *Eurobarometer* 1997 survey, which measured the majority populations' attitudes towards minority groups in each member state of the European Union, 'showed a worrying level of negative attitudes in the 15 EU Member States'; a follow up survey in spring 2000 shows an ambivalent and nevertheless deeply depressing picture: 'in some ways the attitudes ... have changed for the better', e.g., in regard to people favouring new policies to improve coexistence between of majorities and minorities (EUMC 2001: 5), but in 2000 more people in EU states blame their fear of unemployment and loss of welfare on minorities.[68]

EU-wide only 21 percent of the population are classified as belonging to the 'actively tolerant' type of people, meaning that they do not feel disturbed by members of minority groups, see diversity as a richness, do not demand assimilation nor repatriation of immigrants, and show strong support for anti-racist policies; this category is higher educated and represents 'multi-cultural optimism'.[69] Some 14 percent of the EU-population display strong negative attitudes against minorities, support harsh policies against 'foreigners' and are classified as 'intolerant'; these peoples are usually less educated and less optimistic. Comparing EU member states, the Greeks stand out most shockingly with only 29 percent being somewhat tolerant (compared to 60 percent EU-wide), followed by the Belgians (48 percent); the Spanish (77 percent) and the Swedes (76 percent) see themselves as the most tolerant EU citizens. However, the most telling of the dimension of 'xenophobic concerns' has been excluded.[70]

As regards the rather positive classification of a majority 60 percent of European citizens being actively or passively tolerant, serious doubts are cast on such an assessment when looking at the replies on a series of four questions, in which the majority of respondents blame members of minority groups of being responsible for decreasing standards in schools (32–76 percent, EU average 52), abusing of social welfare (37–66 percent, EU 52 percent), increasing of unemployment (36–85 percent; EU 51 percent) and being more often involved in criminality (30–81 percent, EU 58 percent). Only between 30 percent and 37 percent actually disagree with these potentially racist judgements.

The blaming minorities for social deterioration such as unemployment, crime, social insecurity, loss of welfare and drop in educational standards— or the fear of it—felt by large proportions of majority populations, provides right-wing extremists and racists with unlimited recruiting grounds. The persistent threat that—in addition to the notoriously known right-wing political parties in most EU states—more radical racist parties and movements would arise and establish themselves, became more salient.

The shift came all of a sudden in 2002. In 2000 social democrats and a few left-centre parties governed the large majority of the 15 EU states; only in three countries right-wing extremists and racists had a certain influence of central governments: in Spain, since 1996 governed by a conservative government, in Austria, with pro-fascist elements in the central government (Haider's *FPÖ*) since spring 2000, and, unfortunately Italy again, as a result of the May 2001 elections, that brought Berlusconi back to power.[71]

Threats that the power-balance between the democratic parties in the four largest EU countries, Germany, France, United Kingdom could be destabilized by a higher turnout of votes for right-wing populists seemed reduced since the 1990s, with little impact on the extreme fringe groups, which in turn became more radicalised than ever. Established right-wing parties gave a mixed showing in Europe.[72] A plausible threat seemed the undermining of established right-wing parties by new 'modern' racist political agendas, which will pressure established parties to shift their position, and block or reverse institutional re-alignment in favour of pluralism, equality, and justice. And precisely this happened, in rapid course, throughout Western Europe. Within two years, until mid 2002, the political power-balance in the EU states was almost reversed. After Italy (May 2001) the social-democrats lost in Denmark (Nov 2001), Portugal (March 2002), the Netherlands (May 2002) and France (June 2002).[73] The fall 2002 elections in Germany will be decisive for the future of anti-racism in the EU.

It is the institutionalized discrimination and the institutionalisation of racist exclusion practices that are the most worrying aspects of racism and xenophobia in Europe.[74] Ambivalence and conflict are characteristic features of the relationship between immigrants and host societies as well as between indigenous groups and dominant groups. Uncertainties rule the dialectics between 'hosts' and 'guests'. The term of xenophobia, the 'fear of others', mirrors these uncertainties, with 'xenos' in Greek meaning both, alien and guest. The task to explore policy strategies and measures to address these problems starts with rethinking definitions and core concepts. Instead of looking at racism as complex of 'prejudices' a good approach would be to say that 'racism is not an opinion, it is a crime' (ENAR 2000).

Combating Racism and Xenophobia

Ambivalence and conflict are characteristic features of the relationship between immigrants and host societies as well as between indigenous groups and dominant groups. Uncertainties rule the dialectics between 'hosts' and 'guests'.[75] The term of xenophobia, the 'fear of others', mirrors these uncertainties, with 'xenos' in Greek meaning both, alien and guest. This ambiguity lies at the base of 'other-ism'.

The task to explore policy strategies and measures to address these problems starts with rethinking definitions and core concepts. Instead of looking at racism as complex of 'prejudices' a strong approach would be to say that 'racism is not an opinion, it is a crime' (ENAR 2000). Racism against minority group members can be both individual and structural, and it may constitute what Galtung calls 'cultural violence'. Structural elements in racism and xenophobia are greatly reinforced in situations where certain victim groups are facing multiple discrimination on the basis of race, ethnicity, gender, and other factors. Issues of gender or class are inseparable from those of racism and other forms of institutionalized intolerance, be it based on ethnicity, descent, social class or caste, age, disability, nationality, citizenship, immigration status, or other factors.

Multiple discrimination should become a priority area to be addressed by anti-racist policies;[76] this is of particular importance due to particular structural impediments enhancing victimization and vulnerability, aggravated by legal systems and mores.[77] Such structural, often culturally deeply ingrained racism is of particular concern; it explains the common tendency (of which evidence was given based on the findings of the *Eurobarometers*) to blame—and even 'criminalize' or violently attack—migrants, foreigners, racial and ethnic minorities or racialised 'others' for all sorts of reasons. I would distinguish xenophobia, which is a matter of ambivalence, weakness of the Self and problematic individual and collective attitudes towards 'others', 'strangers', 'foreigners' and 'aliens', from racism, which only becomes important and dangerous as part of an apparatus, displaying a strong structural and processual character.[78]

Structural racism is generated by economic, political and social institutions. For this subject the works of Michel Foucault about power structures, institutions and the multitude of different techniques they use, should be seen as a source of inspiration.[79] Knowledge and power create what Foucault calls 'rules of formation', an epistemological form he calls a *dispositif*, which discloses reality while at the same time constructing it.[80] Structural racism categorizes and marks people, makes minority members visible, and denies such people equal access to jobs, education, medical facilities, social welfare, leisure, and habitation. Governments, local and state administrations, domestic companies and transnational corporations, the churches, the education system, civil society organizations, and (not least) the media are part of the apparatuses which form a *dispositif* against the different categories of 'others' and 'aliens'; these are the forces producing 'others' and 'aliens' and shaping public attitudes towards 'others', such as national minorities, and 'aliens, such as 'new minorities' (migrants, refugees, asylum seekers, and trafficked people).

The challenges of anti-racist/anti-chauvinist policies and the prevention and law-enforcement regarding criminal activities of militant racists and fascists are great and the matter is urgent. The EU-wide monitoring of gross human rights violations has to be coordinated by a special task force.[81] There is a high need for a Racism Alert and Early Warning System. The imperative to abolish impunity for racist crimes and the consequent prosecution of racist hate-crimes must be enforced. The *laissez-faire* policy in many EU member states is intolerable. A systematic overview on the tasks, procedures, institutions and voids of anti-racist/anti-chauvinist policies is required.

The European Union wants to combat the crime of racism and is in search of appropriate concepts and tools. Social scientists, psychologists and jurists from all EU member states shall be invited to a series of conferences. The main task is to mainstream practical anti-racist policies aiming at immunizing the European society against racism and xenophobia and promoting tolerance against Otherness. As a next measure the EU should establish a commission of experts to refine its arsenal of responses to racism and xenophobia. I propose to form a Task Force Against Racism, possibly within the already existing EUMC.

This overview is focusing on activities, which are essential to combat racism and xenophobia in Europe. Among others a list of essential anti-racist and anti-chauvinist policies has to include the combat against militant racism. The conception of new policies for preventing and combating racism and xenophobia follows strategies, which are targeting the structural, institutionalized and organized forms of racism.

Rethinking Definitions and Core Concepts of Racism and Xenophobia

A workable definition of contemporary racism understands racism as part of the *dispositif* of societal power relations and the activity of the state apparatus and other institutions, aiming at establishing and maintaining surveillance and control mechanisms, creating policy that aims at policing and imposing discipline and control over citizens and non-citizens. Thus, defining contemporary racism contains the following three core elements:

- Its structural, institutionalised nature, which should be highlighted case by case since common patterns are translated into manifold local forms of rejection, whereby discrimination of individuals is always based on their alleged, asserted or voluntary belonging to a social, cultural, ethnic, religious or national minority.

- The negative dynamics of its production / reproduction are characterized by guided notions and encompass the triple processes, in varying concrete permutations, of (a) the process of racialization and/or ethnicization as the construction of 'races' and/or 'ethnic' groups in the social imaginary of xenophobe individuals and groups, by which process prejudices, stereotypes, aspects of cultural or biological 'superiorism' or other elements of 'false consciousness' whatsoever may play a role (with the so-called interactive element seen with extreme caution); (b) the process of victimization along the perpetrator-based definition of the victims, being either 'inferior' or looked at in envy, but in both cases 'threatening members' of minority group; and (c) the process of selected social exclusion and (often) targeted discrimination of members of minority groups in which process the elements of a whole *dispositif* of the state apparatus, its institutions, the schools, churches, official majority culture, labour markets, etc play respective roles.

- Racism is always linked to violence (as direct personal, structural or cultural violence). Racism appears in different forms of intensity and degrees of organization; in its genocidal and terminal form racism becomes extremely dangerous; the racists would not be satisfied with discriminating and scapegoating certain groups of victims but would rather attack, kill, and exterminate the constructed victim groups.

Conventional perceptions of racism as prejudice are misleading in several ways. First, the problem of 'new racism' is beyond a simple question of prejudice as individual errors or more articulated ideologies. Second, racism is not only a sort of pathological anomy, which could be seen as a social dysfunction, but rather functional and structural in nature. (This can be said despite the difficulty for dissent and rational people—and anti-racists in particular—to actually understand the obsessive types of racism and the perception of minority groups as threats we may encounter across Europe and beyond.) The functionality of racism appears as obvious when looking at the racially compartmentalized global labour markets, whereby racial exclusion—as 'integration by exclusion'—follows the logic of harsh economic exploitation for often-undocumented workers.

When looking at political and legal steps to mitigate and pre-empt destructive forms of interaction between majorities and minorities in Europe any attempt to clarify or resolve 'racial', 'ethnic' or other sub-national conflicts must be preceded by the realization that existential questions relating to the survival of an ethnic group and the cultural survival of migrant groups are not factors that are open to negotiation but essential prerequisites to dialogue. There are a number of destructive forms of interaction between states and ethnic communities resulting in the exclusion and persecution of national groups that have not yet been subject to systematic investigation and for which the international community has not yet developed any consistent policy. (This was demonstrated with devastating clarity in the case of the genocide in Rwanda in 1994. The racist hate-crimes not only call for prevention but for its elimination.)

The political-cum-humanitarian concern to find ways of avoiding structural and direct, personal forms of racism and xenophobia leads on to the questions of:

- how ethnic and cultural difference can be acknowledged and recognized,
- how destructive forms of interaction between states and communities and between majorities and minorities can be prevented,
- how violent, militant forms of racism and xenophobia can be effectively combated, and
- which institutions, legal measures and policies are most appropriate for these purposes.

Structurally Preventing Conflicts between Majorities and Minorities

Regarding forms of 'structural prevention' of troubles, I use 'structural' in the sense that new frameworks and institutions are created to avert possible direct violence and reduce structural violence, such as discrimination against non-dominant groups. I am indebted to Johan Galtung, who developed the concept of 'structural violence' in the 1970s, based on his path-breaking distinction between direct personal violence and structural violence; Galtung also reflected on cultural violence, e.g., values that promote or justify violence and superiority complexes that result into aggressive attitudes. Structural prevention aims at ending repression, injustice and racism, which are ingrained in state policies and which are also inherent part of the cultural attitudes held by many dominant groups.

Today it is common knowledge and the declared policy of the European Union since the mid-1990s that it was simpler and cheaper to tackle conflicts preventively and avoid them than to try to put a stop to hostilities that had already broken out. Undeniably there are a number of practical problems politicians face in promoting preventive measures and policies—beyond rhetoric, when it comes to implementing declared policies, the main difficulty is the unspectacular and long-term character of many such measures, which makes them not really attractive if quick results are required.

In preventing 'ethnic unrest' among minority groups and virulent racism and xenophobia among mainstream national societies there are no easy solutions. The great diversity of cultural and political characteristics exhibited by different types of society produce, corresponding to them, different types of claims and regulatory mechanisms. First steps to mitigate and pre-empt destructive forms of interaction between majorities and minorities in Europe are dealt followed by steps to combat racism and xenophobia among the majority societies.

Classic solutions for indigenous minorities range from cultural autonomy, through territorial self-governance, to *de facto* sovereignty. Protection of ethnic and national minorities by means of a variety of autonomy arrangements did not begin until the 20th century, triggered by a worsening of the so-called 'minorities problem' as a result of revolutions and the regroupings that had occurred in the wake of two world wars.

Too little account has been taken of the policies of certain multinational states when it comes to looking for methods of preventing and dealing with latent or open ethno-national conflicts. Many states have been able to pursue active and successful policies of prevention of troubles by making concessions and negotiating offers involving elements of reactive minority protection and proactive nationality policy (e.g., home rule for the Faeroese and the Inuit in the Kingdom of Denmark from 1948 onwards). Others have—often with limited success—used similar offers to try and resolve armed conflicts that have already escalated (e.g., the regionalization and phased granting of autonomy to Basques, Catalonians, Andalusians, and Galicians in post-Franco Spain). Nationality policies are generally not conceived as solutions to conflicts that are smouldering or have already erupted. Some procedures aim more at containment, or pose the nationality question in a purely socio-political context. But such policies are part of the problem, which they claim to be solving. A detailed comparison ought to be made of the different approaches to nationality policy pursued by selected states such as Denmark, Italy, Spain, and the USSR/Russian Federation; this might include comparison with lessons learned from China, India, Australia, Colombia, Panama, Nicaragua, or Ethiopia.

The contribution of research into preventive strategies ought to be strengthened. Practical preventive steps range from initiatives by popular movements to the elaboration of norms and legal instruments within the framework of international organizations. Efforts to change violence-promoting framework conditions through policing and controls of potential perpetrators, the bans of radical organizations and propagation of violence, and the strengthening of civil society were often neglected in the debate about how to deal with or prevent violent intra-societal conflicts. The underdeveloped state of political and institutional consultancy in peaceful dispute-settlement by third parties or 'go-betweens' in the case of 'ethnic' conflicts is lamentable. Conflict mediation and facilitation in such conflicts can undoubtedly be successful as an instrument of international politics and should not be left solely to state and interstate actors. But efforts at go-between mediation by civil actors and initiatives for transforming ethnic conflicts are arduous and hold little attraction for the media. Furthermore, attempts to give a thorough conceptual account of the phenomenon of ethnicity and ethnicization, to work out elements of a theory of inter-ethnic coexistence, investigate the causes for trouble, to distinguish the many different manifestations of ethnic conflict, to highlight its political and empirically assessed potential, to analyze its structural characteristics and the driving forces behind it, and to set the phenomenon of 'ethnic' conflict in a larger context should all be intensified.

This can be read as a call for the reorientation of peace and conflict research towards the 'real existing' conflict-formations, thus a call for the intensification of international attempts to find methods of preventing and resolving conflict. Of major importance in preventing ethnic and national conflicts is the extension not only of international norms and standards of protection for non-dominant minorities and indigenous peoples but also of the rights of these groups in regard to autonomy and self-governance.

The fundamental weakness of the current debate about conflict prevention (better: the prevention of violence) is that the normative, structural and multi-lateral dimensions of prevention are often neglected in favour of more activist approaches and technical aspects. This contradicts the fact that techniques of preventive multi-track diplomacy (such as mediation, facilitation, good offices, arbitration, etc.) and other forms of peaceful conflict settlement by go-betweens are—in regard to their over-all effectiveness—of secondary importance compared to long-term policies for the prevention of violent inter-ethnic and other intra-state conflicts.

More studies should aim to outline and compare various regional and local attempts at conflict resolution within the framework of state policies on minorities and nationalities, to link these up with evolving provisions in international law and human rights and situate them within the international system. The role of multilateral regimes in preventing and resolving violent conflicts should be discussed more systematically in order to draw the 'lessons learned' from it. Critical reviews should focus on the activities undertaken by international humanitarian organizations in ethnic conflicts, the efforts of the Council of Europe in regards to national minorities, similar the efforts of the OSCE as well as the efforts of the UN Human Rights Commission to work out minimum standards for the rights of minorities and indigenous peoples. The observations on multilateral regimes are confined, for the most part, to the 'human dimension'—that is to say, to human-rights mechanisms and minority rights issues. New paths in this direction have been embarked on with the framework convention of the Council of Europe, which laid great emphasis on the protection of national minorities, and the creation of the institution of a High Commissioner for National Minorities within the OSCE. However, speculations about the transposability of such European 'models' must be viewed with scepticism. Legal instruments are not sufficient in themselves in promoting good relations between different communities on the ground. In addition to standard-setting activities (e.g., the Framework Convention for the Protection of National Minorities of Council of Europe), confidence-building and other measures at the grass-roots level aimed at increasing tolerance and understanding between people belonging to different ethnic communities are required.[82]

Increasing Possibilities for Redress in Case of Racial Discrimination

As regards racial discrimination the expert opinion is that according to the law the possibilities for control and redress are limited in most countries. All the mentioned institutions and organisations (governments, local and state administrations, domestic companies and transnational corporations, the churches, the education system, civil society organizations, the media, etc.) should act responsibly in the interests of human rights and protection of vulnerable groups; for some, codes of conduct could be appropriate means to regulate their operations. Protection mechanisms provided for by international law often are not translated into legal provisions within the nation-states that implement the rules of international conventions; hence they remain without direct consequences.

An 'Anti-Discrimination Charter' (ADC), possibly as an amendment to international treaties such as the European Convention on Human Rights, which has a review mechanism and the right for individual petition, would be more effective. Criminal law cases are successful in a few instances only. The burden of proof needs to be shifted in favour of the victims but the principle of due process of law prohibits a shift of the burden of proof in criminal procedures. Hence, the only way for individual redress is a civil court case. The aim is to make violations expensive for the violators.[83]

Monitoring the implementation of Council Directive of 29 June 2000 is a crucial task for Europe's anti-racist movements. The impact of this directive, which is implementing the principle of equal treatment between persons irrespective of racial or ethnic origin as well as the Council Directive of 27 November, establishing a general framework for equal treatment in employment and occupation (CM-EC 2000a and b), have to be explored carefully. In this respect the upcoming incorporation of the EC Racial Equality Directive into the national laws of the EU member states (until June 2002) and of the candidate states (until June 2003) has to be carefully watched by the anti-racist organizations. In a few countries, however, domestic law already guarantees the protection of minorities in a more comprehensive form than the new legislation on EU level.

Combating Organized Racism: the Roles of EUMC and SOS Racism

As follows I will mention some key areas of activities. One of the important tasks to be accomplished by a fully established European Union Monitoring Centre on Racism and Xenophobia (EUMC), based in Vienna, would be the establishment of a Unit for Identifying Common Elements and Patterns of Militant Racism.

Analyzing and comparing racism and xenophobia the 20th century produces a set of common elements and patterns. Patterns can be found by looking at the perpetrators of hate-crimes and their environment. Hence, comparative research must become a core activity at EUMC; research must be greatly reinforced in order to identify and explore:

- the role of racist, fascist and militant organizations (parties, movements, gangs, etc.) and their international networks;
- the core ideologists, organizers, legitimizers and perpetrators of hate-crimes, and their relations to the mass of 'willing executioners', e.g., weekend militants, skinheads, small criminals, etc.;

- the local and regional conditions they find and create;
- the context in which they act, e.g., complicity of parts of the local officials or state authorities, *laissez-faire* by law enforcement agencies;
- the political environment in which they act, e.g., complicity of right-leaning politicians, down-playing of their aims by established parties;
- the way extremists gain influence;
- the type of victims they chose: members of migrant communities and ethnic minorities, members of left-wing parties/movements, vulnerable groups such as social weak, disabled, etc.;
- the xenophobic, racist or even genocidal ideology they use; and
- the way they plan, prepare and execute crimes.

The perpetrators, their ideology, the process of victimization and the way they execute racist hate-crimes are the first focus of attention. A coherent network of right-wing organizations guided by internationally active vicious elites of militant extremists is more likely to gain influence amongst xenophobic elements in the mainstream society and amongst sympathizers in influential positions. The agendas of such elites are to intimidate, harass, attack, or even destroy specific domestic groups, which as a rule are always in non-dominant and minority position.

The EU-wide monitoring of gross human rights violations is a task that has to be coordinated by a special task force, as part of an action plan to prevent racist offenses and hate-crimes. Such a task force would organize efforts at improving early warning and crime prevention by domestic law-enforcement agencies with the aim of strengthening the capacity to closely monitor organized political criminality and prevent and prosecute crimes committed by militant racist organizations and individuals. Specific training should be given to staff of national intelligence and police corps to identify warning signs, analyze them, and translate warnings into appropriate action. For this purpose a new unit at Europol-Interpol named 'Racism Alert Unit' should be created. This new unit would be closely linked to the commanding structure of national police forces.

A special task would be to filter-out indicators for early warning about serious risk of racist hate-crimes. Similarly to indicators of genocide alert such signifiers for 'red alert' of militant racism could be deducted from an indicator box. Translated into practical work this could be done in much the same way as Interpol when assembling and accessing their criminological database in order to trace organized crime. One of the main tasks for applied research on racism is therefore the development of an early warning system. The functioning of such a system is guaranteed only if a rapid reaction mechanism can be institutionalized EU-wide or as part of a regional regime; it should include a broad 'network of cooperation'.[84]

The reason why a future institution for racism alert and early action in case of serious threats should become part of the European Commission is the necessity to have short procedures in cases of alert. The EU member states must agree on new mechanisms of rapid reaction in cases of alert. The European Commission will be chiefly responsible for organizing political will to establish a rapid reaction mechanism which is not depending on political criteria but is a purely professional venture. The concept of neutrality in case of massive human rights violations has to be dismissed. Capacity building at the European Commission must ensure the necessary resources for law-enforcement against militant political extremism.

Enforcing Prosecution and Anticipating Dangers

The 20th century was the age of mass violence and political extremism; in the 21st century militant racism, which was the root cause for the death of millions in the 20th century, has finally to be outlawed. In the spirit of Raphael Lemkin (the father of the 1948 UN Anti-genocide Convention) the international criminal law has to be developed comprehensively in order for the international rule of law to be respected by all states and political actors. New developments such as the Pinochet case, the indictment of some 45 Rwandan *génocidaires* by the International Criminal Tribunal for Rwanda (ICTR) and the prosecution of crimes against humanity committed on Former Yugoslavia have in recent years helped to form public awareness.

The understanding that the international community is responsible for monitoring the mandatory prosecution of massive human rights violations (racial hate-crimes, genocide and crimes against humanity) in any one state is growing.[85] The effect of deterrence would have greatly increased if Lemkin's idea had been applied by the member states of the League of Nations; Nazism could have been stopped.[86] In Europe a Brussels court made for the first time use of this principle of universal justice for crimes against humanity and tried four *génocidaires* from Rwanda (the 'Butare four', among them two nuns); in June 2001 the four were sentenced to long prison terms.

The political will to punish severe human rights violations is increasing lately. It is only today, as a human life-length has gone by, that mankind arrived at the same square. The debate about the International Criminal Court (ICC) and its establishment in due time showed clearly that the time is ripe for systematic international prosecution and deterrence against racism and mass murder. The international system needs a permanent international criminal tribunal specialized to deal with the racism, hate-crimes and gross human rights violations; it shall be institutionalized as part of the UN system. Current trends, however, go toward decentralized responses to make human rights offenders accountable. A second trend can be seen in the tendency that the principle of national sovereignty can no longer be invoked to neutralize accusations of severe human rights violations.[87]

The main problem is the lack of enforcement of the existing laws and instruments. International instruments rarely provide for law enforcement by comprehensive review processes and checks-and-control, as in the case of the European Convention on Human Rights or in the case of the Convention on the Rights of Indigenous Peoples (ILO conventions 169). Law enforcement needs more institution building. The establishing of the International Criminal Court (ICC) in the first years of the 21st century, in order to outlaw gross human rights violations, is one of the noblest tasks for the near future. Establishing an effective and respected International Criminal Court is genuinely among the tasks of global governance. The heart of global governance must be prevention of destructive violence.[88]

The international community can learn many important lessons from past traumatic experiences of militant racism and genocidal ideology. Two generations ago, the German fascists and their willing executioners in many occupied countries committed the worst crimes of the past 20th century. The crime of genocide seems incomparable to the crime of racism, and yet there is no genocide without a racist ideology. Anticipating dangers posed by organized militant racism is a key area of anti-racist policies.

Much more attention should be given to non-spectacular silent work of organizations such as *SOS Racism*. EUMC should assemble a list of organizations and civic movements that combat racism and deserve moral and continuous material support by the European Commission. Civil actors should take the lead in fighting powerlessness and passive response to racism and xenophobia taken by many states. The development of concepts of structural prevention of racism and xenophobia is among the most urgent tasks for good governance and the rule of law in the enlarging Europe. Charitable Funds and scientific funding institutions should prioritise research project in these fields.

In the 21st century, one of the key tasks for human rights organizations, states and international governmental organizations will be to standardize the prevention of elimination of militant racism, genocide and mass violence internationally. Combating racism and outlawing racist crimes should become part of domestic laws and national constitutions as well as of relevant international instruments.

Abolishing or Transforming Racism-producing Institutions

At the end of the day, the struggle against racism has to establish disconti-nuities and abolish those institutions that produce racism and discrimina-tion. Racism today has no scientific platform anymore, since the theory of the races has been found pseudo-scientific, inhumane and criminal. All its remaining strongholds must be abolished, one by one, or being replaced and/or transformed by new practices:

• Starting with racism in schoolbooks being replaced by anti-prejudice educational goals and values of solidarity, conviviality and democratic culture being explicit part of all curricula;
• Replacing racialised or ethnicized citizenship (esp. the continuous anachronistic use of the 'blood law', the *jus sanguinis*, by some countries — a curious reminder of a sort of tribal descendence) by a multicultural and transnational model of European citizenship;[89]
• Racist immigration practices and illegal *refoulement* of refugees being rendered useless by open borders and freedom of movement for EU citizen and non-EU citizen alike; until the full abolition of immigration control, the immigration practices and policies governing non-EU citizen should be on a solid base of due process, the universal human rights principles, and the UN Convention of the Rights of Migrants;
• Abolishing any *laissez-faire* policy of law-enforcement agencies in regards to racisms; establishing comprehensive political control of police performance towards minority group members and intercultural training courses;
• Replacing the production of racial stereotypes in the media by decon-structing myths about 'otherness' and promoting conviviality;
• Developing the idea of conviviality with such conviviality not remaining a rhetoric term but being experienced by tolerant EU citizens, starting with the most attractive parts of it, such as Brazilian-type multicultural carnivals, e.g., the popular Afro-Caribbean Notting Hill carnival in late August.

Speaking in Foucaultian terms, the *dispositif* of the forces that produce and reproduce racism have to be undermined, weakened and destroyed.[90] Its discourse and practices, e.g., institutions, arrangements, regulations, laws, administrative measures, scientific statements, philosophic propositions, morality, etc., form a specific intensified surveillance and control mechanism, creating policy that aims at policing and establishing discipline among 'out-groups', as to increase the state's control over its citizens and non-citizens in a particular area, and which in turn leads to resistance among certain groups. In Foucault's broader view of this production of 'truth' via power, contemporary racism would be symbolic knowledge and part of the regulatory procedures and the techniques of domination, thus part of the *dispositif* or apparatus of power.

Minority Rights and Anti-racism: The EU and Eastward Enlargement

Within the European Union, there are, in addition to the ten working languages, 41 minority languages in use (comprising Romance, Germanic, Celtic, Slavic, Albanian, Greek, Turkic, Basque, and Finno-Ugric tongues). Fifty million EU citizens—about one in seven people—speak a language other than their state's official language(s).[91] Since 1983, there has been a 'mini-lobby' on linguistic issues in Brussels—the European Bureau of Lesser Used Languages (EBLUL)—with its secretariat in Dublin.[92] A European Parliament group on minority languages has been meeting regularly since 1983. The Kuijpers Resolution of 1987 dealt with the language and cultures of regional and ethnic minorities in the European Community. The European Charter for Regional or Minority Languages supplemented and brought together the various ideas that had come to maturity by that time, including the Kililea Resolution of 1994 on cultural and linguistic minorities in the European Community. The linguistic communities have worked at state, regional, and local levels to obtain recognition of their right to use their own language. In 1994, the Council of Europe adopted the Framework Convention for the Protection of National Minorities, which recognizes that linguistic freedom is a fundamental human right.

The idea of a 'Pact on Stability in Europe' has been adopted as a pan-European agreement on issues relating to European security in May 1994. The pact became known under the name 'Plan Balladur'. At the time of the conference horrible atrocities were committed by the French client regime in Rwanda against the Tutsi minority (shown on all TV-stations)—without any interference from outside, rather with the complicity of Balladur's government.[93] Most people seemed unaware of this coincidence and of the profound cynism that characterized this historic moment: While it was actively supporting a regime elsewhere (in Rwanda), which carried out at the same time the most barbaric genocide since the Holocaust, the very same French government was proposing the 'Plan Balladur' that marks the first occasion that the prevention of inter-state conflicts over contentious border-issues has been linked to human-rights issues. Such issues inherently include the solution of 'minority problems'—while in Africa a minority was obliterated. For Europe, perceiving itself as the core of the 'civilized world', this meant that implicit minority-questions were recognized as an international problem, though Balladur was thinking chiefly of so-called 'border minorities'.[94] This is meant to ensure that old conflicts and disputes between states are disposed of 'forever'—at least in Europe.

The 'Pact on Stability in Europe' consists of two parts. The first is a multilateral 'Declaration of Good Neighbourliness', signed in March 1995 and politically binding on all signatories. Its declared aim is to increase co-operation and solidarity in Europe. The obstacles to this are identified as 'all manifestations of intolerance, and especially of aggressive nationalism, racism, chauvinism, xenophobia and anti-Semitism, as well as discrimination between persons and persecution on religious or ideological grounds' (art. 4). The declaration was signed by all OSCE participating states and by the principal multilateral organizations in Europe. The second part of the pact consists of more than 100 bilateral treaties (between prospective and current members of the European Union, between prospective members themselves, and between prospective members and their CIS neighbours). The pact thus seeks to reconcile the eastward expansion of the EU with the maintenance of European unity, through close relations with Russia and in concert with the OSCE—in other words: it seeks a European Union that excludes Russia and most of the other former Soviet republics.

The New Division of Europe

The European Union has created for itself a, as yet, not fully standardised admission-regime. Among hundreds of more or less precise regulations the principled issues of settlement of 'minority problems', combating racism and border disputes between the twelve states that want to join the union are stipulated as a condition of entry.[95] This means that the new borders of the EU are officially being drawn mainly according to criteria of stability, and thus also according to human-rights criteria. Unfortunately, this division of Europe, with its exclusion of the former Soviet Union (except for the tiny Baltic states), represents the present Western consensus.

The states that would be accepted as new members of the enlarged European Union on these conditions of entry are: two island states in the Mediterranean (Malta and Cyprus), the six states of the old Soviet-dominated Eastern bloc (from Poland to Romania); a single Balkan state—Slovenia (but not Croatia, Bosnia, Serbia, Montenegro, Macedonia, or Albania); and the three former Baltic republics of the Soviet Union. However, Estonia was so far the only Baltic state, which started pre-negotiations with the EU in November 1998, thus theoretically in time for the 2004 accession of an unknown number of candidate countries.

Excluded for as far as 2006 (and beyond) would be the remaining twelve successor-states of the USSR, including the Visegrad group's direct neighbours—Belarus, Moldova, and the Ukraine. Turkey would also be left in the cold. In addition to human-rights considerations, there are a number of other reasons for this; the late Turkish president Turgut Özal had mentioned one: the 'Christian club of the EU' would not easily accept a predominantly Muslim country.

The case of Cyprus is incomparable with the problems Turkey is going to face as a candidate country (provided its political will to go for it). However, the plight of Cyprus is closely linked with the Turkish-Greek relationship and the ability of the Greek Cypriots to accommodate the Turkish minority; here, the EU membership negotiations might facilitate re-establishing the Cypriot Federative Republic—if only the EU would use its mighty arsenal of incentives and disincentives skilfully.[96]

The Central and Eastern European states have been called on to settle the problem of the Hungarian minorities outside Hungary (numbering 3.5 to 4 million); and the Baltic states to settle that of the Russian and Russian speaking minorities living there (3.5 million).[97] Another test (especially in regard to the implementation of the Racial Equality Directive) will be the treatment of the most marginalized people in Europe, the 10–15 million Roma, who live scattered throughout almost every state on the continent.[98]

The European Parliament has continued to produce country reports tackling individual issues (such as the granting of asylum or the abolition of the death penalty) and violations against human and minority rights. Work in this latter area has recently been concerned chiefly with the conflicts in former Yugoslavia. Other cases were Turkey and the Kurds, the Syrian regime, and (since Rwanda 1994) the terrible occurrence of genocide in Burma, East Timor / Indonesia, and the Sudan.

One possible sanctions-instrument available to the European Parliament is the withholding of assent to financial protocols (as in the case of Syria and Morocco). In relations with ASEAN and the ACP states, human-rights issues have so far played a secondary role. In September 1992, a joint parliamentary assembly of representatives of the EU and the ACP states met together for the first time to debate human rights, democratization, and development assistance. However, the debate produced no follow-on, and it revealed some unbridgeable positions on the question of the impact, which human-rights considerations should have on development assistance. At bilateral level, sometimes in concerted actions by Western development-agencies (e.g. before the elections in Kenya), there is generally a more informal approach.

In February 1992, the European Union signed a treaty covering certain elements of a future EU constitution. In this treaty, human rights figure as basic principles of EU law. In common EU foreign, trade, and development (aid) policy *vis-à-vis* third countries—not only at the level of bilateral relations—human-rights considerations and the treatment of minorities are to play a more important role in future. So far, however, there has been little sign of this. Instead, pressure of a 'money for human rights' kind is being used—where it is being used at all—in an arbitrary and biased manner. And in any case, considerations of commercial opportuneness generally take priority.

The 'Patchwork of Minorities' and a New Configuration for Europe

In the search for a new configuration for Europe—one that goes beyond the old nation-states—the issues of membership, transnational citizenship, democratic representation and demographic representativeness, minority rights, conflict prevention and peaceful coexistence, and social welfare pose themselves in an entirely different light. Remembering the violent past that has seen Europe as the world's major theatre of wars and slaughter, the EU enlargement process, or the 'Europeanization', bears a strong promise for a stable peaceful order in Europe. Recalling that even the enlarged European Union is far from representing a genuine unification of Europe, for the time being the 'stable peace' ought to be questioned. The same applies to the idea of EU enlargement as a sort of 'conflict resolution process', not least for internal or minority 'problems'.[99]

Regarding minority rights and the very notion of 'minority' the conditions for the possibility of a change of paradigm may soon be ready-made: the end to majority rule. The future Europe will not have a 'majority' anymore, hence we are approaching a situation Jean-Francois Lyotard dubbed the 'patchwork of minorities', characterizing the state of art of modernity in its ripeness. Not necessarily a utopia, such a conglomerate of cultures, religions, races, fashions, and lifestyles that constitutes—in amalgamation—the world of 'minorities', would be enabled to dump the dominance of a 'majority' and its *Leitkultur* to the rubbish bin of history.

Europe can no longer be a puzzle of nation states and the ongoing debate about a federal new Europe is hugely important for the future orientation of the union. Will there be a sort of 'Enlarged Switzerland without Switzerland' as a genuinely federal entity or will there be some sort of 'devolution of powers' model with an upgrading of the regions. So far unitary, decentralized and federal concepts co-exist, as a broad spectrum of administrative, legislative and regulatory arrangements, whereby laws and regulations mean different things in each state. Despite marked dissimilarities in their political structures, with a range of characteristic institutional and conceptual variations in each state, similar practices prevail in the federal states such as Germany and Belgium, in the unitary nations Italy and Spain, and in the multinational United Kingdom.

In France many fear that—following Joseph Fischer's advocacy for federalism in 2000, duplicated by the German chancellor end April 2001— Germany aims at transforming the European Union according to their own model, with the addition of a European constitution.[100] However, even in France, with its long-standing traditional centralization model (nurtured as a Jacobinist-Gaullist essential feature of the state apparatus) already being somewhat revised by devolution of powers in the case of Corsica (as pacification measure), a genuine change of attitude is being detected in the form of 'a widespread wish for decisions to be taken closer to the grass roots and for further decentralisation on the lines of other European countries' (Rémond 2001).[101] In France, after more than 200 years of rigid centralization, some notion of decentralization (starting with local governance) became more acceptable only in the 1990s. Paradigmatic changes take time. Currently the French-German 'tandem'—which was for decades of decisive importance for the European experience, in concert with the Benelux countries since the times of the European Economic Community, to the building-up of the European Community, and its further development what became today's European Union—seems somewhat weakened.

The European Union will have to sort out what kind of decision-making process is appropriate. Federations and unitary states follow different ways, with power shared in a federal structure because its units wish it to be that way or with powers in a unitary model transferred to the peripheral authorities and the responsibility for the scope and strength of those powers being determined by the centre in Brussels. Opting for a federal administrative arrangement with more grass-roots decentralization ('Europe of the Regions') and the subsidiarity principle in operation as presently would certainly reduce some of the in-built weaknesses of the European Union— its decision making taking place above its citizen and its fundamental democracy deficit—and a new configuration along these lines would have a profound impact on the emerging European identity.

The 'EU semantics' have created many incomprehensible terms. The coinage 'external identity', which means a special European identity *vis-à-vis* the outside, is devoid of content to many citizens. For the Eurocrats, 'external identity' is something to be created. The guiding notion, they say, is not the US ideology of the melting-pot, whose alleged success they much admired, but the development of a 'European facet' to existing multi-layered identities—all the while preserving national, regional, cultural, and ethnic identities.[102]

Europe will be the only continent where borders will be continuously changing during the next decades of enlargement; borders will be shifting eastwards. Nobody knows where the official EU borders will end—at the gates of the Orient and at the borders of the Ukrainian *Rus*? —certainly, according to the unwritten but not unanimous consensus, at the borders of Russia, and nobody knows when the process will stop, probably around the year 2020. The challenge is how to cater for diversity while trying to avoid exclusion within the future enlarged membership.[103] To give more shape to a 'European facet' of identity the decision makers must think about a process towards European citizenship, as a healthy counterweight and binding framework to the existing cultural pluralism.

The new concept of multicultural transnational citizenship—decoupled from nationality and ethnicity—will greatly contribute to a project, which aspires at more than 'external identity' or a 'European facet' of identity but aims at constituting an emerging European identity. This long-term open-ended project of identity formation will produce social cohesion, identification with democratic culture, and a new sense of belonging to a Europe beyond the old nation states. The new Europe must be, in equal measure, a Europe of the citizen and a Europe of the peoples.

Human-Rights Regimes in Regional and UN Organizations

Regional organizations will be increasingly putting the issue of the protection and the rights of national minorities onto their agendas—for example, within the framework of the OCSE, the OAS, the OAU and the envisaged African Union, the Arab League, the SAARC, ASEAN, the ACP system, the SADC, and ECOWAS. The increasing willingness to pursue international co-operation at the regional level is a positive phenomenon. And conversely, greater responsibility at the level of regional organizations would facilitate the work of the United Nations.

As for Europe, two institutions—the Council of Europe and the OSCE, have recognized the importance of the protection of human and minority rights as integral factors in the prevention or resolution of ethno-national conflicts in Europe; and they are prepared to take further steps to improve the situation of endangered populations. In the area of minority rights, there is a healthy duplication of the kind of efforts being made by the OSCE— which can only have positive effects. Both institutions reaffirm the principle of complementarity[104] and the aspiration to translate the political undertakings made within the framework of the C/OSCE into legal obligations. Any problems about competency that arise with the OSCE's Conflict Prevention Centre in Vienna or with the OSCE Human Rights Bureau in Warsaw can be pragmatically resolved. The competition between the two institutions for the laudable role of peacemaker and protector of minorities can only be of benefit to the cause. Also, it should be borne in mind that the area covered by the OSCE—57 member states right around the Northern Hemisphere—is much more extensive than that covered by the Council of Europe and covers the largest area of all regional organizations.

The official end of bloc confrontation and the need for greater co-operation and convergence resulted—particularly on the part of the front-line Cold War states—in a revalorisation of multilateral regimes. It was the Conference on Security and Co-operation in Europe (CSCE), which began in the 1970s with the Helsinki Act, which profited most from the 'peace dividend'. It was only in January 1990, when the CSCE (as it then was) endowed itself with a permanent though very modest secretariat (based in Prague). However, even now, the meagre resources expended on the running of the OSCE in no way match its huge political importance.

One new feature is the growing conviction that condemnations of member states that have violated minimum standards in regard to minority rights should no longer be regarded as interference in internal affairs. A CSCE meeting on the problems of national minorities held in July 1990 in Geneva unfortunately produced disappointing results.[105] The immediate motive for the meeting was the dramatic increase in violent minority and nationality conflicts in the fragmented multinational USSR and Yugoslavia, and—so far at a level below armed engagement—in Romania, Hungary, Slovakia, and Bulgaria.

The CSCE's Helsinki II follow-up meeting (from March to June 1992 in Helsinki) made possible, amongst other things, the creation of a High Commission on National Minorities, to identify and resolve conflicts at an early stage, through early warning and hearings. However, the human-rights process lacks the ability to enforce its objectives, because the two-yearly OSCE meetings are not empowered to draw up binding resolutions on the implementation of human rights, and cannot send experts to investigate human-rights violations. Amnesty International saw no real improvement in the C/OSCE: its work, claimed Amnesty, continued to be impenetrable; and Helsinki II had not resulted in open, issue-oriented relations between governments and non-governmental organizations.[106]

Convention 169 of the International Labour Organization

The resistance of many states to the extension of the right of peoples to self-determination manifests itself in their non-signature of the International Labour Organization's pioneering Convention 169 of 1989. Only 14 of 193 states have signed the convention, which is a shame. Convention 169 is the only international instrument addressing indigenous peoples which has a binding effect, but of course only upon the governments of the state parties which have ratified it.[107] This short list contains a high proportion of Latin

American countries (10 of 14). In recent years, governments in that region have come to recognize the multi-ethnic and multicultural character of their societies. However, certain of these governments have signed but have only reluctantly revised their anti-Indian policies as a result (see Mexico in Chiapas). The recognition of diversity would greatly contribute to ensure political stability in Latin America and would further social progress for all ethnic groups. Most European countries are still hesitating. Some states— Germany, for example—claim, without batting an eyelid, that they have no indigenous peoples; but the Sorbs and Friesians are just as indigenous as the Saami in the Nordic countries.

The ILO convention 169 is the first instrument of international law that talks not about indigenous populations but about indigenous peoples, without stipulating a right to self-determination.[108] The convention created a series of procedures that work on the assumption of the continued existence of indigenous peoples (not of their integration or assimilation). A series of laws are set down formally for the first time. They relate, amongst other things, to participation in the benefits deriving from economic development within the framework of the preservation of, and respect for, cultural difference.

The ILO has an exemplary mechanism for monitoring observance of the convention and the related recommendations. Every five years—or more often if requested—governments submit reports to the ILO on how they are implementing the convention both in law and in practice. The Committee of Experts on the Application of Conventions and Recommendations, a body of independent experts in law and social sciences, then reviews the situation and either makes comments to, or requests further information from, the governments concerned. The committee produces annual reports of its findings. The Standards Committee of the annual International Labour Conference may then invite the governments concerned to appear before it to discuss the situation. The Conference Committee's report includes a detailed account of each discussion, and any remaining questions are followed up by the Committee of Experts. Governments usually review their position in the light of these comments. The ILO continues its monitoring until the situation is resolved. Mention should also be made of the 'direct contacts' procedure between a representative of the ILO's director-general and governments facing special difficulties with, or obstacles to, the application of ratified standards. Studies assessing the compatibility of the national framework and ILO conventions are undertaken.

The convention directly affects the situation of indigenous peoples and can also influence legislation on indigenous rights. In 1995, for the first time in the history of the two conventions on the protection of indigenous and tribal peoples, a state called on the ILO to make contact with represen-

tatives of an indigenous people. Norway granted the ILO the right to nego-
tiate with the parliament of the Saami people. The government report on the
application of Convention 169, which Norway had been the first state to
sign, as early as 1990, was first sent to the Saami and took the latter's views
into account in the formulation of government policy.[109] The Duma, the
Russian parliament, asked the ILO for advice in its legislative debate on
protective provisions for the indigenous peoples of Russia (but refrained
from ratifying convention 169).[110]

Convention 169 is a revised version of Convention 107 of 1957 (Indigenous and Tribal Populations Convention), which already recognized
collective and individual land-rights and stipulated that there must be compensation for confiscated land. Forcible resettlement is to be outlawed in
future (art. 16.2).[111] Criticism of the wording of the text by indigenous
organizations was one of the reasons for its revision.[112] However, the
convention remains fixated on the state in a number of its articles; representatives of indigenous peoples criticized it along these lines.

ILO Convention 169 affirms the right of indigenous nations to determine their own development, to control their own institutions, and to
dispose of the land which they have traditionally settled and claimed as
their own. States with sizeable indigenous populations—like Mexico,
Colombia, Bolivia, Paraguay, and Peru (but not Brazil, for example)—have
now ratified the convention. The latter requires governments to recognize
indigenous peoples' rights of ownership and use in regard to state territory
(pt. II: Land, arts. 13–19). However, this requirement relates only to surface
land rights and not, to a full extent, to the right to resources lying under the
land. The convention does talk of the right to the use, management, and
preservation of the resources (art. 15. 1). Even under ILO Convention 169,
natural resources on indigenous peoples' land can continue to be exploited,
and dams for producing hydroelectric energy can continue to be built.

The UN Human Rights Commission and Endangered Peoples

The opposition of most states to improvements in the rights of indigenous
peoples also manifests itself in the status and evolution of the Working
Group on Indigenous Populations (UNWGIP), set up in September 1981.
The Working Group is a subsection of the Sub-Commission on Prevention
of Discrimination and Protection of (nationalities which states define as)
Minorities, which, in its turn, comes under the Economic and Social Council's Commission on Human Rights.[113]

The Working Group's tasks as determined by ECOSOC are: (a) to
monitor world-wide developments affecting the situation of indigenous
peoples and their protection from the point of view of the observance of

human rights and fundamental freedoms; (b) to keep a close watch on regulations affecting the rights of indigenous peoples; (c) to contribute to the standard-setting of such rights and to conduct studies into the matter.[114]

The membership of the Sub-Commission on the Protection of Minorities is made up of jurists and others specializing on these and more general human-rights affairs; that of the Human Rights Commission, on the other hand, is made up of government representatives, as is the case for almost all United Nations bodies. The Commission consists of five regional country-groups with a fixed number of members and alternating representation.[115] On matters concerning the rights of indigenous peoples, the Asian states traditionally adopt a negative position.

The Working Group on Indigenous Populations is made up of five members of the Sub-Commission with knowledge and experience in the field of indigenous rights. All the group's studies and proposals—which the Human Rights Commission is required to pass on to the UN General Assembly (the forum of government representatives)—expressly represent only the consensus of a body of experts on their own perception of indigenous rights. What then happens to this material in the Commission or the General Assembly is determined exclusively by government represen-tatives. In case of disagreement, the Commission's proposals are generally sent back to it to be worked on further. The regulatory procedure thus provides governments with a host of possibilities for getting disagreeable initiatives shelved. For this reason, the World Conference on Human Rights which took place in Vienna in summer 1993 recommended to the UN General Assembly that it set up within the UN system a permanent, independent forum for indigenous peoples, with more options and more authority than the existing Working Group.[116]

The UN Working Group on Indigenous Populations has now become the major forum through which representatives of endangered ethnic minorities and indigenous peoples address world opinion, from within the UN system.[117] The number of representatives of endangered peoples and also of government representatives/NGO observers, and inter-state or inter-national organizations and other institutions, has greatly increased. To begin with, those involved were mainly representatives of indigenous peoples from former settler-colonies (the two Americas, Australia, and New Zealand). Umbrella organizations that had emerged in the United States in the 1970s—organizations such as the International Indian Treaty Council, the World Council of Indigenous Peoples, and the Inuit Circum-polar Conference—held a prominent position.

The circle of participants from endangered and indigenous peoples steadily widened to include other regions. 1989 saw the advent, for the first time, of delegates from Africa; and 1990 that of delegates from the USSR.

In recent years, there has also been a stronger female presence, with women particularly prominent amongst the Inuit, the Maya, certain North American Indian organizations, and the Australian islanders. Indigenous umbrella-organizations attend sessions with their own jurists, and indigenous delegations can avail themselves of the support of staff from research institutes specializing in issues of indigenous rights. Together with other NGOs, they form an active lobby for indigenous interests.[118]

The UNWGIP is a forum to which complaints about government discrimination against indigenous peoples can be brought. Delegates of indigenous peoples often give deeply distressing reports about gross crimes against humanity—massacres, torture, persecution, and actual ethnocide (cultural genocide)—committed by governments and government forces of repression against 'their own' indigenous inhabitants; but they must sometimes also bear final witness to the silent passing of whole ethnic groups and their cultures. The complaints brought by representatives of the Yanomami Indians in Brazil, the Papuans in Irian Jaya, the Jumma in Bangladesh, and the Karen, Rohingya, and other peoples in Burma, all had an effect, either direct or indirect.[119] This is evidenced most notably in the condemnation of the Burmese regime by a number of UN bodies.[120]

The Struggles of the Indian Peoples of the Americas

The European colonization in the last 500 years resulted in widespread, coercive and rapid change. There were a few exceptions; unlike most parts of Latin America, much of the Caribbean coast of Central America,[121] of the southern most areas of South America and of Amazonia were never really colonized. As a result of the Spanish Conquest in the 16th century, a huge percentage of the indigenous population was wiped out by genocide and disease. The Indians of the Americas were reduced by the Spaniards in the South and by European settlers in the North from eighty million in 1492 to 3.5 million in 1750.

Genocide against Indians continued until today, e.g. in Paraguay, Guatemala, and Brazil. From 1500 onwards Africa lost 100 million people to slavery and raiding; most enslaved Africans died under genocidal conditions during mass transportation from Africa to the Americas. Large Indian groups were also subjected to slavery and forced into submission. European conquest and colonization ultimately led to the disappearance of many American Indian groups and to radical changes in the groups that survived. In Mexico, under the royal Laws of the Indies and under conditions of total neglect and segregation, indigenous peoples were able to retain some degree of collective autonomy and some property rights within their communities. Some Mexican Indian groups, mainly in the South amongst the many populous Mayan groups, were able to maintain pre-conquest self-government. The same applies to the Andes.

Amerindian Struggles for Autonomy, Recognition and Social Justice

Today nations and nationalities increasingly refuse assimilation and subjugation by dominant state societies. Central American indigenous peoples survived 500 years of genocide, assimilation and demanded integration into the Hispano-American (Mestizo or Ladino) society. Some native peoples are fighting for self-determination in the form of autonomy, self-governance or a degree of independence. There were several cases of armed ethnic conflict in the region: The Kuna in Panama in 1927, the Miskitu and Sumu in Nicaragua 1981–1987, during the times of the Sandinistas, the indigenous peoples of Chiapas, mainly from among Mayan Tzotzil and Tzeltal, since the 1994 revolt of the Zapatistas (Zapatista Front for National Liberation, EZLN), the Popular Revolutionary Army EPR-ELN in Guerrero and Oaxaca since June 1996 and the URNG (1960–96), based on strong support from indigenous communities, all fought in arms and attained some limited degree of autonomy, recognition or political reforms.

The organic mixture of ethno-nationalist and Indian issues with genuine left-wing issues is characteristic for most of these movements. It is noteworthy that the ethnic conflict of the Indian vs. Hispanic oligarchy and state is also a social class conflict, due to the simple fact that the Indian population is synonymous with the most impoverished and suppressed section of the population. All the three movement (EZNL, URNG and EPR) have ambitious and elaborate programs for a complete national overhaul, including recognition of indigenous rights, including self-rule, social and economic reform, and state, army and judicial reforms.

Their main aim was to do away with the absolute power of the small class of (land) owners, which exploit the mass of the Indian and Mestizo *campesinos* (small farmers) and farm workers and keep them in harsh socio-economic and political confinement. The oligarchy is the only group of beneficiaries within Central American society and economy. This privileged group holds most of the assets while the majority live in abject poverty and ignorance, deprived of any political participation.

The low level of support for the political and institutional system among the Indians reflects the humiliation and general neglect they continue to suffer. No surprise that absenteeism from elections and mistrust of state institutions is extremely high among Indians. Structural and institutionalized racism is based on a doctrine of Ladino superiority and 'Indio' inferiority. The indigenous peoples' right to self-determination, self-rule, and own juridical powers is not respected by any Central American state. The states' assertion of sovereignty over unconsenting peoples produced the main source of conflict.

Causes of Violent Conflict and Genocide: Hybrid Identity and Racism

The root-cause of conflict is the (neo-) colonial mission of spreading *Hispanidad*, a hybrid European-type of civilization, which was inherited by the *new states*. It included the idea of centralizing power and aimed at erecting homogenous nation states, based on assimilation of non-Hispanic groups. But in reality there is no single homogenous nation-state existing in the Americas. Recognizing multiplicity includes recognizing the dilemma of the Ladino societies' self-identification: It implies to accept the paradigm of cultural distance from the familiar Hispanic-based values and configurations, in order to overcome the blind spot of 'the Indian inside'. Recognizing multiplicity would consequently lead to a relationship of mutual respect between Ladinos, Indians and Blacks in Latin America. But instead the endless search for a so-called 'national identity' became the permanent project of the ruling classes in Latin America.

Structural and institutionalized racism is a basic explanatory factor for the indiscriminate nature and particular brutality with which military operations were carried out against Mayan communities in Chiapas, following the Zapatista revolt of 1994, and in western Guatemala, especially between 1981 and 1983, when more than half the massacres and scorched earth operations occurred. Similar to other Latin American cases the militarization of state and society was a strategic objective which was defined, planned and executed institutionally by the security forces (in Guatemala) or jointly with paramilitary gangs (Mexico). Pipil and Lenca (probably 20 percent of El Salvador's population) have suffered very high casualties in the war between FMLN guerrillas and the US-supported regime. 'Peasant disappearances' were systematically caused by state security and death squads. Pipil lands of high fertility were expropriated by 'land reforms'. Pipils are well above one million, but remain almost 'invisible'. Some Indian peoples struggled for survival. In Guatemala they suffered genocidal politics exercised by the small ruling oligarchy through its instrument, the armed forces, regardless of the form of governance (military or civilian).

Counter-insurgency against leftist guerrilla forces (EGP, FAR, ORPA; URNG) imposed 'total war' on the Indian peoples, with mass relocation into so-called model villages and forced recruiting of 'civilian self-defence patrols' (PAC), which were invented to confront Indians with their own people. Mayan Indians made up a large part of the guerrilla force. The Nobel prize for Rigoberta Menchù drew some attention of the western media on the sad situation of the indigenous peoples of Guatemala. In 1996, after internal armed conflict for 36 years, the guerrillas were made to sign a peace accord after a long negotiation process. But the accomplishments of the accord remained very limited. The outcome of the 1999 report of the Guatemalan truth commission, which was established through the Accord of Oslo on 23 June 1994, between the Guatemalan government and the rebels, and acted with support by the United Nations Verification Mission in Guatemala (MINUGUA), was minimal. The report describes atrocities committed by the armed forces 1962–1996 and how the Mayan peoples had become the collective enemy of the Guatemalan state in the years of the most bloody military confrontations (1978–1985). The gravity of the abuses suffered by Indian people has yet to become part of the national consciousness.[122] One of the chief organizers of the Guatemalan genocide, general Rios Montt, became president of parliament and so-far enjoys impunity.

Descendants of Old Civilizations

Mesoamerican Indian civilizations of the Maya, Mixtec, Zapotec, Olmec, Aztec and others look back on thousands of years of history, magnificent cultural development and political sophistication. Contrary to contemporary Amerindian societies these old civilizations were based on rigid class societies of large and complexly organized empires with a social division into nobles, priests, commoners, and slaves. Today's Indian societies in Mesoamerica are oscillating between a communitarian model and a political system that knows elders or caciques as leader. The Mayas transcend the territory of today's states; they represent an ancient civilization as well as a cluster of contemporary peoples living in southern Mexico, Belize, Guatemala, El Salvador and Honduras.[123] The Mixtec and Zapotec are ancient civilizations and peoples of southwestern Mexico. Mesoamerica is a region with common cultural elements stretching from actual Sinaloa (Mexico) to the gulf of Nicoya (Pacific) and Puerto Limon (Caribbean). The Mayan territory is some 325,000 square km, 900 km long and 500 km wide, covering much of the southern part of Mesoamerica.

Minority and Majority Indian Populations at the Edge

Population numbers for non-Mestizos depend on who is counting them and based on what criteria. Governments tend to minimize numbers while some indigenous peoples' organizations do the contrary. Mexico has 48 indigenous groups with above thirty million people among its population of over one hundred million; this is by far the largest Amerindian population in the Americas (higher than 40 percent) of the estimated seventy million Indians in twenty states of mainland Latin America. Underneath the seven Central American states of Guatemala, Belize, El Salvador, Honduras, Nicaragua, Costa Rica and Panama are over 50 indigenous nations and nationalities with a population of about ten million people, which are very unequally distributed. They live on 40 percent of the entire territory.[124] Arbitrary boundaries of today's American states often cut across the homelands of Indian peoples. The Miskitu and Sumu Indians are a special case since they were divided as late as in 1960. The traumatic developments from 1980 to 1984 renewed, rather than disrupted, the sense of common ethnicity among these two Indian peoples in Nicaragua.[125]

The **Ngobe** or Guaymíes (120,000) live in western Panama (2,500 in Coast Rica). The delimitations of the proposed autonomous area (*comarca*) are still under negotiation (since the 1980s); Latin settlers have invaded a part of their lands. Some Ngobe (Guaymí) work on banana plantations of United Brands, a US-based transnational corporation. The **Kuna** (70,000) live along the Caribbean of south-eastern Panama. An armed uprising in 1925 forced the new state of Panama to recognize the first autonomous Indian area (*Comarca* San Blas) in Latin America. The Kuna call their lands Kuna Yala. The state of Panama has developed a reasonably successful nationality policy for its indigenous peoples (15 percent of Panama's population) since the 1960s. The Kuna uprising in the 1920s gave way to the creation of autonomous areas (*comarcas*) for Panama's indigenous peoples such as for the Huahunán or Emberá Choco (18,000), Terribe-Buglede (2,500), and Bribri (reserve in Panama and Costa Rica), but not for the more populous Ngobe.

Whites Rule in All But a Few Countries—Indians Nowhere

In the region we find the four large macro-groups of Mestizos, White-Europeans, Afro-Americans and Amerindians. The most populous are the 380 million Ladinos followed by 230 million white Europeans and 120 million Afro-Americans (including 35 million in the USA). From Brazil through the Caribbean Basin to the Southern part of the USA, there is one more or less contiguous cultural space of Black America. Indigenous Americans are the fourth macro-group, numbering some 75 million people, more than half of it in Mexico and Central America. (North America contributes 2.5 million or 3.3 percent). Even though they are the majority of the citizen in four of twenty Latin American states, they rule nowhere: Not in Bolivia (an estimated 70–75 percent are Indians), not in Paraguay (70 percent), in Peru (52 percent) nor in Guatemala (50 percent). Additionally there are large Indian minorities in several states such as Ecuador (40 percent), El Salvador and Mexico 30 percent; Chile, Panama and Belize (10–15 percent). In Mexico the indigenous population makes up 75 percent in central and southern provinces. On January 1, 1994, Mayan Indians, organized by the Zapatista Liberation Army (*Ejercito Zapatista de Liberación Nacional*, EZLN), started to revolt and fight against 'a state of submission and almost colonial oppression' (4th Russell Tribunal).

Pan-Ladino nationalism could not unite 380 million Ibero-Americans in some 20 states; half of the *ladino*-dominated states are in Meso-Central America and the Caribbean, the other half in South America. However, European descendants continue to exert almost total hegemony on the Americas. Most Latin countries are still ruled by a small white minority. Although Whites are only a majority in a few countries (USA, Canada, Costa Rica, Chile and Argentina) they rule almost all countries.[126]

Until recently, no country and no region was ruled by Indigenous Americans. They continue to be at the bottom of the ethnic hierarchy. They had no power, anywhere, for none. In May 1990, the very first Indian government took an oath in Bilwi, capital of Yapti Tasba (the Región Autónoma Atlántico Norte, RAAN), Eastern Nicaragua.

Autonomy and Self-rule as Conflict Resolution

States hesitate to grant autonomy. This also has an economic rationale. Many Indian territories are of great strategic importance to the economies of the respective states they belong to. The reason is that these territories contain reserves of raw materials. The examples mentioned here involve special legal provisions for populations, which are of a relatively small size (ranging from 70,000 up to 500,000) but which in some cases inhabit and husband large stretches of land. As may be demonstrated by the example of the Nicaraguan region of Mosquitia, the ethnic composition of a population has a decisive influence on the political model that develops in each case. Along with eastern Nicaragua, Greenland represents the only model of indigenous self-governance with a Western-style parliamentary system and a multi-party set-up.

Issues of (collective) ownership of land by indigenous peoples, and the related issue of who has power over natural resources, were the subject of political debate in Nicaragua and also externally, within the framework of the international Indian movement. In the case of Mosquitia, the land issue was one of the factors that directly contributed to the outbreak of war. In the autonomy law issued in 1987 it has been agreed that revenues from natural resources will be distributed 'in just proportion'.

Nicaragua's scheme of regional autonomy for its two Caribbean areas (Región Autónoma Atlántico Norte: RAAN, and Región Autónoma Atlántico Sur: RAAS) embraces almost 50 percent of the national territory but only 9.5 percent of the population. The division into two regions precludes dominance by one ethnic group (the *Mestizos*). The two regions are multi-cultural in composition, comprising four indigenous communities, a somewhat largish African diaspora (mainly in RAAS), and a number of *Mestizos* who have immigrated to both regions. Land is the Indians' major resource (along with fishing). Conflicts over it have been going on for decades.

Autonomy in the two Caribbean regions is mentioned in the constitution and has existed on paper since September 1987 (law no. 28: *Estatuto de la Autonomía de las Regiones de la Costa Atlántica de Nicaragua*) and in concrete shape in a few pilot projects.[127] The rights and guarantees set out in law no. 28 are the confirmation of the multi-ethnic, pluricultural, and multilingual character of the *costeños* (coastal inhabitants) and stipulation of non-discrimination against them (in article 11.1), with well developed cultural rights (bilingualism in education and administration). Important is the recognition of the communal property of the indigenous communities (225 Miskitu, 32 Sumu and four Rama settlements), including the land, waters, and forests which they 'traditionally work'. Two autonomous regions were established and are independently administered by elected regional parliaments and executives appointed by these, with the parliaments having jurisdiction over the territory.[128] The right to self-identification was laid down in law; and the system is based on a balancing and combination of demographic representation and the formal principle of equality *vis-à-vis* the six ethnic communities benefiting from the law.[129]

The full implementation of the autonomy law was hampered by political conflicts and conflicts of interests from 1990 onwards. The political struggles between Sandinistas and the right parties in Managua are in a way continuing in eastern Nicaragua. Conservatives in central government regard the autonomy arrangement as going too far. One serious setback for the Indian movement was the dissension and infighting.

The Nicaraguan autonomy law is undoubtedly imperfect, but qualitatively speaking it is the best so far produced in Latin America; how much influence it will have, however, depends on whether and to what extent it is ignored or dismantled by Managua. Clear regulations to preclude non-action or obstruction on the part of the government are lacking. The weak-point lies in the area of regional council control over territory and resources: neither the respective competencies nor the share of revenues between regional and central government is clearly laid down. But the process of rectifying the legal weak-points and obscurities has been dragged out.

The case of Panama is also worth mentioning. Panama is regarded as progressive when it comes to recognition of certain Indian rights and the granting of cultural autonomy (though not bilingual instruction in schools). Territorial self-governance existed for years for the Kuna and Emberá Choco, but not for the more numerous Ngobe (Guaymí) Indians, whose area—due to be designated a *comarca*—has been overrun by large numbers of *Mestizo* settlers and banana-companies.

The best-known area is Kuna Yala, the 'land of the Kuna' (official name Comarca San Blas), with its reservation-style system of autonomy and self-governance for 45,000 Kuna Indians. They inhabit a territory extending from El Porvenir up to the Colombian border—where there are also Kuna Indians living—and including some 400 Caribbean coral islands. In Kuna Yala, too, penetration by *Mestizo* settlers, loggers, and drug-dealers (from Columbia) is difficult to halt. The Kuna largely manage their own affairs, only the school system is still run in Spanish. Thanks to their being relatively sealed off from the outside world, their rigid socio-cultural community has survived. Their subsistence system is intact but the economy is partly dependent on external factors; unequal bartering goes on.

Native inhabitants have guaranteed representation in the Panamanian parliament; this applies to the Kuna and Ngobe (Guaymí). However, the *caciques/congreso* system of internal Indian organization has its shortcomings. Where necessary, it can be manipulated more easily by the authorities than can an elected representative body (such as those in Mosquitia in Nicaragua); on the other hand, it keeps traditions alive.

In the case of the Ngobe (Guaymí) Indians, the authorities have dragged their feet over autonomy negotiations in a series of protracted conflicts over land and in tussles over the division of political-cum-administrative competencies. Contributing factors have included, on the one hand, the size of the territory claimed, which extends over several provinces, and, on the other, the disunity, poor organization, and lack of militancy among the Ngobe. The indigenous peoples responded to the government's 'divide and rule' policy, and the various Indian congresses in Panama formed a union.

In Mexico the response to the 1994 Indian revolt has not yet brought autonomy for the Indians, except the *de facto* autonomy they gained in the struggle. A main root-cause of the ongoing struggle lies in the unequal distribution of land. In the southernmost Mexican state of Chiapas the big cattle ranchers use almost half of the territory as pastureland. In contrast, a large number of campesinos work on small plots of generally unfertile land. The constitution of 1917 enshrined land reform. Small peasants were promised *ejidos*, pieces of the communal farming land. In Chiapas much less land was redistributed than in the rest of the country. In the 1960s the struggle for the promised but never distributed land became violent.

At the beginning of 1994, the primarily indigenous Zapatista Army of National Liberation (EZLN) staged an armed uprising in the south-eastern Mexican state of Chiapas, demanding democracy, liberty, and justice for all Mexicans. The EZLN issued the first of many *Declarations from the Lacandon Jungle*. Six municipalities around San Cristóbal de las Casas were taken by the rebels. After two weeks of heavy fighting, with high casualties a cease-fire was declared. Direct talks between the EZLN and the federal government, moderated by San Cristóbal's bishop, reached an agreements to 24 demands of the EZLN but excluded political issues on a national level. Talks and repression and a build-up of the Mexican armed forces were on and off. After the failure of the military operation in 1995, the Mexican Congress approved dialogue with EZLN. From fall 1995 talks started on Indigenous Rights and Culture in San Andrés Sacamch'en de los Pobres (Larrainzar), a Tzotzil Zapatista community in the highlands north of San Cristóbal. In August 1996 the talks were suspended. The tentative agreement was not implemented. Militarization once again replaced dialogue. About 30 percent of the national army (60,000 soldiers) is based in Chiapas.

With the loss of the July 2000 election the Party of the Institutionalized Revolution, PRI, left after 71 years in power, but the chance for a just solution was not used. The winner, Vicente Fox of the Party of National Action, PAN, admitted international observers into the country and ordered the withdrawal of Mexican Army from different parts of Chiapas. The EZLN accepted to resume negotiations for peace and indigenous rights. Although they reached some agreement on the rights of indigenous communities, they still had to face the PRI majority in Congress in order to ratify any legislation for indigenous rights. In March 2001 a large group of the indigenous people marched to Mexico, in support for constitutional reforms. EZLN spokesman, Sub-commander Marcos, spoke to a huge crowd at Mexico City's revolution square. The April 2001 a constitutional reform on indigenous rights and culture was approved by the Congress of the Union. The EZLN rejected the reform, saying it went behind the agreement reached in San Andres and does not answer the demands of the Indian peoples of Mexico. The reform serves to block the exercise of indigenous rights; it disregards the mobilization and the unprecedented consensus, which the indigenous struggle achieved at that time.

The Zapatistas brought to the forefront what is the ugly side of Mexico: poverty, social inequality and racism. This primarily indigenous organization rose up in arms for democracy, liberty and justice for all Mexicans. Of all the Mexican peoples, the indigenous are the most forgotten. EZLN raised the recognition of indigenous rights and culture as an important demand, which found echo throughout the country and internationally. The indigenous issue signifies, for the EZLN, an unfinished debt of Mexico. The Zapatistas do not want independence from Mexico; they want to be part of Mexico, to be Mexican indigenous. Up until now, the Indians were treated as second-class citizens, or as a hindrance for the country, but they want to be first-class citizens and to be part of the country's development, without ceasing to be indigenous.

Protection of Indigenous Peoples: The Paradigm of Collective Rights

The concerns and problems of indigenous peoples are now part of the United Nations agenda. Indigenous issues reach a broader public through large-scale UN conferences such as those on world ecology (the 'Earth Summit' in Rio de Janeiro 1992), human rights (Vienna 1993), world population (Cairo 1994), social development (Copenhagen 1995), the situation of women (Beijing 1995), the housing issue ('Habitat II', Istanbul 1996), the millennium gathering 2000, anti-racism (Durban 2001) and sustainable development (Johannesburg 2002). Unfortunately the outcomes of the latter two world summits were weak; in both cases (as in many other summits, as in Rio 1992) the United States and a few allies went against the rest of the world and blocked progress in the critically important fields of human rights protection and environmentally friendly development.

A whole series of resolutions and declarations have now been passed on matters of concern (or partial concern) to indigenous peoples; but unlike the International Labour Organization, with its Convention 169 in favour of indigenous peoples, the United Nations still does not have its own, comparable instrument of international law for protecting members of indigenous nationalities.

The standard-setting activities that are part of WGIP sessions involve publicly conducted normative debates about the problem of discrimination against indigenous peoples—as documented, for example, in the five-volume study by José R. Martínez Cobo.[130] Legal norms are also elaborated via concrete projects concerned with regulating the rights of indigenous peoples. The UNWGIP also discharges its functions via large-scale projects lasting several years. Within the context of new instruments of international law, its most important task has been the drafting of a 'Universal Declaration on the Rights of Indigenous Peoples', which has involved direct participation by delegates from indigenous peoples and also support from relevant experts. The status of the declaration—as far as those affected is concerned—is reminiscent of that of the Universal Declaration of Human

Rights.[131] One particularly significant feature is the paradigm of collective rights. As the ten years of work on the declaration came to an end, the chairperson commented, with some emotion, that: 'Indigenous participants are the life blood of our work'.[132]

In spring 1995 the progressive line pursued by the UN Sub-Commission on Prevention of Discrimination and Protection of Minorities suffered a severe set-back. Contrary to the usual consensus-based conventions of the UN system, the member states represented in the Human Rights Commissions took a majority decision in favour of what amounted to an act of sabotage. The draft declaration was not forwarded, as expected (with whatever modifications there might have had to be), to the General Assembly to be voted on; instead, a second working group was charged with carrying out further 'revisions'. Access to this second working group was intended to be managed in a more restrictive way. Furthermore, no time-limit was specified, which would seem to indicate that the project is to be put on the back burner.[133] And this is what actually happened; in December 2002 this working group will have its 8th annual secession—and no end is in sight.

The decision to create a new working group on minorities, with an initial budget for 1995, was probably also taken with a view to diminishing the strength of the Working Group on Indigenous Populations.[134] The latter had become too large and influential for some states' liking. That states should have reacted in this way to a promising UN project in the field of human rights and the rights of peoples demonstrates, yet again, the great divide between states and peoples, and the huge fears which any kind of aspiration to sovereignty arouses in many states.[135] The opposition line-up was familiar: most countries in Asia and Latin America were against acceptance of the declaration. The Latin American group (especially Chile, Peru, and Bolivia) expressed concern about 'far-reaching' demands by indigenous peoples; in this they were supported by all the colonial powers (especially France) and the former white settler-colonies, the USA, Canada, Australia, New Zealand; the latter three otherwise liked to see themselves as protectors of indigenous peoples. Australia explained that it was against the right to self-determination because it could lead to 'modification of national territories';[136] following the positive outcome of the Mabo case, this may happen via another route.

The recognition of indigenous peoples' right to self-determination marked a watershed; that right is unequivocally opposed by these states because they are afraid of losing something. In contrast, the African states concede more rights to indigenous peoples because they themselves were colonized. The Nordic countries maintain an open attitude on indigenous issues but do not openly promote the right to self-determination. Only Liechtenstein, Switzerland, and Ethiopia have spoken in favour of recognition of the right to self-determination, including the possibility of the creation of new states—on Geneva, behind closed doors.[137] Ethiopia, it is known, denies the Oromo and Somali their right to self-determination.

Another on-going long-term project of the UNWGIP is a global study on treaties between indigenous peoples and states. The final report for this, originally due in 1996, could not be published before the 1997 session and was finally tabled at the UNWGIP 16th session in July 1998.[138] The study's analysis of 'modern' agreements—especially those concluded in recent decades in Canada and Australia—is one feature in particular that could have direct effects.

Idea and Reality of a 'Permanent Forum for Indigenous Peoples'

Ideas for a permanent forum for indigenous peoples have been under consideration for many years but entered a critical phase in 1995. Following an expert meeting on this theme, held in Copenhagen in June 1995, the ideas were translated into more concrete terms.[139] Questions about the constitution of such a forum—its mandate, structure, composition (or eligibility), institutional status, activities, and funding—were discussed.[140]

The consensus over the years was that any future forum for indigenous peoples should come directly under the United Nations Economic and Social Council. It should have a broad mandate, with one of the central tasks being to co-ordinate all UN activities relating to indigenous peoples. An annual report by the forum on the situation of indigenous peoples across the world could become a highly regarded publication. If there were an open membership, romantic notions of a 'Universal Council of Indigenous Peoples' would not be so outlandish. The best that could be hoped for, however, was that the forum should be composed of equal numbers of representatives of indigenous peoples and representatives of UN member states with equal power. This, however, did not materialize. Another question that had to be resolved is whether the indigenous organizations and the NGOs could nominate the representatives of the indigenous peoples or whether states would do this; the result was a bad compromise, giving the indigenous peoples' representatives consultative voice.[141]

The General Assembly's 'Decade of the World's Indigenous Peoples' in 1995 should have begun with a positive resolution of these questions.[142] The decision came five years later with the Economic and Social Council (ECOSOC) Resolution 2000/22 of 28 July 2000 under the title 'Establishment of a Permanent Forum on Indigenous Issues'. The forum's change of name soon turned out to be quite a wholesale programmatic change. The forum deals with issues of concern for indigenous peoples, without acknowledging their existence; it's a forum on indigenous issues as seen by experts, not a forum for indigenous peoples to convey their issues to the UN system. Positive changes, if any, are symbolic, e.g. the seating order.[143]

Though the forum is an organ of the ECOSOC (not the Commission on Human Rights) it is nevertheless composed of representatives of Member States as any other UN body; representatives of indigenous organizations continue to be admitted selectively as observers who are entitled to make statements but not decisions—that remains the unchallenged right of states. Accompanied by high expectations, after years of waiting for such a forum, the outcome seems meagre and merely symbolic. In order to function the forum needs a secretariat and its own budget.

Draft Universal Declaration on the Rights of Indigenous Peoples

A path-breaking clear-worded declaration was to have been given its final reading in July 1994, at the Working Group's 12th session, and was to have been adopted by the General Assembly in New York after the group's 13th session, towards the end of 1995/beginning of 1996.[144] The General Assembly had already adopted a wide-ranging, generally phrased resolution on the Decade of the World's Indigenous Peoples in December 1994; it meticulously avoided the term 'peoples' (implying a right to self-determination)—'people' refers only to human beings.[145] Unlike treaties and pacts, declarations by the community of states as a whole do not have to be ratified. The assent of the General Assembly would have been the last staging-post before the declaration of principles came into effect. Hopes were flying high, only to be dashed by the member states of the Human Rights Commission, after ten years of hard work. Ten years of work were not thrown in the dustbin directly but the draft was given to an open-ended new working group with the sole task to revise the draft, thus to water it down; it did so for seven years already and there is no end in sight.

The drafting of a Universal Declaration on the Rights of Indigenous Peoples was a complex and ambitious project that occupied whole teams of experts. The adoption planned for 1992 was rendered impossible by the antagonistic positions of indigenous peoples and states. Even in 1993 —the United Nations 'Year of the World's Indigenous People'—the official motto about 'New Partnership' was shown to be hollow. When representatives of over 200 indigenous peoples gathered for the UNWGIP session in Geneva in August 1993, the version of the declaration with which they were presented for revision was one that fell below the standards of 1990 and 1991.[146] Despite numerous delaying tactics (beginning in 1988), and despite further ugly manœuvres and the severe setback of 1995, UNWGIP standard-setting will continue to exert a direct influence on political decision-making and legislation in a whole series of states. A few isolated states made no attempt at all to oppose the 1992 draft, and indeed went beyond the proposals of the legal experts and, in some cases, of the indigenous delegates themselves.[147]

Yet a General Assembly resolution of March 1993 on the 'Year of Indigenous People' contained only platitudes.[148] It talks only of 'persons belonging to national or ethnic, religious and linguistic minorities'. Problems pertaining to group rights continue to be viewed from the perspective not of collective but of individual rights.[149] The preservation of traditional customs in the folkloristic sense is one thing; the right to retain one's own culture (cultural autonomy), to speak, and be taught, in one's own language (the resolution talks ambiguously of instruction in the mother tongue), to run one's own radio-stations, and not to be forced to deny one's identity, is quite another; these poles delimit the range of possible 'concessions' on the part of states. On the central issue of political co-determination by minorities (art. 3.3), the resolution refers to compatibility with the legal provisions of the country concerned, instead of setting out guidelines for these.

The Paradigm of Collective Rights

Concrete demands relating to the principle of self-determination are much more difficult to enforce. This is especially true of the paradigm of the collective rights of indigenous peoples, their right to dissent or assent, the safeguarding of their ownership of land and resources, and respect for the spirit and content of signed agreements—something that is of particular relevance for North American Indians. More account should be taken of the original contribution which indigenous peoples can make to the debate about communitarism.[150] The far-reaching implications of the indigenous paradigm of collective rights, which runs counter to the modern Eurocentric conception of law, merit particular attention.

Collective rights (e.g. in relation to the ownership of land) are a centuries-old tradition in the political struggles of indigenous peoples, especially the Indians of Latin America. To have them sanctioned in law would constitute a milestone on the path to acknowledgement of these peoples' otherness. The community law of indigenous peoples is both an alternative and a counter-position to positive law, which structurally denies traditional laws. In many countries of Asia and Latin America, community law functions in practice as an additional source for legal interpretations.

Indian movements in the Andean states of Chile, Bolivia, Peru, Ecuador, and Columbia, which have high percentages of Indians in their populations (e.g. 85 percent in Bolivia), are fighting for recognition of collective land-rights and village self-government. This will not remain without its effects on the structure of the state and on methods of production.[151] A central role in this struggle is being played by the two great Indian peoples of the Quichua and Aymara, who have a combined population of over 30 million. In response, the Bolivian state is reforming its constitution and others of its laws.[152] This adjustment from colonial to present-day realities was overdue.

The concept of ethno-development (*etno-desarrollo*) was elaborated in the late 1970s, mainly in Mexico, as a concrete expression of the paradigm of collective rights. It took shape under the influence of the Latin American debate about ethnicity and of the increasing strength of the Indian movements. Buvollen supposes that the term developed in reaction to the traditionally indigenist, Marxist, and ethno-political variants of the highly developed ethnicity debate in Mexico. It was taken up by the ecological movement, which did not emerge until later in Latin America; it implies a balanced traditional relationship to nature, as opposed to the exploitative Western (or colonial) ideology of development.[153] The roots of the concept are to be found in Gramsci and his notion of national culture.[154]

The concept had already been introduced as part of the San José declaration of December 1981 (art. 3). In this, ethno-development is understood to mean extending and consolidating the cultural spheres of culturally distinct (or non-dominant) societies by strengthening these societies' autonomous power of decision over their own development, in the sense of practical self-determination at every level, ranging from (self-) governance to secession. This concept sees every ethnic group as a nation in the sense that it represents its own political-cum-administrative unit, decides on its territory collectively, and secures more and more decision-making power and autonomy for itself.

Collective rights are already acknowledged in the constitutions of some states; in practice, this gives rise to a variety of types of law on autonomy.[155] To many observers, it seems only a matter of time before the paradigm of collective rights finds similar recognition in international law. The question that begins to dawn with the paradigm notion, however, is whether such an approach would be compatible with the Euro-centric way of thinking on which international law is based, or whether the law would not then acquire a different 'face'.

Constructive Regulations between States and Peoples

The conduct of a global study on treaties, accords, agreements, and other constructive arrangements between states and indigenous peoples is one of the UNWGIP's major on-going projects. The theme is potentially a far-reaching one: regulations providing for autonomy or a federal system, for example, could be constructive. The study was recommended at the Working Group's fifth session, in summer 1987, and, after persistent obstruction by certain governments, was finally commissioned by the UN Human Rights Commission in March 1988.[156] The Special Rapporteur for the study is the Cuban jurist Miguel Alfonso Martínez.

In 1990, a working paper and two questionnaires were produced. As expected, states' willingness to co-operate was limited. The Sub-Commission on the Protection of Minorities did decide, in 1991, to present governments with questionnaires a second time, but the outcome was extremely disheartening.[157] In 1992 came an initial report, containing substantial information on the history of the contractual process (with numerous examples); and in 1995 a second report, in which Martínez made observations on the minorities/indigenous peoples distinction and on the disempowerment, assimilation, and marginalization to which both, but more especially the latter, were subject.[158] Because of the tardy response of states and the mass of material made available by the indigenous peoples, the Martínez study could not be completed as planned.

Finally in mid 1999, after working on the treaty study for nine years, the Special Rapporteur delivered his 3-parts final report.[159] In a rare attempt to synthesise his findings, Martínez first analysed the origins of the treaty process and the role of treaties in the history of the European colonial expansion. Secondly, he then explored the contemporary significance of these instruments of international law, 'including questions regarding the succession of states, national recognition of treaties, and the views of indigenous peoples in these issues'.[160] Thirdly, he went further to address the 'potential value of all those instruments as the base for governing the future relationships between indigenous peoples and states'. The Special Rapporteur did not stop here but recommended mechanisms of control, which shall be institutionalized in the future in order to secure the implementation of such treaties and constructive arrangements.

Constitutional conflict-resolution, conventions, and treaties—so historical experience would seem to indicate—afford only inadequate protection to indigenous peoples. This is because such agreements, when not simply violated, as they have been, repeatedly and blatantly, in the past, get reinterpreted to accord with the requirements of *realpolitik*. (Neo-) Colonial power politics were leading to a 'gradual but incessant erosion of the indigenous peoples' original sovereignty', transforming the 'rule of law' into the 'law of the rulers'.[161] The European states and their settler colonies, later co-operating in the framework of the League of Nations, practically determined what was the 'rule of law' and played the decisive part resulting in the devaluation of the treaty process between states and peoples.

Therefore, one of the noblest future tasks of the United Nations is to safeguard that past and present agreements between states and peoples will be enabled to take their rightful place in international law. This primarily applies to pacts granting autonomy, and to regulations laying down forms of self-determination. The inability of modern international law to recognize such agreements betrays the presence of Euro-centric, or indeed racist, conceptions of tribalism, as mediated by positivist jurisprudence. The concept of sovereignty was applied only to 'civilized nations'; tribal territories were therefore *terra nullius*.

In the part of America colonized by the Spanish and Portuguese, notions of 'inferior societies'[162] led to the most brutal oppression and extermination of the Indians in the areas that were reached first (Cuba, Haiti, the Dominican Republic). In the areas reached last, on the southern tip of Latin America, agreements—such as that with the Mapuche—were concluded. The same pattern is found, on an east-to-west scale, in the English (and, I believe, the French and Spanish) colonization of North America.

The discriminatory nature of international law finds blatant expression in almost all the agreements between European powers and indigenous peoples on three continents—in the criteria used, in the general conceptions of law, and in the institutions created. The sole purpose of these kinds of discriminatory concepts was to confer a measure of 'legal authority' on the economic and political interests of the dominant societies, and to lend the European looting expeditions abroad some semblance of legitimacy.

Concepts of law are, by nature, bound up with the time in which they occur; they are adapted to the prevailing conditions, the dominant interests, and the spirit of the age. In this connection, medieval, mostly fictitious, legal concepts[163] such as papal 'donation', 'first settlement' or 'discovery', which were based on straightforward violence, extortion, or deception, contrast with later, paternalistic, 'fiduciary' approaches.[164] The contrast with the older Enlightenment traditions that was present in 19th century philosophy of law, which upheld the status of indigenous peoples as legal subjects, was also manifest in the new technocratic paternalism of trusteeship.[165] Yet medieval conceptions of law—such as conquest and cession, or relations regulated by settlement—continue, to this day, to characterize the extremes of behaviour towards extra-European and indigenous peoples, and still represent the full spectrum of state activity.

Notes

1. A reformed OAU would lie, structurally speaking, somewhere between a community shaped into a free-trade area (similar to ASEAN) and an integrated African economic area (rather like the EU after full implementation of the Maastricht treaties).
2. The figure 58 was an estimate proposed by Freedom House: 'Related Territories', *Freedom Review* (1995), 2: 17. The only land-based territories mentioned in the list (in addition to the many islands) are: Kashmir, Tibet, Nagorno-Karabakh (now part of

Armenia), Iraqi Kurdistan, Palestine, Western Sahara, and former autonomous territories of Serbia (Kosovo, Vojvodina). Russia's 20 autonomous republics do not figure.

3. See details in Scherrer 1998*a*: ch. 1. On Oromo diaspora see Scherrer/Bulcha 2002.

4. The war in Chad was also brought to an end. Here, one minority-regime with a narrow ethnic base in the north replaced another (Idris Déby replaced Hissein Habré).

5. George Philip, *Weltatlas* (Hamburg: Xenos), 1998; National Geographic, *Atlas of the World* (Washington, D.C.: NGS); *Encyclopaedia Britannica*, online.

6. The suggestion of a minimum population of 10,000–100,000 has met with criticism (Emile Payne *et al.*, 'Report', unpub., SEF Symposium on Global Governance, 1992).

7. The notion of completeness is often taken to entail that of self-sufficiency or even autarky. Within the framework of the international division of labour, and often also in terms of the domestic economy, this makes little sense.

8. Under the influence of various major Western powers (the USA, France), the UN has up to now tolerated the scandalous disregard of its resolutions. Instead of the planned 3,000–strong MINURSO, only 400 UN troops were deployed, and these were neutralized by Morocco's army. After 17 years of war, Morocco was still refusing to engage in direct negotiations with the Frente Polisario, was playing for time, and continued to bring in settlers unhindered into the Sahara (in preparation for the referendum!). The UN asked for the old civil registry to be taken as basis to determine who would be eligible to vote. After this blow Morocco, with tacit support by the USA and France, managed to block the decolonization process completely.

9. The Luba (18 percent of the population) already ruled themselves as a state-nation in pre-colonial times—as did the Bakongo (16 percent of population in Congo-DR, 50 percent in Congo)—in the form of well-organized multi-ethnic kingdoms. The Bakongo traded with the Portuguese, and the latter's emissaries told of the flourishing kingdom of the Bakongo.

10. Gellner's passing remark about stateless societies, for whom the problem of nationalism allegedly does not pose itself, belongs in this context: Gellner 1983: 4.

11. Numbers of UNHCR cared refugees 1990–2001: 1990: 14,916,498; 1991: 17,209,722; 1992: 17,007,483; 1993: 18,998,777; 1994: 23,033,000; 1995: 27,437,000; 1996: 26,103,200; 1997: 22,729,000; 1998: 22,376,300; 1999: 21,459,620; 2000: 22,257,340; 2001: 21,793,300; The rise to a record 27.4 million in 1995 was due to a succession of large-scale movements caused by regional conflicts (mainly in the Great Lakes region, Bosnia and the Caucasus) and a surge in the repatriation of refugees from the Cold War period (Cambodia, El Salvador, Guatemala, Mozambique). See http://www.unhcr.ch/ See also UNHCR, *The State of the World's Refugees*. Biannual reports. Geneva: UNHCR var. years.

12. The 3.8 million Palestinians are covered by a separate mandate of the U.N. Relief and Works Agency for Palestine Refugees in the Near East (UNRWA); hence, they are not included in the UNHCR reports. A smaller number of Palestinians outside the UNWRA area of operations, such as those in Iraq or Libya, are considered to be of concern to UNHCR and show up in the world refugee reports.

13. The main cause of refugee movements is still civil war. (Nuscheler 1994: 32). The focal point of the world-wide flow of refugees in the mid 1990s was Africa, esp. Central Africa, i.e. Rwanda and Burundi (ibid. 30–3). In addition to millions cross-border refugees officially recognized by the UNHCR (ibid. Table 4 , also 34) and the millions ('much greater number') of internally displaced persons, 'there are between 20 and 25 million refugees…on the move' (mainly in West Africa).

14. Afghanistan: 3,580,400; Burundi: 568,000; Iraq: 512,800; Sudan: 490,400; Bosnia-Herzegovina: 478,300; Somalia: 447,800; Angola: 432,700; Sierra Leone: 400,800; Eritrea: 376,400; Viet Nam: 370,300. See 'Origin of Major Refugee populations in 2000', in UNHCR: *The State of the World's Refugees*. Geneva: UNHCR 2000.

15. Maurice Torrelli, *Le Droit international humanitaire* (Paris: Presses universitaires de France, 1985).
16. A UN General Assembly resolution of 12 Dec. 1973 declared such wars to be legitimate and fully in accord with the principles of international law because they constitute a realization of the right to self-determination, which is one of the supreme principles in the UN Charter.
17. The first set of regulations was drafted by representatives of 26 states, the second by representatives of 44.
18. The four Geneva Conventions of 1949 were created to deal with international armed conflicts. They stipulate that civilians and people no longer taking an active part in hostilities (e.g. wounded or captured combatants) must be spared. They also set out the role of the International Committee of the Red Cross. Article 3, common to all four conventions, authorizes the ICRC to offer its services in the event of non-international armed conflict and accords basic protection to the victims of such situations. The protection provided by the conventions applies to the different categories of persons suggested in their titles: Convention (I) for the Amelioration of the Condition of the Wounded and Sick in Armed Forces in the Field (Geneva, 12 Aug. 1949); Convention (II) for the Amelioration of the Condition of Wounded, Sick and Shipwrecked Members of the Armed Forces at Sea (Geneva, 12 Aug. 1949); Convention (III) relative to the Treatment of Prisoners of War (Geneva, 12 Aug. 1949); Convention (IV) relative to the Protection of Civilian Persons in Time of War (Geneva, 12 Aug. 1949). The 2 additional protocols of 1977 are the most important supplement to the conventions. Of especial importance is the 'Protocol Additional to the Geneva Conventions of 12 August 1949, and relating to the Protection of Victims of Non-international Armed Conflicts' (Protocol II) (8 June 1977). Protocol II was elaborated by state representatives in four sessions of the 'Diplomatic Conference on the Reaffirmation and Development of International Humanitarian Law applicable in Armed Conflicts' (Geneva, 1974–7). Instead of the 47 articles proposed by the ICRC, the conference adopted only 28. Protocol II entered into force on 7 Dec. 1978. Its aim is to limit the use of violence and protect the civilian population by strengthening the rules governing the conduct of hostilities in cases of intra-state mass violence—which has produced about 80 percent of all victims of violent conflicts since 1945. As of 15 May 1998, the number of states party to the Geneva Conventions of 1949 was 188 and the number party to Additional Protocol I was 150. The number having made the declaration under art. 90 of Protocol I was only 53 (the latest to declare was Greece, on 4 Feb. 1998) and the number of state parties to the Additional Protocol II was 142. By comparison, the United Nations has 190 member states.
19. See 'ICRC Action outside the Context of Non-international Armed Conflicts and Internal Disturbances' in the CICR, *Manuel*.
20. Comité International de la Croix-Rouge (CICR), Les protocoles additionnels aux conventions de Genève du 12 août 1949 (Geneva, 1977).
21. 'Conflits de caractère interne', in CICR, *Manuel du délégué* (Geneva, 1982), 222–30.
22. National Red Cross Societies deal with health provision, mostly in an auxiliary capacity, and more rarely as service-providers (this latter function is exercised by the Red Cross in the CIS states, where it supplies much of the health care). As the Red Cross umbrella organization, the League co-ordinates international disaster-relief.
23. CICR, *Manuel*, 29–30 (n. 23).
24. In the case of the extremely brutal war of terror conducted by RENAMO against the civilian population and the FRELIMO-led central government, it was the ICRC that established the first informal contacts between the parties, via its chief delegate in Nairobi, and these led to secret negotiations lasting several months. The Catholic church subsequently figured as the official mediator. The UN worked on the base thus provided

and was able to record a much-needed success (following the disasters in Angola and Western Sahara).

25. This is my simplified quintessence about a complex juridical mechanism.

26. The wars in Africa were the main reason for the flight of over one third of refugees (see countries of origin in UNHCR 2000; in addition, 35 to 40 million cross-border migrants (half the world total) were on the move in sub-Saharan Africa alone. See Nuscheler 1994: 30.

27. Nuscheler 1994: 46–7.

28. Art. 33. 1 of the 1951 Geneva convention on refugees states that: 'No Contracting State shall expel or return ('refouler') a refugee in any manner whatsoever to [somewhere] where his life or freedom would be threatened on account of his race, religion, nationality, membership of a particular social group or political opinion.'

29. CICR, *Manuel*, 160 ff. (POWs), 185 ff. (search/tracing), 194 ff. (aid/humanitarian aid).

30. 'UNPO offers an international forum for occupied nations, indigenous peoples, minorities, and even oppressed majorities who are struggling to regain their lost countries, preserve their cultural identities, protect their basic human and economic rights and safeguard the natural environment.' (See: http://www.unpo.org/)

31. See interview with Dr Michael van Walt van Praag, Secretary-General of UNPO, Geneva 1994, in: 'The struggle for Self-Determination and the role of international NGOs'; in ECOR: *Struggle for Survival in the Decade of the World's Indigenous Peoples. Analysis and Reports from the Frontiers.* ECOR 17. Moers: IEFK-IRECOR 1998, 60–66. Also: ECOR 9. 1997: 177–83. UNPO 1993 and Walt van Praag 1993.

32. Only two of UNPO's members are American Indian nations: the Mapuche (Chile/Argentina) and the Lakota (USA). There are four members from Africa: Zanzibar/Pemba; the Ogoni in south-eastern Nigeria; the Batwa pygmies in Rwanda, and—since April 1997—Cabinda (see: UNPO 1997).

33. Four of the members are so-called minorities from eastern Europe: Albanians in Kosovo/Serbia; Greeks in Albania; Hungarians in Romania; and the Muslim Sanjak between Serbia and Montenegro. From western Europe, there are the Danes of Skåneland or Scania in southern Sweden (comprising Halland, Skåne, and Blekinge) and the Inkeri. Certain CIS areas with indigenous populations, often of multi-ethnic composition and mostly former Soviet republics in the European part of the former USSR, are represented: the Abkhaz (now *de facto* independent from Georgia); the Chechens, Ingushetians, Chuvash, Komi, Mari, Udmurts, and Volga Tatars (Tatarstan), all seven of whom are located in the Russian Federation; and the Tatars of the Crimea (part of the Ukraine).

34. About half the members of UNPO (total number 1998–2002 was 52) come from Asia and the Asia-Pacific area. There are: three members from western Asia (Kurdistan, the Turkomans of Iraq, and the Assyrians in Iraq and the Middle East; four members from British India (Karen in Burma, Naga (NSCN) in north-east India, the Jumma—a group of indigenous peoples— of the Chittagong Hill Tracts, and the Shan of Burma); the Sakha-Yakutians in Siberia; two minority nationalities in China (the Tibetans and the Uighur); the indigenous peoples of Taiwan; the Cordillera peoples in the Philippines; Melanesian areas (Bougainville—part of Papua-New Guinea, the Southern Moluccas, and West Papua); East Timor (became independent 2002) and Acheh (ANLF)—these last four were colonized by Indonesia; the indigenous peoples of Australia; two Polynesian South Sea peoples, the Kanaka Maoli in Hawai and the Maohi in French Polynesia (temporarily also Belau, bound by treaty to the USA but now UN member).

35. After the founding general-secretary Dr van Walt van Praag left, a representative of the Australian Aboriginal peoples followed but was largely mismanaging the office. UNPO stagnated and was almost bankrupt when Erkin Alptekin, representative of the Uyghur people, who was living in exile in Germany, took over and revamped the organization. In January 2002 the UNPO Steering Committee, at its 28th meeting held in The Hague,

appointed Karl von Habsburg, a scion of Austrian nobility and Christian Democratic politician (formerly with the right-wing Pan European Movement), as director general.

36. See UNPO 1991: 7. In 'Who can be a UNPO member?', there is a 5-point list, point 4 of which calls for the 'promotion of non-violence'.

37. UNPO should make greater use of experts and independent observers in considering applications for membership. The standards in regard to democracy and human rights called for by members should also be expanded. The responsible bodies in this connection are the 8–member UNPO steering committee and the secretariat. Both sometimes seem overworked.

38. Zanzibar was admitted by UNPO as an under-represented nation, which makes little sense: it is the smaller part of the only functioning federation in Africa—Tanzania—which was formed from the islands of Zanzibar and the mainland, Tanganyika. Both the president of Tanzania (Ali Hassan Mwinyi) and of the OAU (Salim Ahmed Salim) are Zanzibaris. Zanzibaris hold leading positions in the ruling CCM party and the army. The islands (Zanzibar and Pemba) have received substantial transfer-payments since their major export (cloves) suffered a dramatic fall in price on the world market. Kiswahili, widely spoken on Zanzibar, was made the national language, and language for school and official purposes in Tanzania. There is now a multi-party system in force. The former opposition Zanzibar Democratic Alliance (ZADA) is meanwhile in alliance with the Civic United Front (CUF).

39. See UNPO 1996. The lengthy report focuses on the election process, which the presidential candidate for the opposition party Seif Sharif Hamad (who was at that time UNPO president and a former CCM top leader) lost to Salmin Amour of the ever ruling Chama Cha Mapinduzi (CCM) party. The outcome of the presidential elections of Zanzibar has been contested from several sides. The results showed a narrow victory of 165,271 votes for the incumbent President of CCM, Salmin Amour, to 163,706 for the opposition candidate of Civic United Front, CUF, Seif Sharif Hamad. The number of 'spoiled votes' was almost 5,000. Out of the 'unspoiled' votes Amour got 50.2 percent and Hamad 49.8 percent. Supporters of the main opposition party (CUF) were harassed and charged with possessing seditious materials and with organising illegal assemblies. Obstruction affected the elections. Despite alleged rigging, the CUF holds 24 of 50 seats in parliament and on the island of Pemba CUF even won all seats (21). Pemba is said to be more 'Arab' then 'African'. The OAU declared the elections as 'free and fair'.

40. Chechen leaders, even some who were in leading positions in the local government, have been notorious for advocating 'terrorism as an instrument of policy', something which according to the UNPO Charter should be excluded. It became common knowledge that some thousand Chechens fighters were trained in terrorist commando actions by the Islamist Jihad network of al-Qaeda. In spring 2002, the US-led coalition in Afghanistan (for the first time) used ground forces against al-Qaeda strongholds in the south, which were fiercely defended. Several hundred Chechens, Uzbek and Arabs died in fighting against much larger and better equipped forces composed of US, other Western forces and Afghan Northern Alliance forces.

41. Interview with Luithui Luingam, 'The Naga Movement from the 1970s', in ECOR 1995c: 78–84.

42. Ratification of the most important UN treaties has not progressed rapidly: as at 10 August 1998, 132 states were party to the International Covenant on Economic, Social and Cultural Rights (ICESCR); 131 to the International Covenant on Civil and Political Rights (ICCPR). This is only a slow progress compared to the state of ratification at the end of 1992 when the ICCPR was ratified by 115 states and ICESCR by 118; first protocol ratified by 67 states, second protocol by 12 (see *amnesty international report 1993*, app. VI). Until Aug. 1998 some 143 states had ratified the International

Convention on the Elimination of All Forms of Racial Discrimination; and 141 the Convention on the Elimination of All Forms of Discrimination against Women. But in 8/98 only 90 States had ratified the Convention against Torture and Other Cruel, Inhuman or Degrading Treatment or Punishment. See United Nations 1998 ('Report of the Secretary-General'; on www.un.org/Docs/SG/SG-Rpt/ch4c.htm). Democratic Switzerland, for example, has so far only signed the Covenant on Political Rights and the Convention against Torture, whereas the Nordic countries have signed and ratified the two covenants, the protocols and the anti-torture convention.

43. The Nuclear Non-Proliferation Treaty (NPT) has had for years 178 states parties, 'commanding virtually universal adherence'. (Report of UN-SG, ibid.). The 'indefinite extension' of NPT, decided upon 1995, mislead the public as well as the experts that this would have 'strengthened the nuclear non-proliferation regime' and would have made 'a substantial contribution to the maintenance of international peace and security' (ibid.). The shocking new nuclear policy and missile defence under president Bush Jr. made it soon clear that even conventions that seemed 'untouchable' are put into question. Under these circumstances the Comprehensive Nuclear Test Ban Treaty (adopted on 10 September 1996 by the United Nations General Assembly) will hardly be ratified by a sufficient number of the 44 nuclear-capable States.

44. By the new administration in the USA, its announcement in spring 2001 that it plans to accelerate the development of 'missile defense' (Reagan's star war) and its unilateral withdrawal in Dec 2001 from the 1972 Anti-Ballistic Missile Treaty (between USA and USSR), has re-ignited a decade-old debate. Bush's government is playing with the fire. A missile defense system would destabilize the entire structure of strategic deterrence.

45. 'There has never been a system at the international level that provides for enforcement of international law. The UN is not a world government; it has no authority over the different states' (Berman in Scherrer 1993*b*: 9).

46. At their summit in Cyprus in Oct. 1993, the 50 states belonging to the Commonwealth also had confirmed their commitment to democracy, basic rights, and the rule of law. All the member states were called upon (finally) to ratify the two international UN covenants. The Commonwealth imposed conditions on Cameroon's admission (northeast Cameroon was a British colony), the stipulation being that it must create a democratic system. One can only warmly recommend this move to other communities of states. See *amnesty International report 1994*. At the summit of Francophone countries in 1994, exactly the opposite occurred: the French president and accompanying longstanding dictators re-embraced *realpolitik*. The process of democratization in the neocolonies (dubbed 'Paristroika'), which had been announced in 1990 appeared already to have been abandoned.

47. Over 20,000 complaints have been heard to date. Violations were found to have occurred in 360 cases. Even Switzerland has been condemned on 9 occasions.

48. The publication of previously confidential reports also helped generate a real humanrights campaign against Turkey. See *amnesty international report 1993*. Also Amnesty International, *Turkey: Torture, Extrajudicial Executions and 'Disappearances'* (London, 1992) and *Turkey: Walls of Glass* (London, 1992).

49. The committee must notify the state concerned but need not specify the period between notification and the actual visit, which, in exceptional circumstances, may be carried out immediately after notification. Governmental objections to the time or place of a visit can only be justified on grounds of national defence, public safety, serious disorder, the medical condition of a person, or urgent interrogation relating to a serious crime. In such cases, the state must immediately take steps to enable the committee to visit as soon as possible. See also the UN Convention against Torture and Other Cruel, Inhuman or Degrading Treatment or Punishment, opened for signature on 4 Feb. 1985.

50. The anti-torture measures include: informing the third party (e.g. relatives) in the case of arrest or police custody; the right to a lawyer; the right to a medical examination, with a free choice of doctor. In every annual report human rights organizations disclose that more than half of the world's states practice institutionalized torture of 'state enemies'!
51. Council of Europe 1994.
52. See also Council of Europe press release of 10 Nov. 1994.
53. In Recommendation 1255 (1995) the Assembly held that the Convention is soft worded; it formulates a number of rather vaguely defined objectives and principles. The observation of principles will be an obligation of the contracting parties, but not a right which individuals may appeal to. In the Assembly's Recommendations 1285 (1996) and 1300 (1996), it made a series of strategic proposals to improve the monitoring procedure to be set up.
54. Council of Europe 1997a: I.4. The rapporteur mentioned that like the Framework Convention, the intergovernmental Confidence-Building Measures in the minority field are a follow-up to the Council of Europe's 1993 Vienna Summit. So far, only six member states have made voluntary contributions to finance projects. On European minorities and languages see Trifunovska/Varennes, eds., 2001.
55. European Commission 1996. FUEN argued that the EU should take the Spanish constitution, as a good example, which grants the languages of minority nationalities in their respective autonomous regions an official status; see *pogrom*, no. 194 (June 1997), extra page.
56. Council of Ministers of the European Communities (CM-EC) 2000a and 2000b.
57. Programme of Action, in UNHCHR 2001 (A/CONF.189/5), as it was adopted on 8 September 2001 in Durban, South Africa. Three months later, however, still only an unedited version was available on the UN website http://www.un.org/WCAR/, also on www1.umn.edu/humanrts/instree/wcardeclaration.html; the same goes for the UNHCHR.
58. The state parties recognized 'that colonialism has led to racism, racial discrimination, xenophobia and related intolerance, and that Africans and peoples of African descent, and peoples of Asian descent and indigenous peoples were victims of colonialism and continue to be victims of its consequences'. The participants further recognizes 'the consequences of past and contemporary forms of racism, racial discrimination, xenophobia and related intolerance as serious challenges to global peace and security, human dignity and the realization of human rights and fundamental freedoms of many people in the world, in particular to Africans, peoples of African descent, people of Asian descent and indigenous peoples'. As regards to the issue of reparation the Durban declaration (in §90) said, 'We acknowledge and profoundly regret the untold, suffering and evils inflicted on millions of men, women and children as a result of slavery, slave trade, transatlantic slave trade, apartheid, genocide and past tragedies. We further note that some States have taken the initiative to apologize and have paid reparation where appropriate, for grave and massive violations committed'. It is difficult to conceive any obligation for reparations on the base of this text.
59. Some EU states, in particular Germany, Austria and Italy, fear a wave of workers from Eastern and Central Europe. Poland and other countries oppose the German proposal of a 7–years delay of the 'free movement of persons' because of the fear of wage dumping; obviously, the Poles could not enjoy the prospects of becoming second-class EU citizen.
60. Of the forty recommendations only a few have been fully implemented so far and—until the year 2001—none has led to significant changes in anti-racism legislation.
61. The European Commission's Targeted Socio-Economic Research (TSER) Programme commissioned several studies on social exclusion and inclusion.

62. The EUMC has a staff of twenty but only one single researcher. The centre does not monitor racism but coordinates what is being done by others (including the NGO community). For this purpose, as of end 2001, some seven (of 15) national focal points could be established. It seems mandatory that in all EU member states as well as in the candidate states such focal points are established. In order to promote and monitor this process the EUMC needs a much larger budget and should triple its workforce.

63. Ruzza (1999: 1) did 'field research' in Brussels; his data was drawn from observation, personal interviews, and analysis of archive materials. The paper analyses the role of different concepts of anti-racism and their implications in the policy process. Diverging definitions of the nature, causes and ideal solutions of racism co-existed but '[a]ll together these conceptions give identity and professionalism to the relevant policy network, but in a fragmented and contested fashion' (Ibid.). Some of Ruzza's conclusions are now obsolete since the report was written before the breakthrough. Not at all obsolete is his inquiry into the anti-racism lobby.

64. Anti-racist movements became first prominent in France, where the problems were monumental (along with the rise of FN and other extremist parties) already in the 1980s; broad-based anti-racist groups such as *SOS Racisme* have been supported by left parties, mostly by the socialists. Today *SOS Racisme* exists in several countries and *SOS Racisme International* has an office in Brussels.

65. The anti-racist movement overlaps with a variety of other movements concerned with social exclusion; the largest networks are the Social Platform (which co-ordinates two dozen umbrella organisations, some with several hundred member groups), *Solidar*, the Youth Forum, the European Federation for Intercultural Learning, the European Human Rights Foundation, and a number of religious organisations.

66. Disappointing is that the EC Racial Equality Directive (art. 13) establishes no independent bodies or ombudsman for receiving complains about racial discrimination (as existing in UK Race Relations Act 1976 and amendments, the Dutch and Swedish laws) and places the burden and the financial risk on the plaintiff. See Chopin *et al.* 2001: 47–48.

67. The EU has already spent some €10 billion (besides €16 billion in EBRD loans) to prepare candidate countries for the 'EU shock' and will spend €3 billion annually during first accessions. This seems 'peanuts' compared to the €40 billion annual cost of the Common Agricultural Policy, which still has the largest share of all items. See: James, Barry: 'Recasting Europe', *IHT*, April 23, 2001: 16.

68. *Eurobarometers* are an EU polling tool. The aim is to monitor change of values and attitudes twice a year; the sample size is usually 1.000 (which is rather low). Responsible for the *Eurobarometer* is the 'Public Opinion Analysis Unit' of the DG Education and Culture of the European Commission. For earlier surveys see Commission of the European Communities: Eurobarometers 30, 1988; no. 39, 1993; and no. 47.1, 1997 (*Racism and Xenophobia*).

69. The relative majority of EU citizens belong to the 'passively tolerant' type, who have positive attitudes but do not support policies in favour of minorities or anti-racist polities. A quarter of the EU population is described as 'ambivalent'; they do not see positive inputs by minority groups, desire their assimilation but do not feel disturbed.

70. See EUMC 2001: 24–25. The typology is based on six of seven dimensions of measuring attitudes towards minorities; exactly the most telling of the dimension (of xenophobic concerns about the alleged negative social impact of minorities), labelled as 'blaming minorities', which is 'the most important set of question asked in the survey ... [that] seems to constitute the core attitude within the set of negative and positive attitudes' (ibid., 9). The reason given is 'poor comparability'; my concern that the result could be very different. Apart from critics about the way questions were asked the evaluation seems to be flawed.

71. The 'great communicator', TV-tycoon Silvio Berlusconi, promised almost everything—and won. His *Forza Italia* party conglomerate contains fascist MSI remnants as well as xenophobic *Lega Norte* elements (with Umberto Bossi's Northern League weakened at the ballot box). Berlusconi soon behaved miserably, blocked several EU initiatives and became the problem figure no. 1 in Europe.

72. Some established right-wing racist parties crumbled at the polls while some others, such as the Vlaams Block, the Swiss SVP and the Italian fascists AI-MSI recently got more votes and support. The French *Front National*, led by its ardent anti-Semitic and racist leader Jean-Marie Le Pen, was once the strongest extremist group in Europe, with some 20 percent of the vote nation-wide, and was able to conquer cities like Toulon, Orange, and Marignane in the June 1995 communal elections. The 'Front' seemed in decay due to factionalism, a split in 1999, and 'disciplinary' measures taken against Le Pen, but that was unfortunately a wrong impression. In Germany the right-wing parties were split (*NPD, DVA*, and *Republikaner*) and remained under the critical 5 percent line for the most part; much more threatening are the activities of the organized underground of criminal racist, fascist groupings, who are ready for violence, and election campaigns launched around xenophobic themes by the mainstream Christian democrats.

73. In the 2002 presidential election Le Pen came back strongly (17 percent), just a bit more than the spitted socialist vote, and—shockingly—became the challenger of Chirac in the second and final round of the election. The right-wing gained a comfortable majority in the parliament. Even more shocking was the change in Europe's most liberal country: the Netherlands. The assassination of a 'modern' racist triggered a wholesale political change in the wake of a shocking report on Srebrenica, which was forcing the government to step down and to hold elections. Christian Democrats and right-wingers got a majority in parliament and govern the country with a middle-right coalition.

74. Lately there is a legally workable definition of institutional racism: '...the collective failure of an organisation to provide appropriate and professional services to people because of their colour, culture or ethnic origin. It can be seen or detected in the processes, attitudes and behaviour which amount to discrimination through unwitting prejudice, ignorance, thoughtlessness, and racial stereotyping which disadvantage minority ethnic people.' (McPherson Report on the Metropolitan police investigation into the death of Stephen Lawrence. London, in April 2000: § 6.34)

75. 'Identity formation and reformation take place as a result of societal developments as well as interactions between host and immigrant populations. Ambivalence on the part of host populations relates to, for instance, the value of immigrants as workers, entrepreneurs or human capital versus alleged socio-cultural and economic threats as foreigners and/or potential deviants. The ambivalence of immigrant populations to the host society relates to the dilemmas and difficulties of 'integrating' or 'remaining distinct, thus separate'—in either case, not without feelings of hostility and resentment.' See Burns, Tom R.: 'Racism and Xenophobia: Key Issues, Mechanisms, and Policy Opportunities.' European Community Research Programme. Brussels, April 5–6, 2001.

76. Women, more than men, are subjected to double or multiple manifestations of human rights violations. Hence, sex and gender should not be left out in the discussions of anti-racist strategies. Gender discrimination is a human rights violation intersecting almost all forms of discriminations.

77. Women often are further hindered by a lack of access to remedies and complaint mechanisms for racial discrimination due to structural gender-related impediments, e.g., gender bias in some legal systems and the general discrimination in all spheres of life.

78. Compare the critical approach to, definition of and expertise about racism by Mark Terkessidis (2001: 40), inspired by Robert Miles and Michel Foucault. Terkessidis is presently the best reading in Germany; he comprehensively presents and criticizes the

specific German approach to the problem of racism. Some of his lines of thought should be developed further, esp. in regards to the processual and structural character of contemporary racism (with much inspiration from Galtung).

79. Michel Foucault, 1926–1984, French historian, philosopher beyond structuralism and Marxism, psychologist and social scientist; student at the elite school *Ecole Normale Supérieure* (ENS), professor at several universities, became a member of the Collège de France at the age of 43; a political chameleon and human rights activist; always a non-conformist and controversial character.

80. The *dispositif* is almost synonymous to what Louis Althusser 'apparatus', which rather camouflages reality while at the same time constructing it. For a good Foucaultian discussion of racism and the 'racial knowledge' see Terkessidis 2001: 38–41.

81. EUMC in Vienna does not do any monitoring itself but is supposed to coordinate it.

82. Surprisingly very few sociologists and social anthropologists are contributing to increase the competence of peace and conflict research—and, most importantly, its application by practitioners of conflict management—in regard to the types of conflicts driven by ethnic, national, cultural, and in some cases economic factors, or struggles for power. This lack of interest seems to prevail despite of such research being a highly topical and fundamentally problem-oriented field of labour. Its themes and methods overlap with similarly problem-oriented areas of research dealing with major contemporary issues such as migration, racism, and multiculturalism. The preoccupation with such neglected topical problem-areas has nevertheless become a new feature of studies, concepts, and analyses of a growing body of research since the end of the Cold War.

83. ADC as proposed by Rainer Nickel (2000). 'Criminal law ... when it comes to racist or anti-Semitic hate speech or racist defamation. But many forms of discrimination cannot be fought effectively by criminal law as it is almost impossible to prove certain facts before the courts. It takes a higher degree of proof for a criminal sentencing than it takes for a civil claim to succeed ... In case of discriminations civil courts should be enabled to award reasonably high compensations ... to the victims and/or to victim support groups.'

84. This could work much the same way as the UN Action Plan to Prevent Genocide, as recommended by Carlsson *et al.* 1999. It should 'establish networks of cooperation with humanitarian organisations, academic institutions and other non-governmental organisations with the aim of enhancing early warning and early response capacity'. Carlsson *et al.* recommended 'intensified dialogue' that would not only involve the UN Secretariat and the UN Security Council, but also INGOs, IGOs and regional organizations such as OSCE, OAU, OAS, ASEAN, and others.

85. The attempt of the Spanish prosecutor Garçon in Madrid, who issued an international arrest order against the Chilean dictator Augusto Pinochet, arrested in England 1999 but freed on health grounds in 2000, failed but it will greatly influence future prosecution of large crimes. Garçon may have got the idea from Raphael Lemkin, the father of the anti-genocide convention. The Pinochet case already developed its African version: early 2000 a judge in Dakar interrogated Hissène Habré, former French supported tyrant of Chad who lost power in 1990 and currently lives in Senegal, on charges of torture and 'barbarity' committed against the Chadian opposition in the 1980s.

86. Raphael Lemkin's idea was to outlaw Nazism, fascism and other exterminatory ideologies by punishing its leaders and agitators in anyone state they may enter. Lemkin was an international lawyer, former League of Nations legal expert and member of the International Bureau for Unification of Criminal Law. In Madrid 1933 he introduced the first proposal ever made to outlaw Nazism by declaring it a crime. In Lemkin's words: 'since the consequences of genocide are international in their implications, the repression of genocide should be internationalized. The culprit should be liable not only

in the country in which the crime was committed, but in the country where he might be apprehended. The country where he is found may itself try him or extradite him'. (See Lemkin 1945, *Free World*, on www.preventgenocide.org).

87. It might be more than premature to state 'human rights norms have reached consensual (prescriptive) status on the international level by now' (Risse, Ropp, and Sikkink, eds.: The power of human rights: International norms and domestic change. Cambridge, Melbourne: Cambridge University Press 1999); too many countries such as North Korea, Iraq, Iran, Afghanistan, Turkey, Congo, Nigeria until recently, Ethiopia and a number of other African countries defy and ignore the claimed consensus. Although, for instance, torture is universally condemned and outlawed by a convention, it is according to the Amnesty International annual report very much part of state crimes in more than hundred states in 1999! The convention against torture is signed by a conspicuously little number of states.

88. The ICC is an important step into that direction. Unfortunately the ICC has already met strong resistance by great powers; amongst the hardest resistors were countries known for an intensive official Human Rights discourse such as the USA!

89. See good ideas developed by Delanty; the author believes that 'The Canadian model has much to offer European trans-nationalism, namely the need to separate three domains of group rights: national determination, rights for national minorities and special representations rights. Only by devising a multi-tiered citizenship that is capable of responding to these three realities, will a genuinely democratic multiculturalism be possible. But beyond this the US and Canadian experience is limited.' Delanty 2001: 10.

90. According to Foucault the concept of a paradigm (*episteme* as governing discourse) is insufficient and the concept of *dispositif* fills the gap. The term *dispositif* links theory with practice, thus discursive knowledge with social practices and techniques of power. Foucault was interested in themes such as sexuality; power structures and its multitude of different techniques; different kinds of knowledge; death, madness, disease in general; asylums, the hospitals, the prisons system; the ways to produce discipline and docile people, etc.

91. See Auke van der Goot, 'Sprachliche Vielfalt wahren', *pogrom*, 174 (1994), 17.

92. One of the major tasks of the EBLUL has been, and continues to be, the creation and administration of data banks on important relevant issues (media, education system, legislation on minority languages, smaller cultures). The bureau co-ordinates the Mercator network, which links bureaux in Wales, Catalonia, Friesland, and southern France. (See *EBLUL Contact Bulletin Quarterly*.)

93. The plan was presented by the French prime minister of the day, Edouard Balladur, to a 41–country conference on 'Conflict Prevention in Europe' held in Paris. At the time of the conference horrible atrocities were committed by the French client regime in Rwanda against the Tutsi minority (shown on all TV-stations)—without any interference from outside, rather with the complicity of Balladur's government.

94. This became clear when he mentioned the importance of agreements based on good-neighbourliness: the issue of the recognition of the Oder-Neiße border between Poland and Germany. He also talked of 'very close relations with Russia' (AFP, 26. May 1994).

95. These kinds of conditions do not apply in the case of the three northern countries—Austria, Switzerland, and Iceland. Alain Juppé (then French foreign minister) made it clear that the EU is not willing to take new sources of conflict on board.

96. A 12–point peace plan for Cyprus; see Scherrer 1998*h*. Also see Baier-Allen 1999.

97. Hungarians in Romania/Transylvania (1.6–2 million) and Slovakia (0.4–0.6 million) are seeking improvements in their rights. Things have improved after the main Hungarian party joined the governing coalition in Rumania. The same will most probably happen in Slovakia where Meciar lost the elections in autumn 1998, and the Hungarian minority

party joined the new government. The Hungarians in Voyvodina region of Serbia (0.4 million) and the Carpathian region of the Ukraine do not come under the EU conditions of entry. In the Ukraine the situation of the Hungarians was first regarded as satisfactory (see GfbV 1994, also *pogrom*, 174 (1994), 21).

98. There are thirty countries in which the Roma number over 2,000. In Europe, there may be as many as twelve million Roma between Paris and Vladivostok; in some countries, they represent some 10 percent of the population. Roma life expectancy, educational levels, employment rates, accesses to acceptable housing and citizenship lag far behind national averages. The Roma were the victims of the *Porrajmos* (the Nazi genocide against Roma) and continue to this day to be victims of racial prejudice and social exclusion—on an everyday basis. Only lately the crimes of the past come to surface, even in countries which seemingly have a decent human rights record and which apply minority rights for several domestic minorities or indigenous peoples (such as Sweden or Switzerland). Especially in the Central and Eastern European countries Roma are often the victims of organized violence.

99. 'In assessing *Europeanisation* as a method for conflict resolution, at this level of generality, the answer remains ambiguous. The uncertainty about the eventual shape of European integration undermines the credibility of the EU in playing this role.' (Trimikliniotis 2001: 58–59).

100. In Germany the *Länder* (almost as in Switzerland the *Cantons*) are responsible for drafting and applying local legislation, with each *Land* being free to draft its own constitution within the ideological and institutional framework and principles of the 1949 Basic Law (*Grundgesetz*), and the *Länder* even participate in the federal legislative process through the *Bundesrat* (Federal Council). The *Bundesrat* has a right of veto, which can only be overturned by a majority vote of the federal parliament (the *Bundestag*). Compared with the German Chancellor's ideas of a federal Europe the French press reacted by rejecting it: 'L'Europe qu'envisage Gerhard Schröder serait une réplique exacte du modèle fédéral allemand, couronnée par une Constitution europeenne.' (*Le Figaro*, April 30, 2001: 4). In fact, what Schröder presented (see *Der Spiegel* 22, April 27 2001) was not exactly a copy of the German model described above. The reaction of that time French Prime Minister Leonel Jospin at the end-May 2001 was, as expected, rather defensive and certainly cautious about federalism.

101. According to Rémond, judging from the point of view of French state traditions, it was 'noticeable that territorial autonomy [as administrative autonomy introduced on the unruly island of Corsica, my addition] does not always imply self-determination, nor does it necessarily entail independence'.

102. The new slogan might be 'Diversity and Coexistence in Prosperity'. The European Union is already the strongest economic block worldwide. Enlargement will make sure that the European economic hegemon will defend its position into the 21st century before China will retake the place it had lost to the Europeans some 250 years ago.

103. Sedelmeier, Ulrich: 'Enlarging Europe', in European Commission / Liberatore, Angela 1999: 77–79, this ref. 78.

104. The Council of Europe explicitly highlights the complementarity with the C/OSCE in the explanatory report on the Framework Convention for the Protection of Minorities. Reaching a compromise between the conflicting opinions of all 55 OSCE member states often necessitates so many reservations that it weakens the original intentions of documents or initiatives (as was the case with the mandate establishing the High Commissioner on Minorities).

105. This CSCE meeting took place at Switzerland's suggestion. In the view of the Swiss foreign minister of the time, René Felber, Swiss federalism (and the integration of four national cultures in one state) may serve as a 'model'. Felber suggested to the

disconcerted representative of the former USSR that Swiss experts of federalism be dispatched to his country.

106. AI 1996.

107. When a country ratifies the convention, the state commits itself to improve the laws and take appropriate actions in accordance with the provisions the new instrument contains. As of end 2001, the convention had only been ratified by 14 countries: Norway, 19–06–1990; Mexico, 05–09–1990; Colombia, 07–08–1991; Bolivia, 11–12–1991; Costa Rica, 02–04–1993; Paraguay, 10–08–1993; Peru, 02–02–1994; Honduras, 29–03–1995; Denmark, 22–02–1996; Guatemala, 05–06–1996; Netherlands, 02–02–1998; Fiji, 03–03–1998; Ecuador, 15–05–1998; Argentina, 03–07–2000.

108. However, the use of the term 'people' does not automatically confer a legal right in international law (notably the right to self-determination); this is expressly mentioned in the ILO Convention. See ILO, Convention concerning indigenous and tribal peoples in independent countries' (Geneva, 1989). Art. 1.3.

109. Lee Swepston, 'Indigenous and Tribal Peoples: Recent Developments in the ILO 1995', *doCIP Update*, June 1995, 21.

110. An ILO expert mission appeared before the Duma in Nov. 1994, and following this, in Sept. 1995, the Russian Ministry for Nationalities organized a meeting, in Moscow, of experts on, and representatives of, indigenous peoples. (See Swepston, 'Indigenous and Tribal Peoples', 20.) Russia is the only successor state to the USSR that declares itself to be multi-ethnic in its constitution.

111. The text of ILO 169, art. 16.1–2 runs as follows: 1. 'Subject to the following paragraphs of this Article, the peoples concerned shall not be removed from the lands which they occupy. 2. Where the relocation of these peoples is considered necessary as an exceptional measure, such relocation shall take place only with their free and informed consent. Where their consent cannot be obtained, such relocation shall take place only following appropriate procedures established by national laws and regulations, including public inquiries where appropriate, which provide the opportunity for effective representation of the peoples concerned'.

112. Barsh 1994.

113. Indigenous organizations played a major part in the creation of the Working Group and in drafting international law where this safeguards the legitimate rights of indigenous populations. See Tim Coulter, 'International Law and Indian Nations', in Minugh 1989: 42–8. Also id., 'A Wave of Change: The UN and the Indigenous Peoples', *Cultural Survival Quarterly*, 18 (1994), 2–3: 35–70; and Inger Sjørslev, 'Politics and Performance: Reflections on the UN Working Group on Indigenous Populations', *Indigenous Affairs*, 3 (1994), 38–49.

114. The Working Group makes a very colourful sight. But coverage of its sessions often focuses solely on the 'exotic' aspects. This was the case, for example, when (in 1987) Chief Vernon Bellegarde of the Canadian plains Cree appeared in full feather head-dress; and again when the Mohawks held a ceremony in the park in front of the UN headquarters (1990), and when the Malaccan delegation turned out in (rather fig-leaf-style) traditional costume.

115. The five groups are made up as follows: Africa 15 members; Asia 12; Latin America 11, Western Europe and others 10; Eastern Europe 5. Voting positions are generally agreed in advance in the regional groups. Decisions are normally taken according to the principle of consensus.

116. Erica Daes, chairperson of the UNWGIP, stated, in 1994, that: 'The World Conference on Human Rights [Vienna 1993], as we have repeatedly said today, recommended that consideration be given to the establishment of a permanent body for Indigenous peoples within the UN. These recommendations, together with the UN General

Assembly to proclaim an international decade for indigenous peoples, means that all of us need to consider carefully the directions, structures and mechanisms to ensure that the indigenous peoples will take their rightful place in the international community and family of nations.' (ECOR 12: 6.)

117. Details of UN human-rights activities are given in *United Nations Action in the Field of Human Rights* (New York, 1988). (This 350–page tome makes very little mention of the rights of indigenous peoples: the UNWGIP is dealt with in 20 lines (p. 18).)

118. The UNWGIP is chaired by the Greek jurist Erica I. Daes. Its secretary is Julian Burger, the author of the only existing handbook on the situation of indigenous peoples world-wide. On the history of the UNWGIP, see the outline in Burger 1987: 266–72.

119. The Yanomami Indians now enjoy a kind of autonomy in their settlement-area in Brazil (though not in Venezuela); but for years the government failed to act to stop a massive and aggressive invasion of the area by gold-prospectors. What is going on in West Papua is a decolonization conflict (Indonesia annexed the former Dutch part of the island of New Guinea); a solution to this dispute, which has been smouldering for decades, must be sought by the UN and the international community. Complaints brought by the Jumma have led to negotiations with the new, elected government of Bangladesh. See also the report of the Chittagong Hill Tracts Commission '*Life is Not Ours*': *Land and Human Rights in the CHT of Bangladesh* (Copenhagen/Amsterdam, 1991). Reports such as this have created more awareness about the war in the CHT and made (indirectly) a critical contribution to the peace process, which started soon after.

120. Following the complaints brought by the representatives of the Karen (1990–4) and Kachin (1991) to the Sub-Commission and the UNWGIP in Geneva, and after the visit to New York of the government-in-exile under Sein Win, another Rapporteur was despatched, but he too encountered massive sabotage. Burma has repeatedly been sharply criticized by the UN Human Rights Commission and the General Assembly. The 1993 General Assembly resolution on Burma called on Secretary-General Boutros-Ghali to adopt a more active approach. See the chapter 'Non-active Role of UN in Burma's Internal Conflicts', ECOR 10: 32–42, esp. pp. 35–7 'United Nations Should Observe Peace Talks in Burma', interview with Dr Em Marta, Manerplaw 1994.

121. In Central America, while the subjugation was equally ferocious but mainly concentrated on the more accessible lands along the western coast, manifold indigenous groups on the Caribbean side remained out of reach for the Spanish colonizers or even fought them fiercely, as the Miskitu did over centuries.

122. Most threatened were the Ixil, Chuj, Jacalteco, Karjobal, and Mam. Massacres eliminated entire Mayan rural communities as well as the urban political opposition, trade union leaders and priests. Military operations were concentrated in Quiché, Huehuetenango, Chimaltenango, Alta and Baja Verapaz, the south coast and the capital, the victims being principally Mayan and to a lesser extent Ladino. During the final period, 1986–1996, repressive action was selective, affecting the Mayan and Ladino population to a similar extent.

123. The majority of the Indian peoples of Mesoamerica are the Mayan peoples. Their epicentre is Southern Mexico and the *altiplano* of Guatemala. The large majority of the Mayas are small-scale peasants. Mayan peoples live throughout Mesoamerica, in today's Mexico (states of Chiapas, Tabasco, Campéche and Yucatan), Guatemala, Belize, El Salvador and Honduras. Seven millions of Guatemalan citizens speak 23 Indian tongues, predominantly Maya-Kiché languages. Most populous are the Kiché, Kaqchikel, Mam, Quekchi, Chol and Chorti, in Mexico the Yucatec, Mam, Tzotzil, Huastec, Chol, Kanjobal Tzeltal, Itza, Mopan and Tlapanec. The Mayans form a larger population than any Central American state. The single largest group in Mexico are the Aztec in central and Southern Mexico, numbering 1.2 million people. Major other

peoples include the Zapotec, Otomi, Mixtec, Totonac and Mazatec, all numbering between 200,000 and half a million.

124. In the most populous Central American country of Guatemala, native nations (Maya-Quiché peoples) demographically constitute a 50 percent majority; with a population of almost 7 million (of a population of 13 million as of 2001) members of various indigenous peoples. The other five countries have a combined population of 25 million people of which 2 million are Amerindians and 1.5 million are Afro-Americans (Creoles and Garifuna).

125. They took up arms against the Sandinistas from 1981 up to 1988/89. The indigenous Miskitu (150,000; 120,000 in Nicaragua) and Sumu (13,000; 10,000 in Nicaragua) are living along the Caribbean coast (only Miskitu) and the rivers of North-eastern Nicaragua and South-eastern Honduras. (The term *Miskitu* is used instead of *Miskito*, since the Miskitu do not have the vocal o in their language. The same is valid for Sumu instead of Sumo.)

126. Afro-Americans dominate demographically and/or rule in 12 smaller states of the Caribbean region. Black rule exists mainly on the islands (Haiti, Jamaica, most Caribbean micro-states) and on the continent (Belize, one of three Guayanas). Blacks have large numbers in a several Ladino-dominated states such as Brazil (over 40 million), Columbia, all along the Caribbean, also in Ecuador, etc.

127. The provisions for territorial autonomy do mention the indigenous peoples' settlement-areas but afford them no further legal protection, as indigenous territories, against *Mestizo* immigrants. In practice, the agricultural border is being constantly shifted eastwards as a result of immigration by impoverished *campesinos*; this has mostly occurred to the detriment of the Sumu Indians from Musawas, and of the mining areas.

128. The law brought a pluralist system of parliamentary democracy, but with elements of a presidential system, since not only a *junta executiva* but also a *coordinador* is elected, who, significantly, is called 'governor' by the population.

129. The obvious aim was to reduce inter-ethnic tensions and protect the rights of the small ethnic groups (Sumu, Rama, and Garifuna) against the disproportionate influence of the Hispanic *Mestizos* in the West and the Afro-American Creoles in the South and the Miskitu Indians in the North. Of major importance (though not stipulated in the law) is the fact that radio channels may broadcast in indigenous languages. The radio is either under the direct control of the Indian movement (Radio Miskut in Bilwi) or else is made active use of by it (Radio Caribe).

130. J. R. Martínez Cobo (Special Rapporteur for the Sub-Commission on Prevention of Discrimination and Protection of Minorities), *Study of the Problem of Discrimination against Indigenous Populations* (5 vols.; New York, 1986–7).

131. UN Commission on Human Rights/Sub.2/UNWGIP, Draft declaration on the rights of indigenous peoples, (E/CN.4/Sub.2/AC.4/1993/CRP.4; Geneva, 22 June 1993). The Working Group made its final editorial changes to the draft in Jan. and Apr. 1994. See Erica Daes, First revised text of the draft Universal Declaration on Rights of Indigenous Peoples, Geneva June 1989; ead., Document de travail révisé, Geneva June 1991, and Working Paper, Apr. 1993, 26.

132. ECOR 12: 7.

133. For a current version of Draft Declaration on the Rights of Indigenous Peoples see http://www.itpcentre.org/legislation/english/undeclar.htm. It will most probably be watered-down further.

134. Commission on Human Rights, Resolution 1995/24, Geneva Mar. 1995.

135. The opposition line-up was headed by Chile. After some mollifying introductory remarks, the latter's representative got down to brass tacks, claiming there was a lack of 'political realism', notably in regard to the right to self-determination. The text of the declaration, he said, must be revised in order to safeguard the territorial integrity and sovereignty of internationally recognized states (*doCip Update* , June 1995, 3).

136. Claims to sovereignty are feared by a number of states. The Asian group (e.g. India) considered itself unaffected, since, it said, the whole of Asia was indigenous (*doCip Update*, June 1995, 9.
137. This was in Geneva in February 1995; see *doCip Update*, June 1995, 9. Switzerland talked of 'transition into a state' and advocated acceptance of the declaration in its entirety; as—that time—a non-member of the UN, however, it had only observer status. (Switzerland joint the UN in 2002; the only non-member state is the Vatican).
138. Martínez 1998. Also compare: UNPO 1998 (UNWGIP session monitor).
139. UNWGIP/E.I.A. Daes/Rodolfo Stavenhagen, Considerations of a Permanent Forum for Indigenous People (E/CN.4/Sub.2/AC.4/1995/7/Add.2; Geneva, June 1995).
140. Observations on these matters had already been made by UNWGIP chairperson Erica Irene A. Daes, in the annexe to her report on the 12th session of the Working Group in 1994: see E. I. Daes, Report of the Working Group on its 12th session (E/CN.4/Sub.2/1994/30; Geneva, Aug. 1994), 35.
141. Daes June 1995, 6.
142. On the activities planned for the Decade, see also WGIP, International Decade of the World's Indigenous Peoples (E/CN.4/Sub.2/AC.4/1995/5; Geneva, July 1995).
143. 'Mary Robinson spoke of "partnership", and noted that, for the first time in a UN meeting, the seating arrangements had been changed so as to reflect this new spirit of partnership.' She also spoke of 'the body's potential to address indigenous issues in a truly holistic and comprehensive manner'. Morgan, Rhiannon: 'Daily notes from the Permanent Forum on Indigenous Issues New York, 13-24 May 2002', on http://www.dialoguebetweennations.com/N2N/PFII/English/DailyNotes.htm.
144. Daes, Report on 12th session, Aug. 1994. Her remarks in 'Closing Speech of the 11th Session of UNWGIP, Geneva, July 1993', in ECOR 12: 5–9: 'The work of the UNWGIP: structures and mechanisms to ensure that the indigenous peoples will take their rightful place in the international community'. The chair of the Working Group announced her will to 'provide Indigenous peoples with the possibility of holding informal consultations about the text of the draft declaration, and try to find formal ground'. The promise was honoured. From this point on, unfortunately, the fate of the text once again depended solely on the good will of the UN member states.
145. United Nations/General Assembly, International Decade of the World's Indigenous People: Resolution (A/RES/49/214; New York, Feb. 1995).
146. The text of the declaration as adopted after the 11th session (of 1993) continues to serve as a standard. See ECOSOC, Technical review of the UN Draft Declaration on the Rights of Indigenous Peoples (E/CN.4/Sub.2/1994/2/Add.1; Geneva, Apr. 1994).
147. This was true of Finland in relation to access to mass media (including privately run mass-media; art. 13/1992), land-use (ILO Convention 169 to be taken as the standard; art. 16/1992); and protection in situations of war (extension of art. 36 'special protection in periods of armed conflict'). See E/CN.4/Sub.2/AC.4/1993/1, pp. 2–4.
148. Resolution 47/75 spoke, without being specific, of international co-operation to solve the problems of indigenous 'groups' (not 'peoples'), acknowledged the value and diversity of cultures of the world's indigenous peoples, and pointed to the latter's contribution to sustainable, 'national'—i.e. state—development. See A/RES/47/75.
149. See UN 1992*b* (A/C.3/47/L.66 of 1. 12. 92, 1–7; declaration containing 9 articles).
150. Latin American authors such as Machado or Stavenhagen see the struggle of the Indians in the South as being more (pragmatically) aimed at self-government and the preservation of collective rights, whereas the Indians of the North link the claim to self-determination to the claim to sovereignty. See Lia Z. Machado, 'Indigenous Communitarianism as a Critique of Modernity and its Juridical Implication', IWGIA 76: 73–92; also, Stavenhagen, ibid. 9–30.

151. At the moment, the major disputes are centred on Bolivia where there is a concentration of Indian inhabitants. For example, the Movimiento Campesino Tupak Katari (MCTK) and the Katarista liberation front run by the Aymara, Quichua, and Warami in Bolivia are demanding recognition of the *ayllu*, thus combining a confederal model (new territorial division) and new methods of production (ethno-development).

152. In the 1995 law on *participación popular*, the indigenous peoples are recognized as legal subjects; popular bodies and traditional institutions are also recognized. The newly reformed constitution declares Bolivia to be a 'free, sovereign, multi-ethnic and multi-cultural country' (art. 1). Educational reform is to establish bilingualism officially across the whole country (cf. *doCip Update*, June 1995, 5).

153. Hans Petter Buvollen, 'Nationality, Ethnicity and Self-determination', mimeo (Managua, 1993), 91.

154. Buvollen (op. cit.) cites Guillermo B. Batalla (1982), who places the need for control over one's own culture at the heart of his deliberations. The question (which Buvollen raises) is: Who controls what? Who controls development projects compatible with the indigenous culture? Will it be the collectivity (e.g. the village assembly or an indigenous organization) that exercises control, in place of the individual—rather like the police as a 'moral institution' (Hegel), acting as an instrument of the state to exert control over the individual (Buvollen 1983: 92). This marks a clash between Western individualist values and ideas and Indian ones, which as a rule are collectively oriented.

155. Brazil's 1988 constitution (like Nicaragua's of 1987) recognized a new configuration of collective rights based on the autonomy of indigenous communities. These included, most notably, cultural rights and land rights for 'areas which [such communities] have traditionally and/or permanently inhabited' (the formulation is identical in the Brazilian and Nicaraguan laws). From the point of view of the indigenous peoples, however, the land rights concerned relate to only a small part of their territory. The laws have been applied in a variety of ways. In Brazil, the *silvícolas* had reservations assigned to them; in Nicaragua, two autonomous multi-ethnic regions were created and designed so that the Indians dominate to the north of the Caribbean coast and the Creoles to the south.

156. UNCHR 1992a: 17–20.

157. By mid-1992, questionnaires on the situation of indigenous peoples sent out by Martínez in 1990 and again in 1991 had elicited responses from only seven of (at that time) 175 states. See UNCHR 1992a: 4.

158. UNCHR 1998, 1995b, 1992a.

159. UNCHR/Martínez 1999 (Study on treaties. Final Report. E/CN.4/Sub.2/1999/20).

160. Martínez 1999, § 18; based on the unedited version (WGIP, Aug. 1998).

161. For the Special Rapporteur's strongest remarks about this miserable process, which transformed the 'rule of law' into the 'law of the rulers', see Martínez 1999, § 195–198.

162. UNCHR 1992a: 22.

163. See Howard R. Berman, 'Perspectives on American Indian Sovereignty and International Law, 1600 to 1776', in Lyons and Mohawk 1992: 133 ff.

164. The terms that are used in this context reduce indigenous peoples to the status of minors or imbeciles: 'trusteeship', 'wardship', guardship', 'domestic dependent nations', 'tutorial duties of civilized states towards aborigines', 'tutelage', 'pupillage', etc. Cf. 'Indigenous Peoples, Euro-centrism and the Law of the Nations', UNCHR 1992a: 20 ff. Also 'De soberanos a vasallos, pupilos, asimilados o marginados' (ch. 3/Report 2), UNCHR 1995b: 23–56.

165. See e.g. Vitoria, Suarez, Gentili, Grotius, Pufendorf, and others.

Chapter 7

Multilateral Regimes for Regulating Intra-state Conflict

The theory of international regimes is concerned with the permanent institutionalization and co-operative regulation of conflicts by a number of states.[1] Conflict regulation takes places on the basis of recognized principles, norms, rules, and codes of conduct, which are embodied, according to jointly agreed (usually consensus-based) procedures, in resolutions and in the enactment of these. This requires the participating states to subordinate certain of their own interests and selected areas in which they previously had sole responsibility to the norms and rules of an international regime—in other words, it requires a surrender of sovereignty 'upwards'.

The purpose of multilateral regimes as institutions is to create the framework conditions in which (new) political agreements are concluded. Where necessary, such regimes may develop either into actual organizations, as is the case within the UN system, with a host of subsidiary bodies and associated establishments, or into supra-national entities (like the EU after Maastricht). The logical outcome of such a process of integration and co-operation would in the long run be the self-dissolution of states (Mietzsch 1993: 166). If this is going to happen—and in what period of time—will be highlighted by the restructuring and 'deepening' of the European Community into a full-fledged European Union. This process is not forcibly leading to a situation where the EU super-state would grow uncontrollable. As the gradual emancipation of the European Parliament in recent years showed, the rising tyranny of the 'new eurocracy' produced a strong opposition among the elected deputies. For instance, provoked by mismanagement and corruption in the EU governing body, the European Parliament went, in March 1999, as far as dismissing the entire European Commission.

Existing multilateral regimes function exclusively as inter-state diplomatic processes between governments.[2] However, the euphoria at the start of the 1990s that might have led to a speedy intensification of co-operation in *Greater Europe* (encompassing its eastern and western parts) has now evaporated. Whereas Russia continued to view the OSCE as the most important continental and regional organization, and was keen to enhance its status and upgrade the organization as a whole, certain Western European states inclined towards expanding the military organizations of NATO and the WEU eastwards in time with European Union eastward enlargement, even in the face of Russian resistance, thus devaluing the OSCE. It is clear that the eastward expansion of NATO and the development of the OCSE are basically mutually exclusive. And yet the OSCE is the organization which is expected to play the major role as regards European security issues in the twenty-first century. It is the only forum of its kind in which the NATO and CIS states work together on an equal footing. What other organization would be better-suited for dialogue between eastern and western Europe?

In the domains of foreign and security policy, confidence, reliability, and continuity are especially important elements, producing security of expectation. Confidence-building measures are also central components of every piece of conflict management, particularly in the containment of ethno-national conflicts, which many states regard as the main source of instability (Senghaas 1993: 75). For this reason, conflict resolution has been an integral part of regime processes since the end of the Cold War.

The end of the Cold War brought about an acceleration in regime formation (UN, Council of Europe, C/OSCE), particularly in Europe. Despite the alleged failure in resolving follow-up conflicts during the break-up of Yugoslavia, and despite the loss of image suffered by the OSCE, thought is being given to transposing elements of this multilateral process to other regions of the world (Middle East, South-East Asia, Africa, Central America). The elements particularly concerned here are the methods and techniques that have been evolved for peaceful dispute-settlement and the standards established for the protection of minorities.[3]

Multilateral co-operation can be viewed as a (more or less) permanent process that begins to operate spontaneously, mostly after wars, on the basis of regional and global links, and/or accelerates as a result of pressure or negotiation. Co-operation can generate dynamics that effect a (slow) change in attitudes and ultimately lead to a balancing of interests between the states involved (reciprocal concessions) and to forms of conflict resolution in various political domains. Within the global UN system and the pan-European/Atlantic OSCE, a range of regimes of differing pace, orientation, and compulsoriness have developed.[4]

The OSCE: A Step Towards Permanent Co-operation in Europe?

The creation of a cross-state culture of conflict regulation and the move towards co-operation in vital areas such as security, international relations, minimum democratic provisions on minority protection and human rights, ecology and environmental protection can generate (their own) momentum. Co-operative processes release normative forces from which no state can (permanently) abstract itself without fear of disadvantage.

It is this calculation which, for example, underlies some unexpected concessions which individual states have made within the OSCE framework on the nationality question or the question of national minorities. Both the United Nations and the OSCE now make inter- and intra-state conditions the object of political control by the particular multilateral institutions concerned.

The CSCE was a product of the Cold War, or of European civil society's revolt against this threat. It grew up out of the awareness of a growing number of people who, having been stirred from their slumbers by the 1970s peace movement, recognized the extermination of the human race as a monstrous technological possibility, and realized that all our lives had suddenly become dependent on decisions made by a tiny power-élite in East and West. This horrendous vision produced the realization amongst Western (civil) societies, on an ever more massive scale, that there had to be dialogue between the blocs—a point of view which the politicians in Europe, the main potential nuclear theatre, were also forced, reluctantly and belatedly, to adopt in 1972. The signature of the Helsinki Final Act in 1975 by all the states who would be involved in any war that might break out in Europe marked the start of the so-called Helsinki process. The existence of civil-society actors and structures resulted in pressure from public opinion and an attitude of expectation that gave rise to this diplomatic process between state actors and subsequently accompanied and promoted it from outside and 'from below'. The formation of Helsinki Citizen Assemblies in East and West had lasting effects.[5]

The CSCE's transition from loose, informal, *ad hoc* co-operation by a large number of states to regulated and permanent co-operation only came about with the advent of *Perestroika* in the 'empire of evil' (Ronald Reagan's term for the former Soviet Union) at the end of the 1980s, increasing in intensity at the start of the 1990s—after the silent collapse of the Soviet Union—in parallel with the efforts being made within the framework of the Council of Europe. In the 1980s, interests—and the bartering that derived from these—were bloc-determined.

Ranged against Western demands in the domain of human rights and other basic rights—demands that were sometimes specially staged for propaganda purposes—were the East's interests in security guarantees (recognition of the territorial status quo) and an emphasis on state sovereignty and the principle of non-intervention. Gradual acceptance of minimum democratic and humanitarian standards, defined in accordance with the circumstances of the time, began to accelerate in the USSR after 1985, with the start of *Perestroika*, and in Eastern Europe after the upheavals of 1990. This in its turn had repercussions on Western obstructionist states via what was then the CSCE (now OSCE). A whole series of conflicts of values that had not been susceptible to transformation before this point were now radically and unilaterally altered, not by the conflict-resolution efforts within the CSCE or other international regimes, but by the profound changes in Eastern Europe and the former USSR.

The Institutionalization of the CSCE Process and the OSCE

The Charter of Paris of November 1990 is seen as marking the start of a new era in Europe. The institutionalization of the CSCE process and, today, of the OSCE, has been accelerated by the creation of a variety of executive bodies. The only parliamentary component, which has been in existence since July 1992, is a quasi-independent entity body which calls itself a Parliamentary Assembly, runs a small office in Copenhagen, and comes together once a year in one of the 55 OSCE capitals. However, its resolutions have neither legal force nor any influence on the policies of the OSCE executive bodies. The permanent structure is strictly hierarchical (even more obviously than in the UN system): the C/OSCE consists of the 'Conference' or periodic assembly of the heads of state of all the member states; three hierarchically organized executive bodies; a permanent secretariat; two permanent institutions for human rights and violence prevention; and two other, lower-ranking, small-scale, minimally integrated institutions—the High Commission on National Minorities and the Parliamentary Assembly.[6]

The conference process continues in the form of the two-yearly Review Conference and the summits of heads of state that follow these. This gathering approves the OSCE's activities, particularly the implementation of the decisions of the previous summit, and decides on future priorities.

The three executive bodies are the Council, the Committee of Senior Officials, and the Troika assisting the Chairman-in-Office.[7] The chairman is empowered to send personal *rapporteurs* to areas of conflict or crisis. The Secretariat, based in Prague, is headed by a secretary-general, who has a mixture of administrative and political tasks. The first secretary-general, the German Wilhelm Höynck, took up his office in mid-1993. In June 1996 he was succeeded by Giancarlo Aragona of Italy. From June 1999 to June

2002 the Slovak Jan Kubiš has headed the OSCE; before that he served four years as the director of the Conflict Prevention Centre, which oversees OSCE operations and long-term missions. The Portuguese chairmanship, with Foreign Minister Antonio Martins da Cruz, took over from Kubiš and looks after several hot spots in the OSCE area, among them the 'problem areas' in the Caucasus and the Balkans.[8]

The OSCE Secretariat is responsible for administration, logistics, and dissemination (storage and dispatch of OSCE documentation), and also for relations with non-governmental organizations. The two permanent OSCE institutions are the Office for Democratic Institutions and Human Rights (ODIHR) in Warsaw and the Conflict Prevention Centre (CPC) in Vienna. The end of 1992 (Helsinki II) saw the creation of the High Commission on National Minorities, with its headquarters in The Hague.

Monitoring Compliance with Humanitarian Commitments

The Helsinki II agreements of 1992 charged the Office for Democratic Institutions and Human Rights in Warsaw with monitoring respect for human rights and compliance with commitments in the member states. It also investigates political developments (e.g. crises and emergencies).

More far-reaching demands in the domain of human and minority rights, as made within the framework of the CSCE of the time, subsequently encountered increased resistance from—ironically—the Western side, notably certain 'obstructionist' countries (such as France, Britain, and Greece). In a historic role-reversal, at the Moscow CSCE meeting in September 1991, the 'Eastern Bloc' was making proposals on the monitoring of human rights that 'put Western suggestions in the shade'.[9] Together with the Neutral and Non-aligned (NNA) states, the ex-USSR was of the view that missions to monitor implementation of humanitarian provisions agreed at the CSCE must in future be carried out even in the face of opposition from the states concerned. But this point of view took a long time to be accepted.

The dispatch of observers to areas of ethno-national crisis should be made possible without restriction. An improvement in the possibilities for verification was effected by making experts from each of the current total of 55 OSCE members (formerly 38) available for fact-finding missions in other participating countries.[10] However, such missions only take place at the invitation or application of a country, or of several OSCE members. If necessary, five states can decide to dispatch a *Rapporteur*, on the UN model. In 'particularly serious' cases, a minimum of nine states can send one or more such *Rapporteurs* directly to a country without prior warning. Their reports can then be placed on the agenda of the Committee of Senior Officials in Prague.

This scheme, introduced in 1991, represented the first breakthrough on the verification question, and also the first departure from the principle of consensus within the CSCE. This obstructive principle was done away with by the Prague Council meeting of January 1992, for cases where there was crass violation of commitments by a member state. To begin with, there was no mention of sanctions. Since then, it is the C/OSCE human-rights regime that has undergone the most dynamic development, whereas co-operation in economics, technology, and the environment has lagged behind.[11]

Creation of a Conflict Prevention Centre

The former USSR had called for a system of collective security since the 1950s. Helsinki embodied a ban, in principle, on the use of violence. Beginning in 1973, Switzerland made several unsuccessful attempts to introduce an Agreement on the Peaceful Settlement of Disputes into what was then the CSCE.[12] It was only in 1989, with Gorbachov's new thinking, that the compulsory involvement of a third party in disputes and conflicts between member states, or in conflicts within individual member states (now numbering 55, from Vancouver to Vladivostok), became possible.

The institutionalization of the CSCE process included the creation of the Conflict Prevention Centre (CPC) in Vienna. However, the schemes for a dispute-settlement mechanism (as formulated in February 1991 in La Valletta, Malta) were confined to conflicts between states. Even within these limits, they excluded most kinds of disputes—on the grounds that outside intervention would violate territorial integrity and sovereignty—and assigned no active role to the CPC. A somewhat more extended mechanism for consultation and co-operation in crisis situations was agreed by the CSCE Council meeting in June 1991 in Berlin. Member states can ask for urgent clarification and can call on the CSO in Prague, which can then *recommend* solutions. A military crisis mechanism, created in November 1991, provides for consultations on 'unusual military activities'. The principle of consensus was partially revoked.

Originally, it was the wish of certain states that the Conflict Prevention Centre in Vienna should be given as many competencies as the CSO in its capacity as the executive organ of the CSCE Council.[13] However, this proposal did not win general acceptance: the activities of the CPC are confined chiefly to investigating political and military issues and problems that might present a threat to European security, and to implementing programmes of conflict prevention and resolution.

Misunderstood Prevention: the Birth of OSCE Long-term Missions

With the dispatch of various C/OSCE long-term missions, first to Yugo-slavia and then in greater numbers to various ethno-national trouble-spots in the former USSR, the CPC was unexpectedly able to enhance its role, as it assumed part of the responsibility for the operational direction and logistics of these missions. To begin with, the CSCE, as it was, did not talk of 'long-term missions'—in other words, the concept of having C/OSCE staff observing crisis situations for lengthy periods on the spot sprang not from some theoretical 'idea', but from the practical situation on the ground. The work of these missions was and is characterized by incalculable risks and an oscillation between costly but 'helpless' crisis management' and an arduous and time-consuming process of a peacekeeping presence, observation, negotiation, and proposed solution. In many instances, the OSCE was sucked into conflicts and—unwillingly—became part of it.

Ever since 1993 such mission consumed the bulk of the OSCE budget (with an average of 85 percent). Initially, OSCE long-term missions were developed as an 'alternative model' of conflict containment, alongside mediation at the highest political levels—i.e. classical shuttle and negotiation-based diplomacy (track 1), at moderate costs.[14] Ethnicization and violence in the former Yugoslavia and Soviet Union translated into a 'cost explosion' for the OSCE. In the years 1993–97 the budget quadrupled from 12 to 48 million Euro; in the period of 1997–2000 it quadrupled again from 48 to over 200 million Euro, reaching 209 million Euro in 2001 and slightly decreasing to 180 million in 2002. As already stated, this includes the operational costs for long-time missions. Compared to armed missions by NATO or UNDPKO the costs of these missions are extremely modest.

The whole concept of preventing violent conflict, which hardly does apply to already escalated conflicts, was badly misunderstood. Prevention typically aims at timely averting the turn into destructive violence by peaceful intervention in the early stages of dormant and emerging conflict. The following phases of a conflict cycle, those of escalation and open violence, are the domain of 'fire-fighting', costly military intervention and peacekeeping operations, rather that prevention.

The OSCE had established itself as a major European instrument for early warning, conflict prevention, crisis management, and post-conflict rehabilitation—despite its alleged failure in Yugoslavia. The OECE had a dozen long-term missions (field operations) in progress in various countries including: Bosnia and Herzegovina, Croatia, Estonia, Georgia, Latvia, the Former Yugoslav Republic of Macedonia, Moldova, Tajikistan, and the Ukraine. It has also sent an Assistance Group to Chechnya (Russian Federation) and Georgia, and it has a presence in Albania and a Monitoring

Group in Belarus.[15] Russia was the first big power to agree to the OSCE's acting in a conflict that has been declared to be internal (Chechnya). This is a significant concession, and one hopes it will set a precedent, though this may prove a headache for certain states in the future. A Liaison Office in Central Asia, located in Tashkent, provided a link between the offices in Vienna and Prague and the five OSCE 'participating states' in Central Asia. The largest OSCE mission was that to Bosnia and Herzegovina, which, as of March 1998, had 190 internationally seconded members and an authorized strength of 246. Besides the head office in Sarajevo, it had regional centres in Banja Luka, Bihac, Mostar, Tuzla, and Sokolac. The mission opened 20 field-offices in the two entities of Bosnia and Herzegovina, as well as an additional office in Breko. The OSCE mission to Croatia began in July 1997.[16] Of the OSCE long-term missions, six were in former Yugoslavia (in Sarajevo, Bosnia and Herzegovina, Kosovo, Sanjak and Vojvodina, Croatia, Kosovo in 1999, plus a 'Spillover Monitor Mission' in Macedonia, based in Skopje, which came to real relevance in 2001 and 2002) and six operated in the former Soviet Union (Estonia, Latvia, Moldova, the Ukraine, Georgia, Tajikistan). As of 2002, five missions were closed (two in the Balkans and three in the FSU). The cost in manpower and materials to date has been relatively modest compared with the potential benefits. To begin with, the OSCE had difficulty finding well-trained, properly prepared diplomats and experts who were willing to put up with the very unattractive conditions.[17] This was the reason for increased training efforts being launched in 1999.

On account of political sensibilities, there are as yet no additional OSCE peace-troops (analogous to the UN's blue helmets). A deployment of such troops *had* been planned in—of all situations—an intractable conflict to which neither OSCE diplomacy nor the Russian peace-keeping troops were equal. The task of the troops was to monitor the (so far successful) cease-fire between Armenia and Azerbaijan (in and around Nagorno-Karabakh). To date, no solution has been found to the basic problem—namely, the occupation of a quarter of the territory of Azerbaijan by Armenia. A transformation of the conflict could have been sought in the form of a withdrawal of the Armenian forces from Azeri territory in exchange for Nagorno-Karabakh's becoming part of Armenia, with a demilitarized corridor linking the two. Such 'solutions' may appear dangerous, since they could have a 'domino effect' on other separatist regions. The scenario for Nagorno-Karabakh does not seem to chime with the intentions of Kacharian and other radical leaders who ousted Ter-Petrosyan (after his decision to accept the Minsk group's peace proposals).[18] The presence of the OSCE in this potentially virulent conflict is almost invisible, confined to running three offices (in Baku, Yerevan and Stepanakert/Khankendi).

The use of OSCE troops in the Southern Caucasus would have been an important test for future activities of this kind. But that test (fortunately) never took place: internationally speaking, there has been a sobering-down of attitudes towards the usefulness—indeed, the abysmal failure—of military interventions. Meanwhile the number of UN peacekeeping missions was rising again, with two critical problems being highlighted: (1) the lack of political will in the UN Security Council for some operations and its most appalling double standards (e.g., comparing the large KFOR operation in tiny Kosovo with the tiny UN peacekeeping operation of MONUC in the huge Congo), and, (2) the lack of consent and cooperation on the ground by the parties to the conflict.[19] For the OSCE, the legal justification for these kinds of military ventures is contained in the Helsinki II document of 1992, which mentions the possibility of OSCE measures in line with chapter VII of the UN Charter.

Institutional Protection for Europe's Minorities

Declarations by the then CSCE on the 'human dimension' in the decisive period of 1989–91[20]—departing, characteristically, from the principle of consensus—mention the rights of national minorities to their own ethnic, cultural, and religious identity and to freedom of expression ('free of any attempts at assimilation against their will'). The expert meeting of the CSCE on minority questions in July 1991 in Geneva brought disappointing results overall. However, it was officially established for the first time that minority questions were legitimate international concerns and could not therefore be the (exclusively) internal affair of a state.[21]

The creation of a High Commissioner on National Minorities was agreed at the Helsinki II meeting (March–June 1992). Max van der Stoel, the former Dutch foreign minister, was appointed High Commissioner by consensus decision of the CSO in December 1992, for a three-year period renewable for one further term. This new commitment was welcomed by human-rights organizations but judged to be inadequate.[22]

The High Commissioner on National Minorities can only operate on a restricted, very specific, and, in most concrete cases, inadequate mandate, always on a 'short leash' controlled by the Committee of Senior Officials and the Chairman. These executive bodies also contain officials and representatives of countries responsible for the 'problems' under investigation because they have minorities that may be discriminated against or openly oppressed.

The Mandate of the OSCE High Commissioner on Minorities

As an objective, independent authority, the High Commissioner has an international mandate from the C/OSCE to investigate as yet non-violent 'tensions' between states and national minorities at the early stage, to issue early warnings where appropriate, and to promote dialogue (CSCE 1992: II, 19–24,19):

- He can issue an 'early warning' (§13) if there is a prima facie risk of escalation to conflict or if the 'tensions' have the potential to develop into a conflict (§2), in which case the warning will be discussed at the next meeting of the CSO and any affected state may activate the 'emergency mechanism' (§14).
- The High Commissioner must take the availability of (local) democratic means and international instruments into account and have recourse to these in cases where insufficient use is made of them by the parties involved (§6).
- During his inspection visits, which are notifiable in advance, the High Commissioner will gather information from all those involved (§26), notably state, regional, and local authorities, organizations representing minorities, and NGOs (against whom the state concerned must refrain from taking any punitive action: §30).
- The High Commissioner can only act if empowered to do so by the CSO. Since consensus decision-making is the norm in the CSO, undesired activities by the High Commissioner could easily be blocked by the affected state. The mandate is particularly restrictive on this point (Early Action, §16–26); at the same time, it lacks concrete provisions. 'Action' is evidently understood to mean instituting confidence-building measures and calling on those involved to engage in dialogue and co-operation ('preventive diplomacy').[23]
- After completing his work, the High Commissioner passes his confidential report, including his findings, results, and conclusions, to the Chairman. The latter then consults with the OSCE state concerned and passes the report to the CSO (§19) within a period of one month.
- If a conflict escalates, the High Commissioner informs the CSO via the Chairman, and the CSO or another institution takes action; at the behest of the CSO, the High Commissioner will provide information to CSCE implementation meetings on human-dimension issues (§§21, 22).

These latter provisions are intended to enhance the responsibility and accountability of the states on minority issues. There are a whole series of regulations prohibiting contact between the High Commissioner and ethno-national organizations that advocate violence (here typically labelled 'terrorism').[24] The High Commissioner is also not empowered to investigate minority issues that have developed into armed conflicts (in other words, the situations he deals with must 'not yet [have] developed beyond an early warning stage': §3). This clearly lies more within the province of the Conflict Prevention Centre (CPC).

Neither a Human-Rights Mechanism nor an Ombudsman

The High Commissioner is expressly forbidden to act in situations involving 'organized acts of terrorism'. States usually define any kind of politically motivated anti-state use of force as 'terrorist'. If a state fears investigation by the High Commissioner on its territory, or fears his making contact with an organization representing a minority that is subject to discrimination, it would probably not be difficult for it to fabricate 'terrorist activities' by the organization concerned, or to claim that individual representatives of the minority supported such activities (verbally). In such a case, the organization would not be eligible to join in talks.[25]

Neither the High Commissioner nor the Office for Democratic Institutions and Human Rights in Warsaw (from which the Commissioner is meant to gather the relevant information) probably have the power to determine what is regarded as terrorism in the OSCE. Huber mentions a ban on contact with people who advocate or use violence.[26] In order to attempt to bring about a peaceful settlement to a dispute, the Commissioner has to make a request and obtain a specific mandate from the CSO (§7). The work and findings of the High Commissioner are not accessible to the public because they are 'confidential'.

The upshot of all this is that those conflicts that most urgently need the good offices of the High Commissioner are expressly excluded from his mandate. The real mandate could equally be fulfilled by human-rights organizations in (ideal) conjunction with the media—in other words, by a kind of Greenpeace (or 'Colouredpeace') for minorities.

None the less, positive effects would still be expected for the situation of nationalities that suffer from discrimination if future High Commissioners act like van der Stoel (1973–2001) who was prepared and able to make full use his mandate as a 'lone fighter' (initially with a team of just three diplomats and a small number of advisers from the FIER).[27] The new High Commissioner Rolf Ekéus (since mid 2001) will have to give proof that he lives up to the profile given to the institution by Max van der Stoel.[28] Ekéus already made it clear that quiet diplomacy and discretion are the bedrock of conflict prevention (OSCE-HCNM 2001). After pointing out that the mandate obliges him to focus on the prevention of violent conflict, the new

High Commissioner mentioned that 'in fulfilling this task, I must address discrimination, injustice or exclusion ... The persistence of such conditions can breed extremism and sometimes terrorism' (ibid.). The meeting of experts, already referred to, came to the conclusion that the High Commissioner's mandate, which could, they said, be seen as 'limited and weak', actually proved 'effective' in (non-violent) inter-ethnic conflicts (Conflict Management Group 1993: 3, 10). What was ultimately needed to solve conflicts of the minority–majority type, or to avoid acute escalation, was, they said, a long-term process of dialogue between minorities and governments in the actual countries concerned. Recommendations of the HCNM, made to governments of OSCE participating States regarding the treatment of their national minorities, concerned the policies of certain countries or general themes, such as the Roma question[29] or the packages of recommendations delivered in The Hague 1996, Oslo 1998 and Lund 1999.

According to the experts, four elements had contributed to the relative success of the High Commissioner's preventive diplomacy: the adoption of a non-evaluative or non-judgmental approach by the Commissioner, who saw himself not as a 'policeman' but as a mediator; the fact that proceedings were geared to resolving differences as part of a government–minority interaction aimed at establishing rights and duties; the position of independence and confidentiality (as in classical secret diplomacy); and the backing of the OSCE (ibid., 2–3). This assessment was, however, tempered by the statement that the OSCE 'success story' had more to do with the person of the High Commissioner (van der Stoel, 1973–2001) than with his mandate (ibid., 43). Notwithstanding this positive assessment, a total overhaul of the mandate seems essential in the medium term if the future activity of the High Commissioner is to be successful.

Out of concern about possible resistance by national minorities to encroachments by the state, and out of fear of eroding state authority (even) in Europe, the High Commissioner can only operate under a cloak of silence, and his reports are 'strictly confidential' (§18). The office of High Commissioner is not a human-rights mechanism. He has neither the institutional options nor the mandate to initiate peacekeeping measures or to suggest ways of resolving conflicts; he can only make confidential recommendations. But no state is obliged to follow those recommendations—or even to take official cognizance of them! The OSCE framework does not provide a sufficiently far-reaching mandate for the High Commissioner and CPC, nor the appropriate infrastructure, resources, or funding[30]—despite increased awareness of the explosive nature of the ethno-national factor.

It is not surprising that the High Commissioner is not meant to function as an ombudsman for persecuted minorities (Huber 1993: 31). That he may only consider general violations of OSCE minimum standards and that he is not allowed to investigate concrete cases (§5c), let alone serve as an appellate authority for persecuted minorities, are regrettable concessions to the representatives of certain member states who have their own unsolved ethnic-cum-national problems. What was a good idea has thus been deprived of its teeth.

Minorities Suffering Discrimination in the OSCE Area

The High Commissioner's area of operation in principle extends over much of the northern hemisphere—from western Europe, through eastern Europe, to the former USSR, over the Bering straits to Alaska, Canada, and the USA, via Greenland, Iceland, and the Faeroe islands, back to the European mainland. Within this area, comprising the 55 member states of the OSCE, lives a multiversity of between 800 and 900 nations, nationalities, and peoples.

The OSCE area is inhabited by peoples as varied as the Hopi-Pueblo Indians of the south-west USA, the Basque minority of southern France, the Inuit across four states, the native Siberian peoples in the Far East, the Sami, the Finno-Ugric Mansi and Komi in Russia, the Yakut in Siberia, the Sardinians, the Slovenes in Friuli, the Koreans in Uzbekistan, the French in the Valle d'Aosta, and so on.

The number of communities described as 'minorities' has grown rapidly in recent times and probably now accounts for a large proportion of all ethnic groups—i.e. 2,000 to 3,000 'minorities' in the OSCE area. The growth in the number of internationally recognized states by a figure of 20 has produced perhaps hundreds of new minorities (Yamskov 1994: 58–61). Not only the Russians in the Baltic or the Ukraine, but also, conversely, the Ukrainians in Russia and Kazakhstan, the Estonians in Saint Petersburg, and the Slovaks in the Czech Republic became new minorities almost overnight.[31]

Putting a figure on the minorities subject to discrimination in the OSCE area is a difficult undertaking: one or two facts will give an idea of the dimensions of the problem. Even in the reputedly ethnically and culturally homogeneous nation-states of Western Europe, the diversity beneath the thin 'national' veneer is enormous. As mentioned before, some 50 million EU citizens—about one in seven people—speak a language other than their state's official language(s).[32] And yet most states stubbornly resist making concessions on the language-question or doing anything more than paying lip-service to the maintenance of endangered cultures.[33]

About 100 million Europeans belong to one or other of the more than 200 minority nationalities of Europe.[34] Within the 15 EU member states alone, there are 'more than 40 autochthonous languages in everyday use'.[35]

The enormous complexity of the minority question becomes especially apparent when one lists the ten most populous 'minorities' subject to discrimination or endangerment in the OSCE area. These nations, nationalities, and peoples will be at the heart of current and future conflicts if their legitimate rights to autonomy and self-governance are not dealt with.

The concerns of certain large minorities seem to have been comparatively satisfactorily dealt with—the Québécois (of Canada), for example, or the Bashkirs (in the Russian Federation).[36] The largest OSCE minorities subject to discrimination are, in descending size of population from 35 to 3.5 million: Afro-Americans, Russians, *Chicanos*, Jews, Roma and Sinti, Germans, Turks, Albanians, Magyars, and Serbs. The populations of the first three (Afro-Americans, Russians, and Hispano-American or *Latinos*) are each greater than those of a larger-sized OSCE state. The populations of each of the ten largest OSCE minorities (listed below) exceed those of a number of small European states.[37]

- The largest proportion of the minority population in the OSCE area is accounted for by the more than 35 million Afro-Americans; they are the largest minority in the USA, making up 12–14 percent of the total population. In addition, many blacks live on the territories of former colonial powers.[38]
- Almost 18 percent of all Russians—that is to say, about 26 million— live as minorities in 14 new OSCE states (successors to the USSR), including 11 million (21 percent) in the Ukraine alone.
- The third-largest minority in the OSCE area is that of the 25 million Spanish-speaking people (*Hispanics* and *Chicanos*) in the USA.
- Over 15 million Roma (including Sinti groups) live scattered throughout almost all the states of Europe, the majority in the east and south-east.
- About 11 million Jews live scattered over almost the whole OSCE area, most of them in the USA, followed by Russia, France, and various eastern states.
- About 5 million German-speaking peoples live in more than a dozen states (5 of them in the CIS).[39]
- 4.5 million Turks live in Europe, including 2.5 million living as migrants, chiefly in the FRG.[40]
- Almost 4 million Albanians lived (until May 1999) in difficult circumstances outside the state of Albania (3.3 million).[41]
- 3.5 million Hungarians live as minorities in four states. Only in the Ukraine and in Romania can their situation be regarded as satisfactory; Serbia and Slovakia refuse to accord them adequate minority rights.[42]

- 3.5 million Serbs live outside Serbia, as new endangered minorities in Croatia, Bosnia and Kosovo (with many others becoming refugees in Serbia), and as migrants in Western Europe.[43]

The Activities of the High Commissioner on Minorities

From the middle of 1993 until now, the High Commissioner has been active mainly in Eastern Europe and the former Soviet Union (OSCE-HCNM 1998 and 1998b). The groups concerned, in terms of my demographic ranking of the largest OSCE minorities, were: the Russians (2nd); the so-called 'gypsies'—that is to say, the Roma (5th); the Albanians (8th); and the Magyars (9th). Van der Stoel visited Latvia and Estonia, both of which had passed apartheid-style laws entailing massive discrimination against Russians, Byelorussians, Poles, and other minorities.

The High Commissioner offered the governments of the three Baltic republics (and five other eastern states) advisory services. One cannot say that this on-the-spot mission was a success. In Estonia (where Estonians account for 54 percent of the population), the 'ethnically cleansed', almost purely Estonian parliament passed a racist law on citizenship in July 1993 which was the target of massive advance criticism from Russia, the United Nations, the Council of Europe, and several international human-rights organizations (such as Amnesty International). Following intervention by the High Commissioner, the government is said to have declared itself willing to hold referendums on autonomy in Russian-inhabited parts of the country, including Narva.[44] But a unilateral declaration of sovereignty by the Russian area around the industrial city of Narva had already been made in 1991, following a referendum in which there was 98 percent support for the idea.

In response to the 'problem' of the Roma and Sinti in the OSCE area, the High Commissioner requested in 1993 to be allowed to study the situation of the (semi-)nomadic Roma; until 2000 he delivered several reports on the situation of Europe's most threatened people.[45] Van der Stoel has carried out on-site investigations into the situation of the Hungarian minorities in Slovakia and Romania, and the situation of Roma suffering discrimination in Hungary;[46] from 1993 to 2000 several more reports on the situation of the Roma appeared.[47] Van der Stoel reported about the 'phenomenon of prejudice against Roma' as singular. 'Romani communities are the subject of hostile perceptions across an extraordinary range of countries.'[48]

The situation of the Albanians in Macedonia, unwarrantedly judged by the United Nations to be critical, was also on the High Commissioner's agenda. The UN sent peacekeeping forces to Macedonia as a preventive measure to ensure that any uprising by the Kosovo Albanians against Serb discrimination (after the abrogation of the Kosovar's autonomy already in 1989) did not spread to the Macedonian Albanians and Albania itself. Macedonia seemed under threat.[49] Since then, the situation in the 'heart of the Balkans' has grown more acute but has, until 1998, not been directed at the Albanian minority. This minority soon turned the tables—under NATO protection and cared for by a UN administration. The 1999 NATO war against Yugoslavia, with its unprecedented military intervention in favour of an armed group (several factions of KLA-UÇK elements) combated by government forces in the Kosovo, consisted of eleven weeks of heavy bombardments against Yugoslavia (mainly its Serbian part), and ended as a full-blown disaster. As a result, the 'ethnic cleansing' of Albanians by Serbs was simply reversed. Under the eyes of NATO forces, Serbs and Roma were killed or driven out of Kosovo by the UÇK. In 2000 Macedonia began to become the target of military attacks by UÇK elements, which infiltrated from NATO-occupied Kosovo. Rapid escalation could be broken by Macedonia's new constitutional arrangements for its Albanian minority in 2001 but the situation remained volatile.

Macedonia has not many friends in the area since it became independent. In February 1994, Papandreou's Greek government had imposed a total trade, transport, and communications embargo on Macedonia.[50] These actions had also shed a sombre light on Greece's policy of assimilation *vis-à-vis* its minorities, e.g., the forcibly assimilated Slav-Macedonian minority in northern Greece—a policy that also belonged on the High Commissioner's agenda.[51] In a situation of ethno-national tension, even research-work—such as that by Anastasía Karakasidou on the Greek Macedonians—can trigger hysterical reactions and drive a reputed publisher to abstain from publishing a book on minority rights issues.[52]

Reversal in the Treatment of Minorities

Within the Council of Europe and the OSCE, it was for decades Greece, Turkey, France, and Britain who pursued a backward-looking, hyper-centralist line in regard to nationality policy and the protection of minorities. Under a conservative government, Spain does also belong to this group.[53] Meanwhile, Britain, under a new Labour government, made a complete U-turn towards internal *devolution of powers* in 1997–99, with what was described as a 'quiet revolution'.[54] Even France, with a partial autonomy statute granted to Corsica end of 2001, seemed to distance itself from its centralist-Jacobinist traditions; devolution will allow Corsica only limited self-government but represents a historic peace-building project, for which the left-wing Jospin government sadly paid with the loss of power.[55]

All these five states have a large proportion of minorities or other historical nationalities on their territory and, under the influence of the overriding national chauvinism (of the state classes), they continue to cling to their policies of hyper-centralism and assimilation. In Italy, one of the 'big four' in the EU, regionalization is decades old but was recently complemented by the October 2001 referendum on shifting power from the central government to the country's regions. More than 60 percent of voters backed the proposals put forward by the previous centre-left government; this gives regional authorities more say over taxes, education and environmental policy.

In Eastern Europe since 1990, the treatment of minorities seems quite contrary to the recent developments in Western Europe, which reversed the earlier positioning in both parts of Europe. If there have been any results from the High Commissioner's missions in the three serious cases of the Russians (and other minorities) in the Baltic, the Roma and Sinti throughout Europe, and the Macedonians in Greece, nothing substantial has so far emerged about them. The High Commission has been in existence since the beginning of 1993, and Max van der Stoel has been exclusively active in Eastern Europe throughout the period until retirement in mid-2001, when the new high commissioner Rolf Ekéus took over.[56] After the first period of four years there was an analysis of van der Stoel's efforts;[57] due to the OSCE's discreet policy, assuring affected states of 'absolute' confidentiality, the relevant information is still largely lacking. The age of secret diplomacy in minority matters is not over in Europe.

The Call for a Minorities Charter and an Appeal Body

For nations without a state, the distinction between the right to self-determination and the right to secession continues to represent the real watershed.[58] Such nations make up the bulk of the membership of the Unrepresented Nations and Peoples Organization. The establishment of a minorities' charter or convention has been proposed by various sides as a method of preventing destructive conflict. Respect for such a charter should be made a precondition for the recognition of further secessions by former constituent states in their old administrative, but highly conflictive, borders (this is usually the bone of contention). An OSCE convention on minority rights would be a more binding arrangement for this legally. In November 1994, the Committee of Ministers of the Council of Europe issued a framework convention for ratification by its then 33 member states. The framework convention only went into force in 1998. But a legally binding minority rights convention in the 55 OSCE states would be a much more important step in the direction of a binding multilateral regulation of minority protection.

In the run-up to the creation of the High Commission on National Minorities, Senghaas had proposed a 'CSCE institution for minority protection', whose monitoring functions would ensure respect for the convention (or charter)—for example, by a requirement on the European states to present a yearly report. This new institution could act as an appeal body for endangered or disadvantaged minorities (Senghaas 1992: 132–4). The OSCE should create an institutional framework and co-ordination centre for regional and sub-regional conflict-resolution forums.

Respect for the collective rights of nationalities that are defined by states as minorities and of endangered indigenous peoples has so far not been laid down in binding form. The weak UN declaration on minorities passed by the General Assembly at the end of 1992 does, it is true, represent the start of the process of embodiment of minority rights in international law; but it is hedged around with too many compromises, is not very comprehensive (it contains only nine articles), deals only with individual rights, and, as a declaration, is a long way from being a legally binding document.[59] Up to now, only the text of Art. 27 of the International Covenant on Civil and Political Rights had pointed clearly in the direction of collective rights.[60] Certain states (such as France and Turkey) that behave notoriously badly in regard to minority rights reacted true to type.[61] The accompanying UN resolution 47/135 of December 1992 talks of the increased attention being paid by human-rights organization to minority protection and calls on these and other NGOs to help disseminate the new declaration and ensure understanding of it.

The declaration on the rights of indigenous stateless peoples which has been in the process of elaboration since the mid-1980s (but a decade of deliberations was transferred to a Human Rights Commission working-group specially created for this purpose) goes beyond the individual rights recognized by the OSCE (then CSCE) as being part of the 'human dimension' (notably in the Copenhagen Document). It is in the domain of collective rights that the planned Universal Declaration of the Rights of Indigenous Peoples (draft of 1994) would have made its greatest contribution to the extension of international law. This trend began in 1989, with ILO Convention 169. Initial (theoretical) steps towards establishing these kinds of rights in international law began as far back as the Moscow meeting of the CSCE in October 1991. The aim is to create mechanisms that will make it possible to intervene in the internal affairs of states in cases where minority nationalities are in danger or are being persecuted.

There is a need both for protective regulations in the constitutions of the individual states and for an international guarantee of those regulations by supra-regional organizations and multilateral regimes (the Council of Europe or the OSCE in the case of Europe), including appropriate powers in regard to legal protection that 'impose an obligation on governments to give an account of themselves'.[62] Parties to a conflict (e.g., endangered nationalities) could use this kind of supra-state institution as an independent European court of arbitration (like the Permanent Court of Arbitration in The Hague) and an extra-legal forum for the resolution of conflicts.

The Explosive Nature of the Ethno-national Factor in Europe

In the early 1990s in ten out of 13 ongoing wars in Europe, ethno-national problems played a crucial role—and in some cases had done so for decades. At its peak, 14 percent of all ongoing violent conflicts were taking place in Europe. Some of these conflicts have since been resolved or successfully transformed; others remain precariously balanced; and yet others continue as before, with the propensity to violence and the military infrastructure remaining in place.

In Western Europe, there have been three armed conflicts since 1945, one of which is still in progress:

- Spain vs. the Basque nationalists in Euzkal Herria / Euzkadi: guerrilla war waged since 1937; since 1968 by the nationalist underground army of Euzkadi Ta Askatasuna (ETA, Basque Fatherland and Liberty); no serious negotiations with ETA took place since Aznar came to power, despite 14 month of cease-fire by ETA; fighting and terrorist attacks continue throughout Spain—despite (full) regional autonomy of Basque country; escalation after ban of nationalist party Batasuna in Aug. 2002.
- France vs. nationalist Corsicans: the Corsican National Liberation Front, FLNC, in operation since 1950, split in several factions, with some having links to organized crime; attacks and sporadic incidents continue despite limited self-governance granted in December 2001.
- Britain and Northern Irish Protestant 'settlers' vs. Catholic Republicans in Northern Ireland: armed struggle by IRA, armed wing of Sinn Fein party, since 1960; cease-fire September 1994; peace talks between Britain and Ireland, with the involvement of Sinn Fein, ran into delays; pressure applied by former US President Clinton; other actors such as Protestant death-squads are mainly attacking Catholic civilians (UVF, 1961, 1969, 1986–October 1994; UFF; their maximum objective—preservation of the status quo—a source of conflict). A historic agreement seemed possible since successful direct negotiations began. The breakthrough came in spring 1998 but uncertainties remained until the decommissioning of IRA weapons, which began in 2001.

In Eastern Europe, there have been six armed conflicts; two Yugoslavian ones remain virulent and have only been settled superficially, under pressure from an outside power (NATO):

- Croatia vs. Serb minorities: in Krajina and Slavonia since July 1991; Krajina captured by Croatian troops in August 1995; almost whole Serb population driven out; acts of revenge; the incorporation of eastern Slavonia into Croatian state in Paris accord of December 1995 was accompanied by various guarantees.
- In tripartite Bosnia: Chetniki, Muslims, and HOS from March 1992; 5,000 Mujaheddin mercenaries and al-Qaeda operatives involved from 1993;[63] NATO involved against Bosnian Serbs end of August 1995; Serb moratorium (following US promise that economic sanctions would be lifted); change in the balance of forces; planned division unclear in the Paris accord (December 1995).[64]
- Moldova vs. Dniester Republic: Russians, Ukrainians, and Cossacks March–August 1992; autonomy obtained, sovereignty of Moldova recognized; minority rights for Gagauz also acknowledged.
- Romania vs. Hungary: acts of terror by Securitate (internal secret police) against Hungarians in Timisoara (December 1989); overthrow of dictator, change of government and limited democratization; minority issues unresolved; emigration of Banat Germans to FRG.
- The Kosovo crisis: the 1999 NATO intervention and months-long bombardment of Yugoslavia were seen as a new type of 'humanitarian intervention'. Its consequences were disastrous. The former multi-ethnic Kosovo became an almost mono-ethnic place, with non-Albanian minorities persecuted and driven out.
- Despite the NATO presence in Kosovo, Macedonia was in 2000–2001 aggressed by Albanian armed elements, which infiltrated from Kosovo. Outside intervention forced Macedonia to up-grade the rights of its Albanian minority in exchange for disarmament of UÇK elements.

In south-eastern Europe (the Caucasus) there were a large number of armed conflicts under way:

- Russian army vs. Yandarbijev's Chechen separatists: war started in December 1994; acts of terror by Chechen commandos in Russia; cease-fire from mid-1995; resumption of negotiations in autumn 1995; intensi-fication of violence before parliamentary elections of December 1995 until the truce of August 1996; bomb explosions in Moscow and resumptions of war in October 1999, provoked by hard-line Chechens attacking Dagestan, led to destruction of Grozny and large refugee flows; the growing influence of al-Qaeda trained extremists had become obvious since the later 1990s; the conflict is unsolved and Chechnya's future status in the Russian Federation remains unclear.

- Armenia and Nagorno-Karabakh vs. Azerbaijan: 1988–May 1994; since then, lasting cease-fire despite continuing occupation of Azeri areas by Armenians; intervention of regional powers (Russian 'neutrality'; West and Iran support Armenians; Turkey supports Azeris); mediation and initiatives by CIS, since both states again full members of CIS.
- Georgia vs. Abkhazia: abrogation of autonomy led to war of secession (August 1992–July 1993); defeat of Georgia; threats of war by Georgia (confirmed by Shevardnadze November 1995).[65]
- Georgia vs. South Ossetia: abrogation of autonomy leads to war December 1990 – July 1992; repressive 'pacification' by Georgia; continuing division of Ossetia; continued existence of irredentist movement amongst Ossetians (who want to join Russia).
- Chechnya: Chechens vs. Ingushetians (December 1991–March 1992); separation and division of joint republic.
- Georgia vs. Gamsakhurdia rebels (September 1991–January 1992); rebellion crushed by new government; continuing instability in Georgia.

If such armed conflicts are to be avoided in future in Europe, a multilateral minority-regime must be established forthwith. The creation of the High Commission on National Minorities, as a result of increased awareness of the ethnic factor following a large number of new ethno-national conflicts in Europe, came late and with an insufficient mandate.

Stages in Failure and Reasons for OSCE Reform

As a regional institution for violence prevention and dispute-settlement, the OSCE—as was rapidly demonstrated by the six-year ethno-national war between the Armenians and Azeris in 1988–94 and by the Yugoslavian conflict from 1991—is in need of an 'integrated scheme' for the organization of non-violent conflict resolution' (Mietzsch 1992: 115).

As a product of the Cold War, the former CSCE had neither the mandate nor the institutional capacity to deal with 'internal' conflicts. As a result of the precipitate recognition of the USSR's successor states and the secession of Slovenia and Croatia, these internal conflicts were transformed overnight into 'international' ones. This provided the Conflict Prevention Centre, created shortly before this, with a mandate, but not with the necessary capacity and effectiveness.

The secession of Slovenia and Croatia in summer 1991 resulted in an outbreak of armed hostilities, beginning in the northern part of Yugoslavia.

The fear of the Serb minority in Slavonia and Krajina (in the new Croatian state) that there would be a renewed genocide against them played an important part in the escalation of the war.[66] In the Caucasus, the endemic war between Turkish Azeris and Armenians took an unexpected turn in spring 1993, developing into an undeclared war of conquest and triggering a further humanitarian catastrophe and the mass flight of over a million Azeris in western Azerbaijan.

The C/OSCE's failure in Bosnia in 1992–3 and in the Southern Caucasus in 1993 pointed to continuing shortcomings, given that the institutional measures taken up to that date had no effect. The hectic and ultimately vain efforts of the C/OSCE in the Yugoslavian conflict hampered, or indeed blocked, the work of long-term reform.

The weak points of the OSCE regime continue to be:

- the inadequate development of the Conflict Prevention Centre and considerable confusion about a basic understanding of the concept of preventive policies
- inadequate monitoring of compliance with the human-rights obligations entered into by member states within the framework of the OSCE (verification)
- the inadequate mandate and budget of the High Commission on National Minorities and the poor protection afforded to minorities
- the minimal participation by non-governmental organizations
- the lack of transparency and the poor access to information.[67]

The OSCE as a Third Party in Ethno-national Conflicts

Many authors accuse the C/OSCE of failure in the Yugoslavian conflict, at least as regards the ability to provide an anticipatory analysis of the conflict and to respond in time with appropriate measures. But this failure applies not just to the case of Yugoslavia, but also to that of Nagorno-Karabakh and ten other armed conflicts in Europe, three of them in the west. The conflict in former Yugoslavia dominated many of the CSCE meetings in 1992–3. Certain resolutions reveal the Conference's helplessness in coping with this challenge. From July 1992, in a measure not used even during the Cold War, the CSCE itself cut off channels of communication and consultation: its major interlocutor, the Federal Republic of Yugoslavia (Serbia and Montenegro) was formally excluded from all meetings.[68]

The abrogation of autonomy rights was the trigger to violence in more than half the wars in the former USSR and in Yugoslavia. The CSCE sent several fact-finding missions to the Balkan region and to a number of the

Soviet Union's successor states. It had some degree of success with a long-term monitoring mission, begun in mid–1992, in three areas where national minorities were potentially under threat—in former Yugoslavia, in two formerly autonomous regions of Serbia (Kosovo, with its Albanian majority, and Vojvodina, with its Hungarian and other minorities), and in Muslim Sanjak.[69] The C/OSCE also involved itself in several of the conflicts named above. It sent missions to trouble-spots in south-eastern Europe, to Armenia and Azerbaijan (Nagorno-Karabakh/south-west Azerbaijan), Georgia (South Ossetia and Abkhazia), and Moldova (Dniester Republic).[70] In April 1995, the OSCE for the first time sent a permanent mission to the territory of one of the big powers, namely an autonomous region of the Russian Federation, the war-zone of Chechnya, setting up its headquarters in the war-ravaged city of Grozny. The OSCE was involved in the peace talks in mid-1995;[71] up to now, no peace-agreement has been concluded.

As regards the problem of the (former) Armenian enclave of Nagorno-Karabakh, the CSCE also took some unusual steps and initiated a multilateral conference-process. The original objectives of this process were: negotiations on a peaceful solution of what was (after Tajikistan) the bloodiest conflict in the former USSR, and on the status of this area of Azerbaijan, with its two-thirds Armenian population.[72] The OSCE mediation took place sometimes in competition and sometimes in co-operation with similar endeavours by Russia and the UN.

As the war progressed, the objectives originally formulated by the C/OSCE quickly and unexpectedly became obsolete. In a large-scale offensive conducted between March and August 1993, regular troops from the smaller republic of Armenia and the Karabakh militia (self-defence forces), reputedly acting with the support of CIS military personnel on the ground and with economic aid and arms supplies from *Islamic* Iran (*sic*), conquered between one quarter and one third of the territory of Azerbaijan (which, with 8 million inhabitants has double the population of Armenia). The ccase-fire of September 1993 failed, and with it the mediation and negotiation process instituted by the various third parties. Not until May 1994 was another cease-fire concluded, under pressure from Russia and as a result of the war-weariness of the various parties. To date the situation remains pending and the conflict unresolved.

The OSCE inadvertently became involved in a conflict that grew dangerously acute and which implicated forces, such as the Islamic Republic of Iran, which lay outside its area of operation. The Armenian war of aggression triggered a true 'exchange of populations'—with indescribable consequences for the civilian populations affected.[73] The internationalization of the conflict between Armenia and the Turkish-speaking Azeris, which the C/OSCE initiative had unintentionally promoted, had devastating effects and contributed to the unprecedented escalation and spread of this endemic ethno-national conflict. The cease-fire of May 1994 seemed fragile, having become even more so with the change of leadership in Yerevan (elections of March 1998). The negotiations that have taken place so far in regard to the occupied territory of south-west Azerbaijan, the return of the refugees, and the lifting of the economic blockade against the Armenian republic have produced no results. Enforced recruitment continued on both sides.

In September 1995, with the tentative agreement of Russia, the OSCE decided to send the first multilateral OSCE peace-troops to monitor the cease-fire in the southern Caucasus. This mission could have developed into a dangerous enterprise; however, because of the general sobering-down of attitudes that followed the failure of a number of UN interventions, it did not take place. It seems certain that Azerbaijan, the larger and severely humiliated party, will not be able to agree to permanent separation from parts of its territory. Armenia hopes to persuade Azerbaijan to renounce sovereignty over Nagorno-Karabakh by offering the possibility of a return of Azeri areas. Secret negotiations have reputedly taken place on this deal in Moscow, but they have not produced any results. It is unlikely that the OSCE could achieve any more in the Armenian–Azeri conflict than has been achieved by Russia—which continues to be in a position to exert the greatest influence on both parties to the war.

Proposed Reforms to Improve the OSCE's Capacity for Action

Russia's proposals that the OSCE should be massively upgraded as an organization and should be given a higher status ought to be responded to positively by the Western member states. The OSCE is still the most appropriate forum, in that it allows NATO and CIS states to stay in dialogue. As remarked at the outset, the inadequate budget and meagre resourcing of the OSCE conflict-preventive institutions raises justified questions as to the West's political interest in developing this, the potentially most important organization of the states of the northern hemisphere.

A number of reform proposals pointing the way forward have been available for quite some time, but have not been implemented because of a lack of political will:

- The OSCE should be given an internationally legally binding form.
- The principle of majority decision-making should be instituted in all OSCE bodies; this promises a dynamic effect on the organization's activities.

- Various new structures have been proposed, including an executive general-secretariat, the formation of a security council (like that of the United Nations but with a more representative composition), and the creation of a parliamentary component.
- The new security council's brief would include supervision of OSCE peace-keeping troops.
- The organization's deplorable resource base (relative to its considerable political significance) must be improved. There should be a marked increase in its annual budget (not including long-term missions) in order to strengthen the OSCE's capacities in the prevention of violent conflict.

From its origins in June 1973 to the Charter of Paris in late 1990 the C/OSCE was run with a tiny budget. Since the early 1990s the development of the OSCE budget reflects the return of war and mass violence to Europe and the efforts to contain it. The budget rapidly rose from one million Euro in 1991 to 24 million in 1995, doubled to 48 million Euro in 1997, tripled the next year (1998) to 148 million and passed 200 million Euro in 2000.[74] Although, within a decade, the OSCE budget has with a decade increased from 1 million Euro to 209.3 million Euro, it is still grossly inappropriate,[75] especially regarding the distribution of the funds for the different tasks.

The OSCE institutions with highest preventive force, such as the High Commissioner on National Minorities, HCNM (2 million Euro or 1 percent) and the Office for Democratic Institutions and Human Rights (ODIHR) in Warsaw (6.5 million Euro or 3.1 percent) and the Conflict Prevention Centre (CPC) in Vienna (budget not specified), continue to receive only a tiny fraction of the over-all budget. The greater part of the OSCE budget goes towards missions and field activities; also in 2001 they accounted for 84 percent of the budget. For instance in 1998 some 56 percent was spent in Bosnia alone; 33.8 percent of the total OSCE budget was invested 'unprofitably'—that is to say, in elections that were irregular and from which the narrow nationalist parties emerged ever-triumphant! In short: what is needed is no longer just more money, but more money for sustainable activities aimed at securing peace and co-operation.

An increase in the activities of the OSCE as a third party in ethno-national conflicts is not the only thing that is required; there must also be a functional political concept. This must include properly developed OSCE policies on minority issues, conflict prevention, and peace dispute-settlement, and on the reorganization needed to create the necessary infra-structure.

The following are six proposals for reform in the areas of minority protection, violence prevention, and peaceful dispute-settlement:

1. In order to give teeth to the proscription of violence in the OSCE area, there must be a comprehensive expansion of the Conflict Prevention Centre, including the creation of a centre for proper operational planning, a research unit, and a department for research, which will draw up the necessary policies.
2. Policies aimed at winning acceptance for comprehensive medium- and long-term violence prevention must be elaborated (plural democracy, federalism, autonomy arrangements, and strict protective provisions); there should be appropriate measures to promote its implementation.
3. New procedures and resolutions are needed for regulating intra-state ethno-national conflicts, including sanctions in cases where a member state violates minimum OSCE standards. Where there is a lack of co-operation by a member state, or a failure to implement minimum standards or negotiated settlements, the High Commission on National Minorities should be able to suggest appropriate sanctions via the CSO.
4. The High Commission on National Minorities should have its mandate extended, in order, in particular, to be able to investigate and publicize violations against the standards of minority law by a member state, to give all the parties a hearing, to organize negotiations, and to propose solutions to the conflict.
5. The High Commission on National Minorities should not only develop methods for giving early warning of ethno-national conflicts, but also serve as an appeal body for endangered and persecuted national minorities (thus ensuring pre-emptive conflict-prevention and a circumspect treatment of ethnic conflicts).
6. Going beyond the standards of the Council of Europe's convention on minority protection of November 1994, minority rights should be comprehensively extended (e.g. at the request of the High Commission), within the framework of a legally binding OSCE convention on the protection of minorities.

In this way, the OSCE could be generally upgraded and the OSCE 'model' could really live up to this appellation in the domains of violence prevention, peaceful dispute-settlement, and minority rights.

On the Question of the Transferability of the OSCE Model

The success of the CSCE–OSCE in setting a political mood is beyond question. As a result of the CSCE's undisputed (but hardly measurable) contribution to the easing of tensions in the East–West conflict, and to the ultimate dissipation of that conflict, those who followed the 'learn from Europe' line and talked once again of a 'model' gained fresh impetus. But one needs to take a cautious and circumspect look at the preconditions for transferring a model of regional regime-formation to other areas of the world such as America (OAS), Africa (OAU, now AU), or South-East Asia (ASEAN). This very process of reflection would put the notion of transferability in perspective. Two basic preconditions for transferability deriving from the genesis and operation of the C/OSCE would be:

1. the existence of 'complementary' or shared interest-related structures (economic incentives, collective security)[76]
2. the existence of a developed, organized, and dynamic civil society that exerts pressure, assumes a controlling function, and observes and promotes diplomatic processes between state actors from outside and 'from below'.[77]

Other preconditions for the transferability of the OSCE model would be:

3. the existence of one central actor (e.g. the United Nations or a regional power) or of several major state actors who would take the initiative (i.e. mediate and provide funding)
4. clear limits, sufficient common identity and inward orientation of a region (all of which can in the case of OSCE be seen as missing or put at disposition, as dramatically demonstrated in its mediation initiative in Nagorno-Karabakh)
5. only relative socio-cultural unity of the region; there is, for example, a degree of fuzziness in the 'Christian Occident vs. Islamic Orient' image in the OSCE area; institutional racism, e.g., against African-Americans and other 'people of colour'[78] as well as against Muslim communities in Europe[79]
6. the willingness to resolve conflicts by non-military means (or the realization that the use of violence is fruitless); this is something which, even in Europe, is neither self-evident nor, if one looks at the historical experiences of the past centuries, corresponds to the norm.

One should not only test to see whether certain mechanisms that have proved their worth within the OSCE framework are transferable. One should, conversely, also see whether certain innovations from the context of other regional organizations or from the UN system (e.g. measures relating to the rights of indigenous peoples) might be adopted by the OSCE.

The Organization of American States and its Shortcomings

Speculation as to the OSCE's ability to serve as a model might be encouraged by observing the example of the Organization of American States. Recently, there have been a number of events that indicate that the OAS is beginning to develop an unexpected life of its own.

The Contadora initiative and the Esquipulas peace process, which were started during the Cold War under the banner of hysterical Reaganite intimidation (Nicaragua 1979–85), proved that it was possible for the South to break through 'real existing' power imbalances and the differing interest-structures of North and South by creative collective initiatives.[80] By operating in this way, the OAS has rightly become (something of) a regional organization that can claim to bridge the North–South divide.[81]

The main objectives of the OAS are: the maintenance of peace, the peaceful settlement of disputes, and joint efforts to solve the social and economic problems of the continent.

Because of the unequal distribution of power and wealth (North–South conflict), this last objective remains rhetorical in nature. Interim assessments of NAFTA, the first free-trade agreement in the Americas that links the North (USA and Canada) to a country in the South (Mexico), have a negative ring to them as far as the South is concerned. And in the associated Caribbean area (CARICOM), there have been no signs of an economic breakthrough—only a number of trends towards increased dependence. The general impression is that free-trade areas profit the rich countries, whereas economic co-operation (economic communities) could also bring benefits to the poor countries.[82]

Deficiencies in Regard to Democratization and Human Rights

What most observers criticize are not so much the shortcomings of OAS in the domain of economic co-operation, but its shortcomings in the domain of human rights. The discourse about democracy and human rights (combined sticks and carrots including in the economic sphere) is traditionally one of the sharpest weapons in the US foreign-policy arsenal and, where political opportuneness dictates it, is used against the impoverished 'cousins' in the South, most vociferously against Cuba. The human-rights regime within the framework of the OAS continues to be marked by weakness, even though the overall conditions for it are more favourable than ever before, and even though it was possible to talk of a 'wave of democratization' in 1980s Latin America.[83] One example will suffice to illustrate this: up to now, 24 states have acceded to the American Convention on

Human rights, whereas the Inter-American Convention to Prevent and Punish Torture has been ratified by only half this number of states.[84]

As early as the mid-1990s there began to be talk about the destructive effects of neo-liberalism and the return of authoritarian rule—el retorno de los caudillos.[85] Oscillation between democracy and dictatorship is seen as an inherent characteristic of Latin America. The kind of 'wave of democratization' that took place in the 1980s, and previously during the 1950s and early 1960s, was followed in each case by a wave of regression to dictatorships, military regimes, and grave violations of human rights—such as that which took place in the late 1960s and 1970s, bringing repressive military dictatorships to power in Latin America, in some cases with the active support of the USA. The liquidation of democracy in Chile in 1973 by means of a bloody military coup followed by a murderous wave of repression against all left-wing and democratic forces, was only one extreme example amongst many.

Participatory Democracy is Seen as 'Subversive'

However, the end of the Cold War has led to positive changes in the political climate in Latin America as well, even though recent US measures against Cuba—further tightening of the total boycott on trade, an all-out propagandistic 'television war', toleration of provocative acts of extremist Cuban exiles and the use of the Guantanamo base as detention facility for suspected terrorists—may lead one to doubt it. In order further to isolate unloved Cuba, a 'democracy hurdle' was built into the OAS charter as a condition of membership. Its unbiased application would reduce the OAS membership dramatically. The US depiction of Cuba as a 'rogue state' does not stick in continent that has seen 240 US military interventions, among them US-engineered coups against the democratically elected presidents Arbenz (Guatemala) and Allende (Chile); the latter was murdered by an act of terrorism—bombing of the presidential palace—on September 11, 1973.

The OAS is reportedly the only regional organization with a democracy clause in its charter and with a subsidiary organization whose job is to 'promote democracy'. This organization began to be set up following a decision of the OAS' general assembly in Paraguay in 1990. Democratic institutions and processes are to be deliberately promoted in the member states. The relevant texts make reference to a specific model of democracy, namely representative democracy.[86] Participatory democracy continues to be regarded as 'subversive' in many OAS states. Collective actions to 'defend or preserve democracy' are planned in countries where the democratic process has suffered setbacks or been halted (Villagrán de León 1994: 146).

What 'democracy' means and which states are 'democratic' is generally decided by the United States. The fetish of elections, which no other state celebrates in so overpowering and media-oriented a way as the USA, has become one of the OAS' principal vocations. Missions to observe election —such as those in Nicaragua in 1989–90, continued in 1996 and 2001–2, in Costa Rica, the Dominican Republic, Guatemala, Honduras, and Panama in 1990, Haiti in 1990–91, and El Salvador, Surinam, and Paraguay in 1991— were declared a permanent task of the OAS and were 'institutionalized'.[87] Since then, more systematic programmes have been developed on the basis of short-term missions. But with resolution 1080, the OAS had only limited options for intervention where there are undemocratic developments. The new 'mechanism' was applied in the cases of Haiti, trade embargo from October 1991, and Peru, in response to Fujimori's *autogolpe* of 1992 (see Villagrán de León 1994: 150–1).

A working group of the permanent council of the OAS was working on a controversial scheme to combat one of the most burning human-rights problems of Latin America—the murder or 'disappearance' of dissidents at the hands of state and semi-state bodies (e.g. so-called 'death squads' of active or former security personnel).[88] There are built-in weak points in the scheme: it makes exonerating comments about the 'expected or mandatory obedience' of those who carry out the 'disappearing' at the behest of their superiors; it does not define the 'disappearing' as a crime against humanity; and it proposes no special procedure of the Inter-American Human-Rights Commission in the matter of 'disappearance'. Amnesty International called on the OAS general assembly to put in place an *ad hoc* consultative mechanism via which non-governmental organizations (e.g. the relatives of the 'disappeared') could contribute to the scheme. But an added weak point is the fact that the role of non-governmental organizations in the OAS falls way behind what is conventional in the UN system, the OSCE, or the OAU.

The OAS and the Situation of the Indigenous Peoples of the Americas

The global trend towards increasing multilateralization corresponds to that towards the transformation of the 'sacred' principles of sovereignty and non-intervention. Of the four 'holy cows' of modern statehood—national sovereignty, territorial integrity, more or less systematic secularity, and constitutive modernity—the first could soon be led out to slaughter. The intervention of international and regional organizations in matters concerning the protection of democratic rights, individual human rights, and collective minority-rights, and in matters concerning intervention in cases of conflict has so far been most manifest within the framework of related endeavours on the part of the UN system, the OSCE, and the OAU-

AU. Nor will the OAS and ASEAN be able to abstract themselves permanently from this global trend. In the mid 1990s an expert committee took up its work on an OAS mechanism for violence prevention.[89] There were and are deficiencies in all the areas mentioned, the clearest being the lack of respect for the rights of minorities and indigenous peoples. A belated debate about multiculturalism in Latin America was triggered in the mid 1990s by Jürgen Habermas' essay on struggles for recognition in democratic states.[90]

It is the UN system that sets the trend in regard to the problem of minorities and the issue of indigenous peoples; and leading the field is the International Labour Organization. The ratification of the ground-breaking ILO convention no. 169 (Indigenous and Tribal Peoples Convention, 1989) by a number of American states will result (and, in a number of states has already resulted) in appropriate adjustments to a whole range of laws in individual states. The comparatively rigid ILO controls force states to abandon previous repressive and undemocratic practices of discrimination against indigenous peoples. In the medium term, the convention will have a positive effect on the legal and social situation of indigenous peoples.

The OAU, its Charter and the Project of the African Union

In the case of Africa, the transference of European standards on democracy, minorities, and human rights comes across as particularly forced and hypocritical, given that European colonial and trade policy can claim a large measure of responsibility for the problems that are the subject of complaint. Despite this, in what follows here I shall focus chiefly on the human-rights regime and the mechanism for resolving conflicts. Yet the Organization of African Unity is the continental organization in which contradictions between potentially far-reaching possibilities for development and the actual degree of organization and limited resources emerge most clearly. The OAU was founded as a continent-wide organization in April 1963 in Addis Ababa, where it continues to have its headquarters. Like the OAS, it was based on existing organizations (the Casablanca, Monrovia, and Brazzaville groups). Its members include both states and liberation movements.[91]

Demands issued by the OAU are generally either rejected or ignored by the West. At its summit in Nigeria in 1991, the OAU called for compensation and reparations for the centuries of enslavement suffered by 100 million Africans at the hands of the European colonial powers. On the occasion of the conference on 'Reparation for Africa and the Africans in the Diaspora' held in December 1990, the Nigerian Chinweizu had already worked out a figure of 2000 dollars for compensation, based on the precedent of Japanese reparations to Korea. Part of this could be settled by cancelling Africa's external debt; the rest could be paid over in a kind of Marshall Plan for Africa. There is no knowledge of any official reaction to the OAU demand. The question of reparations for Africa was subject to hot debate in the run-up to the 2001 World Conference against Racism in Durban, South Africa. During the conference, however, this key issue did not receive the required attention and the adequate mentioning in the final declaration.[92]

The African Charter on Human and Peoples' Rights

With the African Charter, the Organization of African Unity has created an instrument that is potentially verifiable, capable of being expanded, and comprehensive.[93] The charter has been ratified by 49 of the 51 member states of the OAU (not by Ethiopia).[94] Some of its articles go further than the UN instruments.[95] In line with a decision by the highest organ of the OAU, the Assembly of Heads of State and Government, in July 1992, all the states party to the charter are required (§62) to submit regular reports on the implementation of the charter's provisions in national law and practice.

The African Commission on Human and Peoples' Rights (African Commission) is working on various resolutions concerning the democratic process and certain crucial rights such as freedom of assembly. It organizes various seminars on these issues and sends observer to major democratic elections (like those in Mali in April 1992 and the crucial South African election in May 1994). However, the body that monitors the charter, the African Commission—like the OAU as a whole—suffers from an acute shortage of financial resources and specialist staff.

In its capacity as an instrument of sanction, the African Commission would have the option—and has already made use of it—of issuing public declarations on the situation of human and minority rights in states that have acceded to the charter. Condemnation of the murder of dissidents by Banda's despotic regime in Malawi may have contributed to restrictions on development aid by Western donor-countries and ultimately also to the dictator's departure in 1994.

The charter could become the basis for a more stringent human-rights regime within the OAU if its authors' calls for a strengthening of human-rights guarantees and implementation provisions are followed. Pan-African seminars on these issues are taking place on an ongoing basis. Lively debates during the March 2002 African Development Forum III, hosted by the Economic Commission for Africa in Addis Ababa, included all important issues around the coming integrating of Africa and the question of 'What Priorities for the African Union?' Important contributions for the side of African NGOs dealt with diverse key issues such as human rights, the accountability of African leaders as well as the question of 'How to Create a Security Community in Africa' (Mohammed *et al.* 2002), whereby rejecting to treat security issues as the sole preserve of governments and arguing in favour of ideas of 'common security based upon an international or cosmopolitan community of citizens, bound together by multiple ties of common interest and a commitment to basic values' (ibid., 3).

OAU Conflict Settlement, UN Peacekeeping and the Rwanda Shock

An OAU conflict-settlement mechanism was agreed at the summit in Dakar in 1992 and was formally adopted in Cairo in 1993. A permanent secretariat was to be created as part of the secretary-general's office at OAU headquarters in Addis Ababa. When there was an urgent need for this kind of authority, as was the case in Rwanda in April 1994, following the lamentable failure of the UN—despite the presence of its 2,500 well-armed UNAMIR troops in the capital, Kigali, right next to the site of horrendous massacres, the OAU secretariat had not yet come into being because the necessary funds were lacking!

None the less, the OAU was active during the genocide in Rwanda: it called, unsuccessfully, for immediate UN intervention. More successfully, it pressed the Tutsi-dominated RPF guerrilla movement (Rwandese Patriotic Front), which had emerged triumphant from the state-organized genocide, to implement the Arusha peace accord, originally mediated by Tanzania and regarded by many observers as having already failed or become obsolete. To the astonishment of all, the accord was indeed implemented, down to the last letter.

The OAU was also active on the ground in neighbouring Burundi, which seems to be on the point of exploding. Through their presence in all ten provinces, OAU observers were trying to prevent a repetition of the kind of genocide that occurred in Rwanda from April to July 1994.

The OAU lacks the resources, staff, and infrastructure to enforce its resolutions on various vital issues. As mentioned above, the declaration (prepared by then OAU Secretary-General Salim Ahmed Salim) providing for the establishment of a 'mechanism for the prevention, management and settlement of conflicts' within the OAU was unanimously approved in June 1993 in Cairo. A special 'Fund for Peace' was set up as part of the mechanism. However, the annual Conference of Heads of State and Government (CHSG), the OAU's highest decision-making body, decided, in June 1995, that 'because of huge financial and logistical problems',[96] the

OAU should concentrate solely on prevention—leaving the costly peacekeeping to the UN.

The United Nations, however, started after Somali 1993 cutting down—temporarily—on blue-helmets to barely 15 percent of its peak period, delegating peacekeeping to CIS, NATO and other organizations.[97] The number of personnel in UN operations fell from its 1993 peak of 76,000 blue helmets to a low of 14,453 peacekeepers serving in seventeen UN missions, as of mid–1998. The drop was the result of the Rwanda shock and failed Chapter VII operations to enforce peace on warring parties. In the mid–1990's the bitter experiences in Somalia, Rwanda and the former Yugoslavia have led to a temporary reluctance by the UN Security Council to authorize new peacekeeping and—even less so—peace enforcement operations.[98] However, in the later 1990s the mood began to change. The number of blue helmets doubled again and reached 45,000 troops serving in 15 UN military operations under way as of mid–2002, although there were three UN operations less than in 2000.[99] Today the number of blue helmets is far from its 1993 peak, and there is a conspicuous selectivity of where peacekeepers are sent and where not. There was no single preventive UN deployment in Africa. The delayed UN operation in Congo and the resulting non-implementation of the Lusaka agreement are just the last example for this appalling selectivity and reluctance to sent UN troops to Africa.[100] The shock at the total failure of the OAU and UN attempts to avert genocide in Rwanda 1994 led to the OAU's trying to devise a complementary peace-maintenance mechanism, discussed at several summits. Progress has been slow, but the mechanism has attracted world-wide interest.[101]

Peaceful Dispute-Settlement Ailing for Lack of Resources

The OAU charter mentions the traditional methods of peaceful dispute-settlement (mediation and reconciliation) and provides for the creation of a 'Mediation, Conciliation and Arbitration Commission' (MCAC)—though the work of this latter body has been rendered difficult, and, unlike the mechanism, it is not a permanent organ of the OAU. In contrast, the charter contains no provisions on internal conflicts: the Mediation Commission is empowered only to deal with conflicts between states; and the parties to the dispute must agree to the arbitration.[102]

Apart from border disputes between members, the OAU has been unable of itself to settle a single one of the many violent conflicts in Africa. (But the OSCE has not managed to do this either, in its own sphere of influence, despite a superior infrastructure, a far larger financial input, and the threat of NATO intervention.) The OAU peace-troops in Chad were not successful either. That said, the ECOWAS operation in Liberia did meet with more success thanks to the indirect intervention of the OAU.

The African initiative in Liberia comes off well compared with the United Nations' fiascos in Somalia, in Angola in 1993–94, Rwanda 1994 and in the Western Sahara ever since. However, in some conflict areas of Africa (such as Mozambique), the OAU is overshadowed by the UN. Where the necessary preconditions are satisfied, the global-scale UN is able, thanks to its financial clout, to fly in thousands of blue helmets and to accelerate the reconstruction of war-torn societies.

Non-governmental organizations play a prominent role within the OAU. They can become involved in activities as members of various committees in the continent-wide organization. NGO conferences held before the sessions of the African Commission and organized by the African Study Centre for Democracy and Human Rights, the International Commission of Jurists, and other human-rights organizations, can exert a positive influence on the commission's work, and make it more effective, by providing detailed information on the human-rights situation in individual countries and by making recommendations on particular issues.[103]

Promoting Joint Development in Africa

Amongst the declared aims of the OAU are: the promotion of unity, solidarity, and joint development in Africa; combating colonialism, racism, and neo-colonialism; defending the independence and sovereignty of states; and ensuring respect for human rights. Originally, this was meant to happen on the basis of territorial integrity in accordance with colonial borders, but this position could not be maintained, as the recognition and admission of Eritrea reveals.[104] As mentioned before, the territorial jigsaw-puzzle of the new states, though European-made, was preserved after decolonization and later declared sacrosanct by the OAU. The independence of Eritrea in 1993 was the first case of deviation. For some observers the costly fraternal war between Ethiopia and Eritrea from May 1998 to mid 2000 seems to confirm that such a policy was adequate. The proliferation of 'endless' internal wars, such as the one in South Sudan, tells the contrary.

In order to realize its goals, the OAU seeks to strengthen co-operation in all areas (politics, the economy, education and health, defence and security). As it will be argued in the next section, the European Union would certainly be a better model here—if there is need of one—than the OSCE, which displays important defects in some of the areas mentioned, notably economic co-operation. Numerous differences of opinion within the OAU over strategic and routine political issues have so far prevented any more intensive economic co-operation. Some of the member states are in competition with one another on the world market, and this played an important role in the collapse in prices for agricultural exports.

The political will to set a confrontational course in the OAU, in concert with other regional organizations in the Third World, or within the framework of the Non-aligned Movement, with a view to forming a cartel that could effect changes in global imbalances and in the African economies' meagre chances on the world market, has so far been lacking. Here too, any notion of taking the OSCE as a model would be misplaced. As far as economic agreements (co-operation) and cartel-formation is concerned, the most obvious candidate to act as a model would be the loose conference and consultation process of the G7 states, which projects the idea of a power-based cartel of the Western industrial states against the rest of the world. Raw-materials cartels by Third World countries would conflict directly with the interests of most OSCE states, and would clash head-on with the G7 states' interest in having access to cheap raw materials for their industries.

By April 1994, 35 member states had already ratified the treaty on the establishment of an African economic community. Former OAU Secretary-General Salim declared that it was part of the post-colonial dependency syndrome that there should be a lot of talk in Africa about economic co-operation, but that very little would be done. Almost 12,000 laws and provisions of a kind that hamper mutual trade reputedly still exist in Africa and urgently need to be done away with.[105] According to Salim, the tasks were to put Africa's enormous resources, such as minerals, raw materials of all kinds, and a huge hydroelectric potential, to sensible use. Precisely because of the fragility of African societies, the weakness of states, and the widespread poverty, Africa, must pull together that much more closely.[106]

The Long March Towards the African Union

Panafricanism became strong in the decolonizing Africa of the 1950s and 1960s. Some 40 years of independence show a sobering result: Africa is the home of most of the world's poorest nations, underdevelopment and indebtness are increasing rather than diminishing, AIDS is spreading rapidly and the continent is the theatre for most of the world's major conflicts. There are enough good reasons for *Afro pessimism* but there is some reason for optimism. Much of the crisis is imported, such as the legacies of Africa's partition into over 50 European properties and its vertical integration as producer of cheap raw material into the Western dominated world market,[107] and there is growing awareness about these basic facts and the political will for change is growing, with the African political class coming under increasing pressure of the common folks. The

OAU's *Treaty Establishing the African Economic Community*, signed in June 1991 in Abuja, Nigeria, by 51 African heads of state, was the most significant declaration of political will for regional integration.[108] The model for it was clearly the European Economic Community.

More than half a century ago, what finally became the European Union, the most powerful and significant development of regional integration world-wide, which created an emerging transnational European super-state and the world's strongest economic and monetary unit, took its humble beginning in May 1950. French Foreign Minister Robert Schuman announced a plan, thought out by the economist Jean Monnet, that proposed pooling European coal and steel production under a common authority. Economic integration was launched in the wake of the Second World War, when a devastated and impoverished Western Europe sought to rebuild its economy or what was left of it.

Similarly to the Europe of the 1940s and 1950s, today's Africa is partly devastated and seriously impoverished. Fifty years ago Europe was in fears about growing economic dependency (after becoming the recipient of aid such as the Marshall plan), political instability and insecurity of the region when faced with the realities of the superpowers having divided up Europe in spheres of influence. In the emerging bipolar system, Europe saw its chance for survival by uniting. Similarly to Europe in 1951, when the unification process began with six countries, whose leaders signed the original treaties establishing the first form of European integration,[109] dealing with matters of coal and steel production, trade, and nuclear energy, which meant to bring the raw materials of war under common control, the plan of the African Union is also a peace project, in a continent that is most seriously affected by the scourge of mass violence.[110]

Europe after World War II was situated between two integrated nations of regional size, the United States of America (USA) and the former Union of Soviet Socialist Republics (USSR). Today, Africa is non-integrated but the neighbour of regions that embarked on different stages of advanced block formation: an ever more united Western Europe, a strong NAFTA, a unified fast growing China, a prospering India and an emerging Asia in general, besides two stagnating blocks, the CIS and Latin America.

It took the European Economic Community (EEC), formed in 1957, more than a decade to achieve a customs union between six countries, and the EEC began to grow only in 1973 (over 20 years after its humble commencement); in 1979 the Europeans started to build a monetary system (EMS).[111] Many African countries have already started to join in sub-regional customs unions, such as the Southern Africa Customs Union, the East African Community or ECOWAS; the latter plans the introduction of a single currency, as the EU has undertaken on January 1, 2002, by introducing the Euro as the new common currency in most EU countries. The Preferential Trade Area (PTA) was transformed into the Common Market for Eastern and Southern Africa (COMESA) in 1994 with 20 countries as members, with the (failed) objective to attain completely free trade by year 2000, followed by a customs union in 2004. The SADC is another sub-regional organisation of economic co-operation and security that shall be enhanced in diverse areas such as water issues, rules for migration, fighting drug and weapon smuggling and promoting trade and economic cooperation. The African Union may make a good start by building on these efforts and interlinking them.

Problems that have frustrated the African political and economic inte-gration in the past can be grouped into seven broad areas: (1) the self-interests of corrupt, politically short-sighted or bellicose African leaders, and the lack of accountability, (2) the democracy deficit in most African countries, lack of possibilities of popular participation and the under-development of civil society, (3) political-cum-social diversity, ranging from the legacies of different colonial backgrounds and the use of different official languages to some contradictions resulting from the politicization of cultural-civilizational and ethnic or national differences (mainly between North Africa and Sub-Saharan Africa), (4) the current grave economic problems most African countries are facing, including the situation of com-peting as raw material producers on the world market, (5) sub-regional power struggles and the support of armed rebellion in other (neighbouring) states, (6) the weakness of security and human rights regimes as well as the ineffectiveness of OAU's scheme of prevention of violent conflict, and (7) the lack of strong, visionary leadership. These problems create serious con-straints and may frustrate positive attempts to unification. However, such obstacles will not prevent Africa from unifying; it may just take more time.

Not Enough Global Dispute-Settlement Institutions

The procedures and institutions for peaceful dispute-settlement that have existed up to now within the framework of the UN system are inadequate and concerned mainly with conflicts between states. Dispute settlement has always been a core issue in international treaties, conventions, and (since the time of the League of Nations) global organizations. International legal measures aimed at establishing peaceful dispute-settlement as part of the global framework have been undertaken since as far back as 1899:

- creation of the Permanent Court of Arbitration in 1899, on the occasion of the First Peace Conference in The Hague, as set out in the Convention on the Peaceful Settlement of International Disputes (CPSID)
- establishment of the rules of land warfare and revision of the CPSID in The Hague, 1907
- statute of League of Nations (with its partial proscription of war), 1919
- establishment of the Permanent International Court of Justice in The Hague, 1920 (now part of the United Nations system)
- Briand–Kellogg Pact, 1928 (proscribing war as a continuation of politics)
- UN Charter, 1945 (with its general proscription of violence and its call for peaceful dispute settlement, as stipulated in art. 33)[112]
- competence of the International Court of Justice (ICJ)
- Manila declaration on the peaceful settlement of disputes, 1988.

Since the Second World War, approximately sixty states have had recourse to the International Court of Justice in The Hague. However, intra-state conflicts do not fall within the ambit of this supreme court. States have to recognize the competence and binding nature of the ICJ's rulings in advance or on an *ad hoc* basis. General requirements on Third World states in respect of accountability take concrete shape in the call for new procedures.

Legitimate demands of indigenous and endangered peoples for national self-determination ought to be made objects of complaints to the International Court of Justice in The Hague. Wars between states and non-dominant national groups should, like wars between states, also be objects of negotiating efforts and rulings by international courts.[113]

The Long Sleep of the Permanent Court of Arbitration

The continued existence of the Permanent Court of Arbitration, created in 1899 on the occasion of the First Peace Conference in The Hague, passes almost unnoticed. Up to now, there have been no institutional links between the UN system and the Court of Arbitration. However, in future, the PCA is to become part of a new international dispute-settlement system under the aegis of the United Nations.[114]

This international court, headed by a secretary-general (P.J.H. Jonkman) continues, like the International Court of Justice, to be based in the Peace Palace in The Hague.[115] It is made up of about 250 legal experts appointed by the states that are signatories to the Hague Convention; so far, however, these experts have only met together once—93 years after the institution was founded. The Court of Arbitration has at its disposal a world-wide network of political-cum-legal arbitrators consisting of 'wise men' from the member states of the Hague Convention. The steps required for arbitration are: establishment of facts, detailed investigation where appropriate, 'good offices', mediation, reconciliation, and/or arbitration.

In 1962, because of the growth in the number of international disputes involving not only states but, to an increasing extent, non-state parties also, the Permanent Court of Arbitration developed a negotiating procedure for intra-state conflicts—in other words, conflicts between states and nations / nationalities.[116] Since the International Court of Justice is active solely in the inter-state domain, the Permanent Court of Arbitration could develop into a complementary institution that is also active on a global scale.[117]

Most provisions for arbitration procedures are optional—that is to say, freely chosen by the parties. One precondition for setting an arbitration procedure in motion is the agreement of two or more parties that they will submit to the binding arbitration-ruling.[118] The arbitrators and their number are a matter of free choice, the rules are freely determined, the parties have autonomy in their decision-making, and the provisions of the model clause for arbitration procedures is marked by a high degree of flexibility.[119]

Despite these favourable (because easily adaptable) provisions and despite the low costs of the involvement of the arbitrating third party, the option of independent arbitration has only been taken up by states acting against other states, but not in cases where (at least) one party is a non-state entity. This perhaps has something to do with the fact that each party, including the state, by accepting to submit to the procedure, is obliged to accept the ruling as binding and implement it without delay (art. 32.2), thus renouncing the right to sovereign immunity against the legal rulings of outside judges. For most states, this constitutes a case of *lèse-majesté*.

The United Nations Charter Imposes an Obligation to Settle Disputes by Peaceful Means

The UN Charter of 1945 (arts. 2, 3, 33) for the first time imposed an obligation on all member states to settle disputes peacefully by means of negotiation, mediation, conciliation, arbitration, judicial settlement, resort to regional agencies, arrangements, or other means (see Unser 1988). However, these provisions had little influence on two dozen of inter-state and some 300 intra-state wars that have taken place since 1945.

The Security Council, whose permanent membership is made up of old colonial powers and new superpowers, is accorded disproportionate influence as regards the 'maintenance of peace' and the management of geopolitics (art. 24.1). The Council's activity was blocked for almost 50 years by the right of veto of its permanent members. The permanent peace-keeping and peace-restoration forces provided for in the Charter never came into being. And forces for the purposes of peace-enforcement in any case lay outside any kind of consensus. The Security Council can put a conflict on its agenda, make recommendations, issue proposals for resolution, and take forcible measures of a civilian or military kind (sanctions and intervention). Because of mutual blocking, this latter measure was only implemented in exceptional circumstances until 1990. The General Assembly appoints a whole range of committees, including Committee No. 6 on the peaceful settlement of disputes.

One of the greatest obstacles to the peaceful settlement of disputes is the politically absurd provision according to which only states (not peoples) may bring their concerns before the International Court of Justice in The Hague. This is not true of the Permanent Court of Arbitration, also based in The Hague. The Charter (art. 52) also cites regional arrangements for maintaining peace (e.g. the OSCE, OAU, OAS, etc.).

The negative results so far obtained with all these formally existing options for dispute settlement has helped stimulate the debate about the reform of the OSCE, the Council of Europe, and the UN system.

Therapeutic Intervention or Violence Prevention?

Consideration of future United Nations conduct and of regional arrangements such as the OSCE in relation to ethno-national conflicts run the risk—under the influence of war atrocities or worse crimes, such as genocide—of degenerating into idle talk about 'sticking plaster' operations. Assuming a general lack of knowledge about the causes and course of armed nationalist conflicts, the model of cause-oriented therapeutic conflict-intervention (Senghaas) was seen by some authors as 'the only chance' of containing ethno-national conflicts.[120] Third parties, they believed, could assume the main 'midwife function'.

By way of general trends, Senghaas cited the process of relative autonomization of the Third World and the emergence of preventive power or chaos-power as a result of ethno-nationalist politicization and mobilization. Both trends were visible in modified form in the Yugoslavian and Soviet successor states. The interventionism of the world powers (and of regional and international organizations) has had the rug pulled out from under its feet (Senghaas 1988: 110). In Eurasia the high tide of ethno-nationalist mobilization seems behind us but the threat of ethnicization and its mixing with militant religious fundamentalisms is far from over, as the lessons learned from Kosovo, Macedonia, Chechnya and Central Asia are teaching us.

The chronicle of US military intervention in Latin America and the Caribbean is not complete. In Haiti (in September 1994), the USA sought a broad 'coalition' with its Hispanic neighbours, under the superpower's own indisputable control. [121] But interventions ought to be increasingly politically underpinned by the UN, as was the case in a number of interventions since the UN regime in Iraq after the Gulf war until the Afghanistan war 2001–02 and the take-over by a UN peacekeeping mission. In the case of failure or an unsatisfactory result, responsibility by a single state can be shifted elsewhere. The costs are charged to the account of the United Nations or the major powers standing on the sidelines (Germany and Japan), as it happened in the Gulf war.

In the case of ethno-national conflicts in particular, military intervention and attempts at containment are extremely cost-intensive and risky. The Kosovo adventure will teach NATO a lesson. What seemed to be an easy game turned out to become a messy situation and a permanent engagement in the Balkans. Even under the eyes of KFOR troops the UÇK operatives could attack a neighbouring country. A decade ago, Senghaas rejected attempts at containment because they produced only short-term 'tranquillization', and did so only where the 'scuffle' was not very politicized. As an intra-state counterpart to inter-state policies, Senghaas advocates the use of confidence-building measures and measures to increase understanding in inter-ethnic conflicts. This would include, for example, 'monitoring the security apparatuses of the parties to the conflict', demilitarization, non-offensive defence, peaceful dispute-settlement, collective security measures, and the promotion of a 'productive culture of conflict' capable of generating empathy for the other party. [122]

In the medium term, constitutional and institutional measures appropriate to the particular situation should be initiated as a means of solving ethno-national conflicts:

- federalism and democracy based on concordance (taking a leaf out of the Swiss book?)
- self-governance for indigenous peoples (as in Greenland, Nicaragua, the Faeroe Islands)
- creation of new state (geographical) entities for territorial autonomy (e.g. the model of the ethnic-cum-linguistic constituent states of India and the ethno-national minority republics in the Russian Federation)
- guaranteed protection before the law, full cultural autonomy, subsidizing of media run by and for national minorities
- multiculturalism or active minority-protection through the promotion of the identities of ostracized minorities
- positive discrimination as a form of affirmative action on behalf of previously disadvantaged groups
- other measures likely to avert conflict.

Prophylactic measures are ultimately more than 'rewarded', as Boutros Boutros-Ghali was compelled to conclude following a series of costly and partially ineffective UN military interventions. When it comes to measures to avert conflict, the proverb says: 'An ounce of prevention is worth a pound of cure'.

Notes

1. Regime theory developed as part of the discipline of International Politics in the USA in the 1980s; see S. D. Krasner (ed.), *International Regimes* (Ithaca NY: Cornell University Press, 1983). For the C/OSCE process see Ropers and Schlotter 1989, 1992.
2. This is the greatest drawback to these kinds of regimes, because their staff is restricted to government members, high-ranking officials, party colleagues, and other 'cronies' who often have no political vision or professional qualities and are driven by particularistic interests.
3. Ropers and Schlotter 1992: 36–42. The usefulness of the CSCE as a model, say the authors, lies in its 'discursive design', which means that 'individual regional peace-strategies each with their own profile can be developed' (40).
4. According to Ropers and Schlotter, a range of regimes of differing quality have developed within the framework of the C/OSCE. These were initially related chiefly to the problem of the division of Europe into the two bloc-systems but, since the coming-to-power of Gorbachov in 1985, and even more so since the upheavals of 1989–90, they have been leading to the 'deregulation' of new political domains.
5. Such groups were formed in the East (Charter 77 in Czechoslovakia, the dissident movement in the GDR) and the West (especially by circles with religious/socio-political concerns and in minority areas such as Catalonia). They formed links with one another and continue to operate (see Calließ and Merkel eds. 1993). One of their areas of operation continues to be mediation in conflicts (incl. those of an ethno-national kind).
6. See Milada Vachudova, *The CSCE Institutional Framework* (Radio Free Europe Research Report, 2 (1993) 31: 33–5.
7. The Council of Foreign Ministers (nominally) has the greatest decision-making power and meets at least once a year for political consultations. The Committee of Senior Officials (CSO), comprising representatives from all 55 member states, meets at least four times a year in Prague; the CSO is the highest-ranking decision-making body for the periods between Conferences; it prepares the meetings of the Council (of Foreign Ministers) and implements the latter's decisions. A smaller, more properly executive form of the CSO meets weekly in Vienna. The OSCE Troika consists essentially of an annual rotating Chairman-in-Office plus his or her predecessor and successor. It is responsible for co-ordinating the OSCE's activities, organizes consultations on ongoing matters, and passes on the decisions of the Council and CSO to the secretariat and the four OSCE institutions so far in existence.
8. Currently the hot spots in the Caucasus are Georgia and Chechnya, with terrorists using Georgian territory to attack, and potentially also the unsolved conflict between Armenia and Azerbaijan. In the Balkans the conflict focus remains on Kosovo and the export of its problems into Macedonia and the Federal Republic of Yugoslavia. Early in 2000 the southern border of Serbia became a problem area and soon after Macedonia got invaded.
9. 'Vertauschte Rollen an der KSZE-Tagung' was the headline in the *NZZ* report (30 Sept. 1991) on the CSCE 'human dimension' meeting in Moscow. 'The Soviet side' suddenly took a driving role in the human rights matters.'

10. Out of the 55 OSCE participating states one was suspended. Yugoslavia was suspended from participation from 8 July 1992 until 2001.

11. For a long time, the Helsinki agreements on these matters 'had no more than a declamatory function' (Mietzsch 1993: 35).

12. These efforts initially introduced 'no new quality' as compared with the UN Charter (Mietzsch 1992: 97–101 (100)). In Athens (Apr. 1984), third parties were at least mentioned as an element.

13. See Vachudova, *The CSCE Institutional Framework* 35.

14. On the conceptional rationale of early OSCE long-term missions, see Rolf Welberts, 'Friedliche Streitbeilegung als gemeinsame Aufgabe von Internationalen Organisationen, staatlichen Regierungen und Civil society: Optionen der OSCE', in Calließ and Merkel eds. 1995: 560–2.

15. See OSCE homepage: http://www.osceprag.cz/

16. It had a ceiling of 250 expatriates to be deployed by October 1998, but as of March 1998, the number of mission members stood at 155.

17. J. Gottschlich, 'Soft power soll Sicherheit in Europa garantieren', *taz*, 11 Sept. 1995.

18. Ter-Petrosyan's last press conference as Armenian president in 1997 eventually led to his resignation. It contained a number of clearly expressed ideas about, *inter alia*, the need for political compromise on Nagorno-Karabakh and the Armenian-occupied territories of Azerbaijan. The tragedy of the Armenian occupation of Azerbaijan means that every seventh resident of Azerbaijan is now a refugee or internally displaced person (IDP). Lately, there have been a number of interesting and encouraging developments in internal Azerbaijani politics. However, the elected Armenian president, Robert Kacharian, is a radical hard-liner. The 'visions' he expresses may well be shared by the majority of the population that voted for him in the 1997 elections.

19. For the latter, the UN Secretary-General wrote: 'The limits of peace-keeping in ongoing hostilities starkly highlighted by the distressing course of events in the former Yugoslavia have become clearer, as the Organization has come to realize that a mix of peace-keeping and enforcement is not the answer to a lack of consent and cooperation by the parties to the conflict' (Kofi Annan, 'Peace-keeping in a changing context'; in: 1998 Report of the Secretary-general, www.un.org/Docs/SG/).

20. Vienna 1989, Copenhagen June 1990, Moscow Oct. 1991.

21. CSCE, *Report of the CSCE Meeting of Experts on National Minorities in Geneva of July 19, 1991* (Geneva, 1991), ch. 2. Cf. Huber 1993: 31 ('The CSCE and Ethnic Conflict in the East'). The title also indicates that the CSCE had not yet been active in ethnic conflicts in the West. Konrad J. Huber is co-director, with Prof. Ari Bloedt (University of Utrecht), of the Foundation for Inter-Ethnic Relations (FIER) in The Hague. The FIER was founded in 1993 and provides advice to the OSCE's High Commissioner on National Minorities.

22. *Amnesty International Report 1993*, 43.

23. There was talk of a 'consensus of the participating states' as a precondition for action by the OSCE High Commissioner for National Minorities, HCNM. (See Huber 1993: 'Lack of CSO backing...greatly limit[s]...mediatory efforts', 32, 35.) The HCNM does not propose any solutions himself; these are, rather, the result of the process of dialogue that has to be initiated between the parties to the conflict. At an expert meeting held to analyse the work of the HKNM in his first year of operation (Dec. 1993, Rome) precisely this approach, an inevitable result of the weak mandate, was described as 'non-coercive and non-judgmental' (Conflict Management Group 1993: 10); it had, it was claimed, made a major contribution to the capacity and effectiveness of the HCNM in preventing conflicts. The HCNM's mediation on nationality legislation in Estonia was cited as an example of success in this area (see Huber 1994*a*).

24. The mandate of the C/OSCE-HCNM says: 'The High Commissioner will not consider national minority issues in situations involving organized acts of terrorism'. The HCNM is not allowed to communicate with and will not acknowledge communications from any party (whether person or organization) that 'practices or publicly condones terrorism or violence' (§25). The OSCE homepage information says 'The Office of the OSCE High Commissioner on National Minorities was established in 1992 to identify and seek early resolution of ethnic tensions that might endanger peace, stability or friendly relations between OSCE participating States.' (www.osce.org/).

25. If it 'publicly condones...violence' (§25), i.e. 'excuses' violence or does not expressly condemn it. This creates a grey area that is open to manipulation.

26. The ban, says Huber, is the result of objections by a number of member states and reflects the sort of compromise solution which the High Commissioner represents.

27. The Foundation for Inter-Ethnic Relations (FIER) in The Hague was set up as an independent private institution for the purpose of advising the High Commissioner on National Minorities. It organizes international meetings of experts on topics with which the High Commissioner deals (minority rights, regional security, prevention of ethnic conflicts), co-ordinates basic research, and organizes informal seminars at which representatives of governments and minorities can engage in joint discussion of political options. Foundation for Inter-Ethnic Relations 1999, 1994. Also, FIER, *Mission and Program* (The Hague, 1994).

28. The Swedish and UN diplomat Rolf Ekéus was active in the Conference on Security and Co-operation in Europe (CSCE) during the period of Gorbatchov's reforms and the end of the Cold War as the head of the Swedish delegation 1988–92 and played a key role in drafting the Charter of Paris for a New Europe (1990). His main theme has not been national minorities and their protection but (since 1983) arms control and disarmament. Ekéus was Executive Chairman of the United Nations Special Commission on Iraq (UNSCOM) where he led the weapons inspectors between 1991 and 1997.

29. See recommendations to respond to the fate of Europe's most repressed national group made 1993–2000 on www.osce.org/hcnm/documents/recommendations/roma/.

30. Huber talks of a 'shoe-string budget with a handful of staff' (1993: 35).

31. New states in Europe: five ex-Yugoslavian (inc. the Yugoslavian Federation), 17 ex-Soviet, and two ex-Czechoslovakian in place of three multinational states.

32. Certain major languages that are not official EU languages—like Catalonian, Basque, or Welsh—have official status in their area of distribution. Only in Switzerland (not an EU member) is this also true of 'minor languages' such as Rhaeto-Romanic, which is only spoken or understood by 50,000 people.

33. Many EU states are 'either unwilling or unable' to provide useful information to the competent EU office (EBLUL) about 'their' minorities.

34. Every sixth western European belongs to a minority: Wolfgang Mayr, 'Im Western nichts Neues: Europa tut sich schwer mit den Minderheiten', *pogrom*, 174 (1994), 11.

35. European Bureau for Lesser Used Languages, *Unity in Diversity* (Brussels, Dublin and Luxemburg: EBLUL, 1997) (map of EU lesser-used languages).

36. Over 7 million Canadians belong to the Francophone minority of 27 percent. Most of them live in the federated constituent state of Quebec. In 1995 Quebec held a referendum about whether it should remain part of Canada, and narrow 51 percent voted to stay in! The Bashkirs, numbering 3.5 million, are also a minority nationality but they are unknown, though their population is higher than those of many OSCE states; there are 2.5 million of them living in the Republic of Bashkortestan at the southern end of the Urals, marking the geographic dividing line between Asia and Europe.

37. These figures are based on estimates. See *Internationaler Weltatlas* (London: George Philip, 1993, 1998); PIOOM 1994*a*; GfbV var. years; *pogrom*, 174 and others.

38. There are sizeable African minorities living in Europe (some of them have been there for decades) or belonging to it politically. They include, most notably, 1.2 million in France (including in French overseas *départements*—800,000 in Guadeloupe, Martinique, and Guyana) and over one million in Britain. In the United Kingdom, 6 percent of the population—that is, 3.3 million—are members of ethnic minorities; most are British citizens. Next to Indians and Pakistanis, the largest group are blacks from the Caribbean. The main population-centre for ethnic minorities is multicultural London, where about half the Britons whose forefathers emigrated from the British colonies are domiciled. Until 1962, members of the Commonwealth had the right to settle in Britain, and they enjoyed equal political rights. There are said to be members of 37 different ethnic groups living in London (Chris Myant, spokesperson, Commission for Racial Equality, in *taz*, 22 Aug. 1995, 15). There are over 100,000 black Africans living as migrants in Italy, and tens of thousands in Spain, some of them in very precarious conditions.
39. German-speakers enjoy satisfactory minority rights in Denmark, Belgium/Wallonia (Eupen, St Vith), Hungary, Russia/the Kaliningrad *oblast*, and Italy/South Tyrol.
40. There are 800,000 Turks and 200,000 Pomaks (Muslim Bulgarians) living as indigenous minorities in Bulgaria. They represent a critical mass and hold the balance of power between the political parties. There are also indigenous Turkish minorities in Greece and the Ukraine/Crimea, as well as in ex-Yugoslavia and Romania, in the latter areas as a result of 500 years of Ottoman rule.
41. 1.8 million Albanians lived—until May 1999, bereft of all rights, in the formerly autonomous Kosovo (Serbia); since May 1999 the Albanians, now the dominant group in a NATO protectorate, deprived all 20 or so non-Albanian minorities in Kosovo of their basic rights and violently drove out most Serbs and Roma, who were living in the Kosovo since centuries. Another 500,000 Albanians (25 percent) live in Western Macedonia, with borders open to Albania but without autonomous status (until 2001). About 1.5 million live as migrants, of whom until the mid 1990s just under 1 million are to be found in the Yugoslavian successor-states (not including Kosovo and Macedonia) and the rest (increasingly) in western Europe. Several hundred thousand Albanians enjoy full cultural autonomy as a minority in Calabria, Southern Italy.
42. Hungarians are to be found in five states; besides Hungary in Romania/Transylvania, southern Slovakia, Vojvodina/Serbia, and the Carpathian area of the Ukraine.
43. Serbs are living as new minorities in Bosnia (40 percent) and Croatia (25–30 percent). In the Serb republic of Krajina (until the time of the so-called 'liberation' of Krajina by the Croatian army and the mass flight of the resident Serbs in Aug. 1995) and in Slavonia (Croatia's next declared target), the Serbs were, and still are, endangered. This is not the case in other Yugoslavian successor-states (notably Macedonia). About one million Serb labour-migrants live permanently in western Europe.
44. Huber 1994*a*. Also Huber 1993: 34.
45. In connection with the 'gypsies', Huber (1993: 32) mentioned a 'review [of] the relevance of the mandate to their complex situation'.
46. Recommendations of the High Commissioner see: OSCE-HCNM 1998 ('Statement of the HCNM on his study of the Roma in the CSCE region'. Meeting of the Committee of Senior Officials (CSO), Prague, The Czech Republic (21–23 September 1993); 'Roma (Gypsies) in the CSCE Region', Report of the High Commissioner on National Minorities 1994; 'Introductory remarks', CSCE Human Dimension Seminar on 'Roma in the CSCE region', Warsaw, Poland, 20 September 1994).
47. OSCE High Commissioner on National Minorities Max van der Stoel: Report on the situation of Roma and Sinti in the OSCE Area. The Hague: HCNM 10 March 2000. (This outstanding 180–page report of the High Commissioner on National Minorities

elaborates that racial discrimination and exclusion are fundamental features of the Roma experience across Europe. Important are its recommendations, ibid., 163–166.)

48. See the Report of the OSCE High Commissioner on National Minorities To Session 3 ('Roma and Sinti') of the Human Dimension Section of the OSCE Review Conference, 22 September 1999, Vienna: OSCE, p 3.

49. Three out of the four neighbouring states were hostile to the state set up in Nov. 1991. Greece and Bulgaria were fearful (without grounds) of an irredentist upsurge amongst 'its' Macedonians. Maps which showed Macedonia divided into three and which therefore acted as a spur to reunification had allegedly been circulated within the largest party in Macedonia (the VMRO). Kiro Gligorov (a social democrat and ex-communist) made vain attempts to establish dialogue with the larger neighbouring states.

50. Because of Greece's almost hysterical reaction, the state was not admitted to the UN until the end of 1992, under the absurd appellation of 'former Yugoslavian republic of Macedonia'. The successive Greek governments allegedly took offence at the symbolism of the name (the Macedonia of Philip II, the native land of Alexander the Great) and at the flag (a sun with 16 rays on a red background), although Macedonia had borne this name as a Yugoslavian republic since 1948.

51. Obvious motives for Greece's reaction are Macedonia's role in the Greek civil war of 1948 and—even more important—the situation of the forcibly assimilated Slav-Macedonian minority in northern Greece. Greece and Macedonia have a common 500–year history as part of the Ottoman Empire; both societies have been shaped by a Christian Orthodox past. The area around Lake Ohrid is of great significance in this history (it is regarded as the cradle of Christianity amongst the Slav peoples). On this basis, an initiative by Macedonian and Greek intellectuals, launched by a Macedonian professor, Janovich, aims to get the log-jam moving; the two sides met in Ohrid.

52. Karakasidou, who lives in the USA, received death-threats after collecting data in a place not far from Thessaloniki. The planned book, *Macedonia in Northern Greece: Conflict of Identity and Nationality*, to be published by Cambridge University Press, was blocked by a process of international pan-Hellenic string-pulling. The Greek lobby in the USA (like its Jewish counterpart) is by tradition quite influential; it is, at any rate, clearly in a position engineer a serious piece of censorship in a respected publishing-house (*ARD Kulturweltspiegel*, 10 Mar. 1996).

53. The Aznar government depended in its first term on the parliamentary support by both, the Catalan deputies and the Basque deputies. Hence the space of manoeuvre concerning national questions of Aznar's government was narrow. His Popular Party (PP) for the first time defeated the socialist opposition (PSOE); PP narrowly became the largest party and obtained a tricky majority (PP won 156 out of 350 seats and formed a coalition with the Catalan CiU and two other parties). This changed in March 2000, after Jose M. Aznar won a second term; the conservatives got the first majority since Spain became a democracy after the death of dictator Franco in 1975 (PP got 183 seats).

54. Devolution means that Scotland, Wales and Northern Ireland are still constituent parts of the United Kingdom (UK) but now have their 'own governments and parliaments', comparable to Swiss *cantons* or German *Länder*. Websites, greeting you in Gaelic with 'Fàilte ort a dh'Albainn' (www.geo.ed.ac.uk/home/scotland/scotland.html), became common place. Of the five million Scots only a faction understands the original language; as in N Ireland and about 20 percent Welsh-speakers of the 2.8 million inhabitants of Cymru or Wales. Contrary to Scotland only half of the population in Wales, or a narrow 50.3 percent, voted in favour of a Welsh Assembly, with a turnout of only 50 percent (see 'The quiet revolution', on http://elt.britcoun.org.pl/i_revol.htm). In Northern Ireland, the Belfast ('Good Friday') Agreement of 1998 provided, amongst other elements, for the establishment of an elected Assembly.

55. This move was a risky one for PM Léonel Jospin, who wanted to succeed president Chirac in 2002. A former defence minister, hard-line Jacobinist and left-socialist maverick, J.P. Chevènement, had demanded greater guarantees of peace before concessions were made to Corsican nationalists. Chevènement decided to run for president. This move split the socialist vote and had a shocking impact: the socialists lost not only the presidential elections in April/May 2002 but also the parliamentary elections in June, hence, the power altogether. A low turnout combined with a large number of minority candidates weakened Jospin's support and almost certain victory; it even allowed the extreme right-winger Le Pen to translate his usual third place into second. Under shock, Jospin retreated from public life. Autonomy for Corsica triggered the fall of its chief promoter. — Corsica has suffered more than 20 years of political violence involving several factions of separatist paramilitaries (said to belong to different 'clans' with its long tradition of vendetta and links to the criminal underworld). J-M Rossi, a nationalist leader who supported the plan, was gunned down in broad daylight after turning against the underground FNLC. The island's assembly would be allowed to gain partial jurisdiction to pass some of their own laws from 2004.

56. After the CSCE decided in 1992 to establish the post of High Commissioner on National Minorities, the Netherlands Minister of State Max van der Stoel was appointed as the first High Commissioner in December 1992 and took up his post in January 1993.

57. The Conflict Management Group (at Harvard University) already gave a positive interim assessment after barely one year (see Conflict Management Group 1993: 43–4).

58. To UNPO founder Michael van Walt van Praag, this makes little sense, either practically or from the legal point of view; Mietzsch, on the other hand, sees it as a step towards the operationalization of the rights of nationalities. (See Walt van Praag 1994.)

59. See Phillips and Rosas eds. 1993.

60. 'In those states in which ethnic, religious or linguistic minorities exist [something often denied by these states], persons belonging to such minorities shall not be denied the right, *in community* [my italics] with the other members of their group, to enjoy their own culture, to profess and practise their own religion, or to use their own language.'

61. The wording was taken over in the UN Convention on the Rights of the Child in 1989. France was the only one to venture a comment—to the effect that Art. 27 was not applicable to the French republic! See the commentary on the UN minorities declaration by Patrick Thornberry in Phillips and Rosas 1993: 19 and 65 (n. 40). Once again, it was France and Turkey who expressed reservations in regard to signature of the Convention on the Rights of the Child.

62. Senghaas 1993: 80–1. The German term *Volksgruppen* ('population groups') which Senghaas uses needs to be replaced by (the German equivalent of) 'nationalities'. The basic meaning of *Volksgruppen* was that of nationalities that have a kin state somewhere else, especially in neighbouring countries. In the First and Second World War, German nationalities abroad became 'fifth columns' of German expansionism.

63. A first contingent of NATO troops was deployed a few days after the signing of the Paris accord (Dec. 1995). In Tuzla, the US troops were, ironically, almost 'neighbours' to the 5,000 'warriors of God' ('Afghan' Mujaheddin, al-Qaeda trained Islamists and Iranian Pasdaran) who had been fighting on the Muslim side in central Bosnia for more than two years, financed by the Arab oil-states. Osama bin Laden has been visiting Bosnia several times. This fact was withheld from the public for several years, and only confirmed after the signature of the Paris accord, in a confidential study carried out by a Pentagon think-tank. (See Foreign Military Studies Office and John E. Stray, *Mujaheddin Operations in Bosnia* (Fort Leavensworth, Kan.: 1995).

64. Yeltsin talked of 'genocide' against the Bosnian Serbs after heavy US/NATO bombings. The Russian foreign ministry observed that there had been an 'unprecedented out-of-

area use of the Western military machine' which, it said, was not covered (as NATO hinted) by UN resolutions. The outcome of the NATO 'peace mission' was uncertain, and it soon became clear that the NATO troops would be staying beyond 1996. One party (the Bosnian Serbs) felt cheated and without adequate guarantees for the Serb civilian population, not only in Sarajevo. Serbs (according to a French UN general) are left with a choice 'between a coffin and a suitcase'. However, the remaining state of Yugoslavia has already taken in over a million refugees. The withdrawal of the foreign soldiers (i.e. the Mujaheddin, trained in terrorist and guerrilla tactics and deployed in Iran, Afghanistan, Turkey, and the Sudan) within 80 days is provided for in the Paris accord of Dec. 1995 but is hardly feasible.

65. Interview with Shevardnadze in *Der Spiegel* (no. 12) 1995.

66. On the conduct of the CSCE in the Yugoslavian conflict, see also Mietzsch 1992: 109–14, n. 62.

67. Compare Amnesty International *Human Rights in the New Europe: The CSCE in Search of a Role* (London: 1992).

68. Serbia was subsequently largely isolated internationally. In addition, there was a real 'economic war'. The UN embargo imposed by the UN has not been lifted since, despite the unexpectedly moderate policy of Serbia towards the armed conflicts in Croatia and Bosnia, despite the unprecedented scale of intervention by NATO (weeks of continuous bombardment, use of cruise missiles, attacks by Croatians and Muslims under cover of NATO), and despite the UN taking sides in this previously geopolitically autonomous area. The attempts at mediation by the post-communist regime in Belgrade and Belgrade's increasing pressure on the Serb nationalists in Krajina (until the 'ethnic cleansing' of Aug. 1995) and in Bosnia were, however, acknowledged by a partial lifting of economic sanctions in Dec. 1995.

69. Sanjak, a Muslim enclave in Serbia and Montenegro, has been calling for a long time, without success, for a special status for this formerly separate entity of the Ottoman Empire. Sanjak lies right in the middle of a very sensitive zone, and also has common borders with Bosnia and Kosovo. It is a member of the UNPO. See Muslim National Council of Sanjak, *Sanjak Muslims of Former Yugoslavia: What Will Be Their Fate?* (Novi Pazar, 1993). The MNC became a member of UNPO.

70. This latter mission was particularly delicate, given that the 14th Soviet Army was involved. This army (led until 1995 by General Alexander Lebed) subsequently made a decisive contribution to de-escalating the conflict. Lebed was regarded as one of the likeliest candidates to succeed Yeltsin (after the front-runner Zyuganov). Yeltsin recruited Lebed to his camp in the fight against Zyuganov, and this helped him secure re-election. Soon afterwards, however, he excluded him from the leadership-circle. Lebed's triumphal comeback in the elections to the governorship of the Krasnoyarsk *oblast* in spring 1998 should put him back in a good starting-position to achieve his federal political ambitions. The Dniester area's continued association with Moldova has produced what has so far been a stable settlement to the conflict thanks to the *de facto* autonomy of the (former) Dniester Republic. The ethnicization of politics in Moldova has, so it is claimed by Bächler, been 'hugely exaggerated by the Russian side', and the Moldovan government has given in to Russian pressure (in Schiemann-Rittri *et al.* 1995: pp. xiv–xv). In fact, the autonomous status of the Dniester area had to be re-established. In the course of the highly ethnicized creation of the state of Moldova, the autonomy rights of the various minorities were abrogated by the Romanian-speaking majority.

71. The mission originally consisted of only six members (*Tagesanzeiger* (Zurich), 20 Apr. 1995, 7). The taking of more than 2,000 mainly ethnic Russian civilian hostages outside Chechnya by Chechen fighters in June 1995 resulted in over 200 civilians being killed (some of them in cold blood by the Chechen Islamists) and led to conflicts within the

Federation leadership; the Chernomyrdin government went against the declared position of the army leadership and Yeltsin and concluded a cease-fire with the rebels.

72. 250,000 Azeris in Armenia and Nagorno-Karabkh (50,000 out of the enclave's 120,000 inhabitants) fled to Azerbaijan, and about 10,000 to Russia. Meanwhile, 260,000 Armenians from Azerbaijan fled in the opposite direction, and half a million to Russia. See PIOOM 1994*a*: 14.

73. The situation in broad areas around the enclave of Nagorno-Karabakh, and at some points deep into Azerbaijan, took a dramatic turn, with over a million people fleeing (figures from PIOOM 1994*a*: 14, also *ak*, 21 Sept. 1994, 29–32).

74. 'OSCE unified budget in million Euro 1991–2002', see www.osce.org/general/budget/.

75. The entire OSCE budget is less than a third of the cost of one single B-2 'Stealth' bomber, as the one shot down by the Yugoslav army during the months of NATO bombardments in 1999. The B-2 'Stealth' is a strategic aircraft first delivered 1993, a high subsonic long-range low-observable heavy bomber; its estimated cost per piece was US$ 750 million.

76. Ropers and Schlotter (1992: 38–40) mention four preconditions for transferability of the C/OSCE model.

77. Although the CSCE was (at least indirectly) also a product of the Western European peace movement, which during the 1970s and early 1980s acquired the capacity for mass mobilization, the conference diplomacy of the C/OSCE for its part 'promoted civil-society actors and structures' mainly in the East. The civil-rights movement in the East, and the Helsinki Citizens Assemblies, which also came into being in the West (and are still in existence today), in their turn influenced and reinforced the CSCE process. On this, see Calließ and Merkel eds. 1993.

78. US statistics speak of stark disparities: 'African-Americans have an unemployment rate of 7.3 percent and are incarcerated at seven times the rate of whites. Thirteen percent of black males in the U.S. cannot vote due to felony convictions. 23 percent of African-Americans live in poverty and live shorter lives than their white counterparts. The African-American infant mortality rate is on par with developing countries with 14.2 per 1,000 live births which is more than double of that of 6 per 1,000 births for white Americans.' See Clarence Lusane (author of *Contemporary Racism and African Americans*) in *Report on the IMADR Symposium Forms of Discrimination, Racism and Anti-Semitism*. New York City, Nov. 28, 2000.

79. Among the worst example for cultural and structural violence in the occident would be the enhanced exclusion many among the ten million Muslims have to face everyday in Christian-occidental Europe (2 millions in USA). The Barcelona process (starting in November 1995) is important for reconciling Europe with the Islamic Southern Mediterranean. The question is: will there be Islamic ghettoes or Euro-Islam?

80. The Organization of American States was created in 1948 in Bogotá, through the amalgamation of various existing pan-American institutions. Its predecessors were the IUAR (1890), the UAR (1910), and the 1947 Rio Pact. The OAS organs are the general assembly, the conference of foreign ministers, and the OAS council.

81. The dominant influence of the USA was demonstrated in 1962, in the exclusion of Cuba from the OAS. However, there are limits to the way in which the OAS can be utilized by the USA to preserve its influence in Latin America and the Caribbean—as was demonstrated by the Contadora group and the Esquipulas peace-initiative.

82. The example of the southern member states of the EU highlights the situation: thanks to transfer payments and comparative cost-advantages, the southern countries of Spain, Portugal, and Greece underwent massive economic development within a very short period (15–20 years), considerably narrowing the gap with the richer EC/EU countries.

83. As in Africa, there have since been numerous indications of a 'return of the dictators'. Initially admired, 'democratically elected' *caudillos* such as Menem and Fujimori give Latin American democratization a bad name.

84. Details from *amnesty international report 1993*, 344.

85. 'El retorno de los caudillos', Tierra Nuestra 1995.

86. The Cartagena Protocol of the OAS charter talks of the 'effective exercise of representative democracy'. This was followed, in 1991, by OAS resolution 1080 of Santiago de Chile 'On Representative Democracy'. At the OAS summit in Nassau in 1992, the possibility of suspending membership because of transgressions against democracy was discussed.

87. Arturo Díaz Córdova, 'El proceso de paz en El Salvador', *Revista del IRIPAZ*, 5 (1994), 9: 85–104.

88. Sensibilities are different. Even the increasing number of murders of street children in the huge cities of South America are not branded as crimes against humanity by the OAS, or made into a subject of discussion by it.

89. See the article by Ronald J. Fisher on the potential of peace-building: *Revista del IRIPAZ*, 5 (1994), 9: 37–48.

90. 'Struggles for recognition under democratic rule of law': essay and responses in *Revista del IRIPAZ*, 5 (1994), 9: 1–37.

91. Currently only one liberation movement: the Polisario front for the independence of Western Sahara.

92. See UNHCHR: 'World Conference against Racism, Racial Discrimination, Xenophobia and Related Intolerance. Declaration and Programme of Action', online on http://www.unhchr.ch/html/racism/Durban.htm. For the OAU reparation claims see: Werena Rosenke, 'Reparationen für Afrika', *Ökozid-Journal*, 3 (1992), 1: 37–44.

93. African Charter on Human and Peoples' Rights, in: Teztlaff 1993 (Eng.): 285–92.

94. One prominent non-signatory is, of all countries, the crisis-ridden multinational state of Ethiopia. Another is the mini-state of Swaziland, a Bantu kingdom and one of the few ethnically homogeneous nation-states in Africa. There are also three smaller states that have so far not become members of the OAU. Apartheid South Africa was excluded; the new South Africa became a member and was immediately requested to provide Nelson Mandela as a mediator in Angola. The ANC and PAC had previously represented South Africa in the OAU.

95. 'All forms of exploitation and degradation of man…shall be prohibited' (art. 5). Certain articles relating to social policy—namely, art. 12 (freedom of movement, right to asylum), 13 (public policy: access and participation), 16 (health), 17 (education), and 18 (family)—are exemplary. Of relevance to peoples' rights are arts. 20–6: 'Colonized and oppressed peoples shall have the right to free themselves from the bonds of domination' (art. 20 on self-determination); 'states parties to the present Charter shall undertake to eliminate all forms of foreign economic exploitation particularly that practised by international monopolies' (art. 21 on the distribution of resources).

96. Wawa Ossay Leba, 'Conflict Management in Africa', *The Courier*, 168, Mar.–Apr. 1998, 76–7.

97. The number fell from its 1994 peak of 76,000 blue helmets to barely 15,000 in 1998.

98. Since 1945 there have been over fifty United Nations peacekeeping operations. Between 1988 and 1999, the Security Council instituted 40 such operations. The drop in 1999 was the result of the UN disaster in Somalia, the Rwanda shock and several failed chapter VII operations to enforce peace on warring parties. Largely successful operations, as the ones in Mozambique and Namibia, could not change the general picture. The development of a 'UN rapid deployment capacity' never materialized. There is a lack of political will; some UN Member States wanted to go on their own.

99. Among the fifteen UN peacekeeping operations in June 2002 are still five operations from the 1970s or older; two 'endless mission' are as old as the United Nations themselves, dating from 1948 and 1949, the ones in Palestine (UNTSO) and Kashmir (UNMOGIP), next was Cyprus 1964 (UNFICYP) and two others in the Middle East: the UNDOF on the Golan Heights (Israel/Syria) since 1974 and UNIFIL in Lebanon since 1978. The other ten UN operations are five from the early 1990s (Iraq, West Sahara, Georgia, Bosnia, and Croatia-Pevlaka), four from 1999 (Sierra Leone, Kosovo, East Timor, and Congo DR), and one from end-2000 (Ethiopia/Eritrea). The force in East Timor changed the name. The dates given do not necessarily mean that there was a deployment of troops in that year, as the example of Congo DR illustrates, where troops were only deployed in spring 2001. The three UN missions terminated in the year 2000 were the ones in Tajikistan, Haiti, and Central African Republic; in two of these countries (Tajikistan and Central African Republic) the United Nations did not achieve anything that comes near to peace. UN peacekeeping cost stood at $2.6 billion in 2000; this about 0.3 percent of the $750 billion UN member states spent on arms.

100. Annan wrote that 'providing support for regional and sub-regional initiatives in Africa is both necessary and desirable' (Annan 1998, § 41); some 15 months later a regional initiative brought about the Lusaka agreement but no UN support has been seen since. Annan also admitted that 'This reluctance appears to go well beyond the lessons that Somalia offers, and it has had a particularly harsh impact upon Africa.' (UN Secretary-General 1998: § 29).

101. The Harvard-based Conflict Management Group has been contracted by the OAU to train the necessary staff and propose new, realistic strategies. CMG seemed having capacity problems.

102. See Kieh Klay, 'Resolving African Conflicts', *Peace Review*, 5 (1993), 4: 447–54.

103. See *amnesty international report 1993*, 39.

104. Eritrea's struggle for independence was directed against the problem of internal colonialism (and annexation by Ethiopia).

105. Al Imfeld in debate about 'Africa's Future' with C.P. Scherrer, Zurich, 21 Sept. 1995.

106. Salim Ahmed Salim accused Europe of 'double standards and hypocrisy': 'Many talk of corrupt dictatorial regimes—governments, with which they themselves have co-operated for years and with the help of which they secure advantages for themselves' ('Nicht auf den Norden warten', interview with OAU Secretary-General Salim Ahmed Salim, *taz*, 16 June 1994, 3).

107. The terms of trade worsened for the world's primary products producers (most African countries), while it improved for the producers of manufactured goods. African countries are facing ever harder condition, characterized by declining GDP, high stagflation pressures, food crisis and heavy burden of external debts.

108. The OAU treaty is an elaborated text consisting of 12 chapters and 106 articles. It built on the 1980 OAU Lagos Plan of Action, which declared the need for all-African economic cooperation and integration. At the African Development Forum III (ADF II), hosted by the UN Economic Commission for Africa, interesting debates about the way towards the African Union took place; see: OAU-ADF III 2002, www.uneca.org. Also see InterAfrica Group 2002, Amponsah 2002. NISER 2002. UN ECA 2002.

109. In April 1951 the European Coal and Steel Community Treaty was signed in Paris by the heads of state of France, Germany, Italy, Belgium, Luxembourg, and Netherlands. Six years later, in March 1957 the European Economic Community (EEC) and European Atomic Energy Community (EURATOM) Treaties were signed in Rome.

110. See OAU 1991, chapter XVIII: Settlement of Disputes.

111. In January 1973 Denmark, Ireland, and the United Kingdom had joined the Community. The 'Big Four' of western Europe were finally joining together. In February 1975,

the community signed the First Lomé Convention with African, Caribbean, and Pacific (ACP) countries. In March 1979 the European Monetary System (EMS) started to operate; thus it took 23 years for the Euro to become the only currency to permanently replace national currencies in twelve countries of the fifteen EU countries.

112. Art. 33, para. 1 of the UN Charter cites the competence of the regional organizations in disputes between states.

113. The recommendations made by the 'Voices of the Earth Congress' call for the European Union and the Dutch government to create procedures making it possible to invoke the International Court. See NCIV 1993.

114. Since 1993 the PCS has had observer status in the General Assembly. The development of institutional links with the UN is intended to make the PCA better known and to awaken the interest of UN members in the Hague Convention (see P. J. H. Jonkman, 'The Future of the Permanent Court of Arbitration', in: PCA 1993*a*: 57–61 (60)).

115. The court consists of (member) states and is a private-law, non-commercial, independent institution. See PCA 1992: Introduction.

116. PCA 1993. Jonkman has disputes between states and international organizations in mind, and between states and private companies (TNCs), rather than disputes between states and national entities.

117. See Jonkman in PCA 1993*a*: 60 (the PCA is to resolve 'certain types of inter-state disputes' and 'disputes which fall outside the jurisdiction of the ICJ').

118. The most important statement in the model clause for arbitration procedures is that 'either party may submit the dispute to final and binding arbitration' (PCA 1993: 23).

119. In general, three arbitrators are chosen—one chosen by each party and one appointed by the secretary-general. The arbitrators may but do not have to be members of the PCA's 250-strong body of experts. The parties may agree on another elective authority—e.g. the president of the International Court of Justice or a specialized expert-forum; it is also possible for an *ad hoc* group of experts assembled by the parties, or an NGO, or a specially appointed individual to determine the composition of the panel of arbitrators. One of the parties is the state, but not necessarily a member-state of the Hague Convention on 1899 or 1907. In addition, the timetable and deadlines for reply, the venue or headquarters of the Court of Arbitration (if not The Hague), the experts to be called upon (appointed by the arbitrators), the format and conclusion of the hearings, the form, nature, and possible publication of the ruling ('interim, interlocutory or partial awards'—PCA 1993: 16), and other provisions or conditions are also a matter of free choice.

120. The importance of economic and diplomatic sanctions is also underlined by Mietzsch (1992: 13). Military intervention is seen only as a last resort. Ropers and Schlotter (1992: 41–2) argue along similar lines. Senghaas (1993: 75) draws an 'unavoidable lesson' from protracted conflicts: 'Anyone who does not…intervene preventively in good time will be overrun by the dynamics of escalation'.

121. But for the first time, it was not purely internal political interests (such as stemming tiresome inflows of refugees) that were decisive; there were also democratic factors at stake, such as the reinstallation of an elected left-wing president who had been forcibly ousted in a *coup*. This is probably the really innovative aspect. On the chronology of US intervention between 1947 and 1994, see Johnny Norden, 'United Killers of Pentagon', *konkret* (1994), 10: 24–6.

122. Mutual acknowledgement of co-existence, says Senghaas, remains the one way in which compromise can eventually be achieved (Senghaas 1992: 126–8).

Chapter 8

Conflict Management and a New Role for the United Nations

Debates were going on for some time about whether the United Nations should become more involved or intervene more in the case of intra-state conflicts. It took Saddam Hussein's persecution of the Kurds and the civil war in Yugoslavia to trigger this debate and to enable us belatedly to see that ethnic conflicts inside sovereign states must be regarded as a threat to international peace and security. Since the United Nations first came into existence, there have been repeated object-lessons as to the violent nature and persistence of ethnicized conflicts. The Burmese conflict, for example, began before the United Nations was founded and continues to this day. The consequences of violent ethno-nationalist conflicts—even more so in case of conflicts ethnicized from above—are horrendously widespread suffering, death on a massive scale, and the destabilization of whole regions.

Invoking the right to self-determination may lead to ethno-national and secessionist conflicts. Since 1948 repressive state action caused ethno-nationalism and secession; protracted and bloody intra-state wars were the well known consequences. Because recognition of the latest set of new states depends, amongst other things, on their admission to the UN, and this is decided on by the UN General Assembly, at the request of the Security Council, there is a potential bar to the continued propagation of states. Up to now, nothing of this kind has happened; in fact, the opposite has occurred, as in the case of the by-products of the collapse of Yugoslavia and the USSR—though not of Somaliland. The recognition of states is geared in each case to (geo-)political interests, not considerations of international law or human rights. Since 1990, over 20 new states have been admitted to the UN.

There is broad agreement on the necessity of UN intervention in the case of genocide or state-organized mass murder. Since the events of 1994 in Rwanda, the need for such intervention has ceased to be hypothetical. An act of barbaric extermination took place before our very eyes. It was by no means unexpected: repeated notice of it had come from various quarters. The Rwanda-Burundi region has been a highly sensitive trouble-spot since colonial times and particularly since the first ever slaughter of Tutsis by

Hutus in Rwanda 1959 and the 'selective genocide' of the Hutus évolués by the Tutsis in Burundi in 1972. The mass murder of the Tutsis in Rwanda went on for a hundred days, from 6 April to 15 July 1994. The world looked on as thousands of defenceless old people, women, and children were hounded by gangs and hacked to death with machetes.

The Apocalypse in Rwanda and the Role of the United Nations

During the state-organized mass murder perpetrated by the presidential guard, elements of Rwanda's former unity-party, the fascist death-squads of the Interahamwe,[1] and the forces of repression (army and police) against the Tutsis and members of the political opposition, the UN troops stationed in Kigali could have prevented the genocide (according to the UNAMIR commander, General Dallaire) but had to stay by and did nothing, and were eventually actually withdrawn on the orders of the UN Security Council!

The apocalypse in Rwanda[2] cost a million people their lives and precipitated the largest flow of refugees in modern history. The real refugees were held as hostages until November 1996 by the regrouped army—rearmed by the Mobutu regime and France—and the genocidal militia of the Interahamwe. It was only the revolt of the Banyamulenge, backed by members of the Rwandan and Ugandan military, that brought about the defeat of the perpetrators of genocide, the return of most of the refugees to Rwanda, and—after seven months of fighting—the fall of the Mobutu regime. In all, half the Rwandan population either died or fled in 1994.[3]

At the same time that the Rwandan dictator Habyarimana died, on 6 April 1994, and the extremists around Bagosora seized power and ordered the carrying-out of the long-planned, centrally organized mass extermination of the Tutsi minority and mass murder of the Hutu opposition, the Seventh Pan-African Congress, on the theme of conflict settlement, was, coincidentally, taking place only a few hundred kilometres away in Kampala.[4] The congress—clearly with good justification—was critical of the idea of UN interventions in Africa.

Where was the United Nations when hundreds of thousands were slaughtered in the space of a few weeks in Rwanda? Critics have condemned the blatant double standards that operate in UN interventions. That criticism ought to be extended to the failure to provide assistance. The assumption must be that racial prejudice played a part in the UN's non-intervention, for which the Security Council, chiefly its members France and United States, bear responsibility. The failure to provide any kind of help at all to the defenceless victims was an incomprehensible scandal.

Those responsible for the state-organized genocide are known and should have been arraigned before a UN tribunal at the beginning of 1995, like the Nazi war criminals in Nuremberg. But the international tribunal struggled with budgetary problems to contend with, and until four years after the genocide, despite parallel efforts by the Rwandan courts, the apocalypse remained unexpiated. The most infamous perpetrators were the *Akazu* élite and the regime ideologues that systematically fuelled anti-Tutsi feeling via the press and radio after the RPF attack out of Uganda in 1990. (Most of these individuals have been living so far undisturbed in countries such as Gabon, Ivory Coast, and France. A few are now on trail at Arusha, less than a dozen principal perpetrators of genocide have been convicted and sentenced by the UN tribunal while the overtaxed Rwandan courts were able to trial thousands of *génocidaires*.)

In June 1994, the Council decided to send UN troops to Rwanda again, and to double their number of 5,500. The guerrilla forces of the Rwandese Patriotic Front, dominated by the Tutsi diaspora, was now in control of the north-eastern half of the country; meanwhile, the murder of the Tutsis in the south-western half continued unhindered. The belated military intervention by the French was aimed more at salvaging a client regime than offering assistance to the victims of the genocide. The RPF halted the killing and, despite its military victory, has—to the astonishment of all informed observers—adhered to the power-sharing arrangement agreed in Arusha in August 1993.[5]

Then UN chief Boutros Boutros-Ghali talked of a scandal. He conceded that the world peace organization had failed in Rwanda and pointed to the fact that, because of the indifference of 'those states that are constantly advocating respect for human rights', nothing could happen.[6] The United Nations did not intervene in Rwanda in 1994, nor has it done so up to now in Burma, and not in southern Sudan either, where other genocides are being committed.[7] There is no personification of evil (such as Saddam Hussein) in these places, nor any strategically important raw materials, and the white man is not dying there. Military interventions took place, rather, in places such as Iraq, where the UN Security Council issued a mandate for the deployment of half a million men under the leadership of the USA,[8] or in Somalia, where the matter seemed a simple one, or in Yugoslavia (Bosnia and Kosovo), which is part of the 'civilized' European world. The murder and the forgotten wars in the South continue, mostly out of the public eye. State-organized mass murder is dealt with in the Western media—if at all—under the rubrics of 'tribalism' or 'bloody tribal feuding'. As a rule the crucial part played by European colonialism in the generation of ethno-nationalist and tribal conflicts is deliberately suppressed.[9]

The devaluation of pre-colonial mechanisms of reconciliation and conflict-resolution, the ethnicization of class differences, and the creation of dichotomies in ethnic classification became sources of violent social

conflict.[10] The two factors of, on the one hand, the destructive colonial policies underlying the violent conflicts in Rwanda and Burundi and in a large
number of other trouble-spots in the South, and, on the other, the manipulation of collective identities for the purposes of preserving the power of
particular ruling élites, are inextricably bound up with one another.

Since 1994 the Rwandan genocide and its spill over effects have
profoundly destabilized the entire African Great Lakes region. French politicians played an extremely ambivalent role in these events. The French
republic carries a heavy burden of responsibility in the Rwandan apocalypse. France saved the genocidal regime of Habyarimana from collapsing
from late–1990 to mid–1994; French personnel trained and equipped the
'willing executioners'.[11] And, the worst, France delivered weapons and
ammunition to the Rwandan *génocidaires* before, during and after they
committed genocide. According to the ruling of the Convention for
Prevention and Punishment of the Crime of Genocide article 3e, complicity
in genocide is a punishable act.[12] The International Criminal Tribunal for
Rwanda has so far not even indicted a single member of the French
government of the time, led by Edouard Balladur and Alain Juppé.

The 'land of human rights' is not the only one now in the dock. The
United States had delayed any rapid response for months and months. The
U.S. government imposed the infamous regulations for civil servants not to
use the term *genocide* in connection with Rwanda—in order to avoid any
obligations stipulated by the Anti-Genocide Convention. The Clinton administration imposed an arms embargo on Rwanda only at the end of May
1994—when hundreds of thousands had already been brutally murdered.[13]
In a heated discussion about the co-responsibility of the United States in
causing the deadly UN non-action, Clinton's ambassador for war crimes
admitted that the United States could have reacted two or three weeks
earlier.[14] If so, a rapid response in May 1994 led by the United States could
have saved hundred thousands of lives.

Major developments have taken place since, such as the installation of a
coalition government of national unity in Rwanda; the continuation of the
civil war in Burundi, despite a promising peace process since 1997, and, the
explosion, in fall 1996 and again in mid 1999, of an internationalised war in
Congo, dubbed Africa War I.[15] The situation evolved after the forcible
return in 1996 and 1997 of roughly two million Hutus, who had fled or
were pushed into than Congo-Zaire and other countries, when the RPF and a
new government of national unity installed itself in Rwanda, with the start of
human rights investigations, and the first trials inside Rwanda as well as the
slow start of the International Criminal Tribunal for Rwanda (ICTR), and
the progress made after introducing new mechanism during 2000. There are
noticeable achievements reached in Rwanda, against all odds, in its struggle

for reconstructing governance, starting democratization from the commune-level and applying justice from the sector-level upwards (a system called *gachacha* to be introduced country-wide in the later part of 2002). Rwanda is progressing economically at a fast rate, and the country is moving toward reconciling society—after one of the worst disasters in modern times.

In Rwanda, for the first time in history, a total genocide of huge magnitude took place before the very eyes of UN forces. The commander of that force stated publicly that the genocide could have been prevented. More than five years after the disaster this was finally admitted in the Carlsson report on the role of the United Nations in Rwanda between 1993 and 1994, published on December 15, 1999 (Carlsson *et al.* 1999).[16] The Carlsson report on UN non-action in Rwanda hit the UN headquarters in New York like a bombshell and its importance and similarities for Burundi seems evident: the report underlined that genocide prevention has to be firmly established in the entire region, as a key task for the United Nations. The inquiry report fully acknowledged the UN's responsibility 'for not having done enough to prevent or stop the genocide in Rwanda'.[17] On the ground different sections of the UN system only began in mid 1994—when one million people were dead and the country devastated—with their largely inappropriate responses to one of the worst tragedies in modern history.[18] In 1994 the United Nations' reputation had suffered lasting damage. During the months of terror, the international community failed utterly.

UN Peacekeeping Needs Clear and Legitimate Objectives

Since 1945, there have been 45 United Nations peacekeeping operations. The number of personnel in UN operations fell dramatically from its 1994 peak of 76,000 blue helmets to less than 15,000 in 1995 and up again to 47,000 troops by 2002. The slump was the result of the Rwanda shock and several failed Chapter VII operations to enforce peace on warring parties. On January 1, 2002, there were 16 UN military operations under way; one mission soon ended and 15 went on.[19] While between 1988 and 1997, 30 such operations were instituted by the Security Council, seven UN peacekeeping operations ended since 1998.[20] Two of the current operations are more than 50 years old (UNTSO since 1948 and UNMOGIP since 1949) and three are more than 20 years old (UNFICYP 1964, UNDOF 1974 and UNIFIL 1978; all except one of this long-term operations are deployed in the Middle East.

Peacekeeping constitutes, amongst other things, a considerable financial burden on an international organization that periodically teeters on the edge of financial ruin. Annual cost of UN peacekeeping peaked at $3.6 billion in

1993, mainly due to operations in the former Yugoslavia and the failed mission in Somalia. Peacekeeping costs fell in 1996 to $1.4 billion, $1.3 billion in 1997 and reached to just under $1 billion by 1998. With the resurgence of larger-scale operations, costs for UN peacekeeping rose again to $1.7 billion in 1999 and $2.5–2.6 billion for the year 2000 and 2001.[21] But the peacekeeping troops have managed to prevent the worst in many conflicts; they have broken the spiral of escalation; and they have prevented conflicts from continuing or erupting anew. In other cases, UN troops have failed in their mission (as was recently the case with UNAMIR in Rwanda and with UNOMUR in Uganda and Rwanda).[22]

The short-term doubling of expenses had also to do with the new character of UN interventions. Peacekeeping has traditionally relied on the consent of opposing parties. In the case of enforcement, the Security Council gives certain member states the authority to take measures to achieve an objective decided upon by itself; the consent of the parties is not required. Enforcement has been used in many recent cases, including the second Gulf war, Somalia, Haiti, Bosnia, Kosovo/Yugoslavia and East Timor in 1999, and Macedonia (by NATO) and Afghanistan in 2000. Most enforcement operations were not under UN control but directed by a single country, which was in all but one case the United States, often in coalition with other countries. The exception was the Australian-led effort in East Timor. A NATO-led multinational force, for example, followed the UN peace-keeping operation in Bosnia.

It was before most failures happened, early in 1992 at a presidential-level meeting of the states belonging to the Security Council, when probably the most momentous signal in regard to the future of UN peace-keeping was given: then UN Secretary-General Boutros Boutros-Ghali was asked to work out proposals on peace enforcement, particularly the creation of a rapid response force. The idea was to use it mainly in the Third World. However, the proposed UN rapid deployment force never materialized.

Non-interference or Legitimate Intervention?

The principle of non-interference in internal affairs—which in practice has not prevented large states from interfering in the affairs of smaller ones—was coming under international pressure for loftier (humanitarian) reasons. The enforcement of human and minority rights by other states or by supra-state organizations—for example, within the framework of the OSCE—will in future not count any longer as interference in internal affairs. The OSCE and the Council of Europe have formulated binding minimum measures for the protection of minorities, though up to now their provisions have not been applied or adhered to by all states.[23]

Third World countries fear that new regulations could give a boost to future attempts at intervention of a general kind, and could provide the power-politics which the West pursues *vis-à-vis* the Third World with new instruments for legitimating military interventions. Instead of the instruments needed for violence prevention and settlement being developed or even being identified, there will, so they fear, be more direct intervention in future. As against this, Dieter Senghaas has offered a 'casuistry' of intervention, as a contribution to the development of a 'political culture of legitimate intervention'.[24] His thinking on a model of 'therapeutic conflict-intervention' and the more far-reaching casuistry of intervention was triggered by the shock of the new barbarism in former Yugoslavia and the 'failure' (or alleged passive bystander role) of the Europeans and the United Nations.

The number of military interventions that have taken place since 1945 is considerable. The parties most often doing the intervening were, depending on the criteria used for calculation, the three Western powers of the USA, Britain, and France. They have intervened militarily many times more often than the United Nations; with the United States having a clear lead since 1945. Statistics very much depend on the exact criteria used for the count.[25] An open debate about the usefulness, non-usefulness or (il)legitimacy of military interventions could help establish generally binding criteria; such a debate should also take place within the framework of the UN.

The NATO as an Instrument of the United Nations?

A casuistry of intervention written by Senghaas was also a contribution to the debate that was going on in Germany at that time about military 'humanitarian intervention'. This should be viewed against the background of the discussion in the mid-1990s about the role of the Federal Army in so-called out-of-area operations by NATO and about the possibility of its taking part in offensive UN operations.[26] The crunch came as early as summer 1995, when the German army was used for the first time outside the NATO area.[27] In September of that year, NATO launched its biggest-ever war operation—with a UN endorsement that could be interpreted in a number of different ways.[28] The USA sought (as it had done in the second Gulf war against Iraq) to bomb its way to a negotiated settlement by inflicting weeks of bombing raids against one of the three parties to the war; Russia was ignored, with Yeltsin even talking of 'genocide' against the Bosnian Serbs.

Intervention by the United Nations should (said Senghaas) be declared legitimate in the cases of genocide, mass expulsion, civil war, grave violations of human and minority rights, ecological warfare, and the proliferation of weapons of mass destruction.[29] This leaves too many doors open for old-style big power intervention as it has been experienced in many parts of the world since decades. Even the imperative of action in the face of genocide has to be qualified, as the Kosovo case and NATO's war against Yugoslavia in 1999 has clearly shown. Representatives and dissidents from Third World countries have criticized the plans of intervention on so-called humanitarian grounds; because they leave the door wide open to selectivity and double standards.[30] No one, they have said, can point to an example of 'successful' intervention—with the possible exception of the later UN intervention in East Timor 1999 (though it came 24 years too late!). The 1993 Somalia intervention was a case in point, only to be magnified by the non-action in Rwanda 1994.[31] One should keep in mind that UN peace-keeping can be as good or bad as the permanent members of the Security Council want it to be.

Instances of military interventions not bound up with interests of one kind or another are hardly conceivable. However, the case of Haiti could be mentioned, which became to be known as the first truly humanitarian intervention of United States thanks to the negotiation skills of former president Carter. Some experts viewed the UN operation in Cambodia as an example of a reasonably successful UN intervention,[32] unfortunately without having solved the question of bringing the genocidal Khmer Rouge leaders to justice. And, as mentioned, so was—apart from deadly delays before and after the referendum on independence and a series of diplomatic failures of the United Nations in Jakarta—the UN Chapter VII peace-enforcement intervention in East Timor 1999. The island became the first territory to be directly administered by the United Nations. The making of independent East Timor in turn contributed to the democratization of Indonesia.

Successes and Failures

An analysis shows that only two operations can be seen as successful (Haiti and East Timor), while most other enforcement operations showed mixed results, others used excessive violence even against civilians or were outright failures. Among them the second Gulf war against Iraq, which was 'not a UN operation' according to that time Secretary-General Javier Perez de Cuellar (who left in 1992, after serving two terms), Somalia, which was ill conceived from the beginning (as discussed below) and came to grief, and the NATO operation against Kosovo/Yugoslavia, which was justified with fabricated accusations of a Serb genocide against Albanians and turned out to spread violence even further. In these three cases almost nothing substantial was achieved for world peace—on the contrary, huge destruction and gross violations of international law were committed.

In cases, where enforcement would have been a legitimate option, such as in Rwanda 1994 and in the Congo since 2000, nothing at all was done (as in Rwanda) to stop the announced genocide or very little was done to follow-up a regional agreement (as in the Congo)—and almost three million people died as a consequence of non-action. To fulfil the task of disarming a large number of 'negative elements' (genocidal elements and killer militias) the United Nations would have needed a well-armed professional military force of at least 50,000 men for a peace-enforcement mission to the Congo. But the Security Council would only send 5,000 troops. It is remembered that in Bosnia some 20,000 were not enough, in Somalia 28,000 could not do the job and in Kosovo even 48,000 could not stop the violence and its spill-over into Macedonia. After two years of 'wait and see' tactics, by February 2001, the UN Security Council even cut down the number of MONUC troops to be deployed in the Congo from March onward to only 3,000, equal to the proposal by the United States. They again reduced deployment in a country the size of Western Europe has drawn strong criticism and confirmed doubts about the United Nations' ability and seriousness in dealing with the world's most deadly conflict.

Some operations carried out under the banner of traditional UN peace-keeping also turned out to be spectacular disasters, particularly in Africa, among them peacekeeping operations in the Western Sahara, Angola, Liberia and, as mentioned already, Rwanda and the Congo. MINURSO in the Western Sahara also failed lamentably to deliver the promised referendum on the future of this territory due to destructive manoeuvring of the Moroccan king Hassan II and his son.[33] In Angola, the UN Verification Mission (UNAVEM) was a complete failure.[34] The elections were indeed observed 'by the book' but the United Nations did nothing to prevent a return to arms by UNITA.[35] A meagre 350 military observers were meant to monitor the withdrawal of South Africans and Cubans from Namibia and Angola (as laid down in the Namibia agreement) and the partial demobilization of 150,000 armed men—in a huge area with no properly functioning transport or communications system! UNITA was allowed to declare a figure of only 14,000 armed troops—less than half its real strength—and concealed extensive arsenals of weapons.

The Failure of the 1993 Intervention in Somalia

These UN operations came to grief because of a lack of clearly defined objectives and of precise stipulations as to the nature of the intervention.[36] The intervention in Somalia was decided on just at the time when the UN Special Envoy, Ambassador Mohammed Sahnoun, working through the clan elders, had secured a peaceful settlement and agreement on all the key issues.[37] Sahnoun had a blueprint for the settlement, and Meles Zenawi, the strongman of Ethiopia, was providing his 'good offices'. That time Zenawi hosted the conference of all the parties to the conflict in Addis Ababa. However, the Ethiopian government has since become notorious for repeatedly aggressing Somali territory. The EPRDF cross-border raids aimed at combating Ethiopian armed opposition groups, such as OLF, IFLO and al-Ittihad al-Islami, and persecuting Ethiopian refugees. The conflict could have been overcome by the forces in the region itself and with the assistance of international experts such as Sahnoun. The staging of the Somalia invasion was geared to outside interests, not to any need on the ground. Playing up military operations as media events (as was done in the case of UNOSOM in Somalia) fuelled emotions and proved counterproductive.

The painful failure of the UN intervention in Somalia was a turning point. In 1994, the Security Council was informed that 35,000 troops would be needed to deter attacks on the 'safe areas' in Bosnia (created by the same Security Council). Member states authorized 7,600 troops and it took a year to provide them. The lessons from the lately completed report 'Srebrenica – a "safe" area' by the Netherlands Institute for War Documentation (NIOD 2002) must be drawn, which has caused the Dutch government to resign.[38]

Lessons have not yet been drawn from the UN (Carlsson *et al.* 1999) and OAU (Masire *et al.* 2000) reports on Rwanda. In Rwanda in 1994, after pulling back a 2,500–strong UN force in the midst of a wave of genocide, the Security Council unanimously decided that 5,500 peacekeepers were urgently needed. But it took nearly six months and the death of one million defenceless victims for UN member states to provide the troops—despite the fact that 19 governments had earlier pledged to keep more than 30,000 troops on stand-by for UN peacekeeping.

Comparing Kosovo and the Congo: Appalling Double-standards

The comparison between tiny Kosovo and the huge Democratic Republic of Congo is telling a story of unreserved double standards and Eurocentrism (at best, some say outright racism). In early 2001 there were almost 38 thousand peacekeepers of NATO's Kosovo Force (KFOR) deployed in this province of Serbia as well as a large UN administration, on a population of just over two million. Nevertheless, under their eyes, Serbs and Gypsies in Kosovo became the targets of Albanian 'counter ethnic cleansing'; disturbing insecurity and disorder characterizes the situation in Kosovo. The Security Council resolution 1244 was not implemented.

KFOR failed to restore peace and co-existence: new hostilities were started by non-demobilized KLA terrorists driving out more than 400,000 non-Albanians (330,000 until Oct, according to FRY sources), primarily

Serbs (est. 250,000), Roma (according to the Roma World Council 150,000), Turks, Muslims, Gorani, Croats, Egyptians and members of other ethnic groups, due to revenge and terror unleashed by KLA and armed Albanian gangs.[39] Compared to 38 thousand KFOR peacekeepers on a population of 1.8 million Kosovars (and a dwindling number of people from originally over 40 different nationalities) the huge Congo with one hundred times larger territory (in which the whole of Western Europe fits) and a population of some 60 million should get a tiny force of 5,537 military personnel. The UN Security Council decided this mini-force in its resolution 1291 of February 2000, following on a proposition made by Annan with the support of the United States. A year later it was even cut down and almost halved to 3,000 men.

Double standards characterized the official discourse the Western leaders about the problems at stake in Kosovo. Former U.S. president Clinton was talking about 'deliberate and systematic acts of genocide';[40] it should be recalled that in 1994 he prohibited the use of 'genocide' in connection with Rwanda. The NATO bombing of Yugoslavia was started in March 1999 with the expressed aim to 'stop a genocide' in Kosovo and received an unprecedented media attention; the result looks like an outright failure, and it will become expensive for the United Nations (and, in the end, for the European Union).[41]

The result was highly questionable: the 'elected dictator' Slobodan Milosevic remained in power in Belgrade; while the suffering of the Kosovar Albanians ended mid-1999, and the refugees returned, the Serbs and Roma (Gypsies) living in Kosovo had in turn been forced to leave. In the Kosovo the remaining non-Albanians live under death threats to be killed by UÇK—even under the eyes of NATO troops—ever since the 1999 war (Chomski 2000). Milosevic, the man presented by the media as the 'new Saddam Hussein', was only chased away by a popular uprising of the Serbian people in October 2000; he was arrested in April 2001 and detained for series of crimes. Under increasing international pressure Milosevic was extradited on June 28, 2001, to be tried by the International Tribunal for the Former Yugoslavia, ICTY, in The Hague. His trial started in Feb 2002 and developed quite unexpectedly, with Milosevic defending himself, defiantly accusing NATO of having committed war crimes in Yugoslavia.[42] Meanwhile, from their bases in the Kosovo, armed UÇK gangs were allowed to attack another state—Macedonia, in May 2001—again under the eyes of the NATO troops.

There was genocide in Central Africa. New massacres took and still take place in different regions of the Congo. Was there 'genocide' in Kosovo? Realities on the ground turned out to be radically different than reported: the ICTY found no genocide; investigators announced to have found some

2,018 dead bodies; however, many of those might well be Serbs and Roma killed by UÇK elements, despite the massive presence of KFOR (NATO).[43] The U.S. State Department had put Kosovo to the size of the Rwandan genocide (!). At the time the Rwandan genocide was even unacknowledged by the Clinton government. Ministers and high U.S. officials have grossly inflated the real number of death in Kosovo—as nine months later announced by ICTY—by a factor of 250.[44] In Congo and its neighbour states to the east the threat of genocide—contrary to the case of Kosovo—is real and potentially on massive scale. Recalling the Western discourse on genocide prevention, the fact that no Western country—contrary to Kosovo—had promised to contribute troops and equipment seems most disturbing. The largest contingents came from African countries; five countries contributed the bulk (83 percent) of the 2,366 peacekeepers deployed in mid-2001.[45] Only a few Western countries contributed minor numbers of staff that makes just about 1 percent of MONUC.[46]

It is certain that the UN Security Council was aware and well-informed (through abundant reports by the UN military observers on the spot) that the government of Kabila Jr. and his allies continued to supply arms and give support to FAR-Interahamwe elements and use them against their foes (as did the late Laurent Kabila before)—in outright breach of the Lusaka agreement and international law instruments, such as the anti-genocide convention and the Geneva conventions. The silence of the Security Council about these criminal activities and the non-action against the rulers in Kinshasa is contradicting the spirit of the United Nations as the world's organization to work for peace and makes the council share the responsibility for the havoc the 'negative forces' create in eastern Congo and in Burundi, resulting in massive death among the civilian populations. The council ought to stop the killings by rapidly deploying a UN force under chapter VII.

Conclusion: The Need for Legitimate Intervention

The debate about the need for intervention is ultimately also an expression of the search for new enemy-images and possible areas of activity for the now-idle Western armies. For the majority of the world's population, however, armed interventions in the Third World are inextricably bound up with the tragic history of colonialism and imperialist power-politics. Intervention carried out in the name of the community of nations must be clearly distinguishable from these latter in both form and content. In my view, the only type of military intervention, whose legitimacy can hardly be questioned, is the intervention in case of genocide or imminent genocide; in the latter case the threat of genocide must be assessed or qualified, e.g., through warnings issued by the UN Human Rights Commission, reports of Special Rapporteurs or assessments delivered by UN independent experts. Legitimate military interventions ought to be adequately mandated by the United Nations and implemented under UN command according to predefined objectives. UN peacekeeping and peace-enforcement operations (under chapter VII) ought to be periodically evaluated and re-evaluated.

Combating International Terrorism: a Task for the United Nations

The assessment is that the only truly new element about international terrorism is its direction (see chapter 2). Terrorist gang wars and state terrorism were present in a number of countries; some of the affected countries were new states created as products of the decay of the USSR and Yugoslavia. Long since the United Nations have tried to rally its member states behind a policy of containing and outlawing terrorism. The Organization and its agencies (in particular the International Civil Aviation Organization, ICAO, the International Maritime Organization, OMP, and the International Atomic Energy Agency, IAEA) have developed a range of international legal instruments to enable action by the international community to suppress terrorism and bring those responsible to justice. Dating back to 1963, several agreements provide the basic legal tools to combat international terrorism. There are ten UN conventions, two protocols, one declaration and a number of resolutions dealing with the threat of terrorism; the first three conventions, elaborated by ICAO between 1963 and 1971 deal with security aboard of aircrafts, are almost globally supported (with above 170 state parties each); another convention deals with security in airports (1988, 107 state parties).[47] The 1999 *Convention for the Suppression of the Financing of Terrorism* is not yet in force. The problem with the majority of the ten treaties is that many states are not yet party to these legal instruments (half of the treaties are ratified by less than half of the UN member states) or the states are not implementing what they have ratified.

The UN General Assembly, on September 12, 2001, passed a resolution that '[u]rgently calls for international cooperation to bring to justice the perpetrators, organizers, and sponsors of the outrages of 11 September 2001'. The General Assembly further called for 'international cooperation to prevent and eradicate acts of terrorism, and stresses that those responsible for aiding, supporting, or harbouring the perpetrators, organizers and sponsors of such acts will be held accountable'.[48] There was a broad consensus among the UN member states that the perpetrators of the massacre of 11 September must be brought to justice. They did not call for any one state to take justice in its own hands. Indeed, the UN's legislative bodies responded rapidly to the terrorist attack, so too did its specialized agencies.

'War against Terrorism' is Inappropriate and Combating Symptoms Only

As soon as the dust settled after the Manhattan twin towers' collapse and the first shock had passed, a bewildering cacophony of embarrassing 'war of words' started. Then, early in October 2001, B-52 and other long-range heavy bombers attacked Afghanistan in the name of a 'war against terrorism', as it was officially and incomprehensively called. Senior US officials, including President Bush, did not stop short of calling this 'war' a 'crusade', a moral and military enterprise at once. While most of the war effort in Afghanistan was carried out by the Afghan Northern Alliance, the US forces were, until the ill conceived *Operation Anaconda* in March 2002, rarely in any exposed position on the ground, but US air force was simply bombing with everything US military industries could produce (including huge-sized depleted uranium bombs). Nevertheless the US claimed 'victory' against the Taliban regime and al-Qaeda.

There was nothing much won in USA's strange 'war on terrorism'. None of the original war aims, to capture the leaders of the Taliban regime and al-Qaeda, 'dead or alive' (Bush), was achieved. A long conspicuous silence followed initial hard talk as regards bin Laden and his lieutenants. Instead we witnessed a military operation with ever-shifting aims. Growing confident, the US president vowed to declare war against a whole 'axis of evil', in which he groups the very heterogeneous group of nations such as Iraq, Iran, North Korea and others. Without a shred of evidence all of these states were accused of aiding al-Qaeda terrorism. Military assaults on other states such as Yemen, Somalia and Sudan were also publicly discussed. Not since the times of Ronald Reagan's obsessive anti-communism, or even back to the US copy of 'Stalinism' in the 1950s, has Washington's political rhetoric about the fight between *Good* (America, its British assistant, Israel and few more) and *Evil* (all the above mentioned evil states and some not mentioned states) reached such a pathological fury. The US administration hoped to build on justified fears of the population in the wake of a ruthless terrorist attack.

War-mongering was the most disturbing element of a whole-sale policy change in the United States, designed (as in the 1950s and the 1980s) to capitalize on growing patriotism and spur domestic popular support for a government obeying to the 'military-industrial complex',[49] as well as to quash progressive dissent at home and to openly support pro-US dictatorships and regimes with abysmal human rights record. Playing on the fear of 'Islamic' (Islamist) terrorism was to advance an ideological agenda not very different from that of the Reagan era, but with an almost unrestrained desire to advance an aggressive brand of US global hegemony and supremacy.[50]

Terrorism as a Catalyst for Increasing Military Spending and Aggressiveness

US military spending of an incredible US$350 billion, already larger as those of the next six states combined (*sic*), was expanded by another US$50 billion 'to fight terrorism', as if terrorism could be fought with more sophisticated bombs, 'missile defence' (a renewed version of Reagan's star wars project) and a new generation of nuclear weapons.[51] Before even he moved into the White House, the new American president-elect Bush made it (end 2000) clear what policy he stands for: he placed highest priority on 'restoring' US military force, which he has described as 'overworked, under-funded (*sic*) and in need of new direction'. Expanding the military was assessed as 'difficult' without a 'new daunting challenge'.[52]

Globalizing terrorism was conveniently delivering the 'new daunting challenge' the Pentagon was searching for. How else would the USA legitimize the growth of the US armed forces and its ever-sophisticated equipment? US military growth is in stark contrast to the planned further reduction of 600,000 by 2005 of the Russian armed forces (SIPRI 2001, 321–22) and the past massive reduction of weapons of mass destruction by the former USSR since 1991. The Pentagon's 2001 Nuclear Posture Review has already raised fears about lowering of the threshold for using nuclear arms. Nuclear weapons, it is obvious, will not help to fight terrorism; rather it is nuclear terrorism—the ultimate threat—that has to be prevented.

The Lack of an Accepted Definition

The Legal Committee of the UN General Assembly has started elaborating a convention for the suppression of acts of nuclear terrorism and a comprehensive convention on the elimination of terrorism. The latter convention is blocked by a row among the UN member states about four areas, with the main issue being the lack of an accepted definition of terrorism.[53] So far the problem has been circumvented due to the fact that the existing UN treaties on terrorism have only aspired at an 'operational definition' of terrorism in a specific circumstance. This was possible because each treaty has dealt exclusively with a particular manifestation of terrorist activity such as bombings, hijackings, hostage-taking or covert financing. The lack of agreement on a definition of terrorism has been among the major obstacles to meaningful international countermeasures. As common legacy of the Cold War era one state's 'terrorist' is another state's 'freedom fighter'. It seems a matter of urgency to identify types of political violence that the international community regards as 'unacceptable' and 'unjustifiable'. Such types of political violence require the application of both, preventive and repressive measures consistent with international law.

The international community has been unable to arrive at any agreed meaning of how to define terrorism, though there have been proposals and attempts at maximalist and minimalist definition; even the latter remained expert definitions. An example for a minimalist definition was the proposal of Alex P. Schmid 1993 that the point of departure for a minimal definition could be the existing consensus on what constitutes 'war crimes', whereby these crimes are committed in 'peace times'. Common understanding what constitutes war crimes is rather diverse; definitions based on codification by the Geneva Conventions (among other bodies of international humanitarian law) are multi-dimensional.[54]

The Misery of Lists of Terrorist Organizations

Terrorism is defined by the United States government in Title 22 of the United States Code, Section 2656f(d) as 'premeditated, politically moti-vated violence perpetrated against non-combatant targets by sub-national groups or clandestine agents, usually intended to influence an audience'. This 'definition' is not operational; it typically excludes state actors and the type of activity; additionally it avoids the question of legitimacy. Lists of terrorist organizations compiled by state agencies expose clear differences from state to state. Due to its importance the latest biannual list compiled by the US Department of State, containing 28 primarily 'designated Foreign Terrorist Organizations' (as of October 5, 2001), has been chosen and comprehensively analyzed.[55] The result is shattering: of the US State Department's October 2001 list of 28 organizations accused to be terrorist, less then half or 12 are indeed terrorist organizations, 16 are not.[56] Of the 16 wrongly accused organizations 11 are non-terrorist but violent or illegitimate groups;[57] and five are genuine movements struggling for self-determination or liberation but may have an anti-US bias.[58]

The law also allows groups to be added 'at any time following a decision by the Secretary'. This has occurred within six months (Oct 2001 to March 2002) and seems to be a very much conjunctural choice, which has to fit into current political developments; five organizations were added, making up a list of 33 prime terrorist organizations (as of March 27, 2002), and these five were, unsurprisingly without exception, Islamic or Islamist organizations; one of the five is clearly a legitimate organization.[59]

When analysing the broader list of 66 groups described in *Patterns of Global Terrorism, 2000*, published by the United States Department of State, April 2001, the result was equally disturbing: of the most recent list of 42 organizations [and an additional 24] said to be terrorist groups, less then half or 19 [+6 = 25] can be said to be more or less clear-cut cases of terrorist organizations.[60] But 23 groups [+18 = 41] seem to have been falsely accused. Of these latter group, 13 [+8 = 21] of 23 [41] non-terrorist are in the grey area. This means they fight for a just cause but show a lack of legitimacy, either by their performance or by targets or aims. A group of ten organizations [+10 = 20] are genuine liberation, self-determination or social revolutionary movements; some of them have taken or may take legal action against their categorization as 'terrorists'.

Combating Terrorism as a Multi-lateral Effort

Ahead of the attack on America the UN Security Council has undertaken several unprecedented steps. Already in October 15, 1999, and probably for the first time ever, a UN Security Council Resolution (1267) demanded that a government (the Taliban regime in Afghanistan) turn over an individual (Osama bin Laden) 'without further delay to appropriate authorities in a country where he has been indicted, or ... where he will be effectively brought to justice'. For this purpose the council adopted sanctions, which were increased on December 19, 2000, by UNSC Resolution 1333.

The UN response to terrorism has been consistent over decades. The organization has not only elaborated an arsenal of legal instruments but also several institutions dealing with terrorism. Within the United Nations Office for Drug Control and Crime Prevention (UNODCCP), which is dealing with the menace of organized crime, three bodies were established. The Centre for International Crime Prevention (CICP) is the UN office responsible for crime prevention, criminal justice and criminal law reform; it implements global programmes such as combating transnational organized crime, corruption and trafficking in human beings; despite its importance the professional staff only numbers 25. Linked with the CICP is the Terrorism Prevention Branch, a small think tank established by the General Assembly in 1999, which is also based in Vienna.[61]

The worst possible scenario of a terrorist attack is, as Secretary-General Kofi Annan explained in his address to the General Assembly debate on measures to combat international terrorism, '... a single attack involving a nuclear or biological weapon could have killed millions', adding, 'there is much that we can do to help prevent future terrorist acts carried out with weapons of mass destruction'.[62] Henry Kelly, in his testimony on 'Terrorist Nuclear Threat', given at a US Senate Foreign Relations Committee hearing in March 6, 2002, pointed out that this threat is an ultimate one and has to be dealt with by all responsible actors.[63]

The underlying strategy of the response of United Nations to the threat of globalizing terrorism has been twofold: On the one side building up a framework of legal instruments to combat terrorism (since the 1960s) and creating institutions to prevent and combat terrorism (mainly done in the

1980s and 1990s), on the other side fighting terrorism through disarmament and preventing a worst scale scenario by creating political will and the necessary instruments for the comprehensive universal abolition of all 'weapons of mass destruction'.[64]

Developing Structural Prevention of Mass Violence

In formerly proud non-aligned Yugoslavia, people have once again been fighting and dying for the nation, an idea that seemed to have been transcended within the framework of the 'highly industrialized nations'. Because of the brutalization of the war in Bosnia, UN military intervention in internal ethno-national conflicts is once again up for debate. The conflict in former Yugoslavia cannot be understood as a genuinely ethnic conflict; it needs to be seen, rather, as a political conflict that exploited a hybrid ethnicization of religious and confessional groups.[65] But the majority of current conflicts, and in particular most ethno-national conflicts, cannot be either influenced or controlled to any significant extent, let alone resolved, using the instrument of military intervention.

Any promising method of conflict resolution requires, first and foremost, political solutions that are geared to the concrete situation, that have been worked out in consultation with all parties to the conflict, and are enforced with the aid of a graduated set of non-military instruments for applying pressure. This set of instruments ranges from preventive diplomacy, through peaceful dispute-settlement via official channels and condemnation by the UN General Assembly, to political and economic sanctions and armed peace-enforcement operations—as a last resort and in cases of genocidal activity. Genocide such as was perpetrated in Rwanda in April 1994 is not an 'internal affair' to be dealt with by states. In such cases, direct intervention becomes a moral duty of the world community. The immediate triggers for it can be resolutions of the Security Council or General Assembly.

The affairs of minorities must become the affairs of the international community. The systematic violation of human and minority rights by individual states must be denounced and investigated by the UN. A state's refusal to accept a UN fact-finding delegation, and moves to hinder or actually preclude this kind of activity, should in future entail severe sanctions. The UN Human Rights Commission's condemnation of Burma, for example, was not followed up by economic sanctions on the part of the UN. Where there is a suspicion of genocide, or where there are findings to this effect by independent authorities, the options of a strict timetable and a shortening of the usual procedures must come into play. Every delay brings untold suffering.

There is a whole range of forms of structural conflict-prevention that are currently largely ignored because they are unspectacular. The operationalization of measures of conflict-prevention of a political, economic, and military kind, and the promotion of a culture of peace (for example, within the framework of UNESCO), would be urgent tasks for an international organization devoted to the preservation of peace.

The instrument of sanctions, first used by the United Nations as far back as 1966 (against Rhodesia), should be further developed and transformed into a graduated UN regime of operative constraint and a standard means of international intervention capable of replacing the military option.[66] Legitimate forms of intervention can be justified on the basis of Chapter VII, of the Charter of the United Nations, titled 'Action with Respect to Threats to the Peace, Breaches of the Peace, and Acts of Aggression'. It is only since 1990 that Chapter VII (peace enforcement) was rediscovered.[67] In contrast to most military intervention, non-military intervention and some economic sanctions had proved to be cost-effective and 'relatively successful'.[68]

The term 'humanitarian intervention' should be reserved for use in relation to the Red Cross and other humanitarian organizations.[69] This also makes it clear that every humanitarian intervention conducted by the ICRC, Amnesty International, or other human-rights organizations, precludes the use of military means and includes the activity of national and international non-governmental organizations.

Developing Structural Prevention of Genocide

The challenges of genocide prevention are great and a matter of urgency. A systematic overview on the tasks, procedures, institutions and voids of genocide prevention is required.[70] A toolbox (on the next page) covers the most important areas to reduce, prevent and eliminate genocide. Today effective instruments, practical procedures and respected institutions necessary to achieve these noble goals are only partly in place: most instruments and institutions for averting, preventing and outlawing genocide have yet to be created. The questions to be asked are:

1. What deficits of scientific research on the origin and nature of genocide and its practical applications can be identified?
2. What policies, procedures and institutions shall be developed that can effectively prevent genocide in the local and global space?
3. What can be done to enforce the existing international law on the punishment of the crime of genocide (i.e. UN 1948 convention)?

4. What instruments, practical procedures and institutions can be strengthened or created that are effectively reducing?
5. How can the media be influenced to provide current and comprehensive information on the crime of genocide?
6. What can the global civil society do against the crime of genocide? How can the public be mobilized to prevent or halt an outbreak of genocide?[71]
7. How can governments, international organizations and the United Nations be urged and pressured to act against the genocide?

The overview on genocide prevention hereafter is focusing on activities, which are essential to combat and eliminate genocide. I believe that different actors shall collaborate to that end. The synergies between the organizations of states in general and the United Nations in particular, the world's 193 states, international non-governmental organizations and locally active NGOs could be used. However, genocide prevention is among the most important tasks for global governance: the global monitoring of gross human rights violations is a task that has to be coordinated by a special United Nations task force. The world organization is called to implement the recommendations made by the remarkably candid and forward looking Carlsson inquiry report 1999. Table 8.1 is exploring six areas of activities to combat the crime of genocide.

Deadly threats and the vulnerability of civilian populations in intra-state conflicts and particularly in genocides were growing at a fast rate in the past 20th century. Civilians are seen by many actors as soft targets, easy to assault; they are murdered, tortured, terrorized, starved, pillaged, put at high risks for their health, chased, expulsed, displaced, rather than protected. Violence is more often used without any purpose than destruction of lives and livelihood. International law and international humanitarian law are not enforced. There are generally no sanctions linked to gross violations of international law. Perpetrators of large crimes still have a chance to get away with it. This is an invitation for others to act the same way.[72] The establishment of the International Criminal Court (ICC) later in 2002 provides the international community with a new tool to counteract and establish universal prosecution of genocide and crimes against humanity.

As part of an 'Action Plan to Prevent Genocide' a UN commission of inquiry headed by Ingvar Carlsson recommended end of 1999 that 'efforts at improving early warning and preventive capacity should include the prevention of genocide as a particular component'.[73] A 'Genocide Alert Unit' should have a short link to the Security Council and the Secretariat. The unit would be closely linked to the commanding structure of a future 'Rapid Reaction Force'; the unit could share some offices with the existing 'Lessons Learned Unit' of the UN Department of Peacekeeping Operations.

Table 8.1: Systematic Overview on Genocide Prevention: A Tool Box

1 Genocide Alert and Early Warning	2 Early Action and Rapid Reaction Mechanism
• Global monitoring of gross human rights violations shall be coordinated • Clear-cut indicators for early warning about serious risk of genocide • Development of an integrated early warning and early response system • Special UN task force for processing data on minorities-at-risk and change of behavior of dangerous regimes • Permanent information of UN Security Council and other key decision makers about high-risk situations	• High level diplomacy in cases of alert • Development of new mechanisms of rapid reaction in cases of 'red alert' • Organizing political will for averting genocide • Organizing political will for mandatory military intervention of UN and protection of the victims in case of genocide
3 Prosecution and Deterrence	4 Enforcing International Law
• Mandatory prosecution of perpetrators of genocide in anyone state • Establishment of special prosecution institutions to end impunity for mass murder • An international tribunal for the crime of genocide to be institutionalized as integral part of the UN system • The International Criminal Court (ICC) to be established in due time; • International criminal law has to be developed comprehensively in order for the rule of law to be respected by all states and political actors	• By comprehensive review processes and checks-and-control, as in the cases of the European Convention on Human Rights or ILO convention 169 • By institution building, e.g. the OSCE High Commissioner for Minorities • By establishing an International Criminal Court (ICC), in order to outlaw gross human rights violations such as genocide and crimes against humanity (ICC met strong resistance by large powers, esp. by USA) • By refining an arsenal of sanctions that shall hurt regimes not the people
5 Pressure, Vigilance, Protection	6 Lessons Learned
• UN, regional organizations and donors to impose conditionality on aid in cases of abuse, violations, threats, state criminality • Incentives shall promote democratization, respect for basic human rights and minority rights, rule of law, good governance • Monitoring risk areas and minorities at risk by INGOs, local NGOs, IGOs • Averting and breaking escalation through presence and media coverage • Rapid and broad system of protection of possible victims	• Learning from experience of genocide-free world regions (such as East Asia) • Fighting powerlessness and passive response on genocide • Development of concepts of structural prevention of genocide • Writing genocide prevention into statutes, domestic laws, constitutions, international conventions, pacts, etc. • Standardizing prevention of genocide and mass violence internationally

There are already a number of independent early warning systems; globally active are PIOOM in Leiden, the Carter Center in Atlanta and the London-based FEWER network. However, the sharing of early warning information amongst governmental organizations and NGOs is not formalized and synergies are not used. Comparative genocide research may decisively contribute to the development of a global early warning system, chiefly by working on reliable indicators. The objective is to establish effective structural prevention of genocide.[74] The main reason why a future institution for genocide alert and early action should become part of the UN General Secretariat is the idea to have short procedures and solid facilitation of high-level diplomacy in cases of alert.

Annan has put it clear by saying that 'without early action, early warning is of little use'.[75] The UN member states must agree on new mechanisms of rapid reaction; in cases of 'red genocide alert' traditional UN diplomacy is not the appropriate means. In case of 'red genocide alert' only the plausible threat of a UN military intervention will be appropriate. Averting genocide is in principle the duty of all signatory states of the UN Anti-Genocide Convention; this was 'forgotten' for almost fifty years.

The UN Secretariat will be chiefly responsible for organizing political will to establish a rapid reaction mechanism which shall not depend on political criteria but a purely professional venture. To create the political will to stop genocide within the system of the United Nations is also to prevent unilateral interventions, which usually have their own agendas. Reforming the UN anti-genocide convention should include organizing the political will for the mandatory military intervention of UN in case of genocide alert. The Rwanda shock made clear: the protection of the victims in case of genocide is a key duty the United Nations must accept.

Over Fifty Years of United Nations: Attempts at Instrumentalization

More than 50 years of history of the United Nations has included several phases during which attempts were made to instrumentalize it, notably by the United States. Even at its birth, in 1945, this international organization was seen as a means by which the USA could underpin the post-war order.[76] Until 1955, the United Nations came under almost absolute Western dominance, leaving the USSR only the right of veto. The Korean war, fought under the UN flag in 1950, was only possible because the USSR absented itself from the Security Council (in protest at the exclusion of China). This made it easier for the USA and the Western majority of the time to utilize the United Nations, between 1950 and 1953, to take sides within their own Cold War camp. The West waged a bloc war but under the guise of the international body, created for the purpose of promoting 'peace between nations'.

It was in the domain of security that the roles that the United Nations were to play over the next decades were defined. Bertrand identifies four roles: as a stage for East–West confrontation; as a 'sounding-board' for decolonization; as a dumping-ground for 'insoluble problems' (which the big powers wanted to be rid of); and as a cloak for punitive measures carried out in the interests of the USA or its allies (Bertrand 1995: 41). The UN functioned not as a forum in which the aspirations of the *peoples* (in reality the member *states*) could be balanced, as a forum for peaceful conflict-settlement, but as a 'battle-ground' on which the big powers publicly arraigned their opponents and beat the propaganda drum (if not the war drum).[77]

Subsequently, the UN Security Council became unable to function, first on account of the USSR (77 vetoes in the period 1945–55), then, in 1970–90, on account of the USA, which made use of its blocking powers even more frequently than the USSR. In the meantime, the composition of the General Assembly had undergone fundamental change. The influx of Asian and African countries, which increased dramatically from 1960, after decolonization, and the growing importance of non-alignment, neutralized the hegemonial plans of the two superpowers. Governments of the new states, meanwhile, often saw the United Nations merely as an instrument by means of which they could legitimate themselves and their power (especially when they were not the product of democratic elections). A number of Third World states sought to use the United Nations as a forum to secure development opportunities for all and to remove the injustices in an economic order dominated by the North. However, the United Nations' contribution to the development of the poor countries remained limited. Many resolutions had no effect because they were systematically sabotaged by the Western industrial states.

From 1975, the United States as the leading power repeatedly sought to extract concessions from the United Nations by means of economic 'extortion' or to influence decision-making.[78] In 1986 the United Nations were forced to grant the USA a *de facto* right of veto on budgetary matters. Disruptive financial tactics and a policy of high arrears in payment continued.[79] The collapse of the Soviet Union also brought a change in relations between the USA and the UN. Multilateralism once again became a prospect for the USA. The second Gulf crisis brought the first unequivocal condemnation of a Third World country by the big powers, as well as invocation of Article 42 of the Charter, on the use of military force (for the first time since the conflict in Korea in 1950), and, subsequently, in the case of the Iraq, the abrogation of its sovereignty in parts of its territory.

In the area of international politics, restrictions on state sovereignty of a kind not previously practised by the United Nations have recently been imposed in the case of Iraq. The third intervention by Western troops in Zaire (in September 1991) and the US intervention (of December 1992) in Somalia (and also the punitive action in June 1993) prompted a discussion about the temporary suspension of the sovereignty of individual states and about their administration as UN trusteeships. The activity of the Trusteeship Council, one of the six principal organs of the UN,[80] which seemed to have become increasingly irrelevant, could be revived on a different basis and with a new organizational profile. However, the military interventions that have taken place up to now have served not humanitarian causes, but the maintenance and underpinning of vital interests of the G7 states.[81]

Changed Scenarios of Threat and Global Security

With the system of global security, the scenarios of threat have undergone fundamental change. Big powers now generally do not lay direct claim to the territories of other states. The borders of the 'free West' and the 'communist East' no longer exist in this form and are no longer defended collectively, or else have shifted—due to the unexpected survival of NATO, one of the two Cold War military alliances, and its dangerous eastward expansion, right to the borders of Russia. Most disturbing are the growing global military imbalance and the spread of nuclear weapons.

Wars between states are rare, wars within states more and more frequent. But zones of intra-state conflict lie at the edges of the rich OECD world—in Yugoslavia, the Maghreb, the Caucasus, Korea, or Mexico. The West now feels threatened by migratory movements, rebellions, civil wars, and fundamentalist currents rather than by the nuclear arsenals and armies of other states. The United Nations millennium summit 2000 called back to memory that 'the need for a more human-centred approach to security is reinforced by the continuing dangers that weapons of mass destruction, most notably nuclear weapons, pose to humanity: their very name reveals their scope and their intended objective, if they were ever used' (UNDPI 2000: 5). After the nuclear arms race in South Asia it once again became clear that nuclear non-proliferation has totally failed. It should be recalled that besides 'new' and undeclared nuclear powers the old nuclear powers are still armed to the teeth. Their super-armament and the exorbitant associated costs are less and less justifiable.[82]

Past massive reduction of weapons of mass destruction by the former USSR since 1991 strikingly contrast with developments in the USA. The Pentagon's 2001 Nuclear Posture Review has raised fears about the Bush administration's lowering of the threshold for using nuclear arms. The

Pentagon declared a 'need for new nuclear arms that could have a lower yield and produce less nuclear fallout.'[83] The targets of such new weapons might even be non-nuclear states. To prepare the ground for such scenarios the Pentagon created a shadowy new *Office of Strategic Influence* for disinformation.[84] Large lower radiation DU bombs were tested in combat situation in Afghanistan (as earlier in Iraq and Yugoslavia); reports describe a frightening vision of a kind of local-level nuclear war fits well into the Pentagon's new aggressive strategy for US supremacy.[85] Bush's USA is not only pushing for the development of new types of nuclear weapons but seemed also to broaden the circumstances in which they might be used.

The growing military imbalance is the single greatest threat to global peace and security. Never in modern history has military force and global military expenditure been so dangerously imbalanced as today. The member states of the North Atlantic Treaty Organization (NATO), already making-up the world's strongest and—after the demise of its counterpart, the Warsaw Pact, from 1955 to 1991—only remaining supra-regional military alliance, representing hardly 10 percent of the world's population, according to SIPRI spent US$471 billion in 2000, which is 62.3 percent of the world's total military expenditure of US$756 billion.[86]

NATO Sidelining United Nations: a Threat to World Peace

The search for new operational options for NATO has been frustrated. The Bosnia operation reactivated old fears amongst the Russians and had the effect of prolonging the war.[87] Intervention by Western armies in the war between the Yugoslavian factions proved, over four years, to be too dangerous for ground forces, too expensive, and difficult to justify. The enforced Dayton peace-accord (of November 1995) did, in the end, give NATO the opportunity to use ground forces.[88] The first joint venture by NATO and Russian troops (and the tussle over supreme command) was meant to stifle the fundamental question of the justification for NATO's existence, and to project an image of yesterday's Cold War organization as tomorrow's 'peace force'.

This image was completely shattered by the second NATO intervention in Yugoslavia in 1999. Sustained NATO bombing of Yugoslavia was started in March 1999 with the expressed aim to 'stop a genocide' in Kosovo and received an unprecedented media attention; the result of a 78–days bombardment looks like an outright failure, and it will become expensive for United Nations, though the world organization has never given a mandate to NATO for going to war. Serbia has been bombed into pre-industrial times; life chances for the population dropped dramatically.

There is no end to violence inside Kosovo, as Mitrovica, the last multi-ethnic city showed. War from Kosovo even spilled-over into Macedonia.[89]

The term 'genocide' was abused by NATO for the purpose of war propaganda. Realities on the ground turned out to be radically different than reported: the International Criminal Tribunal for the Former Yugoslavia (ICTY), found no genocide.[90] Not even the war aims of NATO itself were achieved. Soon after the result proved indeed questionable: the 'elected dictator' Slobodan Milosevic remained in power in Belgrade; he was only chased away more than a year after the NATO war by a popular uprising of the Serbian people in October 2000 and is currently on trial at the International Tribunal (ICTY) for a series of crimes.[91] While the suffering of the Kosovar Albanians ended mid–1999, and the refugees returned, the Serbs, Roma (Gypsies) and other nationalities living in Kosovo had in turn been forced by the Albanians to leave or to live in KFOR-protected ghettos.

Lessons from the Outright Disaster of NATO in the Kosovo

In the Kosovo the remaining non-Albanians live under death threats—even under the eyes of NATO troops—ever since the 1999 war.[92] Since 1999 38,000 to 45,000 KFOR peacekeepers were stationed in Kosovo, as well as a large UN administration, on a population of two million. Nevertheless, under their eyes, Serbs and Roma Gypsies in Kosovo became the targets of Albanian 'counter ethnic cleansing'; since 1999 disturbing insecurity and disorder characterizes the situation in Kosovo and beyond. In May 2001 Macedonia was attacked by a supposedly 'disarmed' UÇK from the NATO-occupied Kosovo. The Security Council resolution 1244 was not implemented. NATO bears full responsibility for this appalling situation.[93]

The responsibilities of KFOR are defined in § 9, among others, (a) 'Deterring renewed hostilities', (b) 'Demilitarising KLA', (c) 'Establishing a secure environment', (d) 'Ensuring public safety and order'. KFOR failed to implement all the mentioned points in their entirety: new hostilities were started by non-demobilized KLA (UÇK) terrorists driving out more than 400,000 non-Albanians (330,000 until October 1999, according to FRY government sources), primarily Serbs (est. 250,000), Roma (according to the Romani World Council some 150,000 were driven out of Kosovo in 1999), as well as Turks, Muslims, Gorani, Croats, Egyptians and members of other ethnic groups, due to revenge killings and terror unleashed by UÇK and other armed Albanian gangs.[94]

The 'Kosovo war' was not only an American war. The European Union, which has adopted prevention as official policy since 1997, has given little proof for its will to implement such policies in practice. Kosovo comprehensively questioned the greatest benefit to NATO itself: being a Cold War organization, it had lost all justification for its existence after 1990, following the break-up of the Warsaw Pact, but now it was free to assume 'new tasks'. However, the uselessness of highly developed military technology has become evident since the attempt to enforce peace in under-developed Somalia, ravaged by feuding between clans, and in the attempts to enforce human rights. The mess NATO created in Kosovo became clearly visible when in May 2001 UÇK commandos attacked the neighbour state of Macedonia—under the eyes of NATO's seemingly powerless 'Kosovo Force' (KFOR).

To conclude, NATO's sidelining of the United Nations raised a number of questions for future global security assessments and the very meaning of security as a multi-layered concept itself. The UN millennium summit 2000 declared that 'security begins with prevention' of deadly conflicts. In the wake of the world's 50 ongoing conflicts a new concept of security need a new understanding of global threats and risks. The concept of security has evolved considerably since the end of the Cold War and attention has been given to the slow disappearance of the classic Clausewitzean warfare and the surge of intra-state conflicts on global scale. Once synonymous with the state-centred view of 'national defence' of territory from 'external attack', the requirements of security ought to have come to embrace the protection of civilians and vulnerable groups from predominantly intra-state violence.

The Policy of Violence Prevention: A Challenge of Political Leadership

For the world organization its declared policy of violence prevention is also a 'challenge of political leadership'.[95] Rightly so the millennium summit declaration stated that 'not all wars are alike; therefore no single strategy will be universally effective' (ibid.). One of the main problems politicians face in promoting preventive measures and policies are threefold: (1) the unspectacular and long-term character of many such measures makes them not really attractive if quick results are required, (2) the difficulty to measure their effectiveness is adding to confusion about the subject matter, and (3) a number of rather diverse institutions, measures and policies have preventive character but they often remain unrelated or only partially implemented. In preventing violence there are no 'easy solutions'. The great diversity of cultural and political characteristics exhibited by different types of society produce, corresponding to them, different types of claims to autonomy and regulatory mechanisms, ranging from cultural autonomy, through territorial self-governance, to *de facto* sovereignty.

As an instrument of prevention the world organization has developed since the 1950s its peacekeeping capabilities. However, double standards are still more the rule as the exception. The latest example would be the delayed and inadequate peacekeeping operation in the Democratic Republic of Congo. Compared to 38,000 KFOR peacekeepers on a population of 2 million Kosovars the huge Congo with one hundred times larger territory (in which the whole of western Europe fits) and a population of some 50 million should get a tiny force of 5,537 military personnel.

An exclusively military conception of international security is in conflict with the image of the United Nations as a peacemaker but dominates whole sections of the UN Charter. This one-sided conception, which is supposed to have proved its worth in the Cold War, has increasingly shown itself to be useless and to be a great obstacle to settling conflict (if not actually conducive to it). Meanwhile, after a phase of intensive UN interventionism up to the mid 1990s, the numbers of blue helmet troops deployed dropped dramatically from 75,000 to less than 15,000.

When intervention was the only way to save the lives of hundreds of thousands, as in Rwanda 1994, the United Nations remained paralysed. A Nordic initiative provided the first infrastructure to a 'Multinational United Nations Stand-By Force High Readiness Brigade', which could be used in case of imminent acts of genocide.[96] This high-readiness brigade was a regional rapid-reaction arrangement organized by Nordic countries in 1996 in support of United Nations missions authorized by the Security Council; this project was one of the many products of the Rwanda shock, which will make a difference in future complex crisis situations.

Despite such positive aspects, it shall be recalled that the military-style thinking on security, when applied to the changed global political parameters and conflict-scenarios, generally hinders new policies of prevention of violence and tends to create more violence—as NATO's Kosovo debacle has exhibited most drastically. Against the general background of military-style thinking on security, the constant UN evocations of preventive diplomacy have proved to be pure illusion, suitable as conceptual gloss in official speeches by foreign ministers and in reports by UN diplomats.

UN Reform and an Agenda for Peace—Driven by Geopolitical Change

The chances of the UN Charter being revised in the next few years, or of its actually being replaced by a completely new text, seem slim. The big powers are privileged in the existing order of global institutions, and they will—out of vested interests and political short-sightedness—resist any serious reform for some time to come. And yet global governance and the necessary strengthening of the United Nations are not possible without certain radical changes to the UN Charter (DGVN 1995a: 15). Growing geopolitical changes will break the deadlock sooner or later and overthrow the present largely Euro-centric power structure.

The discussion that has been under way since the 1980s about the administrative and financial reform of the UN system has meanwhile spread a bit further. Since the euphoria following the ending of the Cold War in 1989–90, the international political climate has once again deteriorated. Academic studies on ways of renewing the United Nations thus largely continue to occupy an area half in utopia and half in reality.

An independent working-party's report on the future of the United Nations, submitted in May 1995, emphasizes the need for the United Nations to be 'improved and adapted, in order to be better able to cope with the challenges of the coming decades'.[97] For this, new institutional mechanisms are needed, so that the chief goals can be achieved.[98] These goals, according to the working-party, are: 'to combat conflicts both within and between states' and 'to promote sustainable economic and social progress' (DGVN 1995*b*: 56). The former is evidently to be achieved by means of a UN rapid intervention force, operating at the behest of an only slightly modified Security Council (with the right of veto retained for measures set out in chapter VII of the UN Charter). Boutros Boutros-Ghali had already suggested such a rapid intervention force in 1992, in his *Agenda for Peace*. The *Agenda for Peace* 'was greatly overestimated as far as its innovatory content was concerned': only the element of creating permanent special UN forces was really new; the rest was provided for in the charter but was never realized. The new forces were to consist of volunteers, better trained and better armed than the classic blue-helmet (-beret) troops.[99]

The legal basis for rapid intervention force in cases of genocide or verified threats of genocide, once again, would be art. 40 of the UN Charter, according to which the Security Council may take preventive measures—including military measures, which would be justified in cases of genocide or serious threats of genocide, verified by independent experts dispatched by UNCHR—in order to preserve world peace. As a highlight of his second term Kofi Annan should write a new and more appropriate *Agenda for Peace*. This could be done on the basis of the UN millennium summit declaration as well as the reports by Carlsson *et al.* 1999 and Brahimi *et al.* 2000. Most importantly, Annan will only be remembered as one of the most capable UN leaders if he moves from rhetoric to action.

As remarkable steps towards a more comprehensive UN policy on prevention, the findings and recommendations of several path-breaking reports by UN, OAU, and NGOs should be mainstreamed into new policy: Annan's 1998 report on 'The Causes of Conflict and the Promotion of Durable Peace and Sustainable Development in Africa', the deliberations of May 1999 'Appeal for Peace' conference in The Hague, the devastating report on the role of the United Nations in Rwanda 1993 to 1994 and the far-reaching recommendations by Carlsson *et al.* 1999, as well as the OAU report on the Rwanda disaster written by Masire *et al.* 2000, both dealing with the imperative of genocide prevention in the twenty-first century, the NGO programme of action *An Agenda for Peace, Security and Development in the 21st Century* developed by over thousand NGOs in Seoul, Korea, late 1999, the UN millennium declaration '*WE, the peoples'- The Role of the United Nations in the 21st Century: New Century, New Challenges* of 2000, the 2000 report on the protection on civilians in armed conflicts, the Optional Protocol to stop the use of child soldiers, the reports submitted by the Special Representative to the Secretary General on Children and Armed Conflict on this issue, and the 'Global Report on Child Soldiers 2001'. (More than half a million children are recruited into government forces and armed groups in 87 countries.)[100] All these recent reports contain important information and policy options to be considered for the elaboration of a comprehensive *UN Agenda for Peace*, including what might add up to, a *UN Agenda for Peace, Security and Sustainable Development in the 21st Century*.

Reforming the United Nations and Giving it a New Role

Reflections on a possible new role for the United Nations have not yet reached the required stage of political ripeness. The procedures for reform currently in force (arts. 108 and 109 of the UN Charter) require both a two-thirds majority of the member-states and the assent of the five permanent members of the Security Council. The UN Charter thus leaves little scope for changes.

The major challenges of world society are well known. They are: the need for peaceful dispute-settlement in intra-state conflicts, given the restricted possibilities allowed by international law (principle of non-interference); the incalculable risks of an irreparable destabilization of the world economy if poverty continues to grow in the Third World or if the OECD world continues to grow richer; and the urgency of measures to avert a global climate catastrophe. In all three named areas, the danger lies in the fact that effective responses get blocked and ultimately come too late.[101]

The main obstacles to much-needed reforms also seem clearly identifiable: in the UN Security Council, the right of veto is still held only by the older nuclear powers (three Western countries and former colonial powers—the USA, Britain, and France—plus Russia/the CIS and China), but not by India, Japan, Indonesia, Brazil, or Nigeria. The call for reforms to the UN system is coming mainly from Third World countries, as a way of preventing future attempts of instrumentalizing the United Nations by the big powers. The idea is that the collusion amongst the big powers should be terminated and replaced by a system of permanent collective

security comprising states with equal rights acting under the overall aegis
of the United Nations.

The Dominance of the Northern Minority over the Southern Majority

In recent years, the UN Security Council and the Bretton-Woods institutions (International Monetary Fund and World Bank) have laid claim to
certain sovereign rights in the practical political domain which were previously the exclusive prerogative of states. An example of this kind of trend
would be the gradual undermining of state sovereignty through IMF
structural adjustment programmes and through constantly expanding credit
conditionality. The IMF has been accused of neo-colonialism by the South
and has acted as a 'drill-sergeant of the political order'.[102] The IMF's structural adjustment programmes constitute an infringement of the sovereignty
of peripheral states and represent a threat to their security. What is more,
they contain measures that run blatantly counter to the type of social policy
recommended by the International Labour Organization, the United Nations
Children's Fund, and other specialist organizations. One cannot talk of
there being any co-ordination in the development domain.[103]

Connoisseurs and critics of the UN system such as Erskine Childers and
Maurice Bertrand have traced the development of the United Nations since
1945;[104]they have convincingly demonstrated the crushing dominance of
the Northern minority over the Southern majority in almost every domain,
notably in regard to the economic agenda. An International Trade Organization (ITO) was meant to be set up within the framework of the UN
system, to assume various major functions alongside the IMF (the future
world central bank). However, the ITO charter was rejected by the United
States. Only two-thirds of the UN member states were represented in
GATT. Today the World Trade Organization (WTO) is an instrument of the
'club of the rich' (the G7 and the OECD states). After almost 40 years of
existence, 'the (Northern) powers largely ignored and have now eviscerated
it' concludes Childers about the United Nations Conference on Trade and
Development, all that is left of the much more representative UNCTAD is a
ruin, despite it being the principal organ of the United Nations General
Assembly dealing with trade, investment and development issues and
commanding global membership (191 states).[105]

The creation of UNCTAD in 1964 has been politically motivated: the
Third World countries wanted a body that would look after their interests
better than the Economic and Social Council. It is the ECOSOC which (in
accordance with the UN Charter) is the principal organ in this broad area of
responsibility and which is supposed to co-ordinate the activities of numerous specialist organizations within the UN.[106] To have a separate body in

the crucial area of world trade and development would be very helpful. Despite the existence of UNCTAD, concludes Bertrand, the United Nations were excluded from treatment of 'all the basic economic issues such as currency matters, credit-grants, investments, and world trade' because of deep conflicts of interest between North and South (and earlier between West and East).[107]

Proposed Reforms and Political Upgrading

Radical proposals for reform call for a political upgrading and fundamental 'democratization' of the UN system and for an increase in its efficiency. The United Nations Organization is not to be 'reinvented'; it is simply to be adjusted in line with the new requirements. Up to now, however, there has been no proposal containing clear practical modalities that would make it possible to overcome the obstacles to reform (Bertrand 1994: 3).

That said, even an incomplete list of proposed reforms shows that that the whole of the UN system is affected. The key proposals, here taken in no particular order, contain the following elements:

- Removal of the right of veto in the Security Council and admission of new permanent members; approximately 20 countries or regional bodies (such as the European Union and the African Union) from all major areas of the world).
- Upgrading of the Economic and Social Council through:
  1. Creation of a world welfare organization; establishment and enforcement of global minimum standards for human existence;
  2. Creation of a world currency and financial system;
  3. Creation of a world central bank and introduction of a single world currency (precluding currency speculation on the financial markets);
  4. Complete overhaul and incorporation of the functions of the Bretton-Woods institutions (IMF, IBRD) under the direction of ECOSOC.
- Strengthening of the General Assembly/introduction of democratically legitimated components into the UN system—e.g. the creation of a world parliament with elected representatives (and the power to approve the annual budget).
- An independent resource-base, fed by global taxes on financial transactions (e.g. at 0.1 percent) and on environmental emissions (5 US dollars per barrel of crude oil, per airline ticket, or per 100 km of lorry travel); the watchword would be 'taxes instead of contributions'; this would cure even the worst cases of defaulting.[108]
- Expansion of the International Court of Justice, reactivation of the Trusteeship Council, and renewal and strengthening of the Secretariat.

- Promotion of conflict-prevention measures as core element of global governance and the creation of a culture of peace to replace repressive measures and military sanctions.
- Global abolition of nuclear weapons and other weapons of mass destruction; ban on arms sales.
- Promotion and increased incorporation of regional arrangements, which ought to be an integral part of the UN system; these include:
  1. Regional security councils;
  2. Regional conflict-regulation mechanisms;
  3. Regional peace-troops—as a last resort, as long discussed in relation to Africa's problems with destabilizing conflicts.[109]
- Increased involvement of non-governmental organizations (NGOs and INGOs) in all global bodies; high budgets and large staffs underline the fact that INGOs became major global players in the 1990s and that they will continue to increase their influence in the 21st century.[110]
- Constitution of a world ecology and environmental council with the power to impose moral-cum-legal and economic sanctions.

The example of the International Labour Organization (ILO) could point the way for future reforms of the whole UN system: the ILO's constitution, which came into force as long ago as April 1919, following the Treaty of Versailles and the creation of the League of Nations, emphasized the link between peace and social justice.[111] In it, the question of the involvement of non-governmental groups, trades unions, and employers' organizations is, as it were, organically resolved; there is an underlying trend towards abolishing the claim of governments to be the sole legitimate representatives of *their* peoples or nations; and the principles of universality and the equal rights of members have unconditional validity.[112] Where international legal minimum standards are not observed, the ILO has no direct sanctions-options to call on; the only possibility open to it is to publish reports on its experts' monitoring missions and to discuss these reports at its annual meetings. As in the issues of democratization and minority protection, efforts are directed towards getting a social clause incorporated into bilateral agreements.

Creation of New Procedures and International Institutions

Two important open questions need to be resolved in this connection:

- How should one go about designing and creating international institutions of a kind that would be capable of coping with the current challenges of world society?

- What binding procedures are there that would open up new options for institutional reform? Or to put it another way: What can be done to prevent the blocking of reforms or their deferment by the currently privileged big powers?

The preconditions for the project of reform are, firstly, binding agreement as to the range and function of international institutions, and, secondly, the selection of a *modus operandi*. The existing UN Charter is dismissed by some critics as 'useless' because it allows little scope for eliminating structural weaknesses. Suggestions have been made for a stage-by-stage creation of new institutions—outside the existing system. This would seem to be necessary, but such an approach overall harbours the risk of creating added complexity.

But uncertainties in the international system are fraught with dangers and ultimately detrimental to reform, and they must therefore be excluded as far as possible. The step-by-step creation of a multi-track world—to use the parlance of European unification—is a practical political option. The alternative would be to abandon the principle of consensus.[113]

Reform schemes envisaging the reorganization or re-creation of the United Nations would have to pose the question of the basic functions of such an organization in new terms. Important functions of global governance would need to be grouped by theme, as part of an open-ended list:[114]

General Functions and Conditions

- Democratic control of the activities of the UN
- Permanent negotiations on problems of global interest; yearly reports on world security and the world economy to serve as a starting-point for future activities of the various UN organs
- Synthesis rather than division of the domains of international security, the world economy, world ecology, e.g. via the imposition of environmental conditions in the allocation of credits
- Involvement of, and consultation with, the major representatives of civil society in the member states; promotion of intercultural communication.

Conflict Management and Peace Policy

- Crisis management within the framework of a comprehensive system of violence prevention
- Allocation of sufficient resources for promoting world peace[115]
- Progressive realization of a global consensus on common principles and procedures in regard to human rights, international law and creation of democratic regimes; disarmament and abolition of dangerous weapons

- Global consensus on massive cuts in the military apparatus (verification and acceptance of a monitoring system) and the reallocation of funds
- Universal abolition of weapons of mass destruction (nuclear, chemical and biological)
- New geo-ecological policies will aim at giving teeth to the Kyoto Protocol, based on the Marrakesh compromise; unilateral non-compliance must be prevented by a regime of trade sanctions
- A 'World Minorities Council' and the 'Permanent Forum of the World's Indigenous Peoples' to mediate in intra-state disputes.

Regional Policy

- Support for, and promotion of, the development of regional organizations and monitoring of measures instituted by regional alliances or powers with a view to preserving peace
- Linkage of regional security to systematic regional economic development and co-operation
- Compatibility between universal representation and population size: introduction of a new system of regional representation for medium-sized and small countries.

Global Governance Needs Economic Teeth

So far my list of important functions of global governance could be said to depend mainly on the mobilization of political will. The continuation of this list, to include the domain of economy, will depend from both, political will and adequate resources. In order to make the idea of United Nations activities in global governance more concrete the list also includes a few key objectives (as voiced in the UN millennium declaration), additional to policies and functions.

Economy/Political Economy: Policy, Functions and Objectives

- Monitoring and political control by the UN General Assembly of the global priorities of policies applied by the international institutions for trade and finance (chiefly the WTO, IMF and IBRD-World Bank)
- The policy of the Bretton Woods institutions must be transparent and its representatives ought to be made accountable for their activities (secrecy and corruption must be done away with)[116]
- The introduction of a global Tobin-type tax on capital transfers to finance the UN system of global governance (as already recommended by the highest representatives of several countries, among them France)
- For securing the establishment of the financial instruments above the self-interests of member states and above the influence of global

economic players (such as large banks and TNCs), the UN would buy the shares of public and private capital owners in IMF-IBRD

- Monitoring the problems that result from integration into the capitalist world economy: globalization requires an international regulatory policy against speculative capital movements ('casino capitalism')[117]
- Establishing a functioning world currency system, creation of a world central bank and a world audit office (undercutting fatal currency speculations)
- Monitoring of the world financial system and regulated access to the capital market for countries that have previously been excluded
- Technical co-operation between countries in all domains and sectors; humanitarian aid; organization of joint global projects, in which the scientific/technological domain could play a pilot function
- 'Marshall Plans' aimed at eradicating absolute poverty (currently the lot of 850 million people) and reversing the trend towards increasing global unemployment; to be financed, for example, through global taxation of speculative transactions (Tobin-type of tax).
- Implementing an integrated world poverty eradication programme
- Defining a 'global humanitarian minimum life quality'
- Implementing integrated development programmes by the UN system (WHO, FAO, UNDP and UNEP) to reach the 'global humanitarian minimum life quality' everywhere on the globe until the year 2020
- Free exchange of information and technology to reach these objectives
- Promotion of global public health standards, eradication campaigns against diseases, and the supply of clean water on global scale until the year 2010
- Urgent promotion of food security programmes and guarantees for the realization of the right to food as defined by the UN Special Rapporteur for the right to food until the year 2005.[118]

The current budget of the United Nations is totally inadequate. The necessary budget coverage for new functions has to be secured by a new 'world tax system'. As Dietrich Fischer has put it, 'the UN budget is now about what New York City spends for garbage collection, and with that it is expected to solve every problem in the world'.[119]

The United Nations may find a way of giving adequate voice to the anti-globalization movement. This 'new movement', since the éclat in Seattle portrayed by Western media 'as students and anarchists' from the rich and prosperous North, is neither new nor just an affair of the North. In fact, this movement, in a rather scattered but truly global form, has for decades existed all over the South. The anti-globalization movement in the South is a 'far deeper and wide-ranging movement has been developing for years, largely ignored by the media' (Woodroff/Ellis-Jones 2001, 1); its protests aim at the policies of the IMF, the WTO and the World Bank in particular countries, more precisely, it usually aims at the dire consequences of such policies on the lives of common folks in the South. The 'bread revolts' after IMF *dictates* (later called 'structural adjustments') became a common feature of popular unrest in the South since the 1970s.

There has to be a fundamental reform of a world order that cements the position of the rich countries against the mass of the poor countries. This 'global apartheid' is based on three morally appalling principles: (1) the promotion of export sectors in the South (in order to pay back unplayable debts) with the effect that the poor countries compete against each other and drive the prices for their commodities down; (2) the Northern countries impose high taxes and build other fences around their markets against products from the South, precisely in those sectors were the South would be competitive, while further distorting the market by heavily subsidizing their agriculture; and (3) Southern countries got trapped by receiving credits for 'white elephant' projects and arms purchases of their elites (for which there is no use and no consent of the citizen) but for these credits the South is forced to pay several times higher interest rates than customers from the North. The dept burden is the main tool to further impoverish the South. An economic order based on such appalling principles must be rejected.

Complete Overhaul of the UN Charter

The 50th anniversary of the foundation of the United Nations prompted a flurry of proposals for reform. Even in his *Agenda for Peace*, the former UN secretary-general had not closed his mind to moderate demands.[120] On the other hand, his observations on the democratization of the UN—a difficult notion given the non-existence of options for exerting democratic influence—remain silent on a number of core issues.[121] No details were given about the thorny issue of its new composition or of future curtailments in the competencies of the all-powerful Security Council. Any reorganization ought to include the imposition of limits on the far-reaching decision-making powers of the Security Council and the transfer of powers to the General Assembly. This would require a renunciation of privileges and a curtailment of the decision-making power by the old nuclear powers.

One innovation introduced by the charter (chapter VII) was a system of international security allowing economic sanctions (art. 41) or military intervention (art. 42) to be used as repressive measures when peaceful dispute-settlement (chapter VI) and regional arrangements (chapter VIII) had been exhausted. But the system thus constituted was never able to prove its functionality because the East–West conflict and the institution of the veto paralysed it. The creation of the UN peacekeeping forces by Dag Hammarskjöld during the Suez crisis in 1956 did little to change this.

The reform of the UN system is an undertaking, which—irrespective of future political developments—could last between ten and 20 years. The proposals so far made have concentrated on the way in which the existing UN Charter might be better utilized; but the prospects offered by this approach can hardly be described as promising.

The questions that the international community must ask itself today have deeper, more far-reaching implications. One of the core questions is whether the UN Charter is really a 'respectable vestige' (Bertrand) of a big-power compromise necessitated by the events of World War II, or whether it is, rather, an outdated platform, a specific product of the Cold War which blocks effective crisis-management in the modern world.

To sum up, the justified and urgent calls for the protection of minorities at risk and of vulnerable civilians in general—as past calls for UN-supervised military intervention in ethno-national and other crisis regions arising out of dramatic circumstances (previously Somalia, Bosnia, Haiti, Kosovo, and currently Sierra Leone, Burma, Sudan, Congo and many other countries)—have to ask with which United Nations this could legitimately be achieved—the present one, with its San Francisco spirit and its legacy of the Cold War logic, and its almost absolute domination by the old nuclear aristocracy; or a reformed, more democratic world organization. A reformed United Nations would have to break free from its particularistic and Eurocentric origins, in order to do justice to the geopolitical realities and requirements of the present times.

The World in the Year 2030

As we reach the year 2030, the world will have changed significantly. Today's superpowers will be less 'super', while some of today's medium powers will have become great powers in a truly multi-polar world. China will become the world's largest economy (already in 2020) and may soon after retake its position it had lost some 250 years ago to the Europeans, as the world most powerful nation. Its power will be based on economic and cultural strength and will therefore be more civilized and less militarily-based and aggressive than the posture of present great powers.

A fully enlarged European Federation, rather a Eurasian one, including today's Russian Federation, will lose its position as the (currently) largest economy and become the second largest but culturally still influential unit. This reflects the fact that after the collapse of state-socialism the trans-formation trajectories of the former nominally socialist states were significantly different, with a depression in Central Europe followed by a West European-leaning orientation to join the European Union, an even deeper depression and serious state- and identity-crisis experienced in Russia and most other former republics of the Soviet Union both trajectories being entirely different from the evolutionary-gradualist, state-guided and high-growth path followed by China since 1980 and imitated by Vietnam.

As a heterogeneous state of regional size, India, again based on the inherent strength of an old civilization, will become the third largest economy, ahead of the multicultural United States, probably still followed by a homogenous Japan, now a medium-sized compact nation of only 80 million people, in alliance with a unified Korea, followed by the 'rest of the world'—which will by 2030 appear in entirely different fashion—in the form of large regionally integrated blocks, based on relative cultural commonalities and geography, such as the African Union, United Latin America, a Southeast Asian Federation, Indonesia-Island Asia and an emerging West Asian Islamic block.

The nation-state, the mother of world disorder, will have transformed or disappeared for a good part, and so will have most violent conflicts, interstate and intra-state alike. Sovereignty will be a shared common good, shared in global governance and shared with the people in a genuinely democratic fashion. By the year 2030—with any alternative being mutually (self-)destructive—global governance will have made the multi-polar world a more peaceful and pleasant place.

Notes

1. The death-squads of the *Amasasu*, the *Interahamwe* killer militias, associated with the Mouvement National Républicain pour la Démocracie (MNRD, headed by dictator Habyarimana) and of the Mupuza Mugambi militia, associated with the Coalition pour la Défense de la République (CDR—a fascist organization banned after 1994), repeatedly provoked violent confrontations with opposition parties, using hand-grenades and bombs. Their members were outside the law and were never brought to account for their crimes. There had been a state of emergency in force in Rwanda from 1 October 1990, the date of the RPF attack launched from Uganda.

2. Rwanda is a little more than half the size (26,340 km^2) of Switzerland but until 1994 had a comparable population (7.5 million). According to official thus doubtful figures, before 1994 85 percent of the population were Hutus, 14 percent Tutsis, and 1 percent Twa. All three groups speak Kinyarwanda. The borders between the groups are fluid. Besides these three named groups, there are three others: the Gogwe, the Hima, and the Nyambo or Mbo. Prior to April 1994, 96 percent of the population lived in rural areas. Rwanda is one of the poorest and most densely populated countries in the world (it is classified as a LLDC, population density is 272 per km^2—cf. Japan 327 km^2). Illiteracy stood at 53 percent, and life-expectancy was 49–53 years. GDP was $310. The gap between GDP growth (1 percent in 1980–90) and population growth (3.3 percent—average for Africa 3.1 percent) has since be closed.

3. About five times as many people died in Rwanda as have died in the whole of the conflict in former Yugoslavia.). The UN sent 20,000 troops to Bosnia alone, several thousand to Croatia, 28,000 to Somalia, and 38,000 NATO troops to Kosovo 1999 (without UN mandate). That time UN secretary-general Boutros-Boutros Ghali commented in 1994 (*Der Spiegel*, 94/23, 138–9) that he could not see why, if this were the case, 5,000 could not be found for Rwanda. In June 1994, probably as many as half the population—estimated at 8 million—were in the process of running away.

4. Gabriel Sebyeza, 'Conflicts and Mediation in Africa', paper for the 7th Pan-African Congress in Kampala, Uganda, 3–8 Apr. 1994.

5. The Arusha agreement was arrived at with the Tanzanian government and an OAU delegation (under Mohammed Sahnoun) acting as go-betweens; it provided for a broad-based coalition-government, elections in 2 years, and the fusion of the RPF and the government forces to form a new army.

6. *Der Spiegel*, 94/23, 138–9. The media, instead of attacking those responsible for the failure of the UN—i.e. the USA, France and other Western countries (who had refused to equip a UN intervention force in good time before April 1994 and to assemble a chapter VII force after April 6), put the blame on others.

7. Admittedly so in the case of Sudan, as Committee on Conscience of the US Holocaust Memorial Museum made it public by its late but dramatic genocide warning in October 2000 (see on http://www.ushmm.org/conscience/sudan.htm). The creeping genocide in Burma is even less visible than the one in Sudan though it is going on for a much longer time. For both cases there is ample evidence and documentation (among it ECOR 1992 and 1997c on Sudan as well as ECOR 1991, 1995b and 1997a on Burma).

8. This huge army was only deployed in the final phase, after the Iraqis had withdrawn from Kuwait and after the Iraqi capital, along with other cities and Iraqi army positions, had been bombed for months by B52s (a pattern of indiscriminate bombing seen in Vietnam until mid 1975 and in a number of other places, and again in Yugoslavia 1999 and in Afghanistan 2001–2).

9. The Germans and Belgians, their colonial administrations, and the Catholic missionaries had fabricated the Hamitic theses (which posited foreign domination by the Tutsi minority). This colonial construct became a decisive ideological and legitimacy factor in the Hutu rebellion of 1959–62. Colonization played a major part in the transformation of the Tutsi kingdom into an ethnocracy.

10. On colonial and post-colonial ethnicization in Central Africa see Scherrer 2002b, 1–64: René Lemarchand, 'The Apocalypse in Rwanda', *Cultural Survival Quarterly*, 18 (1994), 2–3, 29–33, 30 ff; Thomas Laely, Ethnien à la burundaise', in Müller 1994: 236.

11. See Assemblée Nationale de la République Française *et al.* 1998 : part 2, sections II A (*operation Noroît*) to II D (two French military operations in 1993), V (operation Amaryllis to evacuate nationals and take control of the airport by April 9, 1994), VII (operation Turquoise from June 22 to August 21, 1994, and exfiltration of *génocidaires*).

12. Article III, Anti-Genocide Convention: 'The following acts shall be punishable: (a) Genocide; (b) Conspiracy to commit genocide; (c) Direct and public incitement to commit genocide; (d) Attempt to commit genocide; (e) Complicity in genocide.'

13. Clinton prohibited: 'The sale or supply to Rwanda of arms and related material of all types, including weapons and ammunition, military vehicles and equipment, para-military police equipment, and spare parts for the aforementioned, irrespective of origin.' See William J. Clinton: EO 12918 order, Washington DC, May 26, 1994.

14. Talk with David J. Scheffer, then US Ambassador at Large for War Crimes Issues, and company, at the Stockholm International Forum on the Holocaust, January 27, 2000.

15. See Scherrer 2002b; my book is exploring the genocide and its consequences in the context of ongoing developments. The objective was to take a regional view, not a

narrow view on Rwanda; hence, the book covers events in Rwanda, Burundi, Congo and the wider spill-over effects which cast a shadow over Uganda, Tanzania, Angola, Southern Africa and beyond.

16. UN Secretary-General Kofi Annan, who at the time of the genocide was responsible for UNAMIR and the UN response on the ground (as the former head of UN Peacekeeping Operations), received a competent, uncensored and devastating report.

17. The UN Secretary-General should actively seek ways to launch a new beginning in the relationship between the United Nations and Rwanda. (Carlsson *et al.* 1999, IV. Recommendations, 14)

18. S/1994/1125 of 4 October 1994. Genocide in the meaning of article II of the Convention on the Prevention and Punishment of the Crime of Genocide. The secretary-general stated that 'acts of genocide against the Tutsi group were perpetrated by Hutu elements in a concerted, planned, systematic and methodical way'. Some UN Member States seem to be willing to forget about one of the worst genocides of the 20th century.

19. Sixteen UN peacekeeping missions as of January 2002: Africa: 1. Western Sahara—MINURSO/United Nations Mission for the Referendum in the Western Sahara, Apr. 1991–. 2. The Americas: 4. Haiti—MIPONUH/United Nations Civilian Police Mission in Haiti, Dec. 1997–. Asia: 5. India/Pakistan—UNMOGIP, United Nations Military Observer Group in India and Pakistan, Jan. 1949–; 6. Tajikistan—UNMOT, United Nations Mission of Observers in Tajikistan, December 1994–. Europe: 7. Bosnia and Herzegovina—UNMIBH/United Nations Mission in Bosnia and Herzegovina, Dec. 1995–; 8. Croatia—UNMOP, United Nations Mission of Observers in Prevlaka, Jan. 1996–; 9. Croatia—UN CIVILIAN POLICE SUPPORT GROUP, Jan. 1998–; 10. Cyprus—UNFICYP/United Nations Peacekeeping Force in Cyprus, Mar. 1964–; 11. Former Yugoslav Republic of Macedonia—UNPREDEP/United Nations Preventive Deployment Force, Mar. 1995–; 12. Georgia—UNOMIG, United Nations Observer Mission in Georgia, Aug. 1993–. Middle East: 13. Golan Heights—UNDOF/United Nations Disengagement Observer Force, June 1974–; 14. Iraq/Kuwait—UNIKOM, United Nations Iraq-Kuwait Observation Mission, Apr. 1991–; 15. Lebanon—UNIFIL/United Nations Interim Force in Lebanon, Mar. 1978–; 16. Middle East—UNTSO, United Nations Truce Supervision Organization, June 1948–. (See UN Dept. Public Information, http://www.un.org/Depts/dpko/)

20. In the past four years several PKOs ended, such as three in Africa: 1) Angola—MONUA/United Nations Observer Mission in Angola, July 1997–Feb. 1999 (and before that UNAVEM I-III, 1991–7), 2) Central African Republic—MINURCA/United Nations Mission in the Central African Republic, Apr. 1998–Feb. 2000; 3) Sierra Leone—UNOSIL, July 1998–October 1999; in the Americas: 4) Haiti—MIPONUH, December 1997–March 2000; in Asia: 4) Tajikistan—UNMOT, December 1994–May 2000; and three in Europe: 5) Croatia—UNTAES, January 1996 to January 1998, 6) Croatia—UNPSG, January 1998 to October 1998, 7) Macedonia—UNPREDEP, March 1995 to February 1999 (prematurely, soon later substituted by NATO troops); in the Middle East: none (the last was UNIIMOG).

21. The costs for UN peacekeeping and enforcement for personnel and equipment decreased from $3.6 billion in 1993 to $US 2.8 billion in 1995; the high costs were mainly due to expenditure on peacekeeping in former Yugoslavia. Peacekeeping costs fell to $US 1.4 billion in 1996 (1992 level), $US 1.3 billion in 1997 to the lowest costs of under $1 billion by 1998. From then on the costs climbed again to some $2.6 billion spent on peacekeeping in 2000 and as much in 2001. All UN members are obligated to pay their share of peacekeeping costs according to a formula that they themselves have agreed upon. But member states often owed the large amounts in peacekeeping dues (UN $US 1.6 billion as of 1997), with the USA as the largest debtor, owing a total of over $US

1 billion. It was only in October 2001, just before the start of a 'war against terrorism' in Afghanistan, when the USA finally paid most of its dues.

22. 'Frieden schaffen mit Blauhelmen?', *der überblick*, 28 (1992), 4: 5–66.

23. Shocked by exploding communal violence in Easter Europe, minority protection was also the theme of the first meeting of the Council of Europe at presidential level, which took place in Oct. 1993 in Vienna. See also: Hofmann 1992; Ropers and Schlotter 1992; *Blätter des iz3w*, 190 (1993) 17–36 (spec. issue on human rights). On this question of minority protection, there are points in common with the UN Human Rights Commission Working Group on Indigenous Populations (UNWGIP). See Scherrer 1991*a*: 43.

24. Dieter Senghaas, 'Interventionskasuistik', unpub. conference paper, 1992, 15–18. This paper was presented at a meeting organized by the Development and Peace Foundation in Bonn (Nov. 1992) and was criticized by a number of participants (particularly from Third World countries). During the 1970s, Senghaas was a radical development theoretician and peace researcher; he was a specialist at a government think-tank (the Stiftung Wissenschaft und Politik), and as such devoted himself to political consultancy. Critics accused him of having moved away from some of the previous areas of operation, methods, and goals of German peace research.

25. Isabelle Duyvesteyn calculated there have been 690 overt and covert interventions since 1945 (USA 111, UK 75, France 49); Pearson arrives at a figure of 213 military interventions for the period up to 1994 (USA 71, UK 38, Israel 37, France 33, UN 33) (AKUF 1995, 18–19). Zoltan Grossman's (2001) list deals with the USA only but seems most accurate, due to clear definition of criteria for counting; he counted 117 US direct military interventions in the 20th century, whereby excluding 'demonstration duty by military police, mobilizations of the National Guard, offshore shows of naval strength, reinforcements of embassy personnel, the use of non-Defense Department personnel (such as the Drug Enforcement Agency, DEA), military exercises, non-combat mobilizations (such as replacing postal strikers), the permanent stationing of armed forces, covert actions where the U.S. did not play a command and control role, the use of small hostage rescue units, most uses of proxy troops, U.S. piloting of foreign warplanes, foreign disaster assistance, military training and advisory programs not involving direct combat, civic action programs, and many other military activities' (ibid., 2001). William Blum (2001) counted based on a range of specific criteria; he has a list of 67 'global interventions from 1945' (Grossman has 71 until 2001); Blum also includes non-military interventions and much indirect, US-supported violence. For instance, US interventions took the form of bombings in 25 cases; US assassination attempts of political leaders including heads of state were tried in 35 cases; US assistance in torture in 11 countries; furthermore the US were 'perverting elections' and interfering with a democratic process in 23 countries.

26. This debate may become to be seen as a turning-point in German post-war history. The *force majeure* invented by officialdom to justify the move was that the UN was expecting Germany to play a more active role as an international (deputy) policeman. Outside the FRG (and probably amongst most German citizens), the FRG's abstention from world politics—particularly potential military permutations of it—was seen as beneficial and appropriate.

27. At the end of Aug. 1995, after several preliminary experiments, FRG citizens took part for the first time in an out-of-area operation—which very rapidly developed into an armed action. What is more, the operation took place in, of all countries, former Yugoslavia, in areas and against people that had been victims of a fascist German war of aggression and its attendant policy of eradication during the Second World War. German Tornado fighters took part in weeks of bombing raids by NATO against Serb positions in Bosnia, allegedly 'only' as part of reconnaissance or escort missions.

28. The operation reignited the war in Bosnia. Croats and Muslims seized the opportunity to attack their weakened opponent and to conquer huge areas of Bosnia. By September, 10,000 Serb civilians were once again in flight; this followed the expulsion of 300,000 of them from Krajina by the Croatian army in August. Civilian targets (a hospital, residential areas, the Bosnian Serb television station) were either deliberately or accidentally hit in the NATO air-attacks.

29. According to art. 39 of the UN Charter, UN military operations may be sanctioned by the Security Council. Because of the growing 'sensitivity of international public opinion', the danger of the kind of abuse characteristic of the old imperialist policy of intervention is (according to Senghaas 1992: 18), is much less now than it used to be. This claim was contradicted by Third World participants at the above-mentioned symposium on 'Global Governance' held in Bonn (Nov. 1992) and Loccum (June 1993).

30. In a remark tailored to fit the Senghaasian casuistry and the notion of abuse, Kader Asmal (a member of the ANC and an adviser to Nelson Mandela) talked of the 'CNN-ization' of human-rights issues.

31. Mohammed Suliman (speaking in June 1993 in Loccum) criticized the fact that there had not been sufficient grounds for the US intervention in Somalia. The operation, he said, had been mounted as a US-marines PR exercise and media spectacle; it soon ended in a mess.

32. The Cambodia operation was also one of the most costly in UN history and on several occasions it looked as if it would fail. The intervention followed a positive course thanks to a secret agreement between Sihanouk and the Khmer Rouge, which envisaged this criminal organization having a share in government. Subsequently, however, the government sought to crush the Khmer Rouge militarily—which it almost succeeded in doing when it captured its major bases in 1993–4. The interests of the Thai business community and the high-ranking military in the continued existence of the lucrative booty-based economy run by the Cambodian mercenaries (precious stones and tropical wood in return for weapons) preserved the Khmer Rouge from extinction.

33. On this UN mission, see Waltraut Schütz, 'Westsahara', *überblick*, 28 (1992) 4: 48–9.

34. After the 1992 elections, which had been declared free and fair by the UN, UNITA was able (with impunity) to deny its defeat at the polls and return to warfare. One thousand election observers briefly flown into the country confirmed Savimbi's defeat at the polls.

35. Negotiations failed. The South African army, in collusion with the USA, continued to fly in supplies for the UNITA contras, despite protests from most of the neighbouring countries (except Zaire).

36. Françoise Manfrass-Sirjacques, 'Entwicklung und Operationalisierung des Instruments der humanitären Intervention', unpub. paper.

37. Interview with Ambassador Mohammed Sahnoun, Beurs van Berlage, Amsterdam 1992. Sahnoun is a former vice-president of the OAU, Algerian ambassador and one of the most skilful diplomats of our time. For the (French but not the US) public it was obvious since Sahnoun's interview about the intervention in Somalia on the French television channel TV 5 (in March 1992) that crucial mistakes had been made. Sahnoun is one of the experts involved in the International Resource Group on Disarmament and Security, which investigates issues relating to the Horn of Africa. He later became active as Kofi Annan's special envoy for the Great Lakes Region, followed by shuttle diplomacy in 1998–9 in order to find a peaceful conflict settlement between Eritrea and Ethiopia.

38. NIOD 2002 concluded that 'in 1993 a combination of humanitarian motivation and political ambitions led the Dutch cabinet ... to make an Air Mobile Battalion available for the UNPROFOR mission in Bosnia. This took place ... without a proper analysis of the far-reaching consequences beforehand. These were among the factors which led to Dutchbat being destined for Srebrenica, which had been turned down by other countries

with arguments to back up their refusal, and being given the task of keeping the peace in a so-called 'safe' area where there was no peace. By playing down the possible risks of the behaviour of the warring parties so much, a large circle of those involved in this policy, and in particular its advocates, took on a large responsibility for an ill-conceived and virtually impossible mission.' The government, receiving the report with this conclusion in April 2002, was not the same as the government which made an ill-conceived decision in 1993; nevertheless it stepped down. (Tragically, subsequent elections brought a right-wing racist coalition into power, for the first time in post-war Netherlands). – The NIOD inquiry further concluded that 'after the attack on the enclave at the beginning of July 1995, from a military perspective Dutchbat had few grounds for mounting a counterattack on its own initiative', that active defence of the enclave by military means was not in accordance with the mandate, the UN policy (the maintenance of impartiality) or the Rules of Engagement, and 'the military balance of power was such that, without outside support, Dutchbat (200 lightly armed combat soldiers) would have been defenceless (against the VRS) in a serious confrontation'.

39. After the Military Technical Agreement between KFOR and the government of the Federal Republic of Yugoslavia was signed in Kumanovo on June 9, 1999, NATO took over Kosovo (and a small Russian contingent was first). KFOR had to implement the UN Security Council resolution 1244, adopted the day after (June 10, 1999). The responsibilities of KFOR are defined in § 9. Massacres of Serbs took place: between June and October 1999 some 447 persons have been killed and 648 disappeared.

40. *The New Statesmen*, November 15, 1998.

41. Blair was even talking about a 'racial genocide' committed by Milosevic (*The Guardian*, October 28, 1998).

42. The UN tribunal indicted Milosevic in 1999 (see ICTY 1999) but at that time his arrest and extradition seemed remote. It was only after the revolt of the Serbian people, protesting irregularities at the polls in October 2000 that the regime collapsed almost peacefully. Milosevic was extradited to The Hague in April 2001. He called the tribunal 'unfair, infantile and a farce' (New York Times, October 31, 2001). His trial started in February 2002 and is termed to last two years. The trial, however, soon developed unexpectedly. Milosevic defended himself and used the trial to accuse NATO war crimes committed in Yugoslavia 1999. The genocide charges against Milosevic might backlash, and in fact there is little evidence for such a drastic charge. It taints a tribunal that enjoys little legitimacy as a 'NATO court' in the eyes of most Serbian people. With Milosevic quite unexpectedly 'turning the tables' the massive presence and initial interest of the Western media for this trial rapidly evaporated.

43. Inquiries by the ICTY tribunal, other international bodies, and by a number of journalists, 'show a radically different train of events' then the one presented in the media.

44. During the campaign to justify the ongoing NATO bombing the *New York Times* (April 4, 1999) wrote that there could be 50 *Srebrenicas* (equal to 150,000 deaths). ABC (on April 18) announced that tens of thousands of young men could be executed; the next day the U.S. State Department announced that half a million Kosovars 'are missing and thought to be killed'; a month later William Cohen, minister of defence, corrected to hundred thousand 'disappeared' who could be 'assassinated' (CBS, *Face the Nation*, May 16, 1999). The truth is that the ICTY has found some 2,018 bodies. On the media reporting and disinformation campaign about the Kosovo case see Halimi and Vidal 2000: 10–11.

45. The five countries are Morocco (618), Senegal (566), Uruguay (444), Tunisia (243), and South Africa (96). This total of 2,366 military personnel includes 497 liaison officers and military observers (MLOs). Until February 2000 no single Western

country had promised to contribute personnel; (IRIN-CEA: 'DRC: Security Council approves troop deployment', Weekly Round-up 8, February 25, 2000).

46. As of June 2001 the contingent from Western stood at 27 of a total of 2,366: Belgium (5), Canada (7), Denmark (2), France (6), Italy (1), Switzerland (1), and United Kingdom (5); all but three of them were staff officers or MLOs (UN Security Council 2001b: Annex).

47. For a commented list of UN Conventions Against Terrorism, see website of United Nations (www.un.org) or of UNODCCP, United Nations Office for Drug Control and Crime Prevention, http://www.undcp.org/terrorism_conventions.html.

48. UN General Assembly Resolution 56/1 (2001). New York: UN, 12 September 2001, §3 and §4.

49. The term 'military industrial complex' was prominently used by US president Eisenhower as a warning before he left office. As of 2001, seven of the ten world's largest arms-producing companies are based in the USA: Lockheed Martin, 70 percent of US$ 17.6 billon turn-over, no.1; Boeing, 27 percent of 15.3b, no.2; Raytheon 58 percent of 11.3b, no. 4; Northrop Grumman, 79 percent of 7.0b, no. 5; General Dynamics, 62 percent of 5.5b, no. 6; Litton, 70 percent of 3.8b, no.8; United Technologies, 14 percent of 3.4b, no. 9); the other three are based in UK and France. See SIPRI 2001, 304.

50. Indeed, one believes to have travelled back to the early 1980s, with Ronald Reagan's foreign policy of supporting 'freedom fighters' as proxies in so-called 'regional war' of the Cold War, which became hot in a number of countries in the South (which meant propping up counterrevolutionary destabilization forces such as the *contras* in Nicaragua, Savimbi's UNITA in Angola, RENAMO in Mozambique, or the Mujaheddin terrorists such as al-Qaeda against the USSR, while creating havoc and bloody civil wars in most targeted countries), all of it conceived as part of a crusade against the 'evil empire', the ideology of a rollback of 'communism', and the advertisement of free market democracy, based on IMF 'adjustments' and military aid for repressive regimes around the world. For an instant analysis of Bush's State of the Union speech on 28 January 2002, see Stephen Zunes: 'Deconstructing George W. Bush: A Critical Analysis of the 2002 State of the Union Address'. Washington DC: FRIP, January 31, 2002.

51. Military spending by the USA stood at 'US$343 billion in the year 2000 [increased further in 2001] which is 69 percent greater than that of the next five highest nations combined. Russia, which has the second largest military budget, spends less than one-sixth what the United States does. Iraq, Libya, North Korea, Cuba, Sudan, Iran, and Syria spend $14.4 billion combined; Iran accounts for 52 percent of this total' (Grossmann 2001, 1).

52. See Stratfor: 'Promises And Reality: America's Military in 2001', Washington 27 December 2000, http://www.stratfor.com/home/giu/archive/122700. The analysts suggested that Bush may face 'a global landscape that will make it difficult, if not impossible, to immediately implement the improvements he wants in the American military'. He had to wait less than a year for greatly boosting the military expenditure. 'Bush and his advisors argued that 'future U.S. military supremacy in a world fraught with new and daunting challenges' were 'at risk'.'

53. Though there is agreement on the wording of the majority of the draft treaty's 27 articles, the entire project of a comprehensive convention against terrorism is on hold due to four areas that remain in dispute. Otherwise the convention would enter into force 30 days after ratification by 22 states. The areas of dispute are the preamble to the treaty, article 1 (on definitions of terms used in the treaty), article 2 (defining terrorism) and dissent on the wording of article 18 of the draft dealing with exemptions from the treaty's jurisdiction. According to the Australian diplomat Richard Rowe (informing

the General Assembly's *Ad Hoc Committee on Terrorism* in February 2002) the debate continued about whether article 18 should refer to 'parties' or 'armed forces', whether to include a reference to peoples under foreign occupation, and about subtleties such as whether military forces acting in their official capacities should be described as 'governed' by international law or called on to act 'in conformity' with it. Again, some states have to arrogance to ask for their military forces to be above the law. The completion of the *Convention on Nuclear Terrorism* is also blocked; the disagreement is on the treaty's scope.

54. Alex P. Schmid: *The Definition of Terrorism*. Report. Vienna: United Nations Crime Prevention and Criminal Justice Branch, 1993. 'If the core of war crimes—deliberate attacks on civilians, hostage taking and the killing of prisoners—is extended to peacetime, we could simply define acts of terrorism as 'peacetime equivalents of war crimes'.' See 'Definitions of Terrorism' on http://www.undcp.org/terrorism.html. Also: Alex P. Schmid: 'The Problems of Defining Terrorism,' in: Crenshaw, Martha and John Pimlott (eds.), *Encyclopedia of World Terrorism*. Armonk, N.Y., 1997, 12–22.

55. The list of 'Foreign Terrorist Organizations' is compiled every two years by the Office of the Coordinator for Counterterrorism. 'Under the statute, this report is subject to judicial review. The Secretary of State makes designations following an exhaustive interagency effort. The designations expire in two years unless renewed.' Explanations see http://www.state.gov/s/ct/rls/rpt/fto/

56. These twelve terrorist organizations listed by US-DS are al-Qaeda; Armed Islamic Group (GIA); Gama'a al-Islamiya (Islamic Group); Harakat al-Mujaheddin (HUM); Islamic Movement of Uzbekistan (IMU); al-Jihad (Egyptian Islamic Jihad); Kahane Chai (Kach); Hamas (Islamic Resistance Movement); Palestinian Islamic Jihad (PIJ); United Self-Defense Forces of Colombia (AUC); Aum Shinrikyo, Japan; and, Abu Sayyaf Group, Philippines.

57. The eleven non-terrorist but violent or illegitimate groups are: ; Hizb'Allah (Party of God); Abu Nidal Organization (ANO); Popular Front for the Liberation of Palestine (PFLP); Palestine Liberation Front (PLF); PFLP-General Command (PFLP-GC); Liberation Tigers of Tamil Eelam (LTTE); Shining Path (Sendero Luminoso, SL); Real IRA ; Revolutionary Nuclei (formerly ELA); Greece; Revolutionary Organization 17 November, Greece; and, Basque Fatherland and Liberty (ETA), Basque Country/Spain.

58. The five genuine liberation movements are the Kurdistan Workers' Party (PKK), Turkey; Revolutionary People's Liberation Army/Front (DHKP/C), Devrimci Sol, Turkey; Mujaheddin-e Khalq Organization (MEK), Iran; National Liberation Army (ELN), Colombia; and, the Revolutionary Armed Forces of Colombia (FARC).

59. The five new groups are the Al-Aqsa Martyrs Brigade; Asbat al-Ansar; Jaish-e-Mohammed (JEM) (Army of Mohammed); Lashkar-e-Tayyiba (LT) (Army of the Righteous); and, Salafi Group for Call and Combat (GSPC-GIA). The first mentioned group (al-Aqsa Martyrs Brigade) is probably not a terrorist group but a liberation movement; Israel claimed that they are using indiscriminate means (such as suicide bombings) but this is unclear; the fights against the 'illegal occupation of Palestine' (UN wording) is legitimate even according to international law. The latter expression was used by Kofi Annan on March 13, 2002, the day after the adoption of UN Security Council Resolution 1397, adopted by vote of 14 in favour to none against, which for the first time clearly mentioned 'a vision of a region where two States, Israel and Palestine, lived side by side within secure and recognized borders'.

60. Of these 19 terrorist groups seven are extremely dangerous organizations: two are genocidal gangs (ALIR and RUF), two are democidal gangs (AUC and Aum Sect) and three are democidal Islamist gangs (al-Qaeda, GIA and Al-Gama'a al-Islamiyya). Ten others are fundamentalist terrorist groups and two are communal violent groups. Several other

terrorist groups are conspicuously missing if compared, for instance, with the regularly updated list of 370 'Liberation Movements, Terrorist Organizations, Substance Cartels, and Other Para-State Entities' compiled by the Federation of American Scientists, Intelligence Resource Program, www.fas.org/irp/world/para/index.html.

61. The TPB, led by Alex P. Schmid (former head of PIOOM), chiefly carries out research on terrorism and its (new) trends; its mandate includes assisting states in upgrading their capacities to investigate and—primarily—prevent terrorism. TPB promotes international cooperation in addressing this global/globalized phenomenon.

62. See 'Fighting Terrorism through Disarmament', in: 'UN Action Against Terrorism', online http://www.un.org/News/dh/latest/feature_terror_disarm.htm.

63. Kelly is the president of the Federation of American Scientists (FAS). His testimony 'Dirty Bombs and Basement Nukes: The Terrorist Nuclear Threat', given at a Senate Foreign Relations Committee hearing, Washington DC, on March 6, 2002, can be accessed online http://www.fas.org/ssp/docs/kelly_testimony_030602.pdf.

64. The United Nations defines nuclear, chemical and biological weapons as weapons of mass destruction. The UN has been seeking to 'prevent the nightmare scenario of such weapons falling into the hands of terrorists for many years, mainly by promoting multilateral disarmament agreements, which aim to reduce or even eliminate these weapons. The 11 September attacks have given new impetus to this effort.' (ibid.) The legal framework to prevent terrorists from acquiring nuclear, biological and chemical weapons exists (as mentioned), with more than a dozen treaties and protocols, key among which are the Biological Weapons Convention, the Chemical Weapons Convention, and the Treaty on the Non-Proliferation of Nuclear Weapons (NPT). The question is: Is it only after a nuclear device would have killed millions of innocent people in a town like New York that the great powers could be convinced of abolishing all weapons of mass destruction?

65. The media coined the term 'ethnic cleansing'. Religious communities and confessional groups were ethnicized on the basis and in remembrance of the final chapter in an externally imposed barbaric history of genocide that is scarcely two generations old.

66. But sanctions can have catastrophic effects on the civilian population (as in Iraq). A list of 'sanctions in a UN regime of operative constraint' compiled by Schmillen and Schmidt-Eenboom (1993: 6) mentions various types of 'sanctions': economic sanctions (embargoes, transport), currency sanctions (freezing of assets, blocking of credits), international legal sanctions (breaking-off of diplomatic relations, war-crimes tribunals), cultural and social sanctions (sport, cultural exchanges, sciences), electronic sanctions (telecommunications, jamming stations, computer viruses, etc.), and limited military operations (creation of safe zones). See also Achim Schmillen, *Außenpolitik in der globalen Risikogemeinschaft* (Loccum, 1993).

67. According to Article 39 of the UN Charter the Security Council determines what is a 'threat to the peace' or a 'breach of the peace'. The Articles 41 and 42 determine what measures shall be taken to maintain or restore international peace and security. The conference 'Towards Global Governance' organized by the Development and Peace Foundation and the Development and Peace Institute in Loccum (in June 1993) dealt, amongst other things, with the reform of the UN and the problems associated with intervention. The South African constitutional lawyer and adviser to Nelson Mandela Professor Kader Asmal (University of the Western Cape) called Boutros Boutros-Ghali's Agenda 'a very sloppy paper'; it failed to provide an answer to many burning questions, he said. According to Asmal, the UN ought to intervene in cases of 'large-scale oppression', which 'should be an issue for the UN'. One such case would be 'the permanent state of oppression of the majority in South Africa' (during the apartheid era). But the UN, said Asmal, had repeatedly demonstrated its inability to intervene in

conflicts. The unresolved, 'never-ending' cases of UN involvement include: UNTSO in Israel/the Middle East, in operation since 1948; UNMOGIP between India and Pakistan since 1949; Cyprus—UNFICYP from 1964, Turkish occupation of the northern third from 1974; UNDOF in the Golan Heights since 1974; MINURSO in Western Sahara since 1991 (Morocco deferred referendum); MONUA, sent to Angola in July 1997 after failure of power-sharing agreement and subsequent renewed outbreak of intra-state war, with regional spill-over into Namibia, former Zaire/DRC, and Congo/Brazzaville (after 'wrong' election result).

68. Economic sanctions are less spectacular than military ones and need a lot of 'staying power': Karl Meesen, 'Entwicklung und Operationalisierung des Instruments wirtschaftlicher Sanktionen', unpub. paper.

69. In ICRC doctrine, there are two central concepts underpinning humanitarian intervention: that of the 'humanitarian minimum' (which is to be maintained), and that of the '*droit d'initiative*', which was made part of the brief of the ICRC as the body that monitors observance of the Geneva conventions and its protocols by the signatory states. International humanitarian law as contained in the 1949 Geneva Conventions and their Additional Protocols of 1977, which have been accepted by the vast majority of states, recognizes the right of victims to receive assistance, in non-international as well as international conflicts. The 600 or so articles of these conventions and protocols, and the other conventions that form part of international humanitarian law, in fact simply give legal expression to a broad interpretation of the right to initiative and assistance. The ICRC retains the option to take action not just outside the context of non-international armed conflicts and internal disturbances. It may take any necessary initiative to protect persons affected by the conflict concerned. It avails itself of this right of initiative in all armed conflicts, in order to provide material assistance, exchange prisoners of war, and request permission to visit persons deprived of their liberty. (See Yves Sandoz, 'Le Droit d'initiative du Comité international de la Croix-Rouge', *German Yearbook of International Law* (Berlin: Duniker & Humboldt, 1979), xxii. 352–73. D. Schindler, 'The International Committee of the Red Cross and Human Rights', *International Review of the Red Cross*, 208, 1 Jan. 1979, 3–14.)

70. See summary given in table 8.1. The tool box and the related concepts are a result of works since 1994. It was first published in 1998 and presented at the Stockholm early in 2000 ('Teaching and Researching Genocide from a Comparative Perspective'; The Stockholm International Forum on the Holocaust. A Conference on Education, Remembrance and Research. Proceedings. Stockholm: Regeringskansliet 2000, 319–321. www.holocaustforum.gov.se/conference/official_documents/abstracts/scherrer.htm. An edited version 'The Challenge of Genocide Prevention' is available on the website of Prevent Genocide, http://preventgenocide.org/prevent/scherrer.htm.)

71. Prevent Genocide International is an US-based NGO undertaking projects such as the construction of an educational website to inform the global public about the crime of genocide, to use the world wide web to initiate dialogue about how to create an effective rapid response network and how to facilitate genocide eradication, and provide resources for persons and NGOs in over 50 countries which are not yet party to the U.N. Genocide Convention. See 'Mission statement and activities' on http://www.preventgenocide.org/.

72. See Scherrer, C.P.: 'Fundamental Human Rights must be protected.' Working Paper 28. Copenhagen: COPRI 1998.

73. The report on the United Nations during the 1994 Genocide in Rwanda (Carlsson *et al.* 1999) made 14 detailed recommendations, some of which are discussed in Scherrer 2002a, 211–229.

74. The first task is to search for signs of eminent danger. Based on this work the second task is to identify indicators for red alert. Thus, the impending main task for applied

genocide researchers is to develop indicators for a system of effective early warning. Indicators warning of serious risk of genocide or mass violence against vulnerable groups can be deducted from patterns of escalation.

75. 'The critical concern today is no longer lack of early warning of impending crises, but rather the need to follow up early warning with early and effective action.' Annan 1999, § 16 (III. Responding to situations of conflict).

76. The USA was the only nuclear power at that time and had the last word in the General Assembly, to which 51 states (of which only ten were from Africa and Asia) initially belonged. See Gilbert Achcar, 'The United Nations and the United States', *Le Monde diplomatique*, Oct. 1995, 14–15.

77. Assessment of the UN 1945–55 based on Evan Luard, *History of the United Nations*, rev. edn. (2 vols.; London, 1993), quoted in Bertrand 1995: 40.

78. The USA reacted strongly after the General Assembly's 1975 resolution stating that Zionism was a form of racism, and after the condemnation of the USA for mining Nicaraguan ports in 1984, for its bombing raid on Libya in 1986, for its refusal to grant Yassir Arafat a visa in 1988 (the response to which was to move the GA to Geneva!), and its intervention in Panama in Dec. 1989, killing some 2,000 Panamanians.

79. See Achcar, 'Die Vereinten Nationen', 14.

80. The UN's principal organs are: the General Assembly, the Security Council, the Economic and Social Council, the Trusteeship Council, the International Court of Justice, and the Secretariat. These last three organs are to be upgraded as part of a reform of the UN.

81. E.g. oil-production in the Middle East or the exploitation of major raw-materials deposits in Congo-Zaire. A number of other interventions were conducted for strategic reasons (Panama 1989) or to protect tame local potentates (Chad, Mobutu's Zaire, etc.).

82. This was demonstrated by the world-wide outrage at the French nuclear tests on Mururoa in 1995.

83. New nuclear weapons are 'designed to destroy underground complexes, including stores of chemical and biological arms. The targets might be situated in Iraq, Iran, Syria, Libya or North Korea, a reorientation away from cold war scenarios involving Russia.' See Michael R. Gordon: 'Nuclear Arms for Deterrence or Fighting?', *NYT*, March 11, 2002.

84. This office, led by a known PR specialist, is 'plotting to plant deliberately false stories in the foreign press, with both feral and friendly nations' (Maureen Dowd: 'Office of Strategic Mendacity', *NYT*, Febr. 20, 2002).

85. Back in 1999 there were series of warnings about the use of depleted uranium-plutonium during NATO's war against Yugoslavia. A serious investigation was never conducted. An article in *Le Monde Diplomatique* (Robert J. Parsons: 'America's big dirty secret', Paris, LMD March 2002, online http://MondeDiplo.com/2002/03/03uranium) is based on the report of Dai Williams, and it tells why WHO and UNEP mismanaged any serious investigation. Possible threats and health hazards are now going to be of a far greater dimension, several hundred times greater as in Yugoslavia. A bunker breaking bomb GBU-31, carrying a BLU-109 warhead, can weigh as much as one and a half metric tons (so-far the max weight used in SE Europe may have been five kilos for 120mm rounds), thus greatly multiplying nuclear waste from US nuclear plants used in these bombs, thus multiplying the amount of toxic uranium-plutonium dust intoxicating areas in Afghanistan. Already in October 2001, Afghan doctors, citing rapid deaths from internal ailments, were accusing the US-led coalition of using chemical and radioactive weapons. Among the symptoms they reported were haemorrhaging, pulmonary constriction and vomiting, which could have resulted from radiation contamination.

86. See SIPRI Yearbook 2001, 226 and 244. SIPRI does not, however, draw clear-cut conclusions.

87. The massive bombardments against the Bosnian Serbs in Sept. 1995 altered the balance of forces between the parties to the war. There were new hostilities, which had the effect of intensifying and prolonging the war. The Dayton accord of Nov. 1995 was secured under pressure from the USA. The bargaining chip in the hands of the USA was the lifting of the UN sanctions against Serbia, which subsequently, as representative of the Bosnian Serbs (*sic!*), made extensive concessions (although weeks before this Russia had threatened unilaterally to lift the sanctions that were having devastating effects on Serbia).

88. It was foreseeable that the 60,000 NATO troops would (contrary to plan) probably remain deployed for several years.

89. For the purpose of 'stopping genocide' in Kosovo the NATO alliance unleashed (on the night of March 24–25, 1999) air attacks followed by 78 days of bombing on Yugoslavia. End 1999 John Pilger feared that NATO had caused more death than the Serbs.

90. Inquiries by the ICTY, other international bodies, and by a number of journalists, 'show a radically different train of events' then the one presented in the media. The ICTY has announced to have found some 2,018 dead bodies; many of them might be Serbs and Roma.

91. Western 'experts' had not predicted the fall of Milosevic as it happened: as the result of a non-violent mass riot that finally sweep away an authoritarian regime presided over by Slobodan Milosevic for 13 years. Jan Oberg wrote: 'It was a miracle unfolding, minute by minute, in front of our eyes. Unarmed citizens were stronger, finally, than Milosevic' force. They also achieved in about 24 hours what NATO violence could not achieve in 78 days. It's yet another remarkable victory for non-violence.' (in 'The Yugoslav Non-violent Revolution', www.transnational.org, Lund: TFF, October 9, 2000). For a comment on Milosevic's trial also see text and footnote 41.

92. See Noam Chomski: 'Lessons of War: Another way for Kosovo?'; in: *Le Monde Diplomatique*, March 2000.

93. According to the 'Military Technical Agreement' between KFOR and the government of the Federal Republic of Yugoslavia signed in Kumanovo on June 9, 1999, NATO (and a small Russian troop) took over Kosovo. KFOR had to implement the UN Security Council resolution 1244, adopted the day after (June 10, 1999).

94. As the 'Memorandum of the government of the FRY' (dated November 4, 1999) on the non-implementation of S/RES 1244 claimed, this clearly violated S/RES1244, which calls for the maintenance of a multiethnic and multicultural Kosovo. Most parts of Kosovo—under the eyes of KFOR—have been ethnically cleansed of almost all non-Albanians by the UÇK. Massive massacres of Serbs took place: between June and October 1999 some 447 persons have been killed and 648 disappeared!

95. 'Political leaders find it hard to sell prevention policies abroad to their public at home, because the costs are palpable and immediate, while the benefits—an undesirable or tragic future event that does not occur—are more difficult for the leaders to convey and the public to grasp. Thus prevention is, first and foremost, a challenge of political leadership. If we are to be successful at preventing deadly conflicts, we must have a clear understanding of their causes.' UNDPI 2000: 5.

96. While in Copenhagen 1997, the UN Secretary-General visited the military barracks housing the new Planning Element of the Multinational United Nations Stand-By Force High Readiness Brigade. (See: Press Briefing of the spokesman of the UN-SG of 29 Aug. 1997, on: http://www.un.org/). The visit was overshadowed by events in Bosnia where the Stabilization Force in Bosnia and Herzegovina (SFOR) came into trouble.

97. See DGVN 1995*b*.

98. The Qureshi/Weizsäcker working-party proposed creating 'three interrelated councils': a new economic council, a new social council, and a reorganized security council; the

latter would be expanded to include up to 23 members, according to the 'principles of balanced participation and equality' (DGVN 1995*b*: 56), and the right of veto would not be abolished but would be restricted to the military measures provided for in ch. VII. There should be a military authority for carrying out enforcement measures as detailed in art. 42, and it should come directly under 'the supreme command of the United Nations' (ibid. 57). There was also mention of a UN rapid intervention force that could be brought into operation immediately following a decision by the Security Council.

99. He talked of 'peace-enforcement units'. See Heinrich-Böll-Stiftung 1995.
100. As the *Coalition to Stop the Use of Child Soldiers* reported in June 2001 in a new global survey. At least 300,000 of these children are actively fighting in 41 countries. Coalition to Stop the Use of Child Soldiers / Mungoven, Rory *et al.* 2001. Global Report on Child Soldiers 2001. Online on the website of the Coalition, see www.child-soldiers.org/report2001/global_report_contents.htlm. Also child soldiers in today's armed conflicts see www.un.org/special-rep/children-armed-conflict/soldiers.htm.
101. The UN Millennium Summit formulated as priorities for action 'the fight against poverty, ignorance and disease; the fight against violence and terror; and the fight against the degradation and destruction of our common home' (UNDPI 2000: 25).
102. Nohlen and Nuscheler eds. 1992: i: 51.
103. The post of director-general for development created by the General Assembly, whose incumbent was meant to be responsible for co-ordinating the activities of the UN and its special organizations, was done away with by the secretary-general in 1992!
104. Bertrand was an administrative inspector with the UN for 18 years and was for a long time chairman of the UN's Joint Inspection Unit (JIU), which consists of 11 elected financial and administrative inspectors. The JIU conducts investigations to see whether services are effective and how funds are utilized; it can submit reform proposals to the executive organs of the UN (see Bertrand 1995: 84).
105. Erskine Childers, 'The United Nations Seen from the South', paper delivered at a seminar on 'The United Nations and the New World (Dis)order', Ev. Akademie Müllheim, Mar. 1994 (p. 9). UNCTAD's main goals were originally to 'maximize the trade, investment and development opportunities of developing countries and assist them in their efforts to integrate into the world economy on an equitable basis'. In Bangkok, at the 10th UNCTAD conference in February 2000, the Secretary-General of UNCTAD, Rubens Ricupero stated that 'the issue of whether movement towards freer trade on a non-discriminatory basis is consistent with the development aspirations of poor countries still vexes public opinion today. This was evident from the various public demonstrations in Seattle in the name of 'development' and the 'environment', and against the WTO' (see report on an academic round table in Bangkok 2000 titled 'Trade and development directions for the 21st century: the academic perspective', http://www.unctad-10.org/index_en.htm.
106. A split emerged between ECOSOC and UNCTAD in regard to issues dealt with, but in regard to functions, a sensible division of labour was agreed. UNCTAD and the Regional Economic Commissions answer directly to the Secretary-General; the other organizations and programmes concerned with economic and social issues are all inter-dependent.
107. 'Die wirtschaftlichen und sozialen Aktivitäten der UNO', Bertrand 1995: 72–121 (121).
108. The USA and Russia are the biggest UN debtors; the USA alone has chalked up arrears of 1.6 billion dollars. The creditors are often poor developing countries who have assigned troops for UN peacekeeping operations but have then had to wait a long time to be reimbursed. As a transitional solution, the participatory rights of notorious debtor-

countries could be curtailed. Rich countries should also be asked to pay up via appropriate measures.

109. Ali Mazrui, 'Recolonization of Africa', *Sunday Nation*, Feb. 1995.
110. Some INGOs such as Amnesty International, Médecins sans Frontières, and Greenpeace have organizations in dozens of countries, employ hundreds of full-time staff, and have annual budgets that run into hundreds of millions but are subject to sharp fluctuations. E.g., donations to Greenpeace, once an 'environmental enterprise pre-programmed for growth', fell from DM225 million in 1993 to DM200 million in 1995; see *taz*, 25 Sept. 1995, 3. (This was despite the successes it scored against the multinational oil-concern Shell, when it managed, through consumer boycotts and special actions, to prevent the sinking of the Brent Spar oil-platform.)
111. Up to now, the ILO has drafted 173 agreements, including Convention 169, which has acted as a lightship in the area of minority protection. (Most states have so far signed only a faction of that number!)
112. In most ILO bodies, the principle of three-way parity obtains (i.e. between member states, representatives of affected nationalities/minorities/indigenous groups, and ILO experts); both small and large states have a vote.
113. The OSCE does this for decisions on certain issues (such as human and minority rights), according to the formula 'consensus minus one'.
114. See the comments of Bertrand (1994: 22–3, 26 ff.). These have been incorporated into what follows here, after a process of selection and further development.
115. The administrative costs of the IMF and World Bank are currently many times greater (1,000 percent) than the expenditure on the UN's political departments.
116. See late findings of the former chief economist of the World Bank: Stieglitz, Joseph: 'What I learned at the world economic crisis', *The New Republic*, 17 April 2000.
117. 'Counter speculative capital movements and attacks on our currencies, through Tobin-type taxes, capital controls, and prudential and transparency measures imposed on large financial players, particularly hedge funds'; see NGO Conference 1999). SEF 1995: 2.
118. The unspeakable scandal that daily 100,000 people are dying from famine of from the consequences of undernourishment or malnutrition (see Ziegler / UNCHR 2001) cannot continue.
119. Fischer, Dietrich: 2001. 'Strengthening the United Nations: an Ambitious Agenda', online at www.transcend.org.
120. Boutros-Ghali 1992. His prime concern was to adapt UN procedures and mechanisms to the more demanding requirements (art. 15), mainly through: preventive diplomacy (art. 20); early identification of conflicts; fact-finding missions; confidence-building measures; peaceful dispute-settlement; and peacemaking, peacekeeping, and the consolidation of peace (art. 55 ff.). This embraces preventive operations and military intervention (art. 42).
121. Boutros-Ghali believed the UN should be democratized (art. 82 ff.).

Summary

This book deals with the problem of intra-state conflict and mass violence in general and in particular with ethnic conflict, ethno-nationalism and genocide in the international system. The recent proliferation of states was a product of the decline of socialist federations (USSR and Yugoslavia) and does not represent a new paradigm in the context of inter-state relations. Certain efforts by the community of states on the one hand and non-state actors on the other to develop internationally binding standards on the ethno-national question are of a new kind. In order to rise to the ethnic challenge, classic minorities-policy must be reformed and made a province of international law, of regional inter-state regimes (such as OSCE, OAU, and OAS), and of the United Nations. The focus will be on the themes of the prevention of violence, the management and transformation of conflicts.

Part I deals with the challenge intra-state conflict and ethno-nationalism pose to the nation-state. The career of the nation-state has had momentous repercussions. The official nationalism to which it gave rise in developing countries appears to have failed. The ambivalences and violence engendered by nationalism in the process of the creation of nations had manifested themselves early on in Europe as well. Europe became the main theatre of war, on whose battlefields, between the years 1500 and 2000, almost two-thirds of the world-wide total of 160 million victims of violence lost their lives 'in the cause of the nation'; the remaining third was accounted for in large measure by European colonial expansion, beginning in 1500. Historically, colonial expansion also put an end to the autonomous existence of a wide range of social formations and political systems. Attempts to export the idea of the European nation-state to the colonies came up against a host of additional ideological, structural, and practical difficulties. There was no appropriate basis for this 'idea' outside Europe.

Since 1840, a whole series of alternatives to the European colonial legacy have bitten the dust. Projects for regional integration and self-determined development—including as a counterweight to ethno-nationally induced fragmentation—have foundered. The development-based nationalism of the new states was forced to recall its words, because it could not fulfil its promises in regard to development. The 1980s and 1990s were 'lost decades' for the Third World as a whole: it fell deep into debt and forfeited its negotiating power. The legitimacy crisis in peripheral states was accelerated in parallel with economic decline. Advancing capitalist globalization appears to run counter to ethno-national fragmentation but in reality the two elements go together.

Most countries in the South remained for the most part without any successful self-controlled economic growth as base for political stability. The official nationalism failed to satisfy its own aspirations of achieving an acceptable degree of development and to safeguard peace and security. In most countries the struggle against poverty was lost. The sacred cows of statehood had to be slaughtered: IMF dictating economic policies undermined *national sovereignty*. Rebel movements perforated their *territorial integrity*. *Secularity* was given up in many countries, which feared religious fundamentalism and were giving in. The ideology of *modernity* proved hollow compared to the harsh conditions of survival.

Exceptions from the rule are China first, then India, some Asian tiger economies (riddled by the 1997 crisis but not structurally weakened) and socialist Vietnam. The rate of savings is impressive in East Asia, and it is very high compared to Africa and Latin America. Today the former Third World is far from representing a unitary block. Differences between the world regions in the South seem to become greater rather than to diminish. However, the magic term of *self-reliance* is today not often heard; the term of collective self-reliance has almost disappeared. Projects such as an *African Union* (or an *African Economic Community* replacing the OAU) or of an *Islamic Common Market* from Turkey to Pakistan are in an embryonic state. This is in striking contrast to the high and ever increasing degree of co-operation in the framework of the European Union.

The Third World War seems to be in full swing. Violent conflict is neither going on between East and West nor between North and South but being fought and suffered at this very moment inside dozens of states of four continents. The regional distribution of contemporary mass violence shows a clear global trend. Violent conflict is infrequent in the North and West but part of *normality* in the South and some areas of the East. Many wars in the South would not be fought and acts of genocide would not have been committed without involvement of the North. Military intervention and northern complicity with state crimes in the South have not at all been an exception. Since 1945 there have been more than 300 violent conflicts occurring globally—until the late 1980s nearly exclusively in the Third World.

Assertions of 'false' or coercive nation states *vis-à-vis* their own citizen and communities of minority nationalities, non-dominant ethnic groups and indigenous peoples, were put forth in an increasingly aggressive way. Ethnic or ethnicized violence became the single most dangerous source for violence. It influences new types of non-Clausewitzean warfare and modern genocide in the extra-European World, since 1989 also in former socialist multi-ethnic states. Almost in two out of three cases of mass violence we find a component suitable to 'ethnic' interpretation. That means the *ethnic factor* is a dominant or influential component. Because of certain taboos linked with ethnicity there was limited or distorted knowledge about its nature and structural characteristics. Mainstream research replaced the understanding of ethnic phenomena with its denunciation as a 'political pathology'. Such obstacles and the resulting research deficits inhibit adequate understanding and damage strategies for remedy.

Genocide is the most radical and criminal form in which states deal with the 'ethnic question'. All total genocides in the past 20th century targeted domestic minorities as victims. The destructive powers of genocides and their lasting consequences (leading to new violence as in Yugoslavia, Timor and Central Africa) is far greater that those of other forms of mass violence. Comparative genocide and the analysis of patterns of genocide are pivotal to an understanding of genocidal processes and allows the deduction of indicators of alert for an effective early warning system. Warnings as such are meaningless if no early action follows.

The question of whether there are such things as ethnic conflicts *per se* leads to a consideration of the way in which such conflicts arise and the structural features they display. Preferential treatment of particular ethnic groups was an integral part of the techniques of rule used by a number of colonial powers, with devastating effects that are still being felt today. Since decolonization, the 'glitches' of separatism and ethno-nationalism have become a built-in, long-term problem in the Third World—and more recently also in the erstwhile nominally socialist world. Two sets of briefly outlined causes of conflict and crisis in the forgotten wars of the Third World are discussed from the point of view of their history and significance. It emerges, in this connection, that violent ethno-national conflicts are both products and causes of colonial creation and of the inherently unstable existence of peripheral states. Outside Europe, globalization from above and fragmentation from below turn out to be only apparently conflicting processes.

Ethno-national conflicts are still to a large degree 'forgotten wars'. My analysis of the structural features of such conflicts encompasses: potential; agents/actors; causes and (often distant) history; objects of contention; conflictual formation; aims and organization of the opposition; the course of the conflict; the question of outside participation; resources and available military means; structural and other solutions. There is an urgent need for research into the various types of ethno-national conflict. As an illustration of certain conflictual situations, I cite cases that may be regarded as ideal-typical or representative.

The seemingly permanent establishment and globalization of ethno-nationalism in the last fifty years dictates that research efforts ought to be multiplied. However, there is a real cognitive problem here, in that many conflict researchers and security experts have never experienced the horrors of war or of mass violence at close quarters and often have no realistic idea about it. Only detailed, empirical-cum-practical knowledge of the causes of war, its structural characteristics and the forces that drive it—ideally first-hand information combined with personal experience—will turn up the kind of solid findings that are a prerequisite for practical action in concrete instances. Otherwise, well-meaning attempts at prevention, containment, or peaceful intervention by multiple actors risk failing.

Part II deals with the responses of international system on the surge of intra-state conflicts in general and of the challenge of ethno-nationalism in particular. High frequency and huge potential of 'forgotten wars' became decisive regarding the lack of possibilities for structural prevention of violence, conflict management and transformation, as well as regarding the role of multi-lateralism in preventing mass violence. The question of 'What to do in a particular situation?' is linked to the particular type of conflict we are dealing with. The second question of 'When to do what?' underlines the importance of timing in response to conflict. Types of responses have to be related to the different types of violent conflicts we encounter in the real world. Responses have to address the root causes of conflict, in order to safeguard an effective peaceful settlement and accommodation of demands.

Within 20 years, the number of states could have risen further world-wide. Investigation into the question of whether the increase in the number of states that has taken place up to now has made any contribution at all to solving protracted conflicts, and, if so, in what way, produces one crucial observation: Whereas in the first phase of dissolution of the Soviet Union (and also of Czechoslovakia, CSSR), a whole new set of states emerged in an astonishingly peaceful manner and in a very short time, there was a second phase during which the process led to numerous violent conflicts in certain successor states of the USSR and in Yugoslavia. In the Third World, the proliferation of states has often been unavoidable as a means of putting an end to violent conflicts lasting many decades. In an initial phase, this involved belated decolonization conflicts (Bangla Desh, Eritrea, East Timor, Western Sahara), and in a second phase conflicts in multinational entities, often ruled in an ethnocratic way by minority regimes. On the periphery of these repressive ethnocracies—for example, in liberated areas controlled by rebels—*de facto* autonomy and self-rule had long since been wrested from the powers that be. The long list of potential new states over-laps with that of the world's violent conflicts, most of which are susceptible to ethnic interpretation.

There are many ethnicized wars without rules in which the minimum standards of international humanitarian law (Geneva Convention) need to be enforced. The most urgent requirement is for an extension of international law and an improvement in the procedures for enforcing humanitarian and human-rights minimums. In parallel with this, efforts should be made to extend the area of operation of non-state actors. Independent human-rights organizations, indigenous organizations, and the umbrella-organizations of non-dominant and non-represented peoples (the WCIP and UNPO, for example) make an important contribution to the protection of endangered peoples.

More practicable procedures for enforcing human rights for members of non-dominant groups are also being elaborated by organizations composed of state representatives. The European Human Rights Convention is a milestone along this path. Efforts by the Council of Europe and regional organizations to work out so-called human-rights regimes have only just begun. The European Union has recently issued two directives to combat racism, xenophobia and racial discrimination and is about to develop an action plan to implement further anti-racist strategies. Europe-wide polls exhibited the size of the problem and forced the Commission to join hands with the anti-racist movements. In view of the enlargement process being in full swing, issues and tasks such as combating racism, the search for new federal arrangements, closing democracy deficits, developing transnational citizenship and a common European identity gained tremendous importance.

The resistance of many states to an extension of the right of self-determination are reflected in their refusal to sign the International Labour Organization's pioneering Convention 169 of 1989. United Nations are confronted with the dilemma of having to decide between the basic principle of the self-determination of peoples and the claim of states to sovereignty. It was only in 1982 that the United Nations created a (non-permanent) forum in which representatives of minority nationalities and indigenous or endangered peoples had a chance to express their opinions. This working group on indigenous populations serves both as a forum for bringing complaints against repressive states and as an expert body within the framework of the UN Human Rights Commission. A decade of intensive work to produce a universal declaration on the rights of indigenous peoples suffered a severe set-back in the Human Rights Commission in 1995. This shows states' high degree of sensitivity to, or fear of, demands from 'their' nationalities. The development of the rights of indigenous peoples and the systematization of minority protection should be made central tasks by United Nations and its regional organizations.

The contribution that inter- and supra-state regimes can make to the resolution of ethno-national conflicts is still only a modest one but could become significant within the framework of state groupings (such as the UN, the OSCE and other regional organizations). Destructive manifestations of fragmentation in the international system of states could be tempered by new states being integrated into schemes of regional unification and multilateral co-operation. The proliferation of states would then, in the ideal case, be a sort of model of decentralization. The instruments of conflict management should be further developed within the framework of regional regimes (such as the OSCE, OAU or the future AU, ASEAN, and OAS) and within the UN system. The protection of human and minority rights by multilateral bodies and international regimes would guarantee that the enforcement of such rights could in future no longer be rejected as interference in the internal affairs of a state. What has to be addressed is the lack of will on the part of states to prevent conflict or settle a dispute peacefully, e.g., by granting autonomy rights, power sharing, self-governance, or federal solutions. Such solutions are not intrastate matters but have to become part of multilateral regimes.

Progress and problems in subjecting 'ethnic' and ethnicized conflicts to regulation can be illustrated by the transformation of the Conference for Security and Co-operation in Europe (CSCE) into the OSCE. The focal point of my interest is the work done to improve institutional protection for Europe's minorities. One important step was the creation of a High Commission on National Minorities. However, this new institution has only very limited options for intervention. Its mandate and budget are still totally inadequate. Lessons should be learned from the failure of peaceful dispute-settlement in Bosnia and Nagorno-Karabakh. The institutionalisation of long-term missions represents another major step on the part of the OSCE.

The long list of proposed reforms (some of them already familiar) could—following 'failure' in Yugoslavia—help reactivate the debate about the possibilities of the OSCE in regard to peace-policy. The idea that the OSCE model is transferable seems, however, questionable. The Organization of American States (OAS) for instance—unlike the OSCE—is located at the heart of the North–South conflict and suffers from a humanitarian and human rights deficit; it could, however, teach some the lessons from peace initiatives in Central America. The Organization of African Unity (OAU) is faced with unprecedented challenges, which it is resolved to meet with newly created mechanisms, legal procedures and the overriding importance of step-wise implementation of the African Union project. In the past many of its activities and demands failed due to lack of political will, organization and resources. Inhibiting factors on the bumpy road to African Union are manifold but there is no alternative to unification as the only means to avert further disorder, impoverishment and state collapse.

Global and regional conflict-prevention regimes that exist now are, on the whole, still poorly developed. The lack of political will manifests itself most clearly in the meagre material resources and funding accorded to non-military peace measures. The debate about effective sanctions and legitimate military intervention by the United Nations should be conducted in a more thoroughgoing way, against the background of the recent increase in peacekeeping actions and the spectacular failure of some missions. The Brahimi report and its follow-up have brought new dynamics into this debate. It would be naïve to believe that the series of recent cases in which the spectacular failure of the international community was repeatedly and amply demonstrated were due 'only' to deficiencies in fact-finding and poor implementation. Knowledge and interests are seldom compatible in international politics. But ignorance and inadequacy did contribute to the political failure. The threat to the world order emanating from ethno-nationalism, genocide, international terrorism and complex emergencies will make increased efforts to identify and deal with the underlying wrongs unavoidable—within the limitations imposed by practical politics, big-power interests, and the crumbling principles of non-intervention. At the end of the day, the success of attempts at solution depends on whether states can be civilized—that is to say, whether states, which up to now have been the universally privileged protagonists, can be forced to share the sovereignty to which they lay claim in two directions, sharing downwards with 'their' peoples and sharing upwards, to enable global governance.

At the heart of global governance are a world peace order based on comprehensive prevention of violence, poverty eradication, opening up of chances for economic development and a thorough reform of the United Nations as the main instrument of global governance. Priority should be given to the elaboration of effective policies in the field of prevention of violent conflicts in general and of genocide in particular. Here the United Nations policies are largely deficient.

Even if solutions were agreed in a major regional conflict (Middle East 1993) and mediation by a third party (Norway) has produced an agenda for peace, its implementation faced too many obstacles since. In Palestine, the promise of autonomy and statehood seemed to prepare the way to a partial solution but in reality the UN proved impotent and blocked by one member state in the face of a massive breakdown of peace and outright aggressive state terrorism. The United Nations ought to play a more active part—in the sense of effective prevention and/or intervention—among others in Palestine, West Papua, Western Sahara, Kurdistan, Kanaky/Nouvelle Caledonie and other actual or potential hot spots. This is of particular importance also in regard to the role the UN has to play in combating terrorism. Preventive measures are pivotal and shall replace fighting against symptoms. For these important policy fields, which are essentially the fields where global governance must be developed primarily, a number of conceptions and ideas are developed and some recommendations are formulated.

The end of East–West confrontations and the Cold War has already brought the fundamental contradictions between North and South into sharper perspective. The elimination of ideological blocks in international relations has led to more far-reaching demands being made of the United Nations and to attempts to exploit it for particular interests or even to use it to justify wars. The changed international scene has also made reflection on 'global governance' possible and has resulted in proposals for thorough-going reforms of the United Nations system of a kind that are realizable within the medium term. A reformed United Nations would have to break free from its particularistic and Eurocentric origins, in order to do justice to the geopolitical realities and requirements of the present times. The fundamental question to be asked is with which United Nations the challenges of the 21st century could be faced—the present one, with its San Francisco spirit and its almost absolute domination by the old nuclear aristocracy, or a reformed, representative and more democratic world organization.

References and Bibliographic Sources

Abelsen, Emil. (1992), 'Home Rule in Greenland', in UNHCR 1992: 109–16.

ABI (Arnold Bergstraesser Institut) (Braun, Gerald, and Rösel, Jakob). (1988), *Ethnische Konflikte im internationalen System*. Freiburg i.B.: ABI.

AFB (Arbeitsstelle Friedensforschung Bonn). var years. *AFB-Info*, half-yearly newsletter of the Peace Research Information Unit Bonn; *AFB-Texte*, papers on basic issues of peace and conflict research.

——. (1995), 'Fifty Years of UNESCO: Culture of Peace Programme'. *AFB-Info*, 2: 1–3.

Africa Leadership Forum / Arias Foundation for Peace and Human Progress (Brenes, Arnoldo, ed.). (1999), *The leadership challenges of demilitarization in Africa*. Conference Report. San José: Ed. Sanabria.

African Rights (Omar, Rakiya / Waal, Alex de). (1998), *Rwanda: The insurgency in the Northwest*. London: African Rights.

——. (1995), *Facing Genocide: The Nuba of Sudan*. London: AR.

——. (1994), *Rwanda: Death, Despair and Defiance*. London: AR.

——. (1994*b*), *Humanitarianism Unbound? Current Dilemmas Facing Multi-mandate Relief Operations in Political Emergencies*. Discussion Paper 5; London: AR.

AGKED (Arbeitsgemeinschaft Kirchlicher Entwicklungsdienst). (var. years), *der überblick* , quarterly.

AKUF (Arbeitsgruppe Konfliktursachenforschung—University of Hamburg). (var. years), *Das Kriegsgeschehen. Daten und Tendenzen der Kriege und bewaffneten Konflikte*. SEF: Interdependenz, no. 16, 20 and 22.

——. (var. years), Kriege und bewaffnete Konflikte. On website www.sozialwiss.uni-hamburg.de/Ipw/Akuf/home.html.

——. (Rabehl, Thomas, ed.). (2000), *Das Kriegsgeschehen 1999), Daten und Tendenzen der Kriege und bewaffneten Konflikte*. Opladen: Leske und Budrich.

——. (Duyvesteyn, Isabelle). (1995), *Wars and Military Interventions since 1945)*, AKUF-Arbeitspapier 88; Hamburg: AKUF.

Albertini, Rudolf von. (1987), *Europäische Kolonialherrschaft 1880–1940)*, Stuttgart: Steiner.

Amin, Samir. (1994), *L'Ethnie à l'assaut des nations: Yougoslavie, Ethiopie*. Paris: L'Harmattan.

——. (1992), *Das Reich des Chaos: Der neue Vormarsch der Ersten Welt*. Hamburg: VSA-Verlag.

——. (1992*a*), 'Der Kapitalismus ist eine Utopie'. In Koch 1992: 158–66.

Amnesty International. (var. years), Annual Reports.

Amponsah, William A. (2002), *Analytical and Empirical Evidence of Trade Policy Effects of Regional Integration; Implications for Africa*. Addis Ababa: UN ECA.

Anderson, Benedikt. (1991), *Imagined Communities. Reflection on the Origin and Spread of Nationalism*. Rev. Edition. London/New York: Verso [orig. (1983].

——. (1991), 'Die Erschaffung der Nation durch den Kolonialstaat'. *Argument*, 2: 33, 197–212.

Annan, Kofi (U.N. Secretary-General). (1999), *The Causes of Conflict and the Promotion of Durable Peace and Sustainable Development in Africa*. Report of the Secretary-General. New York: United Nations, April 15.

APC-EU, Africa-Caribbean-Pacific-European Union. (1996), 'Lomé Convention'. *The Courier*, 155.

Arnold, Hans. (1995), 'Unvereinte Nationen: Die Weltorganisation und die Friedenssicherung'. *Blätter für deutsche und internationale Politik,* Bonn 10 (1995): 1191–1201.

Ashworth, Georgina, ed. (1980), *World Minorities.* 3 vols. London: Minority Rights Groups, 1977, 1978, 1980.

Asian NGO Forum at 45th Session of the UN Commission on Status of Women. (2001), 'Intersectionality of race and gender in the Asia-Pacific.' Teheran / New York, 17–21 February / 6–16 March .

Asian NGO Forum at 45th Session of the UN Commission on Status of Women. (2001), 'Intersectionality of race and gender in the Asia-Pacific.' Teheran / New York, 17–21 February / 6–16 March.

Asiwaju, A. I. (1985), *Partitioned Africans: Ethnic Relations across Africa's Boundaries 1884–1984),* Lagos: Lagos University Press.

Asmal, Kader. (1993), 'The Democratic Option, Ethnicity and State Power'. Paper, Grahamstown (Rhodes University).

——. (1990), *Developing a Human Rights Culture.* Durban: NADL.

Assies, Willem (1993), 'Self-determination and the 'New Partnership'', in Assies/Hoekema 1994: 31–71.

——, and Hoekema, André J., eds. (1994), *Experiences with Systems of Self-government by Indigenous Peoples.* IWGIA Document 76; Copenhagen.

Aus Politik und Zeitgeschichte. (var. years), Suppl. to weekly *Das Parlament.*

Azar, Edward E. / Burton, John W. (1986), *International Conflict Resolution. Theory and Practice.* Sussex / Boulder: Wheatsheaf/Rienner.

Azar, Edward E. (1990), *The Management of Protracted Social Conflict. Theory and Cases.* Aldershot: Dartmouth.

Bächler, Günther, ed. (1994), *Beitreten oder Trittbrettfahren? Die Zukunft der Neutralität in Europa.* Chur: Rüegger.

—— *et al. (1993), Umweltzerstörung: Krieg oder Kooperation?* Münster: agenda.

Barsh, Russel L. (1994), 'Making the Most of ILO Convention 169', *Cultural Survival Quarterly* , 18, 2–3: 45–7.

Barth, Frederik, ed. (1969), *Ethnic Groups and Boundaries.* Boston: Little.

Bastlund, Carina, *et al.* (1994), *Rethinking Refugee Policies: Issues of Humanitarian Intervention, Relief Development and the UN Refugee Definition.* Denmark: International Development Studies, Roskilde University.

Bauman, Zygmunt. (1991), *Modernity and the Holocaust.* Cambridge: Polity Press.

Bayart, Jean Francois, and Ellis, Stephen, and Hibou Béatrice. (1999), *The Criminalization of the State in Africa.* Oxford: James Currey.

Bayefsky, Anne F., ed. (2000), *Self-Determination in International Law.* Dordrecht, The Hague, New York, London: Kluwer Academic Publishers.

Bélanger, Sarah, and Pinard, Maurice. (1991), 'Ethnic Movements and the Competition Model'. *American Sociological Review,* 56: 446–57.

Bercovitch, Jacob, and Rubin, Jeffrey Z., eds. (1992), *Mediation in International Relations: Multiple Approaches.* London: St Martin's Press.

——, and Anagnoson, Theodore, and Wille, Donette L. (1991), 'Some Conceptual Issues and Empirical Trends in the Study of Successful Mediation in International Relations'. *Journal of Peace Research,* 28/1: 7–17.

Berding, Helmut, ed. (1994), *Nationales Bewusstsein und kollektive Identität.* i and ii. Frankfurt/M.: edition suhrkamp.

Berghof Research Center for Constructive Conflict Management. (2000), The Berghof Handbook for Conflict Transformation. www.berghof-center.org/handbook/.

Berkel, R. van *et al.* / TSER Project Report. (2001), *Inclusion through Participation*. Brussels: TSER.

Bertrand, Maurice. (1995), *UNO: Geschichte und Bilanz*. Frankfurt/M.: Fischer.

——. (1994), 'Une nouvelle Charte pour l'Organisation mondiale? Proposition de réponse à quelques questions', 'Réformer ou refaire l'ONU et les institutions mondiales'. Unpub. paper.

Bienvenue, Rita M. and Goldstein, Jay E. (eds.), *Ethnicity and Ethnic Relations in Canada* (Toronto: Butterworths, 1980; [2nd ed.], (Toronto : Butterworths, 1985).

Billing, Peter. (1992), *Eskalation und Deeskalation internationaler Konflikte: Ein Konflikt-modell auf der Grundlage der empirischen Auswertung von 288 internationalen Kriege seit 1945)*, Berne: Peter Lang.

Birckenbach, Hanne-Margret, Jäger, Uli, and Wellmann, Christian, eds. (var. years), *Jahrbuch Frieden 1995), Konflikte—Abrüstung—Friedensarbeit*. Munich: Beck.

——. (1995*a*), *Jahrbuch Frieden 1994), Konflikte—Abrüstung—Friedensarbeit*. Munich: Beck.

Blätter des iz3w, and Aktion dritte Welt. var years. *blätter des iz3w*. Newsletter of the Informationszentrum Dritte Welt, Freiburg i.B.

——. (1995), *blätter des iz3w:* ''Ethnopoly': Die Konjunktur von Identitätspolitik'.

Blätter für deutsche und internationale Politik, monthly.

Blomert, Reinhard, Kuzmics, Helmut, and Treibel, Annette. (1993), *Transformationen des Wir-Gefühls: Studien zum nationalen Habitus*. Frankfurt/M.: edition suhrkamp.

Blum, William. (2001), *Killing Hope: U.S. Military and CIA Interventions Since World War II*. Monroe, Maine: Common Courage Press (1st ed. (1995).

Bodley, John H. (1988), *Tribal Peoples and Development Issues. A Global Overview*. Mountain View, Cal.: Mayfield.

——. (1983), *Der Weg der Zerstörung: Stammesvölker und die industrielle Zivilisation*. Munich: Trickster.

Bondeli, Martin. (1994), ''Andererseits kann gesagt werden...' Peru: eine alternative Entwicklung?', in Judith Janoska, Martin Bondeli, Marc Hofer, *Das Methodenkapitel von Karl Marx*. Basle: Schwabe, 158–70.

Boutros-Ghali, Boutros. (1992), *An Agenda for Peace: Peacemaking and Peace-Keeping. Report of the Secretary-General Pursuant to the Statement Adopted by the Summit Meeting of the Security Council, January 31)*, New York: United Nations.

Brahimi, Lakhdar *et al.* / UN Independent Panel. (2001), (see also UN General Assembly / Special Committee on Peacekeeping).

2000), *Report of the Panel on United Nations Peace Operations*. (A/55/305–S/2000 /809). New York: UN, August 21), (www.un.org/peace/reports/peace_operations/).

Brass, Paul R. (1991), *Ethnicity and Nationalism: Theory and Comparison*. New Delhi: Sage.

Brock, Lothar. (1995), 'UNO und Dritte Welt: Fünf verlorene Jahrzehnte?', in Deutsches Überseeinstitut 1996: 62–80.

Brosted, Jens and Dahl, Jens (eds.) 1985), *Native Power: The Quest for Autonomy and Nationhood of Indigenous Peoples*. Bergen: Bergen University Press.

Brubaker, Rogers. (1996), *Nationalism reframed. Nationhood and the national question in the New Europe*. Cambridge / New York: Cambridge University Press.

Bund Lausitzer Sorben. (1994), 'Rechtsvorschriften zum Schutz und zur Förderung des sorbischen Volkes'. *Domowina Information* (Bautzen/Budysin).

Burger, Julian. (1991), *Die Wächter der Erde: Vom Leben sterbender Völker*. Reinbek bei Hamburg: Rowohlt.

——. (1987), *Report from the Frontier: The State of the World's Indigenous Peoples*. London: Zed Books.

Burns, Tom R. (2001*a*), Dialogue Workshop: Racism and Xenophobia: Key Issues, Mechanisms, and Policy Opportunities. Brussels, 5–6 April .

———. (2001*b*), Dialogue Workshop: Preventing and Combating Racism and Xenophobia in the Enlarged European Union. Uppsala, 8–9 June .

Burns, Tom R., Kamali, Masoud, and Rydgren, Jens. (2001), 'The social construction of xenophobia and other-isms' (Paper). Uppsala: Uppsala Theory Circle.

Burton, John W. (1996), *Conflict Resolution. Its Language and Processes*. Lanham, Md./London: Scarecrow.

———. (1990), *Conflict: Resolution and Provention*. London: Macmillan.

———. ed. (1990*a*), *Conflict: Human Needs Theory*. London: Macmillan.

———. and Dukes, F., eds. (1990*b*. *Conflict: Practices in Management, Settlement and Resolution*. London: Macmillan.

———. and Dukes, F., eds. (1990*c*. *Readings in Management and Resolution*. London: Macmillan.

Cabral, Amilcar. (1974), *Die Revolution der Verdammten*. Berlin: rotbuch.

Calließ, Jörg, ed. (1994), *Treiben Umweltprobleme in Gewaltkonflikte? Ökologische Konflikte im internationalen System und Möglichkeiten ihrer friedlichen Bearbeitung*. Evangelische Akademie Loccum: Loccumer Protokolle 21; Loccum.

———, and Merkel, Christine M., eds. (1995), *Peaceful Settlement of Conflicts as joint Task for International Organisations, Governments and Civil Society*. Evangelische Akademie Loccum:. Loccumer Protokolle 24 (1 & 2); Loccum.

———, and ———, eds. (1994), *Peaceful Settlement of Conflict: A Task for Civil Society. Third Party Intervention*. Evangelische Akademie Loccum: Loccumer Protokolle 9; Loccum.

———, and ———, eds. (1993), *Peaceful Settlement of Conflict: A Task for Civil Society. Possibilities and Instruments for Conflict Management in Cases of Ethno-national Tension*. Evangelische Akademie Loccum: Loccumer Protokolle 7; Loccum.

———, and Moltmann, Bernhard, eds. (1992), *Jenseits der Bipolarität: Aufbruch in eine 'Neue Weltordnung'*. Loccumer Protokolle 4; Loccum.

Carlsson, Ingvar / Han Sung-Joo / Rufus M Kupolati / United Nations. (1999), *Report of the Independent Inquiry into the actions of the United Nations during the 1994 genocide in Rwanda*. New York: UN.

Carnegie Commission on Preventing Deadly Conflict. (1997), *Preventing Deadly Conflict: Final Report*. Washington, DC: Carnegie.

Cars, Göran *et al.* / TSER Project Report. (1999), *Social Exclusion in European Neighbourhoods. Processes, Experiences and Responses*. Brussels: TSER.

Carter Center of Emory University (Conflict Resolution Program) (Foege, William, ed.). (1992), *Resolving Intra-national Conflicts: A Strengthened Role for Non-governmental Actors*. Atlanta: Carter Center.

Carter, April. (2001), *Political Theory of Global Citizenship*. New York: Routledge.

Cashmore, Ellis. (1996), *Dictionary of Race and Ethnic Relations*. Fourth Edition. London/New York: Routledge [orig. (1984].

Center for World Indigenous Studies (Minugh, Carol J., Morris, Glen T., and Ryster, Rudolph C.). (1989), *Indian Self-governance: Perspectives on the Political Status of Indian Nations in the USA*. Kenmore: CWIS.

Chabal, Patrick and Daloz, Jean Pascal. (1999), *Africa Works. Disorder as Political Instrument*. Oxford: James Currey.

Chamberlayne *et al.* / TSER Project Report. (1999), *SOSTRIS. Social Strategies in Risk Societies*. Brussels: TSER.

Chopin, Isabelle / European Network Against Racism. (1999), *Campaigning against racism and xenophobia from a legislative perspective at European level*. Brussels: ENAR.

Chopin, Isabelle and Jan Niessen / Commission for Racial Equality / Migration Policy Group. (2001), *The Starting Line and the Incorporation of the Racial Equality Directive into the National Laws of the EU Member States and Accession States*. Brussels/London: CRE-MPG, March.

———. (1998), 'Proposal for Legislative Measures to Combat Racism and to Promote Equal Rights in the European Union.' London: Starting Line Group and CRE-UK).

Chrétien, Jean Pierre. (1988), 'Les Ethnies ont une histoire', in id. and G. Prunier, *Les Ethnies ont une histoire*. Paris: Karthala.

Churchill, Ward. (1991), *Critical Issues in Native North America* (ii). IWGIA Document 68; Copenhagen.

———. (1989), *Critical Issues in Native North America*. IWGIA Doc 62; Copenhagen.

Clausewitz, Carl von. (1980), *Vom Kriege. Hinterlassenes Werk. Text der Erstaufl. 1832–1834)*, Frankfurt/M.: Ullstein.

Clauss, Bärbel, Koblitz, Katja, and Richter, Detlef, eds. (1993), *Kriegsansichten— Friedensansichten: Vom Umgang mit Konflikten*. Münster: Lit.

Coalition to Stop the Use of Child Soldiers / Mungoven, Rory *et al.* (2001), 'Global Report on Child Soldiers 2001', www.child-soldiers.org/report2001.htlm.

Commission on Global Governance (Carlsson, Ingvar, and Ramphal, Shridath). (1995), *Our Global Neighbourhood*. Oxford: Oxford University Press.

Confederación de los Pueblos Autóctonos de Honduras. (1993), *Ante-proyecto de decreto de la ley de creación de la reserva de la biosfera Tawahka*. Tegucigalpa.

Conference of NGOs (1999), 'An Agenda for Peace, Security and Development in the 21st Century.' Draft Programme of Action. Seoul, Korea. www.conferenceofngos.org .

Conflict Management Group. (var. years), *CMG Update* , quarterly newsletter.

———. (1994), *Peacekeeping, Peacemaking and Humanitarian Assistance in Areas of Conflict*. Cambridge, Mass.: CMG.

———. (1993), *Methods and Strategies in Conflict Prevention. Report of an Expert Consultation in connection with the Activities of the CSCE High Commissioner on National Minorities*. Rome: CMG.

COPRI (Copenhagen Peace Research Institute. (var. years), Working papers. Copenhagen: COPRI.

Corbin, Jane. (1994), *Gaza First. The Secret Norway Channel to Peace between Israel and the PLO*. London: Bloomsbury.

Cornell University Peace Studies Program (Esman, Milton, and Telhami, Shibley). (1995), *The Role of International Organizations in Ethnic Conflict*. Ithaca, New York: Cornell University Press.

Council of Europe (CoE). (1997), (Henning Gjellerod, Rapporteur) *Protection of National Minorities. Report, Doc. 7899)*, Strasburg: CoE.

———. (1997), *Recommendation 1345 (1997) on the Protection of National Minorities*. Strasburg: CoE.

———. (1994), *Framework Convention for the Protection of National Minorities*. Strasburg: CoE.

Council of Ministers of the European Communities (CM-EC). (2000*a*), *Council Directive 2000/43/EC of 29 June 2000 implementing the principle of equal treatment between persons irrespective of racial or ethnic origin*. Official Journal, OJ L 180/22, 19 July.

———. (2000*b*), *Council Directive 2000/78/EC of 27 November 2000 establishing a general framework for equal treatment in employment and occupation*. Official Journal, OJ L 303/16, December 2.

———. (2000*c*), *Council Decision Establishing a Community Action Programme to Combat Discrimination*. Official Journal, L 303, December 2.

CSCE/OSCE (Conference/Organization on Security and Co-operation in Europe). (1994), Documents/statements on or of the CSCE High Commissioner on National Minorities.

——. (1994*a*), Documents/statements on or of the CSCE High Commissioner on National Minorities.

——. (1992), 'Challenges of Change'. Summit Declaration and Decisions of the 1992 Helsinki Follow-up meeting.

DANIDA (Danish International Development Agency). (1995), *Evaluation of Emergency Assistance to Rwanda:* (1)*Terms of Reference*, (2) *Interim Report*, (3) *Final Report*. Copenhagen: DANIDA.

Delanty, Gerard. (2001), 'Ideas for Multicultural Citizenship In Europe.' Discussion Paper. Brussels/Liverpool.

Deng, Francis M., and Zartmann, I. William, eds. (1991), *Conflict Resolution in Africa*. Washington, D.C.: Brookings Institution.

der überblick: See AGKED (Arbeitsgemeinschaft Kirchlicher Entwicklungsdienst).

Despres, Leo A., ed. (1990), *Ethnicity and Resource Competition in Plural Societies*. The Hague: Mouton.

Destexhe, Alan. (1995), *Rwanda and Genocide in the Twentieth Century*. London/East Haven: Pluto.

Deutsches Überseeinstitut (Hamburg) (Betz, Joachim, and Brüne, Stefan). var years. *Jahrbuch Dritte Welt. Daten, Übersichten, Analysen*. Munich: Beck.

Dinstein, Yoram. (1981), *Models of Autonomy*. New Brunswick: Transaction Books.

Duffield, Mark. (1994), 'The Political Economy of Internal War: Asset Transfer, Complex Emergencies and International Aid', in Macrae and Zwi (eds.) 1994: 50–69.

Eckhardt, William. (1993), 'Wars and Deaths 1945–1992', in Ruth L. Sivard (ed.), *World Military and Social Expenditures 1993)*, Washington, D.C.: World Priorities.

—— 1991), 'Warfare's Toll 1500–1990', in Ruth L. Sivard (ed.), *World Military and Social Expenditures 1991)*, Washington, D.C.: World Priorities.

ECOR (Ethnic Conflicts Research Project). (2003), *Rwanda's Response to Genocide: Establishing Gachacha Jurisdiction*. Report. (ECOR 28). Moers: IFEK–IRECOR.

——. (2002), *Free Nagaland—NE-India's unsolved question*. Compiler of Interviews. ECOR 20; Moers: IFEK-IRECOR.

——. (2001), *War in the Congo and the Role of United Nations*. Study. (ECOR 26). Moers: IFEK–IRECOR.

——. (1999), *Ethnicity and Mass Violence*. Study. ECOR 19; Moers: IFEK-IRECOR.

——. (1998*a*), *Ongoing Crisis in Central Africa. Conflict impact assessment and policy options*. Study. ECOR 18; Moers: IFEK-IRECOR.

——. (1998*b*), *Struggle for Survival in the Decade of the World's Indigenous Peoples. Analysis and reports from the frontiers*. Compiler of Interviews. ECOR 17; Moers: IFEK-IRECOR.

——. (1997*a*), *Ethnicity and State in Former British India*. ECOR 9; Moers: IFEK-IRECOR. (1ˢᵗ ed. (1995).

——. (1997*b*), *Horn of Africa I: Ethiopia versus Oromia*. Moers: IFEK-IRECOR.

——. (1997*c*), *Horn of Africa II: Ethiopia, Eritrea and Sudan between change and civil war*. Compiler of Interviews. ECOR 14; Moers: IFEK-IRECOR.

——. (1997*d*), *Intra-state conflicts and ethnicity: Types, causes, escalation and peace strategies*. Study. ECOR 16; Moers: IFEK-IRECOR.

——. (1997*e*), *Nicaragua's Caribbean coast regions: Recognizing multiplicity—many issues unsolved*. Study. ECOR 15; Moers: IFEK-IRECOR.

——. (1995), *The United Nations in the Decade for the Indigenous Peoples of the World: New Challenges after 50 Years*. ECOR 12; Moers: IFEK-IRECOR.

——. (1995*a*), *Ethnicity and State in Rwanda 1994/95: Conflict Prevention after the*

Genocide. Assessment and Documents. ECOR 11; Moers: IFEK-IRECOR.

———. (1995*b*), *Ethnicity and State in Burma: Ethno-nationalist Revolution and Civil War 1949–1995,* ECOR 10; Moers: IFEK-IRECOR.

———. (1994), *Ethnicity and State in the Third World: UN-WGIP 1989–94: Strengthening Indigenous Movements.* ECOR 8; Moers: IFEK-IRECOR.

———. (1993), *Ethnicity and State in Eastern Nicaragua: Autonomous Governance in Yapti Tasba.* ECOR 6; Moers: IFEK-IRECOR.

———. (1992), *Ethnicity and State in Sudan: Civil War, Politics of Famine, and Dim Prospects for Conflict Resolution.* ECOR 3; Tegelen: ECOR.

———. (1992*a*), *The Liberation of Eritrea.* ECOR 4; Tegelen: ECOR.

———. (1992*b*), Ethnicity *and State in Ethiopia: The Empire Strikes Back.* ECOR 4; Tegelen: ECOR.

———. (1991), *Ethnicity and State in Burma 1990: Ethno-nationalist Revolution Facing Massive Military Onslaught.* ECOR 2; Zurich: ECOR.

———. (1990), *Neue Weltordnung: 'Dialektik zwischen Orient und Okzident'. Ein Gespräch mit Johan Galtung.* ECOR-Papers Series, no. 3), Moers/Tegelen: ECOR.

———. (1989), *Ethnicity and State in Nicaragua: Nicaragua's East Coast Minority Peoples.* ECOR 1; Zurich: ECOR.

ECRI, European Commission against Racism and Intolerance. (2000), *General Policy Recommendation No. 2 on 'Specialist bodies to combat racism, xenophobia, anti-semitism and intolerance on national level' and Appendix.*

———. (1999), *Activities of the Council of Europe with relevance to combating racism and intolerance.* CR(99) 56 final.

Elsenhans, Hartmut. (1985), 'Der periphere Staat: Zum Stand der entwicklungstheoretischen Diskussion', in Franz Nuscheler (ed.), *Dritte Welt-Forschung.* PVS-Sonderheft 16; Opladen.

Elwert, Georg. (1995), 'Gewalt, Gerüchte und das liebe Geld: Kriegsökonomie und ethnische Mobilisierung'. *blätter des iz3w,* 209: 19–19.

———. (1990), 'Nationalismus und Ethnizität'. *Kölner Zeitschrift für Soziologie und Sozialpsychologie,* 3: 404–64.

———, and Waldmann, Peter, eds. (1989), *Ethnizität im Wandel.* Saarbrücken: Breiten-bach.

ENAR, European Network Against Racism. (2000), 'Racism is not an opinion, it is a crime.' Conference Paper. Strasbourg, October (www.icare.to/).

ENCOP (Environment and Conflicts Project) (Böge, Volker). (1992), 'Proposal for an Analytical Framework to Grasp 'Environmental Conflict'', Schweizerische Friedens-stiftung: ENCOP Paper 1; Berne.

——— (Libiszewski, Stephan). (1992), 'What Is an Environmental Conflict?', Schweizerische Friedensstiftung: ENCOP Paper 1; Berne.

Engdahl, F. William. (1992), *Mit der Ölwaffe zur Weltmacht: Der Weg zur neuen Weltordnung.* Wiesbaden: Böttinger.

Engert, Steffi, and Gartenschläger, Uwe. (1989), *Der Aufbruch: Alternative Bewegungen in der Sowjetunion. Perestroika von unten.* Hamburg: Rowohlt.

Esmann, Milton J., and Telhami, Shibley (eds.). (1995), *International Organizations and Ethnic Conflict.* Ithaca, NY/London: Cornell University Press.

———. (1994), *Ethnic Politics.* Ithaca/London: Cornell University Press.

Estel, Bernd, and Mayer, Tilman. (1994), *Das Prinzip Nation in modernen Gesellschaften. Länderdiagnosen und theoretische Perspektiven.* Opladen: Westdeutscher Verlag.

Ethnopolitical Studies Centre (Payne, Emil, ed.) 1993), *Socio-political Situation in the Post-Soviet World.* Moscow: Foreign Policy Association.

EUMC, European Monitoring Centre on Racism and Xenophobia, by SORA / Thalhammer, Eva *et al.* (2001), *Attitudes towards minority groups in the European Union. A special analysis of the Eurobarometer 2000 survey on behalf of EUMC*. Vienna: EUMC, March.

——. (2000), *Annual Report 1999)*, Vienna: EUMC.

European Commission / Liberatore, Angela. (1999), *Governance and Citizenship in Europe. Some Research Directions*. Brussels: Research DG F.4), December.

European Conference against Racism 'All different, all equal: from principle to practice'. (2000), *Conclusions*. Strasburg, October 16.

European Platform for Conflict Prevention and Transformation, EPCPT / Mekenkamp *et al.* (2002), *Searching for Peace in Asia*. Utrecht: EPCPT, forthcoming.

——. (Mekenkamp *et al.*) (1999), *Searching for Peace in Africa. An Overview of Conflict Prevention and Management Activities*. Utrecht: EPCPT.

——. (and PIOOM / Berghof, eds.) (1998), *Prevention and Management of Conflicts. An international directory*. Utrecht: EPCPT.

European Women's Lobby (EWL). (2001), 'Combating Racism and Gender Discrimination in the European Union.' A Contribution from the European Women's Lobby to the World Conference against Racism. Brussels: EWL, March.

Evans-Pritchard, Edward E., and Fortes, Meyer, eds. (1940), *African Political Systems*. London: Oxford University Press, esp. 272–96: 'The Nuer of the Southern Sudan'.

Evers, Hans-Dieter, and Schiel, Tilman. (1988), *Strategische Gruppen: Vergleichende Studien zu Staat, Bürokratie und Klassenbildung*. Berlin. Reimer.

Fairbanks, John K. (1968), *The Chinese World Order*. Cambridge, Mass: Harvard University Press.

Fanon, Frantz. (1963), *The Wretched of the Earth*. New York: Grove Press (translated from *Les damnés de la terre*. Paris: Ed. François Maspéro, 1961).

Faulenbach, Bernd, and Timmermann, Heinz, eds. (1993), *Nationalismus und Demokratie: Gesellschaftliche Modernisierung und nationale Idee in Mittel- und Osteuropa*. Koblenz: Klartext.

Feith, Herb, and Smith, Alan. (1993), 'Self-determination in the 1990s: The Need for UN Guidelines and Machinery to Resolve Ethno-nationalist Conflicts'. Mimeograph, Canberra.

FIER (Foundation on Inter-Ethnic Relations). (1999), *The Lund Recommendations on the Effective Participation of National Minorities in Public Life and Explanatory Note*. The Hague: FIER, September.

——. (1994), *Integrated Research Program in Support of the CSCE High Commissioner on National Minorities*. The Hague: FIER.

Fisher, Roger, and Ury, William. (1987), *Getting to Yes. Negotiating Agreement Without Giving In*. London: Arrow [orig. (1982].

Fisher, Ronald J. (1989), *The Social Psychology of Intergroup and International Conflict*. New York: Springer.

Fitzduff, Mari. (1996), *Beyond Violence: Conflict Resolution Processes in Northern Ireland*. Tokyo: United Nations University.

Förster, Stig and Hirschfeld, Gerhard (eds.). (1999), *Genozid in der modernen Geschichte* (Genocide in Modern History). *Jahrbuch für Historische Friedensforschung*, vol. 7. Münster-Hamburg-London: LIT Verlag.

Foucault, Michel. (1977), *Discipline and Punish: The Birth of the Prison*. Harmondsworth: Penguin.

——. (1973), *The Birth of the Clinic: An Archaeology of Medical Perception*. London: Tavistock.

——. (1972), *The Archeology of Knowledge*. London: Tavistock.

Fourth World Center (Sills, Marc A., and Morris, Glenn T.). (1993), *Indigenous Peoples' Politics: An Introduction*, vol. i. University of Colorado at Denver.

Frank, Andre Gunder. (1980), *Abhängige Akkumulation und Unterentwicklung*. Frankfurt: edition suhrkamp.

Freedom House. (var. years), *Freedom in the World: The Annual Survey of Political Rights and Civil Liberties*. New York: Freedom House.

——. (var. years), *Freedom Review*.

Fritsch-Oppermann, Sybille, ed. (1995), *Minderheiten, Autonomie und Selbstbestimmung: Kollektiv- und Individualrechte von Minderheiten und die Menschenrechte*. Loccumer Protokolle 62; Loccum.

Fürer-Haimendorff, Christoph von. (1982), *Tribes of India: The Struggle for Survival*. London: Oxford University Press.

Furley, Oliver, ed. (1995), *Conflict in Africa*. London/New York: I.B. Tauris.

Gabbert, Wolfgang. (1991), 'Ethnizität—die soziale Organisation kultureller Unterschiede', in id., *Creoles—Afroamerikaner im karibischen Tiefland von Nicaragua*. Münster: Lit., 16–37.

Galtung, Johan. (2002), 'One Hundred Years of Years of German History – A Deep Cilture Perspective', in Schmidt / Trittmann 2002: 203–16.

——. (and Carl G. Jacobson) (2000a), *Searching for Peace. The road to TRANSCEND*. London: Pluto Press.

——. (2000b), 'Friedensvisionen für das 21. Jahrhundert'; Schmidt, Hajo/Institut für Frieden und Demokratie: Kultur und Konflikt. Reader. Hagen:IFD.

——. (1998), *Frieden mit friedlichen Mitteln. Friede und Konflikt, Entwicklung und Kultur*. Opladen: Leske + Budrich.

——. (1998a), *After Violence: 3R, Reconstruction, Reconciliation, Resolution. Coping With Visible and Invisible Effects of War and Violence*. on www.transcend.org.

——. (1997), 'Peace education is only meaningful if it leads to action'. Interview in: UNESCO Courier, January.

——. (1997a), *Conflict Experience 1952–97*. http://www.transcend.org/ [Concrete Proposals for Conflict Resolution in 35 Conflict Cases].

——. (1997b), *Conflict Transformation by Peaceful Means. The Transcend Method*. The Mini-version. A Manual Prepared for the United Nations Disaster Management Training Program. Geneva: UN [online on www.transcend.org].

——. (1996), *Peace by Peaceful Means: Peace and Conflict, Development and Civilization*. London: Sage.

——. (1994), 'Peace and Conflict Research in the Age of Cholera: Ten Pointers to the Future'. Unpub. paper, Malta: IPRA Conference.

——. (1994a), *Menschenrechte—anders gesehen*. Frankfurt/M.: edition suhrkamp.

——. (1994b), 'Conflict Interventions', in Calließ and Merkel (eds.) 1994: 395–417.

——. (1994c), 'Civic Approaches to Conflict', in Calließ and Merkel (eds.): 115–22.

——. (1992), 'Konfliktformationen in der Welt von morgen', in Bächler *et al.*, (eds.) 1992: 229–61.

——. (1992a), 'Conflict Resolution as Conflict Transformation'. *IRIPAZ*, 3/6.

——. (1977–88), *Essays in Methodology*, i–iii (1979, 1988). Copenhagen: Ejlers.

——. (1975–88), *Essays in Peace Research*, i–vi. Copenhagen: Ejlers.

——. (1972), 'Eine strukturelle Theorie des Imperialismus', in Senghaas (ed.), 1972: 29–104.

——. (1964), 'An Editorial'. *Journal of Peace Research*. 1/1: 1–4.

Gantzel, Klaus Jürgen, and Schlichte, Klaus, eds. (1996), *Das Kriegsgeschehen 1995. Daten und Tendenzen der Kriege und bewaffneten Konflikte im Jahre 1995*. SEF: Interdependenz 20; Bonn.

——, and ——. (1994), *Das Kriegsgeschehen 1993. Daten und Tendenzen der Kriege und bewaffneten Konflikte im Jahre 1993*. SEF: Interdependenz 16; Bonn.

——, Schwinghammer, Torsten, and Siegleberg, Jens. (1992), *Kriege der Welt. Ein systematisches Register der kreigerischenKonflikte 1985–1992.* SEF: Interdependenz 13; Bonn.

——, and Siegelberg, Jens. (1990), *Kriege der Welt. Ein systematisches Register der kreigerischenKonflikte 1985–1990.* SEF: Interdependenz 4; Bonn.

Garcia, Ed, Macuja, Julio, and Tolosa, Benjamin. (1994), *Participation in Governance: The People's Right.* Manila: Ateneo University Press.

Gärtner, Heinz. (1992), *Wird Europa sicherer? Zwischen kollektiver und nationaler Sicherheit.* Vienna: Braumüller.

Gellner, Ernest. (1983), *Nation and Nationalism.* Oxford: Blackwell.

——, (and Micaud, Charles, eds.). (1972), *Arabs and Berbers.* London: Lexington Books.

GfbV (Gesellschaft für bedrohte Völker). (var. years), *pogrom.*

—— (Mayr, Wolfgang, and Geismar, Inge). (1994), 'Bedrohte Völker'. Pocket diary, Göttingen: GfbV.

Ghai, Yash. (2001), *Public Participation and Minorities.* London: Minority Rights Group.

Glasl, Friedrich. (1990), *Konfliktmanagment. Ein Handbuch.* Berne: Haupt. (Typologies 47–82, escalation model 215–87.)

Glavanis, Pandeli *et al.* / TSER Project Report. (2001), *'Muslim Voices' in the European Union: The Stranger within Community, Identity and Employment.* Brussels: TSER.

Glazer, Nathan, and Moynihan, Daniel, eds. (1976), *Ethnicity: Theory and Experience.* Cambridge, Mass.: Harvard University Press.

Goldstone, Richard. (1995), 'Exposing the Truth'. Interview with the UN prosecutor for the former Yugoslavia and Rwanda in *The Courier*, 153: 2–5.

Goor, Luc van de, Rupesinghe, Kumar, and Sciarone, Paul (eds.). (1996), *Between Development and Destruction. An Enquiry into the Causes of Conflict in Post- Colonial States.* The Hague, etc.: NIIR (Netherlands Institute of International Relations) Clingendael/Macmillan/St. Martin's.

Greive, Wolfgang, ed. (1994), *Identität und Ethnizität.* Loccumer Protokolle 57; Loccum.

Grimshaw, Allen D. (1999), 'Genocide and Democide', in Kurtz / Turpin (eds.), 1999: Vol. 1, 53–74.

Grossman, Zoltan. (2001), *A Century of U.S. Military Interventions: From Wounded Knee to Afghanistan.* www.zmag.org/CrisesCurEvts/interventions.htm.

Gruiters, Jan, and Tresoldi, Efrem. (1994), *Sudan: A Cry for Peace.* Brussels: Pax Christi.

Guibernau, Monserrat / Hutchinson, John, eds. (2001), *Understanding Nationalism.* Cambridge: Polity Press.

Gurr, Ted Robert *et al.* / CIDCM, University of Maryland, College Park. (2001), *Peace and Conflict 2001), A Global Survey of Armed Conflicts, Self-Determination Movements, and Democracy.* College Park: CIDCM.

——. (2000), *Peoples versus States.* Washington: US Institute of Peace Press (online at Minorities at Risk site www.bsos.umd.edu/cidcm/mar.).

——, (and Barbara Harff). (1996), *Early Warning of Communal Conflicts and Genocide: Linking Empirical Research to International Responses.* Tokyo: United Nations University Press.

——. (1994), 'Peoples against States: Ethnopolitical Conflict and the Changing World System,' *International Studies Quarterly*, 38: 348–77.

——. (1993), *Minorities at Risk. A Global View of Ethnopolitcal Conflict.* Washington, D.C.: US Institute of Peace.

——. (1993a), 'Why Minorities Rebel. A Global Analysis of Communal Mobilization and Conflict since 1945'. *International Political Science Review*, 14/2: 161–201.

——, and Harff, Barbara. (1992), 'Victims of the State: Genocides, Politicides and Group Repression since 1945,' *Revista del IRIPAZ*, 3/6: 96–110.

Haar, Wim De. (1995), 'Ethnic Conflict Management Theory. An Introduction to Theory and Practice: The Case of Bosnia', in Calließ and Merkel (eds.) 1995: 214–33.

Habermas, Jürgen. (1994), 'Annerkennungskämpfe im demokratischen Rechtsstat', *Revista del IRIPAZ*, 5/9: 5–25.

Harff, Barbara. (1999), (with Gurr, Ted R. and Unger, Alan). 'Preconditions of Genocide and Politicide: 1955–1998.' Paper. State Failure Task Force.

——. (and Gurr Ted R.). (1997), *Systematic Early Warning of Humanitarian Emergencies.* Maryland: CIDCM.

——. (1992), 'Recognizing Genocides and Politicides'; in: Fein, Helen (ed.), *Genocide Watch.* New Haven: Yale University Press, 1992: 27–41.

Heinrich-Böll-Stiftung (Büttner, Christian *et al.*). (1995), *Zivile Konfliktbearbeitung und Gewaltprävention: Beiträge gesellschaftlicher Akteure zur Umsetzung der Agenda for Peace,* HBS-Dokumentationen 8; Cologne.

Heintze, Hans-Joachim. (1995), *Autonomie und Völkerrecht: Verwirklichung des Selbsbestimmungsrechtes der Völker innerhalb bestehender Staaten.* SEF: Interdependenz 19; Bonn.

Heinz, Marco. (1993), *Ethnizität und ethnische Identität. Eine Begriffsgeschichte.* Bonn: Holos (diss. University of Bonn).

Henrard, Kristin. (2000), *Devising an Adequate System of Minority Protection: Individual Human Rights, Minority Rights, and the Right to Self-Determination.* Martinus Nijhoff.

Héraud, Guy. (1963), *L'Europe des ethnies.* Paris: Presses d'Europe.

HIIK, Heidelberger Institut für Internationale Konfliktforschung, (var. years), *Conflict barometer.* Online http://www.hiik.de/.

——. (2000), *KOSIMO Manual.* Online http://www.hiik.de.

Hirsch, Klaus, ed. (1996), *Interkulturelle Konflikte. Seminar zu Konzepten und Verfahren interkulturellen Lernens.* Protokoll 9; Bad Boll.

Hobsbawm, Eric J. (1992), *Nations and Nationalism Since 1780), Programme, Myth, Reality.* Second Edition. Cambridge: Cambridge University Press [orig. (1990].

Hobsbawm, Eric J. and Ranger, Terence (eds.). (1983), *The Invention of Tradition.* Cambridge: Cambridge University Press.

Hoekema, André. (1994), *Do Joint Decision-Making Boards Enhance Chances for a New Partnership between State and Indigenous Peoples?* Amsterdam: University of Amsterdam.

Hofmann, Rainer. (1992), 'Minderheitenschutz in Europa. Überblick über die völker- und staatsrechtliche Lage'. *Zeitschrift für ausländisches öffentliches Recht und Völkerrecht,* 52/1: 1–66.

Hofmeier, Rolf, and Matthies, Völker, eds. (1992), *Vergessene Kriege in Afrika.* Göttingen: Lamuv.

Holsti, Kalevi J. (1996), *The State, War, and the State of War.* Cambridge, etc.: Cambridge University Press.

——. (1991), 'War Issues, Attitudes, and Explanations', in id., *Peace and War: Armed Conflicts and International Order 1648–1989),* Cambridge: Cambridge University Press, 306–34.

Hörig, Reiner. (1990), *Selbst die Götter haben sie uns geraubt: Indiens Adivasi kämpfen ums Überleben* Göttingen: GfbV .

Horn, Klaus. (1988), *Gewalt—Aggression—Krieg.* AFK-Schriftenreihe 13; Baden-Baden.

Horowitz, Donald L. (1992), 'Irredentas and Secession: Adjacent Phenomena, Neglected Connections', in A. D. Smith 1992.

——. (1985), *Ethnic Groups in Conflict.* Berkeley: University of California Press.

Huber, Konrad. (1994), *The CSCE's New Role in the East.* (Radio Liberty: Report 3: 31).

——. (1994*a*), *Averting Inter-ethnic Conflict. An Analysis of the CSCE High*

Commissioner on National Minorities in Estonia. (Conflict Resolution Program, Carter Center, Emory University, Atlanta; 1994).

Human Rights Watch (Africa Watch, Americas Watch, Asia Watch, Middle East Watch, Helsinki Watch). (various), *World Report.* New York: Fund for Free Expression.

——. (Des Forges, Alison). (1999), *Leave None to Tell the Story. Genocide in Rwanda.* New York: HRW.

Huntington, Samuel P. (1996), *The Clash of Civilizations and the Remaking of World Order.* New York: Simon & Schuster.

——. (1993*a*), 'The clash of civilizations?' In: Foreign Affairs, Summer 1993, 23–49.

——. (1993*b*), 'If not civilizations, what? Paradigms of the post-cold war world'. Foreign Affairs, Nov.-Dec., 186–194.

IA (International Alert). (var. years), Reports. London: IA.

——. (Atmar, Haneef and Goodhand, Jonathan). (2001), *Aid, Conflict and Peacebuilding in Afghanistan: What Lessons can be Learned?* Report. London: IA.

——. (Clapham, Andrew *et al.*). (2001), *The Mercenary Issue at the UN Commission on Human Rights: The Need for a New Approach.* Report. London: IA.

——. (Goodhand, Jonathan with Philippa Atkinson). (2001), *Conflict and Aid: Enhancing the Peacebuilding Impact of International Engagement. A Synthesis of Findings from Sri Lanka, Liberia and Afghanistan.* Report. London: IA.

——. (Goodhand, Jonathan). (2001), Sri Lanka, Conflict and Aid: Enhancing the Peacebuilding Impact of International Engagement Report. London: IA.

——. (1994), *Self-determination. Report of the Martin Ennals Symposium.* Saskatoon.

——. (Rupesinghe, Kumar). (1994*a*), 'Towards a Policy Framework for Advancing Preventive Diplomacy'. Paper, Amsterdam.

——. (1993), *Conflict in the North Caucasus and Georgia.* Report. London: IA.

ICAR (Institute for Conflict Analysis and Resolution). (var. years), Working Papers. Fairfax: George Mason University.

ICRA (International Commission for the Right of Aboriginal Peoples). (var. years), *Info-Action.*

IISS (International Institute for Strategic Studies). (var. years), *The Military Balance.* London: Brassey's.

——. (var. years), *Strategic Survey.* Oxford, London, etc: Oxford University Press/IISS.

INEF (Institut für Entwicklung und Frieden) (Debiel, Tobias). (1995), 'Die Vereinten Nationen in einer Welt des Umbruchs: Chancen und Grenzen einer kooperativen Friedenspolitik'. *Sozialwisssenschaftliche Informationen*, 24/3: 196–200.

——. (1993), *Krisen, Kriege und Konfliktbewältigung. Daten—Analysen—Schluß-folgerungen.* Duisburg: INEF.

——. (var. years), 'Kriege', in SEF, *Globale Trends. Daten zur Weltentwicklung.* Frankfurt/M.: Fischer.

Institute of Southeast Asian Studies (Chen Lufan *et al.*). (1990), *Proceedings of the 4th International Conference on Thai Studies.* Kunming: ISAS, i–iv.

Instituto Indigenista Interamericano (Stavenhagen, Rodolfo, and Iturralde, Diego, eds.). (1990), *Entre la ley y la costumbre: El derecho consuetudinario indígena en América Latina.* Mexico: Siglo XXI.

InterAfrica Group / Justice Africa. (2002), *The Economic Dimension to the African Union.* Issues Paper for the African Union Symposium. ADF III. Addis Ababa: IAG.

International Commission of Jurists. (1992), *The Events in East Pakistan 1971), A Legal Study.* Geneva: UNCHR 1972

International Social Science Council (Väyrynen, Raimo, ed.). (1991), *New Directions in Conflict Theory: Conflict Resolution and Transformation.* London: Sage.

Isajiw, Wsevolod W. (1999), *Understanding Diversity: Ethnicity and Race in the Canadian Context*. Toronto: Thompson Educational Publishing, Inc.

Ishiyama, John T. and Breuning, Marijke. (1998), *Ethnopolitics in the New Europe*. Boulder / London: Lynne Rienner Publishers.

ISHR (International Service for Human Rights)/MAHR (Minnesota Advocates for Human Rights). (1992), *Orientation Manual: The UN Commission on Human Rights*. Geneva: ISHR.

IWGIA (International Work Group for Indigenous Affairs). (var. years), 82 Docs. 1971–94 on situation of indigenous peoples/newsletters.

——. (1995), *El Mundo indígena 1994–5)*, Copenhagen: IWGIA.

——. (1993), *Yearbook 1992)*, Copenhagen: Scantryk.

——. (1989), *Indigenous Self-government in the Americas*. IWGIA Document 63; Copenhagen.

JEEAR (Joint Evaluation of Emergency Assistance to Rwanda) (David Millwood, chief ed.). (1996), *The International Response to Conflict and Genocide: Lessons from the Rwanda Experience*. 5 vols. Copenhagen: JEEAR.

Jenkins, J. Craig, and Klandermans, Bert (eds.). (1995), *The Politics of Social Protest: Comparative Perspectives on States and Social Movements*. London: UCL Press.

Jentleson, Bruce W. (1998), *Preventive diplomacy and ethnic conflict: possible, difficult, necessary*. Working Paper. Institute on Global Conflict and Cooperation; www.ciaonet.org/.

Johann, Bernd. (1993), *GUS ohne Zukunft? Eine Region zwischen Zerfall und neuen Allianzen*. SEF: Interdependenz 15; Bonn.

Jongman, Albert J., ed. (1996), *Contemporary Genocides: Causes, Cases, Consequences*. Leiden: PIOOM, etc.

Journals of Interest: *AfricAsia*; *Blätter des iz3W*; *The Courier* (Brussels: EU-ACP); *Cultural Survival*;*The Economist*; *Indigenous Affairs* (Copenhagen: IWGIA); *Journal of Peace Research* (Oslo: PRIO/Sage); *Le Monde diplomatique*; *Peace Review*; *pogrom*; *South*; *Der Spiegel*; *Südwind*; *Survival*; *Die Wochenzeitung*.

Kadelbach, Stefan. (1992), 'Zwingende Normen des humanitären Völkerrechts', in Deutsches Rotes Kreuz, *Humanitäres Völkerrecht*. Bonn: DRK, 118–24.

Kamali, Masoud. (2001), 'Conceptualizing the 'Other', Institutionalized Discrimination, and Cultural Racism.' Paper. Uppsala: Dep. for Sociology.

Kawczynski, Rudko. (1997), 'The Politics of Romani Politics'; in *Transitions*, Vol. 4, No. 4, September.

Kelly, Henry. (2002), *'Dirty Bombs and Basement Nukes: The Terrorist Nuclear Threat'. Testimony at a Senate Foreign Relations Committee Hearing*. Washington DC, on March 6; online see http://www.fas.org/ssp/docs/kelly_testimony_030602.pdf

Kelman, Herbert C., and Hamilton, V. Lee. (1989), *Crimes of Obedience: Towards a Social Psychology of Authority and Responsibility*. New Haven: Yale University Press.

Kemp, Walter, ed. *Quiet Diplomacy in Action: The OSCE High Commissioner on National Minorities*. Dordrecht, The Hague, Boston, New York, and London: Kluwer Academic Publishers.

Khader, Bichara. (1997), 'L'imagination collectif occidental sur l'orient arabo-musulman.' In Lehners 1997.

Kidron, Michael, and Segal, Ronald. (1992), *Der politische Weltatlas*. Bonn: Dietz.

Kiernan, Ben. (2000), 'Bringing the Khmer Rouge to Justice.' *Human Rights Review*. 1, 3: 92–108, April-June.

——. (1996), *The Pol Pot Regime. Race, Power, and Genocide in Cambodia under the Khmer Rouge, 1975–79)*, New Haven / London: Yale University Press.

Klute, Georg. (1995), 'Der Tuaregkonflikt in Mali und Niger', in Deutsches Überseeinstitut 1996: 146–61.

Koch, Christine, ed. (1992), *Schöne neue Weltordnung*. Zurich: Rotpunkt.

Koppe, Karlheinz. (1995), *Der unerreichbare Friede: Überlegungen zu einem komplexen Begriff und seinen forschungspolitischen Konsequenzen.* AFB-Texte 1; Bonn.

Kößtler, Reinhart, and Schiel, Tilman. (1995), 'Ethnizität und Ethno-nationalismus'. *Widerspruch*, 30: 47–59.

Kramer, Fritz, and Sigrist, Christian, eds. (1978), *Gesellschaften ohne Staat.* 2 vols. Frankfurt/M.: Syndikat.

Kriesi, Hanspeter. (1995), 'The Political Opportunity Structure of New Social Movements: Its Impact on Their Mobilization', Jenkins and Klandermans (eds.) 1995: 167–198.

Kritz, Neil J., ed. (1995), *Transitional Justice: How Emerging Democracies Reckon with Former Regimes.* Washington, D.C.: US Institute for Peace Press.

Kühne, Winrich. (1992), 'Demokratisierung in Vielvölkerstaaten'. *Nord-Süd aktuell*, 2/VI: 290–300.

Kuper, Leo. (1981), Genocide: Its Political Use in the Twentieth Century. New Haven / London: Yale University Press.

Kurtz, Lester, and Turpin, Jennifer (eds.). (1999), *Encyclodedia of Violence, Peace, and Conflict.* 3 vols. San Diego, London, etc.: Academic Press.

Kymlicka, Will. (1996), *Multicultural Citizenship. A Liberal Theory of Minority Rights.* Oxford etc.: Oxford University Press.

Laely, Thomas. (1994), 'Ethnien à la burundaise', in Müller Co-ord. (1994: 207–47.

Lederach, John Paul. (1998), *Preparing For Peace: Conflict Transformation across Cultures.* Syracuse: Syracuse University Press.

——. (1994), 'Building Peace: Sustainable Reconciliation in Divided Societies'. Draft paper, Tokyo (United Nations University).

Lehners, Jean Paul (ed.). (1997), *L'Islam et l'espace euro-méditerranéen.* Luxembourg: CUL.

Lemarchand, René. (1994), 'The Apocalypse in Rwanda'. *Cultural Survival Quarterly*, 18/2–3: 29–33.

Lenin, Vladimir Ilyich. (1988), 'Zur Frage der Nationalitäten', in *Lenins Vermächtnis.* Moscow: APN.

——. (1961), 'Über das Selbstbestimmungsrecht der Nationen', in *Lenins•Werke*, xx. Berlin: Dietz.

——. (1961a), '§14: Die nationale Frage: Die Aufgaben des Proletariats in unserer Revolution', in *Werke*, xxiv. Berlin: Dietz.

Lentz, Carola. (1995), 'Joker im Spiel. Ethnizität: Moralische Gemeinschaft oder politische Strategie?'. *blätter des iz3w*, 209: 14–17.

Leuzinger, Elsy, ed. (1985), *Kunst der Naturvölker.* Propyläen Kunstgeschichte 22; Frankfurt am M./Berlin/Vienna.

Lijphart, Arend. (1984), *Democracies: Patterns of Majoritarian and Consensus Government.* New Haven: Yale University Press.

——. (1977), *Democracy in Plural Societies. A Comparative Exploration.* New Haven/London: Yale University Press.

Lyons, Gene M., and Michael Mastanduno, eds. (1995), *Beyond Westphalia? State Sovereignty and International Intervention.* Baltimore: Johns Hopkins University Press.

Lyons, Oren and Mohawk, John C. (eds.). (1992), Exiled in the Land of the Free: Democracy, Indian Nations and the U.S. Constitution. Santa Fe, New Mexico: Clear Light Publishers.

Macrae, Joanna, and Zwi, Anthony, eds. (1994), *War and Hunger: Rethinking International Responses to Complex Emergencies.* London: Zed.

Mader, Gerald, Eberwein, Wolf-Dieter, and Vogt, Wolfgang R. / ÖSFK (eds.). (1997), *Europa im Umbruch: Chancen und Risiken der Friedensentwicklung nach dem Ende der Systemkonfrontation.* ÖSFK-Studien, Band 2), Münster (agenda).

Mall, Hugh. (1998), *The Peacemakers: Peaceful Settlements of Disputes Since 1945)*, Houndsmills: Macmillan Press.

Mandal, B.P., Chairman, Backward Classes Commission / Government of India. (1980), *Report of the Backward Classes Commission. First Part. Volumes I & II.* New Delhi: GOI 31/12/80.

Mann, Michael, ed. (1990), *The Rise and Decline of the Nation State.* Oxford: Blackwell.

Mannens, Wolf. (1994), 'Cultural Rights: A Bridge between Individual and Collective Rights'. Mimeograph, The Hague.

Martinelli, Marta. (1998), *Mediation Activities by non-State Actors: an Account of Sant'Egidio's Initiatives.* Working Paper 9), Copenhagen: COPRI.

Martiniello, Marco. (2001), 'Affirmative Action and Racism.' Paper for the Workshop Racism and Xenophobia. Brussels, April 5–6.

Matthies, Volker, ed. (1995), *Vom Krieg zum Frieden: Kriegsbeendigung und Friedenskonsolidierung.* Bremen: Temmen.

———. (1993), *Frieden durch Einmischung?* Bonn: Dietz.

Mazrui, Ali. (1994), 'Global Apartheid: Structural and Overt'. *Alternatives,* 19, 195–93.

Mbaya, Etienne Richard. (1992), 'Relations between Individual and Collective Human Rights', in Hohnholz *et al.* (eds.), *Law and State.* Tübingen: Institut für wissenschaftliche Zusammenarbeit, 7–23.

McCorquodale, Robert, ed. (2000), *Self-Determination in International Law.* Aldershot: Ashgate.

McDonald, John W. / Bendahmane, Diane B. (1987), *Conflict resolution: Track two diplomacy.* Washington D.C.: US Government Printing.

McDowall, David. (1991), *The Kurds.* London: MRG.

McWhinney, Edward. (2000), *The United Nations and the New World Order for a New Millenium: Self-Determination, State Succession, and Humanitarian Intervention.* Dordrecht, etc.: Kluwer Academic .

Medecins Sans Frontieres / Doctors Without Borders. (1997), *World in Crisis. The Politics of Survival at the End of the Twentieth Century.* London/New York: Routledge.

Meillassoux, Claude. (1976), *'Die wilden Früchte der Frau'—Über häusliche Produktion und kapitalistische Wirtschaft.* Frankfurt/M.: Syndikat. (Orig. (1975), *Femmes, greniers et capitaux* Paris: Maspero.).

Memorial Human Right Center, Moscow. (1992), *Annual Report.* Moscow: HRC.

Merkel, Christine M. (1995), *Zivile Konflikttransformation. Gutachten: Zivile Gewaltreduzierung und Streitbeilegung in ethno-nationalen Spannungsfeldern. Aufgaben, Konzepte, Instrumente und Institutionen.* Loccum: Evan. Akademie.

Midlarsky, Manus I., ed. (1992), *The Internationalization of Communal Strife.* New York: Routledge.

Mietzsch, Oliver. (1993), 'Der Beitrag von internationalen Regimen zur Lösung von Konflikten', in Clauss, Koblitz, and Richter (eds.) 1993: 165–80.

———. 'Die KSZE als regionale Institution zur Konfliktverhütung', in Staack (ed.) 1992: 91–117.

Millennium Forum / Weiss, Cora *et al.* (2000), The Priority Actions for Civil Society, Governments and the United Nations. New York: Millennium Forum Committee.

Mitchell, Christopher R. (1997), *Intractable Conflicts: Keys to Treatment.* Work Paper no. 10), Gernika: Gernika Gogoratuz.

———. (and Banks, Michael. eds.). (1996), *Handbook of Conflict Resolution. The Analytical Problem-Solving Approach.* London/New York: Pinter.

———. (1995), *Cutting Losses: Reflections on Appropriate Timing.* Working Paper no. 9), Fairfax: George Mason University, Institute for Conflict Analysis and Resolution.

Modood, Tariq, and Pnina Werbner (eds.). (1997), *The Politics of Multiculturalism in the New Europe: Racism, Identity and Community.* London: Zed.

Mohammed, Abdul / Paulos Tesfagiorgis / Alex de Waal / InterAfrica Group. (2002), Peace and Security Dimensions of the African Union. Addis Ababa: InterAfrica Group/Justice Africa.

Moser, Rupert, ed. (2000), *Die Bedeutung des Ethnischen im Zeitalter der Globalisierung.* Bern etc: Haupt.

——. (1989), 'Kulturelle und interethnische Dissonanzen als Ursache von Migrationen', in W. Kälin and Rupert Moser (eds.), *Migrationen aus der Dritten Welt.* Berne: Haupt.

Moynihan, Daniel P. (1993), *Pandaemonium: Ethnicity in International Politics.* Oxford: Oxford University Press.

MRG (Minority Rights Group). See *ad loc.* for reports and papers.

Müller, Hans-Peter, Co-ord. (1994), *Ethnische Dynamik in der außereuropäischen Welt.* Zürcher Arbeitspapiere zur Ethnologie 4; Zurich.

—— *et al.*, eds. (1992), *Kulturelles Erbe und Entwicklung: Indikatoren zur Bewertung des soziokulturellen Entwicklungsstandes.* BMZ-Forschungsberichte 98; Munich.

Nabudere, Dani W. (1994), 'The African Challenge'. *Alternatives,* 19: 163–71.

Nagel, Joane, and Snipp, Matthew C. (1993), 'Ethnic Reorganization: American Indian Social, Economic, Political and Cultural Strategies for Survival'. *Ethnic and Racial Studies,* 16/2: 201–35.

NCDO (National Committee for Sustainable Development, NL). (1997), *The Amsterdam Appeal 1997. Enhancing European Union conflict prevention. An action plan for European leaders and civil society.* Amsterdam: NCDO.

——. (1997), *Background papers to the European conference on conflict prevention.* Den Haag: RAI.

——. (1996), *Genocide is not a natural catastrophe. Background paper.* Amsterdam: NCDO.

NCIV (Nederlands Center voor Inhemse Volken/Dutch Centre for Indigenous Peoples). (1993), *Outline of the Congress 'Voices of the Earth': Indigenous Peoples, New Partners, and the Right of Self-determination in Practice.* Amsterdam: NCIV.

NGO Conference: 1999), An Agenda for Peace, Security and Development in the 21st Century. Draft Programme of Action. Seoul, Korea. www.conferenceofngos.org .

NGO Working Group on Migration and Xenophobia. (2001), Preparatory Committee Intersessional Working Group. Geneva: UNHCHR, March. www.migrantwatch.org.

Nickel, Rainer. (2000), 'The promises of Equality and Recognition', in *Equality and Difference in Multiethnic Societies—Legal Protection against Discrimination as a Safeguard for Recognition.* Articles written on the official topics of the European Conference Against Racism. www.icare.to/.

Nietschmann, Bernard. (1997), 'Areas of inquiry dealing with extreme problems in the world: State-Nation-Conflicts—A prevented debate'. Interview with Bernard Nietschmann; in: ECOR 17: 37–58.

——. (1987), 'Militarization and Indigenous Peoples'. *Cultural Survival Quarterly,* 11/3: 1–16.

NIOD, Netherlands Institute for War Documentation / Nederlands Instituut voor Oorlogsdocumentatie *et al.* (2002), *Srebrenica – a 'safe' area. Reconstruction, background, consequences and analyses of the fall of a Safe Area.* Amsterdam: NIOD, 10 April.

NISER, Nigerian Institute of Social and Economic Research. (2002), *Reflection on African's Historic and Current Initiatives for Political And Economic Unity.* Ibadan: NISER.

Nispen, Patricia van. (1994), 'International Conflict Prevention and Resolution: Communication Process Agreement'. Unpub. paper.

Nohlen, Dieter, and Nuscheler, Franz eds. (1992–3), *Handbuch der Dritten Welt*. 3rd edn. 8 vols. Bonn: Dietz. And in this, i. 14–30: 'Ende der Dritten Welt?'.

Nuscheler, Franz. (1994), *Internationale Migration: Ein Hauptproblem für Global Governance*. INEF-Report 9; Duisburg.

——. (1992), 'Menschenrechte und Entwicklung', in Nohlen and Nuscheler eds. (1992–3: i. 269–86.

OAU, Organization for African Unity. (2002), Online debates and papers of the African Development Forum III (ADF II), hosted by the UN Economic Commission for Africa. Addis Abeba: ECA, March, www.uneca.org.

——. (2002), *Towards the African Union: A Development Perspective*. Addis Ababa: OAU.

——. (1999), OAU Declarations and Decisions on Good Governance. Yaoundé Summit, July 1996, to Algiers Council of Ministers meeting, July 1999. Addis Ababa: OAU.

——. (1995), *Rules of Procedure of the African Commission on Human and Peoples' Rights, Adopted on 6 October 1995*. Banjul, Gambia: ACHPR.

——. (1993), *The OAU Mechanism for Conflict Prevention, Management and Resolution and Conflict Situations in Africa*. Addis Ababa: OAU.

——. (1991), *Treaty Establishing the African Economic Community*. Abuja: OAU, http://www.oau-oua.org/document/Treaties/Abuja%20Treaty.htm.

——. (1981), *African Charter on Human and Peoples' Rights, adopted June 27, 1981*. (Entry into force Oct. 21, 1986). Addis Ababa: OAU.

Oberg, Jan, (var. years), *Balkan reports*. Lund: TFF (see: www.transnational.org/).

——. (1999), 'Some Ethical Aspects on NATO's Intervention in Kosovo', Lund: TFF.

OECD-DAC (Organization for Economic Co-operation and Development—Development Assistance Committee). (1997), *DAC Guidelines on Conflict, Peace and Development Co-operation*. Paris: OECD/OCDE.

Olzak, Susan, and Nagel, Joane, eds. (1986), *Competitive Ethnic Relations*. New York: Academic Press.

OSCE (Organization for Security and Cooperation in Europe) / CSCE (Conference for Security and Cooperation in Europe). (var. years), *Newsletters*.

——. (2002), 'OSCE High Commissioner praises adoption of 'minority law' in Yugoslavia'. Press Release. The Hague, 28 February.

——. (HCNM/Rolf Ekeus, OSCE High Commissioner on National Minorities). (2001), 'Diplomacy and discretion are bedrock of conflict prevention'. Interview. Online http://www.osce.org/news/profiles/ekeus_profile.php3

——. (1999), *The Lund Recommendations* (see FIER)

——. (CSCE). (1992), *Summit Declaration and Decisions of the 1992 Helsinki Follow-up Meeting: The Challenges of Change*. Geneva: CSCE. [Mandate of the High Commissioner on National Minorities].

Paffenholz, Thania. (1995), 'Vermittlung: Kriegsbeendigung und Konfliktregelung durch Einmischung', in Matthies (ed.) 1995: 39–56.

Palley, C. *et al.* (1991), *Minorities and Autonomy in Western Europe*. London: MRG.

Payne, Emil. (1994), 'Settlement of Ethnic Conflict in Post-Soviet Society', in Calließ and Merkel, eds., 1994: 469–84.

——. ed. (Ethnopolitical Studies Centre). (1993), *Socio-political Situation in the Post-Soviet World*. Moscow: Foreign Policy Association.

PCA (Permanent Court of Arbitration). (1993), *Optional Rules for Arbitrating Disputes between Two Parties of which Only One is a State*. The Hague: International Bureau of the PCA.

——. (1993a), *First Conference of the Members of the Court*. The Hague: PCA/Foundation Asser Institute.

———. (1992), *Optional Rules for Arbitrating Disputes between Two States.* The Hague: International Bureau of the PCA.

Pearson, David. (2001), *The Politics of Ethnicity in Settler Societies: States of Unease.* London: St Martin's Press.

Pfetsch, Frank R., ed. (1991), *Konflikte seit 1945.* 5 vols. (Europe, Arab world/Islam, Sub-Saharan Africa, America, Asia), Freiburg: Ploetz.

Philip, George, ed. (1993), *Weltatlas.* Hamburg: Xenos.

Phillips, Alan, and Rosas, Allan, eds. (1993), *The UN Minority Rights Declaration.* Turku/Åbo: Åbo Academic Printing and London: MRG.

PIOOM (Projecten Interdisciplinair Onderzoek naar de Oorzaken van Mensenrechtenschendigen / Interdisciplinary Research Program on Root Causes of Human Rights Violations: Center for the Study of Social Conflicts) (Jongman, Albert, and Schmid, Alex). (2001), *World Conflict and Human Rights Map 2001 / 2002),* Leiden: PIOOM

———. (Var. years), *World Conflict and Human Rights Map.* Leiden: PIOOM

———. (1997), *World Conflict Map 1996),* Leiden: PIOOM.

———. (1994), 'Contemporary Armed Conflicts. A Global Inventory'. *PIOOM Newsletter,* 6/1: 17–21.

——— (Schermers, Nico J., and Schmid, Alex). (1994*a*), *Prospects for Soviet Successor States based on a Consociational Analysis.* PIOOM Paper 3; Leiden.

Plant, Roger. (1994), *Land Rights and Minorities.* London: MRG.

pogrom: see GfbV.

Prunier, Gerard. (1995), *The Rwanda Crisis 1959–1994. History of a Genocide.* London: Hurst.

Puxon, Grattan. (1987), *Europe's Gypsies.* London: Minority Rights Group.

Rabehl, Thomas, and Trines, Stefan (eds.). (1997), *Das Kriegsgeschehen 1996.* IWP-Arbeitspapier 6. Hamburg: AKUF.

Rashid, Ahmed. (2001), *Jihad: The Rise of Militant Islam in Central Asia.* New Haven / London: Yale University Press

———. (2000), *Taliban: Militant Islam, Oil and Fundamentalism in Central Asia.* New Haven / London: Yale University Press

Reiterer, Albert F. (1988), *Die unvermeidbare Nation: Ethnizität, Nation und nachnationale Gesellschaft.* Frankfurt/M.: Campus.

Rémond, Bruno. (2001), 'How Regions are Governed', in *Le Monde diplomatique,* May, www.en.monde-diplomatique.fr/2001/05/14europe.

Reporter ohne Grenzen (Salgado, Sebastião). (1996), *Die Würde des Menschen. 100 Fotos für die Pressefreiheit.* Frankfurt/M.: Reporter ohne Grenzen.

República de Nicaragua. (1987), Estatuto de la autonomía de las regiones de la Costa Atlántica, Ley No. 28), *La Gaceta, Diario Oficial,* XCI/238: 2833–8.

Requejo, Ferran, ed. (2001), *Democracy and National Pluralism.* New York: Routledge.

Reyneri, Emilio *et al.* / TSER Project Report. (1999), Migrant Insertion in the Informal Economy Deviant Behavior and the Impact on Receiving Societies. Final Report ERB, SOE 2 CT95–3005. Brussels: TSER.

Roberts, Adam. (1994), 'The Crisis in UN Peacekeeping'. *Survival,* 36/3: 93–120.

Ropers, Norbert. (1998), 'Towards a Hippocratic Oath of Conflict Management?'; in: EPCP, PIOOM, Berghof et al, 27–33.

———. (1995), *Friedliche Einmischung: Strukturen, Prozesse und Strategien zur konstruktiven Bearbeitung ethnopolitischer Konflikte.* Berghof Report 1; Berlin.

———. (1995*b*), 'Die friedliche Bearbeitung ethno-politischer Konflikte', in Ropers and Debiel 1995: 197–232.

———, (and Debiel, Tobias, eds.). (1995), *Friedliche Konfliktbearbeitung in der Staaten-*

und Gesellschaftwelt. EINE Welt 13; Bonn.

——, and Schlotter, Peter. (1993), 'Minderheitenschutz und Staatszerfall'. *Blätter für deutsche und internationale Politik,* 38/3: 859–71.

Rosenberg, Tina. (1995), 'Overcoming the Legacies of Dictatorships'. *Foreign Affairs,* 74/3: 134–52.

Rothchild, Donald. (1991), 'An Interactive Model for State–Ethnic Relations', in Deng and Zartmann (eds.) 1991: 190–215.

——, and Olorunsola, Victor A., eds. (1983), *State versus Ethnic Claims: African Policy Dilemmas.* Boulder, Col.: Westview Press.

Rothman, Jay. (1997), *Resolving Identity-Based Conflict in Nations, Organizations, and Communities.* San Francisco: Jossey-Bass Publishers.

——. (1992), *From Confrontation to Cooperation: Resolving Ethnic and Regional Conflict.* London: Sage.

Rothschild, Joseph. (1981), *Ethnopolitics. A Conceptual Framework.* New York: Columbia.

Rottenburg, Richard. (1996), 'Reden über Gewalt-tätigkeiten und Kriege, die andernorts stattfinden', mimeo, Berlin: FU

Rummel, Rudolph J. (1997), *Statistics of Democide: Genocide and Mass Murder since 1900.* New Brunswick, NJ: Transaction.

——. (1994), *Death by Government: Genocide and Mass Murder.* New Brunswick, NJ: Transaction.

——. (1994a), 'Power, Genocide and Mass Murder'. *Journal of Peace Research,* 31/1: 1–10.

Rupesinghe, Kumar, and Mumtaz, Khawar (eds.). (1996), *Internal Conflicts in South Asia.* Oslo/ London: PRIO/Sage.

Rupesinghe, Kumar, and Tishkov, Valery A. (eds.). (1996), *Ethnicity and Power in the Contemporary World.* Tokyo, etc.: United Nations University Press.

Rupesinghe, Kumar. (1992), *Early Warning and Conflict Resolution.* Houndsmills: Macmillan Press/St Martin's Press.

——. (1992a), Internal *Conflict and Governance.* Houndsmills: Macmillan Press; in this, 1–26: 'The Disappearing Boundaries between Internal and External Conflicts'.

——. (1992b), *Ethnicity and Conflict in a Post-Communist World: The Soviet Union, Eastern Europe and China.* Houndsmills: Macmillan Press/St Martin's Press.

Ruzza, Carlo. (1999), 'Anti-racism and EU institutions.' Article prepared for presentation at the 1999 ESA Conference Social Movements Network. Essex University.

Ryan, Stephen. (1993), 'Grass-roots Peacebuilding in Violent Ethnic Conflict', in Calließ and Merkel (eds.) 1993: 313–42.

——. (1990), *Ethnic Conflict and International Relations.* Aldershot: Dartmouth.

Samad, Yunas. (2001), 'Emergence of Islam as Identity rather than Fundamentalism.' Paper. Dialogue Workshop 'Racism and Xenophobia'. Brussels, April.

Sandole, Dennis J.D. (1992), *Conflict Resolution in the Post-Cold War Era: Dealing with Ethnic Violence in the New Europe.* Working Paper No. 6, October 1992. Fairfax: George Mason University, Institute for Conflict Analysis and Resolution (ICAR).

Satha-Anand, Chaiwat. (1985), *Of Imagination and the State.* Paper 6. Bangkok: Thammasat.

Scherrer, Christian P. (2003a), *Ethnizität, Krieg und Staat.* IFEK-Report 4–5. Moers: IFEK-IRECOR, forthcoming.

——. (2003b), *Responses to Genocide.* Westport CT/London: Præger, forthcoming.

——. (2002a), *Genocide and Crisis in Central Africa: Conflict Roots, Mass Violence, and Regional War.* Westport CT/London: Præger.

——. (2002b), *Structural Prevention of Ethnic Violence.* London/Houndmills/New York: Palgrave.

——. (2001a), Free Nagaland—NE-India's Unsolved Question. Analysis and Compiler of Interviews. Moers: IFEK-IRECOR.

——. (2001*b*), *Indigene Völker und Staat: Von Krieg und äußerer Einmischung zum Frieden durch Autonomie. Der Fall Nicaragua.* IFEK-Report 3. Moers: IFEK.

——. (2000*a*), 'The Challenge of Genocide Prevention.' Prevent Genocide, Washington DC 2000 http://preventgenocide.org/prevent/scherrer.htm.

——. (2000*b*), 'Teaching and Researching Genocide from a Comparative Perspective'; in: The Stockholm International Forum on the Holocaust. A Conference on Education, Remembrance and Research. Proceedings. Stockholm: Regeringskansliet 2000, 319–321; www.holocaustforum.gov.se/conference/official_documents/abstracts/scherrer.htm.

——. (2000*c*), 'Ethno-Nationalismus als globales Phänomen'; in: Moser, (ed.), 17–90.

——. (and Wiberg, Håkan (eds.). (1999), *Ethnicity and Intra-state Conflict: Types, Causes and Peace Strategies.* Aldershot: Ashgate.

——. (1999), 'Structural Prevention and Conflict Management, Imperatives of'; in: Kurtz, Lester (ed.-in-chief): *Encyclopedia of Violence, Peace and Conflict. Vol. 3.* San Diego, London, etc.: Academic Press 1999, 381–429.

——. (1999*a*), 'Towards a theory of modern genocide. Comparative genocide research: definitions, criteria, typologies, cases, key elements, patterns and voids'; in: *Journal of Genocide Research* (1999), 1(1): 13–23, Basingstoke: Carfax Publ.

——. (1999*b*), 'Ethnisierung und Völkermord in Zentralafrika: Rwanda und Burundi— Länder der Tausend Massengräber'; Förster/Hirschfeld (Eds.) 1999: 101–129.

——. (1999*c*), 'Feindbild Islam und ‚Kampf der Kulturen'?—Kritik an Huntington und Bemerkungen zur aktuellen Entwicklung in der Türkei'; in: Jean-Paul Lehners (Ed.): L'Islam et l'espace euro-méditerranéen. Luxembourg: Centre Universitaire.

——. (1999*d*), 'Towards a comprehensive analysis of ethnicity and mass violence: Types, dynamics, characteristics and trends'; in: Wiberg, H. and Scherrer, C.P. (eds.), 52–88.

——. (1999*e*), *Peace Research for the 21st Century.* WP 18. Copenhagen: COPRI, online www.copri.dk/copri/downloads/18-1999.doc.

——. (1999*f*), *Rwanda-Burundi: Zur Notwendigkeit von Konfliktprävention und Übergangsjustiz nach dem Genozid.* Moers: IFEK-Report 2.

——. (1999*g*), 'We Need a Notion of Justice as the Base for Reconciliation Policies'. Lund: TFF, www.transnational.org/forum/meet/scherrer_justice-reconc.html.

——. (1998*a*), *Towards a theory of modern full-scale genocide.* Working Paper 22. Copenhagen: COPRI.

——. (1998*b*), *The United Nations and World's Indigenous Peoples.* Working Paper 19.

——. (1998*c*), *Resolving the Crisis in Central Africa I and II.* Working Papers 16 / 31.

——. (1998*d*), *Africa torn by Violent Intra-state Conflict.* Working Paper 12/98.

——. (1998*e*), *The First Indian Government in the Americas: Caught up in Neglect, Confusion and Disunity—Ways out?.* Working Paper. Copenhagen: COPRI.

——. (1997), *Ethno-Nationalismus im Zeitalter der Globalisierung: Ursachen, Strukturmerkmale und Dynamik ethnisch-nationaler Gewaltkonflikte. (Handbuch zu Ethnizität und Staat,* ii). Münster: agenda.

——. (1997*a*), *Ethnisierung und Völkermord in Zentralafrika.* Frankfurt/M.: Campus.

——. (1997*b*), *Intra-state Conflict, Ethnicity and Mass Violence.* Working Paper 22. Copenhagen: COPRI.

——. (1997*c*), Mehrheiten versus Minderheiten: Zur Kritik erklärungswürdiger Konzepte', *Wissenschaft und Frieden,* 15 (1997), 1: 8–13.

——. (1996), *Ethno-Nationalismus im Weltsystem. Handbuch zu Ethnizität und Staat,* i. Münster: agenda.

——. (1996*a*), 'Ursachen und Wahrnehmung von inter-ethnischen und ethno-nationalen Konflikten', in Hirsch 1996: 53–70.

——. (1996*b*), 'Föderalismus für Nigeria'. *pogrom,* 187, 46–8.

——. (1996*c*), 'Ethnisierung und Völkermord in Rwanda'. *Widerspruch,* 30: 61–86.

——. (1996*d*), 'Ein Verbrechen des Gehorsams', in Kinkelbur, Sareika, and Schmidt (eds.), *Peace is a Revolutionary Idea*. Iserlohn: EAI, 29–56.

——. (1996*e*), 'Nunavut-Autonomie', *pogrom*, 189, 42–44.

——. (1996*f*), 'Zur Huntington-Debatte', *Widerspruch*, 32: 99–107.

——. (1996*g*), 'Ethno-Nationalismus als globale Herausforderung', in: Deutsches Überseeinstitut 1997. Munich: Beck, 35–55.

——. (1995), 'Justice and Conflict Prevention after the Genocide: A Primary Task for Rwanda', in Calließ and Merkel (eds.) 1995: i. 351–90.

——. (1995*a*), 'Selbstbestimmung statt Fremdherrschaft: Sezessions- und Autonomieregelungen als Wege zur konstruktiven Bearbeitung ethno-nationaler Konflikte', in Ropers and Debiel (eds.) 1995: 257–83.

——. (1995*b*), 'Burma: Ethno-nationalistische Guerrilla und die letzten großen Teakwälder', in Calließ and Merkel (eds.) 1995: 173–206.

——. (1995*c*), 'Gruppenkonflikte als Krisenherde', in Fritsch (ed.) 1995: 63–101.

——. (1994), *Ethno-Nationalismus als globales Phänomen*. INEF-Report 6; Duisburg: INEF. http://www.uni-duisburg.de/Institute/INEF/publist/report06.PDF.

—— (Buvollen, Hans Petter). (1994), 'Nicaragua: Indians and New Alliances'. *Indigenous Affairs*, 1: 22–35.

——. (1994*a*), 'Ethnische Strukturierung und politische Mobilisierung in Äthiopien', in Müller Co-ord. 1994: 133–205.

——. (1994*b*), 'Ethno-Nationalismus als Interventionsfall?' In Bächler (ed.) 1994: 149–64.

——. (1994*c*), 'Regional Autonomy in Eastern Nicaragua: Self-government Experience in Yapti Tasba', in Assies and Hoekema (eds.) 1994: 109–48.

——. (1994*d*), 'The UNPO: Another Type of NGO', Tegelen: ECOR.

——. (1993), 'Recognizing Multiplicity: Conflict Resolution in Eastern Nicaragua', in Calließ and Merkel (eds.), 1993: 209–80.

——. (1993*a*), 'Der Dritte Weltkrieg'. *Überblick*, 3: 29–33.

——. (1993*b*), 'A Model Process for Indigenous Peoples'. Interview with Howard R. Berman, Amsterdam (mimeo).

——. (1991), 'Dialektik zwischen Orient und Okzident: Thesen von Johan Galtung'. *Dritte Welt*, 4: 101–12.

——. (1991*a*), 'Selbstbestimmung für indigene Völker'. *Widerspruch*, 22: 41–50.

——. (1989), 'Ethnizität und Staat in der Dritten Welt'. Projektbericht. Zürich: Universität Zürich.

——. (1988), *Tourismus und Selbstbestimmung—ein Widerspruch. Das Fallbeipiel Tanzania*. Berlin: Reimer.

Schiemann Rittri, Catherine *et al.* (1995), *Friedensbericht 1995: Tod durch Bomben. Wider den Mythos vom ethnischen Konflikt*. Chur: Rüegger.

Schlichte, Klaus. (1994), 'Is Ethnicity a Cause of War?'. *Peace Review*, 6/1: 59–65.

Schmidt, Hajo, and Trittmann, Uwe, eds. (2002), *Kultur und Konflikt. Dialog mit Johan Galtung*. Münster: agenda Verlag.

SEF (Stiftung Entwicklung und Frieden/Development and Peace Foundation). (var. years), EINE Welt: Texte der SEF, and Interdependenz (listed *ad loc.*).

——. (var. years), *Globale Trends*. Frankfurt/M.: Fischer.

——. (1997), *Policy Paper 5), Auf dem Weg in ein neues Europa*. Bonn.

——. (1996), *Entwicklung Kulturen Frieden. Visionen für eine neue Weltordnung*. Bonn.

——. (1995), *Mit der WTO ins nächste Jahrhundert*. SEF Policy Paper 1; Bonn.

——. (1991), *Gemeinsame Verantwortung in den 90er Jahren: Die Stockholmer Initiative zu globaler Sicherheit und Weltordnung*. EINE Welt 5; Bonn.

——. (1991a), Menschen *auf der Flucht: Fluchtbewegungen und ihre Ursachen*. SEF: Interdependenz 8; Bonn.

Senghaas, Dieter. (1997), 'Die fixe Idee vom Kampf der Kulturen'; in Blätter, Bonn 2/: 213–221.

——. 'Bibliographische Notizen zum zivilisatorischen Hexanon'; in Calließ, Jörg (Ed): *Wodurch und wie konstituiert sich Frieden? Das zivilisatorische Hexanon auf dem Prüfstand.* Papers. Loccum: EAL.

——. (1996), 'Religion—Nation—Europa: Erkenntnisse über gelungene Vergemein-schaftungsprozesse'; in Mader *et al.*: 55–66.

——. (1995), 'Treiben Umweltkonflikte in Gewaltkonflikte? Überlegungen', in Calließ 1994: 301–10.

——. (1995*a*), 'Frieden als Zivilisierungsprojekt', in Vogt (ed.) 1995: 37–54.

——. (1993), 'Einheimische Konflikte oder die Wiederkehr der Nationalismus', in Calließ and Merkel (eds.)1993: 61–81.

——. (1993*a*), 'Global Governance: How Could This Be Conceived', in Jörg Calließ ed., *Auf dem Weg zur Weltinnenpolitik.* Evangelische Akademie Loccum: Loccumer Proto-kolle, 21/93: 103–25.

——. (1992), 'Therapeutische Konfliktintervention in ethnonationalistischen Konflikten', in id., *Friedensprojekt Europa.* Frankfurt/M.: ed. suhrkamp, 116–40.

——. (1990), *Europa 2000: Ein Friedensplan.* Frankfurt/M.: edition suhrkamp.

——. (1989), *Regionalkonflikte in der Dritten Welt: Autonomie und Fremdbestimmung.* Baden-Baden: Nomos.

——. (1988), *Konfliktformationen im internationalen System.* Frankfurt/M.: edition suhrkamp.

——, (ed.). (1978), *Weltwirtschaftordnung und Entwicklungspolitik: Plädoyer für Dissoziation.* Frankfurt/M.: edition suhrkamp.

——, (ed.). (1974), *Periphere Kapitalismus. Amalysen über Abhängigkeit und Unter-entwicklung.* Frankfurt/M.: edition suhrkamp.

——, (ed.). (1972), *Imperialismus und strukturelle Gewalt. Analysen über abhängige Reproduktion.* Frankfurt/M.: edition suhrkamp.

——, (and Zürn, Michael). (1992), 'Kernfragen für die Friedensforschung der neunziger Jahre', in *Politische Vierteljahreszeitschrift*, 33: 455–62.

Seton-Watson, Said, ed. (1977), *Nation and States: An Enquiry into the Origins of Nations and the Politics of Nationalism.* Boulder, Col.: Westview Press.

SFS (Schweizerische Friedensstiftung) (Klingenburg, Konrad, and Mietzsch, Oliver). (1992), *Herausforderung im Wandel: Die KSZE.* Arbeitspapiere der SFS 15; Berne.

Shachar, Ayelet. (2001), *Multicultural Jurisdictions: Cultural Differences and Women's Rights.* Cambridge: Cambridge University Press.

Shearer, David. (1998), *Private Armies and Military Intervention.* IISS Adelphi Paper 316. London: Oxford University Press.

Sheehy, Ann, and Nahaylo, Bohdan. (1980), *The Crimean Tatars, Volga Germans and Meskhetians: Soviet Treatment of Some National Minorities.* Report 6. London: MRG.

Shiels, Frederick, ed. (1984), *Ethnic Separatism and World Politics.* Lanham: University Press of America.

Siebold, Thomas. (1995), *Die soziale Dimension der Strukturanpassung: eine Zwischen-bilanz.* INEF-Report 13; Duisburg.

Siedschlag, Alexander. (1995), 'Konfliktmanagment in der post-bipolaren Welt', in Calließ and Merkel (eds.) 1995 (2): 447–85.

Siegelberg, Jens. (1995), 'Umweltprobleme und Gewaltkonflikte aus Sicht der Kriegsursachenforschung', in Calließ (ed.) 1995: 67–71.

Siim, Birte *et al.* / TSER Project Report. (2000), Gender and Citizenship: Social Integration and Social Exclusion in European Welfare States. Brussels: TSER.

Singer, J. David, and Small, Melvin. (1984), *The Wages of War 1816–1980. A Statistical Handbook, with Disputes and Civil War Data.* Ann Arbor, MI : Inter-university Consortium for Political and Social Research.

SIPRI (Stockholm International Peace Research Institute). (var. years), *SIPRI Yearbooks. Armaments, Disarmament and International Security.* Oxford, etc.: Oxford University Press/SIPRI.

——. (2000), SIPRI Yearbook 2000), http://editors.sipri.se/pubs/yearb.html.

Sisk, Timothy D. / USIP. (1996), *Power Sharing and International Mediation in Ethnic Conflicts.* Washington, DC: United States Institute of Peace Press.

Smith, Anthony David. (1992), 'Ethnicity and Nationalism', in id. (ed.), *Ethnicity and Nationalism.* Leiden: Brill.

——. (1991), *National Identity.* London: Penguin Books [esp. 'The Ethnic Basis of National Identity', 19–42].

Smith, Paul, ed. (1991), *Ethnic Groups in International Relations. Comparative Studies on Governments and Non-dominant Ethnic Groups in Europe, 1850–1940,* v. Aldershot: Dartmouth.

Sollenberg, Margareta and Wallensteen, Peter. (var. years), 'Major armed conflicts,' in: SIPRI Yearbooks.

Soyinka, Wole. (1995), 'Nacht über Nigeria'. Interview with Wole Soyinka. *Tages-Anzeiger Magazin,* 45: 56–63.

Staack, Michael, ed. (1992), *Aufbruch nach Gesamteuropa: Die KSZE nach der Wende im Osten.* Münster: Lit.

Staub, Ervin. (1992), *The Roots of Evil. The origins of Genocide and Other Group Violence.* Cambridge etc.: Cambridge University Press [original 1989].

Stavenhagen, Rodolfo. (1996), *Ethnic Conflict and the Nation-State.* Basingstoke / London: Macmillan.

——. (1994), 'Indigenous Rights: Some Conceptual Problems'. Paper, Amsterdam.

——. (1990), *The Ethnic Question: Conflicts, Development and Human Rights.* Tokyo: United Nations University Press.

Strazzari, Francesco. (1998), *Security-building in Protracted Ethnopolitical Conflict. Third Parties along Southeast European Peripheries.* Unpublished Paper. Florence: EUI.

STT (Survie Touarègue—Temoust). (1994), *Issalan n Temoust,* first issue of newsletter of SST.

Stüben, Peter E., ed. (1988), *Die neuen 'Wilden': Umweltschützer unterstützen Stammesvölker: Theorie und Praxis der Ethno-Ökologie.* Ökozid 4; Gießen.

——, and Thurn, Valentin, eds. (1991), *WüstenErde: Der Kampf gegen Durst, Dürre und Desertifikation.* Ökozid 7; Gießen.

Summer Institute of Linguistics / Grimes, Barbara F. (chief ed.), Pittman, R.S. and Grimes, J.E. (eds.). (1996), *Ethnologue. Languages of the World.* 13th edition. Dallas: SIL. http://www.sil.org/ethnologue/.

Suny, Ronald. (1991), 'Sozialismus und Nationalitätenkonflikt in Transkaukasien', *Argument,* 186: 213–26.

Survival (quarterly of the International Institute for Strategic Studies). (1993), 35/1: 'Ethnic Conflict and International Security'.

Sutter, Alex. (1995), 'Die Fremden und Wir'. Mimeograph.

Swedish Ministry for Foreign Affairs. (1997), *Preventing Violent Conflict. A Study. Executive Summary and Recommendations.* Stockholm: UM.

Tanaka, Yuki. (2002), Japan's Comfort Women. Sexual slavery and prostitution during World War II and the US Occupation. London/New York: Routledge.

——. (1998), Didden Horrors. Japanese War Crimes in World War II. Boulder Col./ Oxford: Westview.

Terkessidis, Mark. (2001), 'Das rassistische Wissen. Wie Wissenschaft und soziale Praxis "Minderwertigkeit" produzieren'; iz3w, no. 253: 38–41.

——. (2000), *Migranten*. Berlin: Rotbuch.

Tetzlaff, Rainer. (1993), *Menschenrechte und Entwicklung*. EINE Welt 11; Bonn. (pub. in English as: *Human Rights and Development*, EINE Welt 12).

——, et al. (1992), 'Politicized Ethnicity: An Underestimated Reality in Post-colonial Africa', in *Law and State* , 24–53), Tübingen: IWZ.

Thompson, Dennis, and Ronen, Dov, eds. (1986), *Ethnicity, Politics, and Development*. Boulder: Lynne Rienner.

Tierra Nuestra—Visiones Latinoamericanas/Agencia de Prensa Internacional Alternativa. (1995), 'El retorno de los caudillos'. *Tierra Nuestra* 11: 1–21.

Tishkov, Valery. (1997), *Ethnicity, Nationalism and Conflict in and after the Soviet Union. The Mind Aflame*. London, etc.: Sage.

Trenin, Dimitri. (1994), 'Russians as Peacemakers'. *Internationale Politik und Gesellschaft*, 257–66.

Trifunovska, Snena / Varennes, Fernand de, eds. (2001), *Minority Rights in Europe. European Minorities and Languages*. The Hague: TMC Asser Press / Dordrecht: Kluwer Law International.

Trimikliniotis, Nicos. (2001), The Role of State Processes in the Production of 'Ethnic' Conflict: The Nation-State Dialectic, *Europeanisation* and Globalisation.' Workshop Paper. Limasol / Brussels.

Tungavik (Inuit of Nunavut), and Canadian Ministry of Indian Affairs and Northern Development. (1993), Agreement between the Inuit of the Nunavut Settlement Area and Her Majesty the Queen in Right of Canada. Ottawa.

UN General Assembly. (2001*a*), *Special Committee on Peacekeeping: Significant Room for Improvement*. (GA/PK/170) [Follow-up on Brahimi]. New York: UN, June 18.

——. (2001*b*), *Special Committee on Peacekeeping Stresses Consultation with Troop Contributors, Exit Strategies, Personnel Protection, Gender Component for Mandates* (GA/PK/172). New York: UN, June 19.

——. (1992), Declaration on the rights of persons belonging to national or ethnic, religious and linguistic minorities. (General Assembly, 47th session).

UN ECA (UN Economic Commission for Africa). (var. years), *Annual Report On Integration in Africa*. Addis Ababa: ECA.

——. (2002), Report On Integration In Africa 2002: One Africa–The Vision. Addis Ababa: ECA. March, www.uneca.org.

UNCHR (United Nations Commission on Human Rights)/ECOSOC. (var. years), Reports of the Working Group on Indigenous Populations. Annual sessions, July/Aug. in Geneva.

——. (2000), Establishment of a Permanent Forum on Indigenous Issues. Decision of UNCHR. E/2000/87. Geneva: UN, 27 April.

——. (Wille, Petter). (2000), Indigenous Issues. Report of the open-ended inter-sessional ad hoc working group on a permanent forum for indigenous people. E/CN.4/2000.86. Geneva: UN, 18 March.

——. (Chávez, Luis-Enrique). (1999), Indigenous Issues. Report of the working group established in accordance with CHR resolution 1995/32), E/CN.4/2000/84. Geneva: UN, 6 December.

——. (Daes, Erica-Irene). (1999), Indigenous people and their relationship to land. Second progress report. E/CN.4/1999/20. Geneva: UNCHR, 22 June.

——. (1999), Report on the Fifty-fifth Session. E/CN.4/1999/167. Geneva: UN.

——. (Martínez, Miguel Alfonso). (1999), Study on treaties, agreements and other constructive arrangements between states and indigenous peoples. Final Report. E/CN.4/Sub.2/1999/20. Geneva: UNCHR, 22 June.

——. (1995), Considerations of a permanent forum for indigenous people. E/CN.4/Sub.2/AC.4/1995/7. Geneva: UNCHR.

——. (1995a), International decade of the world's indigenous people. E/CN.4/Sub.2/AC.4/1995/5. Geneva: UNCHR.

—— (Martínez, Miguel Alfonso). (1995b. Study on treaties, agreements and other constructive arrangements between states and indigenous peoples. Second progress peport. E/CN.4/Sub.2/AC.4/1995/27. Geneva: UNCHR.

——. (1994), Technical review of the UN draft declaration on the rights of indigenous peoples. E/CN.4/Sub.2/AC.4/1994/2/Add.1. Geneva: UNCHR.

——. (1993), Draft declaration on the rights of indigenous peoples. E/CN.4/Sub.2/1993/26. Geneva: UNCHR.

—— (Johansen, L. E. *et al.*). (1992), Report of the meeting of experts to review the experience of countries in the operation of schemes of internal self-government for indigenous peoples, Nuuk, Greenland, Sept. (1991), Statements and background papers. E/CN.4/1992/42/Add.1. Geneva: UNCHR.

—— (Martínez, Miguel Alfonso). (1992a), Discrimination against indigenous peoples: study on treaties. E/CN.4/Sub.2/1992/32. Geneva: UNCHR.

—— (——). (1991), Preliminary report. E/CN.4/Sub.2/AC.4/1991/Misc.2. Geneva: UNCHR.

——. (1980), The right to self-determination. (CHR/SC-PDPM: rapporteur Héctor Gros Espinel).

UNDHA (United Nations Department of Humanitarian Affairs). (var. years), *DHA News*.

——. (1995), *DHA News Special: 1994 in Review*.

UNDP (United Nations Development Programme). (var. years), *Human Development Report*. New York: UNDP.

——. (2001), *Human Development Report. Making new technologies work for human development*. New York / Oxford: Oxford University Press (online from UNDP, http://www.undp.org/hdr2001/complete.pdf).

UNDPI (United Nations Department of Public Information). (2000), (Kofi A. Annan). *'WE, the Peoples'. The Role of the United Nations in the 21st Century. New Century, New Challenges*. Doc E.00.I.16), New York: UN.

——. (1996), *The United Nations and Somalia, 1992–1996)*, New York: UNDPI. [The United Nations Blue Book Series, Vol. VIII].

UNDPKO (United Nations Department for Peacekeeping Operations). (1999), *Strategy Toward Improving African Peacekeeping Training Capacity*, www.un.org/Depts/dpko.

UNESCO (United Nations Educational, Scientific and Cultural Organization). (1994), *First consultative meeting of the Culture of Peace programme, final report* (CPP-94/CONF.601/3). Paris: UNESCO.

——. (1994a), The *Culture of Peace programme: From national programmes to a project of global scope*. Paris: UNESCO.

——. (1994b), *First international forum on the Culture of Peace in San Salvador*, 16–18 Feb. 1994, final report. Paris: UNESCO.

——. (1994c), 'Toward a Culture of Peace', Focus in UNESCO Sources, 62: 7–16.

——. (1993), *Action programme to promote a Culture of Peace*. Paris: UNESCO.

UNHCHR (United Nations High Commissioner for Human Rights). (2001), 'World Conference against Racism, Racial Discrimination, Xenophobia and Related Intolerance. Declaration and Programme of Action', on www.unhchr.ch/html/racism/Durban.htm.

UNHCR (United Nations High Commission for Refugees). (2000), *The State of the World's Refugees*. Biannual report. Geneva: UNHCR (var. years).

UNICEF (United Nations Children's Fund)/Mine Awareness Project. (1993), The UNICEF Mine Awareness Project in El Salvador. San Salvador: UNICEF.

United Nations. (1994), *Seeds of a New Partnership: Indigenous Pepoles and the United Nations*. New York: UN.

—— (Martínez Cobo, José R.) 1986), *Study of the Problem of Discrimination against Indigenous Populations*, i–iv. New York: United Nations. (Doc. E/CN.4/Sub.2/1986/7 and Add. 1–4; vol. v, *Conclusions, Proposals and Recommendations*, was issued as a separate publication.).

UNPD, United Nations Population Division. (1999), *World Population Prospects: The 1998 Revision*, http://www.popin.org/pop1998/.

UNPO (Unrepresented Nations and Peoples Organization). (var. years), Member Fact-sheets and Reports on Members' Human Rights Situations.

——. (1995), *General Assembly IV. Summary Report and Documentation*. The Hague.

——. (1994), *The First Three Years. (1991–1994), Report*. The Hague.

—. (1994a), *UNPO Members 1994)*, The Hague.

——. (1994b), *Conflict Prevention: The Post-Cold War Challenge*. i: Report CSCE. ii: Project. The Hague.

——. (1993), *Self-determination in Relation to Human Rights, Democracy and the Protection of the Environment*. The Hague.

—— (Goldberg, David). (1992), *Human Rights Dimensions of Population Transfer*. Hague.

——. (1992a), *Preventing the Use of Force by States against Peoples under their Rule*. Conference report. The Hague.

——. (1992b), *Summary of the UNPO*. The Hague.

—— (Lord Ennals .). (1992c), *Report of an UNPO Mission to Abkkhazia, Georgia and the Northern Caucasus*. The Hague.

—— 1991), *Covenant of the UNPO* (incl. amendments of Aug. (1991). The Hague.

UNRISD (United Nations Research Institute for Social Development). (var. years), UNRISD Discussion Papers (DP).

——. (var. years), UNRISD Occasional Papers (OP).

——, (WSP: War-torn Societies Project). (var. years), *The Challenge of Peace: An Interactive Newsletter*.

——. (1995a), *Ethnic Violence, Conflict Resolution and Cultural Pluralism. Report*.

——, (Haynes, Jeff). (1995b), *Religion, Fundamentalism and Ethnicity*. UNRISD DP 65; Geneva.

—— (——). (1995c), *Rebuilding War-Torn Societies: An Action-Research Project on Problems of International Assistance in Post-conflict Situations*. Geneva: UNRISD.

—— (Bangura, Yusuf). (1994), *The Search for Identity: Ethnicity, Religion and Political Violence*. UNRISD OP 6; Geneva.

—— (Tischkov, Valery). (1994a), *Nationalities and Conflicting Ethnicity in Post-communist Russia*. UNRISD DP 50; Geneva.

—— (Young, Crawford). (1994b), *Ethnic Diversity and Public Policy: An Overview*. UNRISD OP 8; Geneva.

—— (Premdas, Ralph R.) (1993), *Ethnicity and Development: The Case of Fiji*. UNRISD DO 46; Geneva.

—— (Rashid, Abbas, and Shaheed, Farina). (1993a), *Pakistan: Ethno-politics and Contending Elites*. UNRISD DP 45; Geneva.

Unser, Günther. (1988), *Die UNO: Aufgaben und Strukturen der Vereinigten Nationen*. 4th ed.. Munich: Beck/dtv.

Valdez, Jorge. (2001), *Deliberative Democracy: Political Legitimacy and Self-Determination in Multicultural Societies*. Boulder, Col.: Westview Press.

Väyrynen, Raimo, ed. (1991), *New Directions in Conflict Theory: Conflict Resolution and Conflict Transformation*. London, etc.: Sage.

Villagrán de Leon, Francisco. (1994), 'The OAS and the Democratic Development'. *Revista del IRIPAZ,* 5/9: 145–52.

Vogt, Wolfgang R., ed. (1995), *Frieden als Zivilisierungsprojekt: Neue Herausforderungen an die Friedens- und Konfliktforschung.* AFK-Schriftenreihe 21. Baden-Baden.

——. (1990), 'Positiven Frieden wagen', in id. (ed.), *Mut zum Frieden.* Darmstadt: Wissenschaftliche Buchgesellschaft.

Volger, Helmut. (1995), 'Die vergessenen Völker'. *Blätter für deutsche und internationale Politik,* 11: 1358–66.

Waldmann, Peter. (1988), *Ethnischer Radikalismus: Ursachen und Folgen gewaltsamer Minderheitenkonflikte.* Baden-Baden: Nomos.

Walker, Jenonne. (1993), 'International Mediation of Ethnic Conflicts'. *Survival,* 35/1: 102–17.

Wallensteen, Peter and Margareta Sollenberg. (1998), 'Armed conflict and regional conflict complexes, 1989–97'; in: Journal of Peace Research, 35: 5: 621–634.

——. (1997), 'Armed conflicts, conflict termination and peace agreements, 1989–96'; in: Journal of Peace Research, 34: 3: 339–358.

——, and Karin Axell. (1993), 'Armed Conflict at the End of the Cold War, 1989–92'; in: Journal of Peace Research, 30: 3: 331–346.

Wallerstein, Immanuel. (1995), *Die Sozialwissenschaft 'kaputtdenken': Die Grenzen der paradigmen des 19), Jahrhunderts.* Weinheim: Beltz Athenäum.

Walt van Praag, Michael C. van. (1997), 'The Struggle for Self-determination and the Role of UNPO', in ECOR 9: 197–203.

——. (1994), 'UNPO Was Created and Is Run by the Nations and People that Are not Represented in the UN and in International Fora'. ECOR 12: 49–55.

——1993), 'The Political Rights of Indigenous Peoples and the Political Need for Change'. Unpub. paper.

War Annuals (Laffin, John, ed.). (1985–7), *War Annual: A Guide to Contemporary Wars and Conflicts.* London: Brassey's.

——. (1989–93), *The World in Conflict: War Annuals. Contemporary Warfare Analysed.* London: Brassey's.

Wasmuht, Ulrike C. (1992), *Friedensforschung als Konfliktforschung: Zur Notwendigkeit einer Rückbesinnung auf den Konflikt als zentrale Kategorie.* AFB-Texte 1. Bonn: AFB.

Wearne, Phillip/MRG. (1994), *The Maya of Guatemala.* London: MRG.

Weeks, Dudley. (1994), *The Eight Essential Steps to Conflict Resolution. Preserving Relationships at Work, at Home, and in the Community.* New York: Tarcher/Putnam.

Wegemund, Regina. (1991), *Politisierte Ethnizität in Mauretanien und Senegal.* Arbeiten IAK 79; Hamburg.

Westad, Odd. A. (1992), 'Rethinking Revolutions: The Cold War in the Third World'. *Journal of Peace Research,* 29: 455–64.

Wiberg, Hakan, and Scherrer, Christian P., eds. (1999), *Ethnicity and Intra-state Conflict: Types, Causes and Peace Strategies.* Aldershot: Ashgate .

Widerspruch, half-yearly periodical. (1995), 'Ethnische Politik, Krieg und Völkermord' (30); 1991: 'Neo-Kolonialismus' (22).

Wimmer, Andreas. (1994), 'Der Kampf um den Staat: Zur vergleichenden Analyse ethnischer Konflikte', in Müller (co-ord.) 1994: 511–38.

Winkler, August, and Kaelble, Hartmut, eds. (1993), *Nationalismus, Nationalitäten, Supra-nationalität: Europa nach 1945),* Stuttgart: Klett-Cotta.

Wittfogel, Karl A. (1977), *Die Orientalische Despotie: Eine vergleichende Untersuchung totaler Macht.* Frankfurt/M.: Ullstein.

Woodroffe, Jessica and Mark Ellis-Jones. (2001), *States of Unrest: Resistance to IMF policies in poor countries. World Development Movement Report 2000.* Revised edition. London: WDM. http://www.wdm.org.uk/cambriefs/DEBT/unrest.htm

World Conference of Indigenous Peoples on Territory, Environment and Development (Kari-Oca). (1992), 'Kari-Oca Declaration and Indigenous Peoples Earth Charter', Kari-Oca (Brazil).

Worldwatch Institute (Renner, Michael). (1990), *Konversion zur Friedensökonomie.* Worldwatch Paper 3; Schwalbach.

Wulf, Herbert. (1991), *Waffenexport aus Deutschland: Geschäfte mit dem fernen Tod.* Reinbek bei Hamburg: Rowohlt.

WWC (Woodrow Wilson Center) (Stone, John). (1995), *Problems in Advanced Industrial Societies: Ethnic Conflict in the Post-Cold War Era.* Workshop Paper; Washington D.C.

—— (Tripp, Charles ed.) (1995a), *Sectarianism and the Secular State: Ethnic Conflict in the Post-Cold War Era.* Conference report, Washington D.C.: WWC.

Yamskov, Anatoly N. (1994), 'The 'New Minorities' in Post-Soviet States'. *Cultural Survival Quarterly,* 18/2–3: 58–61.

Yin, Ma. (1989), *China's Minority Nationalities.* Beijing: Foreign Language Press.

Young, Crawford. (1993), *The Rising Tide of Cultural Pluralism: The Nation State at Bay?* Madison, Wisc./London: University of Wisconsin Press.

Zartman, I. William, ed. (1997), *Governance as Conflict Management: Politics and Violence in West Africa.* Washington: Brookings Institution.

——, ed. (1995), *Elusive Peace. Negotiating an End to Civil Wars.* Washington DC: The Brookings Institution.

——. (1992), *Resolving Regional Conflicts. International Perspectives.* London: Sage.

——, and Deng, Francis M., eds. (1991), *Conflict resolution in Africa.* Washington DC: Brookings Institution.

——. (1989), *Ripe for Revolution: Conflict and Intervention in Africa.* Oxford: Oxford University Press.

Ziegler, Jean / UNCHR. (2001), The Right to Food. Report by the Special Rapporteur on the right to food. E/CN.4/2001/53. Geneva: UNCHR, 7 February.

Zimmermann, Klaus. (1992), *Sprachkontakt, ethnische Identität und Identitätsbeschädigung.* Frankfurt/M.: Vervuert.

Appendices

Indexes of Mass Violence

The heterogeneous dynamic character of contemporary violent conflicts has to be expressed adequately. In ECOR's *Indexes of Mass Violence* this has been solved as such: besides pointing at a dominant type secondary and tertiary components were also codified. In order to exclude multiple counting of particular components only the last phase of a war was considered relevant. In the indexes the composition of seven types of wars (A–G) is indicated for each conflict and for each phase of conflict (see Tables A.1 and A.4).

Definitions

Wars and genocide have to be clearly defined and distinguished:

War is defined as a violent mass conflict involving two or more armed forces as combatants and actors in warfare. Regular state armed forces are not involved in all cases. Non-state actors are mainly so-called liberation movements having regular guerrilla or partisan armies, often recruiting along ethnic, national or social class lines. Militias, gangs and other irregular forces have different agendas; they have less or no centralised control or identifiable lines of command. Combat takes place with some degree of continuity.

Major war and mass violence are distinguished from other armed conflicts or massacres by various degrees of medium or high intensity, claiming usually more than an estimated 1,000 victims per annum as an average during the conflict period. In many cases the numbers of victims are contested or otherwise questionable.

Impure types / different components: Combining the basic types can adequately solve the inherent difficulty of all the 'impure' types we find in the real world. By that way we get closer to the 'mixed types' encountered in the field.

Dynamics and change: For a given phase the register shows the primary or dominant type followed (if necessary) by a secondary or tertiary characterisation of a particular conflict.

Types of Conflict Distinguished by the ECOR Index

A   Anti-regime-wars, political conflicts; state versus insurgents
B   Ethno-nationalist conflicts, mostly as intra-state conflicts (state versus nation), often cross-border or spill-over effects
C   Interstate conflicts, state versus state, seen as 'classic wars'
D   Decolonisation wars or Foreign State Occupations
E   Inter-ethnic conflicts, mainly non-state actors
F   Gang wars, non-state actors (mixed with criminal elements), esp. in situations of state failure or state collapse.
G   Genocide, state-organised, mass murder and major crimes

Legend

mixed types	AB, BA, BC, CA, BAD, etc.	first mentioned type in a given period is the dominant type, often with second or less influential component(s)
Foreign actors	+	direct participation of a foreign state or outside power deploying combatants
Phases	/	separating types or periods of time indicate different phases or paradigmatic changes
Period of time	– ...	conflict is continued after the registered periods ending on 31 December 1994 or 31 December 2000
Termination / end	(?)	date or the termination of violence is unknown or questionable
Sources	ECOR, various	own data, evaluation of various compilations and conflict databases.*

Remarks

Register 1 contains violent conflicts including genocide (Rwanda, Central Sudan), wars, armed conflicts, rebellions, etc., taking place 1985 – 1994 in 16 regions of the world. Register 2 contains violent conflicts taking place 1995 – 1996 in now 15 regions of the world (no major conflict in East Asia). Already in 1993/94 there was a slight reduction of the number of ongoing violent conflicts but no reduction of mortality at all occurred. A reason for the slight numeric reduction was the termination of most wars in the former USSR—after the explosion of violence in the period from 1989 to 1994.

---

* Scherrer 1988, 1997, 1999, 2001 and 2002b; ECOR studies, var. years; AKUF, var. years; HIIK *Conflict Barometer*, var. years; SIPRI *Yearbooks*, var. years; Gantzel et al., 1994; 1997; Nietschmann 1987; SEF, *Global Trends*, var. years; Seybolt 2000; Uppsala Conflict Data Project, 'Major Armed Conflicts', in SIPRI *Yearbooks*, var. years; Wallensteen et al., var. years; UNDP, *HD Reports*, var. years; FEWER, *Reports*, var. years.

Table A.1: ECOR Index of Mass Violence in the Decade 1985–1994

no.	Country	Groups / Actors	Conflict Types	Period / Phases
Central-America and the Caribbean				
1.	Guatemala	Maya-Kiché, Ixil, EGP, others	B/GBA/BA	1954 / 1978–85 / 1986 – ...
2.	Guatemala	URNG insurgency coalition	AB	1960 / 1980 – ...
3.	Nicaragua	FDN-Contras / Re-Contras	A+ / AF	April 1981 – 1990 / ...
4.	Nicaragua	Miskitu factions, Sumu, Rama	B+ / B	Feb. 1981–7/1990
5.	El Salvador	FMLN, Pipiles	AB	1980/81 – Feb. 1992 (?)
6.	USA	Panama (LD-RP)	C	20 – 24 Dec. 1989
7.	Haiti	Tonton Macoutes, FRAPH; US	FA / FA+	Sept. 1991 / Sept. 1994 – ...
South America				
8.	Brazil	Gold searchers vs. Yanomami	FE	1986 (?) – ...
9.	Columbia	FARC, EPL; ELN; M-19	AB; A; A	1964/1965/Jan. 1974 – Mar. 1990 / ...
10.	Columbia	Drug syndicates, death squads.	AF	1970 (?) – ...
11.	Columbia	Guajiro	BA	1975 (?) – ...
12.	Suriname	Busi Nengee / Kalinja, Lokono	BA / B	21 June 1986 – 7 June 89
13.	Peru	Sendero Luminoso, militias	ABF	May 1980 – ...
14.	Peru	Aymara, Quichua, MRTA	BA	Nov. 1987 – ...
North Africa				
15.	Morocco	West Sahara: Sahrawi Polisario front	DB	18 Nov. 1975 – 1992 (?)
16.	Sudan	South Sudan: SPLA	BGA	Sept. 1983 – ...
17.	Sudan	SPLA-Dinka, SPLA-Nuer, other factions	BE+	Aug. 1991 – ...
18.	Algeria	GIA, AIS	AF	1991 – ...
19.	Egypt	Islamic Jihad	A	1992 – ...
West Africa				
20.	Senegal	Diola, MFDC	BA	April 1990 – ...
21.	Liberia	NPFL, INPFL	EA / EA+	Dec. 1989 / Aug. 90 – ...
22.	Sierra Leone	RUF, NPFL, ULIMO	AEC	Jan. 1991 – ...
23.	Mali	Burkina Faso	C	21–31 Dec 1985
24.	Mali/Niger	Tuareg: MFUA, MPA, FIAA	BCE / BC	May 1990–2 / June 1994 – ...

Table A.1: ECOR Index of Mass Violence in the Decade 1985–1994 (continued)

no.	Country	Groups / Actors	Conflict Types	Period / Phases
Central Africa				
25.	Chad	FAN, FAP, MPS	E/BAC+/BA+/B	June 1966/79/ 1990 / 1991 – ...
26.	Rwanda	Hutu army, Tutsi rebels FPR/RPA	A+ / BA+	Oct. 1990 / 1992 – July 1994
27.	Rwanda	Interahamwe, CDR, GP, FAR vs. Tutsi	GEF+ / G+	1990 / 6 Apr 1994 – 15 July 1994
28.	Burundi	Tutsi (army), Hutu militias FDD, FNL	G / GE / EAC	1972 / Oct 1993 / 1993 – ...
29.	Zaire	Luba; Hunde, Nyanga, Hutu	EA / GEA	Aug. 1992 / March 1993 – ...
East Africa / Horn of Africa				
30.	Ethiopia	Eritrea: ELF, EPLF	DB / DAB	1962 / 1976 – May 1991
31.	Ethiopia	Tigrai, TLF, TPLF, EPRDF	B / BA	1975 – May 1991
32.	Ethiopia	Oromo: OLF, IFLO, UOPL	BAD / BDA	1976 / May 1991 – ...
33.	Ethiopia	Gojjam, Gondar: EPRP, EDU	A / AB / BA	Mar 1974 / Dec. 1975 / May 1991 – ...
34.	Ethiopia	EPRDF: EPDM, OPDO	AB	Jan 1989 – May 1991
35.	Djibouti	Afar (FRUD, o/a)	BEA / BAE	1981 / Oct 1991 – ...
36.	Eritrea	ELF-Idriss, ELF-GC	EA+	1993 (?) – ...
37.	Somalia	Somaliland: Isaaq, SNM	BA+ / BA	1980 / 1990 – May 1991
38.	Somalia	Marehan, SSDF, SDM, USC	EA / E / E+	1988 / Jan. 1991 / Dec. 1992 – ...
39.	Uganda	NRM, Acholi, Langi, Bari	AB / EA	Feb. 1981 / Feb. 1986 / – ...
Southern Africa				
40.	Angola	MPLA; FLNA, UNITA	D/BAC+/ BAE	1961–75 / 20 June 1991 – ...
41.	Namibia	SWAPO, Herero, !Khoi; TA	BD	1966 – 22 Dec. 1988
42.	Zimbabwe	ZANU, Ndebele-ZAPU	AB / EA	Jan. 1983 / 1987 – May 1988
43.	Mozambique	FRELIMO; RENAMO	D / AC / AE+	1991 / 1975 – Oct. 1992 (?)
44.	South Africa	ANC and PAC vs. Zulu Inkatha, Boers	DA/DAE/EAD	1962 / 1976 / 1990 – ...
Europe – West				
45.	Spain	Euzkadi, ETA, HB	BA	1937 – ...
46.	France	Corsica, FLNC	BA	1950 – ...
47.	Northern Ireland	IRA, UVF, UFF	DB / DEA / EDA	1961–9 / 1986 – Oct 1994

Table A.1: ECOR Index of Mass Violence in the Decade 1985–1994 (continued)

no.	Country	Groups / Actors	Conflict Types	Period / Phases
Europe – East				
48.	Yugoslavia	Slovenia / Croatia	AB / CB	June 1991 – July 91 / Oct 91
49.	Croatia	Serbs (Krajina, Eastern Slavonia)	G / BF+ / EA	1940-44/mid 1991–3 / May 95
50.	Bosnia:	*Tshetnik*i, Muslims, HOS, a/o	EFB+	March 1992 – ...
51.	Moldavia	Russians, Ukrainians, Kosaks	EF+	March – Aug. 1992
52.	Rumania	Securitate, Timisoara Magyar	AE	17. – 28. Dec. 1989
Europe – Southeast / CIS				
53.	Georgia	Gamsachurdia rebels	A / AEF	Sept. 1991/Jan. 1992 – Nov. 1993
54.	Georgia	S-Ossetia	B	Dec. 1990 – July 1992
55.	Georgia	Abkhazia; alliance, Russians	BC / BC+	Aug. 1992 / July 1993 – Dec 1993
56.	Chechnya	Inguschi, North Ossetians	BE	Dec. 1991 – March 1992
57.	Azerbaijan	Nagorno-Karabakh	BE / CBE	1988–90 / 1992 – May 1994
58.	Armenia	SW-Azerbaijan	CBEF	March 1993 – May 1994
59.	Russia	Russian Army vs. Chechen rebels	BEAF	11. Dec. 1994 – ...
West Asia / Middle East				
60.	Lebanon	Maronites, Druses, Shiites / Hisb'Allah	AE/CEA/EAC	April 75 / 78 / 82 – 1993 (?)
61.	Israel	Palestine: PLO / Hamas; Druses	DB	1968 – ...
62.	S-Yemen	Tribes, clans, JSP	AEF	13–29 Jan 1986
63.	N-Yemen	South Yemen	ABC / BAC	Dec. 1991 / March 1994 – July 1994
64.	Turkey	Kurds, PKK, HRK	B / BADF	1970 / 1984 – ...
West Asia / Persian Gulf				
65.	Iran	Azeri, Kurds, Turkmen	BA	July 1979 – 1988 / ...(?)
66.	Iraq	Kurds, PUK, KDP	BA / BAC /BA+	1976 /Feb. 1991 / March 1991 – ...
67.	Iraq	Iran (1st Gulf war), Kurds	CB	Sept. 1980 – 20. Aug. 1988
68.	Iraq	Kuwait	CD	2 – 4 Aug. 1990
69.	USA/GB and others	Iraq (2nd Gulf war)	C	17 Jan – 27 Feb 1991 / ...
70.	Iraq	Shiites	AB/CAB	1990 / Mar 1991 – ...

Table A.1: ECOR Index of Mass Violence in the Decade 1985–1994 (continued)

no.	Country	Groups / Actors	Conflict Types	Period / Phases
Central Asia				
71.	Tajikistan	Tajik clans, Russian troops; Islamists	EAF+	Aug. 1992 – June 1993 (?)
72.	Afghanistan	CP, Pathanen, Tajik, Usbek, a.	ABE/BAE+/EB	1973 / Oct. 1978 / Apr. 1992 – ...
73.	Pakistan	Sindhi, SNA, Muhajir, Paschtun	BEF	Nov. 1986 – ...
South Asia				
74.	India	Pakistan (Siachen glacier)	C	April 1984 – 1989 (?)
75.	India	Kashmir: Muslim/Jamu/Ladakh	BE / BAE	1986 / 1990 – ...
76.	India	Punjab: Sikhs, KLF, KCF	BAE	July 1982 – ...
77.	India	Bihar: Naxaliten	A	1988 – ... (?)
78.	Sri Lanka	LTTE, EPRLF, Tamils, Muslims	B/BA+/BAE+	July 1983/Sept 1987 / Mar 1990 – ...
79.	Sri Lanka	JVP, Singhalese Youth	AE	July 1987 – Nov 1989 (?)
80.	Bangladesh	CHT-Tribes, Chakma; Shanty Bahini	BAF	1973 – ...
81.	NE-India	Tai-Asom, ULFA, Boro / Bodo	BEA	1990 – ...
82.	NE-India	West Bengal / Himalaya: Gorkha	BA	1987 – 1988 (?)
Southeast Asia				
83.	NE-India	Naga: RGN, NNC, NSCN	BD/BEA/AB/BA	1954 / 1963 / 1972 / Nov 1975 – ...
84.	NE-India	Manipur: KNA, NSCN, Meitei	BA / BEA / BAE	1960 / 1975 / 1984 / May 1992 – ...
85.	NE-India	Mizo: MNF, u.a.	BAE	1966 – June 1986
86.	Burma	Karen: KNDO, KNU	BEA / B / BA	1947 / 1950 / 1988 – ...
87.	Burma	CPB (PVO, Red Flag), DPA	A / A+ / AB	1948 / 1962 / March 1989 – ...
88.	Burma	KIO, Mon; NDF; Pa-O, KNPP	B / BAE / BA	1962 / 1976 / Nov. 1988 – ...
89.	Burma	Shan, Da'an, ALF, Wa, a, a.	EA / EBA	1970 (?) / 1988 – ...
90.	Burma	DAB: NDF, ABSDF, PPP, a.	AB	Nov. 1988 – ...
91.	Burma	opium guerrilla: MTA, Wa	EA+/EFA/FE	1950 / 1976 / March 1989 – ...
92.	Thailand	Laos	C	Nov. 1987 – Febr. 1988

Table A.1: ECOR Index of Mass Violence in the Decade 1985–1994 (continued)

no.	Country	Groups / Actors	Conflict Types	Period / Phases
Southeast Asia (continued)				
93.	Laos	Hmong, LLA, drug warlords	FEC+ / FEA	1970 / 1975 – ...
94.	Cambodia	Khmer Rouge, ANS, Sihanouk	A/CA/G/AB+/A +	1968 / 1970 / 1971 – 1975 / 1979 / 1985 – ...
95.	Vietnam	Montagnards, KPNLA, FULRO	B / BA+ / B	1964 / 1970 / 1975 – Oct. 1992 (?)
East Asia				
96.	China	Vietnam	C	Feb./March 1979 – 1988
Island Asia and Pacific				
97.	Philippines	NPA, Cordillera, CPA, Bontok	AB	1970 – ...
98.	Philippines	Mindanao: Moro, MNLF, MILF	BA+ / BA	1970 / 1989 – ...
99.	Indonesia	Aceh, various groups	B	May 1990 – ...
100	Indonesia	East Timor: army vs. FRETILIN	DBA	Aug. 1975 – ...
101	Indonesia	West Papua, OPM	DGB	1965 – ...
102	Papua New Guinea	Bougainville: BRA vs. PNGDF army	BAE / BAD	1988 / Feb. 1989 – ...

Source: Scherrer / ECOR © 1995

Table A.2: Frequency and Dominance of Conflict Types in Percent 1985–1994

Conflict Types 1985–1994	A anti-regime wars	B ethno-nationalism	C interstate wars	D decolonization conflicts
dominance	19.6 %	44.1 %	11.8 %	4.9 %
mentioning	30.7 %	29.3 %	8.0 %	5.3 %

Conflict Types 1985–1994	E inter-ethnic	F gang wars	G genocide	B+D+E+G *ethnic* conflicts
dominance	13.7 %	3.9 %	2.0 %	64.7 %
mentioning	17.3 %	7.6 %	1.8 %	53.7 %

Result

Conflicts with a dominant ethnic-induced or ethnicized character (types B, D, E, and G) account for nearly two third (64.7 percent) of all contemporary conflicts. According to the number of appearances ethnic components made up 53.7 percent.

Table A.3: Frequency and Dominance of Violent Conflicts 1985–1994

World 1985–1994	A	B	C	D	E	F	G	cases
Latin America 13,7%	6-4-0	5-4-0	1-0-0	0-0-0	0-1-0	2-2-1		14
Central America	3-2-0	2-2-0	1-0-0			1-1-0		7
South America	3-2-0	3-2-0	0-0-0		0-1-0	1-1-1		7
Europe 14,7 %	2-2-2	7-3-1	3-1-0	0-1-0	3-3-2	0-3-1		15
Western Europe	0-2-1	2-0-0	0-0-0	0-1-0	1-0-0			3
Eastern Europe	1-0-0	1-1-1	1-0-0	0-0-0	2-1-0	0-3-0		5
SE: Caucasus	1-0-1	4-2-0	2-1-0	0-0-0	0-2-2	0-0-1		7
Africa 29,4 %	5-16-2	13-1-2	1-1-2	2-2-1	7-6-2	0-1-1	2-1-0	30
N-Africa	2-1-0	2-0-1	0-0-0	1-0-0	0-1-0	0-1-0	0-1-0	5
W-Africa	1-2-0	2-0-0	1-1-1	0-0-0	1-1-0			5
Central Africa	0-3-0	2-0-0	0-0-1	0-0-0	1-3-0	0-0-1	2-0-0	5
E-Africa	1-7-2	5-1-1	0-0-0	1-1-0	3-0-1			10
Southern Africa	1-3-0	2-0-0	0-0-0	0-1-1	2-1-1			5
Asia 42,2 %	7-19-4	20-8-2	7-0-2	3-1-2	4-6-5	2-0-4	0-1-0	43
West Asia	1-6-0	4-2-1	4-0-2	1-1-1	1-1-0	0-0-1		11
Central Asia	0-1-0	1-1-0			2-1-0	0-0-2		3
S-Asia	2-4-0	4-0-0	1-0-0		0-1-3	0-0-1		7
SE-Asia	3-6-3	8-3-0	1-0-0		1-3-2	2-0-0		15
E-Asia	0-0-0	0-0-0	1-0-0					1
Island Asia/Pacific	1-2-1	3-2-1	0-0-0	2-0-1			0-1-0	6
all conflicts 1985 – 1994	20-41-8	45-16-5	12-2-4	5-4-3	14-16-9	4-6-7	2-2-0	225
types of conflict	**A**	**B**	**C**	**D**	**E**	**F**	**G**	**all**
dominance	**20**	**45**	**12**	**5**	**14**	**4**	**2**	**102**
total appearances	**69**	**66**	**18**	**12**	**39**	**17**	**4**	**225**

Source: Scherrer / ECOR © 1995

Table A.4: ECOR Index of Mass Violence 1995–2000

no	State	Groups / Actors	Types	Period / Phases
Central America				
1	Mexico	EZLN (Chiapas), Tzeltal, Tzotzil	BA / AB	Jan. 1994 / 2/1995 – ...
2	Mexico	EPR / ELN (Guerrero, Oaxaca)	BA	June 1996 – ... (new)
3	Guatemala	URNG	GAB / AB	1960 / 1980 – Dec 1996 (end)
4	Haiti	Army/gangs, US force	FA+	Sep 1994 – 95 (end)
South America				
5	Brazil	settler, gold rush vs. indigenous peoples	GE / FE	1986 (?) / 1989 – ...
6	Columbia South	FARC vs. army / alliance with narco cartels	AB; A; A; A	1964/ 1965 / Jan. 1974 – Mar. 1990 / 1992 –...
7	Columbia Northeast	ELN vs. army, TNC, paramilitaries; spill over to Venezuela	AB; A; AEC	1965 / 1974 – 96 / 1997 – ...
8	Columbia	drug syndicates, death squads	F	1970 (?) – ...
9	Peru	Andes/Selva: Sendero Luminoso / Rojo; militias	AB / ABF / AFB	1975 / 1980 – March 1995 / ...
10	Peru	MRTA; support among Aymara and Quichua low	AB / AB	Nov. 1987–92/Dec 96 – Apr 1997 / 1997 – ...
11	Ecuador	Peru	C	Jan–Feb 1995 (end)
North Africa				
12	Algeria	Islamists, MIA, AIS; (platform of Rome 95)	AF / AF	1991–4 / Jan 1995 – Oct 1997 (end)
13	Algeria	GIA vs. army, civilians, intellectuals, France	AF / FAC / FG	1992 – 94 / 1995–6 / 1996 – ...
14	Egypt	Muslim integrists / al-djama'a al-Islamiyya	AF / AF	1992–7 / Nov. 1997 – ...
15	Morocco	W-Sahara; Polisario; MINURSO	DB	Nov. 1975 – 92 / ... (?)
16	Sudan	South Sudan: SPLA vs. army	BA+ / BEA / BA	Sept. 1983 – 1991 / 91–2 / 1992– ...
17	Sudan	SPLA vs. SPLA-U, SSIA, Nuer and others	F / BE+ / EF	Aug. 1991 / 1992 / Sep 92– ...
18	Sudan	Arab militias vs. SPLA and civilians (slavery)	F / FE	1983 / 1991 – ...
19	Sudan	Central Sudan: Nuba genocide	BGA / GBE / GE	1989 / 1991–8 / 1998 – ...
20	Sudan	NDA; North Sudanese + SPLA/M, from Eritrea	AB+ / A+	Oct. 1989 / 1995 – ...

Source: Scherrer / ECOR © 2001

Table A.4: ECOR Index of Mass Violence 1995–2000 (continued)

no	State	Groups / Actors	Types	Period / Phases
West Africa				
21	Liberia	NPFL, ULIMO (K+J), LPC / ECOMOG (end of mission 1997)	EF / EA+ / EAC / EA	1989 / 95 / April 96 – 1997 / 2000 – …
22	Senegal	Diola, MFDC, factions vs. Army ; spill-over to Guinea Bissau	BAD / BA / BDC	1990 – July 93 / Jan. 1995 – Dec 1995 / 1997 – …
23	Sierra Leone	RUF, NPFL (Liberia), ULIMO / EO (SAR) / RUF vs. Kamajors, gov., UN and British troops	EC / AE+ / EFA+	Jan. 1991 – 97 / 1998 / 1999 – …
24	Sierra Leone	RUF and AFRC (army) vs. ECOMOG II (Nigerian)	FCG+	May 1997–8
25	Mali	Tuareg: MPA, FIAA; militias	BAE / BCE	1990–2 / 1994–7 (end)
26	Niger	Tuareg: FLAA	BAE / BCE / BC	May 1990–1 / Oct. 1994 – …
27	Niger	Arabs, others; FDR	BE	1995–8 (new/end)
28	Ghana	Konkomba vs. Nanumba, Gonja	EA	Feb. 1994 – 1996 (?) (end)
29	Nigeria South	Ogoni (MOSOP), others vs. army, TNCs / CHIKOKO	BA / BAD	1990er / 1997–9 (new/end)
30	Nigeria Delta	Ijaw (IYC) vs. Itsekiri, Ilaye, army, TNCs; NDVF	EA	1998 – … (?) (new)
31	Nigeria N/S	Islamists vs. migrants from South/Christians	EF	1998 – … (new)
32	Guinea-Bissau	coup d'état / intervention by Senegal and Guinea, later ECOWAS	AC+	June 1998 – Nov 1998 / Jan – Nov 1999 / 1999 – … (new)
Central Africa				
33	N-Chad	Frolinat, FNT; Libya; MDD, Frolinat-FAP, RAFAD	B/BAC+/B A+/EC+ / EA	June 1966 / 1979–83 / 1983–90 / 1991–4 / 1995 – …
34	S-Chad	CSNPD, FARF	BA / BEA / BA / DA	1985 / 1991 / Aug. 94 – 1997 / 1998 – …
35	Congo R	Ngesso militia vs. army	AE	1997 – Oct 1997 (end)
36	Congo DR-South	Luba; Katangan Tigers; Lumumbist	EA / AE	Aug. 1992 / 1993 – May 1997 (end)
37	Congo DR Zaire-East	Rwandan Hutu, FAZ vs Tutsi; a/o; / RCD	GEF	mid 1994 – Nov. 1996/ Aug 1998 – …
38	Zaire-East	AFDL, Banyamulenge vs. FAR, Rwanda Hutu	EA / A	Sept. 1996 – May 1997 (new/end)
39	Congo DR East-NE-South	RCD with RPA + UPDF vs. FAC+ FAA+ ZDF+ NDF+ Chad, Hutu, Maji-Maji, a/o	AC+	2 Aug 1998 – … (new)

Source: Scherrer / ECOR © 2001

Table A.4: ECOR Index of Mass Violence 1995–2000 (continued)

no	State	Groups / Actors	Types	Period / Phases
Central Africa (continued)				
40	Congo DR North	MLC+UPDF vs. FAC+FAA+ZDF, SA	ACE+	2 Aug 1998 – ... (new)
41	Congo DR Northeast	Lendu+Hutu, ADF, Maji vs. Hema+UPDF	FEG+	1999 – ... (new)
42	Rwanda	post-genocide destabilization by FAR-Interahamwe	EFC+ / G / EA+	Oct. 1990 /1994 / Jul 1994 – 1998 (end)
43	Burundi	Tutsi/Hutu: Army vs. FDD/FNL alliance, support by Kabila/DRC	G / GF / EAC / EGC+	1972 – ... / Oct 1993 / 1993–6 / Oct. 1999 – ...
Eastern Africa and Horn of Africa				
44	Ethiopia Oromia	Oromo: OLF, IFLO, (UOPL)	BAD / BDA	1976 – May 1991 / April 1992 – ...
45	Ethiopia	Eritrea; spill over to OLF, Somalia	C	Mar 1998 – June 2000 (new/end)...
46	Ethiopia Ogaden	Somali, div.; al Ittihad; Somalia-South	B / BEA / BC	1974 / 1992 – 96 / 1997 -...
47	Ethiopia	Gojjam, Gondar: EPRP, EDU	A / AB / BA	Mar 74 /Dec. 1975 – 91 / 1991–5 (end)...
48	Djibouti	Afar (FRUD others.)	BEA/BAE	1981 / Oct. 1991 – ...
49	Eritrea	ELF-Idriss, Jihad, ELF-GC	EA+	1993 – 1997 (end)
50	Somalia	clans; SNA, USC, RRA, UNOSOM / warlords / EPRDF+SNF vs. various	EF/ EA / EF / EFC	1988–90 / Jan. 91 / Dec. 1992 – 1996 / 1997 – 2000.
51	Somalia	UNITAF (USA et al) / UNOSOM II vs. warlords	FC	Dec. 1992 – May 1993 / 1993 – Mar 1995 (end)
52	Somali-land	Issa / other clans	EDC* / EF	May 1988-May 1991/ 1992–7 (?) (end)
53	Uganda NW	LRA, WNBF; a/o; support by Sudan vs. UPDF, SPLA	AB / EA+ / EAC+	Feb. 1981 / Feb. 1986 – 96 / 1996 – ...
54	Uganda North	MIR (Islamic), UDFM; support by Sudan	EA+	1995 – ... (new)
55	Uganda SW	ADF; alliance with Hutu, Maji-Maji, Lendu	ECA / FC	1991 / 1996 – 98 / 1998 – ...
Southern Africa				
56	Angola	UNITA vs. FAA army, supported by SAR, then Zaire; 'final offensive' by FAA late 1999	D / BAC+ / BAE+ / EAB / AE	1961–75/June 1991–4 / 1994– 97 / 1997 – Oct 1999 / Nov 1999 – ...
57	Angola Cabinda	FLEC-FAC, FLEC II vs. FAA, TNCs	AE / AEF / BAF	1975 / 1993–4 / 1997 – ...
58	South Africa	Kwa-Zulu: Inkatha IFP	EA	1990 – ...

Source: Scherrer / ECOR © 2001

Table A.4: ECOR Index of Mass Violence 1995–2000 (continued)

no	State	Groups / Actors	Types	Period / Phases
Western Europe				
59	Spain	Basque Country / Euzkadi, ETA, street fighter kids	BA / BAD	1937 – Sept 1998 / Nov 1999 – ...
60	France	Corsica, FLNC a/o	BA / BA	1950-.../ 1970-...
61	Northern Ireland	IRA, INLA vs. UK (RIR and RUC); UVF, UFF	DB / DEA / EDA / DA	1961–9 / 1986 – Oct 1994 / 1995 – July 1997 / May 1998 (end)
Eastern Europe				
62	Croatia	Expulsion of Serbs from Krajina / Eastern Slavonia	G / BF+ / EA	1940–4 / mid 1991–3 / May 1995 – (end)
63	Bosnia:	Chetniki, Muslims, HOS; NATO bombs against Serbs	ECB+	Mar 1992 / Sept 1995 – Oct. 1995 (end)
64	Russia	Chechen rebels vs. Dagestan; 2nd RF intervention	BEAF / EF+	Dec. 1994 – Aug. 1996 / Oct 1999 – ...
65	Yugoslavia Kosovo	UÇK-KLA vs. Serbian Police, army, militias	BFE+/ FE+	mid 1998 – March 1999 / May 1999 – ... (new)
66	Yugoslavia Kosovo	NATO bombardments vs. FRY (for 78 days)	C	March 99 – May 1999 (new/end)
67	Serbia South / Presevo Kosovo	UCK vs. Serb civilians, Roma, Egyptians, a/o / UCPMB vs. Serbs; in presence of KFOR	FE+ FEC+	May 1999 – 2000 / 2000 – (new)
West Asia / Middle East				
68	Lebanon South IDF Zone	Israel + SLA vs. Hisb'Allah, Amal, PFLP, a/o supported by Syria / Iran	EC / EC+	1982–93 / 1993 – 2000 (end)
69	Lebanon South	Israel IDF vs. Hisb'Allah a/o supported by Syria / Iran	ECF+	2000 (new)
70	Israel	Palestine: PLO / Hamas / Jihad Islami, Intifada II (Sharon on Temple Mount)	DB / DBA / DBC	1968 – May 1994 / 1994 – Sep 2000 / 28 Sep 2000 – ...
71	Georgia	Abkhazia; army +Georgian militias vs. Abkhaz militias + Kosaks + CIS troops/UN	B+ / BE+	Aug 1992 – May 1994 / 1994 – 1998 (new/end)
72	Turkey Southeast	Kurds, PKK-HRK vs. army, militias	B / BADF / BAF/ BAFC	1970 / Aug 1984 – 1991 / 1991–7 / 1997 – ....
73	Turkey	Iraq: Turkish Army + KDP vs. PKK + PUK in security zone (Kurdish proxy war)	BC	Mar 1997 – May 1997 / Sep 1997 – Oct 1997 / Dec 1997–8 (new/end)
74	Iran	Kurds, DPK/I; air raids vs. Kurds in Iraq security zone	BA / BAD	July 1979 – 1988 / 1988 – ...
75	Iraq	Kurds, PUK, KDP; Republican Guards + KDP vs. PUK + supported by Iran	BA/BAG / BAF+ / BF+	1976 / -1988 / March 1990 – 1996 / Aug 1996 – ...

Source: Scherrer / ECOR © 2001

Table A.4: ECOR Index of Mass Violence 1995–2000 (continued)

no	State	Groups / Actors	Types	Period / Phases
West Asia / Middle East (continued)				
76	Iraq	Kurdish proxy war: PUK vs. KDP; Iraq RG + KDP vs. PUK + PKK	BFC+	Aug 1996 – Sep 1996 / 1997 (new/end)
77	Iraq	regimes vs. Shiites / Shia	AB/CAB/ AB	1990 / March 1991 / 1991 – ...
78	Iraq	New sustained bombardments by USA and UK; new attempt of destabilizing Saddam	CA	Dec 1998 – 2000 (new/end)
Central Asia				
79	Kyrgyzstan Ferghana valley	Islamist Uzbeks IMU vs. Kyrgyz and Uzbek army; spill-over from Tajikistan/ Afghanistan	EAC+ / ECF*	Aug–Oct 1999 / Dec 1999 – ... (new/end)
80	Tajikistan	Islamist UTO vs. communists, Clans, CIS/RF troops until 1997; Afghanistan spill-over; Uzbekistan	EAF+ / EA+ / EAF+	Aug. 1992 – June 1993 / 1993 – June 1997 / Nov 1998 – 2000 (end?)
81	Afghanistan	CP, Pashtun, Tajik, Uzbek; Taliban and al-Qaeda vs. Northern alliance	ABE / BAE+/ EB / EBC / EC	1973/ Oct. 1978–89 /1989– 92 / Apr. 1992 – 1996 / 1997 – ...
82	Kazakhstan South	Jihad extremists and mafia, Kazakh-Uzbek border; bomb raids by Hezb ut-Tahrir; Kazakh Russians at risk	FA	Aug 2000 – ...
South Asia				
83	Pakistan	India / Kashmir 'line of control'	C	1999 (new/end)
84	Pakistan Sindh	Sindhi, MQM, Muhajir / Pashtun	BEF / EF	Nov. 1986–90 / 1990 – ...
85	India	Kashmir: Muslim JKLF, Hizb'Allah vs. Jamu/Ladakh	BE / BAE	1986 / 1990 – ...
86	India	Bihar: Naxalites	A	1988 – ...
87	Sri Lanka	LTTE, Tamils	B/BA+/ BAE+	July 1983 /Sept 1987/ Mar 1990 – ...
88	Bangladesh	Chittagong Hill Tracts: Chakma, Shanti Bahini	BAF	1973 – 1997 (end)
89	Nepal	UPF vs. special police forces	A	1998 (?) – ... (new)
Southeast Asia				
90	NE-India	Tai-Asom, ULFA; IBRF	FG / BEA	1983 / 1989 – ...
91	NE-India	Boro; ABSU, BSF, BLTF	BEA / BEF	1967 / 1989 – ...
92	NE-India	Naga: RGN, NNC, NSCN; talks with GoI; cease-fire	BD/BEA/A B/BA	1954 / 1963 / 1972 / Nov 1975–97 (end)

Source: Scherrer / ECOR © 2001

Table A.4: ECOR Index of Mass Violence 1995–2000 (continued)

no	State	Groups / Actors	Types	Period / Phases
Southeast Asia (continued)				
93	NE-India	Manipur: Kuki KNA, Meitei vs NSCN	BA / BEA / BAE / BA	1960 / 1975 / 1984 / May 1992 – ...
94	Burma	Karen / Karenni: KNU, KNPP, DAB vs. Army and DKBA (quislings)	BEA / BD / BAG	1947 / 1950 – 1988 / 1988 – ...
95	Burma	Shan/Tai: SSPP-SSA, SURA, a/o	BAD / BA / BAF	1950s; 1960s –1988 / 1988 – ...
96	Burma	Mon, NMSP	B / BAE / BAG	1962 / 1976 / Nov 1988 – June 1995 (?) (end)
97	Burma	opium guerrilla: MTA, Wa, SSNA	EA+/EFA/F E	1950 / 1976 / Mar 1989 – ...
98	Laos	Hmong, LLA, drug war lords	FEC+/FEA	1970 / 1975 – ... (?)
99	Cambodia	Khmer Rouge; ANS//// / Khmer Rouge+ FUNCINPEC vs. CPP	A / CA / G / AB / A+ / AF+	1968 / 1970 / 1971–5 / 1979–97 / June 1997 – ...
Island Asia and Asia- Pacific				
100	Philippines	NPA, Cordillera, CPA, Bontok / RPP-ABB	AB / ABE	1970 – 1996 / 1997 -.
101	Philippines	Mindanao: Moro, MNLF, MILF; Abu Sayyaf, ICC	BA+ / BA	1970 / 1989 – Sept. 1996 / 1996 – ...
102	Indonesia Aceh	Aceh; GAM vs. Army and paramilitaries	BE / BE	May 1990 – ... / 1999 – ...
103	Indonesia Moluccas	Islamist vs. Christians; locals vs. settlers	FG	1998 – ... (new)
104	Indonesia	East-Timor; 80% of vote in referendum; terror of Quisling militia; UN troops	DBA / DG	Aug. 1975 – ... / Aug 1999 – Oct 2000 (new/end)
105	Indonesia Irian Jaya	West-Papua, OPM vs. army, settlers and TNCs	DGBC / DB	1965 – 1993 / Nov 1995 – ...
106	New Guinea	Bougainville, BRA, BTG, BIG vs. army, quislings, TNCs	BAD / BAD+/BAD	Feb. 1989 – 1990 / 1992 – 1995 / 1995 – Oct 1997 (end)
107	Solomon Islands	Guadalcanal; GLA-IFF militia vs. Malaitan migrants, police	EFA / EF	Dec 1998 – Dec 1999 / 2000 – ... (new)

General Observations

The number of conflicts remained high throughout the period 1985 to 2000. The absolute number of conflicts was not decreasing (or even sharply decreasing) as other sources suggest. There was a constant up and down of the annual number of indexed conflicts. Concerning the virulence of violent conflict in the South (esp. in many regions of Africa and Asia) there is no evidence for a relaxation. Many *endless* civil wars are still being continued and many new ones are started. Some of the new conflicts are linked to older ones (Niger, India, DRC, Yugoslavia, a/o.), others are truly new.

Table A.5: Social-historical Typology of Peace

Type of peace	scope, realm	key principle	period	characteristics / phenomena / aims
1) **original positive peace**	society	stable in itself	very long periods	small(er) communities, intra-focus, harmony
2) **tranquil/silent peace by retreat / fleeing** *!Khoi type peace*	*civitas* traditional societies	dissociation; stable in itself, internal, extremely peaceable	long and very long periods	small(er) communities; conflict prevention by retreat / flight to remote uninhabited or ecologically difficult areas; cases: hunters & gatherers in deserts (!Khoi, Zhu Twasi), rain forests (Aka & Mbuti pygmies, Efe, Amazon tribes), mountain areas (Orang Asli, Aita, Papua tribes), bush land (Hadza), islands (Onge, Negritos)
3) **peace through isolation** **case of traditional societies or modern sub-cultures**	society world traditional communities; modern subcultures	dissociation; stable in itself, internal, peaceful	longer periods	limited-size societies; conflict prevention through isolation in geographically hidden areas / up-country, also areas with difficult communication and access; traditional societies; adaptation to nature; contemporary cases: many traditional societies, modern alternative land communities; aim: survival+ / original life-style
4) dynamic negative peace (peaceful coexistence broken by communities raiding) through high mobility & vigilance **acephality case**	society world: traditional communities clans lineages	dissociation; self-centred, internal, acephalous-segmentary	longer and fairly long periods	bigger-sized decentral (acephalous) tribal societies based on descent; conflict prevention through high mobility / vigilance in open areas (savannah, mountain tracts); some zones unsuitable for farming; traditional (semi-) nomadic communities; contemporary cases: pastoralists (Nilotic peoples, Somali), hill tribes in SE-Asia, Amerindians, etc.; aim: survival in pride/autonomy
5) peace as refuge **acculturation type**	sub-societies / traditional communities	dissociation; self-centred, internal; not closed, adaptable	Medium to longer periods	bigger-sized decentralized ethnic groups; conflict prevention through self-defence by refuge to areas with indigenous people; adaptation / acculturation to other societies; simple mode of production; aim: autonomous survival, option for later return to homeland

Table A.5: Social-historical Typology of Peace (continued)

Type of peace	scope, realm	key principle	Period	characteristics / phenomena / aims
6) silent peace by selective isolation and self-centred culture **irrigation-based society type**	hydraulic societies and states	dissociation; self-centred, internal; not closed	very long periods, cycles	large societies, 'high cultures' (behind 'Chinese walls', save from alien intruders, barbarians; conflict prevention by establishing save areas; sophisticated work intensive production (irrigation, AMP); high degree of organization; aim: peace, security and order
7) peace by civilizational cultural development **great tradition type**	irrigation-based (hydraulic) societies and empires	more dissociative as associative; not expansive, self-centred; receptive	Medium and long periods; dynastic	large class societies, 'high cultures' behind walls, standing armies against barbarians; conflict prevention by self-centred development incl. foreign exchange and trade; sophisticated production (AMP+): high geared organization; aim: security and prosperity
8) coexistence through (peace) agreements, treaties, alliances, **colonial peace**	state / corporate economy primary scope; societal scope	expansive, aggressive (internal / external)	Medium or longer periods; *boom-bust*	class societies / metropolitan states; conflict regulation through agreements with other powers; (arms-) production; security through deterrence; higher degree of organization; aims: prosperity through resource exploitation and dominance
9) coexistence through development / trade, negative peace; capitalist economy; **imperial co-existence**	societies and economies	associative; external expansion	medium or longer periods; intended linearity	class societies, stable state structure; rule of law, elites; conflict avoidance, social containment and normalization (internal); prevention, conflict avoidance through trade, 'inter-dependency' (external); industrial goods; higher degree of organization; power and profit (for a few); aim: security / prosperity
10) dynamic negative peace and coexistence through development / trade **modern society type peace of the rich**	societies and states	associative-dissociative; tends to expansionism; some receptiveness	medium periods linearity	class societies / 'consumer cultures'; conflict containment, dynamic social normalization and integration (internal); conflict prevention by foreign exchange, trade (external); migrants for cheap labour followed by walls against migrants; solid production, innovation; high degree of organization; aim: security for all, prosperity for the upper class

Table A.5: Social-historical Typology of Peace (continued)

Type of peace	scope, realm	key principle	period	characteristics / phenomena / aims
11) negative peace and coexistence through self-centred development and selective trade **Indian co-existence**	poor states and heterogeneous societies	associative-dissociative; tends to isolationism; some receptiveness	medium / longer periods; political cycles; intended continuity	multi-ethnic pluri-cultural class (caste) societies, heterogeneous states (often former civilizations); conflict prevention mechanism, regulation through creation of new union states, cultural/religious rights for non-dominant groups, self-governance; quota system; degree of organization; agriculture, emerging industry; aim: security based on respect of multiplicity (internal); negative peace through strength (external), prosperity for middle and upper class
12) military coexistence through dominated alliances, negative peace broken by wars; settler state type; **pax americana**	state and TNC-economy is the primary scope; societal scope	expansive, interventionist; aggressive (internal / external)	medium and longer periods; linearity; intended continuity	mainstream settler society, strong state structure; (formal) rule of law; regulation through social segregation, welfare programmes; ideology of melting pot, schemes for indigenous minorities (internal), agreements with other powers (external); major wars possible; security through strength and dominance; high degree of organization; sophisticated capitalist mode of production; aims: securing prosperity, free resource exploitation, military strength
13) coexistence through autonomization of nationalities and alliances, case of USSR-FSU: **pax sovietica**	state scope primary; societal scope secondary	non-expansionist, self-centred; active/inter-active (internal, external)	Medium & longer periods; political cycles; stagnation	multi-ethnic pluri-cultural societies / heterogeneous states; structural conflict prevention institutionalized, regulation through dispute resolution with / cultural rights for non-dominant ethno-national entities, autonomous territories / self-governance according to the *Korenisazia*-model; high degree of organization; aim: security based on respect of others (internal) and negative peace through deterrence (external), some prosperity for many
14) positive peace and coexistence through pragmatism, sociability and **pax africana**	societal scope primary; state scope secondary	peaceful non-expansive pattern; local / regional setting	longer periods; no intention of linearity	many diverse societies / weak dependent periphery states; internal societal regulations by hospitality, neo-traditions (rituals, myths), respect for *otherness*, palaver-democracy; peaceful settlement of disputes with neighbours; peasants (subsistence), industry disconnected; lower degree of organization; aim: securing survival+

Table A.5: Social-historical Typology of Peace (continued)

Type of peace	scope, realm	key principle	period	characteristics / phenomena / aims
15) peace and coexistence through integration into the world market; dependent state type **neocolonial co-existence**	state scope primary; societal scope secondary	non expansiv, internal / external	medium periods not much linearity	weak dependent states at the periphery / many societies; internal state-based regulations (political ceremonies, elite co-option and bargaining), lobbying with metropolitan powers; agriculture (subsistence+ / export) and industrialization (weak); low degree of organization; aim: preservation of *status-quo*, development
16) peace / coexistence by vertical integration (foreign dominated) & cultural assimilation **repressive co-existence**	state scope (despotic state) primary; societal scope repressed	forced association; expansive state structure internally	shorter / medium periods; pretension of linearity	manifold multi-ethnic societies / military and despotic periphery states; weak internal state-dominated regulations, lobbying with metropolitan colonial powers or new regional powers; agriculture (subsistence+ / export sector) and weak dissociated industry; aim: preservation of status-quo and elite power
17) coexistence through autonomy/conservation for indigenous nations as well as regional co-operation; Latin American liberal type **neoliberal co-existence**	state scope (primary); catholic clergy, civil society (secondary only)	state-centred; internal colonialism by less repressive means	shorter and longer periods	periphery states; *mestizo* societies searching for identity vs. indigenous communities; autonomy types: *comarca* (Kuna since 1920s), *resguardo* (Columbia), self-rule (Nicaragua 1990); weak economic base for autonomy; non-integration in most states with attempts to assimilation; neglect / paternalism; traditional institutions formal life (*caciques/congreso*-system); Mexico to avert armed conflict by autonomy in Chiapas; aim: control by concessions
18) peace / coexistence by new autonomy concessions (internal) and joining EU / NATO (external) **case of Eastern Europe and former FSU-states**	state scope primary; civil societal scope still under-developed active (external)	non-expansive, West-oriented; reactive (internal), sub- active (external)	medium / longer periods; political decline and stagnation / regression	multi-ethnic pluri-cultural societies with (new) minorities / heterogeneous (partly) new states; structural conflict prevention formerly institutionalized, cultural rights for non-dominant ethno-national entities and autonomy regulations in ethno-nationalist frenzy often unilaterally cancelled / revoked after 1990 (loss of autonomy led to several wars); underdeveloped dispute resolution (exception: *Korenisazzia*-model still valid in Russian Federation); declining degree of organization; some prosperity for a few; aim: security based on control of others (internal) and go-West (external)

Table A.5: Social-historical Typology of Peace (continued)

Type of peace	scope, realm	key principle	period	characteristics / phenomena / aims
19) peaceful coexistence through autonomy for minorities (internal) and alliance / treaties (external); welfare state type, **pax helveto-scandinavica**	state scope and societal scope	non-expansive; active / inter-active (internal)	medium / longer periods; intention of linearity	plural societies / welfare states; structural conflict prevention institutionalized; regulation through democratic dispute and affirmative action / rights for non-dominant ethno-national entities; political concessions, no antagonizing dispute; autonomy / home rule for so-called minorities (Åland-model); high degree of organization; aim: security based on respect of others (internal) and negative peace through neutrality (external), 'prosperity for all' (if funds available)
20) negative peace through global governance with key objective to prevent and outlaw violent conflict on global scale 'eternal peace' **(Kant)**	state scope reduced to global state (*Weltstaat*); societal scope to *state* be fully developed	Utopia establishing one single *world* with manifold societies	medium / long period; some linear thinking	resolving the central problems (nation states' claims of sovereignty; permanent threat of war) by establishing a *world state*; objective: preventing war (containing lawless hostility), *reason* will triumph over anarchy and warfare; base for development of positive peace; every society has its own understanding of peace, no limits to multi-facet peace and the positive idea of a *world republic*; aim: sustainable peace by banning wars on a global scale 'for all times'
21) positive peace by the disappearance of the state and borderless freedom; emancipation of humanity '**positive peace**'	state scope disappeared; societal and individual scope fully developed	Utopia emancipation; egalitarian society	long period; linear thinking to be abolished	*positive peace* would represent a new quality of social interaction; proactive; constant efforts by humanity on individual/group base; to reproduce as a free and emancipated individual everyone shall as a free associated member of a chosen group by respect the freedom and space for personal development of others; aim: positive anarchy; full emancipation and satisfaction for all and everyone
Back to 1)				full cycle forward to original positive peace (type 1)

Remark: Social-historic types of peace taken from different periods of history and regions of world; two types belong to utopia. At present most of these types have their place in reality in somewhat modified form. For instance, one could relate traditional societies of less 'extreme kind' as the case of the !Khoi to (post-) modern sub-cultures. We can learn from existing schemes and the reconstruction of former systems. Through the course of human history different forms and ways of peaceful coexistence of peoples, nations, cultures and civilisations have been experienced.

Abstracts of Related Books

Structural Prevention of Ethnic Violence

The themes of prevention, management, and transformation of ethno-national conflicts are addressed. The main topics are collective rights, self-governance, and nationality policies.[1] The political-cum-humanitarian concern to ensure that all possible means of avoiding violent forms of multi-ethnic interaction are exploited, strengthened, and made more attractive leads on to the question of how ethnic-cum-cultural difference is to be understood and acknowledged, and of the appropriate political and legal steps that need to be taken to pre-empt destructive forms of interaction between states and nations/nationalities.

The rethinking of the basic concepts of 'minority conflicts', the ethnos, nationality, and the politicization of the ethnic seems crucial for a better understanding of the new forms of mass violence we encounter in different world regions. The relationships of ethnicity and mass violence are explored. The task is mapping contemporary conflict. First the lacunae of global surveys on mass violence (usually 'war list') have to be identified. As an example of how to overcome the exclusion of ethnicity and non-war mass violence the ECOR typology of contemporary violent conflicts is introduced. Briefly the main actors, conflict causes, driving forces, and colonial legacies are mentioned. The main trends and perspectives in contemporary mass violence are identified. Correlating frequency and dominance of conflict types shows high dominance for ethno-nationalism. Significant trends are the reduction or even 'disappearance' of interstate wars, while foreign interventions increase, and the rise of non-Clausewitzean wars and mass violence. The regional distribution of conflicts has changed dramatically within one decade, exhibiting a decrease in Asia but a marked increase in Africa, particularly a dramatic increase of most deadly conflicts in Africa. Recent trends point to an increase of complex crisis situations and state collapse in the future. This has direct consequences for the task to avert violence and prevent destructive conflict.

Existential factors relating to the survival of an ethnic group are not open to negotiation; they are fundamental prerequisites to interaction between states and nations. There are a number of highly destructive forms of interaction between states and nations/nationalities that have not yet been subject to systematic investigation and for which the international community has not yet developed any consistent policy—in the shape, for example, of regimes for recognition or secession. But the concept of minority rights so often used in the context of the avoidance of ethno-national conflicts seems in need of elucidation on a number of counts.

The overdue reorientation of conflict research away from unfruitful and distorting East–West thinking has cleared the view onto the global phenomenon of intra-state conflicts. The virulence of the ethnic factor had previously been underestimated, but the need for research in this area has now been recognized. The new research priorities involve, first and foremost, greater attention to causes. My critique of some of the approaches—notably, in regard to tempering state-centredness and to correcting the over-simplified 'competition for resources' approach—is intended to broaden the debate about the potential for conflict/conflict resolution of certain types of regime. A combination of urgent need and an increasing awareness of the problems involved have led to an intensification of research-activities in the area of mediation and of the development of preventive and practical political capabilities. My account of the current state of research indicates both deficiencies and positive developments. The most important tasks for conflict research in future lie in the investigation of causes, prevention of mass violence and destruction, and a more practical orientation in general.

Several lacunae are grappling activities in the field of peaceful conflict settlement and add to the various difficulties go-betweens are facing. There is a general lack of systematic analysis and comparative studies in the field of peaceful conflict settlement. This contrasts with the many competing approaches to conflict resolution and theoretical works covering the field. Dispute-settlement is a traditional instrument of international politics but rarely such questions as who facilitates or mediates, what are the aims and objectives, and who are the beneficiaries are asked. Of special interest are the relationships between mediators and warring parties, and the management of the dynamics of talks. Instead of simply asking the question of success or failure a processual definition of objectives and outcomes seems preferable. Multi-track conflict mediation is in upswing and partly substitutes traditional diplomacy and track-1 mediation. The new role of civic go-betweens and peaceful dispute-settlement using civil actors is explored and illustrated with a selection of actors and cases. The process of six stages of conflict escalation is related to the type of possible responses. The question of the right timing for responses to conflict is crucial. A contribution is made to the debate about complex emergencies and post-conflict peace consolidation, focussing on humanitarian intervention and the role of non-governmental organizations. The task is to move from reactive responses to proactive engagement.

The self-determination of peoples is one of the main planks of ethno-national movements of revolt or resistance. But structurally, international law (esp. the law of the nations) protects states rather than peoples; application of the principle is contentious. From the 1920s, and again since the Second World War, autonomy arrangements of all kinds have helped resolve ethno-national conflicts in Europe. Classic measures include authorization of additional languages for official and educational purposes, protection of cultural independence, political representation, and special electoral regulations. The

creation of special territorial units has produced various forms of self-government by minorities in their traditional territories or by populations in outlying
districts (as in the Faeroese model). I explore various elements of, and evaluation criteria for, self-government which I use as guide-lines in my account of
selected examples.

Outside Europe, the demand of many nationalities for self-governance led
to a broadening and deepening of the classic form of minority protection. In the
case of indigenous peoples, there are lessons to be learned from the contractual
process of the last two centuries. The search for regional ideal-typical
examples of autonomy and self-governance produces a number of more or less
successful 'models' that could become paradigms for the particular regions
concerned and that ought to be subjected to more detailed investigation.
Prevention through autonomy-arrangements and generous nationality-policies
is not only cheaper than intervention; it is the only really ideal method when it
comes to dealing constructively with the problem of ethno-national difference.

Constructive conflict-averting structural elements for multi-ethnic states
entail a turning-away from culturally monopolistic, homogenizing nation-state
ideology and the political centralism that goes with it. The move towards
ethno-political cultural neutrality and the principle of decentralization means a
change of paradigm. There is no simple cure-all here. I explore a number of
examples of constructive structural elements in the global context. Federalization, decentralization, and territorial self-governance have proved themselves
all over the world as a means of averting conflict—as may be shown by a
cursory glance at the various 'models'.

Comparison of the nationality policies of the most populous countries of the
world (the multinational Asiatic states of China and India and the CIS/USSR)
with the minority policies of the former settler-colonies of North America (the
USA and Canada) is of major importance when it comes to positing international legal standards in regard to indigenous and endangered peoples. The
nationality policies of China and India in particular are little known or appreci-
ated. Each of these, in their particular permutations and with their differing
arsenals of collateral measures, have produced a number of successes which, in
regional terms, are not inconsiderable.

**Ethno-nationalism in the Age of Globalization: Causes, Structural Features
and Dynamics of Violent Ethno-national Conflicts**[2]

The global trend to ethno-nationalism has steadily increased over the last few
decades. But ethnicity cannot serve either as a rationale or as a fig-leaf to be
used when other interpretations fail. Ethnic violence is a response to difficult,
protracted crises. The question of what drives it leads on to the question of the
nature of ethnicity itself and of what constitutes the ethnic basis of nations.

Part I of this book deals with concepts and their careers. Given the almost routine mingling of ethnic groups, nations, states, and nation-states that is already taking place in both the conceptual and the real world, there is a need for some basic definition here. The concept of a minority, so often used in the context of ethno-national conflicts, seems in need of elucidation on a number of counts.

To list ten characteristics that enable an ethnic group or an indigenous people to describe itself as a nationality (i.e. a nation without its own state) in search of statehood is no academic exercise. These kinds of definitions acquire more and more political relevance the more clearly the relationship between nationalities, nations, and states is viewed as part of 'high politics' (international relations). Nationalities are distinguished from nations by their degree of political organization, their readiness to fight, and particular external circumstances. Part of the problem here is that only very few states are genuine nation-states. But the definition of individual attributes of ethnicity and their relative weighting is contentious, as is that of the organization, *modus operandi*, tasks, and manifestations of statehood. Different types of regimes have different approaches to the 'problem' of ethnicity.

The search for a new paradigm following the end of the Cold War is ongoing. Whatever it is ultimately called, a questioning of the old order based on the European concept of the nation-state and new dislocations caused by the second round of capitalist globalization will be amongst its hallmarks. This new paradigm is producing a global enhancement of ethnic-cum-cultural and economic driving forces as opposed to ideological-cum-political and military aspects.

The image of a 'war of civilizations' (Tibi) is an expression of fears about declining Western dominance. As a result of the debate about this 'war', the significance of the colonial nation-states as basic monistic actors has, for the very first time (even in the political sciences) been tempered. Irrespective of its shortcomings, this overdue debate has sharpened up awareness of the previously suppressed ethnic-cum-cultural domain. The 'clash of civilizations' (Huntington), in the form of a war of religions or even as nuclear destruction, will not take place. But real wars and mass destruction have been taking place since 1945 almost exclusively on the periphery of states, civilizations, and systems.

Part II of the book addresses the subject of ethnicity and mass violence. Armed conflicts in the Third World have many different causes and are a manifestation of a variety of partly autonomous influences. The difficulties of identifying the various factors in violent conflicts are manifold, stemming from confusing terminology, tendentious accounts by those involved, and a general lack of research into, and elucidation of, intra-state conflicts, which are much more frequent than those between states.

Typologies should not just be drawn up for war; they should also be drawn up for peace. With the aid of a typology of intra-state conflicts based on major driving forces, I discuss some of the problems inherent in attempting to distinguish between various types. Their actual merging in concrete conflicts— for example, where ecological conflicts are overlaid with ethnic ones—has repercussions for both theory and practice. The ECOR index for the ten years 1985–94 contained 102 wars and violent conflicts, reaching some 107 violent conflicts in the six years 1995–2000, the complex formation of which is analysed by a combined process of primary, secondary, and (some) tertiary classification. Since the beginning of the 1990s, political conflicts have been militarized to a degree unknown since the World War II. The hopes for a more peaceful world cherished since the end of the Cold War have come to nought.

The claims which false nation-states or ethnocracies, ruled by dominant ethnic groups who have secured 'possession' of the state, make in regard to ethnically distinct nationalities (so-called 'minorities' who are sometimes in the majority) have shown themselves to be the major source of violent conflict. Evidence of an urgent need for research is discernible for every subspecies of ethnically interpretable conflict. Wars of a predominantly ethnic character account for two-thirds of all armed conflicts. In some indexes of contemporary wars, the major type of conflict is listed under the shameful rubric 'miscellaneous intra-state conflicts'.

Over the last few years there has been a continued decline in the proportion of inter-state conflicts. Compared with the previous decade, this has more than halved and now stands at less than a twentieth of all conflicts. Decolonization conflicts remain at a constant twentieth of all conflicts. One disquieting fact is that the proportion of gang-style wars has almost doubled in the space of ten years. Though endemic chaos and 'war-lordism' continue to be a feature in only a small proportion of all conflicts (one in sixteen), there is a danger that this number will increase, as may be concluded from the higher number of mentions. The number of inter-ethnic conflicts—that is to say, conflicts between ethnic groups, mostly without the involvement of state actors—has increased by a clear third. The trend points towards further fragmentation within existing states and signifies an increasing loss of hegemony on the part of state actors.

Part III of the book attempts to highlight the essential difference between ethno-nationalism from below and ethnicization from above. A comparison of Third World societies with differently structured political systems points to differences in collective behaviour in situations of crisis. Using the example of the CIS states, I point up the consequences of the ethnicization of the political system of the former USSR.

There are differences in the capacities of traditional societies for conflict. Examples of militant acephalous/decentralized societies occur in societies as different from one another as the mountain peoples of the Himalayas, north-east India, Burma, and Indochina, the Oromo and Somalis in the Horn of Africa, the Miskitu, Kuna, Ngobe, and other lowland Indians of Central America, the Papua, fighting against transmigration and deculturation, and the

Nilotic pastoral societies of the Sudan, involved in one of the bloodiest wars of our time.

Another set of examples relates to so-called transitional societies, torn between opposition and integration. This applies in particular to the Masiri (Berbers), caught between Arabization, colonization, and cultural resistance. The Tuareg, a major Berber people in West Africa, is engaged in open opposition. In Mali, their revolt prompted de-escalatory moves, but in Niger it led only to a very fragile peace; outside interests continue to determine what happens to the natural resources on the Tuaregs' territory. Alongside the Oromo and Masiri, the Kurds are the largest stateless people on Europe's periphery. Kurds in five Middle Eastern countries continue even today to be divided and oppressed. Internally, their problem is the collaborators—the agas and warlords. Fratricidal conflicts between different Kurdish 'tribes' are weakening the resistance and delaying nation building among the Kurds. The Turkish élites' 'Sèvres syndrome' is preventing a solution being found. The 'scorched earth' policy pursued by the Turkish army in its fight against the PKK has failed. A solution along the lines of Neo-Osmanism and legal pluralism seems in sight, given that the Kurdish conflict is blocking Turkey's integration into the EU and also Turkey's regional ambitions. That said, all peace-initiatives in the Kurdish conflict have so far remained unsuccessful.

In the case of transitional societies, the colonial policy of indirect rule worked to divisive effect. Crowned heads played a destructive role. Given the history of collaboration, the restitution of kingdoms in Asia and Africa is hard to digest. I cite the Ugandan model as an illustration of the ambivalence of this process: nowadays, Baganda rule comes under the banner of 'cultural preservation'. The way in which traditional institutions are remoulded and utilized for political purposes, as illustrated by the example of the collaborators among the Zulu aristocracy in South Africa, highlights the whole contradictory nature of 'neo-tradition'.

As is shown by the example of the CIS, the structure and dynamics of the fragmentation process in the East follows its own set of rules and displays significant differences from the situation in the South. The thesis is that collapse of the USSR was predetermined and led to further ethnicization and follow-up conflicts. Because ethnicization was a constitutive element in the political system, ethno-nationalism in the former USSR came about quasi organically. Ethnic micro-nationalism may be seen as a non-intentional consequence of Lenin's nationality policy of *korenizatsiya*. The collapse of the Soviet Union was predetermined by the latter's administrative structure and— in total contrast to the collapse of other multinational states—proceeded peacefully to begin with.

However, the revocation of autonomy rights in some of the new states that had just emerged soon led to a second, violent phase of fragmentation. Despite this, in other states the nationalities system continued to demonstrate its flexibility and adaptability. Indeed, for economic reasons and reasons relating to status, there was an increase in the number of *sovereign* republics. The limits of the system were encountered in that firebox, the Caucasus, where there were a series of violent conflicts, ultimately also on the territory of the Russian Federation. In Chechnya, after a war that claimed numerous victims, a peace treaty was negotiated, but no permanent solution acceptable to both sides has yet been found.

The Never-Ending Civil Wars in Burma and Ethiopia: Ethno-national Conflict-Constellations Illustrated and Compared

This studies attempt to set the phenomenon of ethno-national conflict in a global context and to illustrate and compare different permutations of it using examples involving distinct colonial histories and cultural settings.[3]

I. The Horn of Africa: Federalization in Ethiopia and the Collapse of the State in Somalia

The multinational state of Ethiopia is remarkable for its extremely heterogeneous multi-ethnic composition. This came about only in the course of the last hundred years, not through external European colonization but through internal Abyssinian colonization of the south and of the peripheral lowlands and highlands. The Amharic Neftegna settlers in the south were largely disempowered in the 1974 revolution, but it was not until 1991 that the national dilemma of the Amhara became evident, when power was seized by the smaller Tigre minority.

The collapse of military socialism in Ethiopia had far-reaching consequences. The overthrow of the Mengistu regime led for the first time in Africa to a reorganization along ethno-national lines and to successful secession by the 'province' of Eritrea. However, the self-determination of the nations, nationalities, and peoples of Ethiopia—as provided for in the 1991 charter—was in practice immediately curtailed. The recourse to old methods of rule ruined the chances of peaceful dispute-settlement with the Oromo majority and the peoples in revolt on the margins of the kingdom.

II. Ethnicity and the Military State: The Burmese Civil War since 1948

Viewed from an ethnic-cum-cultural standpoint, South-East Asia extends as far as north-east India and south-west China. The region is characterized internally by the contrast between the rice-farmers living in the lowlands and on riverbanks, the urban peoples, and a 'multiverse' of minorities in the hill regions—the so-called 'hill tribes'. This contrast is particularly marked in Burma. The British (as in other colonies) fostered ethnic disputes and the ecological-cultural differences between the lowland and highland peoples as the core elements of their policy of 'divide and rule'.

In the run-up to independence, the Burmese nationalists, under the leadership of the subsequently assassinated Aung Sang, negotiated with the leaders of certain minorities a federal *modus vivendi* in the shape of the Treaty of Panglong, excluding from this the largest minority of the Karen. The post-colonial policy of the Burmese élite soon showed itself to be inflexible and increasingly chauvinistic. The never-ending civil war in Burma began before independence in 1948 and continues to this day. Following the assumption of power by General Ne Win in the 1960s, the war extended to practically all the territories of the minorities. Since the end of the 19th century, a broad national movement (the KNU: Karen National Union) has grown up among the Karen in lower Burma and in the southeast. The KNU and the Kachin in northern Burma had the strongest opposition-organizations and, like the communist rebels, were in possession of large, permanently monitored areas in the hilly border-regions.

The dictatorial military regime never made any serious attempt to find a political solution, was militarily not in a position to beat the rebels, and brought the country to economic ruin. In 1988, a powerful movement for democracy took shape in all the larger cities of Burma. Students, monks, and workers demonstrated together over a period of months (from March to September 1988). A general strike paralysed the country, Ne Win was forced to resign, and the military staged a bloody repression of the revolt. Thousands of students fled to the areas controlled by ethno-national rebels and joined in the armed resistance. The new SLORC (State Law and Order Council) regime decided on a political turn-about. Isolationism and the 'Burmese way to socialism' were abruptly abandoned in favour of a brash style of capitalism involving economic opening-up and a breakneck selling-off of natural resources. Money was pumped into huge arms-purchases and a comprehensive militarization.

The disintegration of the strong communist rebel-movement in the northeast into ethnic fragments in April 1989 brought the regime an unexpected advantage. The SLORC exploited the situation to alter the balance of power. The overwhelming electoral triumph of the opposition in 1990 was a vote against the thirty-year-old military dictatorship but it remained without effect. The generals have coldly ignored the demands for power sharing and federalization since then. Cease-fires arduously secured with several of the more than twenty ethnic guerrilla-armies, and the take-over of most of the opium economy of the Golden Triangle, have ensured the regime's survival for the meantime. The junta intends to consolidate its rule through imitation of the Indonesian model, through privileged relations with China, and through membership of ASEAN.

Ethno-national Conflict-Constellations as a Structural Feature of the New World Order

A prima facie comparison of cases according to selected criteria reveals an astonishingly high degree of structural similarity between conflicts on three different continents. Following decolonization in Asia, Africa, and Latin America, an almost mechanistic connection developed between the failure of catch-up modernization, nation-building, with its monopolistic ethnic-cum-cultural approach, and the two consequences of, on the one hand, political instability in the new states and, on the other, a tendency to ethnic conflict. Comparison between most Third World states and the former USSR highlights a whole series of regional and case-specific peculiarities attaching to ethno-national or ethnicized conflicts. The withdrawal of autonomy, post-colonial ethnocratic forms of rule, and the repression of non-dominant ethnic groups—mostly as a result and long-term effect of colonial conflict-formations—continue to be the main causes of ethno-national wars. In the CIS, questions relating to the political status of autonomous areas—including in regard to the demand for economic privileges and special rights—play an important role.

I offer an overview of regimes in multi-ethnic states, divided into minority and majority ethnocracies. The various types are distinguished according to the particular decision-making structure, the degree of co-operation possible between ethnic élites, and the nature of resource allocation. Although the spectrum of regime types in multi-ethnic states is quite broad, half of all states are dictatorships. Both the uncertain minority-rights and the lack of respect for human rights that exist in 161 states constitute virulent causes of conflict which produce ethno-nationalism from below. The difficulty experienced by the state classes in acknowledging ethnic and cultural diversity is the major obstacle to finding solutions to conflicts worldwide. Following the elimination of bipolarity, a new, multi-polar world order is again taking shape. The level of conflict varies considerably in individual regions of the world, as is demonstrated in regional conflict-scenarios for the twenty-first century.

From War and External Interference to Peace through Autonomy

Indigenous Peoples and State in Nicaragua—An Example of Conflict Resolution in the Central American Context[4]

During the 1980s, Central America was the setting of one of the regional conflicts associated with the Cold War. Amongst the anti-regime conflicts that came to public attention was a first batch of ethno-national movements across the whole region. An overview of events shows that the indigenous question was hardly even partially solved. A key event took place in Nicaragua, even though the non-Hispanic population in that country makes up only one tenth of the total population—compared with Guatemala's two-thirds Indian society. The Sandinista revolution in Nicaragua prompted an aggressive reaction on the part of the United States. An attempt was made to destabilize the revolutionary regime by arming the counter-revolutionaries (*contras*). In the eastern half of Nicaragua, endogenous causes of conflict were exploited for the same purpose. The revolt of the Miskitu Indians on the Caribbean coast, meanwhile, had a different historical background and was geared to quite different objectives.

The Indian Mosquitia was a protectorate until 1894, ruled indirectly by the British via the colonially created Miskitu kingdom. From the mid-19th century, Protestant missionaries from the Moravian church evangelized it. At the time that the east was made a part of Catholic, Hispanic Nicaragua, it was dominated politically by English-speaking Afro-American élites, and even under the dictatorship of the Somoza family, it remained economically dependent on the enclave-economy of US-American companies. The integrating developmental ideology of the Sandinistas began by fostering the nascent nationalism of the Indians, but it soon drove them into opposition. From 1980, the USA under Reagan did everything it could to fuel the process of escalation into an armed conflict.

In autumn 1984, the Sandinistas embarked on a policy of reconciliation. The conclusion of peace with the Indians, with mediation from civilian actors, was independent of the Esquipulas process. The resolution of the conflict was founded mainly on the promise of regional autonomy for both multi-ethnic Caribbean regions. The surprising electoral defeat of the Sandinistas in 1990, the weakness of the rule of law, partial political restoration in Nicaragua, and the disunity in the Indian movement are the reasons why the autonomy solution is so far only functioning *tant bien que mal*. As has been demonstrated by the revolt of the Chiapas in 1994 and the subsequent negotiations between the Zapatistas (EZLN: Ejército Zapatista de Liberación Nacional) and the Mexican PRI (Partido Revolucionario Institucional) regime in 1995–6, the autonomy debate has acquired renewed topicality in Latin America. Following the split in the Indian movement and another electoral defeat for the Sandinistas in 1996, it is uncertain whether autonomy will get a second chance.

Genocide and Crisis in Central Africa:
Genocide in Rwanda, Peace Process in Burundi, Regional War in Congo, and the Role of the International Community[5]

The crucial role played by European colonialism in the generation of ethno-national and alleged tribal conflicts is often deliberately suppressed. Before the arrival of the first Europeans in about 1885, Rwanda and Burundi were two kingdoms whose societies had developed national links transcending more narrow clan-based affinities. As a result of colonial intervention, there was a re-ethnicization or de-nationalization. The drawing of ethnic boundaries served the purposes of indirect rule. German colonialists and Catholic missionaries fabricated 'Hamitic thesis' about alien Tutsi rule. This racial theory became a crucial ideological and justificatory factor in the Hutu rebellion in 1959–62.

The devaluation of precolonial mechanisms for ensuring equity and resolving conflicts led, both in Rwanda and Burundi, to a devastating ethnicization of class differences. The colonialists actively pursued a policy of ethnicization from above and of preference for the Tutsi as the allegedly natural 'masters'. From 1959, this began to have an extremely destructive effect on post-colonial development in Central Africa. Racist colonial policies and the manipulation of collective identities as a means for the respective ruling élites to hold on to power were inextricably linked. Politically manipulated dichotomization and ethnic segregation became a source of violent internal social conflicts.

The genocide in Rwanda in 1994 was a well-advertised and well-prepared attempt to obliterate a minority. The whole state apparatus was mobilized for the purposes of exterminating the Tutsi group. Over a period of months, public and private media (notably radio and television) called upon 'loyal citizens' to do their 'duty' and dispatch their neighbours. The Catholic church and other churches failed disgracefully and, as institutions, kept up a stubborn silence (this does not apply to the Muslims). For the first time in the history of humankind, a population played a direct, active, and massive part in a state-decreed act of genocide to which practically the whole minority of the Tutsi who had remained in the country—including old people, women, children, and even babies—fell victim. The genocide in Rwanda was a colossal crime of subordination and submission to the murderous command of a state. Only half the population remained in the country; the other half either fled or was murdered. The exodus proceeded by community and sector and produced the greatest and most ambivalent refugee-crisis of recent times.

Despite earlier warnings, the United Nations remained disunited, paralysed, and inactive in the case of Rwanda. The weeks of inactivity by the UN—in the face of the horrific organized massacre of Tutsi civilians by militia forces, the police and the army—are an incomprehensible scandal. The new High Commissioner for Human Rights, on the other hand, reacted speedily and non-bureaucratically, dispatching the first UN Human Rights Field Operation to Rwanda (HRFOR). That said, investigation of the genocide and prosecution of the perpetrators has since been very slow getting off the ground. The International Tribunal on Rwanda is struggling with budgetary problems and has too few people on the ground. In dealing with the genocide, the UN seems to be acting without any kind of scheme. The international community is asking itself what can be done.

Without some measure of justice, there can be no thought of reconciliation in Rwanda. The sheer number of murderers and criminals is enough to overtax any judicial system; alternative modes of proceeding are therefore required.

Nuremberg-style tribunals should take place on every one of the thousands of hills in Rwanda and Burundi in order to have a cathartic and preventive effect. Nation-wide truth commissions operating both from below and from above are needed. In many communities, traditional arbitration bodies (*gachacha*) have spontaneously been reactivated. Following the voluntary return of more than a million refugees by the end of 1996, it is particularly urgent that efforts such as these be supported. After the Banyamulenge and Masisi Tutsi had driven the perpetrators of the genocide out of the camps in eastern Congo-Zaire, the refugees flowed back to Rwanda in an orderly fashion. In Tanzania, meanwhile, following attempts at diversion by the Interahamwe, the Tanzanian army broke up most of the camps for Banyarwanda (not for Barundi). Along with the returning refugees came tens of thousands of perpetrators of genocide.

If those mainly responsible for the genocide are not prosecuted, and if no sense of guilt is fostered in the 'smaller' perpetrators, an explosive charge capable of re-igniting violent conflicts in the future will remain in the collective consciousness. In Rwanda the first perpetrators have been convicted and executed while the International Criminal Tribunal for Rwanda (ICTR), based in Arusha, was riddled by scandals. The ICTR took a long period of preparations until the first trials started in summer 1998. However, the guilty plea of former prime minister Kambanda (followed by the sentence of life imprisonment) and the first-ever judgement by an international court that found a perpetrator (Akayesu, September 1998) guilty of genocide and crimes against humanity are positive signs. To ensure that impunity and further violence are avoided, the Rwandan government decided 2001 to launch the country-wide establishment of a modified form of the traditional gachacha jurisdiction. Such popular courts on village level will deal with all perpetrator of genocide except category one cases. The task is overwhelming; there must be co-operation between the Rwandan government and civilian actors and massive support from the international community.

Notes

1. *Structural Prevention of Ethnic Violence*. Houndmills/New York: Palgrave 2002.
2. *Ethno-Nationalismus im Zeitalter der Globalisierung* (Handbook 2 on Ethnicity and State). Münster: agenda Verlag, 1997.
3. Forthcoming as *IFEK-Reports*. Moers: IFEK 2002 and 2003.
4. *Indigene Völker und Staat in Nicaragu: Von Krieg und äußerer Einmischung zum Frieden durch Autonomie, Der Fall Nicaragua*. Moers: IFEK-IRECOR.
5. *Genocide and Crisis in Central Africa: Conflict Roots, Mass Violence, and Regional War*. Westport, CT / London: Praeger 2002. German version published in as *Ethnisierung und Völkermord in Zentralafrika*. Frankfurt/M.: Campus, 1997.

Index